# The Roots and Consequences of Independence Wars

# The Roots and Consequences of Independence Wars

*Conflicts That Changed World History*

Spencer C. Tucker

**ABC-CLIO** ™

An Imprint of ABC-CLIO, LLC
Santa Barbara, California • Denver, Colorado

Copyright © 2018 by ABC-CLIO, LLC

All rights reserved. No part of this publication may be reproduced, stored in a retrieval system, or transmitted, in any form or by any means, electronic, mechanical, photocopying, recording, or otherwise, except for the inclusion of brief quotations in a review, without prior permission in writing from the publisher.

Library of Congress Cataloging in Publication Control Number: 2017042051

ISBN: 978-1-4408-5598-6 (print)
        978-1-4408-5599-3 (ebook)

22 21 20 19 18    1 2 3 4 5

This book is also available as an eBook.

ABC-CLIO
An Imprint of ABC-CLIO, LLC

ABC-CLIO, LLC
130 Cremona Drive, P.O. Box 1911
Santa Barbara, California 93116-1911
www.abc-clio.com

This book is printed on acid-free paper ∞
Manufactured in the United States of America

*To Barbara W. Stephen with great gratitude and affection*

# About the Author

**Spencer C. Tucker, PhD**, has been the senior fellow in military history at ABC-CLIO since 2003. He is the author or editor of 62 monographs, biographies, and encyclopedias, many of which have won prestigious awards. Tucker's last academic position before his retirement from teaching was the John Biggs Chair in Military History at the Virginia Military Institute in Lexington. He has been a Fulbright scholar, a visiting research associate at the Smithsonian Institution, and, as a U.S. Army captain, an intelligence analyst in the Pentagon. His recently published works include *World War II: The Definitive Encyclopedia and Document Collection, The Roots and Consequences of Civil Wars and Revolution: Conflicts That Changed World History, Modern Conflict in the Greater Middle East: A Country-by-Country Guide,* and *Enduring Controversies in Military History: Critical Analyses and Context,* all published by ABC-CLIO.

# Contents

# Chronological Entry List

# Alphabetical Entry List

# Preface

This work treats 26 wars throughout history in which peoples sought independence. The wars begin with the Maccabean Revolt (167–160 BCE) and end with the Tamil War for Independence, fought during 1983–2009. Not all of these conflicts were successful. Among the 26 wars, I have included 8 unsuccessful efforts notable for their scope or historical significance. For the most part, I have used "of" to designate revolution wars that were successful, as in the American War of Independence, and "for" to denote those that were failures, as in the 1848–1849 Hungarian Revolution and War for Independence.

Each of the wars has a causes section followed by a section treating the course of the conflict and another section on the consequences. There are also timeline and further reading sections. I was able to follow this model for the multinational Latin American Wars of Independence, but the one exception is the wars for independence in Portuguese Africa. This entry has an initial essay treating the Portuguese Empire and then the causes, course, and consequences section for each of the three wars: Angola, Guinea-Bissau, and Mozambique in the order they began. The timeline and further reading sections cover all three wars, however.

My collaborator on many projects, Dr. Paul Pierpaoli, put together the tables giving leaders, major battles, and casualties for each of the wars.

SPENCER C. TUCKER

# Introduction

Wars of independence are defined as armed conflicts in which particular peoples seek to establish their own nation-states. War may be said to have begun once a declaration of independence has been issued and the state that previously held sway over a region takes up arms to crush the independence movement and restore its own sovereignty. If a new state is indeed established as a result of the war, that conflict is usually known as a war of independence; if the independence movement is defeated, then it is known as a war for independence. Often wars for or of independence are known by other names, as in the Rif War of 1921–1928 in Morocco and the Arab Revolt of 1916–1918 in the Ottoman territories of the Middle East. Both were indeed wars for independence.

Civil wars are quite different. One broad definition for a civil war is a war between citizens of the same country, but civil wars might best be defined as conflicts in which various factions contest for control of the entire state rather than one part seeking to break free. Some might question the inclusion here of the American Civil War, but it was certainly a war of secession, a war in which the southern states established their own government and declared their independence from the United States of America. The determination of white southerners to maintain the institution of slavery and

the economic factors associated with this were its chief causes.

Of course, many factors come into play in causing a people or region to rebel and declare their independence from a larger state authority. These include inept rule by the central government (or mother country as in the case of colonialism) in the form of tyrannical practices or corruption but also simple neglect of important services such as health care and education. Other factors might be economic exploitation of a particular region by the central government, the play of geography (as in a state divided territorially by another or a vast expanse of ocean), and the clash of religion. Also, from the early 19th century there was a growing sense of nationality: of distinct separateness caused by ethnicity, language, or religion. Utilized so effectively by Napoleon Bonaparte in France in the early 19th century, the success of nationalism in France led other peoples in Europe and then the rest of the world to seek to emulate it.

The same factors that determine the outcome of "regular" wars between already established states and civil wars are at play in struggles for independence. These include manpower, economic strengths and weaknesses to include the availability of strategic raw materials and industrial might as well as financial resources, effective leadership, geography, topography, and superior weaponry and tactics. Peoples seeking independence often have some advantage in high morale (at least initially) and familiarity with the terrain on which the war is fought, often leading to innovative tactics. Those seeking independence are, however, often at a disadvantage in manpower, economic strength, and weaponry. This is not always true, of course. The inability of the French in Indochina and the Portuguese in their African empire to mobilize large military forces had a decided impact. In both cases, the French and Portuguese were able to control the urban areas but increasingly lost control of the countryside as the wars went on.

Foreign alliances often come to play, as in the critically important aid rendered the American rebels by France in the American War of Independence. Russian military assistance enabled the Austrians to end the Hungarian War for Independence in 1849, while supplies of modern weapons were especially important to rebel forces in the colonial wars of the 20th century. The lack of this was telling in the Rif War in Morocco. Increasingly too, the mobilization of world opinion and the support or lack thereof from other states have helped influence the outcome of these wars.

The 26 wars covered here ranging from the ancient world through the 20th century present all of these factors and are drawn from the diverse geographical regions of Europe, Asia, the Americas, and Africa.

The impact of religion is best seen in the three wars included involving the Jews: the Maccabean Revolt, the Jewish Revolt against Rome, and the Israeli War of Independence. Religion was also a factor in the Dutch Revolt, but linguistic, geographical distance, a tyrannical government, and economic factors were also influential. Geography certainly played a key role in the American War of Independence. Americans were hardly oppressed; indeed, it has been said that it was the freest people in the world who rebelled, but the vast distance across the Atlantic Ocean eventually led to differing world views, estranging the American colonists from the mother country. Economic factors, namely restraints placed on colonial industry and taxes, as well as a perceived lack of representation in Parliament were also at play in the case of America. Geography was also a major factor in the various colonial wars of the 20th century, for it was hard for the imperial powers to bring their superior resources to bear.

Some of the wars discussed here were short in duration, such as the Hungarian War for Independence of 1848–1849. Others were quite protracted, such as the Dutch War of 1568–1648. Some of the wars were especially terrible in terms of casualties. Here the American Civil War, the Biafra War for Independence, and the Tamil War for Independence stand out.

Regardless, these conflicts have much to teach us, and I hope the discussion of them here will prove beneficial.

SPENCER C. TUCKER

# Maccabean Revolt (167–160 BCE)

## Causes

The Maccabean Revolt of 167–143 BCE was a protracted effort by the Jews of Judea to create an independent state from the Seleucid Empire. The land of present-day Israel was then part of the Seleucid Empire of Syria. At the empire's height, the Seleucids ruled over the Levant and territory to the south and east, including Mesopotamia, much of Anatolia, Persia, and what is now Kuwait, Afghanistan, and parts of Pakistan and Turkmenistan. Judea in southern Palestine, while a seemingly unimportant small territory largely devoid of natural resources, was strategically important as a natural transit point between Egypt to the west and major empires to the east.

Unrest in Judea leading to an armed effort to throw off Seleucid rule was directly related to the outcome of the Roman-Seleucid War (192–188 BCE). In 192 growing tensions between the Seleucid Hellenistic Greek king Antiochus III the Great (r. 222–187 BCE) and Rome resulted in armed conflict. In 191 Antiochus

## Maccabean Revolt (167–160 BCE)

| Principal Commanders | |
|---|---|
| **Maccabees (Jews of Judea)** | **Seleucid Empire** |
| Mattathias | Apollonius |
| Judas | Seron |
| Eleazar | Micanor |
| Simon | Gorgias |
| John | Lysias |
| Jonathan | Bacchides |
| | Nicanor |
| | Bacchides |

| Strength of Forces (Approximate), Battle of Beth Zur (164 BCE) | |
|---|---|
| Seleucids | 20,000–25,000 men |
| Maccabees* | 10,000 men |

*Despite being greatly outnumbered, Maccabean forces soundly defeated the Seleucid army, permitting Judas Maccabeus to take over much of Jerusalem by year's end.

**Sources:** Josephus, Flavius. *The Jewish War.* Edited by Martin Goodman, translated by Martin Hammond. Oxford: Oxford University Press, 2017; Skolnik, Fred, and Michael Berenbaum. *Encyclopaedia Judaica,* Vol. 9. Detroit: Macmillan Reference USA in association with Keter Publishing, 2007.

invaded Greece but was defeated and turned back at Thermopylae. That same year the Romans also won a naval battle in the Mediterranean, and in 190 they defeated the Seleucids in two important naval battles. The turning point in the war came on land after the Romans had crossed the Hellespont and invaded Asia Minor. In the Battle of Magnesia in 189, the Romans under Lucius Cornelius Scipio defeated the Seleucids under Antiochus.

Peace was concluded in 188, and the Seleucids now struggled to pay the heavy annual tribute demanded by Rome. These taxes were paid in the temples of the Seleucid territories and were much resented in Judea.

Religion and inept Seleucid policy toward it were certainly important factors in the revolt. The Jews practiced an exclusive monotheism that was unique in the ancient world and brought contempt and scorn from the pantheistic Greeks and Romans. Hellenized Jews—those willing to worship the Greek gods—were a distinct minority. Both Antiochus III and his successor Seleucus IV Philopator (r. 187–175) were anxious to see Judea remain tranquil and have taxes paid on time, and they wisely left the Jews alone in their religious practices, but Antiochus IV Epiphanes (r. 175–164) proved to be a disaster.

In 167 BCE Antiochus arrived in Jerusalem after having sustained a military defeat in Egypt. Eager to raise funds and opposed to Judaism, Antiochus IV sold the office of high priest to an individual not qualified to hold the position under Jewish law. He also outlawed Judaism and ordered establishment of an imperial cult in its place. In addition, he desecrated the Temple by ordering that a statue of himself as Zeus be raised in it. These actions and

his insistence on the Hellenization of the Jews brought on a Jewish revolt.

The revolt was triggered when Seleucid official Appelles, acting in accordance with Antiochus's policies, directed Mattathias the Hasmonean, a prominent citizen and priest in Mod'lin, northwest of Jerusalem, to sacrifice to the Greek gods. He refused, and Mattathias and his sons Judas, Eleazar, Simon, John, and Jonathan then killed a Jew who did make the required sacrifice. They also slews Appeles and possibly some soldiers. This event triggered the protracted Maccabean Revolt (167–143 BCE).

SPENCER C. TUCKER

## Course

Mattathias the Hasmonean and his sons now launched guerrilla warfare against the Seleucids. In a radical departure, they decided to fight every day—that is, on the Sabbath. Mattathias died in 166. His eldest son Judas then assumed leadership of the revolt, which came to be named for him. The surname of Maccabeus (Maccabee) given Judas may mean "hammer," signifying his leadership in battle, although other scholars claim that it means "the one designated by Yahweh [God]."

A natural leader and military commander of considerable ability, Judas Maccabeus at first avoided major engagements with the better-armed Seleucids and employed guerrilla tactics to defeat a succession of their generals sent to Judea, although his military efforts were first directed against Hellenized Jews, of whom there were a great number in Judea.

In 167 at the Ascent of Lebonah, Judas's men annihilated an entire Seleucid unit; in 166 at Nahal el-Haramiah, he defeated a small Seleucid force under Apollonius, the governor of Samaria, who was

Gustave Doré's depiction of Judas Maccabeus before the army of Syrian general Nicanor. (Nicku/Dreamstime)

among the dead. Optimism kindled by this victory led many Jews to join the cause.

Shortly thereafter in 166 BCE, Judas defeated a larger Seleucid force under Seron near Beth-Horon. Judas was then victorious at Emmaus, defeating Seleucid generals Micanor and Gorgias. Judas's defeat of the Seleucids at Beth Zur (Beth-sura) near Hebron in 164 BCE allowed him to take much of Jerusalem that December, including the Temple, although some Seleucids continued to hold out in the Acra (citadel).

The ensuing purification of the Temple is the origin of the Jewish celebration of the Festival of Lights, also known as Hanukkah (Chanukah), meaning "dedication." This celebration in the month of December commemorates the cleansing and rededication of the Temple following the removal of its pagan statuary. Rabbinic tradition holds that the victorious Maccabees could only find a small jug of oil that remained uncontaminated, thanks to a seal. Although the jug contained only enough oil sufficient to sustain the menorah for one day, it miraculously lasted for eight days until further oil was secured.

While continuing the siege of the Acra, Judas expanded his control over the whole of Judea. Judas could be cruel toward his enemies in accordance with the wars of the time, and he at least contemplated killing all males in communities and cites that opposed him. Eleazar, Judas's second-youngest brother, died in 163 reportedly when he stabbed a Seleucid war elephant from underneath and the dying beast collapsed on him.

Antiochus IV Epiphanes died in 164, and Seleucid regent Lysias invaded Judea and defeated Judas at Beth Zachariah

(162 BCE). Lysias was then forced to return to Syria to suppress a revolt there. Later that same year, however, Bacchides, commander of Seleucid forces in Judea, defeated Judas at Jerusalem, driving him from the city.

Judas rallied, however, and in 161 BCE he defeated a Seleucid army in the Battle of Adasa under Syrian general Nicanor, who was among those killed. Judas was said to be negotiating an alliance with the Romans when, that same year, he was defeated and slain in the Battle of Eslasa by a far more numerous Seleucid force, said to number 20,000 men and commanded by Bacchides. Judas is widely praised in the First Book of Maccabees and is acclaimed by Jews as one of the greatest military leaders in their history.

While many scholars date the revolt as ending in 160 BCE, armed resistance against the Seleucids continued under Judas's brother Jonathan, who enjoyed considerable success with the guerrilla tactics first employed by his brother. He was also able to take advantage of an ensuing political struggle between new high priest Alexander I Balas and Sdeleucid king Demetrius I Soter (r. 161–150).

Establishing his headquarters at Jerusalem in 152, Jonathan was recognized as de facto ruler of Judea. He ruled until 143 BCE, when he was captured in an ambush at Ptolemais (Acre, Akko) and killed by dissident Jews. Jonathan was then succeeded by yet another brother, Simon.

SPENCER C. TUCKER

## Consequences

In 142 BCE Simon Hasmonean, who had been elected to succeed Jonathan, secured recognition of Judean independence, with himself as king. The Maccabeean succession was maintained by Simon's son John.

Known later as John Hyrcanus I, he was both high priest and ruler from 135/134 until his death in 104. During his long reign he consolidated and extended Jewish control to include Samaria, Galilee, Iturea, Perea, and Idumea. Some scholars today refer to the Jewish state of this period as the Kingdom of Israel. In 110 with the disintegration of the Seleucid Empire, the kingdom became fully independent.

The independence of Judea ended in 63 BCE, however, with the arrival of the Roman army of general Gnaeus Pompeius Magnus (Pompey the Great). After defeating Mithridates VI of Pontus and Tigranes I of Armenia, Pompey moved to annex Syria and make it a Roman province. He then laid siege to and captured Jerusalem. Roman soldiers secured the Temple and killed its priests. Although Pompey left the Temple intact, he dared to visit the Holy of Holies, where only the high priest was allowed. This disregard for Jewish religious practices typified much of Roman rule thereafter.

Judea was now transformed into a Roman client state, although Hasmoneans continued as rulers for more than two decades. Heavy Roman taxation created considerable anger against Roman rule. Antigonus II Mattathias was king during the tumultuous period 40–37 BCE. Herod, the second son of Antipater the Idumaean, a high-ranking official, having secured the support of Roman leader Mark Antony, was declared by the Roman Senate in 37 as king of Judea. Returning from Rome in 39 he opened a campaign against Antigonus. In the spring of 38, Herod secured control of Galilee and eventually all of Judea as far as Jerusalem, which he besieged. Antigonus took refuge in Jerusalem and held out there in the siege of some three to five months and into 37, when Herod and the Romans captured the city.

Taken prisoner, Antigonus was sent to Anticoh and there executed, ending Hasmonean rule.

The Hasmonean dynasty was now replaced by that of Herod. Known to history as Herod the Great, he attempted to bolster his legitimacy by marrying a Hasmonean princess, Mariamne, and ordering the deaths of any Hasmonean heirs to the throne. Herod ruled until his death in 4 BCE, when his kingdom was divided between his sons as a tetrarchy, which lasted about a decade until 6 CE, when Rome joined Judea, Samaria, and Ideumea (biblical Edom) into the Roman province of Judea. A Roman official, first known as governor and then procurator, ruled alongside the Herodic king until the death of the last Herodian monarch, Agrippa II (probably in 92 CE), when Rome assumed full power.

SPENCER C. TUCKER

## Timeline

| | |
|---|---|
| **192–188 BCE** | The Roman-Seleucid War forces the Seleucids to sharply raise taxes throughout their empire, causing considerable unrest in Judea. |
| **166** | Seleucid ruler Antiochus IV Epiphanes arrives in Jerusalem, where he outlaws Judaism and orders the establishment of an imperial cult. |
| | Refusing Appelles's order to sacrifice to the Greek gods, Mattathias and his sons kill a Jew who made the required sacrifice as well as Appelles, triggering the protracted Maccabean Revolt (167–143). |
| | Matthathias dies and is succeeded by his son Judas. |
| | Judas is victorious at Nahal el-Haramiah, goes on to defeat a larger Seleucid force near Beth-Horon, and is also victorious at Emmaus. |
| **164** | Judas's defeat of the Seleucids at Beth Zur (Bethsura) allows him to take much of Jerusalem that December, including the Temple. The ensuing purification of the Temple is the origin of the Chanukah, the Festival of Lights. |
| | Continuing the siege of Acra, Judas expands his control over the whole of Judea. |
| **162** | Seleucid regent Lysias invades Judea and defeats Judas at Beth Zachariah. Later this same year, General Bacchides defeats Judas at Jerusalem, driving him from the city. |
| **161** | Judas rallies and defeats a Seleucid army in the Battle of Adasa. Later this year, however, he is defeated and slain in the Battle of Eslasa. |
| **152** | Judas's brother Jonathan is recognized as de facto ruler of Judea. |
| **143** | Jonathan's rule ends when he is slain by dissident Jews. His brother Simon succeeds him. |
| **142** | Simon secures recognition of Judean independence, with himself as king. |

**135/134–104**   The Maccabeean succession is maintained by Simon's son John, later known as John Hyrcanus I, who consolidates and extends his kingdom to include Samaria, Galilee, Iturea, Perea, and Idumea.

**110**   With the disintegration of the Seleucid Empire, the Kingdom of Judea becomes fully independent.

**63**   Independence ends with the conquest of Judea and Jerusalem by Roman general Gnaeus Pompeius Magnus (Pompey the Great).

SPENCER C. TUCKER

### Further Reading

de Lange, Nicholas, ed. *The Illustrated History of the Jewish People*. London: Aurum, 1997.

Green, Peter. *Alexander to Actium: The Historical Evolution of the Hellenistic Age*. Berkeley: University of California Press, 1990.

Josephus, Flavius. *The Jewish War*. Edited by Martin Goodman and translated by Martin Hammond. Oxford: Oxford University Press, 2017.

Robinson, Theodore H., and W. O. E. Oesterley. *A History of Israel*. Oxford, UK: Clarendon, 1932.

Schäfer, Peter. *The History of the Jews in the Greco-Roman World*. New York: Routledge, 2003.

Skolnik, Fred, and Michael Berenbaum. *Encyclopaedia Judaica,* Vol. 9. Detroit: Macmillan Reference USA in association with the Keter Publishing House, 2007.

# Jewish Revolt against Rome (66–73)

## Causes

The Jewish Revolt against Rome of 66–73 was an effort by the Jewish people to secure their independence. Modern Israel is a small state territorially, occupying a land area slightly less than the U.S. state of New Jersey. In ancient times this region was poor, bereft of natural resources, and barely able to provide for itself. Thus, it could hardly resist Roman power. Despite the paucity of resources, this area was strategically important because it formed a highway between the larger empires of the Assyrians, Babylonians, and the Persians to the east and the Egyptians and finally the Greeks and Romans to the west.

In 63 BCE Roman consul Pompey Magnus (Pompey the Great), fresh from defeating Mithridates VI of Pontus and Tigranes I of Armenia, moved to annex Syria, making it a Roman province. Pompey next laid siege to and captured Jerusalem. Roman soldiers secured the Temple there, putting its priests to death with the sword. Although he preserved the Temple treasury, Pompey dared to visit the Holy of Holies, where only the high priest was allowed. This disregard for Jewish practices typified much of Roman rule thereafter.

Jews constituted only a small proportion of the population of the Roman Empire, but this did not keep them from being a constant problem. Although it was nominally under Roman rule from 63 BCE on, Judea was integrated into the Roman Empire under client king Herod the Great, who had allied himself first with Marcus Antonius (Mark Antony) and then with Octavian (later Emperor Augustus). Proclaimed king of Judea by the Roman Senate, in 37 BCE Herod became the unchallenged ruler of Judea, a position he maintained for 32 years. Augustus rewarded Herod's loyalty by twice increasing the size of the territory he ruled. This came to include not only Palestine but also parts of what are now the Kingdom of Jordan to the east of the river and southern Lebanon and Syria.

Herod died in 4 BCE, and his kingdom was divided mostly among three of his sons, who became tetrarchs. One of these divisions was Judea, which corresponded to the territory of the earlier Judea plus Samaria and Idumea. Herod's son Herod Archelaus proved so inept as ruler of this territory, however, that Augustus ordered him deposed in 6 CE.

A Roman governor now assumed rule, the title of governor being subsequently changed to procurator. The procurator, who ruled from the capital city of Caesarea (built by Herod as the Mediterranean port city of Caesarea Maritima), had at his disposal a small Roman military force of five cohorts of infantry and one of cavalry, or something less than 3,000 men. The procurator was responsible for the maintenance of order, the collection of taxes, and overseeing building projects. The Herodian client king controlled the Temple at Jerusalem, but the final regional authority was neither the procurator nor the client king but rather the Roman governor of Syria.

The Jewish priestly elites of Jerusalem handled most of the administrative duties. The high priest, appointed by the Herodian king, who from 50 to 92 CE was Agrippa II, had charge of the Temple, which had

**Jewish Revolt against Rome (66–73 CE)**

| Roman and Allied Forces Arrayed against the Jews of Judea (in 66 CE) | |
| --- | --- |
| Military Group/Type of Force | Number of Men |
| XII Fulminata (Thunderbolt) Legion | 4,800 |
| Legionnaires | 6,000 |
| Cavalry | 2,000 |
| Auxiliary infantry (6 cohorts) | 5,000 |
| Slingers and javelin throwers* | 32,000 |
| Greek and Syrian militias | 2,000 |
| **Total strength** | 51,800 |

*Provided by King Antiochus IV of Commagene and King Sohamemus of Emesa.

| Combat Losses, Battle of Beth-Horon (October 66 CE) | |
| --- | --- |
| Roman Forces | Jewish Militia Forces |
| 500 | 22 |

| Siege of Masada (Late 72–Early 73 CE) | | |
| --- | --- | --- |
| | Roman Forces | Besieged Jews on Masada |
| **Strength** | 10,000 men | 960 men, women, and children |
| **Losses** | Unknown | 953 killed, 7 taken prisoner* |

* Two women and five children.

**Sources:** Davis, Paul K. *Besieged: An Encyclopedia of Great Sieges from Ancient Times to the Present.* Santa Barbara, CA: ABC-CLIO, 2001; Tamarin, Alfred H. *Revolt in Judea: The Road to Masada, the Eyewitness Accounts by Flavius Josephus of the Roman Campaign against Judea, the Destruction of the Second Temple, and the Heroism of Masada.* New York: Four Winds Press, 1968.

been restored by Herod and is known as the Second Temple. This project and Herod's construction of new ports had attracted a number of pilgrims and greatly increased the wealth of the Jewish elites involved in Temple management. This in turn led to increased competition for its positions. These overlapping administrative systems and competition between them, however, contributed greatly to the revolt of 66 CE. Economic circumstances may also have played a role, for there is evidence of an increasing population, especially in the urban centers and the problems that came with this.

There was also the matter of religion. The unique contribution of the Jews to the West lies in their development of an exclusive monotheism, the belief in a single all-powerful god, Jehovah, who watched over his chosen people but also demanded a high standard of ethical conduct on pain of severe punishment. Perhaps no people in history were to fight more tenaciously for their liberty against greater odds. The belief of Jews in their uniqueness along with their intolerance of other religions created in the ancient world a sense of separation and widespread animosity against them. Indeed, the disdain felt by most of the pantheistic ancient world toward the Jews cannot be understated. The Romans inherited, and if anything intensified, the hatred of Greeks toward the Jews. Because of their montheism, Jews could not acknowledge the divinity of the emperor at Rome, nor could they be truly loyal to Rome or its symbols thanks to their strict aniconism that prohibited various forms of images linked directly with idolatry.

Unfortunately, this part of the empire attracted the dregs of the Roman civil service. Inept Roman leadership, insensitivity, sacrilege, and plain stupidity produced a number of riots and uprisings that brought savage reprisals. A string of maladroit decrees and a succession of inept Roman administrators fed Jewish extremism and convinced many Jews that a day of reckoning was inevitable. These determined Jews came to be known as Zealots.

Matters came to a head in May 66 under Gessius Florus, Roman procurator of Judea during 64–66 who had great disdain for the Jewish elites and favored Greeks in Caesarea in their ongoing disputes with the Jews. In 66 some Greeks caused a riot in Caesarea when a number supposedly affiliated with a merchant establishment sacrificed birds in front of a synagogue. Jerusalem was already in a state of unrest over taxation. In addition, on the orders of Flrous, Roman soldiers breached the Temple precinct and removed 17 talents from its treasury, with Florus claiming that this was for the emperor. This act led the Zealots in Jerusalem to act, and a number of them in the city went around soliciting money for Florus in a basket as if he were a beggar.

Furious at this, Florus ordered troops into the city to arrest certain Jewish leaders, but the Jews drove both the soldiers and Florus from Jerusalem. Rioting became open rebellion when Zealot and captain of the Temple Eleazar ben Anaias suspended sacrifice for the emperor. Pro-Roman Herodic king Agrippa II and his sister Bernice fled Jerusalem.

SPENCER C. TUCKER

## Course

The Zealots took control in Jerusalem. They promised amnesty to the Roman forces holding the Antonia Fortress that overlooked the Temple precinct. Despite this pledge, on yielding the fortress the Romans there were slaughtered. Roman procurator Gessius Florus soon had lost control of all Judea and appealed for assistance to the Roman governor of Syria, legate Cestius Gallus at Antioch, who had available a much larger force of four legions.

After having expelled the Romans, two anti-Roman factions vied for control of Jerusalem: the Zealots led by Eleazar ben Simon and the Sicarii under Menahem ben Yair. The Zealots turned on the Sicarii, killing Menachem and forcing his followers from Jerusalem. Throughout the cities of Judea also, many Greeks allied themselves with the Romans and attacked the Jews, while the Jews attacked and slew Greeks.

Cestius Gallus took three months to put together an expeditionary force to retake Judea. Centered on the XII Fulminata (Thunderbolt) legion of 4,800 men, it included another 6,000 legionnaires (2,000 from each of the other three legions). Cestius also had some 2,000 cavalry and 5,000 auxiliary infantry in six cohorts. Rome's allies, King Antiochus IV of Commagene and King Sohamemus of Emesa, furnished slingers and javelin throwers, totaling perhaps another 32,000 men. Some 2,000 Greeks in Syrian militias also joined, eager to participate in any action against Jews.

In October 66 Gallus easily subdued Galilee. His men unleashed a terror campaign of widespread destruction in the expectation that this would both remove any threat to his rear area and intimidate the Jewish population along the route to Jerusalem. Leaving moderate forces to hold Galilee, Gallus also detached units to secure the seaport of Joppa. The Romans razed Joppa and slew perhaps 8,000 people there. Additional Roman columns secured other potential rebel strongholds.

These coastal columns rejoined the main force at Caesarea, and Gallus moved against Jerusalem. He expected to conclude the campaign in a few weeks, before the heavy autumnal rains could make quagmires of the roads. To this point, Jewish resistance was sporadic and apparently disorganized.

Gallus believed that his terror campaign had worked. On his approach to Jerusalem through the Beth-Horon gorge (named for two villages 10 and 12 miles northwest of Jerusalem), he therefore failed to follow standard procedure and make an adequate reconnaissance. As a result, the Jews were able to lay an ambush and attack the head of his column before the Romans could deploy from march formation. According to Jewish sources the Romans sustained some 500 dead, while the Jews had only 22 dead.

Gallus recovered and resumed the advance. He set up camp on Mount Scopus, less than a mile from the city. The Zealots refused, however, to treat with any emissaries and even put one to death. After several days of waiting, on October 15 Gallus sent his men into Jerusalem. The Jews fell back to the inner-city wall. The Romans burned the suburb of Betheza, expecting that this would bring submission. It did not. The Romans then launched full-scale attacks but failed to penetrate the Jewish defenses. Following a week of this, Gallus suddenly withdrew. Stiffer than expected Jewish resistance, the approach of winter, and the shortages of supplies and mules for transport were the factors in his decision.

Gallus decided to move back to the coast through the Beth-Horon gorge. Again he failed to post pickets on the hills, allowing the Jews to attack his forces in the narrow defile. Other Jewish forces moved to block the Roman escape. This running engagement, known as the Battle of Beth-Horon, turned into a rout. Gallus and the bulk of his force escaped but at the cost of all of their baggage and nearly 6,000 men killed. The XII Legion also lost its eagle standard. The equipment that the Jews captured would serve them effectively in combating Roman siege operations four years later.

The battle had serious consequences. One immediate effect was the massacre of Jews in Damascus; Greeks there were now confident that this action would have Gallus's support. The Battle of Beth-Horon also meant that the Jewish revolt would not now be immediately put down. Jews hitherto reluctant to commit themselves now joined the Zealots. Many were convinced that the victory was a sign that God favored their cause. By November the Jews had set up an independent secessionist government in Jerusalem.

The Zealot Ananus ben Ananus, the high priest, was now the leader in Jerusalem. An effective speaker and leader who was said to embrace democratic ideals, he ordered military efforts to establish Jewish control throughout Judea. A siege of the port city of Ashkelon failed, while the future historian Flavius Josephus led an effort to organize the defenses of Galilee in order to better resist an anticipated Roman assault. Josephus, however, encountered resistance from the magnate John of Giscgalla, and when the Romans invasion came in 67, Galilee was divided into territory controlled by John, Josephus, and Roman loyalists, as in the city of Sopphoris.

The Romans could not allow the effort by the Jews to break away from the empire to succeed lest it be replicated elsewhere. Emperor Nero (r. 54–68) appointed experienced general Vespasian (Titus Flavius Vespasianus) to command an expeditionary force that would restore Roman control. In April 67, Vespasian landed on the coast at Ptolemais with two legions. Joined by his son Titus with another legion, the Romans then moved into Galilee. Some cities swiftly surrendered. Others, such as Yodfat and Gamla, had to be besieged and taken by force, the inhabitants put to the sword or sold into slavery. During the siege of the small fortified town of Jotapata, Josephus switched sides and joined the Romans. John of Giscgalla then fled with a number of his men to Jerusalem. By 68, Vespasian had reestablished Roman control over Galilee and set up his base of operations at Caesarea.

Nonetheless, a number of Jews who had been driven out of Galilee rebuilt the walls of the port city of Joppa (modern-day Jaffa), which had been destroyed earlier by Cestius Gallus. They then employed small ships to disrupt commerce in the eastern Mediterranean and to intercept grain shipments from Alexandria to Rome.

In 68–69 there was civil strife in Jerusalem. John of Giscgalla joined the faction led by Eleazar ben Simon and they slew Ananus ben Ananus and a number of his supporters. John then formed his own faction. While this was occurring in Jerusalem, Vespasian had extended Roman control over all of Judea and Samaria except Jerusalem. Roman military successes forced the highly effective Jewish general Simon bar Giora to withdraw with his men into Jerusalem. This merely increased division in the city, with factions now led by Eleazar ben Simon and the Zealots, John of Giaschala, and Simon bar Giora.

In 69 Vespasian moved on Jerusalem with two legions, while Titus came up with another legion. Herodic king Agrippa II, who had tried but failed to prevent the Jewish revolt in 66 and then fled Jerusalem, sided with Rome. He provided the Romans some 2,000 men, archers and cavalry. (Agrippa would accompany Titus on some of his campaigns and was wounded at the siege of Gamla. After the capture of Jerusalem, Agrippa and his sister Berenice went to Rome, where he was given the title of praetor and rewarded with additional territory.)

At the same time there had been great political upheaval in Rome. Nero was deposed in 68 and committed suicide. He was followed, in a rapid succession of leaders, by Galbo, Otho, and Vitellius until in the spring of 69 Roman legions first of the Danube and then of Egypt and Syria declared their allegiance to Vespasian as emperor. In the winter of 69 the forces supporting Vespasian defeated those of Vitellius and killed him. Early in 70, Vespasian departed for Rome to secure the position of emperor. Before leaving, however, he ordered Titus to take Jerusalem and end the Jewish revolt as soon as possible.

Titus arrived at Jerusalem in March of 70. The population of the city had swelled with the arrival of numerous refugees seeking the protection of its walls. For his effort to take the city, Titus had at his disposal some 60,000–80,000 men. The Jewish defensive effort was hampered by factionalism, but the defenders nonetheless managed to damage some of the Roman siege engines. The Romans then methodically encircled the city with parapets and cut it off from any supply of food. Then after several unsuccessful attempts, the Romans captured the Antonia Fortress above the Temple, and by mid-August they had managed to take the Temple itself and burn it. By September all Jerusalem was in their hands.

Because Titus was under some pressure to take the city quickly in order to secure a foreign triumph that would strengthen his father's position in Rome, Roman casualties were heavy, and this undoubtedly influenced what occurred thereafter. The

Roman sack of the city was terrible. In his history of events, Josephus estimates that 1.1 million people died in the fighting or of starvation or disease. No doubt this figure is inflated, but certainly losses were heavy indeed.

For all practical purposes, the Roman destruction of Jerusalem ended the Jewish effort to throw off Roman rule. In the spring of 71, Titus returned to Rome. Now military governor Lucilius Bassus conducted mopping-up operations, taking the remaining Jewish fortifications, including both Herodium and Machaereus.

Bassus fell ill, however, and it was left to his replacement, Lucius Flavius Silva, to take the remaining Jewish fortification atop the flat-topped mountain of Masada. The defenders were commanded by the Sicarii rebel leader Elezar ben Yair. Silva had at his disposal some 10,000 men and

Ruins of the ancient Jewish fortress of Masada, scene of the Roman siege of 72–73. (Vander-WolfImages/Dreamstime)

hundreds of siege engines. When Silva's demand for surrender was rejected, the Romans began siege operations beginning in the autumn of 72. Masada fell early in 73. According to Josephus, the Romans discovered that 960 of the men, women, and children there had committed suicide rather than surrender. Only 7 prisoners were taken: 2 women and 5 children.

SPENCER C. TUCKER

## Consequences

The Jewish effort to win their independence from Rome had been a relatively minor affair in an obscure backwater of the Roman Empire, and its outcome had certainly been predictable. Roman leaders simply could not allow part of the empire to break away lest this example be copied elsewhere.

The Jewish state was no more. The Romans annexed it directly in the year 70. Renamed Syria Palestina, it was not completely subject to Roman law, and Jewish law was no longer enforced. This change no doubt contributed to a decline in the number of practicing Jews. The destruction of the Temple and much of Jerusalem meant that the city was no longer a pilgrimage site, and this had a great impact on Jerusalem's economy.

Certainly Vespasian, lacking legitimate claim as emperor, sought to magnify both the danger and the extent of the revolt in order to make his victory that much greater and use this to solidify his rule. Coins bearing the image of the emperor with the inscription IVIDEA CAPTA (Judea Captured) and showing Judea as a weeping woman on the reverse were issued throughout the empire to make clear the result of rebellion.

Vespasian imposed a tax on the Jews in place of that they had paid to the Jerusalem Temple. Monies from the new tax went to pay for the restoration of the Capitoline Temple of Jupiter Optimus Maximus, which had been damaged in the Flavian capture of Rome. Jewish funds were also used to construct new monuments in Rome, including the Arch of Titus and the new Coliseum. All of this was to show Roman supremacy.

The Jewish revolt also had a profound impact on Christianity, now spreading throughout the Near East. Christianity now became distinct from Judaism. The Roman capture of Jerusalem and destruction of the Temple also was regarded as a great symbolic blow to the Jewish religion, and no doubt it was seen by many converts to Christianity as righteous punishment for the Jews having rejected and persecuted Jesus. But much of Syria Palestina now reverted to Greco-Roman paganism. Certainly, the destruction of the Temple strengthened Rabbinic Judaism, the form of Judaism practiced today. Those who practiced Judaism needed some way to do so without the Temple.

Nearly two centuries would pass until there would again be a Jewish nation-state, in 1948.

SPENCER C. TUCKER

## Timeline

| | |
|---|---|
| **63 BCE** | Roman consul Pompey Magnus (Pompey the Great) secures Judea and captures Jerusalem. |
| **37 BCE** | Herod, a staunch ally of Rome, becomes the unchallenged client king of Judea. |

| | |
|---|---|
| **4 BCE** | Herod dies, and his kingdom is divided mostly among three of his sons. |
| **6 CE** | Herod's son Herod Archelaus proves so inept as ruler of Judea that Augustus has him deposed. A Roman governor now assumes the rule of Judea. |
| **50–92** | Agrippa II is the king of Judea. Inept Roman administrators encourage anti-Roman Jewish extremists, known as Zealots. |
| **May 66** | Under Roman procurator of Judea Gessius Florus, Jewish rioting in Jerusalem becomes open rebellion, driving pro-Roman king Agrippa II from the city. Florus appeals for assistance from Roman governor of Syria legate Cestius Gallus. Two anti-Roman factions now vie for control of Jerusalem: the Zealots and the Sicarii. The Zealots turn on the Sicarii, forcing them from Jerusalem. |
| **Oct 15, 66** | Cestius Gallus sends his troops against Jerusalem but soon withdraws. |
| **Late Oct 66** | Gallus moves to the coast back through the Beth-Horon gorge. The Jews attack the Romans, and Gallus's force suffers some 6,000 dead. |
| **Nov 66** | Many Jews rally to the rebels, who establish an independent secessionist government in Jerusalem. |
| | Flavius Josephus leads an effort to organize the defenses of Galilee, but when the Roman invasion comes, a united defense of Galilee proves impossible. |
| **67** | Roman emperor Nero appoints experienced general Vespasian (Titus Flavius Vespasianus) to command an expeditionary force to restore Roman control. |
| **Apr 67** | Vespasian lands at Ptolemais with two legions. Joined by his son Titus with another legion, Vespasian moves into Galilee. Josephus switches sides, while John of Giscgalla and his men seek refuge in Jerusalem. |
| **68** | Vespasian reestablishes Roman control over Galilee and sets up his base of operations at Caesarea. Amid civil strife in Jerusalem, Vespasian secures control of all of Judea and Samaria except Jerusalem. |
| **68–69** | Chaos occurs in Rome as Emperor Nero is deposed. In the spring of 69, a number of legions declare their allegiance to Vespasian as emperor. |
| **Early 70** | Vespasian leaves for Rome, ordering Titus to take Jerusalem and end the Jewish revolt. |
| **Mar 70** | Titus arrives at Jerusalem with some 60,000–80,000 men. |
| **Aug 70** | The Romans, having encircled the city, capture the Antonia Fortress above the Temple and then the Temple itself, which they destroy. |

| | |
|---|---|
| **Sep 70** | The Romans secure all of Jerusalem. Rome assumes direct rule of what is now known as Syreia Palestina, ending the revolt. |
| **Spring 71** | Titus returns to Rome, and new military governor Lucilius Bassus conducts mopping-up operations. |
| **72–73** | Bassus's successor, Lucius Flavius Silva, takes the remaining Jewish fortification of Massada. |

SPENCER C. TUCKER

## Further Reading

Gambash, Gil. *Rome and Provincial Resistance.* London: Routledge, 2015.

Goodman, Martin. *Rome and Jerusalem.* New York: Knopf, 2007.

Goodman, Martin. *Ruling Class of Judaea.* Cambridge: Cambridge University Press, 1987.

Grant, Michael. *The Jews in the Roman World.* New York: Scribner, 1973.

Jones, A. H. M. *The Herods of Judea.* Oxford, UK: Clarendon, 1967.

Jones, A. H. M. *Soldiers and Ghosts: A History of Battle in Classical Antiquity.* New Haven, CT: Yale University Press, 2005.

Josephus, Flavius. *The Jewish War.* Edited by Martin Goodman and translated by Martin Hammond. Oxford: Oxford University Press, 2017.

Lendon, J. E. "Roman Siege of Jerusalem." *MHQ: Quarterly Journal of Military History* 17(4) (Summer 2005): 6–15.

Schürer, E. *The History of the Jewish People in the Age of Jesus Christ.* Rev. ed. 3 vols. Edinburgh, UK: T. & T. Clark, 1973–1987.

Schwartz, Seth. *Imperialism and Jewish Society, 200 B.C.E. to 640 C.E.* Princeton, NJ: Princeton University Press, 2001.

# Scottish Wars of Independence (1296–1328 and 1332–1357)

## Causes

There are two wars of Scottish independence. The first began with an English invasion of Scotland in 1296 and ended with the Treaty of Edinburgh-Northampton in 1328. The second war saw the English support an invasion of Scotland in 1332 by a rival candidate for the Scottish throne. This ended with his defeat and the Treaty of Berwick in 1357. The first war was caused by the internal situation in Scotland, border disputes, and the refusal of King John Balliol of Scotland to aid English king Edward I in his war with France.

The struggle for control of Scotland began in 1286 with the death of King Alexander III (r. 1249–1286). His heir was his three-year-old granddaughter Queen Margaret, daughter of the king of Norway. King Edward I of England (r. 1272–1307), desirous of securing control of Scotland, concluded the Treaty of Birgham (July 18, 1290) with the guardians of Scotland, the men appointed to govern Scotland during the queen's minority. According to this

**Scottish Wars of Independence (1296–1328 and 1332–1357)**

| Battle of Dunbar (April 27, 1296) | |
| --- | --- |
| | Strength |
| Kingdom of Scotland* | 40,000 men |
| Kingdom of England** | 12,000 men |

*Forces commanded by King John Balliol.
**Forces commanded by John de Warrene, sixth Earl of Surrey.

| Battle of Falkirk (July 22, 1298) | | |
| --- | --- | --- |
| | Strength | Approximate Losses |
| Kingdom of Scotland* | 10,000 men | 2,000 killed |
| Kingdom of England** | 14,000 men | 2,000 killed |

*Forces commanded by Guardian of Scotland William Wallace.
**Forces commanded by King Edward I.

| Battle of Halidon Hill (July 19, 1333) | | |
| --- | --- | --- |
| | Strength | Approximate Losses |
| Kingdom of Scotland* | 14,000 men | 4,000 killed |
| Kingdom of England** | 9,000 men | 10–20 killed |

*Forces commanded by Sir Archibald Douglas, who died in the fighting.
**Forces commanded by King Edward III.

| Battle of Neville's Cross (October 17, 1346) | | |
|---|---|---|
| | Strength | Approximate Losses |
| Kingdom of Scotland* | 12,000 men | 1,000–3,000 killed |
| Kingdom of England** | 6,000–7,000 men | Unknown, but light |

*Forces commanded by King David II.
**Forces commanded by Archbishop of York William Zouche.

**Sources:** Fisher, Andrew. *William Wallace*. Edinburgh. UK: Birlinn, 2007; Prestwich, Michael. *Edward I.* New Haven, CT: Yale University Press, 1997; Rollason, David, and Michael Prestwich, eds. *The Battle of Neville's Cross, 1346*. Lincolnshire, UK: Shaun Tyas, 1998; Strickland, Matthew, and Robert Hardy. *The Great Warbow: From Hastings to the Mary Rose*. Stroud, Gloucestershire, UK: History Press, 2005.

treaty, Margaret was to marry King Edward's son, Edward of Caernarvon. The treaty also provided that Scotland would remain "separate, distinct in itself without subjection from the realm of England."

Margaret, however, died in September 1290 shortly after arriving in her new kingdom. This created a chaotic situation regarding the succession, for there were 13 claimants for the Crown. The two strongest claimants were John Balliol, Lord of Galloway, and Robert Bruce, fifth Lord of Amnandale (the grandfather of future king Robert the Bruce).

In order to avoid civil war in Scotland, the guardians called on King Edward to come north and preside over a process that would choose the successor. Edward agreed to meet with the claimants at Norham in 1291 but insisted that before coming north he be recognized as Lord Paramount of Scotland. The guardians rejected this demand, whereupon Edward gave the claimants three weeks to agree, which was sufficient time for him to assemble a military force and impose his will. The guardians were now forced to agree and to accept Edward's decision regarding the succession.

On June 11, 1291, Edward ordered that all castles in Scotland be temporarily placed under his control and that all officials resign and then be reappointed by him. On June 13 at Upsettlington, the guardians of the realm and Scottish nobles swore allegiance to Edward as Lord Paramount.

In what came to be known as the Great Cause, Edward presided over 13 meetings at Berwick between May and August 1291, during which he interviewed the claimants for the Scottish Crown. He rejected all but four as not proving direct descent from King David I. Arbiters were then named to decide the case. Balliol and Bruce each named 40, while Edward had 24. Obviously, this arrangement left the decision with Edward. On November 17, 1292, the majority named Balliol, whom Edward believed to be the more compliant of the two leading contenders, and he was crowned John, King of Scots, on November 30.

Edward then insisted that King John swear fealty to him. On December 26 at Newcastle upon Tyne, John swore homage to Edward, who soon made it clear that he considered Scotland entirely under English control. Edward then demanded that Scotland furnish troops and financial support for his planned invasion of France. Having to contend with the Bruce faction, which strongly opposed this, John rejected Edward's demands. Edward then called

John to appear before him and gave him a deadline of September 1, 1254, to provide the assistance demanded.

On his return to Scotland, John met with his council and, following heated debate, rejected Edward's demands. A Scottish parliament was called and a war council was established to advise the king. John also entered into negotiations with French king Philip IV (r. 1285–1314), and a treaty was concluded whereby the French and Scots allied to make common cause against England were that country to invade either Scotland or France. The treaty was to be accompanied by the marriage of John's son Edward to Joan, the niece of Philip IV. The Scots also sought a treaty with Norway for naval assistance, but it was never concluded. The alliance with France, known as the Auld Alliance, was frequently renewed and remained in effect until 1560.

Edward was not aware of the negotiations between Scotland and France until 1295, whereupon he called on John to relinquish control of certain castles and burghs and ordered forces assembled for an invasion of Scotland. With the English preparations under way, King John ordered all able-bodied Scots to assemble at Caddonlee by March 11. Several prominent Scottish nobles chose to ignore the call to arms, notable among them Robert Bruce. English forces invaded Scotland in March 1296, and the war was on.

SPENCER C. TUCKER

## Course

### *The First War for Scottish Independence (1296–1328)*

King Edward I was prepared, having secured the fealty of a number of Scottish nobles including Robert Bruce, who had never recognized John Balliol's right to the Scottish throne. Edward invaded Scotland with a large army. After taking and sacking Berwick-upon-Tweed, Edward then strengthened its defenses for a month before sending a strong force under John de Warenne, sixth Earl of Surrey, against Dunbar Castle. Its defenders appealed for assistance to king of the Scots John Balliol, camped at nearby Haddington with most of his army. Most of that force, but not King John, then moved to Dunbar.

The two armies came together on April 27, 1296. Surrey commanded some 12,000 men, while the Scots had perhaps 40,000. The Scots occupied high ground, and Surrey mounted a cavalry attack. To reach the Scots, the English had to cross a gully. In the process the English ranks broke up, and the Scots, believing that the English were retreating, abandoned their strong position and charged. The English horsemen then reappeared and routed the Scots in the course of a single charge. Thousands of Scots were slain.

Edward arrived the next day, and the castle surrendered to him. Among the prisoners were three earls and many knights. The Battle of Dunbar effectively ended the war. King John surrendered in early July and was ceremoniously stripped of his vestments of royalty and sent to England in captivity. Most of Scotland was occupied by August, and the Stone of Destiny was removed from Scone Abbey and sent to Westminster Abbey. With Scotland essentially conquered, Edward convened a Scottish parliament at Berwick, and there the Scottish nobles pledged fealty to him as the king of England.

Edward I was fighting in France against King Philip IV for control of Gascony in 1297 when he learned that the Scots had risen against him under young Scottish knight William Wallace. On September 11, Wallace and Andrew Moray led a Scottish force to defeat Edward's northern army under the Earl of Surrey. Hastily concluding a truce with the French king, Edward returned to England and assembled an army for his second invasion of Scotland. He moved the government to York (where it remained for the next six years) and called together all the nobles. None of the Scottish nobles attended and were therefore declared traitors.

Edward invaded Scotland with as many as 10,000 cavalry and 15,000 infantry, the latter including many Welsh longbowmen. The invasion went poorly at first, for Wallace, who was named guardian of Scotland in March 1298, practiced a scorched-earth policy that denied the English supplies and drew them into central Scotland.

With his army near starvation and mutiny and on the point of having to withdraw to Edinburgh, Edward learned that Wallace and the main Scottish army were at Falkirk a dozen miles away, ready to pursue the English. Edward marched to Falkirk, and on July 22, 1298, he attacked the Scots with 2,000 cavalry and 12,000 infantry. The Scots had only about 500 cavalry and 9,500 infantry. The Scottish infantry were formed in four large, tight formations known as schiltrons and armed with the long spear. Between these hedgehog-like formations were archers equipped with the Scottish short bow.

Although the English cavalry defeated the Scottish cavalry and bowmen, they were unable to penetrate and break up the tight schiltrons, and Edward ordered his cavalry to withdraw. He then employed his longbowmen to destroy the schiltrons, the men of which had nowhere to go and no means of taking cover. Advancing only on Edward's command, the English cavalry then finished off the Scots. The Battle of Falkirk was the first great victory for the English longbow but also marked the beginning of the decline of cavalry in European warfare.

A great many Scots were killed in the battle, but Wallace escaped, and the battle was therefore not conclusive. Edward's army, weakened by Wallace's scorched-earth policy, was in no position to conquer all of Scotland. Many in his army deserted, and Edward was forced to withdraw southward, convinced that disloyalty by his barons had robbed him of the fruits of his victory.

Wallace resigned his position as guardian and traveled to France to solicit aid. He later returned to Scotland and evaded capture until August 1305, when a Scottish knight loyal to Edward turned him over to the English. Tried and convicted in London of treason and atrocities against civilians in wartime, on August 23, 1305, Wallace was stripped naked and dragged through the city behind a horse. He was then strangled by hanging but released while still alive and then emasculated and eviscerated and his bowels burned before him. Then beheaded, his body was cut into four parts, and his preserved head (dipped in tar) was placed on a pike atop London Bridge.

Meanwhile, in 1299 Robert Bruce, grandson of the earlier claimant of the same name to the Scottish throne in 1290, again rallied to the English and in 1299 was appointed coregent of Scotland with William Lamberton, bishop of St. Andrews, and John Comyn, who also had claim to the Scottish throne. On the death of his father in April 1304, Robert Bruce inherited his claim to the throne.

Additional campaigns in Scotland by Edward in 1300 and 1301 led to a truce in 1302. A subsequent campaign in 1303–1304 saw the English besiege and capture the last Scottish stronghold of Stirling Castle during April–July 1304. With most of the Scottish nobles paying homage to the English, the war appeared almost over. Although Bruce was present with Edward at the capture of Stirling Castle, he secretly entered into a pact with Lamberton to pursue Scottish independence.

Bruce now set out to secure the Scottish throne. Comyn meanwhile had broken an agreement with Bruce that if either man were to renounce the throne of Scotland he would receive lands from and support the other in his claim. Comyn apparently hoped to secure the throne and lands for himself by betraying Bruce to the English. After Bruce captured a messenger carrying correspondence from Comyn to Edward that plainly implicated the former, Bruce and his associates proceeded to Greyfriar's Kirk in Dumfries and there on February 10, 1306, murdered Comyn. This action earned Bruce excommunication by the Catholic Church. Bruce, however, secured sufficient support from the nobles and prelates of Scotland to have himself declared at Scone on March 27 king of Scots as Robert I (although he was popularly known as Robert the Bruce).

King Robert's position was hardly secure, however, for Edward sent an army north. In the Battle of Methven (June 19, 1306), Aymer de Valence, Comyn's brother-in-law and the future Earl of Pembroke, surprised and defeated Robert, executing many of his supporters. Robert's army, withdrawing westward following Methven, was again defeated and all but destroyed at Dalry (probably on August 11) by the Clan MacDougall, allies of Clan Comyn and the English. Robert managed to escape and, almost alone, sought refuge on the island of Rathlin.

Robert's cause appeared hopeless. His wife and daughter were taken prisoner and held by the English in harsh conditions, and his brother was executed. Robert bided his time, and following the widespread English ravaging of Scotland that roused hatred of the occupiers, he again took the field in 1307 and was victorious over Pembroke in the Battle of Loudoun Hill on May 10, 1307. Although hardly a major battle, Loudoun Hill nonetheless reversed the negative effects of Robert's two earlier defeats. Learning from his earlier mistakes, Robert utilized mostly guerrilla tactics and raids to drive out the English, and the Scots rallied to him.

Edward now again invaded Scotland with a large army but, already ill, died on July 7, 1307. The English throne now passed to his incompetent son, Edward II (r. 1307–1327). By 1314 Robert I controlled all of Scotland except the English-held castles of Stirling, Dunbar, and Berwick.

In the spring of 1314 Edward Bruce, Robert's younger brother, instituted a siege of the major English stronghold of Stirling Castle, held by Sir Philip Mowbray. Edward Bruce and Mowbray eventually concluded an agreement that if no relief appeared by midsummer, June 24, the castle would surrender.

This arrangement forced Edward II to act. Assembling a large force of 20,000 men, he invaded Scotland in mid-June. His stated goal was to end the siege of Stirling Castle, but his actual intention was to reclaim Scotland. Edward's army was probably twice the size of the Scottish force.

King Robert prepared a defensive position of about a mile-wide front on a slope several miles south of Stirling behind the stream of Bannockburn. Flanking the Scottish position were a morass on the Scottish left and woods on their right. There was only one good approach, the old Roman road. The Scots dug pits and then covered these with brush along the approach route as traps for the English cavalry and as a means to force it to bunch up. The Scots' primary armament consisted of long spears. Of their force of some 8,000 men, only 500 were cavalry.

Mowbray knew of the Scottish preparations and warned Edward. Mowbray also informed the English king that battle was not necessary, for the king had already met the technical terms of the relief of the castle, which now would not have to surrender. Mowbray's wise counsel fell on deaf ears, however. Edward had in effect lost control of his large army, which was eager for battle.

Most medieval engagements were of short duration; the Battle of Bannockburn was unusual in that it extended over two days. Skirmishing began on June 23, 1314, as two English cavalry formations advanced, one under the Earl of Gloucester and the Earl of Hereford and the other under Robert Clifford. A celebrated single combat occurred when the English encountered some Scottish cavalry, Bruce among them. Hereford's nephew, Henry de Bohun, lowered his lance and charged Bruce, who avoided him and then split Henry's head with a battle-ax as they passed one another. The Scots halted both English cavalry formations.

The main battle took place the next day, June 24, and from the very beginning it went badly for the English. The English archers, crowded behind the cavalry, were unable to deploy to the flanks and could not employ their weapons effectively. Their arrows hit their own men in the back as often as they hit the Scots. Meanwhile, crowded into the narrow front, the English cavalry became disorganized, and

the Scottish pikemen beat back their charges. The Scots then mounted a general advance against the disorganized mass of the English army, which began to break. Edward was forcibly taken from the field by his bodyguard, but this ended what remained of the army discipline.

The Scots pursued and slew thousands of the English, although there was no accurate count. The Battle of Bannockburn was decisive, as it greatly strengthened Robert's position. Full English recognition of Scottish independence was still more than a decade away, however.

During the next years King Robert mounted a series of raids into northern England, although he was careful to avoid a major battle. Robert was able to take advantage of internal strife in England, where a number of the nobles were in rebellion against Edward.

A Scottish force also invaded Ireland in what was basically an attempt to open a second front against the English. King Robert offered to help the Irish recover their independence from the English in return for his brother Edward being given the throne of the ancient high kings of Ireland. The Irish nobles agreed, and Edward invaded Ireland in 1316 and was crowned king.

The English reestablished their control of Ireland two years later, when a force under John of Birmingham and Edmund Butler invaded and defeated Edward and a combined Scottish-Irish army in the Battle of Faughart (also known as Dundalk) on October 14, 1318. Details of the battle remain sketchy, and the actual strength of the two sides is unknown, but apparently Edward Bruce was the architect of his own defeat when he decided to attack the larger English force without waiting for reinforcements from Scotland. Bruce

Statue of King Robert the Bruce, Stirling, Scotland. (Rachelle Burnside/Dreamstime)

was among those killed. English control over Ireland remained tenuous, however.

King Edward II defeated the rebellious English nobles opposing him in the Battle of Boroughbridge on March 16, 1322. This victory allowed the English king to attempt another invasion of Scotland, but Edward again suffered defeat, in the Battle of Byland, on October 12, 1322. Although the numbers involved were far smaller than at Bannockburn, the Scottish victory was just as decisive. Edward was forced to abdicate on January 25, 1327, following a coup carried out by his wife Queen Isabella of France and her lover Roger Mortimer, who then became the de facto ruler of England. Edward II was murdered on September 21 that same year at Berkeley Castle in Gloucestershire.

The regency government of Edward III made formal peace with Scotland. The Treaty of Edinburgh-Northampton, signed in Edinburgh by King Robert on March 17, 1328, was ratified by the English Parliament at Northampton on May 1, 1328. The treaty recognized the Kingdom of Scotland as fully independent, with Robert the Bruce and his heirs and successors as its rightful rulers, and also set the border between Scotland and England as that recognized during the reign of Alexander III of Scotland. The peace arrangement was strengthened in the marriage of Robert's son and heir David to the sister of Edward III.

King Robert died the next year, in 1329, and was succeeded by David II (r. 1329–1371). As David was then only five years old, Thomas Randolph, Earl of Moray, assumed control of Scottish affairs as guardian.

In 1330 Edward III overthrew Mortimer and assumed his personal rule. One of the strongest rulers in English history, Edward was king for 50 years until his death in 1377. Determined to avenge the English defeat at the hands of the Scots, he was noted for the restoration of royal authority after the disastrous reign of his father and for his considerable military successes. Under Edward III, England became one of the major military powers of Europe, demonstrated in the field during the Hundred Years' War with France.

### The Second War for Scottish Independence (1332–1357)

The Second War for Scottish Independence began in 1332. Although England and Scotland were now technically at peace, the Disinherited, a group of Scottish nobles who had been forced into exile and lost their lands after the first war, accompanied by a number of English adventurers, began the second war by invading Scotland. They were led by Edward Balliol, son of John Balliol, deposed king of Scotland and claimant to the Scottish throne, and Henry Beaumont. The Disinherited numbered some 1,000 knights and men-at-arms and perhaps 1,500 archers.

Edward III undoubtedly supported this effort by the Disinherited and was probably in direct communication with Balliol, but he would not allow the rebels to invade across the Tweed River, as this would be too obvious a violation of the peace treaty. No doubt he agreed to pretend to be unaware of the plan that was carried out, an invasion from the sea.

The Disinherited came ashore unopposed at Kinghorn in Fife on August 6, 1332, then marched inland to Dumferline, planning to move from there against Perth. Their advance was blocked along the Earn River by new Scottish regent Domhnall II, Earl of Mar, successor to the Earl of Moray, who had died on July 20. Mar had some 2,000 heavy cavalry and 20,000 infantry.

Balliol, however, mounted a daring night crossing and attack and routed the Scots. The latter rallied, however, and attacked at dawn on August 12 with overwhelming force. Balliol's knights and men-at-arms dismounted and formed a tight phalanx on a hill, with the archers to the sides and echeloned back toward the center. The Scots attacked but were forced to fight uphill and then came up against the phalanx. Fighting was fierce, but the Scots were unable to break through. Devastated by arrow fire, they then broke and ran. The Earl of Mar was among the some 2,000 Scots slain that day.

The Battle of Dupplin Moor provided Edward III with both an excuse to invade Scotland and the tactics that he would

employ with such great success in his subsequent battles. Edward Balliol now declared himself king of Scotland, but because he yielded southern Scotland to England, he was unpopular with most Scots and was only able to hold the throne for three months. In December Sir Archibald Douglas attacked Balliol at Annan. Although most of Balliol's men were killed in the night attack, Balliol managed to escape and, although naked, rode a horse to Carlisle.

Acting on behalf of his vassal Edward Balliol against the new Scottish king, the five-year-old David II, Edward III now invaded Scotland and in April 1333 laid siege to Berwick-upon-Tweed. With that place close to surrendering, Douglas marched to its relief with up to 14,000 men. The two sides came together on July 19, 1333, on the 600-foot-high Halidon Hill, about two miles west of Berwick.

Edward held the hill with about 9,000 men. His men-at-arms were formed into three "battles," or divisions, with the flanks of each covered by archers. As at Dupplin Moor, the Scots were obliged to attack uphill. The attacking spearmen were no match for the English longbowmen, however, and suffered heavy casualties from the archers as they struggled up the slope, only to be repulsed at its crest by the English men-at-arms. Edward then ordered the men-at-arms to mount, and they rode down the fleeing Scots, slaying them with maces and swords and destroying the Scottish force. Perhaps 4,000 Scots, including Douglas, were slain for only minimal English losses. The English would employ these same tactics with devastating effectiveness against the French during the Hundred Years' War in the battles at Crécy, Poitiers, and Agincourt. Much of Scotland was now occupied by the English forces, and Balliol ceded to Edward eight lowland Scottish counties.

French king Philip VI offered deposed king David II asylum in France, and he settled in Normandy. King Philip effectively derailed negotiations then under way between England and France to resolve disputes by insisting that any arrangement between the two kingdoms would have to include David II.

Some fighting continued in Scotland, however, and in November 1334 Edward again invaded. Failing to bring the Scots to battle and accomplishing little, he withdrew in February 1335. Returning with Balliol in July 1535, Edward advanced all the way to Perth, where he remained for a time as his forces pillaged widely. Scottish resistance was limited to guerrilla warfare, avoiding pitched battles but harassing the English where possible.

After Edward's return to England, the Scots chose as guardian Sir Andrew Murray, who then concluded a truce with Edward to last until April 1336. A peace agreement was hammered out whereby the elderly and childless Edward Balliol would be king on the condition that he be succeeded by David II, who would leave France and live in England. David, however, rejected this and any new truce with England.

With the expiration of the truce, in May Henry of Lancaster led an English army into Scotland. Edward III followed with another army in July, and the two armies ravaged much of northeastern Scotland including Elgin and Aberdeen. A third English army also invaded and laid waste to southwestern Scotland and the Clyde Valley.

These English actions led French king Philip VI to declare that he would do all in his power to aid Scotland. With the French

assembling a large fleet and army for an invasion of England, Edward withdrew from Scotland, and Murray and the Scots secured the English strongholds. Although Edward invaded Scotland again, concerns about a French invasion mitigated his efforts, and by the end of 1336 the English had been cleared from most of Scotland. In 1337 Edward declared himself king of France through the lineage of his mother Isabella of France, beginning the Hundred Years' War (1337–1453). David II returned from France to Scotland in June 1341.

Ignoring truces with England and determined to aid Philip VI, David ordered a series of raids into northern England, forcing Edward to reinforce the border. Philip VI, however, appealed for a true Scottish invasion. Despite Philip's increasingly desperate calls, this did not occur until early October 1346, after Edward III had landed in France and was besieging Calais.

With so many English soldiers in France, David II expected the campaign in northern England to be an easy one. Practicing a scorched-earth policy, the Scottish army of some 12,000 men arrived at Durham on October 16. Unknown to David, however, Edward had prepared for such an eventuality, and an English army promptly assembled at Richmond under William Zouche, the archbishop of York. Given the demands of the fighting in France, however, it was only about half the size of the Scottish force. The Scots first encountered the English on the morning of October 17 during a raid south of Durham in which the Scottish force was mauled.

David then led his army to high ground at Neville's Cross to await the English attack, which occurred later the same day. The ground was not well chosen, and a stalemate ensued until the English sent longbowmen forward to harass the Scots, who then attacked. The bowmen broke up the Scottish formations, and the Scots gradually left the field, leaving David wounded and captured. During David's subsequent imprisonment, Scotland was ruled by his nephew Robert Stewart.

Edward Balliol made a final attempt to recover the throne. Invading with a small force, he was only able to secure some of Galloway. Recognizing the inevitable, in January 1356 he resigned his claim to the Scottish throne. Held in the Tower of London, David II was finally released after 11 years on October 3, 1357, as part of the Treaty of Berwick, which included payment of a enormous ransom.

SPENCER C. TUCKER

## Consequences

The Wars for Scottish Independence saw important tactical changes as well as those in weaponry, with the longbow emerging as one of the most important weapons in medieval warfare.

Scotland was now an independent kingdom. The enormous ransom for King David II's release, while it was to be paid in installments, required heavy taxes, and these alienated many Scots, especially as David diverted considerable sums for his own purposes. When David II died without an heir in 1371, his half nephew became king as Robert II, beginning the Stewart dynasty. Nine Stewart/Stuart monarchs ruled Scotland from 1371 until 1603.

The Scottish alliance with France continued until 1560, and there was some warfare with England. Yet under the Stuarts, Scotland developed from a relatively poor and feudal country into a prosperous, modern, centralized state. Religion and morality played a role, and Mary, queen of Scots, a Catholic and former queen of France who ruled Scotland from 1542, was forced to abdicate in 1567. James VI, her one-year-old son, succeeded her.

In 1603 on the death of English queen Elizabeth I, James VI in the Union of the Crowns inherited the English domains as James I of England and Ireland. Religion again interceded, and following the Glorious Revolution in 1688–1689, there were two Stuart queens: Mary II and Anne. Both were the Protestant daughters of James VII (Scotland) and II (England) by his first wife. Their father had converted to Catholicism, and his new wife gave birth to a son in 1688, who would be brought up a Roman Catholic and would precede his half sisters. Parliament then deposed James in favor of his daughters. But neither had any children who survived to adulthood, so under the terms of the Act of Settlement 1701 and the Act of Security 1704, the throne passed to the German House of Hanover on the death of Queen Anne in 1714.

On July 22, 1706, the Treaty of Union was agreed upon, and in 1707 Acts of Union were passed by both the English and Scottish Parliaments to create the United Kingdom of Great Britain, which came into force on May 1, 1707. The deposed Jacobite Stuart claimants to the throne remained popular in the Highlands and northeastern Scotland, but two major Jacobite uprisings in 1715 and 1745 failed to remove the House of Hanover from the British throne. The Jacobite threat was effectively ended with the decisive Battle of Culloden (April 16, 1746).

The Scottish Enlightenment and the Industrial Revolution beginning in the late 18th century transformed Scotland, which became recognized as an intellectual, commercial, and industrial leader. Scot David Hume was a world-renowned philosopher and historian, and James Watt invented the first commercially successful system engine. Scotland also became the leading shipbuilding center of the world.

From the mid-19th century there were increasing calls for home rule for Scotland and the cabinet post of secretary of state for Scotland was revived. Sir Walter Scott's historical novels had much to do with promoting Scottish nationalism through cultural identity.

Scotland played an important role in the two 20th-century world wars, but Scottish nationalism again came to the fore when in 1989 British prime minister Margaret Thatcher introduced the Community Charge (widely known as the Poll Tax). This intensified demands in Scotland for its control regarding domestic affairs. A referendum on devolution proposals occurred in 1997, and the next year the UK Parliament passed legislation that established a devolved Scottish Parliament and Scottish government that had control of most matters specific to Scotland.

With demands for independence increasing, a referendum was held on the matter in September 2014, but it failed when 55.3 percent voted against it. One of the reasons cited by those opposed to Scottish independence was that it would endanger Scotland being part of the European Union (EU). In May 2015 the Conservatives won the UK general election, and they then set a referendum on UK membership in the EU. The Scottish National Party, which supports Scottish independence, declared that it would consider holding a second independence referendum if there was a material change of circumstances, such as the United Kingdom leaving the EU. In the June 2016 referendum on UK membership in the EU, the Brexit (British exit) side won with 52 percent of the vote, although in Scotland 62 percent of voters favored continued EU membership. There is thus considerable discussion as to whether there should be a second Scottish independence referendum or, alternatively, if it would be possible for Scotland to maintain ties with the EU in some fashion after the UK departure.

SPENCER C. TUCKER

## Timeline

| | |
|---|---|
| **1286** | King Alexander III of Scotland dies and is succeeded by his three-year-old granddaughter, Queen Margaret. |
| **Jul 19, 1290** | Hoping to control Scotland, King Edward I of England concludes the Treaty of Birgham with the guardians, now governing Scotland. |
| **Sep 1290** | Margaret dies shortly after arriving in her new kingdom, leaving 13 possible successors. The two strongest are John Balliol, Lord of Galloway, and Robert Bruce, fifth Lord of Amnandale. |
| **May–Aug 1291** | To avoid civil war, the guardians invite King Edward to preside over a process to choose the monarch. |
| **Nov 30, 1292** | John Balliol is crowned John, King of Scots. |
| **Dec 26, 1292** | Under duress, John swears fealty to Edward but refuses to provide aid for his planned invasion of France. John then concludes a treaty |

with French king Philip IV whereby the two agree to defend each other if England should attack either country.

**Mar 1296** — Edward invades Scotland, beginning the First War of Scottish Independence.

**Apr 12, 1296** — In the Battle of Dunbar the Scots are routed, and Dunbar Castle surrenders the next day. This battle effectively ends the war.

**Early Jul 1296** — King John surrenders. The English then occupy most of Scotland, and the Scottish nobles pledge fealty to Edward.

**Sep 11, 1297** — William Wallace continues the fight in Scotland, defeating Edward's northern army under the Earl of Surrey. Edward, fighting in France, quickly concludes a truce with the French and returns to England to prepare for a second invasion of Scotland.

**Mar 1298** — Wallace is named guardian of Scotland.

**Jul 12, 1298** — Edward defeats Wallace and the Scots in the Battle of Falkirk, but Wallace's scorched-earth policy forces Edward to withdraw.

**1299** — Robert Bruce rallies to the English and is appointed coregent of Scotland with William Lamberton and John Comyn, who also has claim to the Scottish throne.

**1300–1304** — The English capture the last Scottish stronghold, Stirling Castle, in July 1304. Most of the Scottish nobles then pay homage to the English. Although Bruce is with Edward, he secretly enters into a pact with Lamberton to pursue Scottish independence.

**Aug 23, 1305** — Wallace is executed in London after being taken prisoner by the English.

**Feb 10, 1306** — Robert Bruce and associates murder Comyn at Greyfriar's Kirk in Dumfries.

**Mar 27, 1306** — Bruce secures sufficient support from the nobles and prelates of Scotland to have himself declared king as Robert I.

**Jun 19, 1306** — In the Battle of Methven, Aymer de Valence, Comyn's brother-in-law, surprises and defeats Robert.

**Aug 11, 1306** — Robert's army, withdrawing westward, is all but destroyed. Robert escapes, however, and seeks refuge on the island of Rathlin.

**May 10, 1307** — Following widespread English ravaging of Scotland, Robert again takes the field and defeats Pembroke in the Battle of Loudoun Hill. The Scots rally to Robert.

**Jul 7, 1307** — After again having invaded Scotland, Edward dies. The English throne passes to his incompetent son, Edward II.

**1314** — Robert I controls all of Scotland except the English-held castles of Stirling, Dunbar, and Berwick.

| | |
|---|---|
| **Spring 1314** | Edward Bruce, Robert's younger brother, begins a siege of the English stronghold of Stirling Castle, held by Sir Philip Mowbray. Bruce and Mowbray eventually agree that if no relief appears by June 24, the castle will surrender. |
| **Mid-Jun 1314** | As a result Edward II invades Scotland, hoping to reclaim it. Mowbray warns Edward of Scottish preparations. |
| **Jun 23–24, 1314** | The Scots decisively defeat the English in the Battle of Bannockburn. Robert then mounts a series of raids into northern England. |
| **1316** | Robert sends forces to Ireland. |
| **1318** | The English defeat Edward Bruce and a Scottish-Irish army and reestablish their control of Ireland. Bruce is among those killed. |
| **Mar 16, 1322** | King Edward II defeats the rebellious English nobles opposing him in the Battle of Boroughbridge. |
| **Oct 12, 1322** | Edward is defeated in the Battle of Byland. |
| **Jan 25, 1327** | Edward II is forced to abdicate. |
| **Sep 21, 1327** | Edward II is murdered at Berkeley Castle in Gloucestershire. |
| **May 1, 1328** | The regency government of Edward III concludes peace with Scotland in the Treaty of Edinburgh-Northampton, which recognizes Scottish independence and Robert Bruce and his heirs as Scotland's rightful rulers. |
| **Jun 7, 1329** | King Robert I dies and is succeeded by David II. As David is only five years old, Thomas Randolph, Earl of Moray, assumes control of Scottish affairs as guardian. |
| **1330** | King Edward III overthrows Roger Mortimer and assumes personal rule. |
| **Aug 6, 1332** | Edward Balliol invades Scotland and lands unopposed at Kinghorn in Fife. The Second War of Scottish independence begins. |
| **Aug 12, 1332** | The invaders defeat in the Battle of Dupplin Moor a larger Scottish force under new Scottish regent Domhnall II, Earl of Mar. Balliol now declares himself king of Scotland. |
| **Dec 1332** | Sir Archibald Douglas attacks Balliol and followers at Annan, although Balliol himself manages to escape. |
| **Apr 1333** | Acting on behalf of his vassal Balliol against the new Scottish king, Edward III invades Scotland and lays siege to Berwick-upon-Tweed. |
| **Jul 19, 1333** | Douglas marches to the relief of Berwick-upon-Tweed, and in the Battle of Halidon Hill Edward is victorious, permitting the English to occupy much of Scotland. |
| **Nov 1334** | With some fighting continuing in Scotland, Edward again invades but withdraws after three months. |

| | |
|---|---|
| **Jul 1335** | Edward and Balliol again invade Scotland, but a truce and a peace agreement are arranged, which David rejects. |
| **May 1336** | English armies invade Scotland again, but troubles with France force their withdrawal. Murray and the Scots then clear the English from most of Scotland. |
| **1337** | Edward declares himself king of France, beginning the Hundred Years' War (1337–1453). |
| **Jun 1341** | David II returns to Scotland from France and, in an effort to aid Philip VI of France, raids northern England. |
| **Oct 1346** | Finally answering Philip VI's pleas, David II mounts a major invasion of England. |
| **Nov 17, 1346** | David II is defeated and captured in the Battle of Neville's Cross. His nephew Robert Stewart now rules Scotland. |
| **Oct 3, 1357** | After 11 years, David II is released on the signing of the Treaty of Berwick that recognizes Scottish independence. |
| **Feb 22, 1371** | David II dies without an heir, and his half nephew becomes king as Robert II, beginning the Stewart dynasty. |

SPENCER C. TUCKER

## Further Reading

Bevan, Bryand. *Edward III: A Monarch of Chivalry*. London: Rubicon, 1992.

Bingham, Charlotte. *Robert the Bruce*. London: Constable, 1998.

Bothwell, James S. *The Age of Edward III*. Rochester, NY: Boydell and Brewer, 2003.

Brown, Chris. *Robert the Bruce: A Life Chronicled*. Stroud, UK: Tempus, 2004.

Cannon, John, and Ralph Griffiths. *The Oxford Illustrated History of the British Monarchy*. Oxford, UK: Oxford University Press, 1998.

Johnson, Paul. *The Life and Times of Edward III*. London: Weidenfeld and Nicolson, 1973.

Macnamee, Colm. *The Wars of the Bruces: England and Ireland, 1306–1328*. Edinburgh, UK: Donald, 2006.

Morris, John E., and Michael Prestwich. *The Welsh Wars of Edward I*. Oxford, UK: Clarendon, 1999.

Prestwich, Michael. *Edward I*. London: Edwin Methuen, 1988.

Rogers, Clifford J., ed. *The Wars of Edward III: Sources and Interpretation*. Rochester, NY: Boydell and Brewer, 1999.

Walter, Scott. *From Bannockburn to Flodden: Wallace, Bruce, & the Heroes of Medieval Scotland*. Nashville, TN: Cumberland House, 2008.

Webster, Bruce. *Medieval Scotland: The Making of an Identity*. New York: St. Martin's, 1997.

# Dutch War of Independence (1568–1648)

## Causes

The long Dutch War of Independence, also known as the Dutch Revolt, the Eighty Years' War, and the Revolt of the Netherlands, was a protracted struggle by the Dutch to secure their independence from Spain. The Kingdom of the Netherlands is today only about 16,000 square miles in size. Densely populated and with a flat topography, the Netherlands occupies a strategic position on the North Sea between Germany to the east and France and Belgium (formerly the southern Netherlands) to the southeast. Because of their location the people of the Netherlands naturally took the sea, and the wealth of the northern provinces came to be based on deep-sea fishing, while Amsterdam became in the 15th century one of the great entrepôts of Europe and the principal distribution center for grain shipped there from the Baltic region.

In the 16th century the Netherlands, also known as the Low Countries, roughly comprised what is now the Kingdom of the Netherlands, Belgium, the Grand Duchy of Luxembourg, and some adjacent territory in what is now France and Germany. The Netherlands consisted of 17 provinces, which in 1433 had been united in a personal union by Philip the Good, Duke of Burgundy. The Burgundian period began the path to nationhood. Following Philip's death in 1477 of his successor, Duke Charles the Bold, the territories were inherited by Habsburg archduke Maximilian.

There was as yet no Dutch or Belgian nationality. In the northern part of the Netherlands the people spoke German dialects, one of which came to be called Dutch, while in the south the people spoke French or French dialects, including what would be Flemish. The people of the Netherlands identified themselves not by language or region but rather by town, duchy, or county.

The rulers of the Low Countries promoted Dutch seaborne trade, which grew rapidly especially in the northern counties of Holland and Zeeland. Such trade required warships to protect it, and clashes occurred between the fleets of Holland and those of the Hanseatic League, with the warships of Holland emerging victorious.

Under Habsburg king Charles V (ruler of the Netherlands from 1506, the Spanish Empire from 1516, and the Holy Roman Empire from 1519), all fiefs in the current Netherlands region were united into the Seventeen Provinces. Still, each of these provinces was an entity unto itself, with its own government and laws dating from the Middle Ages. On occasion the provinces would be asked to send delegates to a States General, and from these there began to develop a sense of collaboration on a higher (federal) level.

The gradual growth of a separate identity in the Netherlands was greatly speeded up by the accession of King Philip II of Spain, for Charles V abdicated his many thrones in 1556 and retired to a monastery. His vast territorial holdings were divided. Charles's younger brother Ferdinand, who had already been given the Austrian lands in 1521, succeeded Charles as Holy Roman emperor. The Spanish Empire, which included the New World as well the Netherlands and holdings in Italy, went to Charles's son Philip II. A staunch Catholic

# DUTCH REVOLT, 1568–1648

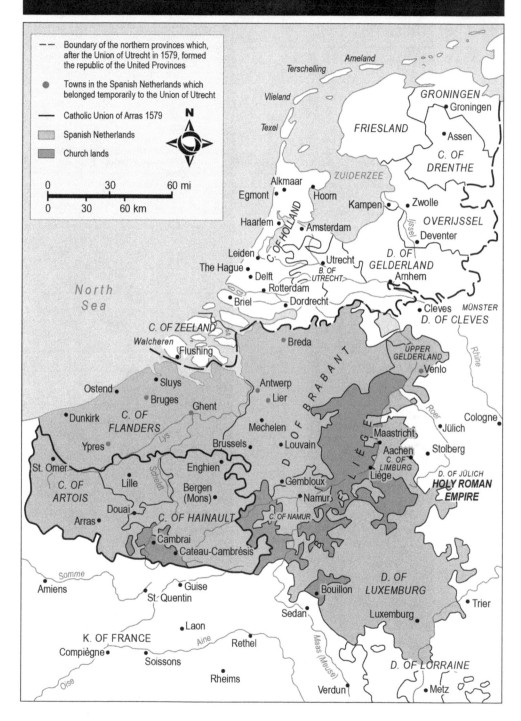

Boundary of the northern provinces which, after the Union of Utrecht in 1579, formed the republic of the United Provinces

Towns in the Spanish Netherlands which belonged temporarily to the Union of Utrecht

Catholic Union of Arras 1579

Spanish Netherlands

Church lands

0      30      60 mi

0      30      60 km

N

North Sea

Terschelling

Ameland

Vlieland

Texel

GRONINGEN
Groningen

FRIESLAND

Assen

C. OF DRENTHE

ZUIDERZEE

Alkmaar

Egmont      Hoorn

Kampen      Zwolle

Haarlem      Amsterdam

OVERIJSSEL

Deventer

Leiden

The Hague      Utrecht

Delft      B. OF UTRECHT

D. OF GELDERLAND

Arnhem

C. OF HOLLAND

IJssel

Rotterdam

Briel      Dordrecht

Cleves      MÜNSTER

D. OF CLEVES

C. OF ZEELAND

Walcheren

Flushing

Breda

UPPER GELDERLAND

Venlo

Rhine

D. OF BRABANT

Sluys

Antwerp

Ostend

Bruges      Ghent

Lier

Dunkirk      C. OF FLANDERS

Lys

Mechelen

Roer

Cologne

Jülich

Maastricht

Stolberg

Ypres

Brussels

Louvain

Aachen

LIÈGE

C. OF LIMBURG

St. Omer

Enghien

Scheldt

Bergen (Mons)

Gembloux

Liège

D. OF JÜLICH

HOLY ROMAN EMPIRE

C. OF ARTOIS

Lille

Namur

Douai

Arras

C. OF HAINAULT

C. OF NAMUR

Cambrai

Cateau-Cambrésis

Somme

Amiens

Guise

St. Quentin

Bouillon

D. OF LUXEMBURG

Trier

Sedan

Luxemburg

Laon

Aisne

Rethel

Maas (Meuse)

K. OF FRANCE

Compiègne

Soissons

Oise

Rheims

Verdun

D. OF LORRAINE

Metz

## Dutch War of Independence (1568–1648)

| Battle of Heiligerlee (May 23, 1568)* | | |
|---|---|---|
| | **Strength** | **Approximate Losses** |
| **Dutch rebels** | 4,100 men | 50 killed |
| **Spanish Friesland Army** | 3,200 men | 1,500–2,000 killed, wounded, or captured |

*First significant military engagement of the war.

| Siege of Antwerp (July–August 17, 1584) | | |
|---|---|---|
| | **Strength** | **Approximate Losses** |
| **States General of the United Provinces** | 60,000 men | 8,000 killed* |
| **Spanish forces** | 20,000 men | Unknown** |

*This figure does not include civilian deaths. As a result of the siege, as many as 50,000 people were forced from the city
**The Spanish managed to compel the surrender of Antwerp on August 17, 1584.

| Battle of Nieuwpoort (July 2, 1600) | | |
|---|---|---|
| | **Strength** | **Approximate Losses** |
| **States General of the United Provinces** | 11,000 men | 2,000 killed |
| **Spanish forces** | 12,000 men | 4,000 killed |

| Naval Battle of Gibraltar (April 25, 1607) | | |
|---|---|---|
| | **Strength** | **Approximate Losses** |
| **United Provinces** | 26 warships | 0 ships, 100 killed, 60 wounded |
| **Spanish forces** | 20 warships | 20 ships, 4,000 killed |

**Sources:** Israel, Jonathan. *The Dutch Republic: Its Rise, Greatness, and Fall, 1477–1806*. Oxford, UK: Clarendon, 2007; Parker, Geoffrey. *The Dutch Revolt*. 2nd ed. London: Penguin Books, 1990; Vere, Francis. *Salt in Their Blood: The Lives of Famous Dutch Admirals*. London: Cassell, 1955.

who spent the early years of his reign in the Netherlands before deciding to return to Spain, Philip was prepared to commit all the resources of his vast realm into preserving the Catholic faith and rooting out Protestantism wherever the latter might be found.

As an entrepôt for trade, the Netherlands was also a center of new ideas, and among these were demands for a long overdue reform of the Catholic Church. The religious revolution of the early 16th century known as the Reformation took hold in the northern Netherlands. The Brothers of the Common Life originated here, while Desiderius Erasmus, the influential advocate for reform in the church, was born in Rotterdam. The calls for religious reforms were strengthened by the arrival in the Netherlands of many French

Calvinists, who fled there after the start in 1560 of the Wars of Religion in France. Thus, initially in the southern provinces there were more adherents of what came to be known as Protestantism than in the northern Netherlands.

The revolt against Spanish rule was both religious and political, but it also came to have a strong economic component as it proceeded. Heavy-handed Spanish rule in all of these areas brought revolt and greatly aided in the development of Netherlands nationalism.

SPENCER C. TUCKER

## Course

### *The First 43 Years (1566–1609)*

The revolt in the Netherlands can be said to have begun in 1566 when some 200 nobles of both Catholic and Protestant persuasion from various provinces established a league with the avowed aim of checking "foreign" (i.e., Spanish) influence. The nobles petitioned Philip II not to introduce the Spanish Inquisition in the Netherlands. They assumed, correctly, that it would be used not only to enforce religious conformity but also to crush political liberties in the Netherlands dating from the Middle Ages.

When this petition was rejected by Philip's administrators in the Netherlands, a mass iconoclastic revolt ensued. Known as the Beeldenstorm and beginning in August 1566, it saw staunch Calvinists break into some 400 Catholic churches across the Netherlands and destroy what they considered symbols of "popery," including religious images, reliquaries, paintings, and stained glass windows. But brigands also made off with gold and silver sacramental vessels. This unrest was mainly centered in the urban industrial areas, and there was certainly an economic element to it.

Appalled at what had transpired, Philip II immediately introduced the Inquisition in the Netherlands. He also ordered there Fernando Álvarez de Toledo, Duke of Alba (Alva), and substantial troop reinforcements with instructions that they restore order. Alba established the Council of Troubles (widely known to the Dutch people as the Council of Blood). Employing torture, it tried thousands of people and sentenced them to death, sharply increased taxes, and confiscated the estates of numerous prominent nobles. These measures, however, had the effect of uniting all classes of people against the Spaniards. The leader of the revolt came to be one of the most prominent nobles of the Netherlands, William of Orange (known as William the Silent), stadtholder (lieutenant or governor) in Holland, Zeeland, Utrecht, and Friesland since 1559. William had been brought up a Lutheran but later became a Catholic. A religious man, he was, however, a staunch advocate for freedom of religion. An early favorite of Philip II, William had nonetheless spoken out in favor of Netherlander rights and had then attempted to mediate between the Spanish Crown and the people. William had retired to Nassau in April 1567 and refused to appear before the Council of Troubles when summoned there. He was declared an outlaw, and his estates were confiscated.

William now assumed in exile the authority of a sovereign. Among his actions was the issuing of letters of marque, or legal instruments for ship captains to make war at sea. Dutch fishing ships as well as ships of other nationalities now received cannon and were transformed into legal privateers. These privateersmen, many of whom were little more than pirates, became known as the Sea Beggars and began attacking Spanish merchant shipping along the coast of the Netherlands as well as on the high seas. They also raided coastal towns, looting, burning, and destroying.

The Spanish administrators in the Netherlands responded by increasing their confiscations and actions against individuals. The whole of the Netherlands was now in chaos, with no clear political or religious lines in the struggle. Gradually, however, a sense of nationalism took hold—of Netherlanders against the Spaniards.

William used his own funds to raise a largely mercenary army in Germany and sent it into the Netherlands under his brother Louis of Nassau. On May 23, 1568, the first battle of the long war occurred. In a predominantly infantry clash at the Heiligerlee monastery, Louis and his brother (also that of William) Adolf of Nassau, leading a force of some 4,100 men, met and defeated the Spanish army of Friesland of about 3,200 men under Johan de Ligne, Duke of Arenberg, the stadtholder of Friesland. The rebels lost some 50 men killed, including Adolf; the Spainards suffered 1,500 to 2,000 killed, wounded, or captured as well as the loss of seven cannon.

Louis then attempted but failed to capture the city of Groningen. Spanish troops under the Duke of Alba drove off his forces and then on July 21 engaged Louis's men in a major battle at Jemmingen (Jemgum) in East Frisia (today a state of Lower Saxony in Germany). Alba had about 12,000 infantry and 3,000 cavalry and some artillery. Louis had 10,000 infantry, some cavalry, and 16 guns.

Following three hours of skirmishing, Louis ordered his infantry to attack, whereupon it was defeated by the Spanish harquebusiers and cavalry. In the battle the rebels sustained 6,000–7,000 dead; the Spanish suffered only 80 killed and 220

wounded. Louis withdrew with the survivors toward the Ems River. For several years the Battle of Jemmingen ended resistance to Spanish rule in the northeastern Netherlands.

This defeat did not end the revolt, however. Gathering an army of some 25,000 men, William the Silent crossed the Meuse River at Stochen. The Duke of Alba had so completely terrorized the local population that few civilians rallied to William. Alba and about 16,000 Spanish troops outmaneuvered William in Brabant and in the Battle of Jodoigne on October 20, 1569, destroyed William's rear guard, forcing him to abandon the invasion and withdraw into first France and then back into Germany. The struggle now was largely limited to the sea.

Meanwhile, England became involved in the war. What occurred in the Netherlands, a natural invasion point just across the English Channel, would always be a concern for England. The revolt in the Netherlands, coupled as it was with Catholicism and Philip II, raised major concerns for English queen Elizabeth I (r. 1558–1603). Philip had been married to Queen Mary I, Elizabeth's predecessor and a staunch Catholic. Although England was now officially Protestant, Catholicism remained strong, and Elizabeth's hold on the throne was hardly secure. Waiting in the wings, although in effect Elizabeth's prisoner in England, was Mary, Queen of Scots, a Catholic who had been queen of France until her husband's premature death and then queen of Scotland until forced to flee south to England. There were real fears that Mary, enjoying the support of the pope, Philip II, and English Catholics, might lead a rebellion and usurp Elizabeth and become queen of England. Although Elizabeth was ambivalent in matters of religion, memories of the religious zeal of Mary I, known as Bloody Mary, were strong in England, and the Protestants were determined to prevent a reoccurrence. Cautious in her approach, Queen Elizabeth gradually moved toward aiding the Dutch rebels. There were calls for Protestant unity, and Elizabeth had to be concerned about the presence of so many Spanish troops just across the channel.

In 1568 the English seized some Spanish bullion ships forced to take refuge in English waters. The gold and silver they carried was to pay Alba's troops in the Netherlands. The Spaniards responded by seizing English merchant ships then in Antwerp. With the deterioration in relations between England and Spain, in the early 1570s Elizabeth lent small sums of money to the rebels and allowed English volunteers to go to their aid, but she was reluctant to commit troops and provoke an open breach with Spain. Clearly Elizabeth did not want direct Spanish control over the Netherlands, nor did she want the French to intervene and gain control of the whole channel coast.

In 1572, however, Elizabeth closed English ports to the Sea Beggars. This action, if intended to improve relations with Spain, had the opposite effect. The commander of the Sea Beggars, William van der Marck, Lord of Luney, then led some 24 Dutch ships from England. Unable to regain the Texel because of contrary winds, the Dutch ships dropped anchor in the Meuse. Van der Marck then sent a message to the leaders of the seaport of Brielle exaggerating the strength of his own force and demanding that Brielle surrender. The townspeople fled, and Van der Marck's men occupied Brielle on April 1. Although militarily insignificant (Brielle was not defended at the time), the capture of that place was a turning point in the uprising of the Netherlands against Spain in that it was the first foothold on land for the rebels at a time when the rebellion was virtually extinguished. During the next several months, uprisings against Alba's repressive rule swept the Netherlands.

During 1572–1573, however, Alba utilized his military skill and horrific practice of massacring both civilians and captured garrisons to great success. He laid siege to and took city after city, reestablishing Spanish control over most of the southern and eastern provinces of the Netherlands.

At sea during October 11–12, 1572, the Dutch Sea Beggars defeated and captured six Spanish ships in the Zuider Zee, although at considerable loss of life to their own side. Because of this Spanish reverse and a repulse in the Spanish siege of Alkmaar led by his son, Don Fadrique, in November, Alba resigned and was replaced by Luis de Requesens.

In October 1573 Spanish forces under Sancho d'Avila began a siege of Leiden. The city was well stocked with food, and its defenses were strong. Meanwhile, a sizable Spanish fleet descended on the Dutch Sea Beggars besieging Middelburg on the Walcheren Peninsula in the Scheldt estuary. The ensuing Battle of Walcheren on January 29, 1574, was hard fought, with no quarter given. It ended in a Spanish defeat with the loss of 15 of their ships.

William the Silent attempted to assist the besieged city of Leiden by sending a relief army under his brother Louis of Nassau. D'Avila then broke off the siege, and on April 14, 1574, the Spanish intercepted and defeated the relief force in the Battle of Mookerheyde near Mook southeast of Mijmegen. Both Louis and Henry of Nassau were among the Dutch killed.

Painting of the Battle of Haarlemmermeer (May 26, 1573) between Dutch and Spanish ships. The Spanish had laid siege to Haarlem in December 1572, but the Dutch naval effort to recapture this supply route to the city failed, forcing the surrender of Haarlem in July 1573 with the slaughter of its garrison by the Spaniards. (Rijksmuseum, Amsterdam)

Following his victory in the Battle of Mookerheide, in June 1574 d'Avila resumed the siege of Leiden. With the city's inhabitants near starvation, the Dutch raised the siege in October but only by cutting the dikes, flooding out the Spanish camps, and enabling Dutch Admiral Louis Boisot's ships to carry provisions to the inhabitants. Spanish commander de Requesens was unable to stop the spread of the revolt from the northern Netherlands to most of the southern provinces. The one significant Spanish success during 1575–1576 was the capture on June 30, 1576, of the Sea Beggar base of Zierikzee on an island off Zeeland.

On October 3, 1576, Spanish troops, their pay long in arrears, mutinied and then took and sacked Antwerp. This action led the northern and southern provinces of the Netherlands to set aside their religious differences. On November 6, 1576, they signed the Declaration of Ghent in which they agreed to make common cause against Spanish rule. The first major expression of national unity in the Netherlands, it called for the expulsion of Spanish troops from the Low Countries, the restoration of provincial and local rights, and an end to the persecution of Calvinists. (Religious differences, however, would bring a split in 1579 between the Calvinist north—the Union of Utrecht—and the Catholic south—the Union of Arras—that ended the union in 1584.)

Also in November 1576, King Philip II named Don Juan of Austria, hero of the great naval victory against the Ottomans in the Battle of Lepanto and his half brother, as viceroy in the Netherlands. Don Juan planned not only to pacify the Netherlands. After consultations with the papacy, his grand design was to invade England with a large Spanish army from the Netherlands; marry Mary Stuart, Queen of Scots; and restore England to Catholicism.

On January 31, 1578, Alessandro Farnese, later the duke of Parma, commanding an advance force of 1,200 men from the main Spanish army of 20,000 under Don Juan of Austria, attacked a mixed force of 20,000 Dutch, Flemish, English, Scottish, German, French, and Walloon soldiers under Antoine de Goignies withdrawing toward Brussels (Bruxelles). In this Battle of Gembloux (Gemblours), Farnese defeated the Netherlander cavalry rear guard, driving it through the infantry columns and panicking the latter. Dutch casualties may have reached 6,000 dead, while Spanish losses were but few. De Goignies was among those taken prisoner.

Don Juan of Austria died on October 1, 1578, and was succeeded by Alessandro Farnese. Thanks to the Battle of Gembloux, the capable Farnese was able to employ a combination of force and persuasion to reestablish firm Spanish control over the southern Netherlands. This was a gradual process, commencing with Masstricht in March 1579 and ending with Antwerp in August 1585. (In 1586 on the death of his father, Farnese succeeded him as the duke of Parma.)

Farnese's successes, however, led the leaders of the provinces of the northern Netherlands to come together, and in the Union of Utrecht signed in that city on January 23, 1579, they established a confederation known as the United Provinces of the Netherlands. This action marks the beginning of what was commonly referred to as

the Dutch Republic and would later become the modern state of the Netherlands. The States General then elected William the Silent as stadtholder (governor) of the northern provinces. A geographic line had now been established between the southern and northern Netherlands, although neither side was prepared to accept it as final.

William the Silent was assassinated on July 10, 1584. The deed was carried out by Burgundian Balthasar Gérard, a staunch Catholic and supporter of Philip II who hoped to claim the 25,000-crown reward promised by the Spanish king for William's death. Gérard was caught before he could escape, however. Tortured and sentenced to death, he was ordered executed in a particularly prolonged and heinous fashion. William's 17-year-old son, Maurice of Nassau, succeeded him as stadtholder.

Also in July 1584, Spanish forces initiated a siege of Antwerp in what became one of the most important battles of the Dutch struggle for independence. Located on the Scheldt River that connects it with the North Sea, Antwerp was in 1584 a large city of about 100,000 people and Northern Europe's most important economic center. The year before Spanish forces had captured both Diest and Westerlo, cutting communications between Antwerp and Brussels, and Farnese now decided to take Antwerp. The Spanish first captured a series of strategic positions that cut the city from the sea. For operations against Antwerp, Farnese had at his disposal some 60,000 men, while Philippe de Marnix, Lord of Sainte-Aldegonde and commander of the Antwerp garrison, commanded about 20,000 men. Antwerp's defenses were strong, leading Farense to believe that it would be next to impossible to take the city by storm. He therefore decided to starve it into submission.

To isolate Antwerp, Farnese caused to be built a series of strongpoints and also a blockading pontoon bridge on the Scheldt River to cut off seaborne supply to the city. Completed in February 1585 and said to have been designed by Farnese himself, the 800-yard-long bridge was an impressive engineering feat. Italian engineers Giambattista Piatti and Properzio Boracci supervised its construction. The bridge had a road running its entire length with parapets on either side to protect against musket fire. Thirty-two barges moored side by side in the Scheldt supported the center portion of the bridge. Each barge mounted two large cannon, one at the bow and another at the stern. The two wings of the bridge, each about 180 yards long, rested on pilings. Two powerful Spanish forts with 10 cannon each guarded the ends of the bridge, and there was also a mobile river defense force of 20 galleys.

The Dutch were not idle, however. They employed Italian engineer Federico Giambelli (or Gianibelli) and a Fleming named den Bosche to develop devices with which to attack the bridge. These included floating casks known as "porcupines" that had sharp metal points on the outside and inflammables within. These and a raft filled with cannon powder to be ignited from the bank when it struck the bridge all failed in their design. Den Bosche then came up with an armed craft filled with 1,000 men and mounting cannon, but Spanish artillery fire drove it ashore, where it was destroyed.

In the spring of 1585 Giambelli designed large flat-bottomed barges with reinforced sides. These were filled with explosives covered with shrapnel. The charges were to be set off by clockwork devices. On April 5 he sent four of these against the bridge. Only one worked, but the resulting explosion blew out nearly 100 yards of the span and killed some 800 Spaniards, with Farnese himself only narrowly escaping death. The Dutch were unable to exploit this temporary advantage, however, and the Spaniards soon repaired the bridge and came up with a system whereby one or more of the pontoon barges could be moved in order to let any floating incendiary device pass through.

With starvation now taking hold in Antwerp, the Dutch attempted sorties from the city as well as several relief expeditions, but Farnese easily defeated these and launched his own attacks. Early in August 1585 the Spanish captured the city's citadel, whereupon Antwerp surrendered on August 17. The Dutch, who controlled both banks of the Scheldt River estuary, then closed off the river to commerce, leading to Antwerp's decline and the exodus of more than half its population.

With the Spanish siege of Antwerp in progress, England entered the fray openly. Queen Elizabeth had sought to prevent an open breach with Spain, but England was now emerging as the Protestant champion, and in 1585 she finally agreed to the pleas of several key advisers and, in the Treaty of Nonsuch signed at Nonsuch Palace in Surrey on August 10, 1585, in the first international treaty by what would become the Dutch Republic, Elizabeth agreed to send to the Netherlands 5,000 foot soldiers and 1,000 cavalry. This action is taken as marking the beginning of the undeclared Anglo-Spanish War of 1585–1604. Elizabeth's favorite, Robert Dudley, Earl of Leicester, had command. Unfortunately for the cause, Leicester proved to be an inept military leader, and the English forces were withdrawn in 1587.

At the Escorial in Spain, Philip II became convinced that the Netherlands could now only be completely restored to Spanish rule by a Spanish invasion and conquest of England. As justification, there was not only the matter of English aid to the Dutch rebels but also Sir Francis Drake's raids against Spanish treasure ships on the high seas. The Spanish plan seemed simple enough. The duke of Parma would collect sufficient shipping and then utilize his battle-hardened troops in the Netherlands for a rapid invasion and conquest of England. To accomplish this, however, the Spaniards needed control, albeit brief, of the English Channel. Toward that end, Philip readied what became known in Spain as the Invincible Armada, a collection of warships that would rendezvous with Parma and convoy his invasion force to England.

The Spanish plans were well known in England, and Elizabeth did what she could to prepare. Mary, Queen of Scots, was executed in 1587, and Francis Drake led an English raid on the Spanish port of Cádiz, effecting considerable damage to the invasion preparations and delaying but not preventing the armada from sailing.

While delayed by Drake's raid, the Spanish Armada of 130 ships, totaling 58,000 tons and carrying 30,000 men and 2,400 pieces of artillery, was the most powerful naval force yet assembled. It sailed north from Spain in May 1588 but in late July and August was harassed by smaller and more nimble English warships in a running fight in the English Channel. The Spanish ships then sought refuge at the French port of Calais but were driven from there and out to sea by English fireships. A great gale known as the Protestant Wind swept the Spanish ships northward. Only two-thirds of them made it back to Spain and only after having to circumnavigate the British Isles. Some 20,000 lives were lost. As a consequence of the armada debacle, England was spared invasion and

the Dutch rebels were emboldened, with their warships now having virtual free range over the Netherlands coast.

Fighting on ground in the Netherlands continued, however. On September 23, 1588, Parma laid siege to Bergen-op-Zoom with 20,0000 men, opposed by an Anglo-Dutch force of only some 5,000 men under Thomas Morgan and Peregrine Bertie. The siege ended on November 13 with the appearance of Dutch forces under Maurice of Nassau, who had taken the offensive. On March 4, 1590, Maurice captured Breda in a surprise attack, the initial assault force being hidden in a peat barge.

Spanish military efforts in the Netherlands ground to a halt when King Philip II ordered Parma to aid the remnants of the Catholic League Army in the ongoing religious wars between Catholics and Protestants in France. Parma advanced on Paris, forcing the Protestant champion Henri of Navarre to raise the siege of that place and allow Parma to resupply and reinforce that Catholic stronghold. Maurice took advantage of the absence of Parma and sizable Spanish forces to expanded Dutch offensive operations in the southern Netherlands. Maurice captured Zutphen after a short siege in June 1591, then took Deventer in July.

Parma returned to the Netherlands in August and threatened Utrecht. Following inconclusive maneuvers between Parma's forces and those of Maurice, King Philip II ordered Parma to return to France to relieve the city of Rouen, then under siege by Protestant forces under Henri. Parma's renewed absence stretched Spanish forces thin in the Netherlands and allowed Maurice to resume offensive operations. In a series of actions marked by rapid movement and excellent use of concentrated artillery fire,

Maurice captured Hulst in September 1591 and Nijmegen that October.

Parma died in France in December 1592, greatly easing Maurice's military efforts. Parma's successor as governor of the Spanish Netherlands from 1592 to 1594 was Count Peter Ernst I von Mansfeld-Vorderortt. A German officer in the employ of Spain, he had seen considerable fighting in the Netherlands since the beginning of the war but proved unable to halt the Dutch under Maurice.

During 1594–1595, Maurice consolidated his control of the northern Netherlands while preparing for operations against the southern Netherlands. On January 24, 1597, commanding a cavalry force of perhaps 7,000 men, Maurice met and defeated an isolated Spanish cavalry force of perhaps 6,000 men under Jean de Ris of Varax at Turnhout in the border area between the northern and southern Netherlands. The Spaniards suffered perhaps 2,000 killed, including Varax, while the Dutch had only some 100 dead.

Philip II died in 1598 a broken man. He had squandered and lost the vast wealth of his kingdoms in his futile religious crusade. Despite this, his successor Philip III (r. 1598–1621) continued the struggle. In 1599 Archduke Albrecht (Albert) of Austria, King Philip II of Spain's son-in-law, became viceroy in the Netherlands. Although Albrecht consolidated Spanish control in the southern Netherlands, he was unable to reconquer the northern Netherlands.

In June 1600, the States General of the United Provinces ordered Maurice to undertake offensive operations to secure a coastal strip of Flanders as far as Nieuwpoort (today in Belgium) and Dunkerque (Dunkirk, in France). Crossing the Scheldt in late June, Maurice drove off Spanish forces blockading Ostend. He then crossed the Yser River and deployed his army among sand dunes along the coast near Nieuwpoort (Nieuport).

On July 2 Archduke Albrecht's army of 12,000 Spanish troops, moving inland from the coast, clashed with Maurice's force of 11,000 in the Battle of Nieuwpoort (also known as the Battle of the Dunes). The Spanish had the best of the early fighting but were tired from several days of hard marching, and the greater mobility and effective artillery fire of the Dutch told. Breaking through the Spanish line, the Dutch forced their enemy to withdraw. Spanish losses approached 4,000 men, while the Dutch lost only half that number. Despite this victory, Maurice was soon forced to raise the siege of Nieuwpoort and withdraw.

Dutch successes at sea helped bring about an armistice, concluded on April 12, 1607, between the United Provinces and the Habsburg southern Netherlands. It was to be valid for eight months and take effect on May 4. The cease-fire was later extended to include operations at sea.

The cease-fire came too late to prevent an important sea battle. With the Spanish having attacked ships of the Dutch East India Company, the Dutch were determined to retaliate and ordered construction of a number of large warships. Jacob van Heenskerk received the command as admiral general and set sail for Spain. On April 24, 1607, Heenskerk, with 26 warships and 4 transports, learned of the approach of 20 Spanish galleons commanded by Admiral Don Juan Alvarez d'Avila headed for Cádiz.

The next afternoon in the Battle of Gibraltar the Dutch intercepted the Spanish ships and engaged them. Both van Heenskerk and Avila were killed in the battle, which ended at dusk in a great Dutch victory. All the Spanish ships were destroyed and more than 4,000 of their seamen killed. The Dutch lost no ships and had only 100 men dead and 60 wounded in what is regarded as the first great sea battle fought by the Dutch Navy.

### The Twelve Year's Truce

On April 9, 1609, the Twelve Years' Truce went into effect. This was the later name for a cease-fire between the United Provinces of the northern Netherlands and the Spanish-controlled southern Netherlands. Mediated by France and England, the cease-fire lasted until August 1621. The line between the two warring parties was drawn farther north than what had been the case under Parma because of the Spaniards having retaken Antwerp and other cities in the middle area. Nonetheless, the truce proved to be of immense advantage to the Dutch, who used this period to consolidate their independent status and greatly expand their military power, especially in the naval sphere.

### Dutch Involvement in the Early Stages of the Thirty Years' War and the Dutch Republic under Siege (1619–1629)

In 1618, the Thirty Years' War (1618–1648) began. This great conflict dominated Europe in the first half of the 19th century. This complex and confusing struggle that engulfed most of continental Europe began essentially as a religious strife in the Holy Roman Empire between Catholics and Protestants. Yet it was also from the beginning entwined with politics, for the great German princes, whether Catholic or Protestant, all sought to retain or even expand their own authority against the centralizing efforts of the Roman emperors, who

sought to establish a unitary state completely under their influence. Increasingly the war shifted from the religious to the political.

The war began in Bohemia, the ruler of which had embraced Protestantism and sought to break away from the Holy Roman Empire, and came to involve the German states. Ultimately it pitted the Habsburg German emperors of Austria, the Catholic German states, and Spain against the Protestant German states, Denmark, Sweden, and France. The latter three states, especially France, sought not only to contain Habsburg power but also to carve off parts of the empire for themselves. The war was incredibly complex, with constantly shifting alliances. It was fought largely on German territory but also in the Netherlands, Denmark, Italy, and France.

The Thirty Years' War devastated Germany. Some historians hold that up to half of the population died either directly in the conflict or from famine and disease related to the fighting. The Westphalia peace settlement of 1648 atomized Germany and created a great political vacuum that invited outside intervention and delayed unification until the second half of the 19th century. Because Spain was forced to dissipate its military efforts, the war greatly aided the Dutch in securing their independence.

Early in the fighting the Dutch provided subsidies to the Protestant side. On August 9, 1621, the Twelve Years' Truce came to an end with a renewal of warfare between the Spanish and Dutch. Prince Maurice of Nassau led the Dutch side, while the great Spanish general Don Ambrogio Spinola Doria, Marques de los Balbases, commanded the Spanish forces.

In the summer of 1622, Spanish forces under Spinola invaded Holland and laid siege to Bergen-op-Zoom. Protestant generals Duke Christian of Brunswick and Count Peter Ernst von Mansfeld, serving under Maurice, marched to the rescue but were intercepted en route at Fleurus in present-day Belgium by Spanish general Gonzalo Fernández de Córdoba. The Protestant side had 14,000 men and 11 guns, the Catholics only 8,000 men and 4 guns. Yet in the ensuing desperate combat of August 29, the Protestants suffered perhaps 5,000 casualties (Christian was among the badly wounded) and the Catholics only 1,200. The remaining Protestant forces escaped under Mansfeld's direction and reached Bergen-op-Zoom, where they surprised Spinola and caused him to raise the siege.

Prominent officials in the court of Spanish king Philip IV (r. 1621–1665), most notably Prime Minister Gaspar Guzmán, Duke of Sanlucar and Count of Olivares, were jealous of Spinola's military successes and may have sought to set him up for failure. In any case, they persuaded Spanish king Philip IV to order Spinola to lay siege to the fortified city of Breda, a Dutch stronghold in northern Brabant that many considered impregnable.

Spinola moved against Breda with the 60,000-man Army of Flanders. Prince Maurice of Nassau had garrisoned Breda with about 9,000 troops, supported by artillery. The Dutch had also improved its defenses with moats, trenches, and revetments. Unlike previous Spanish sieges of Dutch towns (except that of Jülich during 1621–1622), Spinola opted to starve out the city rather than attempt to take it by storm. The siege began on August 28, 1624, and ended on June 5, 1625. Throughout, raising the siege was the focus of all Dutch military efforts.

Spinola made his preparations with great care, mounting his artillery on raised platforms so as to secure maximum effectiveness. He also ordered the construction of barricades to block major egress points from Breda so that his troops would be able to defeat any sorties by the besieged. At the same time, Spinola held back most of his cavalry and infantry in a mobile reserve so as to be able to counter anticipated Dutch relief operations.

The Dutch did attempt sorties from Breda, and Prince Maurice endeavored to get supplies into the city. All met rebuff, including several efforts by Mansfeld. At the same time, Maurice refused Spinola's efforts to draw him into a pitched battle.

The winter of 1624–1625 was severe, and both sides, especially the Spaniards in their improvised field shelters, suffered from the cold, ice, and freezing wind. With the arrival of spring, the Dutch, reinforced by German troops, mounted several unsuccessful attempts to break the siege. Maurice died on April 23, 1625. He was succeeded as stadtholder of Holland by his younger brother Prince Frederik Hendrik (Frederick Henry), who continued his predecessor's policy of refusing decisive battle with Spinola. Frederick Henry did continue efforts to relieve Breda, sending Mansfeld and 12,000 men on a fifth attempt to reach the city with supplies.

On May 12, in an effort to distract the besiegers, 2,000 Dutch sortied from Breda against what they mistakenly perceived to be a weak point in the Spaniards' line. At the same time, Mansfeld approached Breda from the opposite direction. Spinola then beat back both Dutch military efforts, with heavy losses for the latter. Spinola meanwhile had increased the numbers of his artillery pieces and was largely able to silence the guns of the fortress. He then brought up heavy battering guns, and their fire effected breaches in the city walls.

On June 5, 1625, with all hope of relief gone and the Spaniards within the city, Governor Justinius van Nassau surrendered Breda under favorable terms. The defenders were allowed to depart the city with their personal weapons, four artillery pieces, and such personal possessions as they could carry. Four thousand left. Another 5,000 had been killed in the siege. In addition, some 8,000 civilians died, largely from disease and hunger. Breda remained in Spanish hands until the Dutch retook it in 1637.

The Spanish success at Breda was actually a detriment to their overall plans. The city had little strategic value, and the siege was very costly in financial terms. Its heavy drain on troop resources also prevented the Spaniards from pursuing other arguably more profitable goals.

### The Dutch Republic on the Offensive (1629–1648)

A major naval battle occurred between the Spaniards and the Dutch in September 1631, the Spaniards having assembled at Antwerp some 90 small ships to carry 5,500 men. Don Francisco de Moncada, Marquis of Aytona, had nominal command, although actual command was vested in Count Jan van Nassau Siegen. The Spanish planned to sail from Antwerp and land the troops on Goeree and Overflakee islands, presenting the Dutch with a fait accompli. Control of the two large fortresses on each side of the Volkerak Strait would enable the Spanish to blockade the Dutch Hellevoetsluis naval base on Voone Island and cut off the province of Zealand from the remaining Dutch provinces.

Having discovered the Spanish plans, the Dutch sent out 50 ships, most of which were small riverine craft. Vice Admiral Marinus Hollare had command. The Dutch intercepted the Spaniards in the eastern Scheldt on September 12. The subsequent Spanish attempt to capture the more southern island of Tholen was foiled by the timely arrival of 2,000 English mercenaries who were able to wade to the island at low tide.

Van Nassau then decided to attempt to sneak past the Dutch fleet during the night of September 12–13 in hopes of accomplishing his original goal. Having discovered the attempt, the Dutch allowed the Spanish fleet to pass and then suddenly attacked it from behind in the Slaak of Volkerak Channel. Many Spaniards were drowned, and more than 1,000 were taken prisoner. Van Nassau and perhaps only one-third of his fleet managed to regain Antwerp.

On August 22, 1632, Prince Frederik Hendrik captured Masstricht. Peace negotiations then began between the Dutch and Spaniards, but nothing came of the effort. In February 1635, however, the Dutch signed a treaty of alliance with France. This committed the Dutch to a joint invasion with France of the Spanish Netherlands that same year. The treaty provided for a partition of the Spanish Netherlands, with its disposition depending on what transpired. If the inhabitants were to rise up against Spain, the southern Netherlands would be granted independence along the lines of the Swiss cantons, with the exception of the Flemish seacoast, with Namur and Thionville going to France and Breda, Geldern, and Hulst annexed by the Dutch Republic. If the inhabitants of the Spanish Netherlands resisted, however, it would be partitioned, with France receiving the Francophone provinces and western Flanders and the Dutch taking the remainder. This latter opened the prospect that Antwerp would be reunited with the republic and that the Scheldt would be reopened for trade, which Amsterdam greatly opposed. Dutch Calvinists were also unhappy with a provision that the Catholic religion would be preserved in its entirety in those provinces apportioned to the republic.

The joint invasion of the Spanish Netherlands by France and the republic did not go well, however. The Spaniards blocked the French invasion of May 1535 and then concentrated their resources on the Dutch, with the hope of driving them from the war and then treating with the French. After checking the Dutch, the Spaniards captured the strategically important fortress of the Schenkenschans. Located on an island in the Rhine near Cleves, it controlled access to the Dutch heartland along the north bank of the Rhine. Cleves itself was also taken from the Dutch, and Spanish forces overran the Meierij.

The Dutch could not let this Spanish and imperial success stand. Frederick Henry assembled a large force and paid siege to the Schenkenschans, maintaining it even in the winter of 1635–1636. In a major blow for Spain, the Spanish garrison in Schenkenschans surrendered in April 1636.

In 1637 Frederick Henry managed to recapture Breda in the Fourth Siege of Breda (July 21–October 11, 1637). This operation was the stadtholder's last success on land for some time, as the peace party in the republic, despite his objections and an improvement in the Dutch economy, cut expenditures for the war and with it the size of the Dutch Army.

The Dutch did achieve success at sea, however. In the late summer of 1639, Madrid dispatched to Flanders a great armada of 70 ships under Don António Oquendo with the plan to engage and destroy the Dutch fleet, recently reorganized under Admiral Maarten Harpertzsoon Tromp. Oquendo's warships were also escorting 50 transports with up to 24,000 infantry intended for service in the Netherlands.

Tromp met the Spaniards on September 16 with only 17 ships of his own but in fighting extending over three days prevented them from reaching the Netherlands. Indeed, he forced the Spaniards to withdraw. The Spanish ships then anchored in English waters in the Downs roadstead off Kent.

English king Charles I attempted to deal with both sides. He offered the French access to the Spanish fleet in return for the restoration of the Rhenish Palatinate, which they had taken. To the Spaniards he offered protection in return for substantial cash. An English fleet under Admiral John Pennington was to prevent the Dutch from attacking.

While negotiations were in progress, Oquendo managed to get a dozen of his transports across to the Netherlands. Fishing boats also shuttled some of the remaining infantrymen there. At the same time, however, Tromp built up his own strength.

On October 21 Tromp attacked the Spanish fleet in English waters, detaching some of his ships under Admiral Witte Corneliszoon de With to prevent the English from interfering. Oquendo decided to try to reach Dunkerque, but only 16 of his ships succeeded in this. Some 7,000 Spaniards died in this Battle of the Downs. This important Dutch victory ended what remained of Spanish naval power, gave the Dutch undisputed naval supremacy in their conflict with Spain, and seriously weakened the Spanish military position on land. In Asia and in the Americas the war went well for the Dutch, although this was part of the long struggle carried out by proxies in the

Dutch West India and the United East India Company.

General exhaustion brought both the Dutch War of Independence and the Thirty Years' War to an end in 1648. On January 30, the Dutch Republic and the Kingdom of Spain concluded peace in the Treaty of Münster, ratified in that city on May 15, 1648. Spain recognized the independence of the United Provinces of the Netherlands. The Dutch secured some territorial gains in the southern Netherlands, but the rest of the southern Netherlands remained under Spanish control. Warfare in Germany continued into the fall as negotiations involving the other parties proceeded. Two other treaties, both signed on October 24, 1648, joined the May treaty to form the Peace of Westphalia ending the Thirty Years' War: the Treaty of Münster, between the Holy Roman Empire and France and their respective allies, and the Treaty of Osnabrück, between the Holy Roman Empire and Sweden and their respective allies.

SPENCER C. TUCKER

## Consequences

The end result of the long Dutch War for Independence was a permanent split of the former Habsburg Netherlands. The 7 northern provinces of the Dutch Republic constituted roughly the territory comprising the present-day Kingdom of the Netherlands, while the 10 provinces of the Spanish or southern Netherlands (which became the Austrian Netherlands between 1714 and 1797) approximated present-day Belgium, Luxembourg, and the Nord-Pas-de-Calais region of France (since 2016 part of the new region of Hauts-de-France).

The Dutch Republic now was one of the great powers of Europe. Most of the burghers in the Dutch Republic were Calvinist,

which was also the favored state religion, but with perhaps a third of the population remaining Catholic, the Dutch wisely adopted a policy of religious toleration.

Dutch power was based largely on economic wealth as a consequence of the carrying trade and important colonial possessions secured through two Dutch chartered companies: the United East India Company and the Dutch West India Company. Among Dutch overseas efforts, Dutch colonists founded New Amsterdam (the future New York) in 1607 and settled in Southern Africa in midcentury.

The Dutch were a major naval power and dominated the carrying trade of Europe. With the English also taking to the seas and establishing overseas colonies, an intense rivalry ensued between the two states. This in turn led to a series of wars: the First Anglo-Dutch War (1652–1654), the Second Anglo-Dutch War (1665–1667), the Third Anglo-Dutch War (1672–1674), and the Fourth Anglo-Dutch War (1781–1784). Fought largely at sea for world mastery, these wars did not go well for the Dutch.

The Dutch Republic then also became embroiled in the Wars of the French Revolution and Napoleon during 1793–1815. France invaded and made the republic into a satellite as the Batavian Republic. In 1806, Napoleon dissolved the Batavian Republic and established a monarchy with his brother, Louis Bonaparte, as king of the Netherlands. Napoleon removed Louis from power in 1810, and the country was then ruled directly from France until its liberation in 1813.

In 1797 meanwhile, the British conclusively defeated the Dutch at sea in the Battle of Camperdown. Following the French takeover of the Kingdom of the Netherlands, Britain absorbed most of the Dutch colonies. Some of these were returned, but in 1815 the British kept Cape Colony, Gyana, and Ceylon (present-day Sri Lanka). The Dutch were left with the Dutch East Indies (present-day Indonesia), Suriname (which they had captured in May 1804), the Dutch Antilles, and the trading post at Dejima in Japan.

The history of the Spanish Netherlands was quite different. The southern Netherlands had been devastated by the long fighting of the Eighty Years' War, and its great port of Antwerp fell into decline thanks to Dutch control of both banks of the Scheldt River. There was no religious toleration in the south. Protestants there either fled to the north or became Catholics so that the population in the Spanish Netherlands came to be solidly Catholic. In 1714 the Spanish Netherlands became the Austrian Netherlands. This arrangement lasted until 1797, when after the defeat of Austria by France in the Wars of the French Revolution this territory was ceded to France. In the territorial rearrangement of Europe that followed the defeat of Napoleon, Austria ceded its possession to the Dutch, creating the United Kingdom of the Netherlands. This arrangement did not last, however, for the southern Catholics who spoke French or Flemish rather than Dutch resented the heavy-handed Dutch rule. In 1830 a revolution occurred in Brussels, leading to the expulsion of the Dutch. Although the Dutch sought to reconquer the southern Netherlands by force, British and French intervention led to the establishment of the Kingdom of Belgium. Luxembourg also became fully independent.

Spain remained the foremost military power in Europe for another half century, but the long war in the Netherlands and the Thirty Years' War ruined it financially. Its vast holdings of gold and silver taken from the New World all went to pay for the war rather than be invested in the Spanish economy. Inflation, heavy taxes, emigration, and a rigid class structure all took their toll, and Spain entered into a protracted period of decline.

SPENCER C. TUCKER

## Timeline

| | |
|---|---|
| 1433 | The 17 provinces of the Low Countries, what comes to constitute the Spanish Netherlands, are united in a personal union by Philip the Good, Duke of Burgundy. |
| 1477 | The Low Countries pass to the rule of Habsburg archduke Maximilian. |
| 1556 | Holy Roman emperor Charles V dies, and the Netherlands now pass to his son Philip, who also becomes king of Spain as Philip II. |
| | The Dutch Revolt begins when some 200 Catholics and Protestants establish a league with the aim of checking "foreign" (i.e., Spanish) influence. The nobles petition Philip II not to introduce the Spanish Inquisition in the Netherlands. |
| Aug 1566 | When Philip II rejects the petition, a mass iconoclastic revolt known as the Beeldenstorm breaks out. Appalled, Philip II introduces the |

Inquisition in the Netherlands and orders Fernando Álvarez de Toledo, Duke of Alba (Alva), to establish the Council of Troubles, which executes thousands of people and confiscates the nobles' estates. The revolt is led by William of Orange (known as William the Silent). Summoned to appear before the Council of Troubles, he refuses and is declared an outlaw. William now issues letters of marque for seamen to prey on Spanish shipping. Spanish administrators respond with more force, and the whole of the Netherlands lapses into chaos.

| | |
|---|---|
| **May 23, 1568** | In the first land battle of the war, fought at the Heiligerlee monastery, William's brothers Louis of Nassau and Adolf of Nassau defeat a Spanish force under Johan de Ligne. |
| **Jul 21, 1568** | Spanish troops under the duke of Alba defeat the rebels under Louis at Jemmingen (Jemgum) in East Frisia. |
| **Oct 20, 1568** | In the Battle of Jodoigne in Brabant, Alba defeats a rebel army under William the Silent, who withdraws back into Germany. The struggle is now largely limited to the sea. |
| **Early 1570s** | England's Queen Elizabeth extends some covert aid to the Dutch rebels. |
| **Apr 1, 1572** | With 24 Dutch ships, William van der Marck, Lord of Luney, seizes the seaport of Brielle in what is something of a turning point in the war. |
| **1572–1573** | Alba reestablishes Spanish control over most of the southern and eastern provinces of the Netherlands. |
| **Oct 11–12, 1572** | The Sea Beggars capture six Spanish ships in the Zuider Zee. |
| **Nov 1572** | The Spanish reversal in the Zuider Zee and a repulse in the siege of Alkmaar lead Alba to resign. Luis de Requesens replaces him. |
| **Oct 1573** | Spanish forces under Sancho d'Avila besiege Leiden. |
| **Jan 29, 1574** | In the Battle of Walcheren the Spaniards are defeated, losing 15 of their ships. |
| **Apr 14, 1574** | D'Avila intercepts and defeats Louis in the Battle of Mookerheyde. Both Louis and Henry of Nassau are killed. |
| **Oct 3, 1574** | D'Avila resumes the siege of Leiden. With the city near starvation, the Dutch force the Spaniards to end the siege by cutting the dikes. |
| **Jun 30, 1576** | The Spanish capture the Sea Beggar base of Zierikzee on an island off Zeeland. |
| **Oct 3, 1576** | Spanish troops, their pay long in arrears, mutiny and sack Antwerp. |
| **Nov 1576** | King Philip II names his half brother, Don Juan of Austria, as viceroy in the Netherlands. |

| | |
|---|---|
| **Nov 6, 1576** | The northern and southern provinces of the Netherlands sign the Declaration of Ghent in which they agree to jointly fight against Spain. |
| **Jan 31, 1578** | In the Battle of Gembloux (Gemblours), a Spanish force under Alessandro Farnese inflicts a major defeat on a far larger force of Dutch, Flemish, English, Scottish, German, French, and Walloon soldiers. |
| **Oct 1, 1578** | Don Juan of Austria dies. His successor Alessandro Farnese then reestablishes Spanish control over the southern Netherlands. |
| **Jan 23, 1579** | Farnese's successes cause the northern provinces to form the Union of Utrecht, a confederation known as the United Provinces of the Netherlands. This marks the beginning of what was commonly referred to as the Dutch Republic. The States General elects William the Silent stadtholder. |
| **Jul 1584–Aug 17, 1584** | In one of the most important military events of the war, Spanish forces under Farnese besiege Antwerp and force its surrender. |
| **Jul 10, 1584** | William the Silent is assassinated, and his son, Maurice of Nassau, succeeds him as stadtholder. |
| **Aug 10, 1585** | England enters the war openly, beginning the undeclared Anglo-Spanish War of 1585–1604. Philip II orders preparations begun for what will be known in Spain as the Invincible Armada. |
| **Apr–Jul 1587** | Sir Francis Drake leads an English raid on the Spanish port of Cádiz, delaying but not preventing the armada from sailing. |
| **May 1588** | The Spanish Armada of 130 ships sails north from Spain. |
| **Sep 23–Nov 13, 1588** | The siege of Bergen-op-Zoom by Parma occurs. It ends with the arrival of Dutch forces under Maurice of Nassau. |
| **1590–1591** | Spanish military efforts in the Netherlands largely halt when Philip II orders Parma to aid Catholic forces in France. Maurice expands Dutch offensive operations in the southern Netherlands, capturing Zutphen in June 1591 and Deventer in July. Maurice captures Hulst in September 1591 and Nijmegen in October. |
| **Mar 4, 1590** | Maurice captures Breda in a surprise attack. |
| **Dec 3, 1592** | Parma dies in France and is succeeded as governor of the Spanish Netherlands by Count Peter Ernst I von Mansfeld-Vorderortt. |
| **Jan 24, 1597** | Maurice defeats the Spaniards under Jean de Ris of Varax at Turnhout in present-day Belgium. Varax is among the dead. |
| **Sep 13, 1598** | Philip II dies and is succeeded by Philip III, who continues the war. |
| **1599** | Archduke Albrecht (Albert) of Austria, King Philip's son-in-law, becomes viceroy in the Netherlands. |
| **Jul 2, 1600** | In the Battle of Nieuwpoort, also known as the Battle of the Dunes, the Anglo-Dutch forces rally and defeat the Spaniards. Maurice, however, will soon be forced to raise the siege and withdraw. |

| | |
|---|---|
| **Apr 12, 1607** | Dutch successes at sea help bring about an armistice between the United Provinces and the Habsburg southern Netherlands. |
| **Apr 25, 1607** | Although the cease-fire is later extended to include operations at sea, it comes too late to prevent the Battle of Gibraltar on this date. A Dutch fleet of 26 warships under Jacob van Heenskerk defeats 20 Spanish galleons under Admiral Don Juan Alvarez d'Avila. |
| **Apr 9, 1609** | A cease-fire, later known as the Twelve Years' Truce, goes into effect between the United Provinces and the southern Netherlands. It lasts until August 1621. |
| **1618–1648** | The Thirty Years' War occurs. Fought principally in Germany, it draws in most of continental Europe. The war forces Spain to fight on many fronts, greatly aiding the Dutch in securing their independence. |
| **Aug 9, 1621** | The Twelve Years' Truce comes to an end with a renewal of warfare between the Spanish and Dutch. Prince Maurice of Nassau leads the Dutch side, while Spanish general Don Ambrogio Spinola Doria, Marques de los Balbases, commands the Spanish forces. |
| **Mar 31, 1621** | King Philip III of Spain dies and is succeeded by Philip IV. |
| **Aug 29, 1622** | In the Battle of Fleurus, rebel forces under generals Duke Christian of Brunswick and Count Peter Ernst von Mansfeld, moving to relieve Spinola's siege of Bergen-op-Zoom, are intercepted and defeated by Spanish forces under General Gonzalo Fernández de Córdoba. |
| **Aug 28, 1624– Jun 5, 1625** | The Siege of Breda results in a Spanish victory. |
| **Apr 23, 1625** | Maurice of Nassau dies and is succeeded as stadtholder of Holland by his younger brother Prince Frederik Hendrik (Frederick Henry). |
| **Aug 22, 1632** | Prince Frederik Hendrik captures Masstricht. Peace negotiations then begin between the Dutch and Spaniards but end without result. |
| **Sep 16, 1639** | Dutch admiral Maarten Harpertzsoon Tromp intercepts a powerful Spanish fleet under Don António Oquendo, forcing the Spanish, who are bound for the Netherlands, to seek refuge in English waters. |
| **Oct 21, 1639** | In the Battle of the Downs in English waters, Admiral Witte Corneliszoon de With holds the English ships at bay while Tromp attacks the Spanish fleet and destroys some 40 Spanish ships for the loss of only 1 of his own. This important Dutch victory ends what remains of Spanish naval power and seriously weakens the Spanish military position on land. |
| **Jan 30, 1648** | The Dutch Republic and the Kingdom of Spain conclude peace in the Treaty of Münster, ratified at Münster on May 15, 1648. |

SPENCER C. TUCKER

## Further Reading

Arblaste, Paul. *The Dutch Revolt.* Burford, Oxfordshire, UK: Davenant, 2001.

Arnade, Peter. *Beggars, Iconoclasts, and Civic Patriots: The Political Culture of the Dutch Revolt.* Ithaca, NY: Cornell Univertsity Press, 2008.

Bengoa, José. *Historia de los antiguos mapuches del sur.* Santiago: Catalonia, 2003.

Gelderen, Martin van. *The Political Thought of the Dutch Revolt, 1555–1590.* Cambridge: Cambridge University Press, 2002.

Glete, J. *War and the State in Early Modern Europe: Spain, the Dutch Republic and Sweden as Fiscal-Military States, 1500–1660.* London: Routledge, 2002.

Israel, Jonathan. *Dutch Primacy in World Trade, 1585–1740.* Wotton-under-Edge, Gloucestershire, UK: Clarendon, 1989.

Israel, Jonathan. *The Dutch Republic: Its Rise, Greatness, and Fall, 1477–1806.* Oxford, UK: Clarendon, 2007.

Israel, Jonathan. *Empires and Entrepôts: The Dutch, the Spanish Monarchy, and the Jews, 1585–1713.* London: Continuum International, 1990.

Koenigsberger, H. G. *Monarchies, States Generals and Parliaments: The Netherlands in the Fifteenth and Sixteenth Centuries.* Cambridge: Cambridge University Press, 2007.

Parker, Geoffrey. *The Army of Flanders and the Spanish Road, 1567–1659.* 2nd ed. Cambridge: Cambridge University Press, 2004.

Parker, Geoffrey. *The Dutch Revolt.* Ithaca, NY: Cornell University Press, 1977.

Tracy, J. D. *The Founding of the Dutch Republic: War, Finance, and Politics in Holland 1572–1588.* Oxford: Oxford University Press, 2008.

van der Hoeven, Marco, ed. *Exercise of Arms: Warfare in the Netherlands, 1568–1648.* Leiden: Brill, 1997.

# American War of Independence (1775–1783)

## Causes

The American War of Independence, also known as the American Revolutionary War, took place during 1775–1783. Separated as they were by both 3,000 miles of ocean and dissimilar circumstances, it was inevitable that differences in outlook would arise between the ruling class in Britain and the inhabitants of British North America. Statesmen in London did not understand this, and even when they did, they made little or no effort to reconcile the differences. The communities on each side of the Atlantic had been growing apart for some time, but the crushing British victory over France in the French and Indian War (1754–1763) removed the French threat and gave free play to the forces working for separation.

Almost immediately after the war, in 1763 Chief Pontiac of the Ottawa Indians led an intertribal Native American alliance in a rebellion along the western frontier. British regulars put it down, but in these circumstances London decided to station 10,000 regulars along the frontier and require the Americans to pay part of their upkeep. The plan seemed fair, especially as the mother country was hard-pressed for funds following the heavy expenditures of the French and Indian War and the concurrent Seven Years' War (1756–1763) and because the soldiers would be protecting the colonials from both Indian attack and any French resurgence. This decision, however, ignited a long controversy about Parliament's right to tax. Apart from import duties (much of which were evaded through widespread smuggling), Americans paid only those few taxes assessed by their own colonial legislatures. By the same token, Americans did not have any direct representation in the British Parliament.

Parliament's effort began with the American Duties Act of April 1764, commonly known as the Sugar Act. Although it lowered the duty on foreign molasses, the act imposed the duty on all sugar or molasses regardless of its source. The Stamp Act of 1765 was a levy on all paper products. Reaction was such that the act was repealed the next year, as was the Sugar Act. Generally unnoticed in the excitement over the repeal was the Declaratory Act of March 1766, which asserted Parliament's right to bind its American colonies "in all cases whatsoever."

The next effort by Parliament to find some tax that the colonials would pay came in the Townshend Acts of 1767. These imposed customs duties on glass, lead, paint, paper, china earthenware, silk, and tea imported from Britain into the colonies. According to Chancellor of the Exchequer Charles Townshend, the revenues raised would be applied to help pay the salaries of royal governors and judges as well as the cost of defending the colonies. But the act was clearly an attempt to make British officials independent of colonial legislatures to enable them to enforce parliamentary authority. It too was repealed after colonial protests in March 1770, except for the tax on tea. The colonists' primary complaint was that Parliament had no right to levy internal taxes against them because they had no representation in that body.

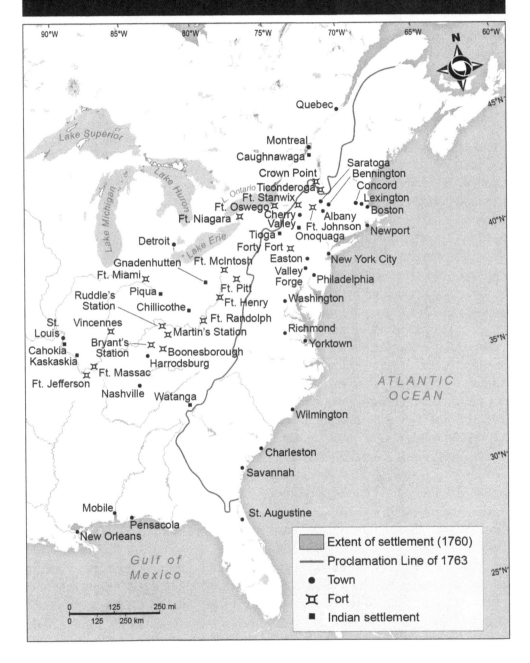

## AMERICAN REVOLUTIONARY WAR, 1775–1783

# SARATOGA CAMPAIGN, 1777

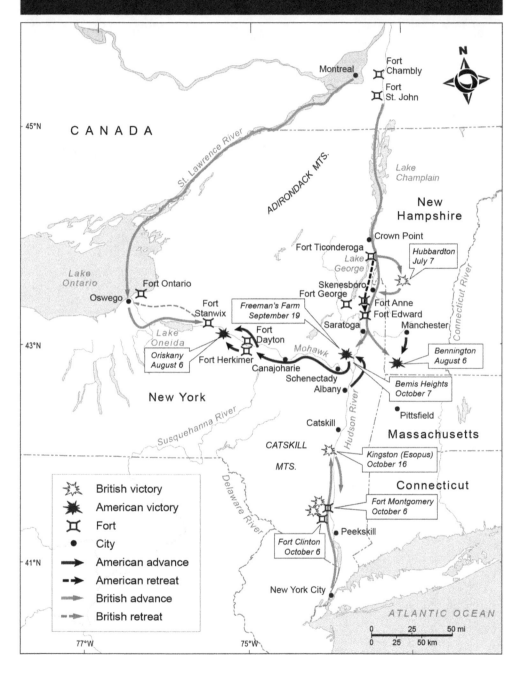

Fort Chambly

Montreal

Fort St. John

CANADA

45°N

St. Lawrence River

ADIRONDACK MTS.

Lake Champlain

New Hampshire

Crown Point

Fort Ticonderoga

Lake George

Hubbardton July 7

Skenesboro

Fort George

Fort Anne

Fort Edward

Manchester

Lake Ontario

Fort Ontario

Oswego

Fort Stanwix

Freeman's Farm September 19

Saratoga

Bennington August 6

Lake Oneida

43°N

Oriskany August 6

Fort Herkimer

Fort Dayton

Canajoharie

Mohawk

Schenectady

Albany

Bemis Heights October 7

New York

Catskill

Pittsfield

Massachusetts

Susquehanna River

CATSKILL MTS.

Kingston (Esopus) October 16

Hudson River

Connecticut

Delaware River

Fort Montgomery October 6

Peekskill

41°N

Fort Clinton October 6

New York City

ATLANTIC OCEAN

British victory
American victory
Fort
City
American advance
American retreat
British advance
British retreat

77°W

75°W

0    25    50 mi
0    25    50 km

# Yorktown Campaign, Aug–Oct 1781

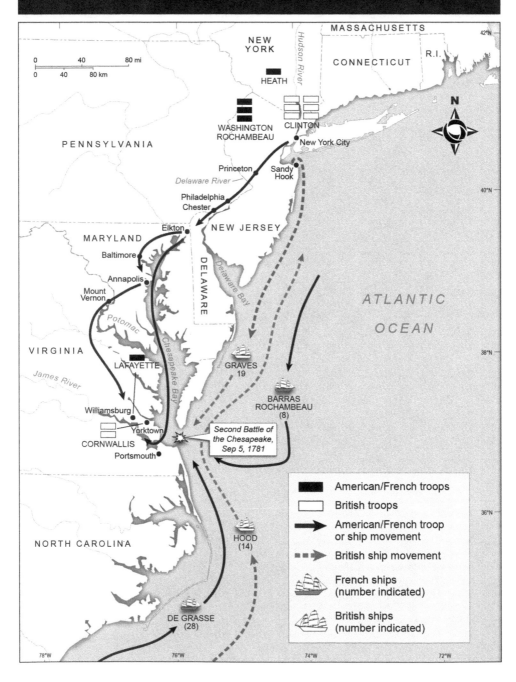

Second Battle of the Chesapeake, Sep 5, 1781

**Legend:**
- American/French troops
- British troops
- American/French troop or ship movement
- British ship movement
- French ships (number indicated)
- British ships (number indicated)

## American War of Independence (1775–1783)

| Estimated Strength and Casualties, American War of Independence (1775–1783) | | | | |
|---|---|---|---|---|
| | **Patriots** | **Britain** | **France** | **Hired German Soldiers** |
| **Total mobilized** | 250,000 | 120,000 | 60,000 | 29,500 |
| **Killed** | 7,000 | 5,500 | 10,000 | 5,000 |
| **Wounded** | 8,400 | 6,000 | Unknown | Unknown |
| **Captured** | 18,150 | 12,000 | Unknown | 4,000 |
| **Missing** | 1,420 | Unknown | Unknown | Unknown |
| **Total losses** | 34,970 | 23,500 | 10,000 | 9,000 |

| Battle of Bunker Hill, Boston, Massachusetts (June 17, 1775) | | |
|---|---|---|
| | **Patriots** | **British-Led Forces** |
| **Strength** | 1,500 | 2,400 |
| **Killed** | 140 | 226 |
| **Wounded** | 380 | 828 |
| **Captured** | 39 | Unknown |
| **Total casualties** | 559 | 1,054 |

| Patriot Advance on Quebec (December 31, 1775) | | |
|---|---|---|
| | **Patriots** | **British Forces** |
| **Strength** | 1,200* | 1,800* |
| **Killed** | 50 | 5 |
| **Wounded** | 34 | 13 |
| **Captured** | 426 | None |
| **Total casualties** | 510 | 18 |

*Regular and militia troops.

| Battle of Bemis Heights, New York (October 7, 1777)* | | |
|---|---|---|
| | **Patriots** | **British-Led Forces** |
| **Strength** | 8,000 | 6,500 |
| **Total casualties**** | 130 | 600 |

*Last major battle of the June 4–October 17, 1777, Saratoga Campaign.
**Includes killed, wounded, and captured. Here British major general John Burgoyne was compelled to surrender his remaining army of 5,895 men.

| Battle of Cowpens, South Carolina (January 17, 1781) | | |
|---|---|---|
| | **Patriots** | **British/Loyalist Forces** |
| **Strength** | 1,900 | 1,150 |
| **Killed** | 12 | 100 |
| **Wounded** | 60 | 229 |
| **Captured** | Unknown | 600 |
| **Total casualties** | 72 | 929 |

| Siege of Yorktown (September 28–October 19, 1781)* | | |
|---|---|---|
| | **Patriot/French Forces** | **British-Led Forces** |
| **Strength** | 17,600** | 8,000–9,000 |
| **Killed** | 75 | 156 |
| **Wounded** | 199 | 326 |
| **Total casualties** | 274 | 482 |

*The British loss at Yorktown prompted a change in Britain's government, paving the way for a negotiated end to the American War of Independence.
**Of this number, 7,800 were French troops and 3,000 were militiamen, the latter of which were not engaged

**Sources:** Clodfelter, Michael. *Warfare and Armed Conflict: A Statistical Reference to Casualty and Other Figures, 1618–1991.* Jefferson, NC: McFarland, 1992; Gabriel, Michal. *Major General Richard Montgomery: The Making of an American Hero.* Madison, NJ: Farleigh Dickinson University Press, 2002; Greene, Jerome A. *The Guns of Independence: The Siege of Yorktown, 1781.* New York: Savas Beattie, 2005; Kennedy, Paul. *The Rise and Fall of the Great Powers.* New York: Random House, 1990; U.S. Department of Defense. *Principal Wars in Which the United States Participated: U.S. Military Personnel Serving and Casualties.* Washington, DC: Washington Headquarters Services, Directorate for Information Operations and Reports, 2003.

Tensions between colonists and British soldiers also had been rising. This was in part for economic reasons (out of need, many British soldiers had taken part-time jobs away from Bostonians). Another problem was the Quartering Act, by which Bostonians were forced to house and feed British troops. These factors led to a bloody confrontation on March 5, 1770, known as the Boston Massacre.

The prolonged British effort to bring the colonies to heel and end colonial resistance to Britain ended with the so-called Boston Tea Party. In May 1773, Parliament attempted to rescue the financially strapped yet politically well-connected British East India Company. The government authorized the company to sell its considerable surplus of tea directly to its own agents in America. The tea would actually be cheaper, even with the tax in place, than smuggled Dutch tea, but the arrangement would cut out colonial middlemen, establishing a monopoly on what was the principal colonial drink and ending a major element of the smuggling trade. Public meetings in New York, Philadelphia, and Boston all condemned the act.

On the evening of December 16, some 8,000 people in Boston met in protest of the arrival there of three ships carrying East India Company tea. Afterward a number of the men, in the guise of Mohawk Indians, boarded the ships and, working throughout the night, emptied them of 342 large chests of tea, which were dumped into Boston Harbor. Further disorders against the landing of tea followed.

This event ended the period of British government patience. Frustrated by its fruitless decadelong effort to tax the colonies and by colonial intransigence and lawlessness, London now adopted a harder line. Determined to teach the rebellious American subjects a lesson, in March 1774 King George III, who was determined to exercise his royal prerogatives, and his ministers pushed through Parliament the first of what became known as the Coercive Acts, measures known in America as the Intolerable Acts. The first of these, the Boston Port Bill, closed the port of Boston, threatening the colony with economic ruin. Other legislation suspended the Charter of Massachusetts, placed that colony under martial law, and gave the new government extensive new powers over town meetings. The Quartering Act required colonial authorities to provide housing and supplies for British troops. If the colonists would make restitution for the destroyed tea, the restrictions would be lifted. Nonetheless, this strong action against a colonial government and the colony's economic livelihood created a firestorm in America, lending credence to arguments by New England's radical leaders that the British were out to crush American liberties.

At the same time, although not part of the coercive program, the Quebec Act of May 1774 seemed to be a gratuitous British insult and one of the "intolerable" measures. Actually one of the most enlightened pieces of imperial legislation of its day, the act sought to reconcile the large number of French Catholics to British rule by granting full civil rights and religious freedom to Canadians. This was anathema to many Protestants in New England. More important for the seaboard colonies, the act defined the borders of the former New France as the French had drawn them, cutting them off from further westward expansion.

After the Intolerable Acts and the Quebec Act, self-authorized groups met in several colonies and sent delegates to the Continental Congress in Philadelphia in September 1774. The delegation adopted the so-called Continental Association that called for nonimportation of English goods after December 1. North American lieutenant general Thomas Gage reported to London that the situation was dangerous and that he lacked sufficient manpower to deal with events if fighting were to break out. This did not affect George III and his ministers, who were determined to pursue a hard line. In February 1775, Parliament declared Massachusetts to be in rebellion.

Gage strongly disagreed with London's approach. In a report sent to London but not shared with Parliament, he estimated that in the event of fighting, it would take a year or two and 20,000 men just to pacify New England. If these men could not be supplied, Gage advocated a naval blockade and economic pressure as the best approach. The ministry in London disagreed. It held that 10,000 troops, supported by Loyalists, would be sufficient. Surely Gage was a defeatist or worse. London was convinced that the vast majority of Americans were loyal to the Crown, that any problems were the work of only a few agitators, and that a show of force and the arrest of the troublemakers would restore order; all would then be well.

The war that London now entered into so blithely caught Britain unprepared. Troops would have to be raised, the navy would have to be rebuilt, and men and supplies would have to be shipped across the Atlantic Ocean. While the Royal Navy, once rebuilt, could enforce a blockade and land troops at any point on the American seaboard and extract them again, campaigning in the interior in a land without adequate roads or strategic centers would be difficult indeed.

SPENCER C. TUCKER

## Course

### Early Fighting (1775–1776)

Fighting began on April 19, 1775, when Gage sent troops from Boston to destroy stores of arms that the radicals had been stockpiling at Concord. Similar operations in the past had been successful, but this time the militia was alerted. At Lexington, the soldiers encountered a hastily assembled small militia force but, in a brief skirmish, brushed them aside. The British then marched on to Concord and completed their mission. The withdrawal to Boston became a nightmare, however, for the local militiamen were then out in force and sniped at the British from along the route. The operation claimed 273 British casualties of some 1,800 engaged and 95 Americans. Some 15,000 New England militiamen then closed around Boston. Commanded by Major General Artemus Ward, they commenced the Siege of Boston (April 19, 1775–March 17, 1776).

In 1775 perhaps a quarter of Americans counted themselves Patriots, another quarter remained loyal to Britain, and half of Americans were neutral. The Patriots were highly motivated, however, and they secured control of most of the local militia formations, using these throughout the war to control local Loyalists (Tories) and the countryside as well as to assist Continental Army formations in combat. In the latter role, however, the poorly trained militiamen often broke and ran.

On May 10, 1775, 83 Patriots led by Connecticut colonel Ethan Allen and Massachusetts colonel Benedict Arnold surprised and seized poorly garrisoned British Forts Ticonderoga and Crown Point on Lake Champlain, securing there 78 serviceable cannon and military supplies.

In late May, British major generals John Burgoyne, Henry Clinton, and William Howe arrived at Boston with 3,500 troops, bringing British strength there to 6,500 men. They carried orders to impose martial law throughout Massachusetts, and they also pressed Gage to undertake offensive action. At the same time, the British government was scouring the German states to hire troops to augment its own small professional army. These auxiliaries, numbering in all some 30,000 men, came to be known collectively as Hessians, as perhaps half of them were from Hesse-Kassel (Hesse-Cassel).

The Second Continental Congress, having in mid-May urged all 13 colonial governments to undertake military preparedness, nonetheless recognized the need for a regular military establishment, and in June it authorized the establishment of 10 rifle companies for the Continental Army (Army of the United Colonies) and named Virginian George Washington as general and its commander. Washington took up his duties at Cambridge, Massachusetts, in early July.

On October 30, Congress also voted to establish a navy. A number of its ships were conversions, and some were secured abroad, although Congress approved construction of 13 frigates. A number of states also raised navies, and Washington authorized armed schooners to disrupt British supplies into Boston. The main Patriot effort at sea during the war was by privateers, however. These captured some 3,087 British ships. Although a number were retaken, 2,208 were left in American hands. The Americans also captured 89 British privateers, of which 75 remained in American hands. (British privateers captured 1,135 American merchantmen, of which 27 were retaken or ransomed. The British also captured 216 privateers.) These figures compare with a total of 196 ships captured by the Continental Navy. The captures of merchantmen drove up insurance rates and helped turn many in the British merchant class against the war. American privateers and Continental Navy ships may also have taken prisoner as many as 16,000 British seamen. This compares to 22,000 British soldiers taken by the Continental Army during the war.

On June 17, 1775, during the Siege of Boston, General Howe led an amphibious operation in Boston Harbor to seize high ground fortified by the Patriots on the Charlestown Peninsula. Instead of simply cutting off the rebel force by taking Charlestown Neck, Howe opted for a frontal assault. The ensuing Battle of Bunker Hill was a British victory but at terrible cost. Of 2,400 British troops engaged, 1,054—including 92 officers—were casualties, with 226 dead. Probably some 1,500 Americans were engaged; of these 140 were killed, 380 were wounded, and 39 were captured. The battle shook Howe and may well have contributed to his later failure to press home attacks.

Fighting worked against reconciliation. At the end of July, the Continental Congress rejected a plan put forward by British prime minister Frederick, Lord North, second Earl of Guilford, for reconciliation. It called for an end to taxes that raised money to pay for British officials and military personnel. The Continental Congress, however, continued to insist that colonial legislatures alone should determine how monies raised might be spent. King George III's Royal Proclamation of Rebellion issued in late August, which pledged severe punishment for all officials deemed treasonous, in effect ended the possibility of reconciliation.

On June 1, the Continental Congress had voted to dispatch expeditionary forces to Canada to seal the backdoor to America. There would be two separate forces: the first would take Montreal, then join the second in capturing Quebec. The first force, initially under Major Philip Schuyler, stalled in a poorly conducted Patriot siege of St. Johns on the Richelieu River. Colonel Benedict Arnold meanwhile led a second force through the Maine wilderness to Quebec. With St. Johns finally taken and Montreal seized, Brigadier General Richard Montgomery joined Arnold at Quebec. With enlistments expiring and supplies running out, the Americans attempted a desperate attack on December 31, 1775. Mounted in a snowstorm, it was a complete failure. Montgomery was killed, and Arnold was wounded. The British captured 426 Americans; another 50 were killed or wounded but not captured. British losses were only 5 killed and 13 wounded. Arnold attempted to maintain a siege with his remaining men, but the arrival in May 1776 of a British supply ship ended it. In the spring of 1776 British reinforcements drove the Americans, belatedly reinforced, from Canada. The Canadian expedition would have succeeded had it been adequately supported from the start.

During the winter of 1775–1776, the Americans transported cannon from Fort Ticonderoga to Boston. In March 1776 they seized undefended Dorchester Heights and fortified it, then placed the cannon there. This led Howe, who had replaced Gage as British commander, to withdraw from Boston, sailing to Halifax, Nova Scotia. Washington permitted the British to depart unmolested on Howe's pledge not to destroy the city.

To counter the likely possibility of a British invasion of New York down Lake Champlain that would cut off New England from the rest of the colonies, Arnold, now a brigadier general, oversaw construction of a small flotilla of gondolas and galleys. In the Battle of Valcour Island on October 11–13, 1776, the more powerful British flotilla destroyed the American vessels, but the delay that Arnold had imposed caused Major General Sir Guy Carleton, British commander in Canada, to call off the planned invasion that year.

Meanwhile, Patriot forces repulsed a British attempt under Major General Henry Clinton to take Charles Town (Charleston), South Carolina. In the Battle of Sullivan's Island (June 28, 1776), the British lost several warships in the effort. On July 4, the Continental Congress voted to approve the Declaration of Independence.

### The British Endeavor to Control the Northern Colonies (1776–1778)

That same month, Howe arrived by sea at New York with 33,000 British and German troops. Washington had anticipated this move but had rejected mounted formations, and his defensive dispositions were poor. However, Howe showed little imagination and lacked drive. The British defeated the Americans in the Battle of Long Island (August 27, 1776), then crossed to Manhattan and pushed Washington's forces northward, taking New York City and then defeating the Americans at Harlem Heights (September 16) and White Plains (October 28).

Washington extracted his forces except for a large garrison, subsequently reinforced, under Colonel Robert Magaw at Fort Washington on the east bank of the Hudson. Washington believed that if necessary it could be evacuated across the river. He also reinforced it to nearly 3,000 men. Howe, however, sent ships up the river and 10,000 men against the fort from the land side on November 16, taking it by assault the same day. The British lost 78 killed and 374 wounded, while 59 Americans died and 96 were wounded. But American losses in prisoners and supplies were staggering. The British captured 230 officers and 2,607 soldiers. They also secured 146 cannon, 2,800 muskets, 12,000 shot and shell, and 400,000 musket cartridges. It was second only to the surrender of Charles Town in 1780 as the worst Patriot defeat of the entire war.

The same thing almost happened to Fort Lee, across the Hudson from Fort Washington, but its garrison was forewarned, and the men got away, although they were forced to abandon military stores. Washington now withdrew across New Jersey, leisurely pursued by Howe. In December the British occupied the port of Rhode Island, securing there a major anchorage for their navy. After setting up a string of outposts in western New Jersey, Howe went into winter quarters.

It looked as if the war was about over. With most Continental Army enlistments set to expire at the end of the year, Washington decided on a daring gamble. He would cross the Delaware River early on December 26 with some 5,500 men in

This famous painting by Emanuel Leutze depicts Continental Army commander General George Washington and his men crossing the Delaware River to attack the Hessian forces manning the British outpost at Trenton, New Jersey, on December 26, 1776. (National Archives)

three bodies and attack Colonel Johann Rall's 1,600 Hessians at Trenton. Only Washington's group of 2,400 made it across in time for the attack. But Washington pressed ahead, and surprise was complete. Artillery, in which the Americans had a considerable advantage, was a major factor. The Hessians had 22 killed, 92 wounded (Rall mortally), and 948 captured. The remaining Hessians would also have been taken had the other American columns gotten into position in time. Americans casualties were 2 men frozen to death and 5 wounded. The Continental Army then withdrew back across the Delaware.

Trenton changed the war. The battle helped end the fear of Hessian troops and added immensely to Washington's prestige, at such a low point a month before.

The battle also restored Patriot morale. Washington had seemingly snatched victory from the jaws of death and restored confidence in the possibility of a Patriot victory.

Washington recrossed the Delaware for an attack on Princeton on January 3, 1777, and was again victorious. He then went into winter quarters at Morristown, New Jersey. During the early months of 1777, Patriot forces harried British communications in New Jersey with guerrilla attacks.

France meanwhile was providing military assistance to the Patriots. Pushed by his foreign minister Charles Gravier, Comte de Vergennes, who was anxious to weaken France's rival Britain but also to avenge France's humiliating defeats of the French and Indian War and the concurrent Seven Years' War, King Louis XVI agreed in 1776 to extend secret aid to the American rebels. This assistance ultimately included more than 200 cannon, 20–30 mortars, 30,000 small arms, 100 tons of gunpowder, and clothing and tents sufficient for 25,000 men. Its importance cannot be overstated.

Meanwhile, British secretary of state for the American Department Lord George Germain, the man actually running the war for the British, approved two different, even opposing, plans for the 1777 campaign. The first would see Howe move against Philadelphia. Howe believed that Washington would be forced to defend the Patriot capital, giving Howe the chance to destroy him.

The second plan would see Lieutenant General John Burgoyne push south from Canada along the Lake Champlain corridor to Albany, New York, where he expected to meet part of Howe's army driving north up the Hudson from New York City. Burgoyne also planned a secondary campaign in conjunction with allied Native Americans in the Mohawk Valley in order to force a dispersion of Patriot resources. British control of the Hudson would cut off New England from the rest of the colonies, but Burgoyne's polycentric plan failed to take into account difficult logistical considerations, problems of coordination and timing, and Howe's own plan, which meant that few troops would be available to move up the Hudson from New York City.

Leaving General Clinton in command at New York, Howe set sail with some 16,000 troops on July 26. The men began coming ashore at the head of the Chesapeake Bay on August 25, then moved toward Philadelphia. On September 11, Howe defeated Washington's army of 11,000 men along Brandywine Creek. Howe fixed the Americans in place with part of his army while marching with the majority around the American right to get in behind Washington and bag his entire force. Howe was again slow, and Washington was able to withdraw in good order. American casualties were some 200 killed, 700–800 wounded, and almost 400 taken prisoner; the British lost 99 killed, 488 wounded, and 6 missing. Howe occupied Philadelphia on September 26.

On October 4, Washington with 11,000 men attempted a complicated night march against the British encampment at Germantown near Philadelphia. It met failure, thanks to poor coordination of the attacking columns and the timely arrival of British reinforcements from Philadelphia. American losses were 152 killed, 521 wounded, and about 400 taken prisoner; the British lost 71 killed, 450 wounded, and 14 missing.

In a series of hard-fought actions and heavy casualties on both sides, Howe took Patriot forts on the Delaware River and thereby opened a supply line for the Royal Navy to Philadelphia. He then settled in at Philadelphia for the winter. Washington also went into winter quarters at nearby Valley Forge, during which German volunteer Wilhelm von Steuben became drillmaster of the army, instilling in it both order and discipline. This enabled the Continentals to fight on equal footing with their British counterparts.

Although Howe had informed Burgoyne of his plans and there was little chance of major assistance, Burgoyne pressed ahead with his own campaign, starting out in June 1777 with some 10,500 men. At first all went well. In early July Burgoyne easily recaptured Fort Ticonderoga, but the advance then slowed owing to both the terrain and the highly effective scorched-earth policy practiced by American commander

Major General Schuyler. At the same time, Burgoyne's secondary effort met rebuff in the Siege of Fort Stanwix (August 2–23, 1777).

With his supply situation becoming desperate, Burgoyne dispatched a foraging expedition of Hessians into Vermont. On August 16, Brigadier General John Stark and some 2,200 militiamen defeated these and a reinforcing unit in the Battle of Bennington. In all, the Hessians sustained 207 killed and 700 captured for American casualties of only 30 killed and 40 wounded. The Patriot side also secured much-needed military supplies and weapons.

Refusing suggestions that he withdraw, Burgoyne crossed the Hudson River and advanced to Bemis Heights, where he came upon defensive works ordered by new American commander Major General Horatio Gates. On September 19 in the Battle of Freeman's Farm (First Battle of Saratoga), some 8,000 defenders rebuffed a British attack. Burgoyne attacked again on October 7 and in the Battle of Bemis Heights (Second Battle of Saratoga) was again halted. Too late, he tried to withdraw but was forced to surrender his army of 5,895 officers and men on October 17.

The surrender of an entire British army was decisive, for it convinced French leaders that the Patriot side could indeed win the war, and on February 6, 1778, the French government signed a treaty of alliance with the United States. Britain declared war on France in June. Spain followed France into the war the next year, hoping to secure Gibraltar, and the Dutch Republic joined when Britain declared war on it in late 1780. The war for American independence had become a world war.

Recognizing the changed situation, London now offered the United States all except independence. This came too late

and was spurned. Howe resigned his command in the spring of 1778 and was replaced by Clinton. Now a lieutenant general, Clinton withdrew British forces from Philadelphia across New Jersey to be conveyed by ship to New York.

Determined to attack Clinton en route, Washington on June 28 fell on Clinton's rear elements in the Battle of Monmouth, the last major engagement of the war in the North. Major General Charles Lee badly managed the Continental attack, and Washington ended up taking command and defending against a British counterattack. American losses were 152 killed and 300 wounded versus British losses of 290 killed, 390 wounded, and 576 captured. Clinton was able to return to New York City, however. Washington took up station at White Plains.

Washington could do little to halt subsequent British raids on Connecticut and New Jersey coastal towns, and he was keenly disappointed that a newly arrived French fleet under Vice Admiral Jean-Baptiste, Comte d'Estaing, with 4,000 ground troops, was unable to attack British ships in New York Harbor largely thanks to Vice Admiral Lord Richard Howe's skillful ship dispositions.

Washington then agreed to a plan for a joint attack by d'Estaing and Patriot ground forces against the British garrison of some 3,000 men at Rhode Island, commanded by Major General Robert Pigot. Major General John Sullivan had command of the Patriot ground element, numbering with militia some 10,000 men. D'Estaing was to provide naval support and land French troops. He secured control of Narragansett Bay, costing the British 5 frigates, 2 sloops, and several galleys, although their guns and ammunition were offloaded and added to the British land defenses. Howe sailed from New York with 13 ships of the line to engage d'Estaing with 12, but the anticipated major naval confrontation did not occur thanks to a hurricane on August 11 that damaged both fleets. Despite Sullivan's pleas to remain even for a few days, d'Estaing insisted on removing his ships to Boston to effect repairs. Sullivan then continued on alone. Sullivan might still have won a victory, but with d'Estaing's departure most of the American militiamen lost heart and decamped. Pigot then sortied from Newport and, with 3,000 troops, attacked the Americans with 5,000.

In the Battle of Newport (August 28–29), the Americans blunted the British attack. Sullivan then withdrew northward, removing his men from the island on the night of August 30. It was a wise decision, for the next day 4,000 British reinforcements arrived.

Thereafter the war in the northern states was largely a stalemate. The British raided New England coastal towns, and the Americans attacked isolated British garrisons. In one such effort, Brigadier General Anthony Wayne attacked the strong British outpost at Stony Point, New York, capturing it with the bayonet alone on July 15, 1779. The Americans lost 15 killed and 80 wounded, but British losses were 63 killed, more than 70 wounded, and 543 captured. Although Wayne was forced to abandon the post several days later, the attack had secured much-needed arms, including 15 cannon, as well as supplies. In October 1779, the British evacuated Rhode Island.

In 1780 Major General Arnold, who had sought command of West Point, turned traitor and endeavored to surrender to the British that key fortification on the Hudson along with Continental Army commander General Washington. The plot was discovered in late September, but Arnold was able to flee to the British. He accepted a British commission as a brigadier general and subsequently campaigned in Virginia. In July 1781, French Army lieutenant general Comte de Rochambeau arrived at Newport with 5,000 French troops to cooperate with Washington.

As the war continued, the American economy sharply deteriorated. With wealth mostly in land and with Congress unable to tax, the central government resorted to printing paper money to pay its bills, and this led to rampant inflation and currency that was all but worthless. Among the consequences were several mutinies in the Continental line.

### The War Shifts to the Southern Colonies (1778–1781)

Fighting now largely shifted to the American South. Germain and other British leaders in London concluded that the South, with a perceived larger Loyalist population, might be more easily conquered, with the plan to secure an area and then raise Loyalist militias to control it. In December 1778 Clinton sent a military force to take the important seaport of Savannah, Georgia. It fell to the British on December 29. American losses were some 550, including 450 captured; the British suffered only 9 men killed and 4 wounded. The British also secured weapons and ships in the harbor.

In early September 1779, d'Estaing arrived off the mouth of the Savannah River with 20 ships of the line, 13 smaller warships, and 3,900 ground troops. However, he was slow to move against the British. Finally disembarking his ground troops, on September 12 he invested Savannah, being joined during the next week by Continental Army commander in the South Major General Benjamin Lincoln, with more than 2,000 Continentals and militia from Charles Town. British commander at Savannah Major General Augustine Prevost had 3,500 men, but he quickly improved the already strong city defenses. Unwilling to wait too long lest his fleet encounter the hurricane season, d'Estaing insisted on an assault, but a deserter alerted the British as to the exact point of the attack, and they repelled the allied assaults of October 9. These cost the allies 244 killed, 584 wounded, and 120 captured. British losses were only 40 killed, 63 wounded, and 52 missing or deserted. Refusing to remain longer, d'Estaing embarked his men and sailed away, while Lincoln returned to Charles Town.

Clinton now prepared a major seaborne assault from New York City on Charles Town by 8,000 British regulars and Loyalist militia. Charles Town's leaders insisted that Lincoln fight for the city, and he allowed his forces to be bottled up there. When the British began shelling the city during the resultant siege of March 29–May 12, 1780, the same city leaders insisted that Lincoln surrender. It was the greatest Continental Army defeat of the war. The siege itself claimed 89 Americans killed and 138 wounded, while the British lost 76 killed and 189 wounded. In the surrender, however, the British captured 5,466 officers and men (including 7 generals), 400 cannon, and 6,000 muskets. They also secured several Continental Navy frigates. British forces soon moved into interior South Carolina, cooperating with Loyalist militias to set up military outposts. Clinton left Lieutenant General Lord Charles Cornwallis as British commander in the South and returned to New York.

Named to replace Lincoln, Major General Gates collected all the forces he could

and rashly marched southward from Hillsborough, North Carolina. Cornwallis rushed northward, and the two forces came together at Camden, South Carolina, on August 16. The Continentals fought well, but the militiamen broke and ran, and Gates was routed. The British suffered 68 killed, 245 wounded, and 11 missing; American losses were some 900 killed or wounded and 1,000 captured. The British also secured artillery, small arms, and all the American stores and baggage. Gates escaped capture, but Washington replaced him with Major General Nathanael Greene.

After Camden, Cornwallis moved northward toward Charlotte, North Carolina, where he hoped to find strong Loyalist support. A virtual civil war now raged in the South between Patriots and Loyalists in which both sides committed atrocities. One large encounter between the two militias, the Battle of King's Mountain on October 7, brought a resounding Patriot victory. British major Patrick Ferguson's Loyalist force of 1,125 men suffered 1,105 dead or captured (refusing surrender, Ferguson was among the slain). Patriot losses were only 40 killed. This defeat of his western flanking force caused Cornwallis to suspend his effort to secure all of North Carolina, and he fell back to Winnsboro, South Carolina, for the winter. The British suffered another defeat on January 17, 1781, when, without reconnoitering, Lieutenant Colonel Banastre Tarleton's legion charged a Continental Army and militia force under Brigadier General Daniel Morgan at Cowpens, South Carolina. Although Tarleton escaped, he lost 90 percent of his force: 100 dead, 229 wounded, and 600 unwounded prisoners. Morgan's losses were only 12 killed and 60 wounded. Morgan also secured some 800 muskets, 2 cannon, 100 horses, and all the British supplies and ammunition. Patriot morale soared.

Determined to bag Morgan, Cornwallis moved against him in force. Greene and his forces now joined Morgan, and a race northward ensued. Greene won the so-called Race to the Dan (the river separating North Carolina and Virginia) during January 19–February 15, 1781, in what is regarded as one of the most masterly withdrawals in U.S. military history. Greene reorganized his forces and again advanced into North Carolina in early 1781.

On March 15, the two sides again came together in the Battle of Guilford Courthouse. Greene had 4,404 men but only 1,490 were Continental troops, and only about 500 of these were trained veterans. The remainder were unreliable militia. Cornwallis had only 1,900 men, but all were regulars, and almost all of these were veterans. The battle was hard-fought, but Greene was unwilling to hazard his forces and withdrew. Cornwallis trumpeted a victory, but it was costly. The Americans sustained 264 casualties: 79 killed and 185 wounded. Another 160 Continentals were missing along with several hundred militia, most of them having simply decamped. British casualties were, however, a quarter of their force: 93 killed and 439 wounded, a number of these mortally.

After retiring to Wilmington to regroup, Cornwallis decided to move with the bulk of his army into Virginia in order to cut the flow of supplies southward to Greene. Lieutenant Colonel Francis, Lord Rawdon, assumed command of British forces in South Carolina. Greene, choosing not to follow Cornwallis, began driving British forces from inland North and South Carolina. Although Greene sustained defeats in the battles at Hobkirk's Hill (April 25) and Eutaw Springs (September 8, 1781), his masterful Southern Campaign secured virtually all of North Carolina, South Carolina, and Georgia, forcing the British into coastal enclaves at Charles Town and Savannah.

Meanwhile, following raids in the Virginia interior, Cornwallis withdrew his forces to the tobacco port of Yorktown shadowed by a smaller American force under Major General Marie Joseph du Motier, Marquis de Lafayette. Washington had hoped that he and Rochambeau might attack New York City but then learned that French vice admiral François-Joseph-Paul, Comte de Grasse, planned to avoid hurricane season in the West Indies by sailing northward with a powerful fleet and 3,300 ground troops for Chesapeake Bay and remain there until October. Seeing the possibility of entrapping Cornwallis, Washington and Rochambeau marched with 7,000 men southward toward Yorktown. Meanwhile on August 30, de Grasse arrived in the Chesapeake with 28 ships of the line and commenced landing his ground forces.

At the same time, Rear Admiral Thomas Graves with 5 ships of the line, reinforced by 14 ships of the line under Rear Admiral Samuel Hood, just arrived from the West Indies, sailed from New York in August in an effort to intercept 8 ships of the line and 18 transports under French commodore Jacques, Comte de Barras, sailing from Newport and correctly presumed to be heading for Chesapeake Bay.

Sailing faster than Barras, Graves arrived in Chesapeake Bay first on September 5 and there discovered de Grasse. Instead of swooping down on the more powerful but unprepared French fleet, Graves formed his ships into line ahead and waited for de Grasse to come out. Shorthanded with many of his men occupied in ferrying French and American troops down the bay, de Grasse nonetheless stood out with

24 ships of the line to meet the British. The resulting engagement was a draw. With no ships lost on either side, the British sustained 336 casualties, the French 221.

Several days of inconclusive maneuvering followed during which Barras arrived. Graves then decided to return to New York to gather additional ships. Thus, this tactically inconclusive Second Battle of the Chesapeake doomed Cornwallis at Yorktown and deserves to be ranked among the most important strategic victories in world history.

On September 28, the allies laid siege to Yorktown. Following some fighting and running out of food, Cornwallis surrendered on October 19, 1781. A total of 8,077 British surrendered—840 seamen, 80 camp followers, and 7,157 soldiers. During the siege the British lost 156 killed and 326 wounded; the allies suffered only 75 killed and 199 wounded. When Parliament learned of this dire event, it voted on March 4, 1782, to end offensive war in America, and peace negotiations commenced in earnest between American and French envoys in Paris.

### End of the War (1781–1783)

Fighting continued in America, including operations in the Ohio Country that helped secure that vast territory for the United States in the peace settlement, but most of the warfare was of low intensity. Overseas there was fighting in India. The British withstood a long siege by the Spaniards and French at Gibraltar (1779–1783), and the French, Spaniards, Dutch, and British all sought to capture islands in the West Indies belonging to the other side. Any French advantage here, however, was lost late in the war with the British naval victory of the Battle of the Saintes (April 12, 1782).

On March 20, 1782, rather than lose a vote of no confidence, Lord North resigned as prime minister. On November 30, 1782, representatives of the United States and the British government signed the Treaty of Paris. This was in violation of the Franco-American alliance stipulating that neither was to sign a separate peace. It also ignored protests by Spain concerning lands east of the Mississippi River. The treaty was not to take effect, however, until the fighting between Britain and France and Spain was also resolved.

SPENCER C. TUCKER

### Consequences

The most important article of the peace treaty was that granting independence to the United States. The Americans also secured territory as far west as the Mississippi River, free navigation of the Mississippi, fishing rights off the Grand Banks, and the removal of British troops from American soil. The treaty was most generous, with the British successfully endeavoring to wean the United States from France.

The British evacuated Charles Town on December 14, 1782, and the French departed America six days later. Britain, France, and Spain agreed to peace terms on January 20, 1783. On February 4, 1783, King George III declared a formal end to hostilities with America, and on January 14, 1784, the Confederation Congress ratified the Treaty of Paris, officially ending the American Revolutionary War. Estimates vary, but perhaps 100,000 Loyalists left the territory of the United States during 1775–1783, most of them settling in the maritime provinces of Canada.

The Articles of Confederation governing the United States proved to be ineffective. In 1786 the nation was confronted with Shays' Rebellion. This unrest in Massachusetts was prompted by dismal economic conditions especially in western New England, where many former Continental Army soldiers found themselves deeply in debt and in danger of losing their lands. Daniel Shays, a former Continental Army captain, became the reluctant leader. In January 1787 the rebels attempted to prevent the Massachusetts Supreme Court from sitting at Springfield and also secure weapons from the federal arsenal there. The rebels, who had not expected confrontation, were dispersed by artillery fire, and the rebellion fizzled and was over by the next February. Fortunately, Massachusetts state leaders had the good sense to recognize the legitimate nature of the grievances and acted with moderation. Only two men were executed in the affair, and these for legitimate charges. Shays' Rebellion greatly strengthened the hands of those who sought to replace the weak Articles of Confederation with a stronger form of government.

By the late 1780s, the young United States faced a host of problems. In addition to the concerns raised by Shays' Rebellion, many American leaders understood that the current political arrangement under the Articles of Confederation was clearly not up to the task of governing the country. These did not permit a chief executive, a bicameral legislature, or a system of checks and balances. Also, the national government was not empowered to levy taxes, leaving that to the individual states. In short, the national government had no effective way to raise revenue or manage the country's large war-related debts. Worse yet, it had no authority to compel the individual states to remit tax receipts. Finally, decision making under the Articles of Confederation essentially

meant leadership by committee, which had proven to be largely unworkable.

In 1787 the Constitutional Convention convened in Philadelphia, and in 1789 the new document received the required state ratifications and was declared in force. It gave more powers to the central government, including the right to levy taxes. Today the world's oldest written instrument of government still in operation, the U.S. Constitution set up a system of checks and balances. The president was the head of the executive branch and commander in chief of the armed forces. The legislative branch of Congress had the right to vote taxes, declare war, and raise armies. There was also a judicial branch, in the form of the U.S. Supreme Court. The United States soon became a beacon of hope for the oppressed of much of the rest of the world who wished that their own nations might be more like it.

For Native Americans, however, the war proved to be disastrous. Without a European power to act as a counter to the triumphant Americans, the Indian nations had little leverage against continued white encroachment of their ancestral lands. A vicious war between the Indians and the American military occurred in the Old Northwest Territory between 1785 and 1795, ending in a Native American defeat. A relentless westward expansionism by settlers resulted in a string of wars between Native Americans and the U.S. government that did not end until 1890, at which time most remaining Native Americans had been herded onto reservations.

Britain suffered little from the loss of its major colonies, as trade promptly resumed and at a greater volume than before. France, for all its considerable efforts and expense, gained virtually nothing except a crushing increase in its national debt that would force the Crown to consider taxing the nobles and the church. This led to the so-called Aristocratic Reaction and the calling of the States General whereby the leaders of the Third Estate (with 97 percent of the nation's population), buoyed by the ideas of popular sovereignty and democracy embodied in the American Revolution, stood firm and produced the French Revolution (1789–1799).

SPENCER C. TUCKER

## Timeline

| | |
|---|---|
| **1754–1756** | French and Indian War. |
| **Nov 20, 1760** | George III becomes king of England. |
| **1763–1765** | Ottawa chief Pontiac leads a revolt by Native Americans against the British. |
| **Feb 10, 1763** | The Treaty of Paris ends the French and Indian War, with France essentially expelled from the Americas. |
| **Oct 7, 1763** | King George III signs the Proclamation Act of 1763 to contain the westward expansion of the American colonies, causing colonial resentment. |
| **Apr 5, 1764** | Parliament passes the Sugar Act to raise revenue for colonial defense and administration. |
| **Mar 22, 1765** | Parliament passes the Stamp Act, a direct tax on the colonies. It meets hostile reaction. |
| **Mar 18, 1766** | Parliament repeals the Stamp Act but passes the Declaratory Act. |
| **Jun 29, 1767** | Parliament passes the Townshend Acts, imposing a new series of colonial taxes. |
| **Oct 28, 1767** | Beginning of the colonial nonimportation movement boycotting British goods. |
| **Mar 5, 1770** | The Boston Massacre occurs in which five colonists are killed. |
| **Apr 12, 1770** | The Townshend Acts are repealed except for that regarding tea. |
| **May 16, 1771** | In the Battle of Alamance Creek in North Carolina, militiamen under Governor William Tryon defeat the Regulators, farmers from the western counties protesting government corruption. |
| **Jun 9–10, 1772** | The British customs vessel *Gaspée* runs aground in Rhode Island and is attacked and destroyed by colonists. |
| **May 10, 1773** | Parliament passes the Tea Act, giving the British East India Company a tea monopoly by underselling American merchants. |
| **Dec 16, 1773** | The Boston Tea Party occurs, during which colonists dump 90,000 pounds of British tea into Boston Harbor in opposition to the Tea Act. |

| | |
|---|---|
| **Mar–Jun 1774** | In response to the Boston Tea Party, Parliament passes the Coercive Acts, known to the colonists as the Intolerable Acts. |
| **Sep 5, 1774** | The First Continental Congress begins. |
| **Apr 19, 1775** | The Battles of Lexington and Concord occur during which British troops and militiamen clash directly for the first time, marking the beginning of the American Revolutionary War. |
| **Apr 19, 1775– Mar 17, 1776** | Colonial forces carry out the Siege of Boston. |
| **May 9–10, 1775** | Patriot forces seize Fort Ticonderoga and Crown Point, securing much-needed matériel and guns. |
| **May 10, 1775** | The Second Continental Congress meets in Philadelphia. |
| **Jun 14, 1775** | The Continental Congress agrees to raise an army and the next day names George Washington commander of the new Continental Army. |
| **Jun 17, 1775** | The Battle of Bunker Hill is fought, the first pitched battle of the war. Although the British win, they suffer nearly three times as many casualties as those of the Patriot side. |
| **Jul 6, 1775** | The Continental Congress issues its Declaration of the Causes and Necessity of Taking Up Arms. |
| **Jul 8, 1775** | The Continental Congress issues its Olive Branch Petition. |
| **Aug 23, 1775** | King George III declares the colonies to be in rebellion. |
| **Sep 5, 1775** | Patriot forces under Major General Philip Schuyler begin an invasion of Canada. |
| **Oct 10, 1775** | General William Howe succeeds Thomas Gage as commander in chief of British forces in North America. |
| **Nov 11, 1775** | Patriot forces under Brigadier General Richard Montgomery take Montreal. |
| **Nov 28, 1775** | The Continental Congress authorizes the formation of the Continental Navy. |
| **Dec 31, 1775** | Patriot forces under Montgomery and Colonel Benedict Arnold attack Quebec but are repelled, and Montgomery is killed. |
| **Mar 17, 1776** | British forces evacuate Boston. |
| **Jun 6, 1776** | British forces defeat the Patriots in the Battle of Trois Rivières in Canada. |
| **Jun 7, 1776** | Richard Henry Lee offers a resolution for independence to the Second Continental Congress. |
| **Jun 17, 1776** | British forces reoccupy Montreal. |
| **Jul 4, 1776** | The Second Continental Congress approves the Declaration of Independence. |

| | |
|---|---|
| **Aug 27, 1776** | British forces invade Long Island, New York, and defeat the Americans, most of whom are able to get away. |
| **Aug 28, 1776** | British forces win the Battle of Brooklyn. |
| **Sep 16, 1776** | British forces win the Battle of Harlem Heights. |
| **Oct 11–13, 1776** | British forces win the Battle of Valcour Island (Lake Champlain), but the American flotilla causes the British to delay their invasion from Canada via Lake Champlain. |
| **Oct 28, 1776** | British forces win the Battle of White Plains. |
| **Nov 16, 1776** | In one of the most costly defeats for the Patriot side in the war, British forces capture Fort Washington. |
| **Nov 20, 1776** | British forces capture Fort Lee, New Jersey. |
| **Dec 26, 1776** | Patriot forces under General Washington, having retreated across New Jersey, turn and defeat a Hessian garrison force in the Battle of Trenton, breathing new life into the Patriot cause. |
| **Jan 3, 1777** | Patriot forces under Washington defeat British forces in the Battle of Princeton in New Jersey. |
| **Jun 17, 1777** | British forces under Lieutenant General John Burgoyne begin their invasion of New York from Canada through Lake Champlain. |
| **Jul 6, 1777** | Burgoyne's forces capture Fort Ticonderoga, but most of its Patriot defenders under Major General Arthur St. Clair escape. |
| **Jul 23, 1777** | Howe sails with a British army from New York bound for the Chesapeake Bay. |
| **Aug 2, 1777** | British forces arrive at Fort Stanwix, a Patriot fort in New York, and commence a siege. |
| **Aug 6, 1777** | In the Battle of Oriskany, Patriot forces hoping to relieve Fort Stanwix are defeated by Iroquois Native Americans and Loyalists. |
| **Aug 16, 1777** | In the Battle of Bennington in New York, the Patriots rout Hessian forces. |
| **Aug 23, 1777** | British forces raise the siege of Fort Stanwix and withdraw. |
| **Sept 11, 1777** | British forces under Howe defeat the Patriots under Washington in the Battle of Brandywine. |
| **Sep 19, 1777** | Patriot forces under Major General Horatio Gates turn back the British under Burgoyne in the First Battle of Saratoga (Freeman's Farm). |
| **Sep 26, 1777** | British troops under Howe occupy the colonial capital of Philadelphia. |
| **Oct 4, 1777** | British forces under Howe turn back a Patriot attack under Washington in the Battle of Germantown. |
| **Oct 6, 1777** | British forces under Clinton capture Forts Clinton and Montgomery, Patriot forts on the Hudson River. |

| | |
|---|---|
| **Oct 7, 1777** | In the Second Battle of Saratoga (Bemis Heights), Patriot forces under Gates again defeat Burgoyne's forces. |
| **Oct 17, 1777** | Burgoyne surrenders his army to Gates. |
| **Nov 15, 1777** | The Second Continental Congress adopts the Articles of Confederation. |
| **Dec 19, 1777** | Washington establishes his winter headquarters at Valley Forge, Pennsylvania. |
| **Feb 6, 1778** | Patriot diplomats, including Benjamin Franklin, sign a treaty of alliance with France. |
| **Mar 16, 1778** | Parliament authorizes Frederick Howard, Earl of Carlisle, to head a peace commission and meet with U.S. representatives. He has broad authority to negotiate except for the granting of independence. |
| **Jun 17, 1778** | Fighting commences at sea between France and Great Britain. |
| **Jun 28, 1778** | In the Battle of Monmouth, Continental Army units attack the British withdrawing from Philadelphia but are turned back. |
| **Jul 20, 1778** | Patriot forces under Virginia Militia lieutenant colonel George Rogers Clark capture the fort at Vincennes (in Indiana). |
| **Jul 29–Aug 31, 1778** | In the Rhode Island Campaign, American and French forces attempt to capture Newport. In the culminating Battle of Newport, the Patriots turn back a British counterattack but then withdraw. |
| **Aug 2, 1778** | France formally declares war on Great Britain. |
| **Sep 2, 1778** | French forces capture the British island of St. Lucia. |
| **Dec 17, 1778** | British forces recapture Fort Vincennes. |
| **Dec 28, 1778** | British forces retake St. Lucia. |
| **Dec 29, 1778** | British forces capture Savannah, Georgia. |
| **Jan 29, 1779** | British forces capture Augusta, Georgia. |
| **Feb 25, 1779** | The Patriots under Clark retake Fort Vincennes. |
| **Apr 20, 1779** | Beginning of the Sullivan-Clinton Campaign, instituted by Washington to break the power of the Iroquois Confederation. |
| **Jun 1, 1779** | The British capture Stony Point, New York. |
| **Jun 18, 1779** | French forces capture the island of St. Vincent. |
| **Jun 21, 1779** | Spain declares war on Great Britain. Spanish and French troops begin the Siege of Gibraltar, which finally fails on February 6, 1783. |
| **Jul 4, 1779** | French forces capture the British island of Grenada. |
| **Jul 6, 1779** | In the naval Battle of Grenada, French forces under Charles Hector, Comte d'Estaing, turn back a British effort by Vice Admiral Sir John Byron to recapture the island. |

| | |
|---|---|
| **Jul 15–16, 1779** | Patriot forces under Brigadier General Anthony Wayne capture the British fort at Stony Point. |
| **Jul 25–Aug 14, 1779** | Massachusetts spearheads a Patriot attempt to capture a British fort on the Bagaduce Peninsula in the bay of the Penobscot River, but the effort ends in disaster. |
| **Aug 17, 1779** | Spanish governor of Louisiana Bernardo de Gález y Madrid departs New Orleans to attack British forts up the Mississippi River. |
| **Aug 19, 1779** | Patriot forces capture the British outpost at Paulus Hook, New Jersey. |
| **Sep 16–Oct 18, 1779** | French and American forces unsuccessfully besiege Savannah, Georgia. |
| **Sep 23, 1779** | In the North Sea, John Paul Jones in the Continental Navy frigate *Bonhomme Richard* defeats the British frigate *Serapis,* commanded by Captain Richard Person. |
| **Dec 1, 1779** | Washington leads the Continental Army into winter quarters at Morristown, New Jersey, where suffering is worse than at Valley Forge. |
| **Mar 14, 1780** | De Gálvez captures the British fort at Mobile following an 11-day siege. |
| **Mar 29, 1780** | British forces under Lieutenant General Sir Henry Clinton besiege Charles Town (Charleston), South Carolina, held by Patriot forces under Major General Benjamin Lincoln. |
| **May 12, 1780** | Lincoln surrenders Charles Town in what is the greatest defeat for the Patriot side in the war in terms of numbers of men lost. |
| **May 18, 1780** | Attempting to pacify the remainder of South Carolina, British lieutenant general Lord Charles Cornwallis marches into the interior. |
| **May 29, 1780** | British lieutenant colonel Banastre Tarleton's force mauls Patriot forces in the Battle of the Waxhaws in South Carolina. |
| **Aug 16, 1780** | Cornwallis soundly defeats Patriot forces under Gates in the Battle of Camden in South Carolina. |
| **Sep 25, 1780** | British major John André is captured with papers revealing the treason of Continental Army general Benedict Arnold. |
| **Oct 7, 1780** | Patriot militia defeat Loyalist militia in the Battle of Kings Mountain in South Carolina. |
| **Dec 2, 1780** | Major General Nathanael Greene arrives at Charlotte, North Carolina, to take command of Patriot forces in the South. |
| **Dec 20, 1780** | In order to end Dutch trade with France and the American rebels, Britain declares war on the Netherlands. |
| **Dec 30, 1780** | British forces, commanded by Benedict Arnold, now a British brigadier general, land at Hampton Roads and commence a campaign in Virginia. |

| | |
|---|---|
| **Jan 5–6, 1781** | British forces raid Richmond, Virginia. |
| **Jan 17, 1781** | Patriot forces under Brigadier General Daniel Morgan soundly defeat Tarleton's legion in the Battle of Cowpens in South Carolina. |
| **Feb 3, 1781** | British forces under Admiral Sir George Brydges Rodney capture the Dutch island of St. Eustatius. |
| **Mar 15, 1781** | British forces under Cornwallis defeat Patriot forces under Greene in the Battle of Guilford Courthouse, but the British sustain heavy casualties, and Cornwallis then relocates to Wilmington. |
| **Apr 23, 1781** | Cornwallis departs North Carolina for Virginia. |
| **Apr 25, 1781** | British forces under Lieutenant Colonel Lord Francis Rawdon defeat Patriot forces under Greene in the Battle of Hobkirk's Hill in South Carolina. |
| **May 10, 1781** | Following a siege, Spanish forces under De Gálvez capture British-held Pensacola. |
| **May 11–Jun 5, 1781** | Patriot forces capture British outposts in South Carolina. |
| **Jun 2, 1781** | French forces capture the island of Tobago. |
| **Jun 3–4, 1781** | British forces raid Charlottesville, Virginia. |
| **Aug 4, 1781** | Cornwallis relocates his forces to the port of Yorktown, Virginia. |
| **Aug 21, 1781** | Washington sets out with Continental Army and French forces under Lieutenant General Jean Baptiste Donatien de Vimeur, Comte de Rochambeau, in forced marches south toward Yorktown. |
| **Sep 5, 1781** | A French fleet under Admiral de Grasse turns back a British fleet in the tactically inconclusive yet strategically critical Second Battle of the Chesapeake. |
| **Sep 6, 1781** | British forces under Arnold raid New London, Connecticut. |
| **Sep 8, 1781** | British forces under Lieutenant Colonel Alexander Steward fight Patriot forces under Greene to a draw in the Battle of Eutaw Springs, near Charleston, South Carolina, in the war's last major engagement in the South. |
| **Oct 19, 1781** | Cornwallis surrenders his army at Yorktown to Patriot and French forces. |
| **Nov 26, 1781** | French forces capture St. Eustatius. |
| **Feb 12, 1782** | French forces capture St. Kitts. |
| **Mar 5, 1782** | The British House of Lords empowers King George III to make peace with the "former colonies." |
| **Mar 20, 1782** | Lord Frederick North, second Earl of Guilford and a strong supporter of the war, resigns as British prime minister. |

| | |
|---|---|
| **Apr 12, 1782** | British forces under Admiral Rodney win a major naval fleet engagement over the French under Admiral de Grasse in the Battle of the Saintes. |
| **Sept 27, 1782** | Representatives of Britain and the United States open peace negotiations in Paris. |
| **Nov 30, 1782** | Conclusion of the Treaty of Paris between the representatives of the United States and the British government. |
| **Dec 14, 1782** | British forces evacuate Charles Town (Charleston). |
| **Jan 20, 1783** | Representatives of Britain, France, and Spain agree to peace terms. |
| **Feb 4, 1783** | King George III declares a formal end to hostilities in America. |
| **Apr 15, 1783** | The Confederation Congress ratifies a preliminary draft of the Treaty of Paris ending the American Revolutionary War. |
| **Jan 14, 1784** | The Confederation Congress ratifies the Treaty of Paris. |
| **Sep 17, 1787** | The U.S. Constitution is signed and submitted to the Continental Congress. |
| **Jun 2, 1788** | The U.S. Constitution goes into effect. |
| **Apr 30, 1789** | George Washington takes the oath of office as the first president of the United States. |

SPENCER C. TUCKER

## Further Reading

Alden, John R. *A History of the American Revolution.* New York: Knopf, 1969.

Black, Jeremy. *War for America: The Fight for Independence, 1775–1783.* Gloucestershire, UK: Alan Sutton, 1991.

Cogliano, Francis D. *Revolutionary America, 1763–1815: A Political History.* New York: Routledge, 2017.

Heimert, Alan. *Religion and the American Mind, from the Great Awakening to the Revolution.* Cambridge, MA: Harvard University Press, 1966.

Higginbotham, Don. *The War of American Independence: Military Attitudes, Policies, and Practice, 1763–1789.* New York: Macmillan, 1971.

Mackesy, Piers, and John W. Shy. *The War for America, 1775–1783.* Lincoln, NE: Bison Books, 2015.

Middlekauff, Robert. *The Glorious Cause: The American Revolution, 1763–1789.* New York: Oxford University Press, 2005.

Miller, John C. *Triumph of Freedom, 1775–1783.* Boston: Little, Brown, 1848.

Ward, Christopher. *The War of the Revolution.* Edited by John Richard Alden. New York: Skyhorse Publishing, 2011.

Wood, Gordon S. *The Creation of the American Republic, 1776–1787.* Chapel Hill: University of North Carolina Press, 1969.

# Haitian Revolution and Wars of Independence (1791–1804)

## Causes

The Republic of Haiti is a sovereign state on the island of Hispaniola in the Greater Antilles archipelago of the Caribbean just to the east of Cuba. Haiti shares the island with the Dominican Republic; Haiti comprises the western three-eighths of the island, while the Dominican Republic comprises the rest. Europeans first arrived in 1492 when Christopher Columbus, sailing for the Spanish Crown, stopped at the island that December, believing he had found Asia.

Spain claimed possession of the island, which remained under Spanish control until the 17th century. The French established settlements in the western part of Hispaniola and on the island of Tortuga by 1659, and in the Treaty of Ryswick of 1697 that ended the War of the League of Augsburg (Nine Years' War), Spain formally ceded to France control both of Tortuga and the western third of Hispaniola, now named Saint-Domingue.

Saint-Domingue had a plantation economy based on slaves brought to the island from Africa. The island's plantations produced coffee, cocoa, and indigo, but the main cash crop was sugarcane. The production of sugar made Saint-Domingue

### Haitian Revolution and Wars of Independence (1791–1804)

| Estimated Total Deaths, Haitian Revolution and Wars of Independence (1791–1804)* | | |
|---|---|---|
| **Black Haitians** | **French and British Soldiers** | **White Colonists** |
| 200,000 | 100,000 | 25,000 |

*Deaths from all causes. Scholars suspect that the majority of deaths were due to yellow fever.

| Statistics of Initial Slave Revolt (ca. August 21, 1791–December 1, 1791) | |
|---|---|
| **Number of slaves revolting** | 100,000 |
| **Number of whites killed** | 4,000 |
| **Number of sugar plantations destroyed** | 180 |
| **Number of coffee plantations destroyed** | 900 |
| **Total monetary damage** | 2,000,000 francs |

| Battle of Ravine-à-Couleuvres (February 23, 1802)* | | |
|---|---|---|
| | **French Forces** | **Haitians** |
| **Strength** | 3,000 infantry | 2,500 infantry + 400 cavalry |
| **Killed in action** | 200 | 800 |

*Also known as the Battle of Snake Gulley.

| Battle of Vertières (November 18, 1803)* | | |
|---|---|---|
| | **French Forces** | **Haitians** |
| **Strength** | 2,000 | 27,000 |
| **Killed or wounded** | 1,200 | 3,200 |

*This was the last major battle of the Haitian Wars of Independence. Even though the Haitians suffered higher casualties, the clash was considered to be a Haitian victory.

**Sources:** Censer, Jack R., and Lynn Hunt. *Liberty, Equality, Fraternity: Exploring the French Revolution.* University Park: Pennsylvania State University Press, 2001; Popkin, Jeremy D. *A Concise History of the Haitian Revolution.* Chichester, West Sussex, UK: Wiley-Blackwell, 2012; Scheina, Robert L. *Latin American Wars: The Age of the Caudillo, 1791–1899,* Vol. 1. Sterling, VA: Potomac Books, 2003.

the most prosperous of France's colonies and the wealthiest of all European colonies in the Caribbean. In 1789 it produced some 60 percent of the world's coffee and 40 percent of the sugar imported by France and Britain. Under the French mercantilist system, Saint-Domingue was not permitted to develop its own industries and was forced to purchase finished goods from France, with all trade carried in French ships. Although many planters became fabulously wealthy, they also harbored resentment against the French government strictures.

The Saint-Dominque economy was based on slavery. Because the plantation owners were only a small fraction of the population next to a very large number of slaves, they employed physical punishment and even castration as a means of keeping the slaves in check. Although the Code Noire issued by King Louis XIV in 1685 was designed to check excesses, it had little practical effect in easing the lot of the slaves.

There were three separate population groups in Saint-Domingue. At the top of the pyramid in 1789 were some 32,000 whites. They held most of the power in the colony. The wealthiest were the plantation owners. Many sought to make their fortune and then retire to France free of the scourge of yellow fever, which regularly swept the island and carried off substantial numbers of people irrespective of their race or social station.

The second group of people were free blacks or mixed bloods, known as mulattoes or *gens de couleur libres* (free people of color). Numbering some 28,000, they occupied an intermediate position in society. Many of this second group were educated and served in the army. Others were artisans or helped run the plantations. A number were wealthy and owned slaves and plantations themselves. Nonetheless, they were systematically discriminated against because of their race by the whites and were excluded from real power. A number of this second group settled in the northern port city of Le Cap Français (also known as Le Cap and today Cap-Haïtien) and, when the revolution occurred, provided a disproportionate number of its leaders.

Most of the population of Saint-Domingue, however, consisted of slaves of African descent; in 1789 they numbered some 452,000 people. Because of their high mortality rate, new slaves were constantly brought to the island from Africa. Those born in the colony were known as Creoles. They and most slaves spoke a mixture of French and West African native languages that came to be known as Creole. Runaway slaves, known as Maroons, attempted to eke out an existence by living off the land or stealing from the plantations or settled in the urban centers where they could hope to blend in with freed blacks and mulattoes. Some of the escaped slaves formed gangs and carried out occasional large-scale raids on the plantations, although they generally lacked the organization, leadership, and weapons to inflict real damage. The fact that the slaves so greatly outnumbered the plantation owners produced considerable fear among the latter of possible slave revolts.

Honoré Gabriel Riqueti, Comte de Mirabeau, a Liberal French noble and influential figure in the early phase of the French Revolution of 1789, summed it up well when he wrote that the whites of Saint-Domonique "slept at the foot of Vesuvius." Indeed, François Mackandal, a voodoo priest, achieved some success in organizing plantation slaves and led a rebellion during 1751–1757. Although Mackandal was captured by French authorities and burned at the stake in 1758, violence continued for some time thereafter.

In addition to the divisions of race and station, Saint-Domingue was also sharply divided by regional differences. Shipping and trading enterprises were concentrated in the northern part of the island. The plantations tended to be concentrated in the west, which grew in importance especially after the capital was relocated from Le Cap Français to Port au Prince in 1781. There were also sharp differences in Saint-Domingue as to national loyalty, for a number of influential people sought either

independence or to join Saint-Domingue to the empires of England or Spain.

In the summer of 1789 Paris was gripped by a revolutionary upheaval. A major event in the history of France and the world, it quickly spread throughout Metropolitan France and to the colonies. In Saint-Domingue, whites were divided between those supporting and those opposing the revolution. Wealthy plantation owners saw it as an opportunity to win independence that would free them from the restrictive trade laws and enhance their own power and influence. Free blacks and mulattoes also took sides. The principal fault line was obviously the matter of racial equality, an obvious threat to the slave owners. This was enhanced by the Declaration of the Rights of Man and the Citizen adopted by France's new National Assembly at Versailles on August 26, 1789, which declared that all men were free and equal.

Fighting soon began in Saint-Dominque. In October 1790 Vincent Ogé, a wealthy man of color who had recently returned to the island from France, believed strongly that the declaration of August 1789 gave full civil rights to wealthy men of color. He now demanded the right to vote from the colonial governor. When the latter refused, Ogé led some 300 free blacks in a brief insurgency in the Cap Français region against the government. Captured early in 1791, Ogé was tried and sentenced to death. Broken on the wheel, he was then beheaded. Although Ogé had not opposed slavery, the brutal treatment he had received at the hands of the authorities was later cited by rebellious slaves when they themselves rose up in August 1791.

In May 1791, the National Assembly in France voted to grant full citizenship to free people of color. When the authorities in Saint-Domingue refused to go along with this, a general slave revolt began.

SPENCER C. TUCKER

## Course

On August 21, 1791, slaves of the Cap Français hinterland rose up in revolt, demanding their freedom. In short order the unrest had spread through the entire Northern Province. Revolutions are often violent affairs, and that of Saint-Domingue was no exception, brought on by longstanding injustice and cruel treatment. Still, in short order the number of slave insurgents had grown to some 100,000. Within two months, some 4,000 whites had been slain and hundreds of plantations had been burned or otherwise destroyed.

Dutty Bookman, a voodoo priest, had issued the call for the revolt. He also named Georges Biassou, Jean François, and a man named Jeannot as its initial leaders. Talks with the French having collapsed, by 1792 the rebel slaves had come to control one-third of Saint-Domingue.

When word of the revolt reached France, members of the Legislative Assembly, which had replaced the National Assembly in October 1791, acted to protect France's economic interests and voted on March 28, 1792, that the free men of color in the colonies be treated as equal citizens under the law. Ths decision shocked many in Europe and the United States, but at the same time the Legislative Assembly was determined to put down the revolt and ordered that 6,000 French soldiers be sent to Saint-Domingue.

After the execution of French king Louis XVI in January 1793, on February 1 France declared war on Great Britain and the Netherlands. A number of white planters in Saint-Domingue then struck an arrangement with the British, inviting in British forces to drive out the French authorities and establish British sovereignty. Spain joined the coalition against France in March. As the Spanish controlled the eastern part of Hispaniola, they now saw an opportunity to control the entire island.

Throughout most of the fighting that followed, the British and Spanish aided the slave rebels against the French, supplying them with arms, supplies, naval support, and military advisers. Slave general Biassou, now de facto leader of the revolt, allied with the Spaniards, and both British and Spanish forces invaded by sea and from Santo Domingo, the eastern two-thirds of the island. With only some 3,500 troops on the island, the French authorities in Saint-Domingue faced a desperate situation. In these circumstances French commissioners Léger-Félicité Sonthonax and Étienne Polvorel granted freedom to all the slaves in Saint-Domingue. This action was subsequently confirmed by yet another government in France, the National Assembly (1792–1794). On February 4, 1794, it abolished slavery in France and in the colonies and granted full civil rights to all black men in the colonies. This provision was retained in the French Constitution of 1795 and was held up by the revolutionaries as an example of idealism and liberty for all.

This decision by the French revolutionaries resinated in Saint-Domingue, and a number of the rebels switched sides back to the French. Among these was François Dominique Toussaint. Born on May 20, 1743, to slave parents on the Breda sugar plantation outside of Cap Français, Toussaint became a domestic worker and then a coachman. Legally freed in 1777, by 1779 Toussaint de Breda, as he was then known, was a free black growing coffee on rented property with a workforce of 12 slaves. A man of considerable intelligence, he also learned to read and write.

Toussaint joined the revolt and is said to have saved the lives of the Breda plantation manager and his family early in the revolution. Toussaint's first recorded activity with the rebels, however, was on December 4, 1791, when he participated in negotiations between the slave leaders and the French. Soon Toussaint was the chief lieutenant to slave general Biassou. Articulate, well organized, and a forceful leader, Toussaint also became an astute practitioner of guerrilla warfare.

With the French government having declared all slaves free men, Toussaint switched sides and joined with the French against the Spanish and British who sought to continue the institution of slavery in Saint-Domingue. In 1793 Tousssaint added Louverture (also spelled L'Ouverture) to his name, becoming Tousssaint Louverture. The word means "opening" and may have been in reference to his military skill. Working with French general Étienne Laveaux, Toussaint officially joined the French side on May 6, 1794. He then defeated those of his former colleagues still allied with the Spanish, including Biassou. (Biassou continued in the service of Spain, but in 1795 he withdrew from Saint-Domingue and settled in Florida, then belonging to the Spanish Crown).

Gradually Toussaint expelled the Spanish forces from the French portion of the island. Fighting continued, however, until the Treaty of Basel on July 22, 1795, which ended the war between France and Spain. The English were also forced to withdraw.

By 1796, the charismatic Toussaint was the leading figure on Saint-Domingue. French governor of Saint-Domingue Étienne Laveaux made him lieutenant governor of the colony, where Toussaint came to be lauded by much of the population for having done much to restore the economy. Ignoring laws passed in France that expropriated the lands of émigré landowners, he allowed them to return to their properties. Many of the French-educated mulatto class sought to replace the largely destroyed white class and take control themselves, but Toussaint was able to limit this for the most part to the southern peninsula of the island. A number of Toussaint's black officers assumed control of plantations, where the former slaves were forced to work but as paid laborers who shared in the profits. At the same time, convinced that the former slaves had to learn European ways, Toussaint worked to calm racial tensions.

In 1796 Toussaint eased Laveaux aside, and new commissioner Léger-Félicité Sonthonax gave him largely free reign and made him governor-general. But Toussaint disliked Sonthonax's radicalism, atheism, coarseness in manner, and immorality and forced him aside in 1797. Despite the continuing war between Britain and France, treaties negotiated by Toussaint with the British in 1798 and 1799 secured their complete withdrawal and led to a lucrative trade with both Britain and its colonies as well as with the United States. Sugar exports paid for the importation into Saint-Domingue of trade goods and weapons. The British even offered to recognize Toussaint as king of an independent Saint-Domingue, but he refused. Toussaint distrusted the British because they still embraced slavery, and he disdained titles.

In 1795 yet another government, that of the Directory, had come to power in France, and in 1798 Gabriel Hédouville arrived in Saint-Domingue as its representative. Knowing that France had no chance of restoring its control as long as war with

Britain continued, Hédouville attempted to pit against Toussaint the mulatto leader André Rigaud, who had established a semi-independent state in the south. Toussaint discovered Hédouville's designs and forced him to flee.

Philippe Roume succeeded Hédouville and gave Toussaint a free hand. In July 1799 in the bloody War of the Knives, also known as the War of the South, Toussaint launched a campaign that drove Rigaud from power and destroyed his quasi state. The ensuing purge in the south that followed, directed by Toussaint's lieutenant brigadier general Jean-Jacques Dessalines, was so brutal, however, that it drove a wedge between the blacks and the mulattoes, making reconciliation impossible.

In November 1799, the government in France changed yet again with the overthrow of the Directory and the establishment of the Consulate. French general Napoleon Bonaparte exercised effective power as first consul. Previously the French Directory had considered a military expedition to restore full French control of Saint-Domingue but was prevented in doing so by the ongoing war with Britain and British control of the seas.

Having now secured control of all of Saint-Domingue, Toussaint turned his attention to Spanish Santo Domingo, where slavery was still in place. Ignoring orders from both Roume and First Consul Bonaparte in Paris, Toussaint invaded the Spanish portion of Hispaniola and easily overran it in January 1801. He then freed the slaves there and treated the former Spanish possession with his magnanimity.

Toussaint was now in command of all of Hispaniola, and on February 4, 1801, the seventh anniversary of the National Assembly's abolition of slavery, he called for the election of a constitutional assembly. A March election returned seven white and three mulatto delegates, who completed the constitution in May. Toussaint signed it in July. Understandably, it was a strong reflection of Toussaint's own views. As Toussaint strongly opposed voodoo, the constitution made Catholicism the official religion. The freed slaves were tied to their workplaces, and Toussaint was named governor-general for life with near-dictatorial powers. But because he considered himself a Frenchman, there was no provision in the document for officials from Metropolitan France. At the same time, however, Toussaint strove to convince Bonaparte of his loyalty, informing one and all of his success in restoring order and prosperity.

Although Bonaparte confirmed Toussaint in his position, he certainly saw Toussaint as an obstacle to the restoration of French control of its most profitable colony and to his dream of creating a great French empire in the New World to include Louisiana. Toussaint was well aware of Bonaparte's dislike of blacks and that he wanted to reestablish slavery in Hispaniola. He was also aware that Bonaparte needed only peace with Britain in order to press Saint-Domingue into compliance with his wishes. Meanwhile, Toussaint did what he could to have excellent relations with France and get all on the island to work together. Not all had his vision. Many whites and mulattoea, fearful of the African majority, wanted to restore the old order, while many blacks wanted nothing less than driving out the Europeans and dividing their considerable holdings.

Bonaparte was able to put his plans into activation with conclusion between France and Britain of the preliminary Peace of Amiens on September 30, 1801 (the actual Treaty of Amiens was signed and went

Depiction of Haitian leader Toussaint L'Ouverture offering a truce to French officers after his guerrillas defeated the French forces in battle. (Hulton Archive/iStockphoto.com)

into effect on March 25, 1802). Bonaparte appointed his brother-in-law General Charles Victor Emmanuel Leclerc to command a 25,000-man expeditionary force.

The first French troops came ashore in Saint-Domingue on January 20, 1802. Some of Toussaint's supporters went over to them, and the French soon controlled most of the south and the coastal towns. A major battle took place at Fort Crête-à-Pierrot east of Saint-Marc in the Artibonite River Valley during March 4–24. The fort was strategically important, as it controlled access to the Cahos Mountains. General Dessalines had command of the fort, while Leclerc directed some 2,000 French troops in the effort to take it. Casualties were heavy on both sides, but the eventual placement of artillery in a commanding position on his ground overlooking the fort led the rebels to abandon it to the French. Casualties were heavy on both sides, and

the battle certainly demonstrated that blacks could fight on a par with regular European forces.

Following the battle, Dessalines temporarily swore allegiance to France and joined forces with Leclerc. Dessalines may also have had a hand in Toussaint's surrender. On May 7, Toussaint capitulated on the pledge from Leclerc of continued freedom for blacks and retired in honor to a plantation. A few weeks later in June, he was invited under false pretenses to a meeting by French general Jean-Baptiste Brunet, With Leclerc's full cooperation and under orders from Bonaparte, Toussaint was seized at Brunet's residence and sent with his family to Fort-de-Joux in the French Jura Mountains, where he was confined and interrogated. He died there of pneumonia on April 7, 1803.

In June also, Bonaparte instructed Leclerc to restore the former French colonial system and slavery, thus violating the pledge made by Leclerc to Toussaint. This brought renewal of the war, as blacks under Dessalines resumed fighting. By August, resistance to the French had sharply increased. By late October, the French controlled only the larger cities. Leclerc died of yellow fever in early November, one of many Frenchmen felled by the disease.

The arrival in April 1803 of reinforcements gave the French their best chance of a military victory, but the Peace of Amiens lasted only 14 months, and war between Britain and France resumed on May 18. A Royal Navy squadron was promptly dispatched from Jamaica, and the French forces found themselves cut off as British warships gradually captured French supply ships and warships and blockaded the Haitian ports. The French forces now suffered increasingly from a lack of supplies and from disease. Most surrendered to the British that November, although a few held out on the Spanish side of the island until 1809.

On January 1, 1804, in the city of Gonaïves, Dessalines declared the former French colony independent, giving it the name Haiti from the indigenous Awawak name in order to emphasize the break with European colonialism. Although figures vary widely, one source claims that between 1791 and 1804 some 200,000 blacks died in Haiti, along with as many as 100,000 French and British soldiers. Yellow fever rather than actual fighting may have claimed the majority.

SPENCER C. TUCKER

## Consequences

The Haitian Revolution leading to independence was a major event in the history of the New World and had profound implications for Africans elsewhere. Not only did it inspire slave revolts in the United States and in the British colonies, but it also challenged the notion of the inferiority of blacks. It also had a profound effect on the development of the United States. With the failure of Bonaparte's effort to reconquer Haiti and create a large French empire in the Western Hemisphere coupled with British domination at sea and the likelihood that war between France and Britain would soon resume, U.S. president Thomas Jefferson was able to arrange to purchase the Louisiana Territory from France. The treaty was signed on May 2, 1803, but antedated to April 30. An incredible undertaking, for only 60 million francs (about $15 million) the infant United States gained 828,000 square miles of territory and doubled its territorial extent.

Dessalines continued Toussaint's policy of forced labor to prevent Haiti from reverting to a subsistence economy. Unlike Toussaint, however, he confiscated the lands of white plantation owners and made it illegal for them to own property. His most extreme measure was a campaign during February–April 1804 to eliminate the white population of Haiti entirely. Personally traveling to various cities of Haiti, he cited French atrocities and then ordered the massacre of all whites. An estimated 3,000–5,000 people were killed, including women and children, and there were numerous instances of rape and pillage. Three categories of whites were excluded from the 1804 massacre: Poles serving with the French forces who had deserted, the small number of Germans, and medical personnel. Thousands fled the island, and whites of French descent on the island were virtually eliminated. Many whites and free people of color settled in New Orleans, with some in both categories owning slaves whom they brought with them.

Dessalines proclaimed himself emperor of Haiti on September 2, 1804. As emperor, he sought to carry out reforms to improve the Haitian economy. He imposed strict regulations on foreign trade, favoring trade with Britain and the United States over that with France. He also placed well-educated Haitians, primarily mulattoes, in key administrative posts. He also built up the strength of the Haitian military, an action that had the adverse effect of drawing labor from the plantations.

Many in Haiti opposed Dessalines's draconian measures and rule. He was assassinated on October 17, 1806, possibly in an ambush led by Alexandre Pétion and Henri Christophe, who later split the country in two and ruled each section separately.

Despite his oppressive rule, the day of Dessalines's death, October 17, is a national holiday in Haiti, and his legacy finds expression in the naming of the Haitian national anthem of 1903, "La Dessalini-enne," in his honor.

The Haitian economy suffered thereafter. In 1825 during the presidency of Jean-Pierre Boyer and abetted by the presence of French warships off the Haitian coast, the Haitian government was forced to agree to indemnify the French slaveholders in the amount of 125 million francs (reduced in 1838 to 68 million francs). This bankrupted Haiti. Haiti then underwent a long history of dictators, kept in place by the large Haitian military establishment. Corrupt and inept rule coupled with natural disasters served to make Haiti the poorest nation in the Western Hemisphere in terms of per capital income.

SPENCER C. TUCKER

## Timeline

| | |
|---|---|
| **Dec 1492** | Christopher Columbus, sailing for Spain, lands on the island subsequently named Hispaniola and claims it for Spain. |
| **1697** | In the Treaty of Ryswick, Spain formally cedes to France control of the western third of Hispaniola, now named Saint-Domingue. Its sugar plantations will make Saint-Domingue France's wealthiest colony. |
| **1751–1757** | François Mackandal, a voodoo priest, leads a rebellion of plantation slaves. The rebellion is put down, and Mackandal is executed. |
| **Jul 1789** | The French Revolution begins in Paris, creating deep racial fault lines in Saint-Domingue. |
| **Aug 26, 1789** | France's new National Assembly enacts the Declaration of the Rights of Man and the Citizen, declaring all men free and equal. |
| **Oct 1790** | Fighting begins in Saint-Domingue when Vincent Ogé, a wealthy man of color, demands the right to vote. When this is refused, Ogé leads some 300 free blacks in a brief insurgency in the Cap Français region. |
| **May 1791** | The National Assembly in France votes to grant full citizenship to free people of color. When authorities in Saint-Domingue refuse to accept this, a slave revolt ensues. |
| **Aug 21, 1791** | Following a call by voodoo priest Dutty Bookman, slaves of the Cap Français hinterland begin a revolt, demanding their freedom. Within several months some 100,000 slave insurgents kill 4,000 whites and burn hundreds of plantations. |
| **Mar 28, 1792** | France's Legislative Assembly votes to grant equal citizenship rights to free men of color in the colonies. At the same time, however, it orders 6,000 French soldiers to Saint-Domingue. |
| **1793** | Britain and Spain aid the rebels in Saint-Domingue. Slave general Georges Biassou, now de facto leader of the revolt, allies with the Spaniards, and British and Spanish forces invade by sea and from |

Santo Domingo. With only some 3,500 troops on the island, French commissioners Léger-Félicité Sonthonax and Étienne Polvorel grant freedom to Saint-Domingue's slaves.

| | |
|---|---|
| **Feb 1, 1793** | France declares war on Great Britain and the Netherlands. |
| **Mar 22, 1793** | Spain joins the coalition of powers at war with revolutionary France. Spain, which controls eastern Hispaniola, sees an opportunity to control the entire island. |
| **Feb 4, 1794** | The French National Assembly abolishes slavery in France and its colonies and grants full civil rights to all black men in the colonies. In consequence, a number of the rebels switch sides back to the French. |
| **May 6, 1794** | François Dominique Toussaint Louverture (also given as L'Ouverture), a Biassou lieutenant, formally joins the French in fighting the British and Spanish. Gradually, Toussaint drives Spanish forces from Saint-Domingue. |
| **Jul 22, 1795** | The Treaty of Basel ends the war between France and Spain. |
| **1796** | Toussaint is now the leading figure on Saint-Domingue. French governor Étienne Laveaux makes him lieutenant governor, and Toussaint does much to restore the economy and ease racial tensions. He then eases Laveaux aside, and new commissioner Léger-Félicité Sonthonax makes Toussaint governor-general. |
| **1798** | The new French government (the Directory), sends Gabriel Hédouville to Saint-Domingue as its representative. He attempts to pit against Toussaint the mulatto leader André Rigaud. Toussaint discovers this and forces Hédouville to flee. Hédouville's successor Philippe Roume gives Toussaint a free hand. |
| **1798, 1799** | Treaties negotiated by Toussaint with the British not only secure their complete withdrawal but also lead to lucrative trade between Saint-Domingue, Britain, and the United States. |
| **Jul 1799** | Toussaint launches an invasion of Rigaud's territory. In the bloody War of the Knives (War of the South), Toussaint drives Rigaud from power and destroys his quasi state. The ensuing brutal purge in the south directed by Toussaint's lieutenant brigadier general Jean-Jacques Dessalines drives a wedge between blacks and mulattoes. |
| **Nov 9–10, 1799** | The Directory is replaced by the Consulate, with French general Napoleon Bonaparte exercising effective power as first consul. |
| **Jan 1800** | Having secured control of all Saint-Domingue and ignoring orders from Roume and Bonaparte, Toussaint invades Spanish Santo Domingo, which still embraces slavery. He easily defeats the Spansh and frees the slaves there. |
| **Feb 4, 1801** | Toussaint calls for the election of an indigenous constitutional assembly. |

| | |
|---|---|
| **Jul 1801** | Elected delegates complete the constitution in May, and Toussaint signs it into law. Toussaint is named governor-general for life with near-dictatorial powers. |
| **Jan 20, 1802** | French troops came ashore in Saint-Domingue. Soon they control most of the south and the coastal towns. |
| **Mar 4–24, 1802** | A major battle occurs at Fort Crête-à-Pierrot, resulting in a costly French victory. Following the battle General Dessalines, who had commanded the fort, switches sides and joins Leclerc. |
| **Mar 25, 1802** | The Peace of Amiens goes into effect, ending the war between France and Britain. This allows Bonaparte to reestablish French control of Saint-Domingue as part of a larger scheme to create a French empire in the New World. Bonaparte names his brother-in-law General Charles Victor Emmanuel Leclerc to lead a 25,000-man expeditionary force to Saint-Domingue. |
| **May 7, 1802** | Toussaint capitulates on the pledge from Leclerc of continued freedom for blacks. |
| **Jun 1802** | Toussaint is arrested and sent to France, where he is interrogated. Bonaparte then orders Leclerc to restore the French colonial system and reinstate slavery, which brings renewal of the fighting. |
| **Oct 1802** | Fighting goes badly for the French, who now control only the larger cities of Saint-Domingue. |
| **Nov 2, 1802** | Leclerc dies in France of yellow fever. |
| **Apr 1803** | French reinforcements in Saint-Domingue. |
| **Apr 7, 1803** | Toussaint dies in France of pneumonia. |
| **May 2, 1803** | With the collapse of Bonaparte's plans in Saint-Dominique and with war with Britain likely to resume, Napoleon completes the Louisiana Purchase with the United States. |
| **May 18, 1803** | Fighting begins again between Britain and France. The Royal Navy shuts down French access to Saint-Domingue, dooming French forces there. |
| **Nov 1803** | Most French forces surrender to the British, although a few hold out on the Spanish side of the island until 1809. |
| **Jan 1, 1804** | In Gonaïves, Dessalines declares Saint-Domingue's independence, proclaiming it to be Haiti. |
| **Feb–Apr 1804** | Dessalines orchestrates the massacre of whites in Haiti. Some 3,000–5,000 are killed. Many emigrate and settle in Louisiana. |
| **Sep 2, 1804** | Dessalines proclaims himself emperor of Haiti. |
| **Oct 17, 1806** | Dessalines is assassinated. |

SPENCER C. TUCKER

## Further Reading

Bellegarde-Smith, Patrick. *Haiti: The Breached Citadel.* Boulder, CO: Westview, 1990.

Blakburn, Robin. "The Force of Example." In *The Impact of the Haitian Revolution in the Atlantic World,* edited by David P. Geggus, 15–21. Columbia: University of South Carolina Press, 2001.

Bryan, Patrick E. *The Haitian Revolution and Its Effects.* Exeter, NH: Heinemann, 1984.

Dubois, Laurent. *Avengers of the New World: The Story of the Haitian Revolution.* Cambridge, MA: Belknap Press of Harvard University Press, 2004.

Fick, Carolyn E. *The Making of Haiti: The Saint Domingue Revolution from below.* Knoxville: University of Tennessee Press, 1990.

Geggus, David Patrick. *The Haitian Revolution: A Documentary History.* Cambridge, MA: Hackett, 2014.

Geggus, David Patrick. *The Impact of the Haitian Revolution in the Atlantic World.* Columbia: University of South Carolina Press, 2002.

Ghachem, Malick W. *The Old Regime and the Haitian Revolution.* Cambridge: Cambridge University Press, 2012.

Girard, Philippe R. "Black Talleyrand: Toussaint Louverture's Secret Diplomacy with England and the United States." *William and Mary Quarterly* 66(1) (January 2009): 87–124.

Girard, Philippe R. "Napoléon Bonaparte and the Emancipation Issue in Saint-Domingue, 1799–1803," *French Historical Studies* 32(4) (Fall 2009): 587–618.

Girard, Philippe R. *The Slaves Who Defeated Napoleon Toussaint Louverture and the Haitian War of Independence, 1801–1804.* Tuscaloosa: University of Alabama Press, 2011.

Heinl, Robert. *Written in Blood: The History of the Haitian People.* New York: Lanham, 1996.

James, Cyril Lionel Robert. *The Black Jacobins Toussaint Louverture and the San Domingo Revolution.* New York: Vintage, 1989.

Nicholls, David. *From Dessalines to Duvalier: Race, Colour, and National Independence in Haiti.* Cambridge: Cambridge University Press, 1979.

Ott, Thomas O. *The Haitian Revolution, 1789–1804.* Knoxville: University of Tennessee Press, 1973.

Parkinson, Wenda. *"This Gilded African": Toussaint L'Ouverture.* New York: Quartet Books, 1978.

Peyre-Ferry, Joseph Elisée. *Journal des opérations militaires de l'armée française à Saint-Domingue 1802–1803 sous les ordres des capitaines-généraux Leclerc et Rochambeau.* Paris: Les Editions de Paris-Max Chaleil, 2006.

Popkin, Jeremy D. *You Are All Free: The Haitian Revolution and the Abolition of Slavery.* New York: Cambridge University Press, 2010.

Tyson, George F., Jr., ed. *Toussaint L'Ouverture.* Englewood Cliffs, NJ: Prentice-Hall, 1973.

# Spanish War of Independence (Peninsular War) (1808–1814)

## Causes

The Spanish War of Independence (Guerra de la Independencia Española as it is known in the Spanish-speaking world or Peninsular War as it appears in English-language history books), is directly linked to French emperor Napoleon Bonaparte's institution of the Continental System. The Battle of Trafalgar (October 21, 1805) had established British supremacy at sea and led Napoleon to try to get at the British by economic means. First announced in the Berlin Decree of November 21, 1806, during the War of the Fourth Coalition (1806–1807), the Continental System prohibited trade between the French Empire, including the German states, and Britain. The system was subsequently strengthened through additional decrees. In 1807 following the entente between France and Russia, the system was extended to Russia; the next year Portugal and Spain were added. Napoleon's intention was to cut off British trade with the European continent, forcing Great Britain into ruinous inflation. He also hoped that with continental Europe deprived of British-manufactured goods, the Continental System would stimulate industry, especially that of France, which received preference.

Napoleon's decision to institute the Continental System was a major blunder. It not only excited great resentment of France in many parts of Europe but also led Napoleon to undertake perhaps the most disastrous decision of his career: a military intervention in the Iberian Peninsula. This "Spanish ulcer," as Napoleon would come to call it, would cost France 300,000 casualties in five years of fighting and have a profound impact on his military operations elsewhere.

On July 7, 1807, the Treaty of Tilsit, concluded between Napoleon and Czar Alexander I of Russia, brought to an end the War of the Fourth Coalition. The treaty solidified Napoleon's hold on continental Europe and caused him to consider ways in which he might strengthen the Continental System against Britain. This in turn led to his intervention in the Iberian Peninsula. Bourbon Spain had long had close relations with France. The so-called Pacte de Famille (Family Compact) between the two states dated from 1733. True, Spain had joined the coalition of powers against revolutionary France in 1793, but this had ended in the Second Treaty of Basel of July 22, 1795, and the next year in the Treaty of San Ildefonso of August 19, 1796, when Spain allied with revolutionary France against Great Britain.

Portugal was another matter altogether, however. It was a major trading partner and the closest continental ally of Britain. Britain was also trading extensively with the Portuguese colony of Brazil, and on occasion British warships engaged against France utilized Portuguese ports. In addition to punishing Portugal and causing it to switch sides, Napoleon also no doubt wanted to secure the Portuguese Navy. Probably also, Napoleon saw French control of Portuguese affairs as furthering his intentions to completely dominate Spain.

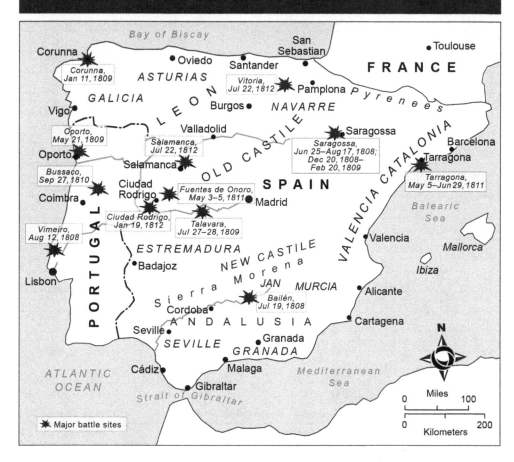

## SPANISH WAR OF INDEPENDENCE, 1808–1814

Ruling Portugal was Prince John of Braganza, regent for his insane mother Queen Maria I. John sought to pursue a neutral course and had refused Portuguese participation in the Continental System. On July 19, 1807, however, Napoleon ordered his ambassador in Lisbon to demand that Portugal close its ports to British shipping by September 1. Anticipating a negative response, on August 2 Napoleon ordered the creation of the I Corps of the Gironde Army of Observation commanded by General of Division Jean-Andoche Junot. Shortly afterward, Napoleon placed all Portuguese shipping in the French Empire under embargo, and on August 12 the French and Spanish ambassadors presented Prince John with a demand that he declare war on Great Britain, place the Portuguese Navy at the disposal of France and Spain, seize all British merchant ships in Portuguese ports, and arrest all British subjects in Portugal. While John agreed to suspend diplomatic relations with Britain and close Portuguese ports to British ships, he rejected the demands that he seize British goods and citizens as probably leading to war with Britain. Declaring John's reply unsatisfactory, the French and Spanish ambassadors departed Portugal on September 30.

## Spanish War of Independence (Peninsular War) (1808–1814)

| Second Siege of Saragoza (Saragossa) (December 20, 1808–February 20, 1809) | | |
|---|---|---|
| | **French and Allied Forces** | **Spanish Forces** |
| **Strength** | 38,000 infantry, 3,000 sappers/ gunners, 3,500 cavalry, 141 artillery guns | 34,000 infantry, 10,000 militiamen, 160 artillery guns |
| **Total killed** | 10,000* | 54,000* |

*Deaths by all causes. Historians estimate that as many as half of the total killed died of disease.

| Battle of Coruña (Corruna) (January 16, 1809) | | |
|---|---|---|
| | **British Forces** | **French Forces** |
| **Strength** | 16,000 infantry, 10 artillery guns | 12,000 infantry, 3,000 cavalry, 20 artillery guns |
| **Killed/wounded** | 1,200 | 650 |

| Battle of Salamanca (July 22, 1812) | | |
|---|---|---|
| | **British, Spanish, Portuguese Forces** | **French Forces** |
| **Strength** | 52,000 | 49,650 |
| **Casualties** | 5,200 | 13,000 |

| Battle of Vitoria (June 21, 1813) | | |
|---|---|---|
| | **British, Spanish, Portuguese Forces** | **French Forces** |
| **Strength** | 80,000 | 60,000 |
| **Casualties** | 5,000 | 8,000 |

**Sources:** Esdaile, Charles. *The Peninsular War.* New York: Palgrave Macmillan, 2003; Fortescue, John. *A History of the British Army, 1807–1809,* Vol. 2. New York: Macmillan, 1910; Gates, David. *The Spanish Ulcer: A History of the Peninsular War.* New York: Da Capo, 2001.

On October 12 Junot's corps began crossing the Bidasoa River into Spain at Irun, and on October 27 Napoleon concluded with King Charles IV of Spain the secret Treaty of Fontainebleau. It provided for the division of Portugal into three separate entities under French and Spanish control. Portugal's extensive overseas empire would also go to France and Spain. On November 19 Junot's corps and 25,000 Spanish troops invaded Portugal. The conquest of that kingdom was easily accomplished, with Junot entering Lisbon on December 1. Learning that Napoleon had announced the deposition of the Braganzas, Prince John and a number of nobles and merchants hastily loaded what possessions they could and sailed in 15 warships and more than 20 transports for Brazil.

Napoleon made Junot a duke and appointed him governor of Portugal. The French seized the property of those who had fled. They also imposed an indemnity of 100 million francs and sent the Portuguese Army to northern Germany, where it was assigned garrison duties. The heavy taxes imposed by the French and the execution of some of the Portuguese citizens who dared to resist the foreign troops caused considerable resentment, but outright revolt against French and Spanish rule would have to await other developments.

With Portugal having been so easily secured, Napoleon set in motion plans to subdue Spain. He now ordered 100,000 French troops into that country under Marshal Joachim Murat, designated lieutenant of the emperor in Spain and commander of the (French) Army of Spain. The first French soldiers crossed into Spain on January 8, 1808. The pretext for this was that the men were to guard the Spanish coasts against the British.

Spain was already in unrest under the rule of King Charles IV. The Family Compact had undergone considerable strain. Napoleon never did understand war at sea, and his decision to order the French and Spanish fleets to Italy brought their decisive defeat by the British in the Battle of Trafalgar, which rankled in Spain. Economic difficulties and Charles's inept rule also brought much discredit to the Crown. The situation was such that Crown Prince Ferdinand had even attempted a coup d'état in 1807. Rioting and a revolt at Aranjuez finally brought Charles IV's abdication on March 19, 1808, in favor of his son as Ferdinand VII. Napoleon distrusted Ferdinand, however, and when Charles appealed to the emperor for assistance in reclaiming the throne, Napoleon summoned both men to meet with him at Bayonne in April 1808 and there forced both to abdicate.

SPENCER C. TUCKER

## Course

### *The French Invasions of Spain and Portugal and British Intervention (1808)*

With the forced abdication of both Charles IV and Ferdinand VII and the arrival in Spain of Marshal Joachim Murat and his 100,000-man (French) Army of Spain, things reached the boiling point. The Spanish War of Independence can be said to have begun on May 2, 1808, in Madrid in an uprising against the correctly perceived French rule of Spain. This event is known as El Dos de Mayo (The Second of May). The rioters killed as many as 150 French soldiers. The French put the uprising down with great savagery, killing as many as 500 Spaniards, and the next day executed 113 of those Spaniards who had been arrested. Those executed were memorialized by Spanish artist Francisco Goya in his famous painting *The Third of May 1808*. There was also rioting in other Spanish cities, albeit on a smaller scale, that ended with the same result. Napoleon welcomed this as a means of securing complete Spanish submission to his authority. He then sent his elder brother Joseph, currently the king of Naples, to Spain as king (from June 6), whereupon Murat took Joseph's place at Naples.

Even before this, guerrilla war commenced in Spain. Indeed, the word "guerrilla" comes from the Spanish word *guerra* and is the diminutive, meaning "small war." The fighting often saw no quarter given by either side. The British provided arms and assistance to insurgents in both Spain and Portugal, and then in July they dispatched an expeditionary force to Portugal under Lieutenant General Sir Arthur Wellesley.

Two French sieges of Zaragoza (Saragossa), during June 25–August 17, 1808, and December 20, 1808–February 20, 1809, illustrate the desperate nature of the warfare in Spain. One of the major centers of resistance against the French and the chief city of Aragon, Zaragoza lies about 200 miles northeast of Madrid on the Ebro River. In 1808 it had a population of about 60,000 people. General Don José Robolledo Palafox y Melzi had charge of the defense. Initially he had only 300 royal dragoons, and only one-third of these had horses, but Palafox recruited volunteers, called up retired and half-pay officers, and organized the city defenses as best he could, including the establishment of a munitions factory. Although he had artillery, few of his men were trained in its use.

The first fighting took place on June 8 at Tudela, where a French force of 5,000 infantry, 1,000 cavalry, and two artillery batteries under the command of General François Joseph Lefèbvre-Desnouettes clashed with some 6,000 Spanish levies and armed peasants who tried to bar the way to Zaragoza. The French soon scattered them. A second and last effort to block the French approach occurred shortly thereafter at Alagon, where Palafox led 650 men and four guns against the French; he was wounded and his force defeated.

On June 15, 1808, Lefèbvre and his men arrived at Zaragoza and commenced military operations against it. Situated on a plain, Zaragoza was protected by the Ebro to the north. Its buildings were sturdy and tightly packed—ideal for defensive purposes—and the city was surrounded by a 12-foot-high stone wall. Palafox now commanded about 10,000 men.

Lefèbvre assumed that a determined attack would soon carry the city and directed his artillery against the west walls, while his infantry and some cavalry attacked the Santa Engracia gate to the south. Several French attacks encountered ferocious Spanish resistance, with the attackers sustaining 700 casualties. Lefèbvre then decided to await reinforcements. Learning that a force of 4,000 Spaniards was en route to the city, Lefèbvre feigned an attack on Zaragoza but slipped away with most of his men, surprising and destroying the Spanish relief column.

On June 29 an additional French division with siege guns arrived at Zaragoza under General Jean Antoine Verdier, who took overall command of operations. Verdier ordered his men to drive 300 Spanish defenders from Mount Torrero, a dominating hill south of the city, where the French then placed their siege guns. From that position at midnight on June 30, 46 French guns opened fire on Zaragoza. Following a 12-hour bombardment, Verdier ordered his infantry forward.

Desperate fighting ensued, during which Agustina Raimunda María Saragossa Domènech, or Agustina of Aragon, made her appearance and became a Spanish heroine. Immortalized by British poet Lord Byron, who was her lover, Agustina carried food to a gun crew and then took the place of one of its members, reportedly firing the gun herself and shouting that she would not leave the gun while she was still alive. At the same time a young boy seized a banner from a wounded standard-bearer and waved it. These actions helped rally the defenders, who were able to drive out those French troops who had gotten inside the city. The attackers sustained 500 casualties.

Verdier now reverted to a conventional siege. With only 13,000 men, he was unable to seal off access to the city, and the Spaniards continued to receive both supplies and reinforcements. Gradually the French pushed their lines forward and continued their bombardment. On August 4 the French made another breach in the walls. That afternoon 3,000 French troops attacked, entered the city, and secured about half of it. No quarter was given by either side. Verdier demanded that Palafox surrender, but he reportedly replied "Guerra á chillo" (War to the knife). Desperate fighting then raged, with priests and monks fighting alongside the people.

On the morning of August 14, Verdier withdrew his troops from the part of the city the French had captured, and on August 17 he broke off the siege entirely. The news of the French defeat in the Battle of Bailén (Anglicized as Baylen) on July 16–19, his inability to seal off the city, and word that additional Spanish reinforcements were en route to Zaragoza all caused Verdier to end siege operations.

After Napoleon had taken personal charge in Spain, on December 20, 1808, the French returned to Zaragoza and again placed it under siege. This time the Spaniards were ready. Palafox had substantially improved the city defenses, which were now manned by 34,000 regular Spanish troops supported by 10,000 armed peasants. He also had 160 artillery pieces. Marshal Bon-Adrien Jannot de Moncey led the French forces, reinforced by troops under Marshal Edouard Mortier. Moncey commanded 38,000 infantry, 3,000 sappers and gunners, 3,500 cavalry, and 144 guns.

Again concentrating on Mount Torrero, the French captured it on December 20, driving its 6,000 defenders into the city and taking seven Spanish guns. Moncey called on Palafox to surrender, but the latter replied "Spanish blood covers us with honor and you with shame." French siege operations began in earnest on December 23.

On January 2, General Jean Androche Junot arrived at Zaragoza to replace Moncey and with orders to detach Mortier and 10,000 men to keep upon the road to Madrid. The French defeated a series of small Spanish sorties directed at spiking the French guns, which now were concentrated against the southeast walls of the city at close range. By January 26 the French had made several breaches in the walls, and the next day infantry assaults penetrated the Spanish defenses.

Learning that 20,000 Aragonese were marching to relieve Zaragoza, Napoleon sent reinforcements to the city and entrusted command of operations to Marshal Jean Lannes, who ordered Mortier to move against the Spanish relief column, which the French surprised and scattered at Nuestra Señora de Magallón.

Inside Zaragoza, bitter house-to-house fighting raged; it continued without letup for the next three weeks. With much of the city reduced to rubble and his main equipment factory destroyed by a mine, Palafox surrendered on February 20, 1809. Zaragoza was by then a smoking ruin, with about a third of the city destroyed. The siege claimed 54,000 Spanish lives, and only 8,000 of the Spanish garrison were still alive. Some 10,000 French had perished: 4,000 killed in action and 6,000 dead of disease.

Zaragoza became a symbol of defiance and a powerful standard for other Spanish cities resisting the invader. Napoleon was never able to solve the problem of Spanish nationalism.

Meanwhile, on July 19, 1808, General Pierre Dupont and some 20,000 French troops were surrounded and after three days were forced to surrender at Bailén by 30,000 Spanish troops under General Francisco Castaños. Although Dupont's men were mostly inexperienced raw recruits, the surrender was the first for a French

Spaniard Francisco de Goya's painting *The Third of May 1808* was one of a number of his works that dramatized the horrific nature of the Peninsular War, and especially atrocities committed by the French against the Spanish people. (Museo del Prado, Madrid)

army under Napoleon and sent shock waves across Europe, invigorating opposition to French rule in other countries, especially Austria. It also served as a tremendous boost to the continued Spanish resistance and to British hopes for it. The Spaniards failed to honor the surrender terms that provided for the 17,000 captured French soldiers to be repatriated to France. With the exception of Dupont and a few other officers, the men were transferred to the island of Cabrera, where most died of starvation.

King Joseph panicked, and on August 1 he and the court quit Madrid, withdrawing his forces north of the Ebro River. A furious Napoleon then decided to go to Spain in person. On August 1 also, a British expeditionary force commanded by Lieutenant General Sir Arthur Wellesley landed north of Lisbon. Junot marched from Lisbon

with 13,000 men to engage Wellesley's 17,000 men at Vimeiro (August 21). Devastating British musket fire against the dense French attack formations gave the British victory. Junot's position was now completely untenable, but the elderly and inept commanders of the British expeditionary force in Portugal, Lieutenant Generals Hew Dalrymple and Harry Burrard, granted Junot generous terms.

In the Convention of Cintra of August 30, 1808, the French army in Portugal was transported back to France by Royal Navy ships, with all its weapons, equipment, and the loot acquired in Portugal. A storm of protest in Britain over this led to the recall of the senior British officers in Portugal, although Wellesley, who had opposed the terms, was exonerated. Lieutenant General Sir John Moore then assumed command of British forces in Portugal.

British forces in Portugal were reinforced to 35,000 men. Moore left 12,000 men there and invaded Spain with the remainder to assist what then numbered some 125,000 Spanish Army and irregular forces. Napoleon also reinforced his forces in Spain. Buoyed by events in Spain, Austrian leaders considered yet another war with France. To prevent this, Napoleon met with Russian czar Alexander I at Erfurt during September 27–October 14, 1808, seeking to secure a pledge that war between Austria and France would necessarily mean war between Austria and Russia. This undoubtedly would have prevented Austria from going to war, but at night Alexander met secretly with Napoleon's chief negotiator, French foreign minister Charles Maurice de Talleyrand, who was working against Napoleon in the hopes of restoring a balance of power in Europe. Talleyrand persuaded Alexander against extending the guarantee and thus was probably more responsible for the war in 1809 between Austria and France than any other individual.

Napoleon arrived in Spain in early November 1808. Moving south of the Ebro River with nearly 200,000 men, he entered Madrid on December 4. Napoleon then abolished monastic orders and the Spanish Inquisition, confiscated rebel property, and ordered the sequestering of goods deemed necessary to France. After restoring Joseph to power, Napoleon departed Madrid on December 22 to deal with Moore.

Taking advantage of his great numerical advantage, Napoleon attempted to destroy Moore's force, but the latter hurriedly withdrew to La Coruña (Corunna), where his men might be evacuated by the Royal Navy. Messages from Paris that the Austrians were mobilizing led Napoleon to quit Spain. On January 16, 1809, French general Nicolas-Jean de Dieu Soult attacked Moore at La Coruña but was repulsed (Moore was mortally wounded). The next day, the Royal Navy evacuated the British force.

Following the Battle of La Coruña, French forces under Soult invaded Portugal, but British forces there, now under Wellesley, had been reinforced. Wellesley surprised Soult at Oporto on May 21 and forced him to withdraw back to Spain.

Believing that the continued combat in Spain meant that other parts of Europe, notably the Germanies, were ready to revolt against French rule, in March 1809 Austria declared a German war of liberation and began the War of the Fifth Coalition (1809). Archduke Charles had rebuilt the Austrian regular army to 300,000 men and the Landwehr to some 150,000, but the troops were still poorly trained, and he had opposed war. Unfortunately for Austria, his wise counsel was overruled. Austrian leaders were disappointed by the response to their declaration of war. Prussia had yet to recover from its defeat at the hands of Napoleon in 1806–1807, and most of the major German princes had benefited greatly from Napoleon's rearrangement of territory and had no incentive to join a war against him. In addition, Russia remained on the sidelines.

Austrian forces invaded Bavaria and Italy. Napoleon quickly departed Spain and took the field. He captured Vienna, but this time no Austrian officials met with him, and on May 21–22 in the Battle of Aspen/Essling, Charles inflicted on Napoleon his first personal military defeat. On July 6, however, in the largest Napoleonic battle to that point (340,000 men engaged), Napoleon won a close-run yet decisive victory over Charles in the Battle of Wagram. Austrian leaders were now forced to sue for peace. The Treaty of Schönbrunn on October 14, 1809, was harsh. Austria was forced to cede extensive territories and now joined Prussia as a second-class power. The French inroads in Poland and in the Balkans were nonetheless alarming to Czar Alexander.

### The British Invade Spain from Portugal (1809–1810)

Warfare continued in the Iberian Peninsula. In June 1809 Wellesley invaded Spain from Portugal with 45,000 men. In July King Joseph devised a plan that, had it been forcefully executed, might have trapped and destroyed Wellesley. It called for 60,000 men to move south from Salamanca and get in behind Wellesley. But the French troops from Salamanca were slow to arrive, so Joseph, Marshal Claude Victor, and troops from Madrid met Wellesley alone.

The ensuing Battle of Talavera, fought some 70 miles southwest of Madrid on July 27–28, was indecisive. Warned of the approach of the Salamanca force, Wellesley retired, forced to withdraw back to Portugal. Shortly thereafter Wellesley was ennobled as Viscount Wellington of Talavera.

Meanwhile, a British force landed in the Low Countries in an effort to seize the port of Antwerp. The operation should have been abandoned upon news of that Austrian defeat but was in any case soon forced to withdraw. The Royal Navy meanwhile continued to secure overseas territories.

From Milan on November 23 and December 17 Napoleon expanded the Continental System, authorizing the seizure of any ships that had called at British ports and the confiscation of cargoes not certified as originating outside of Britain or its colonies. London responded that the Royal Navy would seize any ship that dared sail directly for a European port controlled by Napoleon. These policies directly affected international trade and were a chief cause of war between Britain and the United States in 1812.

Napoleon's Continental System was not only a failure but also a major factor in his ultimate defeat. It forced him to spread thin his limited resources, and it angered Europeans, including the French middle class, who desired trade with Britain and British goods. Exports to Britain were especially important to Russia, where there was growing unrest and pressure on Alexander to eschew the French alliance. Meanwhile, the British did everything they could to pry open the blockade. Some trading continued, on occasion with Napoleon's approval.

In Spain meanwhile, insurgent Spanish forces suffered their worst defeat of the Peninsular War when they were routed by Soult's cavalry at Ocaña near Madrid (November 19, 1809). Soult then conquered all of Andalusia except Cádiz, site of the Spanish naval base and the capital of the free Spanish government, defended by ships of the Royal Navy. On February 5, 1810, Marshal Claude Victor-Perrin commenced a siege of Cádiz; it lasted to August 24, 1812. French general Louis Gabriel Suchet meanwhile established French control over Aragon and Valencia. Spanish guerrillas continued operations in remote regions of Spain, however, attacking small French garrisons and supply columns but being unable to challenge French rule seriously.

Napoleon believed that the key to stabilizing the situation in Spain was to drive the British from Portugal. He gave Masséna command of the 60,000-man Army of Portugal and ordered him to clear the British from Iberia. Following a 24-day siege, Masséna captured Ciudad Rodrigo in Salamanca Province (July 10), then invaded Portugal on September 15. Wellington withdrew before him.

With 25,000 British and a like number of Portuguese troops, Wellington established a strong defensive position at Bussaco, near Luso. Masséna attacked Wellington on September 27. Because Wellington had positioned his men on the reverse slope of a long ridge, Masséna was uncertain as to this strength and dispositions. With their artillery fire largely ineffective, the French were driven off.

Wellington then continued his withdrawal into Portugal, occupying the prepared Torres Vedras line before Lisbon on October 10. Testing the allied position and finding it too strong to attack, Masséna remained in place until, his army starving, he had to withdraw. Deprived of food and harried by British hit-and-run tactics, he lost 25,000 men before regaining Spain early in 1811. Virtually all of Portugal was now free of French control.

Meanwhile, on December 31, 1810, Czar Alexander I announced that Russia was withdrawing from the Continental System. Alexander was alarmed by Napoleon's ambiguous plans regarding Poland, his annexation of Oldenburg without consultation and compensation, and French troop movements in Europe. But Alexander's chief concern was the Continental System, which had caused great unrest among the Russian nobility by cutting off the long-standing and important Russian trade with Britain. The nobles also strongly opposed the Westernizing influences introduced by the French alliance. Alexander was well aware that his father Paul I had been assassinated in a noble conspiracy. Napoleon on his part rejected sound advice from his ministers to offer some concessions to restore the alliance, deciding instead on military action to bring Russia to heel.

### Stalemate (1811–1812)

Napoleon's decision to invade Russia stretched his military assets thin—too thin it turned out, for sizable French forces were still engaged in major combat in the Iberian Peninsula. Masséna attempted to relieve the British siege of Almeida, Spain, but was rebuffed by Wellington in the Battle of Fuentes de Oñoro (May 3–5, 1811). However, following a siege of nearly two months (May 5–June 29), Suchet took the port of Tarragona, held by Spanish forces under General Juan Senen de Contreras. Then in the Battle of Albuera (May 16), British and Spanish forces under Generals William Beresford and Joachin Blake prevented Soult from raising the allied siege of Badajoz.

In early January 1812 Wellington again invaded Spain and laid siege to Ciudad Rodrigo, taking it after a 12-day siege (January 19). For his success, Wellington was elevated to earl. He then moved against Badajoz and, in its third siege of the war (March 17–April 6), captured it as well.

Auguste de Marmont, who in July 1810 had replaced Masséna as commander of French forces in Spain, engaged Wellington in the major battle of Salamanca on July 22, 1812. In his most brilliant victory to date, Wellington, leading British, Spanish, and Portuguese forces, defeated Marmont and the French in the Battle of Salamanca (July 22, 1812). The French sustained 13,000 casualties, including 7,000 prisoners; allied casualties were only about 5,200. This crushing victory opened the way for Wellington to Madrid, and King Joseph fled to Ocaña. Wellington entered Madrid (August 12) to general popular enthusiasm, securing some 180 guns and substantial quantities of military stores in the process.

Moving northward, Wellington hoped to destroy the French Army of Portugal, shattered at Salamanca. Its new commander, French marshal Bertrand Clausel, had reconstituted the army and on August 13 began a counteroffensive, relieving a number of French garrisons. Wellington then advanced on Burgos but failed to take it in siege operations during September 19–October 10.

The French, having built up their forces to 110,000 men, forced Wellington, with 73,000 men, to withdraw. The British abandoned Madrid on October 31 and retreated to Salamanca and then across the Huebra River, where the French abandoned the pursuit. Wellington then went into winter cantonments near Cuidad Rodrigo, receiving reinforcements from Britain, an enhanced subsidy, and appointment as general in chief of the Spanish Army and allied commander in the peninsula (a position previously denied him by his stubborn and on occasion difficult Spanish allies).

Meanwhile Napoleon, having assembled in eastern Germany and Poland a vast force of 611,000 men, 250,000 horses, and 2,000 guns, led it across the Nieman River into Russia on June 24, 1812. This force was the largest army under one command to that point in history. Napoleon entered Russia with but three weeks of supplies, for he planned to live off the land and anticipated winning one big battle in western Russia that would bring the czar to his senses and restore the Russian alliance. Napoleon failed to anticipate the Russians withdrawing deep into their vast territory and embarking on a scorched-earth policy. He also did not take into account the likely difficulties of securing adequate supplies

for his men and fodder for the horses or problems of sickness, stragglers, and the indiscipline of the large allied contingents. In the end it was matters of supply rather than Russian winter and the Cossacks that destroyed him.

Napoleon's advance went well at first. The invaders occupied Vilna (Vilnius) on June 26, Vitebsk on July 29, and Smolensk on August 17. Napoleon had planned to winter at Smolensk, but the ease and speed of his advance led him to decide to proceed to Moscow that autumn, convinced that taking that city would force Czar Alexander to treat with him. The aging Field Marshal Mikhail Kutuzov now assumed command of Russian forces. Ordered to stand and fight, he planned a defensive battle at Borodino, the last natural defense before Moscow. In the Battle of Borodino (September 7, 1812) Napoleon forced a Russian withdrawal. With an estimated combined casualty total of as many as 80,000, it was the bloodiest battle in European history until World War I.

Napoleon entered Moscow a week later, but the city was soon in flames, the fires set by the Russians. He then waited for Alexander to come to terms. Alexander delayed, and Napoleon rejected the wise advice of those who knew the nature of Russian winter. Too late, on October 19 he ordered a withdrawal. The retreat was a disaster. Winter came early and was one of the coldest on record. Napoleon abandoned the army on December 5 and returned to Paris two weeks later. Of some 460,000 men of the Grand Army who had entered Russia in June, only about 100,000 returned. A like number were prisoners in Russia. The same number perished in battle, while the remainder were lost to disease, starvation, and the elements. Napoleon had been unable to conquer all of

Europe. Now it would be seen as if all of Europe could conquer Napoleon.

Prussia now joined Russia against France, and a wave of anti-French sentiment swept the Germanies, beginning the so-called German War of Liberation. Also identified as part of the War of the Sixth Coalition (1813–1814), it would pit Russia, Britain, and Prussia against France and its allies. For the moment Austria remained neutral, but Sweden joined the coalition in June.

In 1813 Napoleon was able to field a force of 300,000 men, but many were young and largely untrained. Particularly serious was the loss in Russia of skilled junior officers and noncommissioned officers as well as trained horses. Equipment and arms were also in short supply. Napoleon might have minimized these shortcomings by standing on the defensive behind the Rhine, but true to form, he took the offensive.

All major battles of the German War of Liberation occurred in Saxony. Napoleon enjoyed victories at Lützen (May 2), Dresden (May 7–8), and Bautzen (May 20–21). Flush with victory, he rejected concessions to Austria, then on the fence, and on August 12, encouraged by French military reverses in Spain, that power again went to war against France. The allies now had four major armies in the field totaling 515,000 men, soon to be 600,000. Napoleon could count on only 370,000.

Although outnumbered, Napoleon scored a brilliant tactical victory at Dresden (August 26–27), but allied numbers told. In the Battle of Leipzig (October 16–19), probably the largest battle in terms of men engaged until the 20th century, the allies fielded 410,000 men to only 195,000 for Napoleon. Defeated, Napoleon was forced to withdraw to the Rhine, where his German allies

defected and threw off the rulers imposed by Napoleon. The liberation of Germany was complete, and the allies were in position to invade France from the northeast, while British forces invaded southwestern France from Spain.

Over British objections, the allies again offered Napoleon generous peace terms. Austria and most of the German rulers feared the expansion of Russian influence into Central Europe and were content solely to end French rule in Germany and Italy. They were willing to see Napoleon remain in power so that France would be a strong counterweight to Russia, which had already taken Poland. Under the peace terms, France was to have its natural boundaries of the Rhine and the Alps. Napoleon foolishly rejected the offer. On December 21, their armies crossed the Rhine.

### British and Spanish Forces Triumphant (1813–1814)

Meanwhile, 1813 saw British and allied Spanish and Portugese forces successful in Spain. Having reorganized his forces, in the spring of 1813 Wellington took the offensive. Commanding some 172,000 men against 200,000 French, in a series of maneuvers he forced the French back. On Napoleon's orders, King Joseph again abandoned Madrid (May 17). Napoleon ordered him to concentrate at Valladolid. Joseph moved too slowly, however, and was outflanked there and forced north of the Ebro River.

With some 60,000 men, Joseph established defensive positions south and west of Vitoria. Outnumbered by Wellington's 80,000 men, Joseph and his chief of staff, Marshal Jean Baptiste Jourdan, compounded the numerical disadvantage by widely dispersing their men. They did, however, have more guns: 150 to 90.

On June 21, Wellington attacked simultaneously in four columns. Exploiting gaps in the allied line, he won a complete victory. The allies sustained 5,000 casualties, the French 8,000, but in a precipitous retreat Joseph abandoned 143 guns, baggage, his treasury, vast amounts of stores, and even his crown. Fortunately for the French, the allies were not prepared for a rapid pursuit.

The Battle of Vitoria was decisive. It marked the end of Napoleonic rule in Spain and enabled Wellington to invade France, and, as already noted, it had profound effect on the vacillating Austrians and the war in Germany.

Wellington now moved against the strategically important port of San Sebastián on the French border but was forced to break off siege operations there on news that French forces, now under Marshal Soult, had returned to Spain and were proceeding against Pamplona. In the Battle of Sorauren northeast of Pamplona (July 27), Soult had a considerable numerical advantage but delayed attacking for a day, giving Wellington time to reinforce and rebuff the French, who withdrew.

Following smaller inconclusive battles, Soult withdrew to France to prepare defenses against the anticipated allied invasion. Wellington then resumed operations against San Sebastián, taking it on August 31 in hard house-to-house fighting. The troops then went on a rampage, destroying most of the city. Fighting also occurred to the east when Soult attempted to relieve San Sebastián, but he was defeated by a largely Spanish force in the Battle of San Marcial (August 31).

Beginning on October 7, Wellington led 24,000 allied troops across the Bidassoa River into France. By early November he had 82,000 men against only 62,000 French, many of therm raw conscripts.

Soult could only hope to delay the allies. On November 10 along the lower Nivelle River, Wellington breached Soult's defensive positions.

On December 10 having secretly concentrated his forces, Soult opened the Battle of Nivelle. Although the French achieved surprise and forced the British back, Soult mismanaged the fighting and, lacking resources to exploit the situation, finally withdrew. Deteriorating weather conditions then drove both sides into winter quarters.

Hostilities resumed in February 1814. Wellington advanced beyond Bayonne, leaving 31,000 men to encircle the city and its 17,000-man French garrison while he drove Soult's remaining men northward. The two commanders clashed again in the hard-fought Battle of Orthez (February 27). The British won, and Soult executed a fighting withdrawal on Toulouse. Wellington then broke off the pursuit to take the important port city of Bordeaux, which surrendered without a fight on March 12.

Meanwhile, major allied armies had also invaded France from the northeast. Although Napoleon conducted a brilliant campaign, it was with rapidly dwindling resources. Paris surrendered on March 30, 1814, and his own marshals forced Napoleon to abdicate. After a failed effort at suicide, he signed the Treaty of Fontainebleau on April 14, 1814. Given the island of Elba to rule, he decided on one last throw of the dice and returned to France. The so-called Hundred Days ended in his defeat by Wellington in the Battle of Waterloo on June 18, 1815. The Napoleonic Wars were over.

SPENCER C. TUCKER

## Consequences

Napoleon said of the Spanish War of Independence that it "overthrew me. All my disasters can be traced back to this initial knot." If this is true, he had only himself to blame, for he alone was responsible for the French intervention in Spain. By invading the Iberian Peninsula with the stated aim of expanding and strengthening the Continental System, Napoleon had not begun the process of strategic overreach that was to cost him dearly in subsequent campaigns. Far from diminishing the power of the British—that "nation of shopkeepers" he had called them—he had significantly strengthened it. The 19th century would see Britain as the preeminent world power.

With the end of the Peninsular War some of the British troops who had fought there returned to England, while others were sent to America to fight in the War of 1812 with the United States (1812–1815). Portuguese and Spanish soldiers left France and returned to their homelands, while the French soldiers still in Spain returned to France.

Spain was reeling. In addition to the human losses, dislocation, and suffering, the country had undergone enormous physical destruction in the war, greatly adding to its prewar financial problems. There was also considerable political turmoil. In 1810 a new revolutionary body, the Cortes (parliament), had come into being at Cádiz and had produced the Spanish Constitution of 1812. Modeled on the French revolutionary Constitution of 1791, it was at the time certainly one of the world's most liberal governing documents. Yet when King Ferdinand VII returned to Spain in 1814, he promptly issued the Manifest of Valencia that annulled the constitution and then instituted an absolutist regime. Determined to stamp out anything that resembled a representative institution, he ruled by decree and even restored the Inquisition, which had been abolished in Spain by King Joseph during the French occupation. Ferdinand also imposed a strict censorship, with all papers prohibited except for the official *Gaceta*.

Ferdinand was also determined to restore Spanish rule in the Americas, where during the war the many Spanish colonies and Portuguese Brazil had taken advantage of the break in ties with their mother countries to declare their independence. These actions had cut off an important revenue stream, adding greatly to financial difficulties in both Spain and Portugal.

Despite Ferdinand's best efforts and the imprisonment or execution of a number of liberals and radicals, opposition to his autocratic rule continued, and a revolt broke out in January 1820 among army units assembling in Cádiz to be sent to end the independence movements in the Spanish colonies. The revolt was made easier because there was great disaffection in the army about being sent on such a mission.

Colonel Rafael Riego was the leader of the rebels, who then marched from Cádiz on Madrid. Parts of northern Spain also rose in revolt, and ultimately the Madrid garrison joined as well. Realizing that in order to retain the throne he must submit, Ferdinand in March 1820 took an oath to the constitution modeled on that of 1812, becoming a virtual prisoner until 1823.

In October 1822 the representatives of France, Prussia, and Austria met at Verona to discuss the situation in Spain. Alarmed by the possible spread of liberalism elsewhere in Europe, they authorized France, now governed by ultraroyalists, to send an army into Spain and restore Ferdinand to full authority. The Duc d'Angoulême then led a large French army of some 200,000 men into Spain. The French troops kept to the conservative countryside, and the revolution was put down. Madrid was secured in May 1823, and the last rebel stronghold of the Trocadero Fortress at Cádiz fell that August.

Ferdinand then abolished the liberal constitution and resumed his absolutist rule. The French soon withdrew, appalled by the speed and ferocity of Ferdinand's reactionary rule. Ferdinand has been held in detestation by Spaniards ever since.

The Congress of Verona had also discussed the matter of restoring Portuguese and Spanish rule in their New World colonies, but no decision regarding this was reached at that meeting. The British government had rejected the absolutist position taken by Austria, Prussia, and Russia and refused to send a representative to Verona or to a meeting called in December 1823 by Ferdinand to discuss the matter of retaking the colonies. Indeed, London was unwilling to see the colonies return to Spanish and Portuguese control, as the British were profiting handsomely from trade with the colonies built up during the Napoleonic Wars. The U.S. government was also anxious to see the former colonies independent.

British foreign secretary George Canning suggested to U.S. minister to Britain Benjamin Rush that if the U.S. president were to make a statement opposing Spanish efforts to recover the colonies, it would have the full support of the British government backed up by the Royal Navy. Secure in this knowledge, in December 1823 President James Monroe issued what became known as the Monroe Doctrine, stating that the United States would consider any such effort as being "dangerous to our peace and safety." Canning later boasted that "I have called the New World into existence to redress the balance of the Old." In 1824 the United Kingdom recognized the independence of Colombia, Mexico, and Argentina. Spain made no further effort to secure its former New World colonies.

Further turmoil lay ahead for Spain. In 1833 on his deathbed Ferdinand revoked the Salic Law of Succession and reverted to traditional Spanish successionist rules when he decreed that his three-year-old daughter succeed him as Queen Isabella II under a regency headed by his wife Maria Christina. Ferdinand thus rejected the claim of his brother Carlos (Charles) who sought the throne as Carlos V on the basis that as a male he was next in line. Needing broader support, Maria Christina issued a decree of amnesty on October 23, 1833. Liberals who had been in exile returned to Spain and dominated its politics for the next decades. Carlos called on his supporters for assistance and began the First Carlist War (1833–1839). Two Carlist Wars followed, in 1868 and 1872. The matter of who occupied the throne was not the sole issue, for the Carlists embraced a return to absolute monarchy. The Carlist Wars, continued financial difficulties, regional divisions, and revolts in Cuba and the Philippines all plagued Spain and led to its continued decline as a world power. In the Spanish-American War of 1898 Spain would lose Cuba, Puerto Rico, and the Philippines.

SPENCER C. TUCKER

## Timeline

**Aug 19, 1796**     In the Treaty of San Ildefonso, Spain allies with France against Great Britain.

| | |
|---|---|
| **Oct 21, 1805** | The British Royal Navy defeats the French and Spanish fleets in the Battle of Trafalgar, establishing British naval supremacy at sea for a century. |
| **Nov 21, 1806** | In Berlin, French emperor Napoleon I proclaims establishment of the Continental System, closing the ports of French-controlled Europe to British goods. |
| **Jul 1807** | Napoleon moves to strengthen the Continental System against Britain, and this brings his intervention in the Iberian Peninsula. |
| **Jul 7, 1807** | The Treaty of Tilsit signed by Napoleon and Russian czar Alexander I ends the War of the Fourth Coalition. |
| **Jul 19, 1807** | Napoleon orders his ambassador in Lisbon to demand that Portugal close its ports to British shipping. |
| **Aug 2, 1807** | Anticipating a negative response, Napoleon establishes a force commanded by General Jean-Andoche Junot to invade Portugal. |
| **Oct 12, 1807** | Junot's troops enter Spain. |
| **Oct 27, 1807** | Napoleon concludes with King Charles IV of Spain the secret Treaty of Fontainebleau, dividing Portugal into three separate political entities under French and Spanish control. |
| **Nov 19, 1807** | Junot's troops and 25,000 Spanish troops invade Portugal. |
| **Dec 1, 1807** | The French enter Lisbon, secure Portugal, and stifle dissent there. |
| **Jan 8, 1808** | Napoleon sets in motion plans to completely control Spain by sending Marshal Joachim Murat and 100,000 troops into that country. |
| **Mar 19, 1808** | Rioting and a revolt at Aranjuez bring Charles IV's abdication in favor of his son as Ferdinand VII. |
| **Apr 1808** | Napoleon forces both Ferdinand and Charles IV to abdicate. |
| **May 2, 1808** | The Spanish War of Independence (Peninsular War) begins with an uprising in Madrid against the French known as El Dos de Mayo (The Second of May). The British provide assistance to the Spaniards. |
| **Jun 6, 1808** | Napoleon sends his brother Joseph, then king of Naples, to Spain as its king. |
| **Jun 25–Aug 17, 1808** | The First Siege of Zaragoza (Saragossa) by the French occurs, but they break off the siege without taking the city. |
| **Jul 16–19, 1808** | In the Battle of Bailén, 30,000 Spanish troops under General Francisco Castaños surround and defeat 20,000 French troops under General Pierre Dupont. |
| **Aug 1, 1808** | King Joseph and his court evacuate Madrid. He also withdraws French forces north of the Ebro River. A British expeditionary force under Lieutenant General Sir Arthur Wellesley lands north of Lisbon. |

| | |
|---|---|
| **Aug 21, 1808** | At Vimeiro, Wellesley defeats Junot's forces. |
| **Aug 30, 1808** | In the Convention of Cintra, British lieutenant generals Hew Dalrymple and Harry Burrard grant Junot generous surrender terms, with the French forces in Portugal to be transported back to France in Royal Navy ships along with all their weapons and loot. |
| **Dec 4, 1808** | Napoleon arrives in Madrid with substantial French forces. He abolishes monastic orders and the Spanish Inquisition, confiscates rebel property, and orders the sequestering of goods deemed necessary to France. |
| **Dec 20, 1808– Feb 20, 1809** | Second French Siege of Zaragossa. Palafox retains command on the Spanish side, with the French led by Marshals Bon-Adrien Jannot de Moncey, Édouard Mortier, and then Jean Lannes. The French take the city, but much of it is destroyed. The siege claims 54,000 Spanish and 10,000 French lives. |
| **Jan 16, 1809** | French forces, now under General Nicolas-Jean de Dieu Soult, attack Sir John Moore at La Coruña but are repulsed. The next day, Royal Navy ships evacuate the British force. |
| **Jan 23, 1809** | Napoleon begins to plan for military action against Austria. |
| **Mar 1809** | Austria calls for the German states to rise up against Napoleon, beginning the War of the Fifth Coalition (1809). |
| **May 21, 1809** | Wellesley surprises Soult at Oporto, Portugal, and forces him back to Spain. |
| **May 21–22, 1809** | Austrian forces under Archduke Charles defeat Napoleon in the Battle of Aspen/Essling. |
| **June 1809** | Wellesley invades Spain from Portugal with 45,000 men. |
| **Jul 6, 1809** | In a decisive victory, Napoleon defeats Charles in the Battle of Wagram. Austria soon sues for peace in the October 14 Treaty of Schönbrunn. |
| **Jul 27–28, 1809** | After an indecisive battle at Talavera, Wellesley withdraws to Portugal. Shortly thereafter, he is ennobled as Viscount Wellington of Talavera. |
| **Nov 19, 1809** | Spanish insurgent forces suffer their worst defeat of the war, routed by Soult's cavalry at Ocaña near Madrid. Soult then conquers all of Andalusia except Cádiz. |
| **Feb 5, 1810** | French marshal Claude Victor-Perrin besieges Cádiz until August 24, 1812. |
| **Jul 10, 1810** | Following a 24-day siege, Masséna, commanding Napoleon's Army of Portugal, captures Ciudad Rodrigo in Salamanca Province. |
| **Sep 15, 1810** | Masséna invades Portugal, and Wellington withdraws. |

| | |
|---|---|
| **Sep 27, 1810** | Masséna attacks British and Portuguese troops under Wellington at Bussaco but is driven off. Wellington then continues his withdrawal into Portugal. |
| **Oct 10, 1810** | Wellington's forces occupy the prepared Torres Vedras line before Lisbon and force Masséna to withdraw. Masséna loses 25,000 men before regaining Spain early in 1811, when nearly all of Portugal is free of the French. |
| **Dec 31, 1810** | Czar Alexander I announces that Russia is leaving the Continental System, compelling Napoleon to take military action against Russia. |
| **May 3–5, 1811** | Masséna, attempting to relieve the British siege of Almeida, Spain, is rebuffed by Wellington in the Battle of Fuentes de Oñoro. |
| **May 16, 1811** | In the Battle of Albuera, British and Spanish forces under generals William Beresford and Joachin Blake prevent Soult from raising the allied siege of Badajoz. |
| **Jan 12–19, 1812** | Having again invaded Spain, Wellington lays siege to and captures Ciudad Rodrigo. |
| **Mar 17–Apr 6, 1812** | Wellington lays siege to and takes Badajoz. |
| **Jun 24, 1812** | Napoleon invades Russia with nearly half a million men. |
| **Jul 22, 1812** | Marshal Auguste de Marmont, who replaced Masséna as commander of French forces in Spain, engages Wellington and British, Spanish, and Portuguese soldiers in the Battle of Salamanca. Wellington is victorious. |
| **Aug 12, 1812** | Wellington enters Madrid to general popular enthusiasm, securing there substantial quantities of military supplies. |
| **Aug 13, 1812** | Having reconstituted his forces after the defeat at Salamanca, new French commander in Spain Marshal Bertrand Clausel begins a counteroffensive. |
| **Sep 7, 1812** | In the bloodiest combat of the Napoleonic Wars, Napoleon wins the Battle of Borodino against the Russians but at high cost. This opens the way to Moscow, which the French take a week later. |
| **Sep 19–Oct 10, 1812** | Wellington besieges but fails to take Burgos. The French force Wellington to withdraw. |
| **Oct 19, 1812** | Napoleon quits Moscow. The ensuing retreat is a disaster. Of some 460,000 who had entered Russia in June, only some 100,000 men return. |
| **Oct 31, 1812** | The British abandon Madrid, then retreat to Salamanca and across the Huebra River. Wellington then receives reinforcements from |

Britain and is appointed general in chief of the Spanish Army and allied commander in the peninsula.

**Dec 19, 1812** Having abandoned his army in Russia, Napoleon returns to Paris.

**May 17, 1813** Reinforced, Wellington takes the offensive in Spain and forces the French back. On this date King Joseph abandons Madrid.

**Jun 21, 1813** Joseph and his chief of staff Marshal Jean Baptiste Jourdan are defeated by Wellington in the Battle of Victoria, marking the end of Napoleonic rule in Spain and enabling Wellington to invade France.

**Jul 27, 1813** In the Battle of Sorauren, Wellington rebuffs the French, who then withdraw.

**Aug 31, 1813** Wellington captures San Sebastián while Soult, attempting to relieve that place, is defeated by a largely Spanish force at San Marcial.

**Oct 7, 1813** Wellington leads 24,000 allied troops across the Bidassoa River into France.

**Oct 16–19, 1813** Napoleon is defeated in the decisive Battle of Leipzig and is forced to withdraw to the Rhine.

**Nov 10, 1813** Wellington breaches Soult's defensive positions along the lower Nivelle River.

**Dec 21, 1813** Overriding British objections, the allies again offer Napoleon generous peace terms, which he rejects. Meanwhile, the allied armies cross the Rhine.

**Feb 1814** Wellington resumes the offensive. Leaving a force to besiege Bayonne, he drives northward with the remainder.

**Feb 27, 1814** Wellington defeats Soult in the hard-fought Battle of Orthez.

**Mar 12, 1814** Wellington captures the important port city of Bordeaux, which surrenders without a fight.

**Mar 30, 1814** Paris surrenders to the allied forces.

**Apr 14, 1814** Napoleon agrees to abdicate and signs the Treaty of Fontainebleau with the allied powers.

**Mar 20–Jul 11, 1815** Napoleon leaves the island of Elba, given him to rule under the terms of the Treaty of Fontainebleau. In one last throw of the dice, he returns to France. The so-called Hundred Days ends with the return of French king Louis XVIII.

**Jun 18, 1815** Wellington and Prussian general Gebhard Leberecht von Blücher defeat Napoleon in the Battle of Waterloo.

SPENCER C. TUCKER

## Further Reading

Bell, David A. *The First Total War: Napoleon's Europe and the Birth of Warfare as We Know It.* Boston: Houghton Mifflin, 2008.

Carr, Raymond. *Spain: A History.* Oxford: Oxford University Press, 2000.

Chandler, David G. *The Campaigns of Napoleon.* New York: Macmillan, 1968.

Clowes, William Laird. *The Royal Navy: A History from the Earliest Times to 1900,* Vol. 5. 1900; reprint, London: Chatham, 1996.

Connelly, Owen. *The Wars of the French Revolution and Napoleon, 1792–1815.* New York: Routledge, 2006.

Crawley, C. W., ed. *The New Cambridge Modern History,* Vol. 9, *War and Peace in an Age of Upheaval, 1793–1830.* Cambridge: Cambridge University Press, 1965.

Dwyer, Philip. *Citizen Emperor: Napoleon in Power.* New Haven, CT: Yale University Press, 2013.

Esdaile, Charles. *The Peninsular War.* New York: Palgrave Macmillan, 2003.

Esdaile, Charles. *The Spanish Army in the Peninsular War.* Manchester, UK: Manchester University Press, 1988.

Fremont-Barnes, Gregory. *The Napoleonic Wars: The Peninsular War, 1807–1814.* New York: Osprey, 2002.

Gates, David. *The Spanish Ulcer: A History of the Peninsular War.* New York: Norton, 1986.

Glover, Michael. *The Peninsular War, 1807–1814: A Concise Military History.* Hamden, CT: Archon Books, 1974.

Haythornthwaite, Philip J. *Napoleon's Military Machine.* London: Hippocrene, 1988.

Lefebvre, Georges. *Napoleon: From Tilsit to Waterloo, 1807–1815.* Translated by J. E. Anderson. New York: Columbia University Press, 1969.

Rothenberg, Gunther E. *The Art of Warfare in the Age of Napoleon.* Bloomington: Indiana University Press, 1978.

# Latin American Wars of Independence (1808–1825)

## Causes

Numerous factors worked to bring about the separation of the Spanish and Portuguese territorial holdings in the New World from the mother countries. Distance certainly played a role. Separated by the vast expanse of the Atlantic ocean, the overseas colonies during the course of some 300 years developed very different outlooks and attitudes than those of the mother country. These included sharp differences on the economy and trade. Rulers in Spain and Portugal expected the colonies to continue to provide treasure in the form of gold and silver and agricultural commodities but to purchase manufactured goods from the mother country. This closed economic system was known as mercantilism and rankled in the colonies, as they were forbidden to purchase less expensive products produced in, say, Britain, which was then leading the world in the Industrial Revolution.

Caste also came into play. At the top in Spanish North America were those born in the Iberian Peninsula (the *peninsulares*).

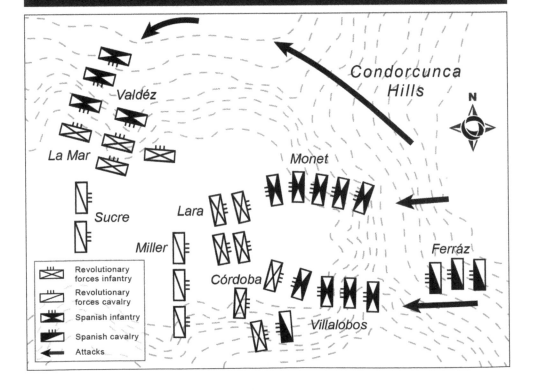

**BATTLE OF AYACUCHO, DEC 9, 1824**

Condorcunca Hills

N

Valdéz

La Mar

Monet

Sucre

Lara

Miller

Córdoba

Ferráz

Villalobos

Revolutionary forces infantry
Revolutionary forces cavalry
Spanish infantry
Spanish cavalry
Attacks

# SOUTH AMERICA, 1810–1914

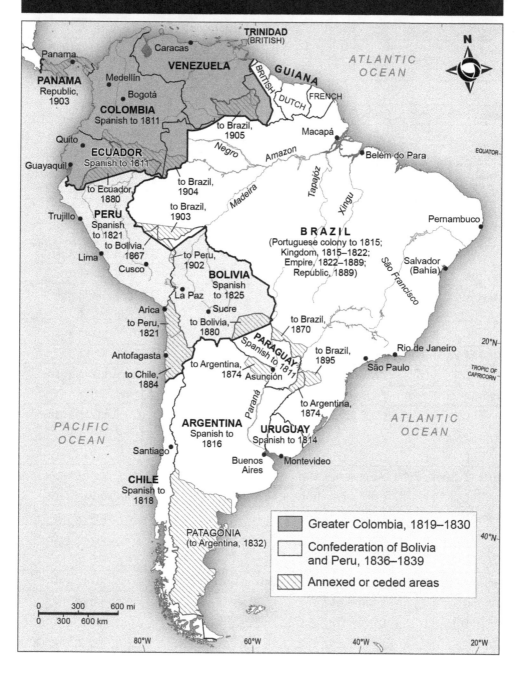

TRINIDAD
(BRITISH)

Panama

Caracas

VENEZUELA

GUIANA

ATLANTIC
OCEAN

N

PANAMA
Republic,
1903

Medellín

Bogotá

BRITISH

DUTCH

FRENCH

COLOMBIA
Spanish to 1811

to Brazil,
1905

Macapá

Quito

Negro

Amazon

Belém do Para

EQUATOR

ECUADOR
Spanish to 1811

Guayaquil

to Ecuador,
1880

to Brazil,
1904

Madeira

Tapajóz

Xingu

Trujillo

PERU
Spanish
to 1821

to Brazil,
1903

Pernambuco

Lima

to Bolivia,
1867

to Peru,
1902

BRAZIL
(Portuguese colony to 1815;
Kingdom, 1815–1822;
Empire, 1822–1889;
Republic, 1889)

São Francisco

Salvador
(Bahía)

Cusco

BOLIVIA
Spanish
to 1825

Arica
to Peru,
1821

La Paz

Sucre

to Bolivia,
1880

to Brazil,
1870

Antofagasta

to Chile,
1884

to Argentina,
1874

PARAGUAY
Spanish to 1811

Asunción

to Brazil,
1895

Rio de Janeiro

São Paulo

20°N

TROPIC OF
CAPRICORN

PACIFIC
OCEAN

Paraná

to Argentina,
1874

ATLANTIC
OCEAN

ARGENTINA
Spanish to
1816

URUGUAY
Spanish to 1814

Santiago

Buenos
Aires

Montevideo

CHILE
Spanish to
1818

PATAGONIA
(to Argentina, 1832)

40°N

| | Greater Colombia, 1819–1830 |
| | Confederation of Bolivia and Peru, 1836–1839 |
| | Annexed or ceded areas |

| 0 | 300 | 600 mi |
| 0 | 300 | 600 km |

80°W          60°W          40°W          20°W

## Latin American Wars of Independence (1808–1825)

| Battle of Cúcuta, New Granada (Modern-Day Colombia) (February 28, 1813) | | |
|---|---|---|
| | **Proindependence Forces** | **Spanish Royalists** |
| **Strength** | 400 | 800 |
| **Killed** | 2 | 20 |
| **Wounded** | 14 | 40 |

| Battle of Chacabuco, Chile (February 12, 1817) | | |
|---|---|---|
| | **Army of the Andes** | **Spanish Royalists** |
| **Strength** | 2,500 infantry, 700 cavalry, 21 guns | 1,500 infantry, 7 guns |
| **Casualties** | 100 killed or wounded | 500 killed or wounded, 600 captured |

| Battle of Carabobo, Venezuela (June 24, 1821) | | |
|---|---|---|
| | **Proindependence Forces** | **Spanish Royalists** |
| **Strength** | 4,000 infantry, 2,500 cavalry | 4,000–5,000 men |
| **Losses** | 200 killed | 2,900 killed, wounded, or captured |

| Battle of Pichincha, Modern-Day Ecuador (May 24, 1822) | | |
|---|---|---|
| | **Insurgents/Liberationists** | **Spanish Royalists** |
| **Strength** | 3,000 | 1,900 |
| **Losses** | 200 killed, 140 wounded | 400 dead, 190 wounded, 1,260 captured |

| Battle of Junín, Peru (August 6, 1824) | | |
|---|---|---|
| | **Proindependence Forces** | **Spanish Royalists** |
| **Strength** | 2,000 cavalry | 2,000 cavalry |
| **Killed** | 150 | 250 |

| Results of the Latin American Wars of Independence | | | |
|---|---|---|---|
| **Colonial Possession** | **Current Nation** | **Gained Independence From** | **Declared Independence On** |
| Brazil | Brazil | Portugal | September 7, 1822 |
| Captaincy-General of Guatemala | Costa Rica | Spain | September 15, 1821 |
| | El Salvador | Spain | September 15, 1821 |
| | Guatemala | Spain | September 15, 1821 |
| | Honduras | Spain | September 15, 1821 |
| | Nicaragua | Spain | September 15, 1821 |

| Saint-Domingue | Haiti | France | January 1, 1804 |
|---|---|---|---|
| Viceroyalty of New Granada | Colombia | Spain | July 20, 1810 |
| | Ecuador | Spain | October 9, 1820 |
| | Panama | Spain; Colombia | November 28, 1821; November 3, 1903 |
| | Venezuela | Spain | July 5, 1811 |
| Viceroyalty of Peru | Chile | Spain | February 12, 1818 |
| | Peru | Spain | July 28, 1821 |
| Viceroyalty of the Rio de la Plata | Argentina | Spain | July 9, 1816 |
| | Bolivia | Spain | August 6, 1825 |
| | Paraguay | Spain | May 17, 1811 |
| | Uruguay | Brazil | August 25, 1825 |

**Sources:** Archer, Christian. *The Wars of Independence in Spanish America.* Wilmington, DE: Scholarly Resources, 2000; Harvey, Robert. *Liberators: Latin America's Struggle for Independence.* New York: Overlook, 2000; McFarland, Anthony. *War and Independence in Spanish America.* New York: Routledge, 2014; Rojas, Ricardo. *San Martín: Knight of the Andes.* New York: Doubleday, Doran, 1945.

Next came the criollos, the locally born people of confirmed European (primarily Spanish) ancestry. These two classes enjoyed preeminence over the other populations of peoples of mixed descent, the Amerindians, and enslaved Africans. The attitudes of the different classes often clashed. There were often inept administrators who failed to understand or were insensitive to the differences that had developed.

New ideas were also a major influence. The Enlightenment of the late 17th century and the 18th century postulated new thinking regarding individual rights. There was also new thinking regarding economics, with advocacy for free trade over the prevailing mercantilism that favored the mother country at the expense of the overseas colonies.

There were also the reforms of the Spanish government introduced in the mid-18th century. In order to more effectively control its overseas possessions and curb corruption, the Crown had reintroduced the practice of appointing outsiders, almost all *peninsulares,* to royal offices throughout the empire. While this had salutary effect in a number of places such as Cuba, the Reio de la Plata (the future Argentina), and New Spain (Mexico), this also led to great resentment, as native-born criollos lost positions they had secured through the practice of the Crown selling offices. Unrest led to open revolt in some areas, such as the Rebellion of Túpac Amaru II in Peru (1780–1872) and the Revolt of the Comuneros in New Granada (now Colombia and parts of Venezuela) in 1781. These did not directly lead to the wars of independence but did reveal a degree of dissatisfaction regarding the caste system.

There was also the powerful examples of the American War for Independence (1775–1783) and the Haitian War of Independence (1791–1804) but also the French Revolution (1789–1799), all of which proclaimed certain rights that should apply to all men regardless of birth.

That the wars for independence in Latin America occurred when they did, however, was largely owing to Napoleon Bonaparte. A successful French general, Bonaparte had come to power in France in 1799 and became emperor Napoleon I in 1804. Although there had been a brief respite in the fighting between Britain and France in 1802, fighting had resumed the next year. In October 1805, the British had defeated a combined French and Spanish fleet in the Battle of Trafalgar. This decisive sea combat would give Britain world naval dominance for the next century. To get at Britain (called by Napoleon "a nation of shopkeepers"), in December 1806 Napoleon announced in his Berlin Decree the Continental System. This order shut the ports of France and French-controlled parts of Europe to British trade. The plan here was to cut off British trade and force Britain into ruinous inflation while also building up European (primarily French) manufacturing.

Napoleon continued to tighten and expand the Continental System. As part of the Treaty of Tilsit in 1807 between France and Russia, Russia agreed to join the system. Napoleon now sought to expand it to both Portugal and Spain. Prince John of Braganza ruled Portugal as regent for his insane mother Queen Maria I. Portugal was a long-standing ally of Britain, and when John, while accepting a number of his demands, refused to accede to all of them, in November 1807 Napoleon sent French and Spanish troops into that country with the plan to divide Portugal and its empire between France and Spain. On December 1, the invaders entered Lisbon. Learning that Napoleon had announced the deposition of the Braganzas, Prince John and a number of nobles and merchants, having hastily loaded what possessions they could, sailed in 15 warships and more than 20 transports from Lisbon for Brazil.

With Portugal apparently easily subdued, in January 1808 Napoleon sent a large army into Spain, claiming that this move was intended to defend its coasts against British attack. In April he summoned to Bayonee to meet with him both former king Charles IV and his son Ferdinand VII, who had unseated his father in a coup d'état in 1807. Distrusting both men, Napoleon secured their abdications with the subsequent plan of installing his brother Joseph on the Spanish throne instead. On May 2, 1808, an uprising occurred in Madrid against the French. Known as the Dos de Mayo (Second of May), it was put down by the French but marks the beginning of the Spanish War of Independence (1808–1814), part of the wider Peninsular War (1807–1808).

The British soon extended aid to the Portuguese and Spanish rebels fighting the French and even dispatched an expeditionary force to the Iberian Peninsula. These events were soon known in the Spanish colonies, where movements favoring independence, sentiment for which had been growing, abetted by the British who sought to secure lucrative trading advantages. The British provided arms and assistance to the insurgents in both Spain and Portugal and then also sent an expeditionary force to the peninsula.

Events in the Iberian Peninsula had a direct effect in the empires of Spain and Portugal. The loosening of ties between the Iberian Peninsula and its overseas empires brought revolt in Latin America. Owing to the vast extent of South America, very different circumstances, and the challenges of topography, especially high mountains, the liberation effort was badly fragmented.

SPENCER C. TUCKER

## Course

### Uprisings against Colonial Rule (1808–1813)

When the fighting began in Latin America, both the British and the Americans profited. In 1812 the U.S. Congress passed legislation that annexed Spanish West Florida from Spain, adding it to the Louisiana Territory, which had been purchased from Napoleon in 1803, itself a consequence of the collapse of his scheme to create a great French empire in the New World owing to the successful Haitian revolt.

During 1808–1809 with British assistance, the Spanish colony of Santo Domingo, occupying the eastern half of the island of Hispaniola, rose in revolt against the rule of the former French colony of Haiti to the west. Then on May 25, 1810, citizens of Buenos Aires created the First Government Junta. Known as the May Revolution, it in effect made the Rio de la Plata (the future Argentina) independent of Spain.

On September 16, 1810, in Mexico, the first true revolt against Spanish rule began. Led by Roman Catholic priest Miguel Hidalgo y Costilla, it was fueled by caste discrimination and calls for reform. Protracted fighting followed, with Mexican independence formally established on September 28, 1821.

On September 18, 1810, led by José Miguel Carrera, Chilean nationalists declared their independence from Spain, and on July 5, 1811, led by Francisco Miranda, Venezuela followed suit. Then on August 4

Simón Bolívar (1783–1830) was, more than any other individual, responsible for the liberation of Venezuela, Colombia, Ecuador, Peru, and Bolivia from Spanish rule. (Library of Congress)

following a popular uprising, Paraguay—a small subdivision of the Río de la Plata viceroyalty—declared its independence from both Spain and the viceroyalty. Paraguay soon passed under the rule of a dictator, José Rodriguez de Francia.

Joining the fight in Venezuela was one of the great figures in Latin American history, Simón Bolívar (1783–1830). Born into a wealthy family in Caracas, he was orphaned at age six and raised by an uncle. Receiving his formal education in Spain, Bolívar traveled back and forth between Venezuela and Spain several times and also visited France before returning to Venezuela in 1807, where he soon joined those seeking independence. Dispatched on a diplomatic mission to Britain by the Venezuelan Junta in 1810, Bolívar was unable to secure British assistance for the Venezuelan revolution and returned home in March 1811 with Francesco Miranda, who had led an unsuccessful revolution in Venezuela in 1806. Bolívar then joined the army of the new republic and received command of the fortress of Porto Cabello. When Miranda was forced to surrender to the Spaniards in July 1811, Bolívar fled into exile to Cartagena de Indias.

Securing a military command in New Granada (now Colombia), Bolívar led a campaign against royalists in New Granada. On January 28, 1813, he captured strategically located Ocaña, a city on the main route to Venezuela, and on February 28, 1813, he defeated the royalists in the Battle of Cúcuta, taking this border city as well.

With royalist forces in Venezuela preparing to invade New Granada, Bolívar secured permission from the leaders of New Granada to cross into Venezuela. On May 14, he began what became known as the Campaña Admirable (Admirable Campaign). After crossing the Andes he won six hard-fought battles, beginning with entry into Mérida on May 23, where he was proclaimed "El Liberador." At Trujillo on June 15, Bolívar made his famous "War to the Death" speech. In it he announced that the liberationist forces would treat *peninsulares* and criollos differently: "Spaniards and Canarians, you can expect death, even if uninvolved, if you do not actively work in favor of the independence of America. Americans, count on life, even if guilty." This remained technically in force until a treaty signed with Spanish general Pablo Morillo at Santa Ana de Trujillo on November 26, 1820, regularizing the rules of engagement. From Trujillo Bolívar continued eastward, defeating his adversaries until the royalist army capitulated in the city of La Victoria, not far from Caracas. Having won control of western Venezuela, Bolívar entered Caracas on August 6.

Civil war soon broke out, however. Although Bolívar won a series of battles against the royalists at Araure (December 5, 1813), La Victoria (February 1814), San Mateo (March 1814), and Carabobo (May 1814), he was then defeated by royalist general José Tomás Boves at La Puerta (July 1814) and forced to flee to New Granada.

With Chilean leader Carrera having proven incompetent, Bernardo O'Higgins replaced him. On October 1 at Rancagua, some 600 Chilean troops under O'Higgins turned back a Spanish expeditionary force of 1,200 men from Peru under Mariana Osorio. The next day the battle resumed, and this time Osorio was victorious. In large part the royalist success was owing to Carrera having refused to lend support to O'Higgins. Several days later, Osorio's troops entered Santiago and reestablished Spanish control of Chile.

### Spain Endeavors to Regain Control (1814–1816)

With the defeat of Emperor Napoleon I in Europe in April 1814, King Ferdinand VII returned to power in Spain and immediately set about efforts to restore Spanish control in the New World by sending out substantial troop reinforcements to South America to crush the liberation movements there. Ferdinand appointed General Pablo Morillo y Morillo expedition commander and captain-general of the Provinces of Venezuela on August 14, 1814. Morillo set sail with 18 warships and 42 cargo ships and disembarked in Carupano and Isla Margarita.

In 1815 Bolívar returned to Venezuela from New Granada with a new army. Following some early successes, however, he was defeated by Morillo, who pacified the port cities of La Guaira, Caracas, Puerto and Cabello (in present-day Venezuela), and Cartagena de Indias (in present-day Colombia). Bolívar again fled this time to Jamaica, from where he mounted several unsuccessful raids against the Venezuelan coast.

### The Revolutionaries on the Offensive (1817–1825)

On July 9, 1816, Argentina formally declared its independence from Spain. Argentinian native José Francisco de San Martín (1778–1850) had served for more than two decades as an officer in the Spanish Army. Distinguishing himself in fighting against the French during the Peninsular War, he ended that conflict as a lieutenant colonel.

Despite his long service in the Spanish Army, San Martín believed that Spain's Latin American colonies should be independent. Learning of the independence movements there, he resigned his commission in 1812 and traveled to South America, where he joined Simón Bolívar as one of the great leaders in the cause of Latin American independence. Arriving in Buenos Aires in March 1812, San Martín associated himself with the revolutionary government. His military experience secured him command of a mounted unit, and in December he joined the revolutionary army in northern Argentina and soon had distinguished himself in the fighting.

Latin American revolutionary leaders believed that their success depended on securing Peru, a center of loyalist support. Royalists there had already defeated three Argentinian invasions of upper Peru (later Bolivia). San Martín planned a cross-Andean invasion to liberate Chile, which could then be used as a base for a seaborne invasion of Peru.

San Martín resigned from the revolutionary army in January 1817 and secured appointment as governor of Cuyo Province in western Argentina at the base of the Andes Mountains. Establishing a base at its capital city of Mendoza, he conferred with Chilean exiles there and built a military force of Argentinians, Chileans, and slaves who had been promised freedom in exchange for their military service.

San Martín's so-called Army of the Andes, numbering some 2,500 infantry, 700 cavalry, and 21 guns, departed Mendoza and made its way north through the Andes passes into Chile during January 18–February 8, 1817. Catching Spanish forces there completely by surprise, San Martín on February 12, 1817, encountered at Chacabuco near Santiago a royalist force of 1,500 infantry and 7 guns under Spanish brigadier general Rafael Maroto. San Martín immediately attacked, well aware that all Maroto had to do was to delay the advance of the Army of the Andes, as Spanish royalist reinforcements were en route.

San Martín ordered General O'Higgins, commanding the Chilean forces in the army, to hold Maroto in place while the other part of the army attempted to turn the defenders' flank. When the flanking attack was delayed, however, O'Higgins disobeyed orders and attacked, breaking the defending line. San Martín then joined the flanking force, which completed the rout of Maroto. The Army of the Andes suffered 100 killed or wounded, while the royalists lost 500 killed or wounded, 600 taken prisoner, and all their guns.

San Martín's forces occupied Santiago on February 15, 1817. San Martín then named O'Higgins to direct political affairs in Chile. On the arrival of a large Spanish force from Peru under General Mariano Osorio in early 1818, San Martín engaged Osorio and was narrowly defeated by him in the Battle of Cancha-Rayada (March 16). San Martín rallied his forces, then struck back and this time routed Osorio in the Battle of Maipo (April 5), for all practical purposes securing Chilean independence, although this was not formally declared its independence until February 12, 1818. Chilean leaders offered San Martín the position of supreme ruler of Chile, but he declined in order to continue the war against the Spaniards in Peru.

Meanwhile, Bolívar had returned to Venezuela in December 1816. Proclaimed commander in chief of liberation forces of both Venezuela and New Granada, he also secured troops from Haitian leader Alexandre Pétion in return for a promise to free the slaves. However, at La Puerta, the same location where he was defeated earlier, Bolívar was again defeated on March 15, 1818, this time by Spanish troops under General Morillo. Bolívar then retired to regroup, deal with challenges to his leadership, and raise a new force, concentrating on the liberation of New Granada, which had been retaken by the Spaniards.

While this was transpiring, Spanish general Mariano Osorio proceeded southward from Peru with 9,000 troops into Chile to engage San Martín's Army of the Andes of Chileans and Argentinians. In the Second Battle of Cancha-Rayada, fought near Linares, Chile, on March 16, 1818, Osorio surprised San Martín and defeated him. The royalist side lost 200 killed or wounded, whereas the Army of the Andes suffered 120 killed and the loss of 22 guns.

Following his defeat, San Martín regrouped his army. On April 5, 1818, he again engaged the royalists under Osorio, attacking them along the Maipo River. In the battle of the same name, San Martín turned the royalist left and routed the Spanish force, which sustained some 1,000

killed, 2,300 taken prisoner, and 12 guns taken. San Martín's army suffered only 100 killed or wounded. General Osorio then abandoned further campaigning in Chile and returned to Peru.

With San Martín enjoying success, Bolívar developed a bold plan to induce the Spaniards to concentrate their forces in Venezuela. He would then cross the Andes, unite with guerrilla forces under General Francisco de Paula Santander, seize Bogotá, and force the Spaniards from New Granada. In June Bolívar led some 2,500 well-armed troops, including a number of Englishmen, across the Andes. Arriving in New Granada, he united with Santander, defeated the Spanards on July 1 in Tunja Province, and entered the town of Tunja on July 23.

On August 7, 1819, Bolívar, now commanding a force of some 3,400 men, defeated Spanish colonel José María Barreiro, with some 3,000 men, in the Battle of Boyacá. In the rout, Bolívar's forces suffered 13 dead and 53 wounded, while Barreiro lost 100 killed, 150 wounded, and 1,600 taken prisoner in addition to much of his equipment. Among those captured, Barreiro was later executed on the order of Santander.

Boyacá proved to be the decisive battle in the liberation of South America from Spanish rule. On August 12, Bolívar made a triumphal entry into Bogotá. All the provinces of New Granada now rose up against the Spaniards, who sought refuge in the fortified town of Mompox. In December 1819 Bolívar appeared before a congress at Angostura and was made president and military dictator. He urged the legislators to proclaim a new state, and three days later the Viceroyalty of New Granada became the Republic of Colombia, usually called Gran Colombia. It consisted of the three departments of New Granada (now the countries of Colombia and Panama), Venezuela, and Quito (Ecuador). Still, most of its territory remained under royalist control.

San Martín spent more than a year preparing to invade Peru, but in order to proceed he had to first end Spanish control of the sea. The liberationist side assembled a small naval squadron, including the Spanish frigate *Reyna Maria Isabel* of 40 guns that they had captured and renamed the *O'Higgins*. Chilean Manuel Blanco Encalada, who had served as an officer in the Spanish Navy, had command of the squadron. In November 1818, however, the revolutionary navy received a significant boost with the arrival of able Royal Navy officer Thomas Cochrane, Earl of Dundonald. Tried and convicted as a conspirator in the Great Stock Exchange Fraud of 1814 and forced to resign from both Parliament and the Royal Navy, Cochrane accepted an offer to command San Martín's naval forces. Now vice admiral, Cochrane set about reorganizing the Chilean Navy and introduced British naval practices.

At the beginning of 1819, Cochrane set sail with his small squadron but was unsuccessful in his efforts to draw the Spanish squadron at Callao and Valdivia into action. Cochranre's attempt to seize the Spanish fortress of Real Felipe at Callao also failed, and he then decided to attack Valdivia.

One of the most strongly fortified locations in South America, Valdivia was also a major Spanish base. On the night of February 3–4, 1820, Cochrane landed 350 men with the intention of capturing its seven forts, with a total of 118 guns and a garrison of some 1,600. Cochrane's men quickly seized two of the forts, and two others promptly surrendered. The next

morning the three remaining Spanish forts also surrendered, followed by Valdivia shortly thereafter. The Chilean side suffered 7 killed and 19 wounded; the Spanish lost 100 killed and 106 men taken prisoner. The remaining Spanish troops sacked the city before departing overland for Osorno. The capture of Valdivia removed the last vestige of Spanish power in Chile and enabled San Martín to proceed with his invasion of Peru.

In August 1820, San Martín sailed for Peru with some 4,500 men in 16 transports escorted by Cochrane's warships. They came ashore at Pisco, some 100 miles south of Lima, on September 8. Cochrane then sailed to Callao, Peru's most important port, where he blockaded the Spanish squadron there. On November 5, Cochrane personally led 250 men in small boats in a daring cutting-out operation against the ships of the Spanish squadron riding at anchor in the harbor. Although the Spanish warships were protected by chains and a great many shore batteries, the attackers succeeded in cutting out the Spanish Navy frigate *Esmeralda* and taking it out of the harbor as a prize. In the operation, Cochrane was badly wounded twice. He had intended to take other warships in the harbor as well, but this effort failed. Nonetheless, the operation ranks as one of the most daring of its kind in naval annals.

With Spanish forces in Peru larger than his own, San Martín refused to accept battle unless it was on favorable terms, hoping that his presence would spark popular uprisings. In the meantime, he planned to whittle down the Spanish through guerrilla warfare. Indeed, the Spanish evacuated Lima in June 1821. Entering Lima on July 9, San Martín declared Peruvian independence on July 21. Callao fell to the liberationist forces on September 21.

Bolívar meanwhile was concentrating on securing Venezuela. After the expiration of an armistice (November 15, 1820–April 28, 1821), he led 6,500 men (2,500 of them cavalry) against Spanish general Miguel de la Torre, with 4,000–5,000 men, in the valley of the Carabobo. Torre made the mistake of dividing his force to meet a flanking attack, allowing Bolívar to defeat him in detail on June 24, 1821. The battle was a rout. Bolívar's side suffered only 200 dead, while Torre lost some 2,900 dead, wounded, or captured. The remnants of Torre's force fled. With the defeat of the main royalist force in Venezuela, the Battle of Carabobo was the decisive engagement in the liberation of Venezuela from Spanish rule. Bolívar entered Caracas in triumph. Cartagena surrendered on October 1, 1821, following a 21-month-long siege.

Bolívar now moved southward to join with his lieutenant, General Antonio José de Sucre. Sucre was campaigning in Quito Province against the royalist forces led by Spanish governor-general Melchior Aymerich. The two sides met on May 24, 1822, in the Battle of Pichincha. Fought on the slopes of Pichincha next to the city of Quito, it pitted an insurgent force of 3,000 men under Sucre against a 1,900-man royalist force under Aymerich and ended with Sucre victorious. The liberationist side suffered 200 dead and 140 wounded, while the royalists lost 400 dead, 190 wounded, and 1,260 captured along with 14 guns. The defeat of the royalists brought the liberation of Quito the next day and secured the independence of the provinces belonging to the Real Audiencia de Quito, which then became the Republic of Ecuador.

In Peru there were sharp political divisions, forcing San Martín to take power as "protector of Peru." He then instituted policies that angered the rich, including the imposition of taxes, an end to Indian tribute, and freedom for children of slaves. Threatened by unrest and the continued presence in Peru of the larger Spanish forces, San Martín met with Bolívar at Guayaquil (July 26–27, 1822). Although there is some disagreement on what actually transpired (no record of the meeting was kept), it appears that the two agreed to join forces, with San Martín handing over to Bolívar the liberation of Peru. Returning to Lima, San Martín resigned in September 1822 and departed for Argentina. He then began a self-imposed European exile and died in Boulogne-sur-Mer, France, on August 17, 1850.

Brazil meanwhile also became independent but by peaceful means. Growing tensions between Brazil and Portugal and Portuguese king John VI and his son Prince Regent Dom Pedro in Brazil led to the proclamation of Brazilian independence on September 7, 1822. The Empire of Brazil was unusual in Latin America as a large, successful, and stable monarchy until 1889, when the monarchy was overthrown following the abolition of slavery and a republic was established.

There was some naval combat between the newly independent Brazil and Portugal. In March 1823 Cochrane left the Chilean Navy to accept command of the Brazilian Navy. With a small squadron of warships, both purchased and captured, he prepared to take on the Portuguese Navy. He first blockaded the port of Bahia on the Atlantic coast of northeastern Brazil, where Portuguese naval strength was concentrated.

On July 2 the Portuguese evacuated Bahia, departing in 60 transports with 17 escorting warships—far too powerful for Cochrane to attack with only 2 frigates. Cochrane pursued, however, and by skillful seamanship in his flagship, the 50-gun frigate *Pedro I,* he managed to cut out several of the transports and take several stragglers, which were sent on to Salvador. Assuming that the Portuguese convoy was bound for Maranhão (São Luiz), Cochrane then raced to that port ahead of the Portuguese and captured it.

As the Brazilian Army had occupied Bahia on July 4, there was no place for the Portuguese to go but on to Portugal. Some Brazilian warships harassed the Portuguese ships as they crossed the Atlantic. Cochrane was rewarded for his success by being made governor of the province of Maranhão and created Marquess of Maranhão by Pedro I. Cochrane soon tired of the political upheaval and returned to Britain, however.

Central America moved to establish its independence from Mexico. Following its declaration of independence from Spain in 1821, Mexico had come to control most of Central America. With the republican revolution in Mexico in March 1823, however, Mexican general Vicente Filosola called a Central American assembly in Guatemala City, and on July 1, 1823, it established the United Provinces of Central America, to include Costa Rica, Guatemala, El Salvador, Honduras, and Nicaragua. Meanwhile, the final struggle for control of Venezuela was being played out. It was fought on Lake Maracaibo on July 24, 1823, between patriot naval forces under Admiral José Prudencio Padilla and the royalists under Captain Ángel Laborde and ended in a patriot victory.

The independence of Latin America was greatly aided by the proclamation on December 2, 1823, of what came to be known of the Monroe Doctrine. Knowing that he had the full support of the British government and the Royal Navy, U.S.

president James Monroe issued his policy statement during the course of his State of the Union address to Congress. Set against the backdrop of the wars in Latin America, Monroe stated that the United States would not tolerate new European colonization, interference in the affairs of the newly independent nations of the Americas, or the transfer of existing colonies from one European nation to another. He said that the United States would remain neutral in the ongoing fighting but also that he expected the European powers not to intervene militarily in the Americas. If that were to occur, the United States would regard it as a hostile act. In effect, Monroe proclaimed that the Western Hemisphere was off limits to European intervention. British foreign secretary Sir George Canning, who had pledged to U.S. minister to Britain Benjamin Rush that such a statement by the American president would have the support of the Royal Navy, would have preferred a joint British-U.S. declaration but nonetheless boasted that he had "called the New World into existence to redress the balance of the Old."

The Viceroyalty of Peru was the last Spanish holding in South America. San Martín had proclaimed Peruvian independence in July 1821, but in February 1824 the royalists regained control. In the absence of San Martín, Bolívar assembled a force of some 9,000 men at Trujillo, and in June he advanced to confront a Spanish force of equal size under General José de Canterac.

The ensuing battle occurred on the Junín plains northwest of the Jauja Valley about 100 miles northeast of Lima on August 6, 1824. The Battle of Junín was a purely cavalry engagement of about an hour's duration, with some 2,000 men on each side. It began when Bolívar attempted to cut off the royalist withdrawal in the direction of Cuzco. The royalist cavalry charged that of Bolívar in an effort to cover the withdrawal of their infantry. The fighting involved close combat with lance and saber but no firearms. The royalist side suffered some 250 dead, while 150 died among the liberationists. The battle greatly enhanced the morale of the revolutionaries. Although the royalist troops continued their withdrawal into the highlands southwest of Lima, they experienced increasing defections. Patriot general Antonio José de Sucre pursued the royalist forces, while Bolívar entered Lima and reorganized the Peruvian government.

By late 1824, royalist forces under Spanish viceroy General José de la Serna y Hirojosa still controlled much of Peru. Sucre continued his military offensive, however. After prolonged maneuvering, the two sides came together in December on the plain of Ayacucho, 186 miles southeast of Lima, at Pampa de La Quinua, close to Ayacucho and near the town of Quinua. The Quechua term *ayacucho* means "dead corner," referring to a slaughter of natives there by the Spanish early in their conquest of Peru. Spanish viceroy José de La Serna y Hinojosa commanded the royalist force of some 9,300 men and seven guns. Sucre had only 5,780 men and two guns. Both sides also possessed some cavalry.

In the precombat maneuvering La Serna managed to position his own forces to the north of Sucre, hoping to cut the patriot forces from the sea and additional forces that Bolívar was raising in Lima. La Serna then attempted to employ his superior numbers to advantage by encircling his opponent. Sucre managed to avoid the latter and took up an excellent defensive position on the plain. La Serna then endeavored to pin Sucre's flanks while finishing off the patriots with a drive into the center of their line. Sucre ceded the initiative, hoping that he would be able to contain that royalist attack and then exploit the situation with a reserve of three battalions of infantry and five cavalry squadrons.

The Battle of Ayacucho (also known as the Battle of La Quinua and the Battle of the Generals) opened early on the morning of December 9, with the royalist left wing advancing against the patriot right commanded by General José Maria Córdoba. This attack failed, as did another royalist assault on the patriot center. A patriot counterattack drove back the royalist left and opened a break in their lines that allowed Sucre to introduce his infantry and cavalry reserves to seal the victory.

The entire battle lasted less than an hour and a half. Despite being outnumbered, Sucre won a complete victory. The royalists lost 1,400 dead and 700 wounded, while the patriots sustained 309 dead and 607 wounded. Particularly grievous for the royalist cause was the large number of senior officers among the 2,500 prisoners taken: 15 generals, 16 colonels, and 68 lieutenant colonels. It is for this reason that it is sometimes called the Battle of the Generals. La Serna, who was wounded half a dozen times, was among those captured.

Under the terms of capitulation, La Serna agreed to withdraw all Spanish forces from Peru. Sucre then moved into upper Peru, and on August 6, 1825, he declared the province of Chuquisaca independent and renamed it Bolivia in Bolívar's honor. Although fighting by small isolated royalist units continued thereafter, the Battle of Ayacucho marked the effective end of the Latin American Wars of Independence.

SPENCER C. TUCKER

## Consequences

Spain's colonies in the Americas were now reduced to only three, all of them in the Caribbean: Cuba, Puerto Rico, and Santo Domingo. Cuba soon experienced revolts, as did another Spanish colony, the Philippines. The strongmen (caudillos) who now ruled most of the new Latin American states were drawn largely from the military, which helped bring about authoritarian rule throughout Latin America, leading in turn to coups d'état, revolts, and wars. Unfortunately for Latin America, it was never able to unite. The wars of independence were soon followed by a number of internecine wars, the result of internal divisions, cultural differences, and territorial disputes.

Bolívar attempted to promote close cooperation and unity and forge a common policy toward Spain. In 1826 he hosted the Congress of Panama. Held in Panama City during June 22–July 15, the conference was attended by representatives of Gran Colombia (comprising the modern-day nations of Colombia, Ecuador, Panama, and Venezuela), Peru, the United Provinces of Central America (Guatemala, El Salvador, Honduras, Nicaragua, and Costa Rica), and Mexico. Bolívar proposed the creation of a league of American republics with a supranational parliamentary assembly and a common military bound by a mutual defense pact. This proved impossible owing to the conflicting interests among the states.

Indeed, war soon broke out. During 1825–1828 Argentina and Brazil went to war. The Argentina-Brazil War, also known as the Cisplatine War, occurred when Argentina lent aid to a revolt against Brazil in the Banda Oriental (Eastern Bank, constituting modern-day Uruguay and known to Brazil as the Provincia Cisplatina), which

Brazil had incorporated into its territory when it achieved independence from Portugal in 1822. Argentina wanted to reacquire the area, with Argentina and the Banda Oriental constituting the United Provinces of the Río de la Plata. Brazilian naval forces blockaded the Río de la Plata, and Argentine forces then invaded Brazilian territory and, in the major battle of the war, engaged and defeated Brazilian forces in the Battle of Ituzaingó (February 20, 1827). The major naval battle, that of Monte Santiago (April 7–8, 1827) was a Brazilian victory, however.

The war exacted a heavy financial toll on both sides, disrupting important foreign trade. With the British and French governments acting as intermediaries, the two sides opened peace talks, and in the Treaty of Montevideo of August 27, 1828, the disputed province of the Banda Oriental became the independent state of Uruguay and was thus permanently lost to both Argentina and Brazil. The eastern portion of territory, known as the Misiones Orientales, was awarded to Brazil. Brazil's loss of the Provincia Cisplatina was a factor in the abdication of Dom Pedro I in 1831.

In yet another war during 1827–1829, Peru embarked on aggressive expansionism and invaded both Bolivia and Ecuador (then part of the Republic of Gran Colombia). A Peruvian naval squadron captured Guayaquil. However, General Antonio José de Sucre, who had taken refuge in Ecuador, combined with Ecuadorian colonel Juan José Flores to defeat the Peruvians in the Battle of Tarqui on February 27, 1829. The Ecuadorian forces then retook Guayaquil the next day, ending Peruvian plans to expand northward. Ecuador, Venezuela, and Colombia then all became separate nations. Disheartened by the secession of Venezuela from the Gran Colombia in

1829, Bolívar, now in failing health, resigned his presidency on April 27, 1830. Intending to travel to Europe, he died near Santa Marta, Colombia, of tuberculosis on December 17, 1830. Tenacious, bold, and resourceful, Bolívar was a great motivator of men. He was a staunch republican who favored limited government, property rights, and the rule of law. Credited with having led the fight for the independence of the present nations of Venezuela, Colombia, Ecuador, Panama, and Bolivia, Bolívar was disappointed in his efforts to achieve continental unity. He is today regarded as one of Latin America's greatest heroes.

In 1835 Bolivian dictator Andreas Santa Cruz and Peruvian president Luis Orbegosa established a confederation of their two countries. Chile and Argentina opposed this, and Chile declared war in November 1836. Although the Chileans were defeated in their first invasion of Bolivia, they went on to win a decisive victory over Bolivia in the Battle of Yungay (January 20, 1839), breaking up the confederation.

SPENCER C. TUCKER

## Timeline

| | |
|---|---|
| **1780–1782** | Rebellion of Túpac Amaru II in Peru. |
| **1781** | Revolt of the Comuneros in New Granada (present-day Colombia and parts of Venezuela). |
| **1806** | Francesco Miranda leads an unsuccessful revolution in Venezuela. |
| **Nov 1807** | Napoleon sends French and Spanish troops into Portugal. |
| **Dec 1, 1807** | French and Spanish troops secure Lisbon. Regent John, informed that Napoleon has declared the deposition of the Braganzas, sails to Brazil. |
| **Jan 1808** | Napoleon sends a large army into Spain, ostensibly to defend its coasts against British attack. |
| **Apr 1808** | Napoleon secures the abdications of former Spanish king Charles IV and his son Ferdinand VII. Napoleon plans to install his brother Joseph on the Spanish throne instead. |
| **May 2, 1808** | An abortive uprising against the French occurs in Madrid, marking the beginning of the Spanish War of Independence (1808–1814), part of the wider Peninsular War (1807–1808). This encourages revolutionary movements in Latin America. |
| **May 25, 1810** | In the May Revolution, citizens of Buenos Aires create the First Government Junta, in effect declaring the Rio de la Plata (Argentina) independent of Spain. |
| **Sep 16, 1810** | The first true revolt against Spanish rule begins in Mexico, which is led by Miguel Hidalgo y Costilla. |
| **Sep 18, 1810** | Chilean nationalists led by José Miguel Carrera declare independence from Spain. |

| | |
|---|---|
| **Jul 1811** | Miranda is forced to surrender to the royalist forces. |
| **Jul 5, 1811** | Led by Francisco Miranda, Venezuela declares independence from Spain. |
| **Aug 4, 1811** | Paraguay—part of the Río de la Plata viceroyalty—declares its independence from both Spain and the viceroyalty. Paraguay is soon ruled by a dictator, José Rodriguez de Francia. |
| **May 9, 1812** | Argentinean native José Francisco de San Martín, an officer in the Spanish Army, returns to Buenos Aires. Supporting the revolutionary cause, he secures a military command in northern Argentina. |
| **Jan 28, 1813** | Venezuelan revolutionary Simón Bolívar, leading a military force against royalists in New Granada, takes Ocaña, a city on the main route to Venezuela. |
| **Feb 3, 1813** | San Martín defeats royalist forces at San Lorenzo, on the Paraná River. |
| **Feb 28, 1813** | Bolívar defeats the royalists in the Battle of Cúcuta, taking that border city. |
| **May 14–Aug 6, 1813** | Bolívar begins what becomes known as the Campaña Admirable (Admirable Campaign). Bolívar wins six hard-fought battles, having secured control of western Venezuela by August 6. |
| **Dec 5, 1813** | Civil war breaks out in Venezuela, but Bolívar defeats the royalists at Araure. |
| **Feb 12, 1814** | Bolívar defeats the royalists at La Victoria. |
| **Mar 25, 1814** | Bolívar is victorious at San Mateo. |
| **Apr 1814** | King Ferdinand VII returns to power in Spain and immediately begins efforts to restore Spanish control in the New World. |
| **May 28, 1814** | Bolívar defeats the royalists at Carabobo. |
| **Jul 6, 1814** | Royalist forces under General José Tomás Boves defeat Bolívar, who is forced to flee to New Granada. |
| **Aug 14, 1814** | Ferdinand VII appoints General Pablo Morillo y Morillo as expedition commander and captain-general of the Provinces of Venezuela. |
| **Oct 1, 1814** | At Rancagua, Chilean leader Bernardo O'Higgins initially turns back a Spanish force under Mariana Osorio that has invaded Chile. Osorio is victorious, however, and several days later Osorio's troops reestablish Spanish control of Chile. |
| **1815** | Bolívar returns to Venezuela from New Granada with a new army. Following some early successes, he is defeated by Morillo, who pacifies major part cities in Venezuela and Cartagena de Indias (present-day Colombia). Bolívar again flees, this time to Jamaica, from where he mounts several unsuccessful raids against the Venezuelan coast. |
| **July 9, 1816** | Argentina formally declares independence from Spain. |

| | |
|---|---|
| **1816** | Peruvian royalists defeat three invasions by the Argentinean revolutionaries into upper Peru (later Bolivia). San Martín plans a cross-Andean invasion to liberate Chile and then use it as a base for a seaborne invasion of Peru. Establishing a base at Mendoza, San Martín establishes the Army of the Andes. |
| **Jan 18–Feb 8, 1817** | San Martín's Army of the Andes departs Mendoza and passes through the Andes northward into Chile. |
| **Feb 12, 1817** | San Martín attacks and defeats a royalist force under General Rafael Maroto at Chacabuco near Santiago, Chile. Three days later, his men occupy Santiago. |
| **Feb 12, 1818** | Chile formally declares its independence. |
| **Mar 15, 1818** | Bolívar suffers a second defeat at La Puerto, this time by Spanish troops under General Morillo. |
| **Mar 16, 1818** | Spanish general Osorio defeats San Martín's Army of the Andes in the Second Battle of Cancha-Rayada in Chile. |
| **Apr 5, 1818** | San Martín again engages the royalists under Osorio, winning the Battle of the Maipo River. For all practical purposes, this battle secures Chilean independence. Osorio is returned to Peru. |
| **Jun 1818** | Bolívar leads an army across the Andes into New Granada. |
| **Jul 1, 1818** | Arriving in New Granada, Bolívar defeats the Spaniards in Tunja Province. |
| **Feb 15, 1819** | Bolívar proclaims the Republic of Colombia and becomes its president. |
| **Aug 7, 1819** | Bolívar routs a loyalist force under Spanish colonel José María Barreiro in the Battle of Boyacá. |
| **Aug 12, 1819** | Bolívar makes a triumphal entry into Bogotá. All the provinces of New Granada now rise up against the Spaniards. |
| **Dec 1819** | A congress at Angostura names Bolívar president and military dictator. Representatives proclaim the Viceroyalty of New Granada as the new Republic of Colombia. |
| **Feb 3–4, 1820** | Former British naval officer Thomas Cochrane, now commanding the Chilean Navy, forces the surrender of Valdivia. This enables San Martín to invade Peru. |
| **Sep 8, 1820** | San Martín's men come ashore at Pisco, some 100 miles south of Lima. |
| **Jul 21, 1821** | San Martín proclaims Peruvian independence. |
| **Sep 21, 1821** | Callao, Peru, falls to the liberationist forces. |
| **Jun 24, 1821** | Bolívar routs a royalist force under Spanish general Miguel de la Torre in the Battle of Carabobo, which is the decisive engagement in the liberation of Venezuela. |

| | |
|---|---|
| **Sep 28, 1821** | Mexico formally declares independence from Spain. |
| **Oct 10, 1821** | Royalist forces under Brigadier General Gabriel Torres surrender Cartagena in New Granada to revolutionary forces under General Mariano Montilla. |
| **May 24, 1822** | In the Battle of Pichincha, General Antonio José de Sucre, Bolívar's lieutenant, defeats royalist forces, ultimately leading to creation of the Republic of Ecuador. |
| **Jul 26–27, 1822** | San Martín and Bolívar meet at Guayaquil and agree to join forces, with San Martín yielding authority to Bolívar. |
| **Sep 1822** | San Martín resigns his position as protector of Peru and departs for Argentina, then begins a self-imposed European exile. |
| **Sep 7, 1822** | Growing tensions between Portuguese king John VI and his son Prince Regent Dom Pedro in Brazil bring a proclamation of Brazilian independence. |
| **Jul 1, 1823** | Following the March 1823 republican revolution in Mexico, Mexican general Vicente Filosola establishes the United Provinces of Central America, to include Costa Rica, Guatemala, El Salvador, Honduras, and Nicaragua. |
| **Jul 24, 1823** | In the Battle of Lake Maracaibo, patriot naval forces under Admiral José Prudencio Padilla defeat royalist naval forces under Captain Ángel Laborde. |
| **Dec 2, 1823** | The Monroe Doctrine is proclaimed. |
| **Feb 1824** | The royalists regain control of Peru. |
| **Jun 1824** | Bolívar assembles an army at Trujillo and advances to confront a royalist force under General José de Canterac. |
| **Aug 6, 1824** | Bolívar is victorious in the Battle of Junín, some 100 miles northeast of Lima. Royalist forces under Spanish viceroy General José de la Serna y Hinojosa still control much of Peru, however. |
| **Dec 9, 1824** | Sucre defeats la Serna in the Battle of Ayacucho, marking the effective end of the Latin American Wars of Independence. |
| **Aug 6, 1825** | Sucre moves into upper Peru and declares the independence of the province of Chuquisaca, renaming it Bolivia in Bolívar's honor. |

SPENCER C. TUCKER

**Further Reading**

Andrien, Kenneth J., and L. Johnson Lyman. *The Political Economy of Spanish America in the Age of Revolution, 1750–1850.* Albuquerque: University of New Mexico Press, 1994.

Archer, Christian. *The Wars of Independence in Spanish America.* Wilmington, DE: Scholarly Resources, 2000.

Bethell, Leslie. *The Cambridge History of Latin America,* Vol. 3, *From Independence to 1870.* Cambridge: Cambridge University Press, 1987.

Brown, Matthew. *Adventuring through Spanish Colonies: Simón Bolívar, Foreign Mercenaries and the Birth of New Nations.* Liverpool: Liverpool University Press, 2006.

Burns, Bradford E. *The Poverty of Progress: Latin America in the Nineteenth Century.* Berkeley: University of California Press, 1980.

Bushnell, David, and Neill Macaulay. *The Emergence of Latin America in the Nineteenth Century.* 2nd ed. Oxford: Oxford University Press, 1994.

Chasteen, John Charles. *Americanos: Latin America's Struggle for Independence.* Oxford: Oxford University Press, 2008.

Costeloe, Michael P. *Response to Revolution: Imperial Spain and the Spanish American Revolutions, 1810–1840.* Cambridge: Cambridge University Press, 1986.

Graham, Richard. *Independence in Latin America: A Comparative Approach.* 2nd ed. New York: McGraw-Hill, 1994.

Harvey, Robert. *Liberators: Latin America's Struggle for Independence, 1810–1830.* London: John Murray, 2000.

Hasbrouck, Alfred. *Foreign Legionaries in the Liberation of Spanish South America.* New York: Octagon Books, 1969.

Humphreys, R. A., and John Lynch, eds. *The Origins of the Latin American Revolutions, 1808–1826.* New York: Knopf, 1965.

Kaufman, William W. *British Policy and the Independence of Latin America, 1804–1828.* New Haven, CT: Yale University Press, 1951.

Kinsbruner, Jay. *Independence in Spanish America: Civil Wars, Revolutions, and Underdevelopment.* Albuquerque: University of New Mexico Press, 1994.

Lynch, John. *The Spanish American Revolutions, 1808–1826.* 2nd ed. New York: Norton, 1986.

McFarland, Anthony. *War and Independence in Spanish America.* New York: Routledge, 2014.

Nicholson, Irene. *The Liberators: A Study of Independence Movements in Spanish America.* New York: Praeger, 1969.

Robertson, William Spence. *France and Latin American Independence.* New York: Octagon, 1967.

Savelle, Max. *Europe and the World in the Age of Expansion,* Vol. 5, *Empires to Nations: Expansion in America, 1713–1824.* Minneapolis: University of Minnesota Press, 1974.

Whitaker, Arthur P. *The United States and the Independence of Latin America, 1800–1830.* Baltimore: Johns Hopkins University Press, 1941.

# Mexican War of Independence (1810–1821)

## Causes

In 1492 Christopher Colombus, sailing for Spain, landed in North America and began the process of creating the oldest European colonial empire in the New World. In 1519 Spaniard Hernán Cortés arrived in Mexico at the head of a 500-man expeditionary force and began the conquest of the powerful Aztec Empire. His small invasion force prevailed largely owing to alliances crafted with natives opposed to the oppressive Aztec rule and the devastation wrought by smallpox that may have claimed as much as half of the native population. Spanish rule lasted some 300 years. Spain's holdings in North America were vast and included the Mexican borderlands, the territory that in the mid-19th century would become the southwestern United States: Texas, New Mexico, Arizona, and California. Spanish officials undertook efforts to protect the border areas against encroachment by the young United States, but the real threat to Spanish rule came from within Mexico itself.

Geography was one factor that worked against Spanish rule in Mexico. The Atlantic Ocean was a highway for commerce, and especially valuable to Spain were the treasure ships laden with gold and silver that made their way from New Spain to the mother country. But given the vast distance involved, divisions in interests were almost certain to develop, as British leaders seeking to control northeastern North America had themselves discovered in 1775. A diversity of interests and loyalty developed over the course of centuries, especially among the generations of Spanish citizens born in the New World.

The conquistadores who had secured Mexico for Spain enjoyed considerable autonomy, but in the 1560s Don Martín Cortés, son of Hernán Cortés and second Marquis of the Valley of Oaxaca, led a conspiracy against the Spanish throne after the latter had sought to eliminate the special privileges enjoyed by the conquistadores. The conspiracy was easily suppressed, and while there were several subsequent instances in which the Mexican elites fomented urban unrest to force replacement of unpopular officials, these did not represent a challenge to the Crown or to the institution of colonial rule. Indeed, there was no substantial threat to royal rule in Mexico until 1810.

The intellectual movement of the Enlightenment of the late 17th century and the 18th century, with its emphasis on reason and individualism rather than tradition, found a ready reception not only in Europe but also in the colonies. But for the forces working for separation in its colonies to succeed, Spanish control would have to be weakened or, better, interrupted. The latter occurred as a consequence of the Napoleonic Wars (1803–1815).

In 1796 Spain had allied with revolutionary France against Britain, but the Royal Navy destroyed a powerful joint Spanish and French fleet in the Mediterranean off Cape Trafalgar, Spain, on October 21, 1805. This battle was decisive, for it established British supremacy at sea for the next century and led to heightened British operations to pry open and even take control of the Spanish overseas colonies, an effort that had been under way since the reign of Queen Elizabeth I (r. 1558–1603).

## Mexican War of Independence (1810–1821)

| Battle of Monte de las Cruces (October 30, 1810) | | |
| --- | --- | --- |
| | Mexican Rebels | Spanish Royalists |
| Strength | 80,000 | 2,700 |
| Casualties | 3,500 | 2,000 |

| Battle of Calderon Bridge (January 17, 1811) | | |
| --- | --- | --- |
| | Mexican Rebels | Spanish Royalists |
| Strength | 100,000 | 6,000 |
| Casualties | 13,000 | 2,000 |

| Battle of Puruarán (January 5, 1814) | | |
| --- | --- | --- |
| | Mexican Rebels | Spanish Royalists |
| Strength | 1,200 | 1,200–1,500 |
| Casualties | 660* | Unknown but few |

*Rebel leader Mariano Matamoros was taken prisoner during this engagement and executed on February 3, 1814.

| Key Commanders and Leaders, Mexican War of Independence (1810–1821) | |
| --- | --- |
| Mexican Rebels | Spanish Officials and Mexican Royalists |
| Miguel Hidalgo (1810–1811) | Francisco Javier Venegas (1810–1813) |
| Ignacio Allende (1810–1811) | Félix María Calleja (1813–1816) |
| Ignacio López Rayón (1810–1811) | Juan Ruiz de Apodaca (1821) |
| José María Morelos (1810–1815) | Francisco Novella Azabal Pérez (1821) |
| Vicente Guerrero (1810–1821) | Juan O'Donojú (1821) |
| Marianm Matamoros (1811–1814) | |
| Martín Francisco Javier Mina (1817) | |
| Agustín de Iturbide (1821) | |

**Sources:** Christon I. Archer, ed. *The Birth of Modern Mexico*. Wilmington, DE: SR Books, 2003; Hamnett, Brian R. *Roots of Insurgency: Mexican Regions, 1750–1824*. Cambridge: Cambridge University Press, 1986; Krause, Enrique. *Mexico: Biography of Power; A History of Modern Mexico, 1810–1896*. New York: HarperCollins, 1998; Rodríguez O., Jaime E., ed. *The Independence of Mexico and the Creation of the New Nation*. Los Angeles: University of California at Los Angeles Latin American Center Publications, 1989.

The Trafalgar defeat had another even more important effect on Spain itself, for it led French emperor Napoleon I to try to get at the British by economic means. His Continental System, first announced at Berlin on November 21, 1806, during the War of the Fourth Coalition (1806–1807), prohibited trade between Britain and the French Empire as well as the states allied to France. The Continental System was subsequently strengthened through additional decrees. In 1807 it was also extended to Russia and the next year to Portugal and Spain. Napoleon's intention here was to cut off British trade with the European continent, forcing Great Britain into ruinous inflation.

A monumental mistake on the part of Napoleon, this decision also led him to undertake one of the most disastrous decisions of his career: military intervention in the Iberian Peninsula. The "Spanish ulcer," as Napoleon would come to call it, cost France some 300,000 casualties and had a profound impact on his military operations elsewhere as well as on developments in the New World.

In 1807 French and Spanish troops invaded Portugal, seeking to divide up its territory and overseas empire. Then in January 1808 Napoleon sent a large number of troops into the territory of his ally Spain, ostensibly to protect its coasts from British attack but in reality to control that country, for he had already secured the abdications of Spanish king Charles IV and his successor Ferdinand VII. A revolt against French rule broke out in Madrid on May 2, 1808, beginning the War of Spanish Independence. Napoleon then revealed his hand by placing his older brother Joseph on the Spanish throne. Portuguese and Spanish resistance to French rule in the Iberian Peninsula received increased British military aid and even a growing British expeditionary force as the fighting wore on.

The ensuing fighting of the Spanish War of Independence (1808–1814) loosened the ties between metropolitan Spain and its overseas empire. In Mexico a rigid caste system was in place. At the top were the Iberian-born *peninsulares*. Next came the criollos, the locally born people of confirmed European (primarily Spanish)

Father Miguel Hidalgo y Costilla delivered the "Grito de Dolores" ("Cry from Dolores"), the passionate speech in his parish church of Dolores on September 16, 1819, that ignited the independence struggle in Mexico. (Library of Congress)

ancestry. These two classes had preeminence over the other populations of peoples of mixed descent, Amerindians, and enslaved Africans.

Roman Catholic priest Miguel Hidalgo y Costilla, a well-educated criollo who in 1803 had become the priest at Dolores, in Guanajuato state, was angered by the effects of the caste system and the extreme poverty of the Mexican peasantry. Steeped in the views of Enlightenment-era writers, he found himself opposed to traditional political and religious views and questioning the absolute authority of the Spanish king and long-held Catholic dogma, including papal authority, the virgin birth, and clerical celibacy. Hidalgo began holding secret gatherings in which the participants discussed whether an armed revolt was justified against a tyrannical governmental system that held the peasantry in check. Among the attendees at these meetings was Ignacio Allende, who had been born into a humble family of indigenous, African, and Spanish descent.

In 1810 Hidalgo and his followers concluded that revolt against the Spanish authorities was both justified and necessary. The rebels planned to launch their military effort that December, but on September 15 Hidalgo and other rebel leaders, including Allende, were meeting in Dolores when they learned that the Spanish authorities had discovered their conspiracy. Early the next day Hidalgo called a gathering of the townspeople at the church and there issued a call for revolution. This Grito de Dolores, or Cry of Dolores, marks the beginning of the Mexican War of Independence.

SPENCER C. TUCKER

## Course

Within a few days Hidalgo had assembled a force of some 600 poorly armed men. Adopting the Virgin of Guadalupe as their symbol and protector, they added additional adherents as they proceeded. Killing all Spaniards they could find, they arrived at the city of Guanajuato on September 28 to find the Spanish royalists there barricaded inside the public granary. The rebels stormed and took the granary, in the process killing a reported 500 people there. They then took the road to the capital of Mexico City.

Learning of the rebel approach, Spanish viceroy Don Francisco Javier Venegas ordered General Torcuato Trujillo to intercept and defeat the rebels. Acting on short notice, Trujillo was able to assemble only some 2,700 men and two artillery pieces to engage as many as 80,000 rebels. The fighting occurred at Monte de las Cruces on October 30. Although the rebels were poorly armed, their vastly superior numbers told, and having managed to capture the royalist artillery pieces, they won the battle. The surviving royalists withdrew to Mexico City. Rebel casualties in the battle have been reported at 3,500 casualties, with royalist losses perhaps 2,000.

Now enjoying nearly every advantage and with Mexico City apparently within his grasp, Hidalgo overruled Allende, who had become the rebel military commander, and ordered a withdrawal. Although the reason for this is unclear, historians generally attribute his decision to Hidalgo's fears that based on what had occurred thus far, there would be a bloodbath should the rebels take the capital city. Whatever the reason, the decision was certainly a mistaken one for the rebel cause.

Hidalgo planned a defensive strategy. With the royalists having assumed the offensive, the decisive encounter occurred on the banks of the Calderón River on January 17, 1811. Despite being heavily outnumbered (some 6,000 royalist soldiers to as many as 100,000 rebels) in the ensuing Battle of Calderón Bridge (the engagement being named for the combatants' objective), the royalist side was victorious. The rebels sustained perhaps 13,000 casualties to only 2,000 for the royalists. Following the battle the rebels dispersed, with many attempting flight across the northern border into the United States. Blaming Hidalgo for their defeat, on January 25, 1811, at Hacienda de Pabellón near Aguascalientes, Allende and other insurgent leaders stripped Hidalgo of military command of the revolutionary forces, although he continued as political head. Allende took over the military command.

Most of the insurgents were intercepted and taken prisoner. Hidalgo himself was captured at the Norias de Baján in Coahuila on March 21. The rebel leaders were all found guilty. One was sentenced to life in prison in Spain, but three others, including Allende, were sentenced to death and executed on June 26, 1811, shot in the back as a symbol of dishonor. As a priest, Hidalgo was brought before the Spanish Inquisition and removed from the priesthood. The civil authorities having found him guilty, he was executed on July 30. The heads of all four executed leaders were then hung from the corners of the Guanajuato granary as a warning to other would-be rebels. Despite his shortcomings as a military leader, Hidalgo is today remembered in Mexico as a national hero, indeed the father of the country.

The fight for Mexican independence did not end with the death of Hidalgo, however. His confederate José María Morelos y Pavón, also a Roman Catholic priest, became the new leader and soon proved himself to be a capable military strategist and field commander. Taking the offensive, he won nearly two dozen victories in just nine months, securing control of almost all of what is now Guerrero state. He captured the city of Acapulco except for the Fort of San Diego, and he won most of the Pacific coast region in what are now the states of Michoacán and Guerrero. On May 24, 1811, he occupied Chilpancingo, and on May 26 he took Tixtla.

On December 24, 1811, the people of Cuautla in the state of Morelos welcomed Morelos and his troops, but on February 2, 1812, some 12,000 royalists under General Félix María Calleja del Rey arrived and laid siege to Cuautla, which was defended by about 17,000 rebels under Morelos, Hermenegildo Galeana, and Mariano

Matamoros. The royalists secured the town after three months on May 2 but only with the rebel forces having broken free. During the siege the rebels suffered perhaps 6,000 casualties, the royalists half that number.

Morelos then embarked on his third military campaign. In 1812 he scored victories over the royalists at Citlalli on June 8, Tehuacán on August 10, and also at Orizaba, where he arrived with 10,000 men on October 28, 1812. With its royalist garrison numbering only 600 men, Orizaba surrendered without bloodshed. Morelos entered Oaxaca on November 25, and Acapulco fell on April 12, 1813, except for its Fort of San Diego, where royalist forces commanded by José Pedro Antonio Vélez de Zúñiga sought refuge. The royalists were able to hold out there until August, when the two sides concluded a truce. On March 4, 1813, Field Marshal Félix María Calleja assumed power as the viceroy of New Spain. He held that position until September 20, 1816.

The Mexican revolutionaries received a boost from the liberals in Spain, for in 1810 during the Peninsular War the Spaniards fighting to expel the French had established under the protection of the British Royal Navy a revolutionary government at the port city of Cádiz. This elected representative body of the Cortes (parliament) produced the Spanish Constitution of 1812. Modeled on the French revolutionary Constitution of 1791 and certainly one of the world's most liberal governing documents of its day, it called for the establishment of representative bodies at both the local and national levels in Spain itself but also in the Spanish colonies.

In 1813 Morelos called for the election of representatives from the areas of Mexico under his control to meet in what became known as the Congress of Chilpancingo. The congress met in the city of that name in Guerrero state from September to November. The delegates endorsed what was called the "sentiments of the nation." This proclaimed Mexico to be an independent republic with a representative form of government that would have executive, legislative, and judicial branches. It also established Catholicism as the state religion and called for the abolition of torture, slavery, and the caste system with its many social distinctions, endorsing the term "American" for all those who were native born. On November 6, 1813, the congress issued the Solemn Act of the Declaration of Independence of Northern America. Offered the title "generalissimo" to be addressed as "your highness," Morelos asked instead that he be known as "siervo de la nación" (servant of the nation).

Fighting continued as the members of the congress organized a meeting in Apatzingán. There on October 22, 1814, they promulgated the Decreto Constitucional para la Libertad de la América Mexicana, known as the Constitution of Apatzingán. Morelos had sought a strong executive, but this document instead called for a powerful legislature and a weak executive. The new constitution never went into effect, however.

Morelos then embarked on his fourth major military campaign. This time the revolutionary side suffered a series of defeats. The first of these came in the Battle of Lomas de Santa María in the municipality of Valladolid (present-day Morelia) during December 23–24, 1813. With the royalist side having refused to surrender Valladolid, on December 23 Morelos's lieutenant Mariano Matamoros y Guridi mounted an assault on the city. The royalist defenders, led by Agustín Cosme Damián de Iturbide y Arámburu, managed to hold off the attackers until the arrival of reinforcements from Mexico City under Ciriaco del Llano, dispatched by viceroy of New Spain Calleja.

Morelos then ordered Matamoros to return to camp with his men with the plan that they would renew the attack the next day. The rebels camped in a heavily forested area known as the Lomas de Santa María. Around midnight, with the royalist commanders having learned the location of the rebel encampment, Llano convinced Iturbide, although they were outnumbered some 1,200 to 5,600, to mount an immediate assault in order to prevent a likely rebel victory the next day. This royalist attack at about 2:00 a.m. on December 24 caught the rebel side by surprise. Owing to confusion in the darkness, the rebel soldiers fired on one another after the royalist troops had already withdrawn. In the fighting for Valladolid the rebels suffered 789 casualties, the royalists only 200. The battle marked the end of Morelos's fourth campaign.

Morelos now withdrew to Puebla and made plans to continue the fight. At Puruarán in Michoacán on January 5, 1814, the royalist force under Iturbide inflicted a major defeat on the rebels under Matamoros in which the rebels sustained some 660 casualties, including Matamoros taken prisoner, and the loss of 23 artillery pieces (royalist losses are unknown). This defeat forced Morelos to retreat to the Hacienda of Santa Lucia. Matamoros was sentenced to death on January 23. Morelos attempted to save his comrade's life by offering to exchange 200 Spanish royalist captured soldiers for him. Viceroy Calleja refused, and Matamoros was executed on February 3, 1814. When he learned of this, Morelos ordered all 200 royalist prisoners held by his side to be killed.

Morelos was elected president of the Supreme Mexican Government on October 24, 1814. While escorting the insurgent congress from Uruapan to Tehuacán, however, he was defeated in Tezmalaca and taken prisoner by royalist forces on November 5. Because he was a Catholic priest the church had jurisdiction, and he was taken to Mexico City and there brought before the Inquisition and civil authorities. Tried and found guilty of treason, he was executed by firing squad on December 22, 1815, in San Cristóbal Ecatepec, north of Mexico City.

From 1815 to 1821 rebel military effort was for the most part limited to guerrilla warfare. Two leaders arose: Guadalupe Victoria (born José Miguel Fernández y Félix) in Puebla and Vicente Guerrero in Oaxaca. Believing the situation to be under control, Juan Ruiz de Apodaca, the new viceroy of New Spain during September 1816–July 1821, issued a general pardon to every rebel who would lay down his arms. Thousands did so, although Victoria and Guerrero refused. Still, after a decade of war and the death of two of its founders, by early 1820 the independence movement was close to collapse. The rebels faced significant military resistance and the apathy of many of the most influential criollos.

In what was assumed to be the final government campaign against the rebels, in December 1820 Apodaca dispatched Colonel Iturbide and a royalist force to defeat Guerrero in Oaxaca. Iturbide, a native of Valladolid, had gained fame for his earlier successes against the rebels. A staunch Catholic, he also embraced conservative criollo values, including upholding property rights and the maintenance of social privileges.

Iturbide's assignment to command the Oaxaca expedition coincided with major events in Spain. Reactionary King Ferdinand VII, who had been restored to his throne on the defeat of the French in 1814, was determined to restore Spanish rule in the Americas. Despite Ferdinand's best efforts and the imprisonment or execution of a number of liberals and radicals, opposition to his autocratic rule from within metropolitan Spain continued, and a revolt broke out in January 1820 among army units assembling in Cádiz to be sent to the New World. The revolt was made easier because there was great disaffection among the soldiers about being ordered on such a mission.

Rebel leader Colonel Rafael Riego then led a march from Cádiz on Madrid. Parts of northern Spain also rose in revolt, and ultimately the Madrid garrison joined in. Realizing that in order to retain the throne he must submit, Ferdinand in March 1820 took an oath to the constitution modeled on that of 1812, becoming a virtual prisoner until 1823.

When news of this reached Mexico, Iturbide saw it as a threat to the status quo and a catalyst to rouse the criollos to gain control of Mexico. In a rather surprising development, the conservative royalist forces in the colonies chose to align themselves against the new liberal regime in Spain. Then after an initial clash with Guerrero's forces, Iturbide assumed command of the army.

At Iguala, Iturbide proclaimed the Three Principles, or "guarantees," regarding Mexican independence from Spain. Mexico would be an independent monarchy governed by King Ferdinand, another Bourbon prince, or some other conservative European prince; criollos would be granted equal rights and privileges to peninsulares; and the Roman Catholic Church in Mexico would retain its position and privileges as the established church of Mexico, with Catholicism the only accepted religion. Iturbide then managed to convince his troops to accept the Three Principles, announced on February 24, 1821, as the Plan of Iguala. Iturbide then persuaded Guerrero to join his forces in support of this conservative independence movement. A new army combining their two forces and known as the Army of the Three Guarantees was then established under Iturbide's command to enforce the Plan of Iguala. The heretofore elusive goal of independence and protection of Roman Catholicism brought together all factions.

Other rebel forces from all over Mexico now professed solidarity with Iturbide, and with a rebel victory all but certain, Viceroy Apodaca resigned. On August 24, 1821, representatives of the Spanish Crown and Iturbide signed the Treaty of Córdoba. This document, although never reatified by the Spanish Cortes, recognized Mexican independence based on the Plan of Iguala. On September 27, 1821, the Army of the Three Guarantees entered Mexico City, and the following day, September 28, Iturbide proclaimed the independence of the Mexican Empire, as New Spain would now be known.

SPENCER C. TUCKER

## Consequences

For decades after achieving independence in 1821, Mexico suffered from chronic political instability, economic stagnation, civil wars, and foreign interventions. In the absence of a central state capable of exercising sovereign political authority throughout the territory of Mexico, regional military strongmen, or caudillos, seized and lost power through military coups.

Between 1821 and 1855 Mexico saw 55 different presidencies, each lasting an average of less than one year and 35 of them held by military men. The most notable of the 19th-century caudillos, General Antonio López de Santa Anna, seized the presidency himself on nine different occasions.

General Agustín Cosme Damián de Iturbide y Arámburu had included in the Treaty of Córdoba of August 1821, which established Mexican independence from Spain, a clause that permitted appointment of a criollo monarch by a Mexican congress if a suitable European royal could not be found to be Mexican emperor. Iturbide used this to proclaim himself emperor on May 19, 1822. His tenure was short-lived, however. A revolt led to his ouster on March 19, 1823, and the establishment of the United Mexican States, and the next year a republican constitution created a presidential regime.

King Ferdinand VII, having been restored to full authority thanks to a French military intervention on his behalf in Spain in 1923 sanctioned by Austria, Prussia, and Russia, then ignored the declaration by U.S. president James Monroe and dispatched an expeditionary force to Mexico in 1828. It landed at Tampico in August but was besieged there and forced to surrender the next month by Mexican forces under Santa Anna. This marked the end of Spain's efforts to reimpose its authority in Mexico.

Unfortunately, the history of the Mexican Republic was marked by continued pronounced disagreements regarding the form of government and internal strife, as in the so-called Pastry War of 1838–1839 and French military intervention. Considerable separatist sentiment in northern Mexico brought the independence of Texas in 1836; it joined the United States in 1845. U.S. president James K. Polk's determination to purchase or otherwise acquire additional Mexican territory, especially California, then led to the U.S. war with Mexico (1846–1848), Mexico's defeat, and the loss of half of its pre-1836 national territory to its northern neighbor.

Throughout this period, liberals and conservatives—the two main political factions in 19th-century Mexico, as elsewhere in Latin America—struggled to establish a central state capable of providing for political stability and economic development. The crux of the difference between the two groups was whether the state would be secular, limited in its powers, and federal in organization, as the liberals would have it, or centralized, powerful, and closely linked to the Catholic Church, as advocated by the conservatives. The liberals gained ascendancy in the Revolution of Ayutla (1854–1855) after ousting Santa Anna from the presidency for the final time and in the wake of Mexico's disastrous defeat in the Mexican-American War.

Beginning in 1855, the liberal government issued a series of far-reaching reforms designed to spark economic growth, radically curtail the power and activities of the Catholic Church, and foster a common national identity rooted in liberal citizenship. The most notable of these reforms was the 1856 Lerdo Law. It mandated that almost all property owned by civil and ecclesiastical corporations—including the Catholic Church, Indian villages, and municipalities—be privatized through sales to occupants and tenants.

The church's extensive properties were ultimately nationalized and sold off in the context of the civil war generated by the liberal reforms. The privatization of municipal and village lands was a much longer, more contested, and more incomplete process. Liberals intended this property to remain in the hands of its mainly peasant cultivators, but in many regions and villages wealthier residents and outsiders were able to acquire municipal and village lands through various types of sales, procedural irregularities, and fraud, giving rise to one of the central grievances that would later fuel the revolution.

The promulgation of the liberal constitution of 1857 set off a civil war between liberals and conservatives known as the War of the Reform (1858–1861). No sooner had the liberals under the leadership of President Benito Juárez defeated their conservative opponents than they faced intervention by the French. Using the excuse of Mexico's failure to meet its foreign debts, the French invaded in 1862 and established the short-lived Second Mexican Empire (1864–1867) under Austrian archduke Maximilian of Habsburg, supported by French bayonets and Mexican Roman Catholic clergy and conservatives. With the defeat and ouster of the imperial armies and the execution of Maximilian in 1867, leading liberals then fought among themselves.

José de la Cruz Porfirio Díaz Mori, a popular liberal general and hero in the war against the French, attempted to oust the increasingly autocratic Juárez from the presidency in the failed Rebellion of La Noria in 1872. Four years later Díaz successfully unseated Juárez's successor, President Sebastián Lerdo de Tejada, in the 1876 Rebellion of Tuxtepec and assumed the presidency himself, although he did not take formal control until early 1877. Díaz ushered in a period of unprecedented political stability and economic development.

The period from 1876 to 1911 is known as the Porfiriato. Apart from a four-year period (1880–1884), Díaz held the presidency throughout. This period, the famed "political peace" of the Porfiriato (*pax porfiriana*) was achieved and maintained through a combination of coercion and patronage politics. It in turn led to the Mexican Revolution of 1910, the end of the dictatorship, and the restoration of a constitutional republic.

JENNIE PURNELL AND
SPENCER C. TUCKER

## Timeline

| | |
|---|---|
| **1519** | Spaniard Hernán Cortés arrives in Mexico and begins the conquest of the Aztec Empire. Spain will rule Mexico for some 300 years. |
| **Nov 1807** | French and allied Spanish troops invade Portugal, seeking to divide up its territory and overseas empire. This begins the Peninsular War of 1807–1814. |
| **Jan 1808** | French emperor Napoleon sends sizable forces into Spain to control that country. He has already secured the abdications of Spanish kings Charles IV and Ferdinand VII. |
| **May 2, 1808** | The Spanish War of Independence begins. The ensuing fighting in Spain during 1808–1814 greatly loosens its ties with the Spanish Empire. |
| **1810** | At Dolores, Guanajuato, Mexico, Miguel Hidalgo y Costilla, angered by the extreme poverty of the Mexican peasantry, meets with other like-minded individuals to discuss undertaking a revolt against the government. |
| **Sep 16, 1810** | Hidalgo brings the townspeople of Dolores together and calls for revolution. Known as the Grito de Dolores, or Cry of Dolores, this marks the beginning of the Mexican War of Independence. |
| **Sep 28, 1810** | Arriving at the city of Guanajuato, the rebels attack and take the public granary before moving toward Mexico City. |
| **Oct 30, 1810** | At the Battle of Monte de las Cruces, the rebels defeat forces under General Torcuato Trujillo. |
| **Jan 17, 1811** | Royalist forces decisively defeat rebel fighters in the Battle of Calderón Bridge. |
| **Mar–Dec 1811** | Hidalgo's confederate José María Morelos y Pavón becomes the new rebel leader. He soon secures control of almost all of what is now Guerrero state. |
| **Mar 21, 1811** | Hidalgo is captured at the Norias de Baján in Coahuila. He and other rebel leaders are executed. |
| **Feb 2–May 2, 1812** | Royalist forces secure Cuautia, but the rebels manage to break free. |

| | |
|---|---|
| **Jun–Nov 1812** | Morelos wins victories over the royalists at Citlalli, Tehuacán, Orizaba, and Oaxaca. |
| **Mar 4, 1813** | Field Marshal Félix María Calleja becomes viceroy of New Spain. |
| **Apr 12, 1813** | Morelos captures Acapulco except for its Fort of San Diego, where royalist forces commanded by José Pedro Antonio Vélez de Zúñiga hold out until August. |
| **Sep–Nov 1813** | The Congress of Chilpancingo, championed by Morelos, proclaims Mexico an independent republic with a representative form of government. It also calls for the abolition of torture, slavery, and the caste system. |
| **Dec 23–24, 1813** | Morales and his lieutenant Mariano Matamoros y Guridi are defeated by royalist forces under Agustín Cosme Damián de Iturbide y Arámburu in the Battle of Lomas de Santa María. |
| **Jan 5, 1814** | At Puruarán, royalists under Iturbide inflict a major defeat on the rebels under Matamoros, who is executed on February 3, 1814. |
| **Oct 24, 1814** | Morelos is elected president of the revolutionary government. |
| **1815–1821** | Rebel military efforts are largely limited to guerrilla warfare. Two leaders arise: Guadalupe Victoria (born José Miguel Fernández y Félix) in Puebla and Vicente Guerrero in Oaxaca. |
| **Nov 5, 1815** | While escorting the insurgent congress from Uruapan to Tehuacán, Morelos is defeated in Tezmalaca by the royalist forces and is executed on December 22. |
| **Sep 26, 1816** | Juan Ruiz de Apodaca becomes viceroy of New Spain and issues a general pardon to rebels laying down their arms. Victoria and Guerrero, however, continue the fight. |
| **Early 1820** | After a decade of war and the death of two of its founders, the independence movement is close to collapse. |
| **Dec 1820** | In what is assumed to be the final campaign against the rebels, Apodaca orders Colonel Iturbide and a royalist force to defeat Guerrero in Oaxaca. |
| **Feb 24, 1821** | At Iguala, Iturbide proclaims the Plan of Iguala, which holds that an independent Mexico will be a monarchy, that criollos will be granted equal rights to *peninsulares,* and that the Roman Catholic Church will remain the established church of Mexico. |
| **March–Jun 1821** | Iturbide persuades Guerrero to join his forces in support of the conservative independence movement. A new force, known as the Army of the Three Guarantees, is established under Iturbide's command to enforce the Plan of Iguala. |
| **Jul 5, 1821** | With rebel forces from all over Mexico professing solidarity with Iturbide, Viceroy Apodaca resigns. |

**Aug 24, 1821**  Representatives of the Spanish Crown and Iturbide sign the Treaty of Córdoba. Although not ratified by the Spanish Cortes, the treaty recognizes Mexican independence based on the Plan of Iguala.

**Sep 28, 1821**  The Army of the Three Guarantees enters Mexico City, and on this day Iturbide proclaims the independence of the Mexican Empire.

**May 19, 1822**  Iturbide declares himself emperor of Mexico.

**Mar 19, 1823**  A revolt ends Iturbide's tenure as emperor.

**Oct 4, 1824**  A republican constitution goes into effect, creating a presidential regime.

SPENCER C. TUCKER

## Further Reading

Archer, Christon I., ed. *The Birth of Modern Mexico.* Willmington, DE: Scholarly Resources, 2003.

Anna, Timothy E. *The Fall of Royal Government in Mexico City.* Lincoln: University of Nebraska Press, 1978.

Benjamin, Thomas. *Revolución: Mexico's Great Revolution as Memory, Myth, and History.* Austin: University of Texas Press, 2000.

Dominguez, Jorge. *Insurrection or Loyalty: The Breakdown of the Spanish American Empire.* Cambridge, MA: Harvard University Press, 1980.

García, Pedro. *Con el cura Hidalgo en la guerra de independencia en México.* Mexico City: Fondo de Cultura Económica 1982.

Hamill, Hugh M., Jr. "Early Psychological Warfare in the Hidalgo Revolt." *Hispanic American Historical Review* 41(2) (1961): 206–235.

Hamill, Hugh M., Jr. *The Hidalgo Revolt: Prelude to Mexican Independence.* Gainesville: University of Florida Press, 1966.

Hamnett, Brian R. *Roots of Insurgency: Mexican Regions, 1750–1824.* Cambridge: Cambridge University Press, 1986.

Hamnett, Brian. "Royalist Counterinsurgency and the Continuity of Rebellion: Guanajuato and Michoacán, 1813–1820." *Hispanic American Historical Review* 62(11) (February 1982): 19–48.

Knight, Alan. *Mexico: The Colonial Era.* Cambridge: Cambridge University Press, 2002.

Krause, Enrique. *Mexico: Biography of Power; A History of Modern Mexico, 1810–1896.* New York: HarperCollins, 1998.

Rodríguez O., Jaime E., ed. *The Independence of Mexico and the Creation of the New Nation.* Los Angeles: University of California at Los Angeles Latin American Center Publications, 1989.

Timmons, Wilbert H. *Morelos: Priest, Soldier, Statesman of Mexico.* El Paso: Texas Western College Press, 1963.

Tutino, John. *From Insurrection to Revolution in Mexico: Social Bases of Agrarian Violence, 1750–1940.* Princeton, NJ: Princeton University Press, 1986.

# Greek War of Independence (1821–1830)

## Causes

The 11-year-long Greek War of Independence (also known as the Greek Revolution and the Greek Uprising) of March 25, 1821, to February 3, 1830, was a watershed event in European history. It was prompted by an insurrection in Wallachia in present-day Romani against the Ottoman Empire, leading to a revolt in the Peloponnese (Morea) in southern Greece against Ottoman rule.

Numerous factors were at play in causing the revolt. Although Greece had been part of the Ottoman Empire since the mid-15th century, the Greeks had retained their national identity under the loose Ottoman rule. Although Orthodox Christians enjoyed certain political rights under the Ottomans and indeed a number held positions of influence, the Greeks were nonetheless regarded as inferior subjects.

This was also hardly an isolated event. There had been a number of revolts in the Balkan region against Ottoman rule. Notable among these in Greece were uprisings in the Peloponnese in the 17th and 18th centuries, including during the Russo-Ottoman War of 1787–1792, and there was a major revolt during 1815–1817 by Serbs against Ottoman rule.

The Greek Orthodox Church had served as a rallying point and had helped keep the Greek identity alive. This was buttressed by the key role played by the ancient Greeks and their myriad contributions to Western civilization in the arts and letters and to the concept of democracy (itself a Greek-derive word). This created great sympathy for the Greeks abroad, particularly in Western Europe.

The period of the French Revolution and the Napoleonic Wars (1789–1815) was also highly influential. It marked the beginning of modern European nationalism and the concept that peoples of the same language and ethnicity should be able to live together in their own nation-state. Greek intellectuals, many of whom had emigrated abroad and been educated in Western Europe, took up the cause of an independent Greek state and promoted it in their writings. Greek nationalists were, however, profoundly disappointed when their appeal for self-determination was rejected by the leaders of the Great Powers meeting in the Congress of Vienna of 1814–1815 to redraw the map of Europe after the defeat of Napoleon.

In 1814 Greeks in Odessa, Russia, founded the Hetairia Philike (Association of Friends) with the avowed aim of expelling the Ottomans from Europe. These nationalists received aid from Greeks living abroad and at least sympathy from Russia. Beginning with Czarina Catherine the Great (r. 1762–1796) and her so-called Greek Scheme, there had been great interest among Russian statesmen for the establishment of an independent Greece under Russian protection as a means to secure access to the Mediterranean. Indeed, Russia had long used its claim to protect the rights of Greek Orthodox Christians to intervene in the Ottoman Empire. Czar Alexander I (r. 1801–1825) was named for Alexander the Great of Macedon, and the czar's younger brother bore the name Constantine. Czar Alexander wanted to weaken the Ottoman Empire and early on lent his support to the Hetairia Philike.

## Greek War of Independence (1821–1830)

| Siege of Tripolitsa (April–October 1821) | | |
|---|---|---|
| | **Greek Revolutionaries** | **Ottomans and Allies, Civilians** |
| **Strength** | 10,000–15,000 troops | 11,000 troops* |
| **Losses** | 100 or less | 10,000** |

*Of this number some 8,000 were Ottoman troops, while about 3,000 were allied Albanian troops.
**This number includes troops and civilians, including many Muslims and a number of Jews.

| Chios Massacre (March 1822)* |
|---|
| 42,000 starved or massacred |
| 50,000 enslaved |
| 23,000 refugees |

*The pillaging of Chios and the massacre that occurred there was perpetrated by Ottoman forces.

| Naval Battle of Navarino Bay (October 20, 1827)* | | |
|---|---|---|
| | **British, Russian, French Forces** | **Ottoman/Egyptian Forces** |
| **Ships of the line** | 11 | 3 |
| **Frigates** | 9 | 19 |
| **Brigs** | 4 | 12 |
| **Corvettes** | 0 | 26 |
| **Schooners** | 2 | 0 |
| **Fire brigs** | 0 | 5–6 |
| **Total ships** | 26 | 65–66 |
| **Killed/wounded** | 646 | 4,000+ |

*This four-hour battle ended in a substantial allied victory over the Ottomans and Egyptians.

**Sources:** Anderson, R. C. *Naval Wars in the Levant, 1559–1853.* Liverpool: University Press of Liverpool, 1952; Beaton, Roderick. *Byron's War: Romantic Rebellion, Greek Revolution.* Cambridge: Cambridge University Press, 2013; St. Clair, William. *That Greece Might Still Be Free: The Philhellenes in the War of Independence.* London: Oxford University Press, 1972.

Alexander Ypsilanti (Ypsilantis), a general officer in the Russian Army from a powerful Greek family in Moldavia, headed the Hetairia Philike. He was in contact with the Russian government through Count Giovanni Capo d'Istria, a close friend of Alexander. Ypsilanti hoped to bring about the establishment of a Greek empire, one that would include other Ottoman territories in Europe, including modern-day Romania.

Spencer C. Tucker

## Course

The revolt against Ottoman rule began first in Wallachia in the Danubian Principalities in February 1821. Although easily put down, it sparked revolt in Greece. On March 17, Maniots in the Peloponnese also revolted against the Ottomans, and by the end of the month the entire Peloponnese was in open rebellion. On March 21 Ypsilanti led an armed force from Ukraine across the Pruth River into Moldavia, then appealed to Russia for assistance in a war to free Greece from Ottoman rule. Influential Austrian first minister Klemens von Metternich, then dominating the affairs of Continental Europe, strongly opposed outside interference and reminded the czar of the danger of revolutions to the established order. The revolt, he said, should be allowed to "burn itself out beyond the pale of civilization." Alexander was then under Metternich's influence and soon disavowed Ypsilanti.

Ottoman forces of Sultan Mahmoud II were thus able to crush Ypsilanti's forces in the Battle of Dragashan (June 26, 1821). Yspilanti fled across the border into Austrian territory, where he was arrested and was imprisoned until 1827. (Released at the insistence of Russian czar Nicolas I [r. 1825–1855], Ypsilanti retired to Vienna, where he died in poverty in 1828.) This was not the end of the unrest in Greece, however.

A wide range of dates have been advanced for the Greek War of Independence. Depending on the source, dates for its beginning settle on February and March 1821, with the war ended at various dates ranging from 1829 or 1831. Perhaps it should begin with Ypsilanti's failed effort in Moldavia, but probably a more suitable date is that of the present Greek Independence Day of March 25. On that day in 1821 Germanos, the archbishop of Pátrai, raised a Greek flag at the Ayia Lavra monastery near Kalávrita.

Turks were in the minority in Greece, but there were a number of scattered Ottoman military garrisons. Greeks led by Theodoros Kolokotronis now laid siege to the Ottoman garrison at Tripolitsa, then the largest city of southern Greece. The attackers stormed that city on October 5, 1821, and during the next several days the Greeks massacred some 10,000 Ottomans, including women and children. Many were tortured to death. Savage Ottoman reprisals followed, and all of Greece then rose up against Ottoman rule. On January 13, 1822, at Epidauros, Greek nationalists proclaimed the independence of Greece. The Peloponnese uprising also brought revolts elsewhere, in Crete, Macedonia, and central Greece.

In March 1822, several hundred armed Greeks from the nearby island of Samos landed on the island of Chios (Scio) off western Anatolia and proceeded to attack Turks living there. While some of the local Greeks joined in, the vast majority realized the precariousness of their position and refused to participate.

A powerful Ottoman naval squadron under Captain Pasha Kara Ali arrived at Chios on March 22. The Ottoman forces came ashore and quickly pillaged and looted Chios, and on March 31 they deliberately burned it. When additional Ottoman troops arrived, they were ordered to kill all Greek infants under the age of 3, all males 12 years and older, and all females 40 and older except those willing to convert to Islam. Although the figures are in dispute, perhaps 23,000 Greeks managed to escape Chios, 50,000 were enslaved, and some 42,000 were massacred or starved to death. Only 2,000 people remained on the island afterward. The event was subsequently immortalized in a famous painting by French artist Eugène

Delacroix. The Greeks did achieve a measure of revenge when on June 19 the Turkish fleet was destroyed by a Greek fleet under Constantine Kanaris.

The plight of the Greeks became the subject of extensive press coverage and led to a wave of sympathy for them in Europe. Known as Philhellenism, it was in part based on the democratic and artistic legacy of ancient Greece. Many Europeans, especially in Britain, France, and Germany, volunteered to fight for Greece, the best known of them being British poet George Gordon Byron, sixth Baron Byron, who died of a fever in Greece in 1824. Ultimately, the foreigners included able British naval officer Lord Thomas Cochrane, who came to command the Greek Navy, and British general Sir George Church. The foreign officers, however, often found their efforts foiled by Greek infighting.

In July 1822 two Ottoman armies invaded and soon overran all of Greece north of the Gulf of Corinth. The Greek government took refuge off the mainland in the Greek islands. Ottoman forces under Omar Vrioni were, however, halted before the strategically located Greek fort of Missolonghi (Messolonghi) guarding the entrance to the Gulf of Corinth. The Ottomans arrived there on October 25, 1822, but made the mistake of entering into negotiations. The Greeks dragged these out and on November 8 were reinforced by sea with more than 1,500 men. The Ottomans realized their mistake too late and resumed siege operations. After a month of bombardment and sorties without success, the Ottomans hoped to catch the Greeks by surprise in an assault on the night of December 24–25. Forewarned, the Greeks beat back the attack, and the Ottomans then withdrew. Missolonghi withstood a second Ottoman siege during September 20–November 30, 1822.

The Greeks failed to take advantage of their military success, however. Rather, they dissipated their energies in leadership struggles as Theodoros Kolokotronis opposed Lazaros Kountouriotis for leadership. This flared into civil war in 1824, during which Kolokotronis was defeated.

With the Ottoman military intervention in Greece going badly, Sultan Mahmud II appealed for assistance to his powerful vassal, Muhammad Ali of Egypt, who then dispatched a considerable fleet and army to Greece under his son Ibrahim Ali. The Egyptian expeditionary force landed in Greece on February 24, 1825, and soon subdued virtually the entire peninsula. As result of this intervention, the Porte formally ceded Crete to Egypt, the forces of which had conquered the island during 1822–1824.

In the spring of 1825, an Ottoman army under Reşid Pasha drove from the north and on April 7 opened a third siege of the strategically important Greek stronghold of Missolonghi guarding access to the Gulf of Corinth. The defenders held out for an entire year, rejecting Ottoman offers of honorable terms. Prolonged resistance was possible only because the Greeks were able to resupply the fortress from the sea. When the besiegers closed this off, starvation and disease took their toll. The defenders attempted a breakout on the night of April 22, 1826, but only some 1,000 of 7,000 managed to reach the forests of Mount Zygos, and most of these later perished there.

On the morning of April 23, the Ottomans entered Missolonghi. Many of the Greeks committed suicide rather than surrender; the rest were slain or sold into slavery. The Ottomans subsequently displayed some 3,000 severed heads on the city walls.

After the fall of Missolonghi in western Greece, Reşid Pasha turned his attention to Athens in eastern Greece. Athens was the only Greek-held stronghold in the mainland outside the Peloponnese, where Yannis Gouras had established virtual independent rule. Reşid's conciliatory policies facilitated his march, and many in the countryside welcomed him as a liberator.

The city of Athens surrendered on the first Ottoman assault on August 25, 1826. The attackers then initiated a close blockade and bombardment of the Acropolis, to which the Greeks had withdrawn. Greek forces there responded with night raids and mining, utilizing the expertise of Konstantinos Chormivitis, who had distinguished himself at Missolonghi.

In these apparently dire circumstances, the Greek government appointed Georgios Karaiskakis as supreme commander of its forces in central Greece. A master of guerrilla warfare, he was a man of great patriotism and courage who led from the front. At Chaidari, the Ottomans defeated the first Greek attempt to relieve Athens. The defenders of the Acropolis were hardpressed, however, especially with the death of Gouras on October 13, but his wife took over the command and inspired the defenders. The siege dragged on as Karaiskakis fought with varying success in the mountains to the south.

On February 3, 1827, Karaiskakis routed Ottoman forces in the Battle of Distomo, and two days later he conducted a surprise night attack on the Ottoman camp, capturing there much-needed supplies and artillery and forcing an Ottoman withdrawal. These were the first major Greek victories since 1825. Karaiskakis, however, was killed in battle on April 23. He was succeeded by British general Church.

The Ottoman victory at Phaleron (Analatos) on April 24 ended the possibility of relief, and the Acropolis garrison, accorded the honors of war, surrendered on May 24. Church and the remaining poorly trained Greek forces were reduced to guerrilla warfare.

With Ottoman and Egyptian forces now controlling virtually all of Greece, Greek nationalists appealed to Britain. The British government, worried that Russia might intervene unilaterally and end up dominating Greece, sought to work out a solution acceptable to all the Great Powers. Indeed, devout Czar Nicholas I (r. 1825–1855) believed it his duty to answer the call of his Orthodox coreligionists in Greece against the Ottomans. Already on April 5, 1826, the Russian government had demanded that the Sublime Porte return to the status quo in the Danubian Principalities and dispatch a special envoy to St. Petersburg to discuss relations. Pressed by France and Austria, the Ottomans had agreed.

The Porte was also distracted by the June 15–16, 1816, destruction of the Janissaries. Sultan Mahmud II (r. 1808–1830) had long planned to move against the Janissaries, their military ineffectiveness having been amply demonstrated. His decree calling for a modern military establishment provoked the expected Janissary revolt in Istanbul (Constantinople). Mahmud was prepared, and the revolt was ruthlessly crushed, with some 6,000–10,000 Janissaries slain.

On July 8, 1827, representatives of the French, British, and Russian governments concluded the Treaty of London. It called on the Ottomans to agree to an armistice and on the Egyptians to withdraw. Should the Porte refuse, the three powers pledged to come to the aid of the Greeks with their naval forces. In the meantime, the British make a strong but ultimately unsuccessful diplomatic effort to get Muhammad Ali to remove his forces from Greece.

On August 16 the same three powers sent a note to the Porte demanding an armistice, which the Ottomans rejected on August 29. With that, the British, French, and Russian governments issued orders to their naval commanders in the Mediterranean to sever waterborne Ottoman and Egyptian resupply to Greece. In late August 1827 despite warnings from the European governments not to do so, Egypt dispatched a large naval squadron with troop reinforcements to Navarino Bay (Pylos) on the west coast of the Peloponnese. On September 8 it joined several Ottoman ships already there.

Four days later, a British squadron under Vice Admiral Sir Edward Codrington arrived off the bay. The French and Russian governments also had dispatched squadrons to Greece. Codrington's instructions called on him to try to secure an armistice and to use force only as a last resort. Codrington strongly supported Greek independence and had been freed regarding force because the Ottoman government had rejected the allied conditions.

On September 25 Codrington and French admiral Henry Gauthier de Rigny met with Egyptian commander in Greece Ibrahim Pasha to discuss a mediation arrangement already accepted by the Greeks. Ibrahim agreed to an armistice while awaiting instructions from the sultan. Leaving a frigate at Navarino Bay to watch the Egyptian and Ottoman ships there, Codrington then withdrew to the British-controlled Ionian island of Zante (Zakynthos).

Ibrahim learned that while he was expected to observe a cease-fire, Greek naval units under British mercenary commanders were continuing operations in the Gulf of Corinth, at Epirus, and at the port of Patras. Then during September 29–30 a Greek steamer warship, the *Karteria,* sank nine Ottoman ships off Salona (Split) in Dalmatia. Codrington sent messages to warn these British officers, who were not under his command, to desist from such operations; this had little effect, however. Ibrahim duly protested and, when nothing changed, decided to act.

On October 1, Ibrahim ordered ships from Navarino Bay to assist the Ottoman garrison at Patras. Codrington's squadron intercepted them and forced the ships to return to Navarino. On the night of October 3–4 Ibrahim personally led another relief effort. Although they managed to avoid detection by the British picket ship at Navarino Bay in the darkness, a strong wind prevented Ibrahim's ships from entering the Gulf of Corinth. Ibrahim was forced to anchor off Papas and await the storm's end. This allowed Codrington time to come up with his squadron. Firing warning shots, he forced Ibrahim to return to Navarino Bay.

Ibrahim continued land operations, which included the wholesale burning of Greek villages and fields, the fires from which were clearly visible from the allied ships. A British landing party also reported that the Greek population of Messenia was close to starvation.

On October 13 Codrington was joined off Navarino Bay by the French squadron under De Rigny and a Russian squadron under Admiral Count L. Heidin (Heyden). Both of these commanders were inferior in rank to Codrington, who also had the most ships, and they agreed to serve under his command.

On October 20, 1827, following futile attempts to contact Ibrahim, Codrington consulted with the other allied commanders and made the decision to enter Navarino Bay with the combined British, French, and Russian squadrons. The allies had 11 ships of the line and 15 other warships. Codrington flew his flag in the ship of the line *Asia* (84 guns). He also had 2 74-gun ships of the line, 4 frigates, and 4 brigs. French admiral de Rigny had 4 74-gun ships of the line, 1 frigate, and 2 schooners. Admiral Count Heidin's Russian squadron consisted of 4 74-gun ships of the line and 4 frigates. The Egyptians and Ottomans had 65 or 66 warships in Navarino Bay: 3 Ottoman ships of the line (2 of 84 guns each and 1 of 76), 4 Egyptian frigates of 64 guns each, 15 Ottoman frigates of 48 guns each, 18 Ottoman and 8 Egyptian corvettes of 14 to 18 guns each, 4 Ottoman and 8 Egyptian brigs of 19 guns each, and 5–6 Egyptian fire brigs. There were also some Ottoman transports and smaller craft.

Around noon on October 20, the allied ships sailed in two lines into Navarino Bay. The British and French formed one line, the Russians the other. The Ottomans demanded that Codrington withdraw, but the British admiral replied that he was there to give orders, not receive them. He threatened that if any shots were fired at the allied ships, he would destroy the Ottoman-Egyptian fleet.

The Egyptian-Ottoman ships were lying at anchor in a long crescent-shape formation, with their flanks protected by shore batteries. At 2:00 p.m. the allied ships began filing into the bay. They then took up position inside the crescent. The British ships faced the center of the Ottoman-Egyptian line, while the French were on the Ottoman left and the Russians were on the Ottoman right. The shore batteries at Fort Navarino (Pylos) made no effort to contest the allied movement. Still, Codrington's plan appeared highly dangerous,

for it invited the Ottomans to surround the allied ships, which with the prevailing wind out of the southwest risked being trapped. The plan simply revealed the complete confidence of the allies in their tactical superiority.

Codrington dispatched the frigate *Dartmouth* to an Ottoman ship in position to command the entrance of the bay with an order that it move. The captain of the *Dartmouth* sent a dispatch boat to the Ottoman ship, which then opened musket fire on it, killing an officer and several seamen. Firing immediately became general, with shore batteries also opening up on the allied ships.

The ensuing four-hour engagement, essentially a series of individual gun duels by floating batteries at close range without an overall plan, was really more of a slaughter than a battle. Three-quarters of the ships in the Ottoman-Egyptian fleet were either destroyed by allied fire or set alight by their own crews to prevent their capture. Only one, the *Sultane,* surrendered. Allied personnel losses were 177 killed and 469 wounded; estimates of the Ottoman and Egyptian killed and wounded are in excess of 4,000 men. The battle led directly to Egypt's withdrawal from the war and to Greek independence. Navarino Bay is also noteworthy as the last major battle by ships of the line in the age of fighting sail.

News of the allied victory was received with great popular enthusiasm in virtually all of Europe. The Porte, furious at what had transpired, demanded reparations. Recalled to Britain, Codrington was subsequently acquitted on a charge of disobeying orders.

The Battle of Navarino Bay removed any impediment to the Russian Black Sea Fleet, and on April 26, 1828, Russia declared war

The destruction of the Egyptian and Ottoman naval forces during the Greek War of Independence by the combined British, French, and Russian squadrons in the Battle of Navarino Bay, October 20, 1827. (Nautical Museum of Greece/Hellenic Ministry of Culture)

on the Ottoman Empire. Although the British were opposed, the French supported the Russian move. On June 28 Russian forces crossed the Danube, but their advance was held up by Ottoman resistance on the southern banks of the river.

On August 9, 1828, the British and French governments concluded a convention with Muhammad Ali in which the Egyptian leader agreed to withdraw his forces from Greece. The French dispatched an expeditionary force, and under its supervision the Egyptian military departed Greece during the winter of 1828–1829. This action virtually ended the war.

On August 20, with Russian forces having crossed the Balkan mountains, they captured the city of Adrianople (present-day Edirne, Turkey). Meanwhile, Russian forces also took Kars and Erzerum on the Asian front. With the collapse of the Ottoman Empire looming, the Porte sued for peace. Russian forces had been decimated by disease, however, and were thus in no position to move against Istanbul.

Moreover, Russian leaders feared possible military intervention by Britain, France, and Austria to assist the Ottomans.

As a consequence, peace was concluded in the Treaty of Adrianople of September 14, 1829, the peace terms of which were lenient on the Ottomans. Russia abandoned most of its conquests beyond the Danube but gained territory at the mouth of the Danube and acquired substantial territory in the Caucasus and southern Georgia. The Porte recognized Russia's possession of western Georgia and of khanates that had been ceded to Russia by Persia in 1828.

The Ottomans also recognized the autonomy of Serbia, the removal of their troops from Serbia, and an end to Ottoman taxes in return for a fixed annual Serbian tribute to the sultan. The treaty also provided for autonomy of Moldavia and Wallachia under Russian protection and fixed the border between the Ottoman Empire and Wallachia on the Danube. The treaty opened the Dardanelles to all commercial vessels, and Russia was granted the same capitulatory rights in the empire as the Western powers.

As regards Greece, the Porte agreed to recognize the London Protocol, concluded on March 22, 1829. The ambassadors of the Great Powers had decided that Greece south of a line from the Gulf of Volo to the Gulf of Arta, with Negroponte (Euboea) and the Cyclades (without Crete), was to be an autonomous tributary kingdom of the Ottoman Empire, with a ruling prince not to be chosen from the royal families of Britain, France, or Russia.

On November 30, 1829, a conference of ambassadors in London decided that Greece was to be fully independent, but the conference participants also moved back the frontier of the new state to the line Aspropotamo–Gulf of Lamia—that is, almost to the Gulf of Corinth. This found formal expression in the London Protocol of February 3, 1830, which, however, was rejected by the Greeks. The Great Powers settled on Prince Leopold of Saxe-Coburg as the new Greek ruler, but he rejected the throne on the grounds that the new Greek frontiers were too restricted. Meanwhile Capo d'Istria ruled, largely as dictator, but was assassinated in March 1831, and civil strife ensued. Finally in March 1832, the representatives of the Great Powers settled on Prince Otto of Bavaria as the ruler of Greece. They also extended the frontiers of Greece to a line between Volo and Arta.

SPENCER C. TUCKER

## Consequences

The Greek War of Independence was a seminal event in the collapse of the Ottoman Empire, an ongoing process that was completed in World War I. It was significant in that it was the first time that a Christian subject people, no matter how insignificant in terms of population and landmass, had achieved independence from the empire. The Greek revolt was the first great triumph for nationalism in Europe since the French Revolution and Napoleon—for the principle that distinct ethnic groups should have their own nation-states. This resonated in many places in Europe: in Poland, in the former Austrian Netherlands (soon to be Belgium), and in the Balkans with Serbia, Romania, and Bulgaria.

The war led to the establishment of a fully independent Greek state, but many problems confronted it, including the destruction of more than a decade of war and the accompanying displacement of much of the population. The sovereignty of the new state was somewhat compromised by the fact that Britain, Russia, and France all exerted a major role in Greek affairs. The new monarch was also a foreigner. Prince Otto of Bavaria, not a native Greek, became king.

Greeks living in the Ottoman Empire, many of whom had occupied important positions, were now suspect and found themselves regarded as little more than traitors. Greek administrators lost their positions, and Greek bankers and merchants, who had enjoyed important roles in the empire, were soon replaced by Armenians and Jews. Many Greeks chose to emigrate, and a great number settled in the United States.

Greece's population at the end of the war was only some 800,000. This was less than a third of the 2.5 million Greeks living in the Ottoman Empire, and for a century thereafter it was a major goal of the Greek government to gather the "unredeemed" Greeks into a larger Greek territorial entity. Considerable success was registered in that regard, for over the course of the next century parts of Macedonia, Crete, Epirus, a number of Aegean Islands, and other Greek-speaking territories would join the new Greek state.

A revolt in September 1843 forced King Otto I to grant constitutional government. Meanwhile, economic problems abounded. Not only was their the widespread destruction caused by the war, but nature had also been cruel to the Greeks, for there was a paucity of natural resources. When the population did increase substantially later in the century, this put even greater strain on the rural economy based on small farms of low productivity. Population pressure also brought greater urbanization. Thus, Athens grew from a population of only 6,000 in 1834, when it became the capital of Greece, to 167,000 in 1907.

SPENCER C. TUCKER

## Timeline

| | |
|---|---|
| **1814** | Greeks in Odessa, Russia, found the Hetairia Philike (Association of Friends) with the aim of expelling the Ottomans from Europe. Alexander Ypsilanti, a Russian Army general from an important Greek family, heads the organization, which is supported by Russian czar Alexander. |
| **Mar 21, 1821** | Ypsilanti leads an armed force into Moldavia and then appeals to Russia for assistance. Pressed by Austria, which warns of possible revolution, Czar Alexander disavows Ypsilanti. |
| **Mar 25, 1821** | Germanos, archbishop of Pátrai, raises a Greek flag at the Ayia Lavra monastery near Kalávrita. This date is celebrated in Greece as its Independence Day. |
| **Jun 26, 1821** | The Ottoman Army defeats Ypsilanti's forces in the Battle of Dragashan. |
| **Jul 27, 1821** | A Russian ultimatum to the Porte demands that the Ottomans restore Christian churches and protect Christians in the empire. The Porte rejects the ultimatum, but a Russian war declaration is prevented through the efforts of Austria's Count Klement von Metternich and British foreign secretary Robert Stewart, Viscount Castlereagh. |
| **Oct 5, 1821** | Greeks in the Peloponnese storm Tripolitsa, massacring some 10,000 Turks. |
| **Jan 13, 1822** | A Greek assembly at Epidauros declares independence. It also draws up a preliminary constitution and establishes a directorate of five individuals. |
| **Mar 1822** | Greeks from Samos land on Chios (Scio) and attack Ottomans living there. |
| **Mar 22, 1822** | A powerful Ottoman naval squadron under Captain Pasha Kara Ali ravages Chios. Only some 2,000 people remain on the island. |
| **Jun 19, 1822** | A Greek fleet under Constantine Kanaris destroys the Ottoman fleet. |

| | |
|---|---|
| **Jul 1822** | Two Ottoman armies invade and soon overrun all of Greece north of the Gulf of Corinth. |
| **Oct 25–Dec 31, 1822** | Ottoman forces under Omar Vrioni besiege the fortress at Missolonghi. Following the failure of an assault on the night of December 24–25, they break off the siege. |
| **1824** | The Greeks dissipate their energies in leadership struggles, with Theodoros Kolokotronis opposing Lazaros Kountouriotis. This flares into civil war in 1824, in which Kolokotronis is defeated. |
| **Feb 24, 1825** | Ottoman sultan Mahmud II sends a powerful Egyptian fleet and army force to Greece under his son Ibrahim Ali, which soon secures virtually the entire peninsula. In return, the Porte cedes Crete to Egypt. |
| **Apr 6, 1826** | The Russian government demands that the Sublime Porte return to the status quo in the Danubian Principalities and also dispatch a special envoy to St. Petersburg to discuss relations. Pressed by France and Austria, the Ottomans agree. |
| **Apr 15, 1825– Apr 23, 1826** | In the spring of 1824 an Ottoman army under Reşid Pasha drives from the north and on April 15, 1825, opens a third siege of strategically important Missolonghi. The defenders hold out for a year. On the night of April 22, 1826, some 7,000 Greeks try to escape, but only 1,000 make it to safety. The next morning, the Ottomans enter the city. |
| **May 1826** | Reşid Pasha now proceeds to Athens, the only remaining Greek-held stronghold on the mainland outside the Peloponnese. |
| **Aug 25, 1826** | Athens surrenders on the first Ottoman assault. The Greek government now appoints Georgios Karaiskakis supreme commander of its forces in central Greece. |
| **Feb 3, 1827** | Karaiskakis routs Ottoman forces in the Battle of Distomo. |
| **Feb 5, 1827** | Karaiskakis mounts a surprise night attack on the Ottoman camp, capturing much-needed supplies and artillery and forcing an Ottoman withdrawal. |
| **Apr 11, 1827** | The feuding Greek factions come together behind Capo d'Istria, who is named president. |
| **Apr 23, 1827** | Karaiskakis is killed in battle. He is succeeded by British general Richard Church. |
| **Apr 24, 1827** | The Ottoman victory at Phaleron (Analatos) ends the possibility of relief for the defenders of the Acropolis in Athens. |
| **May 24, 1827** | The Acropolis garrison surrenders. Church and the remaining poorly trained Greek forces are now reduced to guerrilla warfare. |
| **Jul 6, 1827** | With Ottoman and Egyptian forces now fully in control of Greece, representatives of the French, British, and Russian governments |

|  | conclude the Treaty of London, which calls on the Ottomans to agree to an armistice and on the Egyptians to withdraw. |
|---|---|
| **Aug 16, 1827** | The British, French, and Russian governments send a note to the Porte demanding an armistice. The Ottomans reject this on August 29. The three governments order their naval commanders in the Mediterranean to sever Ottoman and Egyptian resupply routes to Greece. |
| **Sep 8, 1827** | A large Egyptian naval squadron arrives in Navarino Bay, joining several Ottoman ships already there. |
| **Sep 12, 1827** | A British squadron under Vice Admiral Sir Edward Codrington arrives off Navarino Bay. Codrington's instructions call on him to try to secure an armistice. |
| **Sep 25, 1827** | Codrington and French admiral Henry Gauthier de Rigny meet with Egyptian commander Ibrahim Pasha to discuss a mediation arrangement already accepted by the Greeks. Ibrahim agrees to an armistice. |
| **Sep 29–30, 1827** | A Greek steamer warship, the *Karteria,* sinks nine Ottoman ships off Salona (Split) in Dalmatia. |
| **Oct 1, 1827** | Ibrahim orders ships from Navarino Bay to assist the Ottoman garrison at Patras. Codrington's squadron intercepts them and forces their return to Navarino. |
| **Oct 3–4, 1827** | Ibrahim attempts another effort, but a storm prevents the ships from entering the Gulf of Corinth, and Codrington arrives with his squadron and forces Ibrahim to return to Navarino Bay. |
| **Oct 13, 1827** | Codrington is joined off Navarino Bay by the French squadron under De Rigny and a Russian squadron under Admiral Count L. Heidin (Heyden). |
| **Oct 20, 1827** | In the Battle of Navarino Bay, three-quarters of the Ottoman-Egyptian ships are lost. Allied personnel casualties are 469, while Ottoman/Egyptian casualties are estimated to be in excess of 4,000. |
| **Dec 28, 1827** | The allied ambassadors leave Istanbul. |
| **Apr 26, 1828** | Russia declares war on the Ottoman Empire. |
| **Aug 9, 1828** | The British and French governments conclude a convention with Muhammad Ali in which the Egyptian leader agrees to withdraw his forces from Greece. |
| **March 22, 1829** | In the London Protocol, the Great Powers decide that Greece south of a line from the Gulf of Volo to the Gulf of Arta, with Negroponte (Euboea) and the Cyclades (without Crete), is to be an autonomous Ottoman tributary kingdom. The Greeks, however, reject these frontiers. |

**Sep 14, 1829**    The Treaty of Adrianople ends the Russo-Ottoman War.

**Mar 1832**    The Great Powers settle on Prince Otto of Bavaria as Greek ruler. They also extend the frontiers of Greece to a line between Volo and Arta.

SPENCER C. TUCKER

## Further Reading

Anderson, R. C. *Naval Wars in the Levant, 1559–1853.* Liverpool, England: University Press of Liverpool, 1952.

Brewer, David. *The Greek War of Independence: The Struggle for Freedom from Ottoman Oppression and the Birth of the Modern Greek Nation.* Woodstock, NY: Overlook Press, 2001.

Bridge, F. R., and Roger Bullen. *The Great Powers and the European State System 1814–1914.* London: Longman, 1980.

Clogg, Richard. *A Concise History of Greece.* 2nd ed. Cambridge: Cambridge University Press, 2002.

Crawley, C. W. *The Question of Greek Independence: A Study of British Policy in the Near East, 1821–1833.* New York: H. Fertig, 1972.

Dakin, Douglas. *The Greek Struggle for independence, 1821–1833.* Berkeley: University of California Press, 1973.

Howarth, David Amine. *The Greek Adventure: Lord Byron and other Eccentrics in the War of Independence.* New York: Atheneum, 1976.

Jelavich, Barbara. *History of the Balkans: Eighteenth and Nineteenth Centuries.* New York: Cambridge University Press, 1983.

Koliopoulos, John S. *Brigands with a Cause: Brigandage and Irredentism in Modern Greece, 1821–1912.* Oxford, UK: Clarendon, 1987.

Ortzen, Len. *Guns at Sea: The World's Great Naval Battles.* London: Cox & Wyman, 1976.

Phillips, W. Alison. *The Greek War of Independence, 1821–1832.* New York: C. Scribner's Sons, 1897.

Sayyid-Marsot, Afaf Lutfi. *Egypt in the Reign of Muhammad Ali.* Cambridge, England: Cambridge University Press, 1984.

Stavrianos, Leften Stavros. *The Balkans since 1453.* New York: Rinehart, 1953.

St. Clair, William. *That Greece Might Still Be Free: The Philhellenes in the War of Independence.* New York: Oxford University Press, 1972.

Woodhouse, C. W. *The Greek War of Independence: Its Historical Setting.* London: Hutchinson's University Library, 1952.

# Texas War of Independence (October 2, 1835–April 21, 1836)

## Causes

The Texas War of Independence (also known as the Texas Revolution), began on October 2, 1835, and ended on April 21, 1836. The first European in Texas was most probably Alonso Álvarez de Pineda in 1519 while leading an expedition to locate a water passage between the Gulf of Mexico and Asia. The first real effort at European colonization occurred in 1685, when geographical miscalculations by French explorer René-Robert Cavelier de La Salle led him to establish Fort Saint Louis on Matagorda Bay rather than on the Mississippi River as planned. Harsh conditions and hostile natives led to the abandonment of the colony within four years, however.

In 1690 authorities in New Spain, concerned about French exploring expeditions in the region and anxious to create a strong presence there themselves, ordered the establishment of several Catholic missions in present-day eastern Texas. Fierce Native American resistance soon forced the missionaries to return to Mexico. When the French established settlements in southern Louisiana, however, this led Spanish authorities in 1716 to initiate a new effort to establish missions in eastern Texas. In 1718 San Antonio de Béxar became the first Spanish civilian settlement in the region. Texas remained sparsely populated, however. Hostile native tribes, especially the Comanches, and the distance of Texas from other Spanish colonies discouraged European settlers from moving there.

In 1810 Mexican Roman Catholic priest Don Miguel Hidalgo y Costilla began the Mexican War for Independence. Eleven years later in 1821, independence from Spain was achieved through force of arms with the creation of the Empire of Mexico. Meanwhile, the United States concluded with Spain the Adams-Onís Treaty, signed in Washington, D.C., on February 22, 1819. For a cash settlement, Spain renounced all claims to West Florida and agreed to cede East Florida to the United States. The United States renounced all claims to Texas, and the disputed western boundary of the Louisiana Purchase territory, acquired by the United States from France in 1803, was set as running from the mouth of the Sabine River on the Gulf of Mexico northwest along the Red and Arkansas Rivers and then west along the 42nd parallel to the Pacific.

In March 1823, a revolution occurred in Mexico when Emperor Augustín I was forced from the throne, and in October 1824 the revolutionaries established the Federal Republic of the United Mexican States. With the proclamation of a republic, the Central American provinces of Mexico broke away, while the region of Soconusco proclaimed its independence and was annexed by the Federal Republic of Central America. The remaining Mexican territory was nonetheless vast. It included present-day Mexico and the present U.S. states of California, Nevada, New Mexico, Arizona, Colorado, Wyoming, and Texas.

Because of its slight population, in 1823 Mexico made Texas (or Tejas, as it was

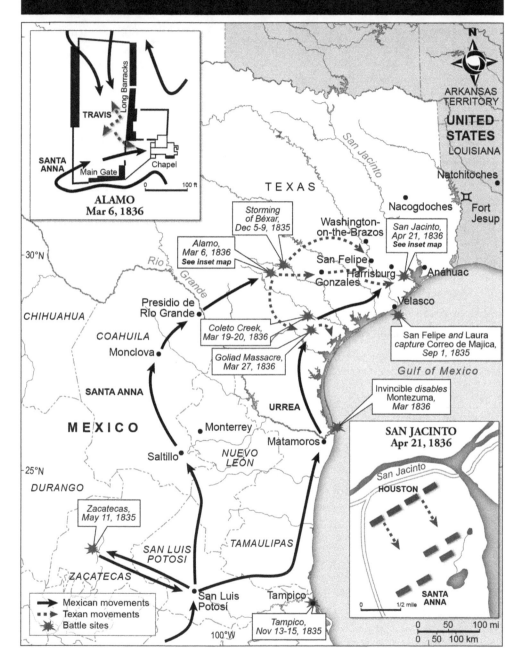

# TEXAS WAR OF INDEPENDENCE, 1835–1836

**ALAMO**
Mar 6, 1836

TRAVIS
SANTA ANNA
Long Barracks
Main Gate
Chapel
0    100 ft

ARKANSAS TERRITORY

UNITED STATES
LOUISIANA

Natchitoches

TEXAS

Nacogdoches
Fort Jesup

Storming of Béxar, Dec 5-9, 1835

Alamo, Mar 6, 1836
See inset map

Washington-on-the-Brazos

San Jacinto, Apr 21, 1836
See inset map

San Felipe
Harrisburg
Anáhuac
Gonzales

Velasco

Rio Grande

30°N

CHIHUAHUA

Presidio de Rio Grande

Coleto Creek, Mar 19-20, 1836

COAHUILA
Monclova

Goliad Massacre, Mar 27, 1836

San Felipe and Laura capture Correo de Majica, Sep 1, 1835

Gulf of Mexico

SANTA ANNA

Invincible disables Montezuma, Mar 1836

MEXICO

URREA

Monterrey

Matamoros

SAN JACINTO
Apr 21, 1836

Saltillo

NUEVO LEÓN

25°N

DURANGO

San Jacinto
HOUSTON

Zacatecas, May 11, 1835

SAN LUIS POTOSI

TAMAULIPAS

SANTA ANNA

0    1/2 mile

ZACATECAS

San Luis Potosí

Tampico

Mexican movements
Texan movements
Battle sites

Tampico, Nov 13-15, 1835

100°W

0    50    100 mi
0    50   100 km

## Texas War of Independence (October 2, 1835–April 21, 1836)

| Battle of the Alamo (March 6, 1836) | | |
|---|---|---|
| | Republic of Texas Forces | Mexican Forces |
| Approximate strength | 187 men | 3,000–4,000 men |
| Approximate losses | 187 men killed | 400–1,600 men killed and wounded |

| Battle of Refugio (March 12–15, 1836) | | |
|---|---|---|
| | Republic of Texas Forces | Mexican Forces |
| Approximate strength | 146 men | 1,500 men |
| Killed | 16 | 150 |
| Executed | 15 | 0 |
| Wounded | Unknown | 50 |
| Captured | 107 | 0 |

| Goliad Massacre (March 27, 1836) | |
|---|---|
| Number of Texan prisoners executed | 342–445* |
| Number of Texan prisoners spared | 20** |

*Estimates vary, but Texan sources have settled on 407.
**The 20 men spared execution were medical doctors, interpreters, orderlies, and mechanics.

| Battle of San Jacinto (April 21, 1836)* | | |
|---|---|---|
| | Republic of Texas Forces | Mexican Forces |
| Strength | 910 men | 1,360 men |
| Artillery pieces | 2 | 1 |
| Killed | 9 | 630 |
| Wounded | 30 | 208 |
| Captured | 0 | 730** |

*This battle is considered the last major engagement of the war. Mexican general Antonio López de Santa Anna managed to escape the debacle but was located and captured the next day.
**Includes wounded men.

**Sources:** Brands, H. W. *Lone Star Nation: How a Ragged Army of Volunteers Won the Battle for Texas Independence—and Changed America.* New York: Doubleday, 2004; Hardin, Stephen L. *Texian Iliad: A Military History of the Texas Revolution.* Austin: University of Texas Press, 1994; Rodríguez-O, Jaime E. *Down from Colonialism: Mexico's Nineteenth Century Crisis.* Los Angeles: University of California at Los Angeles, 1983.

then known, for the Caddo-language term for the area), part of the state of Coahuila y Tejas (Coahuila and Texas), with only a single seat in the state legislature at Saltillo. Following strong complaints from the Mexican-born residents of Texas, state officials agreed to make Texas a department of the new state, with its capital in San Antonio de Béxar.

U.S. citizens had begun to settle in Texas in the 1820s. Because so few Mexican citizens wanted to settle there owing to depredations by American Indians, primarily the Comanches and Kiowas, the Mexican government actively encouraged the settlement efforts. In 1824 impresario Stephen F. Austin led the second, and successful, Anglo colonization of Texas by bringing 300 families there from the United States. A decade later Texians (a term often used for Anglos born in Texas) numbered some 20,000 with 2,000 slaves, and they outnumbered native Mexicans there by four to one. On April 6, 1830, the Mexican government banned additional Anglo immigration into Texas, imposed tariffs and customs duties on Texans, and specifically outlawed slavery there. Mexican officials found it impossible to enforce this legislation, however.

Many factors caused a separation between Texas and the rest of Mexico. Slavery was certainly a major issue and had been banned throughout the Mexican territories. Also, the Mexican government was in constant turmoil, and there were disagreements about tariffs, representation, immigration, and army garrisons.

In 1832, Mexican general Antonio López de Santa Anna y Pérez de Lebrón led a revolt to overthrow the government of President Anastasio Bustamante. Texians, the English-speaking settlers of Texas, took advantage of the situation to take up

arms and expel Mexican troops from East Texas. The Texans then called on the central government to weaken legislation passed in April 1830 that prohibited further immigration to Texas from the United States, increased taxes, and again banned slavery, all acts that the Texans had in any case ignored. In November 1833 the Mexican government made some concessions, including increased representation in the state legislature.

Then in 1835, Santa Anna abolished the federal Constitution of 1824 and proclaimed a new centralist constitution that concentrated power in Mexico City, sweeping away states' rights and doing away with the state legislatures and militias. This caused widespread unrest and led to revolts in the border areas of Yucatan, Zacatecas, Coahuila, and Texas.

Santa Anna did not want a war but knew that he had to crush the unrest, especially in Texas, before it got out of hand and led to possible military intervention by the United States. Mexican leaders were well aware of manifest destiny, the argument by many American leaders that U.S. territory should extend to the Pacific, including the rich prize of Alta (upper) California.

Having enjoyed success in employing force to crush unrest elsewhere, Santa Anna expected the same to be the case in Texas. In early September he ordered his brother-in-law, General Martín Perfecto de Cos, to lead 500 soldiers to Texas and prevent unrest from becoming outright rebellion. Cos and his men landed at the port of Copano on September 20.

Texan leader Austin called on all municipalities to raise militias to defend themselves. Meanwhile, Mexican military commander in Texas Colonel Domingo de Ugartechea ordered the settlers in the community of Gonzales in southeast Texas to return a small cannon given to them by the Mexican authorities to defend against Native American attack. When the settlers at Gonzales rejected the request, Ugartechea dispatched Lieutenant Francisco de Castaneda and 100 dragoons to Gonzales to secure the cannon, ordering Castaneda to avoid force if possible. This order brought on the war.

SPENCER C. TUCKER

## Course

### Early Texas Offensive (1935)

Upon reaching the Guadalupe River near Gonzales on September 29, Mexican lieutenant Castaneda informed the settlers of the town of his intention to speak with the alcalde (mayor). Informed that he was absent, Castaneda said that he would remain on the other side of the Guadalupe until the mayor returned. The delay gave the settlers time to assemble some 140 men, whereupon Castaneda relocated his camp upriver.

Led by John Henry Moore, the Texans crossed the Guadalupe during the night of October 1–2 and the next morning attacked the Mexican camp. In a lull in the fighting, Moore met with Castaneda. Arguing that Santa Anna's policies violated the Mexican Constitution of 1824, Moore demanded that the Mexican soldiers surrender and join the Texans. Castaneda replied that while he too opposed Santa Anna's policies, as a soldier he was obliged to follow orders. Fighting resumed shortly thereafter, with the Texans displaying a white flag with the image of a cannon and the words "Come and Take It." The outnumbered and outgunned Mexicans then withdrew and fell back on San Antonio.

Reportedly one Texan was injured and two Mexican soldiers were killed in the skirmish. Regarded as the opening battle of the Texas War for Independence, the Battle of Gonzales was widely publicized in the United States and brought an influx of Anglo adventurers to Texas eager to join the fight against Mexico.

Informed of the fighting at Gonzales, Mexican general Martín Perfecto de Cos immediately moved his 500 men to San Antonio, the de facto Texas capital. On October 11 the Texan volunteers elected Austin, who had no military experience, as leader of what he referred to as the Army of the People. Once they were organized, Austin planned to move the volunteers to San Antonio.

Unaware of Cos's departure, on October 6 some 125 Texans at Matagorda marched on the Presidio La Bahía in Goliad with the plan of taking Cos prisoner and securing substantial Mexican government funds said to be there. On October 10 the Texans stormed the presidio, and its garrison quickly surrendered. Two Texans were wounded, while three Mexican soldiers were killed and seven others wounded.

Texan captain Philip Dimmitt assumed command of the presidio and sent local volunteers to join Austin for the march to San Antonio. In November, Dimmitt also sent Ira Westover and some men to seize Fort Lipantitlán near San Patricio. The fort was undermanned, and the Texans seized it without a shot being fired. With the fort disarmed, the Texans prepared to return to Goliad. However, when the remainder of the Mexican garrison, who had been out on patrol, returned to Fort Lipantitlán, a brief skirmish occurred, after which the Mexican soldiers withdrew. The small Texan force now controlled virtually the entire Gulf Coast, forcing Mexican commanders in Texas to rely on slower and more difficult land lines of communication.

Dimmitt, however, faced considerable unrest, as many local inhabitants supported the efforts of governor of Coahuila and Texas Agustín Viesca to reconstitute the state government. Dimmitt's declaration of martial law to forestall this alienated many, and fighting ensued between supporters of the rebellion and those backing the government.

Meanwhile, Austin and some 450 men arrived in the vicinity of San Antonio, now held by Cos and some 650 Mexican soldiers. On October 28, a Texan advance party led by James Bowie and James Fannin clashed on the grounds of Mission Concepción, two miles south of what is now downtown San Antonio, with a Mexican force led by Colonel Domingo Ugartechea. Lasting only some 30 minutes, it was the first major engagement of the Texas Revolution. The Texans employed their riles with good effect and forced the attacking Mexicans to withdraw. One Texan was killed. Mexican casualties vary, between 14 and 76 dead, according to sources.

The Texans instituted a loose siege of San Antonio, but both sides suffered difficulties. With food scare and the onset of colder weather, many Texans simply decamped and went home. The besiegers were cheered, however, by the arrival on November 18 of the New Orleans Greys, the first group of volunteers from the United States. Unlike the Texans, they were uniformed, reasonably disciplined, and well armed.

Meanwhile, on November 3, 58 elected representatives from a number of Texas municipalities assembled in San Felipe de Austin in what was known as the Consultation. Following days of debate, the delegates established a provisional government consisting of a governor and a General Council, with one delegate from each municipality. On November 7, 1835, in a declaration of causes, the provisional government declared as its aims the defeat of Santa Anna, the restoration of the Constitution of 1824, and securing statehood for Texas within the Mexican federation. Although they did not declare independence, rejoining Mexico was contingent on the reestablishment of a federal system.

The delegates elected as governor Henry Smith, a fierce champion of independence for Texas. On November 13 they also voted to establish a regular army, with Sam Houston as its commander. Houston, however, did not have authority over Austin's volunteers, and few of them elected to join the new army. In order to secure men for the Texan regular army, the soldiers were promised land. This step showed that the delegates expected Texas to be independent, for in Mexico all land was owned by the government. The delegates also named three men, including Austin, as commissioners to go to the United States to secure volunteers and aid. On November 14 the Consultation adjourned, leaving Smith and the Council in charge.

With Austin now about to leave for the United States, the volunteers at San Antonio elected Edward Burleson as their commander. Learning on November 26 that a Mexican pack train with 50–100 Mexican soldiers was within five miles of San Antonio, Burleson ordered Bowie and William H. Jack to intercept it and secure the supplies. In the resultant engagement the Mexican soldiers withdrew, leaving the supplies behind. Much to the disappointment of the Texans, the supplies consisted only of fodder for the horses, and for this reason the engagement became known as the Grass Fight.

The besiegers voted down several proposals to storm San Antonio. With morale plummeting, on December 4 Burleson proposed that they lift the siege and withdraw to Goliad for the winter. In order to avoid the appearance of retreat, Texan colonel Ben Milam recruited men to mount an attack, and on December 5 he and Colonel Frank W. Johnson led several hundred men into the city. During the next four days the Texans worked their way house by house toward the fortified plazas.

Cos received 650 reinforcements on December 8, but most of the men were raw recruits, and some were convicts still in chains. Indeed, far from being an assist, the new arrivals were simply a drain on the dwindling food stocks. On December 9, Cos and the bulk of his men withdrew into the 18th-century Alamo Mission on the outskirts of San Antonio. When Cos announced plans for a counterattack his cavalry officers rejected it, and perhaps 175 troopers simply deserted, leaving the mission and

riding south. The following morning, Cos surrendered. The terms required that he and his men leave Texas and no longer fight against those supporting the Constitution of 1824.

The departure of Cos and his men meant that there was no longer any organized Mexican military force in Texas. Believing the war for all practical purposes to be over, Burleson resigned his post on December 15 and returned home along with many of his men. Johnson assumed command of the 400 who remained.

Having no funds, the provisional Texas government authorized impressment of supplies. This caused great resentment among the population, especially where the Texan troops were stationed, around Goliad and San Antonio.

With the issue of independence still hanging fire, on December 20 at Presidio La Bahía 91 Texans and Tejanos (those of

The Alamo, an abandoned Catholic mission in San Antonio, where following a 23-day siege on March 6, 1838, the defending Texan garrison was wiped out by Mexican forces under President Santa Anna. The defeat nonetheless served as a rallying cry for Texas independence. (Neonriver/Dreamstime)

Mexican descent living in Texas) in the Gulf Coast settlements signed what became known as the Goliad Declaration of Independence. Unwilling to make this decision themselves, the Council called for a new election for delegates to what would be the Convention of 1836, with voting open to all free white males as well as those Mexicans who supported federalism. Smith tried but failed to veto this, as he wanted all Tejanos excluded from voting. Since it was unclear whether volunteers who had come to Texas to fight would be allowed to vote, there was considerable chaos in the voting process.

Unrest was not limited to Texas. With some leading federalists in northern Mexico urging an attack on centralist forces in Matamoros, on December 25 the Council voted to support this plan in anticipation that it would encourage revolts elsewhere in Mexico as well as shift fighting from Texas. On December 30 Johnson moved with most of the army to Goliad to prepare for the expedition.

Governor Smith strongly opposed the Matamoros scheme and indeed threatened to dismiss the Council unless it revoked its approval. Although it is unclear whether Smith had the authority to do this or whether its response to Smith's threat would be binding, on January 1, 1836, the Council voted to impeach Smith and named James W. Robinson as acting governor.

Acting on orders from Smith, however, Houston was able to dissuade all but 70 men from following Johnson. With his own authority also now in question, Houston, who had earlier also been named a commissioner to the Native Americans, left the army and traveled to Nacogdoches to negotiate a treaty with the Cherokees. There Houston pledged that Texas would recognize Cherokee claims to land in East Texas if the Indians refrained from attacking settlements or assisting the Mexican Army. Now the highest-ranking active regular army officer, Fannin led to Goliad the men who had rejected the Matamoros expedition.

## Mexican Government Offensive (1836)

Mexican president Santa Anna was determined to take action against Texas. Those in authority blamed the Anglos for not conforming to Mexican law, and few members of the Mexican leadership doubted that it would be an easy matter to defeat the disorganized and ill-trained Texas rebels. Santa Anna assumed personal command himself.

Given needs elsewhere, few soldiers were then available, however. The president secured a loan from the Roman Catholic Church specifically for the operation and put together a new military force, which he called the Army of Operations in Texas. In December 1835 Santa Anna and some 6,000 men began their movement northward. Composed principally of raw recruits, the new army was poorly trained and inadequately armed. The men were equipped with the smoothbore Brown Bess musket, which lacked both the accuracy and range of the rifles carried by the Texans. Santa Anna believed, however, that superior numbers, discipline, and better planning would carry the day.

On November 15 General José Antonio Mexía, who opposed Santa Anna's assumption of dictatorial powers, had attacked Tampico with three companies of men enlisted at New Orleans. A number of Mexía's men were captured by forces loyal to Santa Anna. In large measure to discourage Americans from aiding the revolutionaries in Texas, Santa Anna then approved the execution of 28 of the prisoners, whom he characterized as "pirates." The men were shot on December 14. Also on December 30 on Santa Anna's urging, the Mexican Congress passed the Tornel Decree. It declared that foreigners fighting Mexican troops "shall be treated and punished as pirates, since they are not subjects of any nation at war with the republic nor do they militate under any recognized flag." This clearly implied immediate execution upon capture for rebel prisoners.

Santa Anna's march northward was slow and involved considerable suffering for the men owing to shortages of food, transport, and winter clothing. At Saltillo, Cos and his remaining men from San Antonio joined the Army of Operation in Texas. Santa Anna claimed that Cos's pledge not to take up arms in Texas was void because it had been given to rebels.

Santa Anna now ordered General José de Urrea to proceed to Goliad with some 1,500 men while he and the rest of the army advanced on San Antonio. Santa Anna planned to approach San Antonio on the Camino Real from the west. On February 17 his army crossed the Nueces River and officially entered Texas.

Temperature had sharply dropped, and as much as 16 inches of snow fell on February 13, imposing a real hardship on Santa Anna's men, some of whom died of hypothermia while others succumbed to dysentery. As the army advanced, settlers on the route evacuated their homes and fled northward.

Believing San Antonio to be too isolated to defend, Houston sent Bowie there with orders to remove its garrison and artillery. Bowie, however, became convinced that the abandoned mission of San Antonio de Valero, better known as the Alamo and that had served as a barracks for Mexican troops, could withstand attack. The Texas garrison had already begun shoring up its defenses.

Bowie informed Governor Smith that he intended to stay and defend the Alamo. Bowie soon clashed with Alamo garrison commander Colonel William B. Travis, but they reached agreement to share command. Only some 150 men, including legendary frontiersman Davy Crockett, were in the Alamo when Santa Anna arrived there with 1,500 soldiers on February 23.

Santa Anna quickly ordered his army, reinforced on March 2 to some 3,000–4,000 men, to surround the Alamo. He also commenced a round-the-clock artillery bombardment. The defenders could make but slight reply, as they had little powder for their few guns. The siege was a loose one, however, and Travis (who assumed command when Bowie fell ill) dispatched three men on horseback to appeal for assistance. In response, 32 men rode in from Gonzales, reaching the garrison at night.

The final Texan force at the Alamo thus numbered about 187 men, although the exact count is still in dispute. In any case, the defenders were outnumbered at least 16 to 1 and had to defend a fairly long perimeter encompassing the mission church itself and two sets of barracks around a very large open courtyard. The complex's walls, which were built to keep out the Comanches, could not withstand sustained artillery fire.

The Mexican bombardment ended on the night of March 5, and the Mexican soldiers were then moved into position for a dawn assault. Darkness on the morning of March 6 and the inexperience of the Mexican troops combined to make the initial assault unsuccessful, but the Mexicans then re-formed, and their second assault was successful. Having breached the walls, the overwhelming numerical superiority of the attackers ensured victory.

Reportedly Travis died early in the battle, and Bowie fought from his sickbed for a short time. The men inside the church building itself held out the longest. Mexican sources state that many of the defenders, possibly half, fled to the southeast, only to be ridden down by Mexican cavalry anticipating such a move.

By 8:00 a.m. the battle was over, and all the defenders were dead. The attackers spared some 20 women, children, and African American slaves. Mexican Army casualties have been estimated at anywhere from 400 to 1,600. A diary allegedly kept by one of Santa Anna's staff officers claimed that some of the defenders including Crockett were taken prisoner, only to be executed on Santa Anna's order. Although the siege at the Alamo slowed the Mexican campaign in Texas only by some two weeks, "Remember the Alamo!" became a rallying cry for the Texans and a recruiting tool for Houston's army.

Meanwhile, at Washington-on-the-Brazos 45 elected delegates assembled on March 1, and the next day they overwhelmingly passed a declaration of independence. On March 6, a final dispatch from Travis at the Alamo arrived with a pessimistic assessment of the defenders' chances. Although some of the deputies favored adjourning the Convention in order that its members might join the army, Houston convinced them to remain. Now invested by the Convention as the commander of all regular, volunteer, and militia forces in Texas, Houston left to do battle with the invader.

On March 17 the delegates approved a constitution for the new Republic of Texas. Much of the document was drawn verbatim from the U.S. Constitution. It provided

for a chief executive, a bicameral legislature, and a supreme court. While legalizing slavery, it also recognized the right to revolt against government authority. David G. Burnet, who had not been a delegate, was elected president of the republic.

On March 11, Santa Anna had ordered some of his men to join those under Urrea, with instructions that his brother-in-law would move to Brazoria once Fannin had been defeated. General Antonio Gaona and 700 men were to advance along the Camino Real to Mina and then proceed to Nacogdoches, while General Joaquín Ramírez y Sesma would take an additional 700 men to San Felipe. The Mexican columns were thus moving in a northeasterly direction on roughly parallel tracks but separated by 40–50 miles and were thus too far apart to provide mutual support.

General Urrea meanwhile had proceeded northward along the coast, allowing resupply by sea. On March 2 his men ambushed a small force of Texans in the Battle of Agua Dulce. Losing only 1 of their men killed, the Mexicans killed 12–15 Texans and captured another 6. Urrea now commanded some 1,500 men.

Fannin and some 500 Texans were at Goliad's Presidio La Bahía, or Fort Defiance as Fannin renamed it. Fannin had spent considerable time fortifying the post and was reluctant to give it up. His men were also confident and anxious to confront the Mexicans. Yet after the fall of the Alamo on March 6, Houston ordered Fannin to withdraw from Goliad to Guadalupe Victoria, 28 miles distant, "as soon as practical on receipt of this order." Fannin was slow to obey, however.

During March 12–15 at Refugio, Urrea's forces defeated Amon B. King and Lieutenant Colonel William Ward and 146 men. The Mexicans lost some 150 killed and 50 wounded. The Texan side lost 16 killed, 15 executed, and 107 captured. Ten men escaped.

Fannin learned on March 17 of the defeat at Refugio, but he still delayed ordering a withdrawal to Guadalupe Victoria until the next day. Yet no movement occurred until early on March 19. Even then progress was slow, for Fannin insisted on taking along nine cannon and some 1,000 muskets. This decision allowed Urrea's forces to close. Fannin had also failed to take sufficient water, and he had food sufficient for only several meals.

Urrea's flying column caught Fannin and about 300 of his men on the open prairie at a slight depression near Coleto Creek on March 19. In the ensuing battle the Texans managed to repulse several Mexican charges, but they were desperately short of both food and water. When Urrea brought up reinforcements and artillery, Fannin realized that further resistance was futile and agreed to treat with Urrea. What transpired in their meeting is still debated, but Fannin certainly hoped that he would received terms for himself and his men. Urrea said he had made it clear that he could accept only unconditional surrender but that he would also seek to intercede on behalf of the Americans. Still, the extant capitulation documents show that the Texans surrendered "subject to the disposition of the supreme government."

While Urrea continued on to Victoria with the bulk of his forces, the Texan prisoners were returned to Goliad. There they were joined by other prisoners, bringing the number of men held there to more than 350. On March 27 some 342 of the Texans captured during Urrea's Goliad Campaign were executed. This occurred over Urrea's protest and on the direct orders of Santa Anna. "Remember Goliad!" was yet another Texan rallying cry.

Houston meanwhile arrived at Gonzales on March 11 and informed the 374 men gathered there of the declaration of independence. Two days later word arrived of the Alamo defeat and Mexican Army movements northward. A council of war voted on an immediate evacuation and retreat. Civilians joined the trek northward, which was so hasty that supplies that could not be carried had to be burned; the army's only two guns were consigned to the Guadalupe River. Mexican forces under General Ramírez y Sesma reached Gonzales on the morning of March 14.

News of the defeat at the Alamo brought more volunteers to the colors, however. Houston now commanded some 1,400 men. He learned of Fannin's defeat on March 20. Houston understood that his poorly armed and ill-trained force could not survive a prolonged campaign against the better-equipped and more numerous Mexicans. Despite opposition from his men, Houston knew that he must keep what force remained together, avoid envelopment, and withdraw. In what Texans remember as the Runaway Scrape, by March 28 they had withdrawn some 120 miles. Many of his men deserted; others thought Houston a coward and said as much openly.

On March 31, Houston paused his men at Groce's Landing some 15 miles north of San Felipe. For the next two weeks, his army rested and trained. Two cannon, known as the Twin Sisters, arrived from Cincinnati, Ohio. Interim secretary of war Thomas Rusk also came to the encampment with orders from President Burnet to replace Houston if he refused to fight. Houston quickly persuaded Rusk of the correctness of his plans. Still, considerable opposition to Houston remained within the army.

## Houston Turns the Tables

Santa Anna had tarried at San Antonio with a small force. Believing that the Texas Revolution was on its last legs, he intended to complete the job by capturing the Texas interim government at Harrisburg, where it had relocated. On April 14 with some 700 men, Santa Anna set out. His advance units arrived at Harrisburg near midnight on April 15, only to learn that the Texas officials had already left. On April 18 Santa Anna ordered Harrisburg put to the torch and moved to New Washington on the Gulf Coast. There he discovered that Burnet and other Texas government officials had fled to Galveston Island.

Houston meanwhile learned from captured dispatches of Santa Anna's location and that the Mexican general was separated from the main body of his army. Houston now moved swiftly to exploit the situation. On April 20 his men were near Lynch's Ferry on the Lynchburg-Harrisburg road, in position to block Santa Anna from joining his main forces. That afternoon a cavalry skirmish occurred between the two sides, nearly bringing on a full-scale battle. Meanwhile, Santa Anna got word of his situation to General Martín Perfecto de Cos, who joined him on the morning of April 21 with about 540 men. The two encampments were only about three-quarters of a mile apart.

Santa Anna commanded some 1,260 troops, while Houston had only 910. Believing that he had the advantage, Santa Anna decided to rest his army and attack the next day. Meanwhile, shortly before noon on April 21 Houston held a council of war. Despite a majority opinion (four to two, with Houston withholding his opinion)

in favor of remaining on the defensive to await the Mexican attack, Houston decided that he must assault Santa Anna before additional Mexican reinforcements could reach him.

The Battle of San Jacinto began at about 4:30 p.m. on April 21. The initial Texan advance being screened by rising ground and trees, the Texans then charged, shouting "Remember the Alamo!" and "Remember Goliad!" The Texans easily penetrated the inadequate breastworks protecting the Mexican encampment, while Santa Anna's inexplicable failure to post sentries during the traditional Mexican afternoon siesta and decision to set up camp with a swamp to the rear proved fateful.

Houston's assault turned into fierce hand-to-hand combat lasting less than 20 minutes. The bloodshed continued for several hours more, however, the Texans killed hundreds of Mexican soldiers in reprisal for the slaying of prisoners at the Alamo and Goliad. At the end of the battle, 630 Mexicans lay dead; another 730 were prisoners, 208 of them wounded. Surprisingly, the Texans suffered only 9 killed and 30 wounded. Houston was among the latter, badly wounded by being shot in the ankle. San Jacinto was the decisive battle of the Texas Revolution.

Santa Anna had fled the battlefield but was found the next day, dressed in the uniform of a private of dragoons and hiding in a marsh. Recognized, he was brought before Houston while Texan soldiers gathered around and clamored for his immediate execution. Santa Anna bargained with Houston and agreed to send a letter to his second-in-command, General Vicente Filisola, now the senior Mexican official in Texas, and order Mexican forces to withdraw to San Antonio and there await further instructions.

Urrea urged Filisola to continue the fight. Urrea had won all his battles in Texas and was confident that he could defeat Houston as well. But Filisola was unwilling to risk it. Heavy spring rains had rendered the roads almost impassable, food for the troops was in short supply, and a number of men were sick from dysentery and other diseases.

With the war now for all intents and purposes over, during the next several weeks Santa Anna negotiated with the Texans. The two Treaties of Velasco signed on May 14, 1836, required that all Mexican troops withdraw south of the Rio Grande and that all private property (i.e., slaves) be respected and restored. All prisoners of war were to be released, and Santa Anna was to receive immediate passage to Veracruz. Secretly Santa Anna promised to persuade the Mexican Congress to acknowledge the Republic of Texas and to recognize the Rio Grande as the official border between the two countries.

As the Mexican troops withdrew, many of those who had supported the Mexican Army went with them. Urrea also refused to honor the treaty provision calling for the return of slaves, and many of those who had been freed also accompanied the army southward. By late May the Mexican troops had crossed the Nueces.

SPENCER C. TUCKER

## Consequences

In mid-July 1836 in Texas, a group of soldiers attempted a military coup. It failed, but in response David Burnet called for elections to ratify the constitution and elect another congress. It met in October 1836 at Columbia (now West Columbia) and approved the constitution earlier drawn up. Sam Houston was also elected president by a wide margin. Two principal

political factions emerged. Houston and his followers sought the annexation of Texas to the United States and peaceful coexistence with the Indians when possible. Mirabeau B. Lamar, who succeeded Houston as president in 1838, advocated the continued independence of Texas, the expulsion of Native Americans, and territorial expansion.

Lamar's reversal of Houston's policy toward the Native Americans brought considerable bloodshed, principally from Commanche raids on the settlements. When peace talks in 1840 saw the massacre of 34 Comanche leaders in San Antonio, some 500–700 Comanche warriors led by Potsanaquahip (Buffalo Hump) invaded the Guadalupe River Valley, killing and plundering to the Gulf of Mexico, where they sacked Victoria and Linnville. With Houston again president in 1841, peace was reestablished.

Slavery in Texas delayed annexation, which most Texans preferred. Meanwhile, the Republic of Texas built a navy, accumulated a national debt, and received British and French recognition. Southerners in the United States clamored for the addition of Texas to the Union. This finally occurred on March 1, 1855, by joint resolution of Congress because of much opposition to this in the North due to slavery. A joint resolution did not require a two-thirds vote but was of questionable constitutionality. The indecent haste was occasioned by fear on the part of influential southern politicians that Texas would abolish slavery to secure admission. That June a called Texas convention accepted joining the United States, and this was then ratified by a popular vote in October. Texas was formally admitted to the Union on December 29, 1845.

Although the Anglo population of Texas was only some 50,000 people against a

Mexican population of as many as 7 million, Mexico made no major effort to reconquer Texas. Despite the May 1836 Treaties of Velasco pledging recognition of Texas independence and his immediate release, Santa Anna was held as a prisoner in Texas until November 20, when the Texas government guaranteed him safe passage to Veracruz. During his long return journey Santa Anna passed through Washington, D.C., where he met briefly with U.S. president Andrew Jackson. The U.S. Navy warship *Pioneer* delivered him to Veracruz early in 1837.

Santa Anna returned to Mexico in disgrace. A new government in Mexico City had removed him as president and declared the treaty made with Texas null and void. Filisola was much criticized for withdrawing Mexican forces from Texas and was soon replaced by Urrea, who then assembled a 6,000-man army at Matamoros with the plan to reconquer Texas. Instead, his army was directed to put down federalist revolts in other parts of Mexico. On March 3, 1837, the U.S. government recognized the Republic of Texas, a move that greatly angered Mexicans.

Santa Anna recouped his reputation during the war with France (1838–1839). Mexico's failure to pay its foreign debts was the excuse for French military intervention. French warships blockaded Mexico City's principal port, Veracruz, on April 16, 1838, shutting off sizable customs revenues to the Mexican government. With negotiations at an impasse, on November 27 the French warships began a bombardment of Veracruz. French shelling soon secured the surrender of the fortress of San Juan de Ulúa, and the French also occupied the city of Veracruz. Mexico declared war on France on December 1, 1838, beginning what was called the Pastry War

because among the claims mentioned as justification for the French action was one by a French pastry chef in Mexico City.

Given command of the Mexican Army by the government, Santa Anna engaged the French forces occupying Veracruz. During a Mexican withdrawal after a failed assault, he was struck in the left leg and hand by cannon fire. His wounds required amputation of much of the leg (which he ordered buried with full military honors). Despite Mexico's capitulation to French demands that ended the war, his brief war service made Santa Anna a hero in Mexico and restored him politically, and he again became president in March 1939 after the claims of the French were settled and they withdrew. Santa Anna would hold the presidency 11 different times.

For years, Mexican authorities used the stated goal of the reconquest of Texas as an excuse for new taxes and building up the strength of the army, but despite the steadfast refusal of Mexico to recognize the independence of Texas, little came of this. In March 1842, Ráfael Vásquez led some 500 Mexicans in an invasion. Although they briefly occupied San Antonio, they soon withdrew. That September French mercenary general Adrián Woll launched a second invasion, this time with some 1,400 Mexican troops, and again briefly held San Antonio. A Texas militia force retaliated at the Battle of Salado Creek (September 17), while at the same time a mile and a half away Mexican soldiers massacred 53 Texans who had surrendered following a skirmish. That night, the Mexicans withdrew from San Antonio.

Relations between Mexico and the United States remained strained, abetted by efforts by the James K. Polk administration's determination to pursue manifest destiny and secure through purchase additional Mexican territory to the Pacific Ocean and south to at least the Rio Grande. When this tactic failed, Polk goaded Mexico into war in 1846. President Santa Anna, again also his country's military commander, waged war, with disastrous result. In the Treaty of Guadalupe Hidalgo of February 2, 1848, which ended the Mexican-American War, Mexico lost half its territory and was at last obliged to recognize the independence of Texas.

SPENCER C. TUCKER

## Timeline

**1519**
Spanish explorer Alonso Álvarez de Pineda is probably the first European to see Texas.

**1690**
Authorities in New Spain establish several Catholic missions in present-day eastern Texas. Fierce Native American resistance soon brings these to an end, however.

**1718**
Renewed French interest in southern Louisiana leads to a new effort by New Spain officials to establish missions in eastern Texas, and San Antonio de Béxar becomes the first Spanish civilian settlement in the region.

**Feb 22, 1819**
As part of the Adams-Onís Treaty with Spain, the United States renounces all claims to Texas.

**1820s**
U.S. citizens begin to settle in Texas, encouraged by the Mexican government.

**1823**
Owing to its small population, Mexico makes Texas (or Tejas), part of the state of Coahuila y Tejas (Coahuila and Texas). When Tejanos complain about representation, Texas is made a department of the new state.

**1824**
Stephen F. Austin leads the successful Anglo colonization of Texas by bringing 300 families there from the United States.

**Apr 6, 1830**
The Mexican government bans additional Anglo immigration into Texas, imposes tariffs and customs duties on Texas, and specifically outlaws slavery there.

**1835**
Mexican general Antonio López de Santa Anna y Pérez de Lebrón abolishes the federal constitution of 1824 and proclaims a new centralist regime. This brings revolt in Texas.

**Sep 20, 1835**
Mexican general Martín Perfecto de Cos lands troops at Copano on the Gulf Coast, charged with restoring Texas to Mexican authority.

**Oct 2, 1835**
The Texas War of Independence begins with the Battle of Gonzales between Texans under John H. Moore and Mexican dragoons under Lieutenant Francisco de Castaneda.

| | |
|---|---|
| **Oct 10, 1835** | Texans from Matagorda under Captain Philip Dimmitt storm and capture the Presidio La Bahía in Goliad. |
| **Oct 11, 1835** | Texas volunteers elect Austin their leader. |
| **Oct 28, 1835** | The first major engagement of the war sees the Texans driving off the attacking Mexicans at Mission Concepción near San Antonio. |
| **Nov 3, 1835** | Following days of debate known as the Consultation, the delegates from numerous Texas municipalities establish a provisional government consisting of a governor and a General Council. |
| **Nov 4, 1835** | Dimmitt dispatches Ira Westover's small contingent to seize Fort Lipantitlán near San Patricio. The small Texan force now virtually controls the entire Gulf Coast. |
| **Nov 7, 1835** | The Texas provisional government proclaims in a declaration of causes that its aim is to defeat Santa Anna, restore the 1824 Constitution, and obtain statehood for Texas within the Mexican federation. |
| **Nov 13, 1835** | Delegates to the Consultation elect Henry Smith governor and establish a regular army, with Sam Houston as commander. |
| **Dec 1835** | Determined to crush the rebellion in Texas, Santa Anna creates a new force of some 6,000 men known as the Army of Operations in Texas, then assumes personal command and proceeds northward with it. |
| **Dec 5, 1835** | Texan colonels Ben Milam and Frank W. Johnson lead several hundred men in an assault on San Antonio. |
| **Dec 9, 1835** | Having taken up a position in the abandoned mission of the Alamo at San Antonio, Cos surrenders. |
| **Dec 20, 1835** | At Presidio La Bahía 91, Texans and Tejanos sign what becomes known as the Goliad Declaration of Independence. |
| **Dec 30, 1835** | On Santa Anna's urging, the Mexican Congress passes the Tornel Decree, declaring foreigners fighting Mexican troops as "pirates." |
| **Feb 17, 1836** | The Mexican army crosses the Nueces River, officially entering Texas. |
| **Feb 23, 1836** | Santa Anna arrives with his army at the Alamo in San Antonio and orders it surrounded. The defenders will number only some 182 men. |
| **Mar 2, 1836** | At Washington-on-the-Brazos, 45 elected delegates officially declare Texas independence. |
| | The remainder of Santa Anna's army arrives at the Alamo, bringing Mexican strength there up to 3,000–4,000 men. Santa Anna orders an around-the-clock artillery bombardment. |
| | Part of General Urrea's force ambushes a number of Texans in the Battle of Agua Dulce. |

| | |
|---|---|
| **Mar 6, 1835** | Mexican Army forces assault the Alamo, and their vastly superior numbers carry the day. All of the defenders are killed, and "Remember the Alamo!" becomes a Texan rallying cry. |
| **Mar 12–15, 1836** | At Refugio, Urrea's forces defeat Texans led by Amon B. King and Lieutenant Colonel William Ward. |
| **Mar 13, 1836** | At Gonzales, Houston convenes a council of war that decides on an immediate evacuation and retreat. Mexican forces under General Joaquín Ramírez y Sesma arrive at Gonzales the next day. |
| **Mar 17, 1836** | Texas Convention delegates approve a constitution for the new republic, and David G. Burnet is elected president of the republic. |
| **Mar 19–20, 1836** | Fannin's force is caught by Urrea's flying column near Coleto Creek on March 19 and is forced to surrender on March 20. |
| **Mar 27, 1836** | Some 342 of the Texans captured in Urrea's Goliad Campaign are executed. |
| **Apr 14, 1836** | Santa Anna leaves San Antonio with some 700 men to capture the members of the interim Texas government, now in Harrisburg. |
| **Apr 18, 1836** | Santa Anna arrives at Harrisburg, finds it deserted, and orders it burned. He then moves to New Washington on the Gulf Coast. |
| **Apr 20, 1836** | Learning of Santa Anna's location and that his men are separated from the main Mexican Army, Houston's Texans are in position to block Santa Anna from joining his main forces. Skirmishing begins that afternoon. |
| **Apr 21, 1836** | The Battle of San Jacinto ends in a decisive Texan victory. |
| **Apr 22, 1836** | Santa Anna is taken prisoner. |
| **May 14, 1836** | In the two Treaties of Velasco signed by Santa Anna, all Mexican troops are to withdraw south of the Rio Grande, with all private property (i.e., slaves) to be respected and restored. Prisoners of war are to be released, and Santa Anna is to receive immediate passage to Veracruz. |
| **Mar 1, 1845** | A joint resolution of Congress admits Texas to the United States. |
| **Jun 23, 1845** | A Texas convention accepts U.S. statehood. This is ratified by a popular vote in October. |
| **Dec 29, 1845** | Texas is formally admitted to the United States. |
| **Feb 2, 1848** | In the Treaty of Guadalupe Hidalgo ending the Mexican-American War, Mexico cedes 525,000 square miles of land (half its territory) to the United States and is obliged to recognize the independence of Texas. |

SPENCER C. TUCKER

## Further Reading

Barr, Alwyn. *Texans in Revolt: The Battle for San Antonio, 1835.* Austin: University of Texas Press, 1990.

Bauer, K. Jack. *The Mexican War, 1846–1848.* Lincoln: University of Nebraska Press, 1974.

Brands, H. W. *Lone Star Nation: How a Ragged Army of Volunteers Won the Battle for Texas Independence—and Changed America.* New York: Doubleday, 2004.

Clary, David A. *Eagles and Empire: The United States, Mexico, and the Struggle for a Continent.* New York: Bantam Books, 2009.

De la Tejas, Jesús Frank, ed. *Tejano Leadership in Mexican and Revolutionary Texas.* College Station: Texas A&M University Press, 2010.

Dimmick, Gregg J. *Sea of Mud: The Retreat of the Mexican Army after San Jacinto, an Archeological Investigation.* Austin: Texas State Historical Association, 2006.

Hardin, Stephen L. *Texian Iliad: A Military History of the Texas Revolution.* Austin: University of Texas Press, 1993.

Hopewell, Clifford. *Remember Goliad: Their Silent Tents.* Austin, TX: Eakin, 1998.

Huffines, Alan C. *Blood of Noble Men: The Alamo Siege and Battle.* Austin, TX: Eakin, 1999.

Lack, Paul D. *The Texas Revolutionary Experience: A Political and Social History, 1835–1836.* College Station: Texas A&M University Press, 1992.

Long, Jeff. *Duel of Eagles: The Mexican and U.S. Fight for the Alamo.* New York: William Morrow, 1990.

Matovina, Timothy M. *The Alamo Remembered: Tejano Accounts and Perspectives.* Austin: University of Texas Press, 1995.

Moore, Stephen L. *Eighteen Minutes: The Battle of San Jacinto and the Texas Independence Campaign.* Plano: Republic of Texas Press, 2004.

Pohl, James W. *The Battle of San Jacinto.* Austin: Texas State Historical Association, 1989.

Pruett, Jakie L., and Everett B. Cole. *Goliad Massacre: A Tragedy of the Texas Revolution.* Austin, TX: Eakin, 1985.

Robinson, Charles M., III. *Texas and the Mexican War: A History and a Guide.* Austin: Texas State Historical Association, 2004.

Roell, Craig H. *Remember Goliad!* Austin: Texas State Historical Association, 1994.

Winders, Bruce. *Sacrificed at the Alamo: Tragedy and Triumph in the Texas Revolution.* Abilene, TX: State House Press, 2003.

# Hungarian Revolution and War for Independence (1848–1849)

## Causes

In 1848, a wave of revolutions occurred throughout Europe. The chief causes were liberalism and nationalism, which had been spawned by the French Revolution of 1789 abetted by a number of European revolutions in 1830. Political liberalism called for governmental reforms to include written constitutions, responsible governing ministries, and wider suffrage. Nationalism held that peoples of similar language and culture ought to be allowed to form their own nation-states.

Widespread economic distress was also a common factor. This began with the Irish Potato Famine of 1845–1848. Europe as a whole experienced a heat wave followed by a drought and massive grain failures. By late 1847 what had begun as an agricultural crisis had grown into a widespread industrial and economic crisis. Factories shut down, and workers were laid off.

### Hungarian Revolution and War for Independence (1848–1849)

| Battle of Pákozd (September 29, 1848)* | | |
|---|---|---|
| | Hungarian Revolutionary Forces | Austrian-Led Forces |
| Strength | 30,000–35,000 men | 35,000–40,000 men |
| Casualties | 7 | 100–200 |

*Although this battle was little more than a brief skirmish, the Hungarian victory here was seen as a watershed in Hungarian history.

| Battle of Kápolna (February 26–27, 1849)* | | |
|---|---|---|
| | Hungarian Revolutionary Forces | Austrian-Led Forces |
| Strength | 36,000 men, 136 guns | 30,000 men, 165 guns |

*Here Austrian forces decisively defeated revolutionary forces.

| Battle of Temesvár (August 9, 1849) | | |
|---|---|---|
| | Hungarian Revolutionary Forces | Austrian/Russian Forces |
| Strength | 50,000–55,000 men, 112 guns | 90,000 men, 350 guns |
| Casualties | 10,490* | 4,500** |

*Of this number, approximately 6,000 were captured; several hundred more were killed, and the rest were wounded.
**Of this number, approximately 50 were killed; the rest were wounded or captured or deserted.

Sources: Deák, István. *The Lawful Revolution: Louis Kossuth and the Hungarians, 1848–1849*. New York: Columbia University Press, 1979; Sked, Alan. *The Survival of the Habsburg Empire: Radetzky, the Imperial Army and the Class War, 1848*. New York: Longman, 1979.

Unemployment in Europe's major cities soared to as much as 30–40 percent. The displaced and unemployed were thus ready and able to support revolutionary activity. The success of a revolution in one location served as a stimulus to others.

The revolutions of 1848 occurred in short order and were widespread, occurring from Spain to Hungary (notable exceptions were Britain and Portugal in the west of the continent and Russia and Poland in the east). What is perhaps most remarkable about them is how easily they occurred and how quickly they were reversed. A number of factors explain the latter. For one thing, the established regimes were found to be stronger than had been realized. Also, after the revolutionaries had taken power, sharp differences arose among the leaders themselves. Liberals found themselves at odds with democrats and Marxists. These differences certainly made it much easier for the conservatives and reactionaries to overturn the revolutions.

The revolutionaries also proved incapable of sustaining mass public support. Much of Europe was still overwhelmingly rural and agricultural, and the peasantry was largely politically inert. The revolutionaries for the most part were also humanitarians who failed to do away with the opposition leaders. The latter for the most part retained control of the military establishments, as in Prussia and Austria, and the Russian military could be called upon to help crush revolution elsewhere. Economic recovery also helped remove the underpinnings of the revolutions. The 1848 harvests were good ones, and the national economies quickly rebounded. Employed workers had little time or energy for revolutionary activity. Finally, many religious people considered an outbreak of cholera that took place as a sign of divine judgment on revolutionary activity.

There were two principal centers of revolutionary activity: Italy and France. The revolutions actually began first in Italy in late 1847, but the real storm came in France in February 1848 when King Louis Philippe, who had come to power as a consequence of the French Revolution of 1830, was overthrown and a republic proclaimed.

The success of the revolutionaries in France led to a number of revolutions in Central Europe. The Austrian Empire was particularly vulnerable to the forces of nationalism, for it had no ethnic majority. Germans, who dominated the political and economic life of the empire, constituted only 23 percent of the population. Czechs and Slovaks together made up 19 percent; Magyars counted for 14 percent. Other minorities consisted of Rutheniuans, Romanians, and Italians, each 8 percent; Poles, 7 percent; Serbs; 5 percent; Croats, 4 percent; and Slovenes, 4 percent. In parts of the empire these separate populations were in blocs, while in other areas they were intermingled. The Habsburg dynastic system controlling the whole still had a while left to live, but nationalism now threatened to tear it apart.

Chancellor of the Austrian Empire Prince Klemens von Metternich, who had dominated Austrian affairs for some 40 years, attempted to hold the empire together. He clearly understood the threat posed by nationalism but had no answer other than force and repression. In 1835 Austrian emperor Francis I (r. 1792–1835) had been succeeded by Ferdinand I. An epileptic who had apparently suffered brain damage, he was known to his detractors as Ferdinand the Silly. During his reign there was considerable infighting among his principal ministers, leading to a breakdown in the machinery of repression. Indeed, the revolutions of 1848 in the Habsburg Empire occurred not from repression but rather the lack of it.

In 1846 an uprising sparked by nationalism and led by the nobles occurred in Galicia, but the Austrian Army soon put it down. The economic crisis that now came to grip all of Europe by late 1847 posed a greater threat. A large number of industrial workers in Vienna were thrown out of work, and news of the success of the workers in Paris that February, known in Vienna and Budapest at the beginning of March, had an immediate impact.

The Hungarian nobles had long chaffed at control by Vienna. In the Middle Ages an independent Hungarian kingdom had dominated much of Central Europe. The great Hungarian king Matthias I (r. 1458–1490) defeated the Ottomans and conquered Silesia and much of Bohemia. Mathias also laid siege to Vienna and took it in 1485, annexing Austria, Styria, and Carinthia to his domains and transferring his capital to Vienna.

It was not to last. Matthias was a centralizer, and a reaction led by the nobles set in under his successor, greatly weakening the Hungarian state. Emperor Maximilian (r. 1486–1519) took back the Austrian lands, and the Ottomans invaded and annihilated a hastily organized Hungarian army in the 1526 Battle of Mohacs. The Ottomans then took Buda and ravaged a quarter of Hungary, carrying off 100,000 captives. Hungary was soon partitioned between Austrian and Hungarian claimants to the throne. Another Ottoman invasion followed, and this time Hungary was partitioned three ways. The emperor was left in possession of his former share, subject to annual tribute to the sultan;

Transylvania and some adjacent counties went to John Sigismund with the title of prince, while the Ottomans annexed the rich central plain.

This arrangement lasted with some changes for the next 150 years. Transylvania became the center of Hungarian nationalism, with the Ottomans and Habsburgs equally detested. In the late 17th century the Ottomans resolved to conquer the rest of Hungary. A 16-year war followed with one of the great battles of Western history, the 1683 Siege of Vienna in which the Ottomans were defeated. In 1699 Prince Eugene of Savoy routed the Ottomans in the Battle of Zenta, leaving Emperor Leopold in possession of almost all of Hungary.

Heavy-handed rule from Vienna made Hungary ripe for revolution. With Austrian forces largely withdrawn for the War of the Spanish Succession (1702–1715), Hungarian noble Francis II Rákóczy led a lengthy but ultimately unsuccessful effort to throw off Austrian rule, suffering a major defeat in the Battle of Trencsén (1708).

The Habsburgs repeatedly refused to convene the Hungarian Diet, but under reformer Count István Széchenyi the Diet reconvened in 1825, marking the beginning of the so-called Reformkor (Reform Period) of 1825–1848. Much was achieved in this time frame in the way of modernizing Hungary, although Vienna blocked all liberal legislation involving civil and political rights and economic reforms. Indeed, many reformers were imprisoned.

Among the reformers was fiery lawyer Lajos (Louis) Kossuth, who demanded freedom of the press throughout the empire. Charged with treason, Kossuth served five years in prison, which damaged his health but did not diminish his determination. Released in 1840, he found himself a national hero and soon became editor of a new liberal newspaper, *Pesti Hírlap,* which came to enjoy a wide circulation.

Imbued with the liberal ideas espoused by the French Revolution of 1789, Kossuth regarded all inhabitants of Hungarian territory as Hungarians, regardless of the language they spoke and ethnic ancestry. Nonetheless, he argued for rapid Magyarization of Croats, Romanians, Germans, and other minorities in Hungary and for Hungarian as the sole language of public life.

Széchenyi criticized Kossuth for "pitting one nationality against another" and warned publicly that such appeals to popular passions would bring revolution. Kossuth was undaunted. Apart from normal liberal demands, he touted the superiority of the Hungarian culture over that of Austria and went so far as to suggest the possibility of separation from Austria.

Dismissed from *Pesti Hírlap* in 1844, probably a result of government intervention, Kossuth was unable to obtain government permission to start his own newspaper. He rejected an offer from Metternich to enter Austrian government service and held no regular position thereafter. Kossuth advocated the independence of Hungary, with the new state to have its own port at Fiume (Rijeka).

In the autumn of 1847, Kossuth was elected from Pest to the new Hungarian Diet. A brilliant public speaker and also fluent in a number of languages, he immediately became leader of the opposition. Count Széchenyi argued against what he regarded as Kossuth's imprudent approach. According to Széchenyi, economic, political, and social reforms had to be introduced slowly and carefully in order to be

Statue of Lajos Kossuth, leader of the Hungarian Revolution of 1848–1849, Heroes Square, Budapest. (Poeticpenguin/ Dreamstime)

lasting, and Széchenyi was correct in predicting that Kossuth's immediate approach would only bring Habsburg interference and a tragic result for Hungary.

SPENCER C. TUCKER

## Course

The Hungarian Diet had been meeting in Pressburg (present-day Bratislava) and debating reforms when news arrived there of what had transpired in Paris. On March 3 Kossuth delivered a fiery speech in which he attacked heavy-handed Austrian rule, stressed the virtues of liberty, and demanded liberal reforms to include a constitution for the Habsburg Empire and establishment of a responsible ministry in Hungary. This date can be said to mark the beginning of the Hungarian Revolution of 1848.

On March 13 students in Vienna, inspired by events in Paris and in Bratislava, demanded reform in Austria itself, including an end to censorship. Workers soon joined them, and Metternich was forced to resign and soon fled Austria for exile in England. Emperor Ferdinand I promised reforms, but much of the Habsburg Empire now erupted in revolution. Events moved too quickly for Vienna to avoid making concessions.

In Hungary, students and peasants gathered in Budapest for a trade fair in mid-March. On March 15 the radical young poet Sándor (Alexander) Petőfi addressed a large crowd on the steps of the new National Museum. The crowd then crossed to Buda on the other bank of the Danube. Its members took control of city hall and the university. They also marched on the Viceroyal Council building and proceeded to confront the members of the Imperial Governing Council, who were forced to sign a document known as the "12 Points." The 12 Points demanded freedom of the press; the establishment in Budapest of an independent Hungarian government and its annual meeting; an end to censorship; full civil and religious equality before the law; the creation of a Hungarian national army, with its members to take an oath of loyalty to the constitution and with Hungarians serving in the national army to be sent home and "foreign soldiers" serving in Hungary to be recalled; burden sharing; the abolition of socage (the payment of feudal dues); courts and juries based on equal legal representation; the creation of a Hungarian national bank; freedom for political prisoners; and the union of Transylvania (which had a large Magyar population) with Hungary.

The Hungarian Diet then hurriedly convened in Pozsony and, under the leadership of Kossuth, enacted a host of reforms known as the April Laws before it dissolved on April 11. In effect a new constitution, these 31 laws established Hungary as a constitutional monarchy, with the monarchy constrained by an annually convened parliament to which the prime minister, Count Lajos Batthyány, was responsible. Hungarian military forces were to be reorganized as a national guard, with every soldier in Hungary obliged to take an oath of loyalty to the Hungarian government. The April Laws also abolished the institution of serfdom and made peasants owners of the land they worked. The laws also ended the tax-free status of the nobility and brought an end to censorship. They also provided for the complete constitutional separation of Hungary from Austria, although the Austrian emperor would remain king in Hungary.

The whole structure of the Austrian Empire seemed to have been blown apart, for there were also revolutions in the empire in Italy and in Bohemia. In these circumstances, the leadership in Vienna bided its time in a waiting game, hoping that the revolutionary tide would soon pass. At the same time, however, the Crown retained control of the military establishment and was prepared to use it when the time appeared propitious. In late May Ferdinand and the court left Vienna for Innsbruck, where they rallied both the peasantry and the army. Prominent loyal army leaders included Alfred I, Prince of Windisch-Grätz; Field Marshal Count Johann Josef Wenzel Radetzky von Radetz; and Croatian baron Josip Jelačić.

Sure enough, the revolutionary tide began to ebb in June. In the Austrian Empire the masses were more conservative and not as educated as in France. Peasants also made up the bulk of strength in the imperial army, which was largely immune to revolutionary impulses.

Still, things appeared grim at first. As noted, the revolutions that swept much of Europe began first in Italy, where there was great resentment regarding Austrian domination of Italy and its outright control of the northern part of the peninsula. (In the 1815 Vienna settlement following the Napoleonic Wars, Austria had secured Lombardy and Venetia.) Riots in Italy led to monarchs being forced to grant constitutions, and on March 18 revolt flared in Milan, the capital of Lombardy. The so-called Five Days of Milan (May 18–22) ended with 82-year-old field marshal Radetzky withdrawing Austrian troops from the city. With unrest spreading and the seeming success of revolutionaries in Milan and other parts of Italy, King Charles Albert of the Kingdom of Sardinia (Piedmont-Sardinia) sought to lead an Italian war of liberation by declaring war against Austria on March 22, 1848. Revolutionaries then seized control of Venice. In mid-June Radetsky took the offensive and quickly reestablished Habsburg control in Lombardy and in most of Venetia except Venice itself. Radetsky then turned his attention to the forces under Charles Albert, defeating them in the Battle of Custoza (July 23–26).

The Austrian court also had to deal with revolt in Bohemia. An earlier revolt in Bohemia against Habsburg rule had touched off the Thirty Years' War (1618–1648) but had been crushed in 1620, and much of the best lands of Bohemia had then been parceled out to Germans. Despite the reimposition of Habsburg rule, Czech nationalism remained just below the surface, fueled by the University of Prague and the establishment of a Czech national museum in that city.

The Czechs took advantage of the revolution in Vienna to assert their own independence. Leaders in Prague called a Pan-Slav assembly, which had begun meeting in Prague on June 2, with most of the representatives coming from the Austrian Empire. The representatives did not at this point favor a Slavic state, which would be surrounded by hostile powers, but instead demanded autonomy and constitutional rights equal to those of other minorities within the empire.

The situation in Bohemia deteriorated with the surfacing of violence fed by long-held animosity between Czechs and Germans. One of the victims was the wife of the Austrian military commander there, Prince Windisch-Grätz. She had been accidently shot and killed during a demonstration. Windisch-Grätz commenced an artillery bombardment of Prague and took control there on June 17. The Slave Congress abruptly ended, and the Austrian Army soon controlled all of Bohemia.

Hungary's turn came in the fall. Although Kossuth and the other leaders of the Hungarian Revolution were liberals, they were first and foremost Magyar nationalists. The Diet now replaced Latin with Magyar as the official language of Hungary and moved the capital eastward from Pressburg near Vienna to Budapest in central Hungary. Unfortunately for them, in attempting to free themselves from their German connection the Magyars imposed their own cultural hegemony on the many minorities living in Hungary: the Croats, Germans, Slovaks, Romanians, and Serbs. Constituting half of the population, these peoples resisted Magyar control. Anti-Magyar uprisings took place throughout Hungary, the first of these by Serbs on the southern border, who received support from Serbia. The Croats came to take a leading role under one of their own, General Jelačić, who raised the banner of civil war against the Magyars on behalf of the Austrian Empire. Appointed commander of Austrian forces against Hungary, on September 17 Jelačić crossed the Hungarian border with 30,000–35,000 poorly equipped Croatian troops, and Hungary now fell into civil war.

Hungarian units constituted a substantial portion of the imperial army. They made up 15 of 58 infantry regiments, 5 of 20 grenadier battalions, 23 of 37 cavalry regiments, and an additional 18 border guard regiments. But the bulk of these were stationed in other parts of the empire, and it would take time for them to work their way back to Hungary. Initially the Hungarians had available only some 25,000 men to meet the invaders. The government hastily called some 60,000 national guardsmen into active service, but only a quarter of them were armed, and the men also had to be trained.

After a steady withdrawal, on September 29 at Pákozd some 30 miles southwest of Budapest, Hungarian forces led by General János Móga stood and fought, defeating Jelačić's army. Considered by Hungarians a landmark in their history, the Battle of Pákozd, which was actually little more than a skirmish, has been described as Hungary's Valmy in reference to the victory of French revolutionary forces over the invading Prussians in September 1792. Certainly the battle proved that the new Hungarian national army was willing and able to fight.

An armistice was then arranged between the Royal Hungarian Army and the Imperial Royal Croatian Army. Jelačić withdrew toward Vienna and a juncture with the other imperial forces forming under Windisch-Grätz. On October 3,

Habsburg emperor Ferdinand I issued a manifesto that dismissed the Hungarian parliament, subjected Hungary to military rule, and appointed Jelačić its military governor.

Meanwhile, students and other radicals in Vienna, sympathetic with the revolutionaries in Hungary and upset with the imperial court's decision to send Austrian troops to support Jelačić, sought to convince soldiers in Vienna not to obey their orders. On October 6 a grenadier battalion defied an order of minister of war and general Count Theodor Baillet von Latour to move toward the Hungarian border. A bloody clash occurred when troops loyal to Latour and the grenadiers fired on each other.

Within hours, crowds of Viennese drove some 14,000 imperial troops from Vienna. Latuor was hanged from a lamppost, and the court and other government officials fled to Olmütz (Olomouc) in Moravia. The Austrian Reichstag (parliament) remained behind, but power in the city passed into the hands of the revolutionaries.

Hungarian Army troops from the east and Austrian imperial forces from the north under Windisch-Grätz both now advanced on the city of Vienna. Windisch-Grätz assembled 70,000 men and moved swiftly, while the far smaller and less organized Hungarian force was slower to move and in fact halted at the Hungarian-Austrian border because its commander, General Móga, and many of his officers hoped to avoid further inter-Habsburg fighting and war against Hungary's king. The Viennese revolutionaries were also reluctant to call in the Hungarians, so several weeks were lost.

When the Hungarians did cross the border with some 30,000 men and 70 guns, they encountered the united forces of

Windisch-Grätz and Jelačić, with 80,000 men and 210 guns. Attacked at Schwechat just east of Vienna on October 30, the Hungarians encountered a heavy Austrian artillery barrage and were soon in precipitous flight, many not halting until they reached the Hungarian border. Móga, who fell from his horse and was injured during the battle, resigned his command. On November 1 Kossuth, acting as president of the Hungarian National Defense Committee, appointed young Artúr Görgey, born in 1820, as commander of Hungarian forces in the west.

After the Austrian victory at Schwechat, Windisch-Grätz turned westward and marched on Vienna. He took the city with his Czech, Moravian, Galician, and Croatian forces on October 31. The troops embarked on considerable looting there, while a few revolutionaries were executed and others were imprisoned.

In the east, Austrian forces under the general Baron Anton Puchner invaded Transylvania, and on November 17 they captured its capital of Kolozsvár. Kossuth appointed Polish revolutionary hero József Bem as Hungarian military commander in Transylvania. Next to Görgey, Bem proved to be Hungary's most effective military leader of the war. Operating almost independently, he soon secured control of most of that province, allowing Görgey to concentrate on the major Austrian threat from the west. Certainly, without Bem's able leadership the war would have been lost in late 1848. Meanwhile, Kossuth and Görgey assembled an army of some 170,000 men, surpassing in numbers the local Austrian forces.

Within Austria at Olmütz (Olomouc) in Moravia, new Austrian chief minister General Prince Felix zu Schwarzenberg persuaded the weak-willed Emperor Ferdinand I to abdicate. His brother, the mild-mannered Archduke Franz Karl, renounced the throne, and on December 2 Franz Karl's son, 18-year-old Franz Joseph, became emperor of Austria. The reactionary Franz Joseph I would rule as Austrian emperor and king of Bohemia, Croatia, and Hungary until his death in 1916 during World War I.

Imperial forces under Windisch-Grätz now invaded Hungary from the west, while other Austrian forces invaded from the north and south. Only the Hungarian forces under József Bem to the east in Transylvania defended successfully; the other Hungarian armies were driven slowly back, and on December 30 one of them suffered defeat at Mór, west of Budapest. Kossuth and most of the government officials then abandoned Budapest for Debrecen, in far eastern Hungary.

Austrian forces under Windisch-Grätz occupied Budapest on January 5, 1849. General Görgey, his forces now outnumbered two to one, broke with Kossuth and the revolutionary government and withdrew into the mountains to the north, leaving central and eastern Hungary defenseless. Kossuth then named Polish volunteer and general Henryk Dembiński commander of the Hungarian Army. Dembiński had been the principal Polish military commander during the 1830–1831 Polish Revolt against Russia, and his appointment fueled Austrian claims that the Hungarian Revolution was part of an international conspiracy. Windisch-Grätz, however, informed the Austrian court that the Hungarian revolt had been crushed. Indeed, he now concentrated on the administrative reorganization of Hungary.

At Debrecen, Kossuth tried to rally his people to continue the struggle. Although the Hungarian Diet remained in session, most of its members either rallied to the Austrians or chose to remain at home. Kossuth and the National Defense Committee simply issued laws by decree. At the end of January 1849, though, Görgey's army suddenly reappeared from the north, broke through the Austrian forces, and joined the remainder of the Hungarian army in the northeast.

In the Battle of Kápolna northeast of Budapest on February 26–27, 1849, Austrian forces under Windisch-Grätz defeated Dembiński, and despite Kossuth's objection, Görgey resumed command of the army. During April and early May 1849, Görgey outmaneuvered the Austrians and won a series of small military victories: Hatvan on April 2, Tápióbicske on April 4, and Isaszeg on April 6. The Hungarians also fought their way into Budapest, and the Austrians continued to hold Castle Hill on the Buda side of the Danube.

With Austrian forces too strong in Budapest, the Hungarian army moved on to Komárom, at the confluence of the Vág River with the Danube. Komárom was one of the strongest fortresses in the entire Austrian Empire. The Austrians had laid siege to it in March but were now forced to raise the siege and withdraw westward. Soon the Viennese were fortifying the Austrian capital in anticipation of a Hungarian attack, although the Hungarians lacked the population, industrial resources, and military might to win the war.

On April 14, 1849, the Hungarian parliament at Debrecen declared the complete independence of Hungary and elected Kossuth governor-president. The declaration made little difference in the war and led to an even more pronounced split between Kossuth and Hungarian Army commander Görgey, a realist who favored a negotiated settlement.

Although the Hungarians controlled the rest of Budapest, a few thousand Austrian troops under General Heinrich Hentzi held out on Castle Hill in Buda across the Danube from Pest. Görgey moved against Castle Hill, but with the Hungarians lacking heavy artillery, he was forced into siege operations, which took three weeks. Following a tenacious defense, the Austrians surrendered on May 21, and Kossuth entered Budapest that same day. Görgey's decision to take Castle Hill instead of immediately moving against Vienna was his one and only major strategic error of the war. It probably cost the Hungarians their last chance to force the Austrians into negotiations.

Hungarian independence did not last long, as Franz Joseph now called on Russian czar Nicholas I (r. 1825–1855) for assistance. The czar needed no urging, for he was a strong believer that monarchs should aid one another to put down revolutions and, moreover, was angered that Polish generals were serving with the Hungarian forces. Prepared to intervene earlier, he insisted on an Austrian request. The Austrians, humiliated at having to do so, now formally requested Russian assistance, and on May 9 Nicholas agreed.

On June 17 Field Marshal Prince Ivan Paskievich led some 200,000 Russian soldiers in an invasion of Hungary from Poland and the Danubian Principalities. At the same time, Colonel General Julius Jacob von Haynau, who replaced Windisch-Grätz, invaded Hungary from the west with a well-equipped Austrian army of about 175,000 men. Against these two forces the Hungarians were able to muster only about 170,000 men, with perhaps one-third the field artillery of their opponents.

In late June and early July, Austrian forces under Haynau defeated the main

Hungarian army under Görgey in a series of battles near the Komárom Fortress. On July 8 the Hungarian government again abandoned Budapest. Other Hungarian defeats followed. Most of these were at the hands of the Austrians, with the Russian generals proving far less adroit than their Austrian counterparts.

Certainly the Hungarian cause was not helped by squabbling between Görgey and Kossuth. Although maneuvering brilliantly, Görgey managed only to preserve his forces largely intact for the Hungarian defeat. The other Hungarian armies, including that of Bem in Transylvania, were defeated one by one. On July 28 Kossuth and the Hungarian government extended full ethnic rights to all the minorities in Hungary, but this came too late to have any advantage.

By early August 1849 the remaining Hungarian forces were concentrated in southeastern Hungary. Kossuth gave overall command of the army back to Dembiński, whose subsequent poor maneuvering accelerated the date of the final Hungarian defeat. Austrian general Haynau commanded the Austrian side during the final battle at Temesvár on August 9, 1849. Bem commanded the Hungarians, who had only their southern forces available and lost several hundred killed and some 6,000 taken prisoner. The rest of the army simply dissolved. The Austrians lost fewer than 50 killed.

The forces under Görgey were all that remained. These and the government were at Arad. On August 11 Kossuth resigned his position and appointed Görgey military dictator of Hungary. On August 17 Kossuth buried the Crown of St. Stephen near the frontier and then fled in disguise across the southern border into Ottoman territory along with a few thousand Hungarian soldiers, the entire Polish legion, and some civilians. On August 13, meanwhile, Görgey showed his contempt for the Austrians by surrendering to the Russians at Világos (now Şiria, Romania) with some 34,000 officers and men and 144 guns. He evidently hoped that they would be allowed to enter Russian service, but except for Görgey himself, the Russians handed all of the prisoners over to the Austrians, who then executed a number of the leading officers.

The Austrians showed little mercy to the remaining members of the Hungarian Army or, for that matter, the civilian population. With the surrender of their fortress of Komárom on October 5, the Hungarian War of Independence was over. The next day the Austrians commenced the execution of the Hungarian revolutionary leaders in their custody.

SPENCER C. TUCKER

## Consequences

Kossuth subsequently made his way to Britain and then to the United States. He was lionized in both countries as an impassioned advocate of democracy. Kossuth met with President Millard Fillmore and became only the second foreigner after the Marquis de Lafayette to address the U.S. Congress. Disappointed in his efforts to rally immigrants in the United States behind the cause of Hungarian independence, Kossuth returned to England and finally relocated to Italy, where he died in Turin in 1894.

Following the failed Hungarian War for Independence, reaction held sway in Hungary. Prince Feliz zu Schwartzenberg, minister-president and foreign minister of the Austrian Empire during 1848–1852, dominated Austrian affairs. During his tenure the government sought to root out freedom of expression, constitutionalism, and nationalism throughout the Austrian Empire. Under the Bach System, named for Minister of the Interior Alexander von Bach, government was highly centralized in Vienna, and an imperial council of German and Czech officials administered Hungary. Hungary also lost the special rights it had enjoyed before 1848. Although Bach insisted on improving the lot of peasantry and legal reforms as well as doing away with internal tariffs and making the whole of the empire a free trade area, his effort to create a unitary system for the empire failed.

The Austrian Empire was soon reeling, as Emperor Franz Joseph blundered into two wars. In 1859 the Austrian Army suffered battlefield reversals in Italy in war with France and Piedmont-Sardinia in the bloody battles at Magenta and Solferino. Hungary contributed to the defeat in that during the war the Austrian leadership was reluctant to withdraw their military garrisons there. A number of Hungarians also enlisted to fight against Austria.

Then in 1866 the Austrian Empire stumbled into war again, this time with Prussia. The Prussians triumphed in this short war of only seven weeks' duration. The Prussian victory at Königgrätz (also known as the Battle of Sadowa) on July 3, 1866, ended the 140-year-long struggle to see which of the two powers would dominate the Germanies.

The defeat of 1866 forced the German rulers of Austria to seek a power-sharing arrangement with the Magyars of Hungary. In effect, the Germans, with 23 percent of the population, chose to compromise with the next largest minority, the Magyars, with 14 percent, in order to rule the remaining 63 percent. It was thus largely Germans and Magyars cooperating to hold the Slavs in check.

Leading Hungarian statesman Ferenc Deák negotiated with imperial chancellor Count Friedrich Ferdinand von Beust. Deák had supported the 1848 revolution but now broke with the hard-line nationalists such as Kossuth to support a union under the Habsburgs that would ensure full internal independence for Hungary, with only matters of defense and foreign affairs common to both countries. Beust hoped to soon go to war again against Prussia with different results and believed that settling with Hungary would make that possible.

Franz Joseph and Deák signed what was known as the Ausgleich (Compromise), and it was ratified by the restored Diet of Hungary on May 29, 1867. The so-called Dual Monarchy was unique in Europe. It was actually two separate states bound together only in allegiance to Franz Josef as emperor in Austria and king in Hungary. There were common ministries of finance, foreign affairs, and the military, but elaborate safeguards were put in place to prevent evolution into a more unitary state. There was no common cabinet or prime minister (other than Franz Joseph himself). Matters that concerned both Austria and Hungary would be dealt with by the Delegations, representatives from each of the two parliaments. There was also a customs union, a common currency, and a sharing of accounts to be revisited every 10 years.

The vast majority of Hungarians wanted full independence, and the Compromise was approved by only a very small part of the population, for the franchise was restricted to only about 8 percent of the population. Indeed, the Compromise was so unpopular that force was necessary to suppress demonstrations against it. Beust's hopes for speedy revenge against

Prussia came to naught. In 1870 he wanted Austria-Hungary to support France against Prussia, but Hungarian premier Gyula Andrássy would have none of it, and the matter was dropped.

From Italy, Kossuth watched the reconciliation with anger and dismay. He penned the so-called Cassandra Letter, an open letter to Deák in which he condemned both the compromise arrangement and the Hungarian leader himself for giving away Hungarian independence. Kossuth predicted that having now tied their fate to the Germans of Austria, the Hungarians would follow them into a devastating continental war induced by extremist nationalism with disastrous results, leading to "the death of our nation."

Kossuth's words proved prophetic. The Dual Monarchy made sound sense economically but was a racial museum that exploded in World War I. The chain of events that led to war in fact began when Austro-Hungarian leaders decided on a punitive war against Serbia for the assassination by a Slavic terrorist of Archduke Franz Ferdinand. Germany supported Austria-Hungary while Russia backed Serbia, and the war was on. As the so-called Central Powers collapsed in late 1918, liberal noble Count Mihály Károlyi tried to hold Hungary together by promising genuine reforms, but it was too late; the subject peoples wanted their independence. The 1919 Treaty of Trianon drafted by the victors came as a shock. It stripped Hungary of 65 percent of its prewar territory. In these circumstances in March 1919 the communists staged a revolution in Budapest that came to be dominated by a young army captain named Bela Kun. Communist efforts both to transform the economy and hold on to all old Hungarian territory met with failure. The communists were driven out, and a monarchy, minus a king, was set up under Admiral Nicholas Horthy as regent. Twice the former king/emperor Charles tried to return, but each time the Allies forced him to withdraw.

Pressed by German chancellor Adolf Hitler, who promised the return of some of its prewar territory, Hungary joined the Axis side in World War II and again suffered defeat and, this time, Soviet occupation. Soviet tanks crushed a new revolutionary effort in 1956, and Hungary remained part of the Soviet empire. Hungary can be said to have regained full independence only with the end of communism in 1989.

SPENCER C. TUCKER

## Timeline

| | |
|---|---|
| **Jul 1847** | Austrian troops occupy Ferrara, inflaming Italian nationalists. |
| **Late 1847** | An agricultural crisis in much of Europe becomes a widespread economic crisis. |
| **Feb 24, 1848** | French king Louis Philippe I abdicates, and a republic is proclaimed. |
| **Mar 3, 1848** | Hungarian nationalist leader Lajos Kossuth attacks Austrian rule and demands reforms to include the establishment of a constitution and responsible ministry in Hungary. This marks the beginning of the Hungarian Revolution. |

| | |
|---|---|
| **Mar 13, 1848** | In Vienna, inspired by events in Paris and in Bratislava, students demand reform in Austria and are joined by workers. Metternich is forced to resign and flees Vienna. |
| **Mar 15, 1848** | A large crowd in Budapest seizes control of government buildings and demands reforms. They also force Austrian representatives to agree to the 12 Points, which call for Hungarian independence and reforms. |
| **Apr 1848** | A Hungarian Diet convenes in Pozsony and enacts the so-called April Laws, in effect a new constitution that establishes a constitutional monarchy. |
| **May 1848** | Emperor Ferdinand and the Austrian court leave Vienna for Innsbruck, where they rally the peasantry and the army. |
| **Jun 2–12 1848** | A Pan-Slav assembly meets in Prague. |
| **Jun 17, 1848** | Austrian troops led by Alfred I, Prince Windisch-Grätz, take control of Prague. |
| **Sep 17, 1848** | Having been appointed commander of Austrian forces against Hungary, Croatian baron Josip Jelačić leads Croatian forces into Hungary to put down the rebellion there. |
| **Sep 29, 1848** | At Pákozd, Hungarian forces under General János Móga defeat Austrian Crown forces under Jelačić. An armistice is then arranged. |
| **Oct 3, 1848** | Austrian emperor Ferdinand I dismisses the Hungarian parliament, subjects Hungary to military rule, and appoints Jelačić its military governor. |
| **Oct 30, 1848** | Hungarian forces under General Móga are defeated by united Austrian forces under Windisch-Grätz and Jelačić at Schwechat. Móga, who is injured, resigns his command. |
| **Oct 31, 1848** | Windisch-Grätz's troops take control of Vienna. |
| **Nov 1, 1848** | Kossuth, acting as president of the Hungarian National Defense Committee, appoints Artúr Görgey to command Hungarian forces in the west. |
| **Nov 17, 1848** | Austrian forces under General Baron Anton Puchner invade Transylvania and capture its capital. Kossuth then appoints Polish officer Józef Bem as Hungarian military commander in Transylvania. |
| **Dec 2, 1848** | Ferdinand I abdicates, and Franz Josef I becomes Austrian emperor. |
| **Dec 30, 1848** | Austrian forces under Jelačić defeat the Hungarians under Mór Perczel, forcing Kossuth and most Hungarian government officials to abandon Budapest for Debrecen. |
| **Jan 1849** | Kossuth names Polish general Henryk Dembiński commander of the Hungarian Army. |

| | |
|---|---|
| **Jan 5, 1849** | Austrian forces under Windisch-Grätz occupy Budapest. |
| **Feb 26–27, 1849** | In the Battle of Kápolna, Austrian forces under Windisch-Grätz defeat the Hungarians under Dembiński. Görgey resumes command of the army. |
| **Apr–May 1849** | Hungarian general Görgey wins a series of small victories against the Austrians, liberating much of Hungary. |
| **Apr 14, 1849** | The Hungarian parliament declares the complete independence of Hungary and elects Kossuth governor-president. |
| **Apr 22, 1849** | Hungarian forces relieve the Austrian siege of the fortress of Kamárom on the Danube. |
| **May 21, 1849** | Hungarian forces recapture Castle Hill in Budapest. |
| **Jun 17, 1849** | Russian czar Nicholas sends Field Marshal Prince Ivan Paskievich and some 200,000 Russian soldiers into Hungary. At the same time, Colonel General Julius Jacob von Haynau invades Hungary from the west with a well-equipped Austrian army. |
| **Jul 8, 1849** | After Haynau's force defeats the Hungarian army under Görgey near the fortress of Komárom, the Hungarian government again abandons Budapest. |
| **Jul 28, 1849** | Kossuth and the Hungarian government extend full ethnic rights to all Hungarian minorities. |
| **Aug 9, 1849** | Haynau and the Austrians defeat the Hungarians under Bem in the final battle at Temesvár. |
| **Aug 11, 1849** | Kossuth resigns his position and appoints Görgey military dictator of Hungary. |
| **Aug 13, 1849** | Görgey shows his contempt for the Austrians by surrendering to the Russians at Világos (now Şiria, Romania). |
| **Aug 17, 1849** | Kossuth and several thousand other Hungarians and the entire Polish legion flee into Ottoman territory. |
| **Oct 5, 1849** | The Hungarian fortress of Komárom surrenders, bringing to an end the Hungarian War of Independence. |

SPENCER C. TUCKER

## Further Reading

Breunig, Charles. *The Age of Revolution and Reaction, 1789–1850*. New York: Norton, 1970.

Deák, István. *The Lawful Revolution: Louis Kossuth and the Hungarians, 1848–1849*. New York: Columbia University Press, 1979.

Deme, Laszlo. *The Radical Left in the Hungarian Revolution of 1848*. New York: Columbia University Press, 1976.

Dowe, Dieter, ed. *Europe in 1848: Revolution and Reform*. New York: Berghahn Books, 2000.

Duveau, Georges. *1848: The Making of a Revolution*. New York: Pantheon Books, 1987.

Evans, Robert, John Weston, and Hartmut Pogge von Strandmann, eds. *The Revolutions in Europe, 1848–1849: From Reform to Reaction.* New York: Oxford University Press, 2000.

Ginsborg, Paul. *Daniele Manin and the Venetian Revolution of 1848–49.* New York: Cambridge University Press, 1979.

Hahs, Hans J. *The 1848 Revolutions in German-Speaking Europe.* New York: Longman, 2001.

Langer, William. *The Revolutions of 1848.* New York: Harper, 1971.

Pouthas, Charles. "The Revolutions of 1848." In *New Cambridge Modern History: The Zenith of European Power, 1830–70,* edited by J. P. T. Bury, 389–415. Cambridge, UK: Cambridge University Press, 2000.

Rapport, Michael. *1848: Year of Revolution.* New York: Basic Books, 2009.

Robertson, Priscilla Smith. *Revolutions of 1848: A Social History.* Princeton, NJ: Princeton University Press, 1952.

Sked, Alan. *The Survival of the Habsburg Empire: Radetzky, the Imperial Army and the Class War, 1848.* New York: Longman, 1979.

Sperber, Jonathan. *The European Revolutions, 1848–1851.* 2nd ed. New York: Cambridge University Press, 2005.

Stearns, Peter N. *1848: The Revolutionary Tide in Europe.* New York: Norton, 1974.

# Italian Wars of Independence (Wars of Italian Unification) (1848–1849, 1859, and 1866)

## Causes

The Wars of Italian Independence, also known as the Wars of Italian Unification, are usually identified as occurring in 1848–1849, 1859, and 1866. When the wars of the French Revolution and the Napoleonic era began in 1792, Italy was little more than a geographical expression—a patchwork of 15 small states, each in rivalry with, if not openly hostile to, the others. Not since the days of the Roman Empire had the Italian Peninsula been united politically.

The wars of the period 1792–1815 had a profound impact on Italy, however. The French Army of Italy commanded by Napoleon Bonaparte had conquered much of the peninsula and introduced a uniform system of laws and administration. Napoleon had also reduced the number of states to three. Part of northwestern and east-central Italy was incorporated into France, and there was the Kingdom of Italy in the northeast and the Kingdom of Naples in southern Italy. Napoleon, the great practitioner of French nationalism, had also declared at St. Helena that "Italy is one nation."

The example of what the French had accomplished with a more effectively administered nationalist state was not lost on the Italians. The Congress of Vienna of 1814–1815, which met to redraw the map of Europe after the defeat of Napoleon, had resurrected the old Italy of many different monarchial states dominated in the north by Austria. Small nationalist uprisings in the immediate aftermath of the Napoleonic Wars by the so-called Carbonari had been easily crushed. Nonetheless, the peninsula was swept by a new spirit, what came to be called the Risorgimento (Resurgence).

Three men played key roles in the unification of Italy to follow. They were Giuseppe Mazzini (1805–1872), Count Camillo Benso di Cavour (1810–1861), and Giuseppe Garibaldi (1807–1882). English poet George Meredith wrote of them "Cavour, Mazzini, Garibaldi: Three: Her Brain, her Soul, her Sword."

Mazzini devoted his life to the cause of Italian independence and unity. This, he believed, should be entrusted to the young. In 1832 Mazzini organized among Italian exiles in Marseille, France, the first "lodge" of Young Italy. Established in Italy at Genoa, this organization soon spread throughout northern and central Italy and then the entire peninsula. The banner of the organization had the words "Unity and Independence" on the one side and "Liberty, Equality, Humanity" on the other. Members agreed to promote the national ideal, regardless of personal cost.

Mazzini believed strongly that all states should be organized on the basis of nationality and that, in keeping with the dignity of the individual, the only acceptable form of government was a republic. Not all Italian nationalists favored this, however. A number wanted to see Italy united under a limited monarchy; these individuals looked to the Kingdom of Sardinia (most often known at the time and since as Piedmont-Sardinia or Sardinia-Piedmont

## BATTLE OF SOLFERINO, JUNE 24, 1859

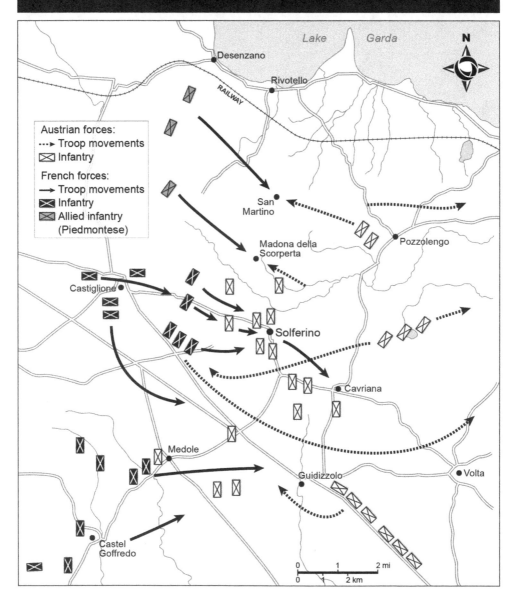

for its two component territories). Others favored a federation of states under the presidency of the pope.

In 1833 Mazzini's plan for revolution in northern Italy was discovered by the authorities before it could be carried out. Many of his followers were arrested, and a dozen were executed. Mazzini himself was tried in absentia and sentenced to death. He tried again the next year. The revolt was in Piedmont, and among its participants was Italian sailor cum nationalist Giuseppe Garibaldi, who had recently joined the movement at Genoa. However,

THE UNIFICATION OF ITALY, 1859–1870

Piedmontese authorities easily crushed the revolt during January 31–February 1, 1834.

In 1846 Giovanni Maria Mastai-Ferretti became pope as Pius IX. The Papal States of central Italy were notorious in their poor government, and Pius IX was soon hailed as a reformer. He released numerous political prisoners, permitted freedom of the press, allowed Rome to have its own city government, and carried out a number of other reforms that endeared him to liberals. Also regarded as an Italian nationalist, Pius IX arranged a customs treaty with Piedmont and Tuscany that could have been the start of political unification for all of Italy, and he adopted a hostile stance toward Austria. Pius began to backtrack, however,

## Italian Wars of Independence (1848–1849, 1859, and 1866)

| Battle of Custoza (July 24–25, 1848)* | | |
|---|---|---|
| | **Piedmont-Sardinian Forces** | **Austrian Forces** |
| **Strength** | 22,000 men | 33,000 men |
| **Total casualties** | 1,507 men | 3,813 men |

*Despite suffering higher losses, the Austrians triumphed at Custoza.

| Battle of Magenta (June 4, 1859) | | |
|---|---|---|
| | **French and Sardinian Forces** | **Austrian Forces** |
| **Strength** | 54,000 men | 58,000 men |
| **Total casualties** | 4,515 men | 10,406 men* |

*Of this number, approximately 4,500 men were taken prisoner.

| Battle of Solferino (June 24, 1859)* | | |
|---|---|---|
| | **French and Sardinian Forces** | **Austrian Forces** |
| **Strength** | 138,000 men, 366 guns | 129,000 men, 429 guns |
| **Total casualties** | 17,191 men | 22,097 men |

*This was the largest battle to occur in Europe since the Battle of Leipzig in 1813.

| Battle of Custoza (June 24, 1866) | | |
|---|---|---|
| | **Italian Forces** | **Austrian Forces** |
| **Strength** | 65,000 men, 122 guns | 75,000 men, 168 guns |
| **Total casualties** | 8,100 men* | 5,600 men** |

*This includes 4,300 men taken prisoner.
**This includes 1,000 men missing or taken prisoner.

| Estimated Battle Deaths during Key Events in the Italian Wars of Independence | | | | | |
|---|---|---|---|---|---|
| Conflict | Papal States | Piedmont-Sardinia | Two Sicilies | Austria | France |
| Austro-Sardinian War (1848–1849) | —* | 3,400 | — | 5,600 | — |
| Sicilian Antigovernment Revolt (1848–1849) | — | — | 1,000 | — | — |
| Defeat of the Roman Republic (1849) | 1,500 | — | 100 | 100 | 500 |
| War of Independence (1859) | — | 2,500 | — | 12,500 | 7,500 |
| Italo-Roman War (1860) | 700 | 300 | — | — | — |
| Italo-Sicilian War (1860) | — | 600 | 400 | — | — |
| Austro-Prussian War (1866) | — | 4,000 | | 20,000 | — |
| Capture of Rome (1870) | 20 | 50 | | — | — |

* Did not participate in the conflict or statistics are unavailable.

**Sources:** Beales, Derek Edward Dawson. *The Risorgimento and the Unification of Italy*. New York: Barnes and Noble, 1971; De Cesare, Raffaele. *The Last Days of Papal Rome*. London: Archibald Constable, 1909; Small, Melvin, and Joel David Singer. *Resort to Arms: International and Civil Wars 1816–1980*. Thousand Oaks, CA: Sage, 1982.

when he realized the full implications of the reform movement, which were at sharp variance with papal sovereignty.

In Vienna there was great concern over the revolutionary agitation in Italy. Old field marshal Joseph Radetsky von Radetz (1756–1868), viceroy of Lombardy-Venetia, then part of the Austrian Empire, favored a strong stand, and in July 1847 following revolutionary agitation and disorders there, Austrian troops occupied Ferrara, one of the papal legations in which Austria had garrisoning rights. This action, however, greatly inflamed Italian nationalism.

In late 1847, Grand Duke Leopold of Tuscany and King Charles Albert of Piedmont-Sardinia were both forced to grant constitutions. In January 1848 the people of Palermo, Sicily, rioted against their reactionary ruler, King Ferdinand II; he too was forced to grant a constitution. Then on March 18 revolt broke out in Milan, the capital of Lombardy. In the so-called Five Days of Milan, Radetsky was forced to withdraw Austrian troops from the city. They retreated to the stronghold at the foot of the Alps known as the Quadrilateral, consisting of the cities of Mantua, Verona, Peschiera, and Legnago.

SPENCER C. TUCKER

## Course

### First Italian War of Independence (1848–1849)

With the unrest and seeming success of revolutionaries in various parts of Italy, on March 22, 1848, King Charles Albert of Piedmont-Sardinia declared war on Austria in what he believed would be a war of national liberation by Italians alone. Indeed, he boasted "Italia fera da se" (Italy will do it by itself). Thousands of volunteers from other parts of Italy, including troops from the Papal States, joined the 60,000-man army of Piedmont-Sardinia. On March 26, 1848, fortified by what had happened in Milan, revolutionaries seized control of the arsenal in Venice and organized both a civic guard and a provisional government. Austrian forces evacuated Venice on March 26, and Venice was declared a republic under the leadership of revolutionary Daniele Manin. In mid-June, however, Radetsky assumed the offensive and soon reestablished Austrian control in Lombardy and in most of Venetia except Venice.

Charles Albert's troops proved to be poorly trained and equipped and ineffectively led. Sharp divisions also developed among the allied Italian contingents, and under heavy Austrian pressure, Pope Pius IX withdrew the papal forces and announced his neutrality in a war with another Catholic power. Radetzky's men were not only better trained but also enjoyed the advantage of numbers (33,000 to 22,000).

The two sides joined battle at Custoza near Verona during June 24–25. The fighting was fierce, and casualties were heavier on the Austrian side (3,813 for the Austrians, 1,507 for Piedmont-Sardinia), but the Austrians triumphed. King Charles Albert now appealed to France for assistance, but the new republican government in Paris was dealing with the massive worker uprising in Paris known as the June Days and was in no position to intervene.

Radetsky then drove Charles Albert's troops from Lombardy, and on August 9 Piedmont-Sardinian Army chief of staff General Carlo Canera di Salasco concluded a six-month armistice, expecting to resume the struggle on its termination. On their part, the Austrians needed to concentrate on crushing the revolution that had swept Hungary.

In November 1848, papal prime minister Pellegrino Rossi, a liberal whose reforms were nonetheless insufficient for many, was assassinated in Rome. A revolt occurred, and Pius IX fled to Gaeta. On February 9, 1849, a constituent assembly declared Rome a republic. The effects of this were great especially in northern Italy, where Charles Albert, under considerable pressure from radicals in Piedmont, renounced the armistice and again took up arms against Austria.

Assembling an army of 75,000 men and 141 guns, Radetzky invaded Piedmont and defeated Charles Albert's army of 87,500 men and 109 guns on March 22–23 in the Battle of Novara. The Piedmont-Sardinian side suffered some 2,000 casualties, the Austrians a bit more. Charles Albert was forced to sign a second armistice and abdicate the throne in favor of his son, Victor Emmanuel II. Piedmont-Sardinia did, however, retain its liberal constitution of 1848. Radetzky's victory also allowed him to send part of his forces north to assist in the battle against the Hungarians. In northern Italy, only the city of Venice now held out against the Austrians. Peace with Piedmont-Sardinia was formally concluded on August 9, with the latter forced to pay an indemnity of 65 million francs. Although Charles Albert's efforts had failed completely, Italian patriots now looked to the Kingdom of Sardinia for leadership in the unification struggle.

The news of the defeat at Novara led revolutionaries in Rome at the end of March to reorganize their government along more moderate, conciliatory lines, with Mazzini being the best-known figure in the new government. Despite this, the new leaders of Austria (Emperor Franz Joseph I) and France (President Louis Napoleon Bonaparte) each considered sending troops to restore Pius IX to power. With the Austrian Army still heavily engaged against the Hungarians, Bonaparte moved first. In April 1849 the French assembly voted funds for a military expedition, supposedly to forestall Austrian intervention but in reality prompted by Bonaparte's hopes of winning the political support of French Catholics.

On April 24, French marshal Nicolas Oudinot and some 8,000 men landed at Città Vecchia, Italy, and then moved against Rome. Believing that the republicans enjoyed only limited support, Oudinot ordered an assault on the city. The defenders, commanded by Garibaldi, repulsed the French attacks of April 29–30. The republicans also deflected attacks by the Neapolitan army at Palestrina (May 9) and at Velletri (May 19).

French government emissary Ferdinand de Lesseps (later the builder of the Suez Canal) reached an understanding with the republican government of Rome that would have allowed French troops into the city in return for French acceptance of the new republic and a guarantee to protect Rome against other foreign intervention. Bonaparte, however, disavowed it. He then reinforced Oudinot and ordered him to take Rome by force.

On June 3, French troops again assaulted Rome and, in desperate fighting, were again repulsed. Oudinot was then forced to commence siege operations. At the request of Pius IX, Spain also sent some 9,000 troops. Realizing that the situation was hopeless, on June 30 Garibaldi came to terms with Oudinot. Garibaldi and some 4,000 volunteers were allowed to march out of the city on July 2. They hoped to join the defenders of the Republic of

Venice but were soon pursued by French, Austrian, Spanish, and Italian loyalist forces, and most were captured, killed, or dispersed. Garibaldi was among those able to escape and ended up in exile in the United States.

Although republican Venice had come under blockade by the Austrians months earlier, on May 26, 1849, the defenders were forced to abandon Fort Marghera. Food was in short supply. On June 19 the powder magazine blew up, and the next month cholera broke out. The Austrians then begin to shell the city, and when the Piedmont-Sardinian fleet withdrew from the Adriatic, the Austrians were also able to attack Venice from the sea.

On August 24, 1849, with food and ammunition exhausted, Manin negotiated the city's capitulation, securing amnesty for all except himself and a few others who were nonetheless allowed to go into exile. Manin departed Venice three days later in a French ship; he died in exile in France in 1857.

## Second Italian War of Independence (1859)

The lessons of 1848–1849 were clear. First, the unification of Italy would not be achieved around the papacy, for when Pius IX returned to Rome it was as a confirmed reactionary. Second, Italy could not "do it by itself." Outside assistance, most likely that of France, would be necessary in throwing off the Austrian yoke. Third, Italian nationalists now regarded Piedmont-Sardinia, which had demonstrated its steadfastness by twice going to war against Austria, as the natural leader in the independence/unification struggle.

Piedmont-Sardinia was now widely regarded as a progressive state. As minister of commerce and agriculture during 1850–1852, Count Cavour did much to transform the state economically and in 1852 was rewarded with appointment as prime minister. Displaying extraordinary political and diplomatic skills, Cavour became the real power in the state, and it was he who now directed the unification struggle until his death in 1861.

Cavour embarked on a series of political, social, and economic reforms to make the kingdom a model of parliamentary monarchy and an exemplar for the rest of Italy. In January 1855 he took his country into the Crimean War (1854–1856) to gain the support of Britain and France, and he used the Congress of Paris at the end of that conflict to expound on the problems of Italy.

In 1856, leading Italian nationalists formed the National Society to support the unification of Italy under the Kingdom of Sardinia. Then on January 14, 1858, Italian nationalist Felice Orsini, angered by the failure of now emperor Napoleon III, a participant in his youth in the Italian revolutionary movement, to support the present unification movement, attempted to assassinate him. This event seems to have goaded Napoleon into action, for on July 20, 1858, he met with Cavour at Plombières in southeastern France and there concluded a secret agreement.

The Pact of Plombières called for the two powers to goad Austria into war against Piedmont-Sardinia, at which point France would come to its assistance with 200,000 men. The two countries would then fight until Italy was "free from sea to sea" and they had established a kingdom of northern Italy consisting of Piedmont-Sardinia, Lombardy, Venetia, Parma, Modena, and the Papal Legations of Ravenna, Ferrara, and Bologna. Napoleon wanted a federation of Italian states under French influence to include the new kingdom of northern Italy as well as a kingdom of central Italy (Tuscany with Umbria and the Marches), Rome and its surrounding territory, and the Kingdom of Naples. All of these would be under the presidency of the pope. In return for French aid against Austria, Piedmont-Sardonoa would then cede Nice and Savoy to France.

To cement the pact, Princess Clotilde, daughter of King Victor Emmanuel II, was betrothed to Prince Joseph Charles Bonaparte, cousin of Napoleon III. (They were married in January 1859.) The formal treaty was signed on December 10, 1858, after Napoleon assured himself of the goodwill of Russian czar Alexander II.

In January 1859 Napoleon III publicly complained about the plight of Italy and unsatisfactory relations with Austria, while articles in the official French press attacked Austrian rule there. Many ardent French Catholics expressed alarm, however, regarding the direction of events and possible threats to the papacy. Finding his Italian policy opposed by his wife Eugénie and a majority of his cabinet ministers, Napoleon wavered.

On March 9 Cavour mobilized his army, calling up reserves and also recruiting volunteers, many of whom were from Lombardy. This was a direct provocation to Austria, and on April 9 Emperor Franz Joseph I authorized mobilization of the Austrian Army. Then, with Napoleon III of France backtracking, on April 20 the Austrian government made a fatal error in sending an ultimatum to Piedmont-Sardinia, giving it three days to demobilize. Cavour, believing that the opportunity for war was lost, had on April 19 already ordered demobilization, but with no direct telegraph link between Turin (Turnio) and Vienna, Austrian leaders were unaware of this. The Austrian ultimatum appeared to be an act of diplomatic bullying and provided Cavour with the excuse he needed for war. Piedmont-Sardinia rejected the ultimatum, and on April 29 Habsburg forces invaded Piedmont.

On May 3, 1859, France declared war on Austria. The ensuing conflict is known as the Franco-Austrian War, the Second War of Italian Independence, and the Austro-Sardinian War. For three weeks inept Austrian commander Field Marshal Count Franz Gyulai marched and countermarched, failing to take advantage of his superior numbers and allowing French troops to come up. Napoleon III arrived at Genoa by sea on May 12 to take personal command.

In the first real engagement of the war, Gyulai, perhaps under prodding from Vienna, ordered General Count Stadion to mount a reconnaissance in force with his corps toward Voghera in Lombardy on May 20. At about noon, this Habsburg force of some 27,000 men encountered near Montebello a French infantry division and some Piedmontese cavalry totaling perhaps 8,000 men. French division commander General Elias Forey audaciously attacked. Only a portion of the Habsburg force took part, and after two hours of fighting the French drove the Austrians from Montebello. Stadion, having sustained 1,300 casualties, withdrew all the way to Stradella. Allied casualties totaled 730. Assuming that the rest of Gyulai's force would resume the attack the next day, Forey also withdrew. Although not a major battle, Montebello brought great prestige to the French and was a major morale boost for the allies and a corresponding depressant for the Austrians.

With all the French troops and their equipment having arrived, the allies now took the offensive, planning to advance on Novara and then to Milan. On the allied right flank, part of the Piedmontese army advanced to Robbio, where on the morning of May 30 it crossed the Sesia River and, following hard fighting, captured Palestro, Confienza, and Vinzaglio. The next day, Habsburg general Fredrick Zobel counterattacked at the village of Palestro with some 14,000 man and 42 guns against the Piedmontese under King Victor Emmanuel II. The previous night the king had called up reinforcements in the form of a French Zouave regiment, so the allies had 21,000 men and 36 guns.

In the Battle of Palestro the allies repulsed the Austrians, suffering some 600 casualties against Austrian losses of 1,600. The allies, however, had 50,000 men within several hours' march and had not used these superior resources, nor did they pursue the retreating Austrians.

On June 4, the two sides clashed at Magenta in one of the two major engagements of the war. This battle pitted 54,000 French troops against 58,000 Austrians. Napoleon III planned a pincer movement against the Austrians by maneuvering the II Corps of General Marie Edme Patrice Maurice MacMahon on the left bank of the Ticino while the Imperial Guard and the III and IV Corps crossed the stream farther south. The French did not expect the Austrians to react prior to the closing of the pincers.

The Austrians, however, had already decided to retreat to the northeast. They were even slower in their withdrawal than MacMahon was in his advance, and the two sides came together on the morning of June 4. MacMahon's corps managed to break through and win the battle, chiefly owing to the élan of the French infantry, the highly effective fire of French rifled artillery, and the inept performance of

Habsburg commander Gyulai. The Austrians, however, withdrew unmolested in good order to Robecco. French casualties totaled 4,515, while the Austrians lost 10,406 (including 4,500 taken prisoner). On June 8, Napoleon III and Victor Emmanuel II made a triumphal entry into Milan.

Napoleon III then ordered Marshal Achille Baraguey d'Hillie, supported on his right by General Adolphe Niel's IV Corps and on his left by MacMahon's II Corps, to attack Austrian forces 18 miles southeast of Milan at Melegnano. Battle was joined in the early evening on June 8.

Poor tactics denied the French the opportunity to trap the isolated Austrians. Failing to wait for McMahon's corps to arrive, Baraguay d'Hilliers immediately launched an infantry attack without adequate artillery support. Habsburg general Ritter Ludwig August von Benedek's VIII Corps was heavily entrenched and barricaded in the small medieval town, and their rifle fire exacted a heavy toll. The French II Corps did not arrive in time for the battle, which ended at nightfall with the Austrians withdrawing in good order. The French sustained 948 casualties, the Austrians 1,480. The French then returned to Milan.

Franz Joseph then dismissed Gyulai. Assuming personal command himself, he moved against the French and Piedmont-Sardinian forces. Thanks to poor reconnaissance, the ensuing battle and culmination of the war came as a surprise to both sides. As with other battles of the war, that of Solferino on June 24 saw little recognition on the part of the generals of the tremendous defensive firepower of the rifled musket behind field entrenchments. It was also marked by poor coordination of forces; men were committed to battle en masse as

Napoleon III (left) at the Battle of Solferino, after a painting by Jean-Louis-Ernest Meissonier. At Solferino, forces from France and Sardinia-Piedmont defeated the Austrians. This bloody fight on June 24, 1859, and suffering of the wounded in the battle, led to the creation of the Red Cross. (Library of Congress)

they arrived, charging in large frontal assaults with the bayonet.

The forces involved were quite large; indeed, Solferino was the biggest battle in Europe since Leipzig in 1813. The French and Piedmontese had some 138,000 men and 366 guns, while the Austrians committed 129,000 men and 429 guns. The allies enjoyed superiority in cavalry, while the Austrians had the advantage of fighting from defensive positions. The battle was concentrated along the Mincio River, centered on the town of Solferino. MacMahon commanded the French forces. Napoleon III, King Victor Emanuel II, and Franz Joseph I were all present.

Fighting began at 4:00 a.m when the advance elements on each side stumbled upon the other. Much of the ensuing combat was hand to hand, with the battle decided by the bravery of the attacking French and Piedmontese infantry. The fighting lasted until about 8:00 p.m. with the collapse of the Austrian center and subsequent general withdrawal, saved from a rout only by the effective leadership of General Benedek.

Although the allies trumpeted a great victory, it was a hollow one. The allies had suffered 17,191 casualties, the Austrians 22,097. The suffering of the wounded was made all the more horrible because of totally inadequate ambulance services. Many lay for days under a hot sun until they were tended to. Swiss businessman Henri Dunant witnessed the battle and its aftermath, and in 1862 he published a small book about his experiences and efforts to tend to the wounded. Dunant suggested that each country form societies to care for wounded from battle, and this led in 1864 to the formation in Geneva of the International Committee of the Red Cross.

The bloodshed of Solferino caused Napoleon misgivings. He was also concerned about a mobilization of forces by Prussia and possible military intervention by that country on the Rhine while the best French troops were committed in Italy. Habsburg troops also now occupied strong defensive positions in the Quadrilateral. And it was apparent that Napoleon III had misread the strength of the Italian unification movement and that the likely result of a total Austrian defeat would be a unitary Italian state rather than the loose confederation under French influence that he had envisioned. Finally, French public opinion had turned against the war.

In light of all of this, Napoleon III abandoned his ally and pledge to free Italy "from sea to sea" and unilaterally concluded an armistice with the Austrians on July 8, 1859. He then met with Franz Josef I at Villafranca on July 11. The Austrian emperor agreed to turn over to France all of Lombardy, except for the fortress cities of Mantua and Peschiera, with the understanding that France would then cede the territory to Piedmont-Sardinia. Austria would retain control of Venetia. The rulers of Modena, Parma, and Tuscany—all unseated by nationalist uprisings during the war—were to be returned to their thrones. The terms were formally ratified by the Treaty of Zurich on November 10, 1859. Italian nationalists were outraged by events, and Cavour foolishly urged Victor Emmanuel II to continue the war alone. When the king refused, Cavour resigned.

In the late summer of 1859 popularly elected assemblies in Parma, Modena, Tuscany, and the Ramagna called for union with Piedmont-Sardinia. The latter was, however, reluctant to agree without the approval of Napoleon III. In January 1860 Cavour returned as prime minister and negotiated the annexation of these states. Napoleon III insisted on and received from Piedmont both Nice and Savoy. In early March, plebiscites in Parma, Modena, Tuscany, and the Ramagna duly approved annexation to Piedmont. Another plebiscite confirmed the transfer of Nice and Savoy to France in the Treaty of Turin on March 24.

## Garibaldi Secures Sicily and Naples (1860)

Meanwhile, following an abortive uprising led by Rosolino Pilo in Sicily against King Francis II on March 4, 1860, Giuseppe Garibaldi handpicked a force of some 1,150 volunteers to continue the work of Italian unification. It was known as the One Thousand (in Italian, Mille) or, for their makeshift uniforms, the Red Shirts. Most had served under Garibaldi in the war against Austria and respected his leadership.

Having received secret financial support and arms from Cavour, Garibaldi sailed from Genoa in two steamers, arriving at Marsala in western Sicily on May 11. Several Neapolitan Navy gunboats appeared and, although delayed by the presence of several British warships, sank one of the steamers and captured the other. Garibaldi, however, was able to get all his men ashore and march inland.

Garibaldi announced that he was assuming the dictatorship of Sicily in the name of Victor Emmanuel II, "King of Italy." Although Bourbon king of the two Sicilies (Naples and Sicily) Francis II had an army of some 100,000 men, he was unpopular with his subjects, and Garibaldi gathered recruits as he proceeded toward Palermo.

At Calatafimi on May 15, Garibaldi did battle with General Francisco Landi and 2,000 men of the Neapolitan Army. In this sharp action Garibaldi recklessly exposed himself to enemy fire in rallying his men, but the One Thousand were victorious. They suffered some 30 dead and 150 wounded, 100 of them so badly that they could not proceed, but the Neapolitan forces fled to Palermo.

Increasing numbers of Sicilians rallied to Garibaldi, who advanced on the Sicilian capital of Palermo, now held by some 22,000 Neapolitan troops under General Ferdinando Lanza. On May 27 although he had only about 750 men able to fight, Garibaldi attacked. A significant portion of Palermo's 180,000 residents rallied to Garibaldi, including some 2,000 prisoners liberated from the local jails, and on the first day of fighting the Neapolitan forces were driven back from a number of key positions. Lanza then shelled that part of the city that had been lost, leading to some 600 civilian deaths during a three-day span. By May 28, though, Garibaldi controlled much of Palermo, and on May 29 the One Thousand defeated a Neapolitan counterattack, and Lanza requested a truce.

With the arrival of two battalions of well-trained and well-equipped Bavarian mercenaries in the employ of the Bourbons, however, the situation looked bleak for Garibaldi, whose men were almost out of ammunition. He was saved by Lanza's decision to surrender on May 30. An armistice was hastily arranged by British admiral George Rodney Mundy, and a convention on June 6 provided for the withdrawal by sea from Palermo of some 22,000 royal troops, to be effected by June 19.

In late June in a bid to win moderate support for his regime, Francis II formed a liberal ministry and adopted the liberal constitution of 1848. This came too late. With the fall of Palermo, only Syracuse, Augusta, Milazzo, and Messina remained under Bourbon control. Cavour, now worried by the pace of Garibaldi's victories and unsure of his intentions, sent an envoy calling for the immediate annexation of Sicily to Piedmont, but Garibaldi rejected this, pending completion of his mission.

Garibaldi then created the Southern Army, reinforced by volunteers from throughout Italy and some regular Piedmontese troops sent by Cavour. Against these, Francis II mustered 24,000 men at Messina and the other fortress cities. Garibaldi also had to contend with lawlessness as peasants revolted against the landowners.

On July 20 Garibaldi and 4,000 of his men attacked Milazzo, held by perhaps 3,000 Bourbon troops under General Bosco. The attackers suffered 750 killed or wounded, while the Neapolitan troops, who were fighting from cover, sustained only 150 casualties, although they were eventually forced to surrender. Under terms of the capitulation, the defenders were allowed to depart on July 24 with the full honors of war, leaving Garibaldi the fortress guns, munitions, and stores. Shortly thereafter, Messina surrendered. All remaining Sicilian strongholds capitulated by the end of September.

Not content to rest on his laurels, Garibaldi was adamant about campaigning in southern Italy and defeating the remaining Neapolitan forces. Cavour at first opposed this but then agreed. On August 22, Garibaldi crossed the narrow Straits of Messina with an initial force of 4,000 men. He faced in southern Calabria perhaps 20,000 well-equipped Neapolitian Army troops. Apart from some relatively minor battles, Garibaldi's progression to Naples was an easy one.

King Francis II still had some 40,000 men. Plans to block Garibaldi on the plain between Eboli and Salerno evaporated, however, and on September 5 the entire Neopolitan cabinet resigned. Two days later Garibaldi entered Naples in triumph, while Francis II fled to the fortress of Gaeta. Garibaldi planned to defeat the remaining Neapolitan troops, then march on Rome and conquer Venetia.

Although Garibaldi had always professed loyalty to King Victor Emmanuel II, Cavour was worried about the international impact of Garibaldi's future plans. Cavour also feared that a march on Rome would bring French intervention, while one on Venetia would assuredly mean a new war with Austria. An uprising in the Papal States on September 8, 1860, however, gave Cavour the opportunity to take leadership of the campaign for Italian unification out of Garibaldi's hands.

When the papacy rejected Cavour's demands that it disband its foreign military force, on September 10 Cavour sent Piedmontese forces south into papal territory. The British government supported the move, fearing a Muratist (French) restoration in Naples. There was other fighting, but the principal battle occurred on September 18 at Castelfidaro, a dozen miles south of Ancona. Although overall the Piedmontese forces were considerably larger than those of the papacy, at Castelfidaro each side deployed only about 3,000 men. The Pedmontese were commanded by General Enrico Cialdini, while the papal side was commanded by expatriate French general and commander of the papal army Louis Christophe Léon Juchault de Lamorcière.

The Piedmontese lost several dozen dead and about 140 wounded. Papal losses were not much greater, but the battle was decisive, for the papal forces dissolved virtually overnight. Piedmontese forces then advanced into Neapolitan territory and linked up with Garibaldi.

King of Naples Francis II meanwhile hoped that with his sizable remaining forces he could defeat Garibaldi before the Piedmontese army could arrive. Battle was joined north of Naples in northern Campania between Capua and Maddaloni along the Volturno River. General Giosuè Ritucci commanded 31,200 Neapolitan troops; Garibaldi had only about 20,000 men.

Ritucci attacked at dawn on October 1. The battle raged for most of the day and ended in a Neapolitan defeat. Garibaldi sustained 2,017 casualties. Bourbon losses are not known with any certainty but were probably no fewer than 1,000 killed or wounded, with 2,000 taken prisoner the next day.

During October 21–22, Naples and Sicily voted by plebiscite to join Piedmont-Sardinia. Similar favorable votes occurred in the Marches (November 4) and Umbria (November 5). On October 26 at Teano in northern Campania, Garibaldi met with King Victor Emmanuel II. Garibaldi requested that he be allowed to remain for one year as dictator of the former Kingdom of the Two Sicilies and that his officers be absorbed into the new Italian Army. Victor Emmanuel, however, refused both requests, whereupon Garibaldi returned to his home at Caprera.

Beginning on November 3, 1860, Piedmontese forces laid siege to Gaeta, where former Neapolitan king Francis II had taken refuge with his remaining forces. The siege was protracted by actions undertaken by the French, as Napoleon III had ordered French Mediterranean Squadron commander Vice Admiral Marie Charles Adelbert Le Barbier de Tinan to position his own ships between those of the Piedmontese and the forts ashore. Under growing British diplomatic pressure, however, the French withdrew their ships on January 10. Gaeta surrendered on February 14, and Francis II went into exile in Austria.

On March 17, 1861, King Victor Emmanuel of Piedmont-Sardinia became Victor Emmanuel I, king of Italy, under a constitution based on that of Piedmont-Sardinia from 1848. Italy was now united except for Rome and the territory around it held by the pope and Venetia, still under Austrian control. Unfortunately for Italy, its brilliant statesman Cavour died on June 6 at only age 51 just when his wise stewardship was most needed.

Agreement was reached between Italy and France on September 15, 1864, regarding the status of Rome. The Italian government promised to protect the Papal States against external menaces (i.e., Garibaldi's nationalists), and the French government promised to withdraw its troops from Rome within two years, allowing sufficient time for the creation of an effective papal army.

## Third War of Italian Unification (1866)

Prussian minister-president Otto von Bismarck, confident in the military reforms enacted in his country, was now actively planning war against Austria to bring about the unification of Germany under Prussian leadership. To proceed, however, he first had to isolate Austria. To secure French neutrality, Bismarck traveled to Biarritz and on October 4, 1865, met with Napoleon III. Promised unspecified "compensation" on the left bank of the Rhine, Napoleon pledged French neutrality. Napoleon was hardly the innocent in this. He expected a protracted struggle (after all, the last war between Austria and Prussia lasted for seven years, during 1756–1763), with France able to step in and dictate a settlement.

To encourage the war that he saw as being to his advantage, Napoleon urged Bismarck to make an ally of Italy. In return for its participation in a war against Austria, Italy would receive compensation in

the form of Venetia. On April 8, 1866, Prussia and Italy concluded a secret alliance whereby Italy promised to join Prussia if war were to begin between Prussia and Austria within three months, with the promise of Venetia as a reward.

With war between Prussia and Austria now looming, on June 12 Napoleon III signed a secret treaty with Austria. France promised to remain neutral in the forthcoming conflict and also to work for Italian neutrality. (Napoleon had, of course, already encouraged Italy to conclude a treaty with Prussia!) In return Austria agreed to cede Venetia to France, which would then hand it over to Italy whether or not Austria won the war. If Austria were to win the war and its reorganization of Germany upset the balance of power, as was bound to be the case, Vienna promised not to object to the organization of a buffer state under French influence in the Rhineland. Napoleon stupidly assumed that he could not lose.

War between Prussia and Austria commenced on June 14, and six days later Italy declared war on Austria in accordance with its secret treaty with Prussia. Italy's strategic plan called for an invasion of Austrian Venetia along the Mincio and Po Rivers by some 200,000 men and 370 guns, an area defended by the Austrian South Army of 75,000 men and 168 guns. The critical battle of the campaign occurred at the old battlefield of Custoza, southwest of Verona. In a major tactical blunder, Italian general Alfonso Ferrero di La Marmora, unaware of the South Army's strength and dispositions, managed to get only 65,000 troops and 122 guns across the Mincio. These confronted virtually the entire Austrian South Army under Field Marshal Archduke Albrecht.

In the daylong Battle of Custozza on June 24, the Austrians defeated the Italian columns piecemeal and drove them back across the Mincio into Lombardy. Albrecht did not pursue. The Italians sustained 3,800 killed or wounded and 4,300 taken prisoner. Austrian casualties totaled 4,600 killed or wounded and 1,000 missing. On July 3 Emperor Napoleon III arranged the transfer of Austrian-held Venetia to France, then ceded it to Italy.

It was fortunate for the Prussians that Archduke Albrecht had been assigned the command in Italy, for Benedekt, who commanded against the Prussians, fumbled away a good chance of victory over them in the decisive battle of the Austro-Prussian War at Königgrätz (also known as the Battle of Sadowa) in Bohemia on July 3.

During July 3–21 meanwhile, Garibaldi, given a general's commission and command of 10,000 men and a flotilla on Lake Garda, fought a series of small indecisive engagements with the Austrians: Monte Asello (July 3), where he was among the wounded; Lodorone (July 7); Darso (July 10); Candino (July 16); Ampola (July 19); and, in the largest engagement of the campaign, Bezzecca (July 21). Garibaldi was about to attack Trent when he was ordered to withdraw. Bismarck had made it clear that he would not permit the Italians to hold part of the Trentine Tirol (Tyrol).

On July 20, 1866, the only naval battle of the war occurred, in the Adriatic between Italy and Austria. Italy had built up its navy before the war, adding ironclads acquired from Britain and the United States. Unfortunately for Italy, at the insistence of Victor Emmanuel II the incompetent Admiral Count Carlo Pellion di Persano commanded the Italian fleet. Energetic young rear admiral Wilhelm von Tegetthoff commanded the Austrian Fleet.

Ordered to sea, Persano sortied on July 15 with virtually the entire Italian Navy but sailed not to Pola, where the Austrian Navy was located, but instead to seek an easy victory against the Austrian Adriatic island of Lissa. For two days the Italian ships bombarded Lissa with little effect, while the Italian ironclad capital ship *Formidabile* of 20 guns was badly damaged by shore fire and suffered 60 casualties.

News of the Italian attack reached Pola, and on July 19 Tegetthoff sortied for Lissa with 21 warships, 7 of them ironclads, with his flag in the ironclad frigate *Erzherzog Ferdinand Maximilian*. In all, his ships displaced 57,300 tons, mounted 532 guns, and carried 7,870 men. Persano commanded 31 ships, 12 of them ironclads. They displaced 86,000 tons, mounted 645 guns, and carried 10,900 men. The Italians thus had the advantage in all except leadership and discipline.

The Austrians were sighted at dawn on July 20. Persano had no contingency plan and, moreover, was engaged in landing troops on Lissa, but by 10:00 a.m. the Italian ships were under way. Tegetthoff ordered his armored ships to charge the Italian vessels and attempt to ram and sink them. Both sides also fired on the other, and some of the Italian ships attempted to ram the Austrian vessels before Persano broke off the action. The Italians lost two ships (one to a ram), and four others were badly damaged. They also suffered 619 dead and 39 wounded. Later another Italian ship foundered in a squall off Ancona, largely because of damage sustained at Lissa. Austrian losses were only several ships damaged, with 38 men killed and 138 wounded.

The Battle of Lissa was notable as the first between oceangoing ironclad fleets at sea. It was also the only major fleet encounter between ironclads and one with the principal tactic being ramming. Even though only one ship was sunk by this method during the battle, for the next three decades the world's navies made the ram standard equipment in battleship construction. Unfortunately for the Austrians, however, their victory at sea went for naught. The Prussian triumph on land at König-gratz (Sadowa) had decided the war. The Treaty of Vienna of October 12, 1866, that formally ended the Austro-Prussian War confirmed Italy's annexation of Venetia.

## The Addition of Rome (1870)

Concerned about open preparations by Garibaldi to raise 10,000 volunteers to march into papal territory and capture Rome and the effect that this would have on his support in France, in October 1967 Napoleon III ordered French forces to return to Rome to preserve the remaining papal territory. Garibaldi had indeed planned both an uprising in Rome and a march on the city. The uprising occurred on October 22 when the rebels seized part of the city but were then defeated by papal forces. The last group of rebels was captured on October 25.

Meanwhile, the 2,000-man French expeditionary force, commanded by General Pierre Louis Charles de Failly, arrived at Civitavecchia on October 26 and prepared to do battle with Garibaldi's ragtag force of some 8,000 men, which had arrived on the outskirts of Rome after defeating a papal force, mostly of foreign volunteers, sent against them at Monte Rotondo on October 24.

On November 3 near the village of Mantana, northeast of Rome, Garibaldi's men joined battle with the French and some 3,000 papal troops under General Hermann Kanzler. Garibaldi was defeated,

in part because of the excellent French chassepot rifle, here making its first battlefield appearance. The allies took some 800 prisoners. Garibaldi and 5,100 men returned to the Kingdom of Italy, where they were arrested.

Rome was added to the Kingdom of Italy in 1870, however. Taking advantage of the withdrawal of French troops on August 19, 1870, as a consequence of the Franco-Prussian War, General Raffaele Cardona led 60,000 Kingdom of Italy troops to invest the city. On September 20 following a short bombardment, his forces effected a breach in the walls at Porta Pia and entered Rome. Pope Pius IX then ordered his troops to lay down their arms.

On October 2 following a plebiscite, the Kingdom of Italy annexed Rome. Italy was at last reunited, and Rome became the capital. Pius IX shut himself up in the Vatican; not until 1929 would the papacy recognize the loss of Rome and be content with the Vatican City.

SPENCER C. TUCKER

## Consequences

For the first time since the destruction of Ostrogoth king Theodoric the Great's kingdom in the sixth century, the Italian Peninsula was now an independent and unified state. A new major power had come into being in Europe, and the unification of Italy and that of Germany in 1871 had profound implications for the European balance of power.

The new Italian government was based on Piedmont-Sardinia's constitution of 1848, itself modeled on the British system of government. The king was largely a figurehead, with a two-house parliament of the Senate and the Chamber of Deputies holding ultimate power. The king appointed the premier, who was then responsible to the Chamber of Deputies. Members of the Senate enjoyed life tenure, while the members of the Chamber of Deputies were elected on a very narrow franchise in which only about 2.5 percent of the population could vote. Rather than a few political parties as in Britain, however, a multiparty system held sway, which produced frequent changes of ministries and considerable instability. In these circumstances, Cavour's masterly political skills were greatly missed.

Unlike the new Germany, which had a federal system (albeit one in which Prussia was supreme), the new Italian state was centralized. With an administrative system similar to that of France, the new nation was rather arbitrarily divided into provinces that ignored the earlier kingdoms and duchies. The various state armies were merged into the national Italian Army, and a uniform tax system and uniform legal codes were introduced.

The high hopes of Italian nationalists were a long time in being realized, however. Rich, arable land for agriculture was in short supply, as much of Italy was mountainous terrain, and there were also numerous low-lying swamp lands. Particularly in southern Italy, scientific methods of agriculture were all but unknown. Illiteracy was also widespread, with the vast majority of the population in the south unable to read or write. Thus, even Italy's agricultural assets were insufficient for its population.

Regional differences were pronounced. Political divisions, set for generations, would have to be broken down and the old state loyalties replaced by that of Italy alone. Not only were the divisions occasioned by geography and history to be broken down, but there was a much broader division in that the north of the country was better educated, much more urban and industrialized, and generally prosperous, while southern Italy was rural, impoverished, and agricultural. In the south, secret criminal organizations such as the Camorra of Naples and the Mafia of Sicily operated unchecked.

Reaching accommodation with the powerful Roman Catholic Church in Italy may have been the most pressing immediate problem. Although the vast majority of Italians were pleased with the seizure of church lands and with Rome as the capital of the new state, Pope Pius IX held that he had been illegally deprived of these and refused to recognize the new state. In 1871 the Italian parliament sought to resolve the matter through domestic legislation. Its Law of Papal Guarantees granted the papacy possession of St. Peter's Cathedral, the Vatican, and the Lateran Palace, all in Rome, and also the villa of Castel Gandolfo some 15 miles from the city. The pope was accorded sovereign rights within these possessions; further granted the use of the Italian telegraph, railway, and postal systems; and guaranteed an annual subsidy from the state. Pius IX refused to recognize this unilateral legislation, however. He and his successors declared themselves "prisoners in the Vatican," with no pope leaving the Vatican until 1929.

Pius IX responded with decrees that first urged and then specifically forbade Roman Catholics from serving in parliament or even voting in national elections. Although most Italians simply ignored the pope's decrees, it did keep some capable individuals who were also devout Catholics from government service. Not until 1929 in the Vatican Accord was the relationship regularized between the Italian government and the Catholic Church.

Nonetheless, the government continued to maintain Roman Catholicism as the state religion and paid the salaries of Catholic clergy. The government also permitted religious instruction to be given in the public schools and supported the church's views regarding divorce. At the same time, however, it confiscated church property, did away with theological faculties in the universities, and introduced civil marriage.

Finance was a major problem. Italy was largely bereft of mineral assets, natural resources, and financial capital. The financial situation was made worse by the fact that the new government was forced to assume the debts of the former states. Transportation systems were also more developed in the north than in the south. Thus, in 1860 the entire Kingdom of Italy had only 60 miles of railroad track.

Considerable investments would be required in education and transportation if the regions of Italy, divided for so long, were to be knit together in one nation and it was to be able to complete with other nations in Europe. Securing the sizable funds required to realize these goals would be a daunting task given the sharp political divisions between the Left and the Right that characterized Italian politics at the national level and the determination of the politicians to sharply increase the size of the army and navy as the mark of Great Power status and then to embark on overseas expansion in imperialist ventures with the goal of securing resources and as an outlet for the nation's surplus population.

In 1870 Italy, with a population of about 26 million, already had a surplus population in the sense that it could not be adequately supported by the existing agriculture and industry of the kingdom. Economic pressures led a great many Italians to immigrate overseas, chiefly to the United States and to South America. Despite improvements, the daunting task of improving economic conditions in Italy remained, while the differences between north and south in economic terms continued.

Nonetheless, much was achieved in infrastructure improvements, in particular the construction of new roads and the improvement of those existing as well as laying more railroad track. Great strides were also made in improving Italian port facilities and adding significantly to merchant shipping tonnages.

Regardless of the myriad problms, a unified Italy was now fact. European diplomatic calculations had to take a new populous nation-state into account, and Italy was to play a major role in World War I.

SPENCER C. TUCKER

## Timeline

**1814–1815**      The Congress of Vienna resurrects the old Italy of many states. Italian nationalism leads to the Carbonari uprisings, which are easily quelled but also foster a new Italian spirit that will be known as the Risorgimento (Resurgence).

**1832**      In Marseille, Italian nationalist Giuseppe Mazzini organizes the first "lodge" of his Young Italy nationalist organization.

**1833**      Mazzini's plan for revolution in northern Italy is discovered, and many of his followers are arrested or executed. Mazzini himself is tried in absentia and sentenced to death.

| | |
|---|---|
| **Jan 31–Feb 1, 1834** | Piedmont-Sardinia crushes another Mazzini-led republican revolt. |
| **Jul 1847** | Following revolutionary agitation, Austrian troops under Field Marshal Joseph Radetsky von Radetznary occupy Ferrara, greatly inflaming Italian nationalism. |
| **Late 1847** | Grand Duke Leopold of Tuscany and King Charles Albert of Piedmont-Sardinia are both forced to grant constitutions. |
| **Jan 1848** | Sicilians in Palermo riot against reactionary Ferdinand II, king of Naples. He too is forced to grant a constitution. |
| **Mar 18, 1848** | Revolt in Milan, capital of Lombardy, forces Radetzky to withdraw Austrian troops from the city. |
| **Mar 22, 1848** | King Charles Albert of Piedmont-Sardinia declares war on Austria. |
| **Mar 26, 1848** | Revolutionaries under Daniele Manin take control of Venice and declare it a republic. |
| **Mid-Jun 1848** | Radetzky reestablishes Austrian control of Lombardy and most of Venetia except Venice. |
| **Jun 24–25, 1848** | In the Battle of Custoza, Radetzky's troops defeat Charles Albert's Piedmont-Sardinian and allied Italian forces. |
| **Aug 9, 1848** | Piedmont-Sardinian Army general Carlo Canera di Salasco concludes a six-month armistice with Radetzky. |
| **Nov 1848** | Papal prime minister Pellegrino Rossi is assassinated in Rome. A revolt occurs, and Pope Pius IX flees to Gaeta. |
| **Feb 9, 1849** | A constituent assembly declares Rome a republic. Learning of this, Charles Albert renounces the armistice with Piedmont and resumes warfare against Austria. |
| **Mar 22–23, 1849** | Radetzky invades Piedmont and defeats the Piedmont-Sardinia army in the Battle of Novara, compelling Charles Albert to abdicate in favor of his son, Victor Emmanuel II. |
| **Apr 24, 1849** | French marshal Nicolas Oudinot lands at Città Vecchia, Italy, with an expeditionary force. He then moves against Rome. |
| **Apr 29–30, 1849** | Led by Giuseppe Garibaldi, the republicans in Rome repulse French assaults. |
| **May 9 and 19, 1949** | Roman republican forces turn back Neapolitan Army attacks at Palestrina and then at Velletri. |
| **Jun 3, 1849** | Forces in Rome defeat yet another French assault. |
| **Jul 2, 1849** | With Oudinot besieging Rome, some 4,000 volunteers march out of the city. Garibaldi escapes capture, however. |
| **Aug 9, 1849** | Peace between Austria and Piedmont-Sardinia is formally concluded. |

**Aug 24, 1849**     Manin negotiates the surrender of Venice and goes into exile in France.

**Jan 26, 1855**     Premier Count Camillo Benso di Cavour takes direction of the unification struggle when he takes Piedmont-Sardinia into the Crimean War (1853–1856).

**Jan 14, 1858**     Italian nationalist Felice Orsini, angered by French emperor Napoleon II's refusal to support Italian unification, attempts to assassinate him. Strangely, this seems to goad Napoleon into action.

**Jul 20, 1858**     Napoleon III concludes the secret Pact of Plombières with Cavour, whereby Austria will be goaded into war against Piedmont-Sardinia, at which point France will come to its assistance. In return for French assistance, Piedmont-Sardinia is to give Nice and Savoy to France.

**Mar 9, 1859**     With Napoleon now wavering in his commitment, Cavour mobilizes the Piedmont-Sardinia Army.

**Apr 9, 1859**     Austrian emperor Franz Joseph I authorizes mobilization of the Austrian Army.

**Apr 20, 1859**     With Napoleon now backtracking, the Austrian government sends an ultimatum to Piedmont-Sardinia giving it three days to demobilize, which Cavour rejects.

**Apr 29, 1859**     Habsburg forces invade Piedmont.

**May 3, 1859**     Honoring its pledge, France declares war on Austria.

**May 20, 1859**     French forces defeat Austrian troops in the Battle of Montebello.

**May 30–31, 1859**     The allies turn back an Austrian attack in the Battle of Palestro.

**Jun 4, 1859**     In the major Battle of Magenta, French and Piedmont-Sardinian forces defeat the Austrians.

**Jun 8, 1859**     Napoleon III and Victor Emmanuel II enter Milan in triumph.

**Jun 24, 1859**     The Battle of Solferino results in a victory for the allies, but both sides suffer heavy casualties.

**Jul 8, 1859**     Napoleon abandons his ally, and the French conclude an armistice with the Austrians at Villafranca.

**Jul 11, 1859**     Napoleon III meets with Franz Josef I at Villafranca and negotiates a settlement that favors France and pays lip service to Italian nationalism.

**Nov 10, 1859**     The terms of Villafranca are formally ratified by the Treaty of Zurich.

**Mar 4, 1860**     Rosolino Pilo leads an uprising in Sicily against King Francis II, but it is put down.

**Mar 24, 1860**     Cavour and Napoleon draw up the Treaty of Turin.

| | |
|---|---|
| **May 11, 1860** | Determined to liberate Sicily, Giuseppe Garibaldi and a volunteer force land at Marsala, Sicily. Garibaldi announces that he is assuming the dictatorship of Sicily in the name of Victor Emmanuel II. |
| **May 15, 1860** | Garibaldi defeats the Neapolitan Army in the Battle of Calatafimi. |
| **May 27–30, 1860** | Garibaldi attacks and takes the Sicilian capital of Palermo. |
| **Jul 20, 1860** | Garibaldi captures the Fortress of Milazzo. Shortly thereafter Messina surrenders, and all remaining Sicilian strongholds capitulate by late September. |
| **Aug 22, 1860** | Garibaldi crosses the narrow Straits of Messina and advances on Naples. |
| **Sep 7, 1860** | Garibaldi enters Naples in triumph. |
| **Sep 8, 1860** | An uprising in Rome gives Cavour the opportunity to take the leadership of Italian unification from Garibaldi. |
| **Sep 10, 1860** | Cavour sends the Piedmont-Sardinia army south into papal territory. |
| **Sep 18, 1860** | Piedmont-Sardinia forces win the Battle of Castelfidaro, and the papal forces almost immediately dissolve. |
| **Oct 21–22, 1860** | Naples and Sicily vote to join Piedmont-Sardinia. Similar votes occur in the Marches (November 4) and Umbria (November 5). |
| **Oct 26, 1860** | Garibaldi meets with King Victor Emmanuel II at Teano. When the king rejects Garibaldi's requests that he remain as dictator of the former Kingdom of the Two Sicilies for a year and that his officers be absorbed into the new Italian Army, Garibaldi retires. |
| **Nov 3, 1860–**<br>**Feb 14, 1861** | Piedmont-Sardinia forces lay siege to and finally take Gaeta, where Francis II had taken refuge with his remaining forces. |
| **Mar 17, 1861** | King Victor Emmanuel of Piedmont-Sardinia becomes Victor Emmanuel I King of Italy. Italy is now united except for Rome and the territory around it, held by the pope, and Venetia, still under Austrian control. |
| **Jun 6, 1861** | Cavour dies. |
| **Sep 15, 1864** | Italy and France reach agreement on the status of Rome. The Italian government promises to protect the Papal States, and France pledges to withdraw its troops from Rome within two years. |
| **Oct 4, 1865** | At Biarritz, Napoleon III pushes Prussian minister-president Otto von Bismarck, who is planning to go to war with Austria, to make an alliance with Italy against Austria. |
| **Apr 8, 1866** | Prussia and Italy conclude a secret alliance whereby Italy promises to join Prussia in a war with Austria within three months, with the promise of Venetia as a reward. |

| | |
|---|---|
| **Jun 12, 1866** | With war between Prussia and Austria looming, Napoleon signs a secret treaty with Austria, promising to remain neutral in the forthcoming conflict and work for Italian neutrality. |
| **Jun 18, 1866** | With war between Prussia and Austria having begun on June 14, Italy declares war on Austria in accordance with its secret treaty with Prussia. |
| **Jun 24, 1866** | Austrian forces under Field Marshal Archduke Albrecht defeat Italian forces under General Alfonso Ferrero di La Marmora in the Battle of Custozza. |
| **Jul 3, 1866** | Napoleon arranges the transfer of Austrian-held Venetia to France, then ceded to Italy. |
| | Prussian forces defeat the Austrians in the decisive Battle of Königgrätz (also known as the Battle of Sadowa) in Bohemia. |
| **Jul 20, 1866** | In the Battle of Lissa, Austrian warships under Rear Admiral Wilhelm von Tegetthoff defeat the Italian fleet under Admiral Count Carlo Pellion di Persano. |
| **Oct 12, 1866** | The Treaty of Vienna formally ends the Austro-Prussian War. |
| **Oct 24, 1867** | Garibaldi's volunteers defeat a papal force at Monte Rotondo. |
| **Nov 3, 1867** | Near the village of Mantana, Garibaldi's men battle French papal forces and are defeated. Garibaldi and his men return to the Kingdom of Italy, where they are arrested. |
| **Aug 19, 1870** | French troops are withdrawn from Rome as a consequence of the Franco-Prussian War. |
| **Sep 20, 1870** | Italian general Raffaele Cardona's forces enter Rome, and Pope Pius IX orders his troops to lay down their arms. |
| **Oct 2, 1870** | The Kingdom of Italy annexes Rome. Italy is at last reunited, and Rome becomes its capital. |

SPENCER C. TUCKER

**Further Reading**

Beales, Derek Edward Dawson. *The Risorgimento and the Unification of Italy.* New York: Barnes and Noble, 1971.

Coppa, Frank J. *Pope Pius IX: Crusader in a Secular Age.* Boston: Twayne, 1979.

Davis, John A., ed. *Italy in the Nineteenth Century, 1796–1900.* Oxford: Oxford University Press, 2000.

Hibbert, Christopher. *Garibaldi and His Enemies: The Clash of Arms and Personalities in the Making of Italy.* Boston: Little, Brown, 1966.

Holt, Edgar. *The Making of Italy, 1815–1870.* New York: Atheneum, 1971.

Idley, Jasper. *Garibaldi.* New York: Viking, 1976.

Mack Smith, Denis. *Cavour.* New York: Knopf, 1985.

Mack Smith, Denis. *Mazzini.* New Haven, CT: Yale University Press, 1994.

Mack Smith, Denis. *Modern Italy: A Political History.* Ann Arbor: University of Michigan Press, 1997.

Matin, George. *The Red Shirt & the Cross of Savoy: The Story of Italy's Risorgimento (1748–1871).* Mew York: Dodd, Mead, 1969.

Thayer, William Roscoe. *The Life and Times of Cavour.* 2 vols. New York: Houghton Mifflin, 1911.

Trevelyan, George Macaulay. *Garibaldi and the Making of Italy.* London: Longmans, Green, 1911.

Turnbull, Patrick. *Solferino: The Birth of a Nation.* New York: St. Martin's, 1985.

# Confederate States War for Independence (1861–1865)

## Causes

The Confederate War for Independence, or the War for Southern Independence as it is still known today by some die-hard southerners in the United States, is more usually referred to as the American Civil War. A war fought by the southern states to break way from the North and form their own state, it was rooted in states' rights founded in slavery. In many ways the first "modern" war, it lasted four years, from 1861 to 1865.

The United States underwent great territorial expansion during the first half of the 19th century as a consequence of the Louisiana Purchase (1803), the acquisition of Florida (1819), and the Mexican-American War (1846–1848). The country also experienced rapid population growth from both a high birthrate and immigration. By 1860 with some 31 million people, the United States was more populous than Great Britain and almost as large as France.

By 1860, however, the nation was coming apart, with the North and South entirely estranged. The South boasted an agricultural economy based on cotton, tobacco, rice, sugarcane, and naval stores. It

THE AMERICAN CIVIL WAR, 1861–1862

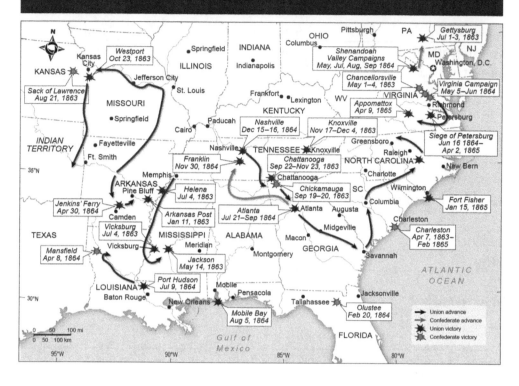

# THE AMERICAN CIVIL WAR, 1863–1865

was the world's largest producer of raw cotton, but seven-eighths of it was exported, chiefly to the United Kingdom. Southerners therefore sought a low tariff in order to be able to purchase cheaper manufactured goods from Britain, then leading the Industrial Revolution. The North, on the other hand, had a balanced economy. It was rapidly industrializing, and northern business interests sought a high tariff to protect their finished goods against cheaper British manufactures. Unlike the economy of the South, capital tended to multiply in the North, and banking, insurance companies, and railroads all concentrated there. Increasingly the railroads were tying the West to the North. There was also a large and growing population imbalance between North and

South; new immigrants were unable to compete with free slave labor and settled primarily in the North. Most whites in the South were also hurt economically by the slavery system.

The Mexican-American War set up the American Civil War, for the chief issue regarding the acquired territories was whether they would be slave or free. The Missouri Compromise of 1820 provided that new states would be admitted to the Union on the basis of one slave and one free in order to maintain rough parity in the U.S. Senate and in presidential elections. But California was admitted singly as a free state in 1850. In the ensuing Compromise of 1850 the North agreed to enforce laws on runaway slaves. This, however, ran counter to increasing abolitionist

## Confederate States War for Independence (1861–1865)

| Prewar Resources, Confederate States versus United States, 1861* | | |
|---|---|---|
| | Confederate States | United States |
| Population | 9 million** | 22 million |
| Naval strength | Fewer than 10 ships | 90 ships*** |
| Railroad mileage | 29% of U.S. total | 71% of U.S. total |
| Manufacturing plants | 10% of U.S. total | 90% of U.S. total |
| Farm acreage | 35% of U.S. total | 65% of U.S. total |

*Figures reflect comparisons made on the eve of war in January 1861.
**Of this number, 3.5 million were enslaved persons who were ineligible for combat duties.
***Of this total, only 40 ships were commissioned, but the U.S. Navy expanded rapidly from 1861 to 1865.

| First Battle of Bull Run, Virginia (July 21, 1861) | | |
|---|---|---|
| | Confederate States | United States |
| Strength* | 18,000 men* | 18,000 men* |
| Killed | 387 | 460 |
| Wounded | 1,582 | 1,124 |
| Captured/missing | 13 | 1,312 |

*Only troops engaged in combat.

| Battle of Pea Ridge, Arkansas (March 7–8, 1862) | | |
|---|---|---|
| | Confederate States | United States |
| Strength | 16,500 men | 10,500 men |
| Total losses* | 4,600 | 1,384 |

* Includes killed, wounded, captured, and missing.

| Battle of Shiloh, Tennessee (April 6–7, 1862)* | | |
|---|---|---|
| | Confederate States | United States |
| Strength | 40,000 men | 63,000 men |
| Killed | 1,723 | 1,745 |
| Wounded | 8,012 | 8,408 |
| Captured/missing | 959 | 2,885 |

*Casualties in this battle exceeded those from all previous U.S. wars combined.

| Battle of Antietam, Maryland (September 17, 1862) | | |
|---|---|---|
| | Confederate States | United States |
| Strength | 41,000 men | 87,000 men |
| Killed | 1,546 | 2,108 |
| Wounded | 7,752 | 9,540 |
| Captured/missing | 1,018 | 753 |

| Battle of Gettysburg, Pennsylvania (July 1–3, 1863) | | |
|---|---|---|
| | **Confederate States** | **United States** |
| **Strength** | 74,000 men | 94,000 men |
| **Killed** | 4,708 | 3,155 |
| **Wounded** | 12,693 | 14,531 |
| **Captured/missing** | 5,830 | 5,369 |

| Overland Campaign, Virginia (May 4–June 12, 1864) | | |
|---|---|---|
| | **Confederate States** | **United States** |
| **Strength** | 60,000 men | 12,000 men |
| **Total losses** | 32,600 | 55,000 |

| Sherman's March to the Sea, Georgia (November 15–December 21, 1864) | |
|---|---|
| **Strength of Sherman's forces** | 62,000 men |
| **Railroad tracks destroyed** | 300 miles |
| **Horses/mules seized** | 9,000 |
| **Head of cattle confiscated** | 13,000 |
| **Total estimated monetary damages** | $100 million |

| Total Casualties and Losses, 1861–1865 | | |
|---|---|---|
| | **Confederate States** | **United States** |
| **Total killed, all causes** | 285,000* | 360,000** |
| **Total wounded** | 100,000 | 275,000 |
| **Total economic costs** | $1 billion*** | $2.3 billion |

*Of this total, 94,000 were killed in action or died of wounds.
**Of this total, 110,000 were killed in action or died of wounds.
***Figure does not include $1.1 billion in Confederate war damages.

**Sources:** Beringer, Richard E., et al. *Why the South Lost the Civil War.* Athens: University of Georgia Press, 1986; Eicher, David J. *The Longest Night: A Military History of the Civil War.* New York: Simon and Schuster, 2001; McPherson, James M. *This Mighty Scourge: Perspectives on the Civil War.* Oxford: Oxford University Press, 2007; Weigley, Frank R. *A Great Civil War: A Military and Political History, 1861–1865.* Bloomington: Indiana University Press, 2004.

sentiment in the North and fueled violence in the territories, especially Kansas.

As abolitionism gained strength in the North, white southerners increasingly saw their way of life threatened. Political parties and churches split along regional lines.

Increasingly there was talk of secession; most southerners believed that a state had the right to secede from the Union, whereas northerners rejected this notion.

In October 1858 militant abolitionist John Brown led a raid on the federal arsenal at Harpers Ferry, Virginia (now West Virginia), with the intention of setting up a base in the Appalachian Mountains for fugitive slaves and using arms from the arsenal to raid the South. The raid was easily put down and Brown was tried and hanged, but the event greatly alarmed southerners, who chose to see in it true northern sentiment, and led to increasing numbers of state militia units in the South.

In November 1860, Republican Party candidate Abraham Lincoln was elected president of the United States with a plurality of the vote and largely because the Democratic Party split on the issue of slavery. The Republican platform called for no more slavery in the territories but promised no interference with slavery in the states. Nonetheless, many southern leaders refused to accept a "black Republican president," and on December 24, 1860, South Carolina voted to secede from the Union.

State conventions in Alabama, Georgia, Florida, Mississippi, Louisiana, and Texas followed South Carolina's lead. On February 8, 1861, representatives from the seven seceded states met in Montgomery, Alabama, and formed the Confederate States of America. The next day the Confederate Congress elected Jefferson Davis president.

U.S. president James Buchanan's Democratic administration had almost a month remaining, but Buchanan was afraid of using force and alienating the border states, chiefly Virginia, and took no action. But Lincoln took office he also did nothing for six weeks. In his March 4, 1861, inauguration address, Lincoln renewed his promise to respect slavery where it existed and to enforce the fugitive slave laws but also said that he would not countenance secession.

The Confederates had now taken control of all federal forts and navy yards in the seceded states except the key installations of Fort Pickens in Pensacola, Florida, and Fort Sumter in Charleston Harbor, South Carolina. Lincoln reluctantly concluded, against the advice of a majority of his cabinet, that he had to send relief expeditions to these two installations even though this would probably bring the secession of Virginia. Lincoln informed Davis that this would be only for provisioning, but Davis ordered Major General P. G. T. Beauregard at Charleston to demand the surrender of Fort Sumter. If refused, he was to reduce the fort. Following an unsatisfactory reply from fort commander Major Robert Anderson, Beauregard ordered fire opened on Fort Sumter before the Union relief expedition could arrive.

Shelling commenced at 4:30 a.m. on April 12, 1861. After 34 hours of bombardment and being short of ammunition and provisions, Anderson surrendered. The only casualty in the shelling itself was a horse.

A whirlwind of patriotic fervor swept the North, and on April 15 Lincoln called for 75,000 volunteers to serve three months, limited constitutionally to the 90-day term for militia in federal service. Claiming that this was an act of war against the South, Virginia seceded. A major blow to the North, this gave the South the important Tredegar Iron Works at Richmond, the largest such enterprise in the South, and the largest prewar navy yard (at Norfolk) as well as many of the South's best officers, including Robert E. Lee. Virginia was closely followed in secession by Arkansas, Tennessee, and North Carolina. In a major blow to the Confederacy, however, Kentucky declared its neutrality.

SPENCER C. TUCKER

## Course

### *Early Expectations Dashed (1861)*

The North enjoyed tremendous advantages. The population of its 23 states was 22 million, a figure that continued to increase during the war thanks to ongoing immigration (some 400,000 foreign-born soldiers served in the Union Army during the war). The North also had a well-balanced economy, with some 90 percent of the prewar manufacturing facilities. Its superior rail network proved to be of immense logistical advantage during the war. The North also had a large merchant marine. Its population was better educated, and it enjoyed superior managerial systems essential in waging modern war. At the start of hostilities the U.S. Army numbered only some 25,000 men, but its 90 ships (40 of which were then in commission) completely eclipsed the navy of the South, which had only a handful of ships.

The 11 seceded states had only 9 million people, but 3.5 million of these were slaves. Although the South's abundant natural resources had not been developed and its manufacturing resources were severely limited, it had only 29 percent of the 1860 railroad track, and this steadily deteriorated during the war owing to the Union blockade. The South was also plagued by states' rights. Having protested federal power, the leaders of the seceded states were now reluctant to yield authority to the Confederate government. The South also had a much higher rate of illiteracy, which adversely impacted war management.

Despite the great advantages lying with the North, the secessionists were convinced that the North would not fight to maintain the Union and that if it did Great Britain and France, dependent on staples from the South, would recognize the Confederacy and provide it material assistance. To encourage this, at the beginning of the war Davis embarked on so-called cotton diplomacy, withholding the South's cotton crop from shipment in order to force European intervention. This did not have the desired result, as other suppliers were found.

Southerners believed that the Confederacy could simply stand on the defensive and wear down the North, which in order to win would have to physically invade and conquer the South. Southerners also assumed that their greater emphasis on outdoor living, familiarity with firearms, and an inclination for military service would give them an advantage.

The Southern war aim was recognition of independence. The North sought restoration of the Union, but after 1862 abolition of slavery became a secondary objective. Yet in proclaiming a blockade of the South on April 19, 1861, and forbidding trade with the seceded states (August 16), Lincoln recognized a state of war.

Lincoln was a superb war leader. Although he had little military experience, he understood the strategic picture clearly and had an excellent sense of what needed to be accomplished and how to go about it. He proved to be singularly adroit at communicating his war aims and the role of adroit diplomacy. He also understood the importance of sea power and a naval blockade and determined that the chief military goal would be the destruction of Confederate armies rather controlling territory. His problem was in finding the right leaders to carry out his plans.

Jefferson Davis was a study in contrast. Aloof and inflexible, he had commanded a regiment with great distinction during the war with Mexico and had been an excellent secretary of war (1853–1857). Because of his supposed expert knowledge, he insisted on intervening in military decisions and made a number of very poor personnel appointments and strategic choices.

U.S. Army commanding general Brevet Lieutenant General Winfield Scott developed the war plan that would defeat the South. Dubbed the "Anaconda Plan" for the South American snake that strangles its victim to death, Scott planned to blockade the Confederacy, build up and train a large Union Army, and then invade and bisect the South via its great rivers. Although Scott soon retired, his was the plan Lincoln followed.

There were three major theaters of war: the eastern theater, the western theater (from the Appalachian Mountains to the Mississippi River), and the Trans-Mississippi West. The eastern theater has received the most attention in part because of the proximity of the two capital cities, the fame of

the generals who fought there, and the concentration of newspapers in the East. Also, some 60 percent of all Civil War battles occurred in Virginia. The western theater, with abundant natural resources and major rivers, deserves to rank in importance with the eastern theater, but the Trans-Mississippi West theater was of little importance, especially after Union forces secured control of the Mississippi River.

During April 15–July 20, 1861, fighting occurred in Kentucky and western Virginia (soon to secede from the rest of Virginia as the new state of West Virginia). Major General George B. McClellan, a West Point–trained officer who was in the railroad business when the war began, led some 20,000 Union troops in securing this area for the Union, with the notable battles being Philippi (June 3, 1861) and Rich Mountain–Carrick's Ford (July 11–14).

A Union artillery position at Fort C.F. Smith, Arlington, Virginia, as published in 1865. Sixty-eight major forts protected Washington, D.C., during the Civil War. (Library of Congress)

Skirmishing between the two sides also occurred at Big Bethel (June 10) near Union-held Fort Monroe in far eastern Virginia.

With the Northern public and press demanding military action and a quick end to the rebellion and with the 90-day enlistments in some volunteer regiments about to expire, Lincoln overruled Scott, who wanted more time to train the men, and ordered Brigadier General Irwin McDowell to advance from southwest of Washington westward with 30,000 men and defeat Confederate brigadier general Beauregard's forces at Manassas Junction, Virginia. Once this had been accomplished, McDowell was to turn south and march on Richmond, now the Confederate capital. Brigadier General Patterson and another Union force were to prevent Confederate brigadier general Joseph E. Johnston from bringing 10,000 Confederates from the Shenandoah Valley to Manassas.

The Battle of Bull Run, also known as the Battle of Manassas (the Union named battles for the nearest body of water, while the Confederates named battles for the nearest telegraph station), began before dawn on July 21. McDowell attacked and seemed to have carried the day by midafternoon. But his plan proved to be overly complicated for the largely untrained troops, and Johnston eluded the inept Patterson and brought his men to Manassas Junction by rail just in time to prevent disaster. A magnificent stand by Confederates under Brigadier General Thomas J. Jackson (now dubbed "Stonewall") turned an apparent Southern rout into victory. McDowell's men began a withdrawal back toward Washington that soon became a rout. The Confederates were equally disorganized, however, and incapable of a pursuit into Washington. Confederate casualties totaled 1,982; the Union lost 2,896 (nearly half of them captured or missing). The Confederates also secured substantial amounts of weapons and supplies.

The battle ended any illusions about the war and brought home to both sides a realization of the resources required to win it. Convinced of the need for more thorough training for the army, Lincoln replaced McDowell with McClellan; upon Scott's retirement, on November 1 McClellan became Union general in chief.

On April 19, Lincoln had proclaimed a naval blockade of the South. To carry this out, U.S. secretary of the navy Gideon Welles requisitioned merchant ships in Northern harbors for conversion into warships and commenced a massive naval construction program. This included many steam warships and soon also ironclads. During the war, the vast majority of the Union ships were employed in blockade duties.

It took time to establish an effective blockade of nearly 3,500 miles of Confederate coastline. To run the blockade, the Confederates counted on speedy, stealthy ships, most of them built in England. Nassau in the Bahamas became a major supply port, with European cargoes offloaded there and at other points in the West Indies for transshipment to the South. Some 800 ships passed through the blockade in its first year of operation, but in 1860 some 6,000 ships had entered and cleared Southern ports. At first the Confederacy did not restrict cargoes, and most blockade-runners carried nonmilitary goods, as the financial return on these were much greater. Joint Union naval and military expeditions secured bases for the North and helped tighten the blockade. Chances of capture of blockade-runners were estimated at 1 in 10 in 1861 but 1 in 3 in 1864.

By 1865 also, the Union Navy, with 700 vessels of all types including 60 ironclads, was the second largest in the world behind only that of Britain.

Confederate secretary of the navy Stephen R. Mallory sought to break the Union blockade by the construction of ironclads, sending raiders to sea against Union merchant shipping and, as the war continued, employing new technology in the form of mines and submarines.

Europeans were divided about what was happening in America. Generally speaking, the upper classes favored the South, while the lower classes identified with the Union. Businessmen saw in the South a lucrative market for finished goods. Yet the British government, followed by France and other nations, dashed Southern hopes by declaring neutrality. This move angered Washington but prohibited the armed ships of either side from bringing their prizes into British ports, a particularly heavy blow to Confederate privateers and government commerce raiders.

### Union Successes in the West but Failures in the East (1862)

In the fighting on land, McClellan repeatedly ignored orders by Lincoln for offensive action in Virginia, but the Union scored victories early in 1862 in Kentucky and Tennessee. Confederate major general Leonidas Polk's mistaken decision to invade Columbus, Kentucky, in September 1861 ended that state's neutrality and turned Kentucky against the Confederacy. There also, Union brigadier general George H. Thomas defeated the Confederates under Major General George B. Crittenden in the Battle of Mill Springs (January 19–20).

In the Battle of Pea Ridge fought in Benton County, Arkansas, during March 7–8, 1862, U.S. major general Samuel R. Curtis, with 10,500 men, won a major victory against 16,500 Confederates under Major General Earl Van Dorn. Union losses were 1,384 against as many as 4,600 Confederates. It was the first major Union victory in the Trans-Mississippi West and ensured Union control of Missouri for more than two years.

In early February 1862, Union brigadier general Ulysses S. Grant and a gunboat flotilla with the first ironclads of the war under Commodore Andrew H. Foote moved against Confederate fortifications on the Tennessee and Cumberland Rivers. Foote captured Confederate-held Fort Henry on the Tennessee (February 6), but most of its garrison marched the short distance to Fort Donelson on the Cumberland. Confederate commander of the Western Department General Albert S. Johnston regarded Donelson as the major defense of Nashville, and he now reinforced it to buy time for his flanking garrisons to withdraw from Bowling Green and Columbus, Kentucky. Grant soon besieged Donelson, and following a failed attack by Foote's gunboats and an unsuccessful effort by the Confederates to break free, it surrendered on February 16. The Union took some 15,000 prisoners plus substantial equipment and supplies. The Confederates suffered some 1,500–3,500 killed or wounded in the battle; Union casualties totaled 2,832.

The capture of Forts Henry and Donelson were the Union's first two significant victories of the war and gave it access to middle Tennessee, with its abundant natural resources. Nashville fell to the Union on February 25, the first Confederate state capital in Union hands.

Grant was prevented from moving immediately against the Confederate key railhead of Corinth, Mississippi, when his superior, Major General Henry W. Halleck, diverted 25,000 men in the Army of Mississippi under Brigadier General John Pope to expel Confederate forces from the upper Mississippi. Pope and Foote's gunboat flotilla besieged Island No. 10 in the Mississippi River on March 16. The Confederates surrendered on April 7, but the delay allowed Johnston time to bring up reinforcements at Corinth. Grant marched with 36,000 men to Pittsburg Landing just across the Tennessee border from Corinth, ordered to wait there for 20,000 reinforcements under Major General Don Carlos Buell. But Buell was delayed, and Grant, who was always offensively minded, chose to drill Union reinforcements rather than erecting fortifications.

Johnston was determined to attack. His 40,000 men struck before dawn on April 6, taking the Union troops by surprise in what became known as the Battle of Shiloh, for the Baptist church there. Confusion reigned on both sides, and Johnston was mortally wounded. The hungry Confederate troops, seemingly on the verge of success, stopped to loot the Union camps, and a fierce Union stand imposed further delay. But then with Union troops close to defeat, Beauregard broke off the assault to reorganize.

That night Buell's Army of the Ohio arrived, and the next day the stronger Union forces attacked. By evening the Confederates were in retreat to Corinth, with Union forces too exhausted to pursue. The battle cost the Union 13,038 casualties of some 63,000 men engaged, while the 40,000 Confederates suffered 10,694. The grim tally of 23,732 causalities from this single battle was more than the United States had suffered in all of its previous wars combined.

While Union forces were steadily working their way southward along the northern Mississippi, other Union forces secured its mouth. Following a two-day largely ineffective bombardment of Confederate forts on the lower river by 13-inch mortars aboard specially constructed river craft, Flag Officer David Farragut would permit no further delay and successfully ran his squadron past the forts and on April 26 took the surrender of New Orleans. Union troops under Major General Benjamin F. Butler then occupied the city.

By now Lincoln had lost confidence in McClellan for his inaction and on March 11, 1862, removed him from command of the entire army, leaving McClellan with its chief field force, the Army of the Potomac (Halleck became general in chief in July). Lincoln ordered McClellan to commence immediate operations against Richmond, but McClellan planned an advance not south from the Washington area, as Lincoln desired, but instead from the east by way of the peninsula between the James and York Rivers. McClellan's opponents persuaded Lincoln to withhold General McDowell's strong corps to protect Washington.

The water route to Richmond up the James as well as Union transports at Hampton Roads now came under threat from the Confederate ironclad ram *Virginia,* formed from the hull of the scuttled U.S. Navy steam warship *Merrimack* at the Norfolk Navy Yard. On March 8 the *Virginia* sallied and sank the Union frigate *Cumberland* and burned the sloop *Congress.* Other Union wooden warships, including the flagship *Minnesota,* ran aground endeavoring to escape. That evening the *Virginia* retired, its crew confident that they would complete destruction of the Union ships the next day. That same evening, however, the revolutionary Union ironclad *Monitor* arrived in Hampton Roads and took up position near the *Minnesota*. The next day the two ironclads did battle in the first clash between such ships in history. It seemed to be an unequal match, with the much larger *Virginia* mounting 10 guns to only 2 for the *Monitor*. The *Monitor*, however, proved far more nimble, and its turret revolved (the first such use in actual warfare), enabling the gun ports to be moved away from enemy fire while its 2 11-inch Dahlgren smoothbores were being reloaded. The battle lasted four hours. Although the *Monitor* got off far fewer shots, most of these told, while most of the shells from the *Virginia* failed to register. The battle ended in a draw, with both vessels retiring, but the *Virginia* had been hit 50 times and was leaking. The *Monitor* had sustained only 21 hits and was virtually undamaged.

Both sides now pushed construction of ironclads. Of 40 laid down by the North during the Civil War, 35 were of the turreted *Monitor* type. The South continued to construct casemated ironclads of the *Virginia* type. The battle also led to an effort on both sides to manufacture more powerful guns capable of penetrating the new iron plating.

On March 17 McClellan's army began its movement south by water from Alexandria, Virginia, to Fort Monroe, and then marched west toward Richmond in the March–August 1862 Peninsula Campaign. McClellan's advance was glacial. On April 5 he commenced siege operations against Yorktown but, despite a sevenfold manpower advantage, did not take it until May 4 upon a Confederate withdrawal. A stubborn Confederate rearguard action at Williamsburg (May 5) prevented McClellan from confronting the bulk of Joseph Johnston's army and its supply train. By May 14, however, the Army of the Potomac had reached the Pamunkey River, some 20 miles from

Richmond. Despite his overwhelming numerical advantage (100,000 Union troops to 60,000 Confederates), McClellan halted to await the arrival of McDowell's 40,000-man corps from Fredericksburg, south of Washington.

General Robert E. Lee, then military adviser to President Davis, had earlier recommended that Major General Thomas J. Jackson in the Shenandoah Valley be reinforced and mount an operation to divert as many Union reinforcements from McClellan as possible. Davis agreed. Union major general Nathaniel P. Banks was supposed to clear the valley as part of McClellan's Richmond Campaign. Upon defeating Jackson, Banks would then cover Washington, releasing McDowell to join McClellan.

Jackson's ensuing Valley Campaign (March 23–June 9, 1862) was one of the most brilliant in military history. Commanding no more than 18,000 men, he parlayed excellent intelligence and rapid movement (his infantrymen were known as foot cavalry) to tie down more than 64,000 Union troops. Jackson engaged three Union armies under Banks, Major General John C. Frémont, and Brigadier General James Shields in a series of battles (Kernstown, March 23; McDowell, May 8; Front Royal, May 23; First Winchester, May 25; Cross Keys, June 8; and Port Republic, June 9) and numerous other actions. The Union suffered some 8,000 casualties, the Confederates fewer than 2,500.

Although Jackson did not have the means to attack Washington, fears of this led Lincoln to detach 20,000 men from McDowell and rush them to the Shenandoah Valley. Jackson meanwhile had left the valley for the critical battles before Richmond.

At the end of May, troops of the Army of the Potomac occupied both sides of the

Chickahominy River, with their northern elements reaching out to meet McDowell and the lower part only some five miles from Richmond, just beyond Fair Oaks Station. In the Battle of Seven Pines (Fair Oaks, May 31–June 1), General Johnston and 39,000 men attacked two Union corps isolated on the south bank by the flooded river from the main part of McClellan's army. The passage of a third corps across the river prevented a Union defeat. Union casualties were under 6,000; Confederate casualties were almost 8,000 including Johnston, severely wounded.

On June 1, President Davis replaced Johnston with Lee in command of the Army of Northern Virginia. During June 12–15, Lee sent his cavalry commander, Major General James E. B. Stuart, and 1,200 men in a ride entirely around McClellan's army, destroying Union supplies and rattling the Union commander, now firmly convinced that he was outnumbered.

Determined to drive McClellan from the peninsula, Lee assembled some 97,000 men (the largest force he would ever command) and sent them against McClellan in what became known as the Seven Days' Campaign (June 25–July 1). Jackson had just arrived, and Lee planned to send Jackson's corps in a flanking attack against Union major general Fitz John Porter's corps on the north side of the Chickahominy, with most of the army under Lee west of Mechanicsville moving against McClellan's center.

The operation was poorly handled. Jackson, physically spent from the Shenandoah Valley Campaign, failed to exercise effective command and moved too slowly, never getting into the fight in the Battle of Mechanicsville on June 26. Porter turned back the Confederate assaults and, learning of Jackson's approach, retired to Gaines' Mill.

Lee again attacked Porter on June 27 in the Battle of Gaines' Mill. Jackson was again late and failed to get in behind Porter's right flank as Lee had planned. Lee managed to penetrate Porter's left, however. In danger of a double envelopment with the approach of Jackson, Porter managed to withdraw in good order thanks to the arrival of Union reinforcements. That night on McClellan's order, Porter withdrew to the south bank of the Chickahominy. Ignoring appeals from his subordinates that Richmond was his for the taking, McClellan withdrew to the James and the protection of Union gunboats.

During June 29–30 Lee pursued, suffering sharp rebuffs in battles at Peach Orchard, Savage's Station, White Oak Swamp, and Glendale-Frayser's Farm. Jackson again failed to envelop the Union right flank. In the Battle of Malvern Hill on July 1 Porter, in the absence of McClellan, exercised command, and the Army of the Potomac, supported by the heavy guns of the Union James River squadron, turned back Lee's desperate attacks, with the Confederates suffering more than 5,000 casualties. Although this was a clear Union victory, an unnerved McClellan ordered an immediate retreat to Harrison's Landing. The next day, the Confederates withdrew toward Richmond. In the Seven Days' Campaign the Union suffered nearly 16,000 casualties, but Confederate losses were more than 20,000.

McClellan had fumbled away victory. He informed Washington during the campaign that he was outnumbered two to one when the reverse was true. A little more energy on his part and the war might have been ended or drastically shortened. On August 3 Lincoln ordered McClellan to return with his army to Washington.

Halleck now consolidated the Armies of Virginia under General Pope. Major

General Ambrose E. Burnside was to march north from Fortress Monroe to Falmouth, and McClellan would bring his army to Alexandria and there join Pope for an overland march south to Richmond. Determined to strike while the Union forces were still divided, Lee ordered Jackson to attack Pope's rear and destroy his headquarters and supply base at Manassas Junction (August 26). Pope then moved to attack Jackson in the belief that he was isolated from the main Confederate army. This led to the Second Battle of Bull Run (August 29–30). Confederate general James Longstreet hit Pope in the flank and sent the Union forces reeling back toward Bull Run. Major General Fitz-John Porter, who had refused to throw his corps into action the first day, was made the scapegoat for Pope's defeat and was cashiered, but McClellan had failed to reinforce Pope in time.

Pope withdrew to the defenses of Washington, and Lincoln reluctantly replaced him with McClellan as commander of the Army of the Potomac. McClellan then reorganized his forces and moved to meet Lee, who in mid-August had begun an invasion of the North in the hope of cutting rail lines and isolating Washington, with Harrisburg as his probable ultimate objective. Again overestimating Confederate strength, McClellan proceeded in customary slow fashion. A fluke brought McClellan to Antietam Creek, Maryland; Lee's entire operational plan had fallen into Union hands. Incredibly, McClellan was slow to take advantage, and it took him two days to cover the 10 miles to the South Mountain passes. On September 14 Confederate forces fought small, intense engagements for the passes, buying precious time for Lee to bring his scattered troops together. Lee ordered his men to concentrate at Sharpsburg.

On the afternoon of September 15, McClellan and some 55,000 men of the Army of the Potomac were within easy striking distance of Lee, just east of Sharpsburg with only 18,000 men. Hilly terrain allowed Lee to conceal his inferior numbers, but had McClellan moved that afternoon he would have enjoyed an overwhelming victory. McClellan delayed, however, and Jackson arrived at midday on July 16, having the day before taken the surrender of Harpers Ferry. That action netted the South 12,419 prisoners, 13,000 small arms, 73 cannon, 200 wagons, and considerable stocks of military equipment in the largest Union surrender of the war. Even with Jackson's corps, however, Lee was still outnumbered more than two to one: 41,000 to 87,000.

The battle began on the morning on September 17. McClellan threw away his great advantage of vastly superior numbers, holding an entire corps in reserve and employing a piecemeal rather than simultaneous form of attack, which was mirrored by subordinate units. McClellan also failed to utilize his cavalry to cut the Confederate lines of communication and prevent reinforcements from reaching the battlefield from the south. Even a delay of an hour or two would have changed the battle, as Lee's remaining three divisions arrived on the battlefield in late morning, with the fighting already under way.

The Battle of Antietam was the bloodiest single day of the war. Union casualties totaled 2,108 dead, 9,540 wounded, and 753 captured or missing. Confederate losses were 1,546 dead, 7,752 wounded, and 1,018 captured or missing. These were fewer than those of the Union but nearly twice as great in percentage of total force engaged: 26 percent to 15 percent. Lee waited a day and then pulled back into Virginia with his prisoners and booty. McClellan trumpeted a victory but failed to pursue Lee effectively.

Although inconclusive, the Battle of Antietam was nonetheless one of the most important engagements of the war. Lee's defeat weakened Confederate hopes of securing recognition from Britain and France. Never again was the Confederacy this close to winning foreign diplomatic recognition. The Union victory also helped ensure that the Democrats did not win control of the U.S. House of Representatives in the November congressional elections. A single percentage's shift in the vote would have brought Democratic control and a push for a negotiated end to the war. Antietam also gave Lincoln the opportunity to issue the Preliminary Emancipation Proclamation, which he did on September 22. This freed all slaves in areas of the South still in rebellion as of January 1, 1863. The proclamation effectively gave the Union the moral high ground and greatly lengthened the odds against foreign recognition of the South. Lincoln, angered by Lee's escape, McClellan's procrastination in pursuing him, and a daring cavalry raid by General Stuart into Pennsylvania around Gettysburg (October 10–12), replaced McClellan with General Burnside on November 7.

## Vicksburg and Gettysburg (1863)

Now under General Burnside, the Army of the Potomac advanced against Lee, arriving at the Rappahannock across from Fredericksburg on November 19, 1862. Pontoon bridges for the crossing had not arrived, but instead of immediately crossing in boats, Burnside elected to wait for the bridges. When they did arrive on November 27, the Confederates had reinforced. The crossing, which did not begin until very early on December 11, came

under heavy Confederate rifle fire, but with massed Union artillery fire and the engineers using the pontoons as makeshift boats, bridges were placed, and the army crossed by nightfall. Burnside spent the next day organizing the attack. Lee's army was now entirely in place and occupying excellent well-prepared defensive positions on high ground just west of the city. Burnside commanded some 120,000 men, Lee 78,000.

On December 13 Burnside ordered two attacks. The first was by Major General G. Gordon Meade on the Confederate right, commanded by Jackson. Meade achieved some success before his men were driven back by Confederate reinforcements, sent by Lee. The second attack, on the Confederate left, came against the heart of Lee's defenses on Marye's Heights directly behind Fredericksburg, where a shoulder-high stone wall ran for some 400 yards and was defended by Confederate infantry two ranks deep. Six hundred yards of open field stretched between the Confederate position and the town, where the Union soldiers were located.

Burnside's assault on Marye's Heights began at noon and promptly came under devastating Confederate artillery fire. Lee also reinforced the defenders at the wall to four ranks deep, allowing the Confederates there to lay down a continuous hail of fire against 14 separate Union attacks, which ended only at nightfall. No Union soldier ever reached the wall, and few got within 50 yards.

The Battle of Fredericksburg was Lee's most lopsided victory of the war. The Union side suffered 12,653 casualties to only 4,201 for the Confederates. The Confederates also recovered 11,000 Union firearms.

On January 25, 1863, Lincoln replaced Burnside as commander of the Army of the

Potomac with Major General Joseph Hooker, who accomplished much in retraining the army and building esprit de corps.

With the increasing need for manpower, both sides resorted to conscription. The Confederacy was first, in April 1862, followed by the North in March 1863. Individuals could avoid service by providing a substitute or making a cash payment. In the South, those owning 20 or more slaves were exempt. Whereas 20 percent of the Confederate Army was conscripted, only 6 percent of the Union Army was. Blacks also fought for the North; some 200,000 served, mostly in labor units and under white officers, but black infantry regiments distinguished themselves in many battles.

On April 27, 1863, Hooker crossed the Rappahannock to the west of Fredericksburg with 130,000 men to attack Lee, with fewer than 60,000 men, at Chancellorsville. Seeking to take advantage of his greatly superior numbers, Hooker planned a double envelopment, with the eastern pincer at Fredericksburg. But then Hooker suddenly halted to see what Lee would do. Hooker also erred in sending 10,000 cavalry in a wide sweep south well below Fredericksburg to destroy Confederate supply depots and lines of communication; this action uncovered the Union right wing and denied Hooker intelligence regarding Lee's intentions.

Lee now staged a double envelopment of a double envelopment, endeavoring with his far smaller force to surround a much larger one. Lee would demonstrate with about 17,000 men in front of the Union line while sending Jackson and 26,000 men in a movement around the Union right flank. Success rested on Hooker's continuing failure to exploit the Confederate separation or determine Jackson's intentions.

Jackson struck on May 2. Although his force had been detected moving off, it was thought that it was retreating; indeed, Union major general Daniel Sickles advanced his men to attack, weakening the Union line. Jackson's attack was a complete surprise and enfiladed the Union lines. Union troops were sent reeling back in confusion. Increasing Union resistance, darkness, and the loss of Confederate unit cohesion in the heavily wooded Wilderness all prevented a Union catastrophe. That evening Jackson was shot by his own men in front of his own lines while reconnoitering and subsequently died of complications. On May 3, however, Stuart, who replaced Jackson, resumed the Confederate attack, further constricting Hooker's lines.

Another part of the battle, often known as the Second Battle of Fredericksburg, occurred on May 3. Major General John Sedgwick and 25,000 men advanced from Fredericksburg against 10,000 Confederates at Salem Church. Lee now feinted again. Leaving just a small force against Hooker, Lee turned east to deal with Sedgwick. Hooker did nothing, and Sedgwick, surrounded on three sides and unaided, retired back across the Rappahannock during the night of May 4.

On May 5 Hooker pulled his battered army back across the Rappahannock. The May 2–4 Battle of Chancellorsville was a military masterpiece but also the South's costliest victory. Union casualties were far higher than those for the Confederates— 17,197 to 12,764—but the Union losses were 13 percent of effectives, while the Confederate casualties were 21 percent. Particularly grievous was the loss of Jackson. The Army of Northern Virginia was never quite the same without him.

Meanwhile, Union forces in the western theater were endeavoring to take the

Confederate fortress of Vicksburg on the Mississippi. Attempts by the navy in May and June 1862 had met rebuff. Grant took command of the Army of the Tennessee in October 1862 and attempted a land assault (October 16–December 20) that had to be called off following a successful Confederate assault on his major supply base. Subsequent joint army-navy efforts to approach Vicksburg from the north via rivers and bayous during early 1863 were also unsuccessful.

Vicksburg, commanded by Lieutenant General John C. Pemberton, was ideally situated for defense and strongly fortified. It was most vulnerable from the south and east, but these were remote from Grant's supply base to the north at Memphis.

On March 29, 1863, Grant cut loose from his base, crossed the Mississippi above Vicksburg, and marched down the Louisiana shore of the river to a point south of the city where Rear Admiral David Dixon Porter's Mississippi Squadron, which ran the Vicksburg batteries on the night of April 16–17, ferried his men across the river (April 30). Grant planned to attack Vicksburg from the rear. Gambling boldly, he ignored Halleck's instructions to await reinforcements, which would also give the Confederates time to reinforce and fortify, and abandoned his river base at Grand Gulf and marched inland, carrying supplies in wagons and living off the land as much as possible.

Grant planned to place his own force between the Confederate forces at Vicksburg and Jackson, Mississippi, then destroy the latter and turn on the former. Following a series of small victories he took Jackson, held by 6,000 Confederates, on May 14. Soon abandoned by Grant, the Confederates reinforced there, but Grant had destroyed it as a transportation and logistics center for Vicksburg. Pemberton now came out of Vicksburg to engage Grant. In a hard-fought battle at Champion's Hill (May 16), Grant with 32,000 men defeated Pemberton with 25,000. Pemberton then retired back into Vicksburg. Outnumbered at the outset although his opponents were divided, Grant had marched 200 miles in less than three weeks, won five battles, and inflicted 8,000 casualties.

After two futile assaults (May 19 and 22) against Vicksburg, Grant began a siege (May 22–July 4). With food running out and after a six-week bombardment, on July 4 Pemberton surrendered the city and more than 30,000 men. The remaining Confederate Mississippi stronghold, Port Hudson, surrendered on July 9. The entire river was now under Union control, and the Confederacy was split north to south.

At the same time as the Siege of Vicksburg was occurring, the most important of Civil War battles took place in the eastern theater. After considerable discussion and Lee's opposition, President Davis dropped plans to reinforce Vicksburg and accepted Lee's plan to invade Pennsylvania. This was not to relieve pressure on Vicksburg or to support a Southern peace offensive. Instead, it was a spoiling attack designed to give Virginia a reprieve, disrupt Northern war plans, and delay the next Union invasion.

At the end of May 1863, Lee's army was south of the Rappahannock River in and near Fredericksburg; Hooker's army was just north of the river. Hooker had some 85,000–90,000 men, and Lee had about 70,000. On June 3 Lee began moving west. He planned to move beyond the Blue Ridge, march north and cross the Potomac River, and then threaten Philadelphia and Baltimore, cutting communications to Washington and putting pressure on Hooker to attack him in circumstances of Lee's choosing. Hooker meanwhile moved parallel to Lee, keeping his own army between Lee and Washington.

By the end of June, Lee's infantry and artillery crossed the Potomac. Lee, however, had heard nothing from his cavalry. Stuart, charged with screening the Confederate right flank and keeping Lee informed of Hooker's movements, had been forced farther east than planned, and as a result Hooker was able to get his entire army north of the Potomac unreported to Lee. Lee assumed that the Army of the Potomac was still in Virginia. Lee's own army was spread over 45 miles when on the evening of June 28 Lee learned that Hooker's entire army was in the vicinity of Frederick, Maryland, and much closer to the separate pieces of his army than those were to each other.

Lee ordered an immediate concentration at the road hub town of Gettysburg. The leading divisions of the Army of the Potomac were also headed there, but Hooker no longer had command. In what seemed to be a dangerous move with a major battle looming, on June 28 Lincoln named General Meade as the fifth commander of the Army of the Potomac in 10 months. Meade was solid and dependable, unlikely to be rattled by Lee.

Preliminary contact between the two armies occurred on June 30 at Gettysburg, with both sides rushing men forward. Lee was not happy that battle had been forced on him here by a premature engagement with Union troops. He had hoped to fight from prepared defensive positions at Cashtown to the northwest.

The Battle of Gettysburg, probably the most famous battle in American history, lasted three days (July 1–3). The two sides were about evenly matched. The Army of the Potomac had an advantage in manpower (some 94,000 to 72,000), but the men were exhausted and hungry after their forced marches to the battlefield. Meade also had an edge in artillery.

On July 1 the Confederates drove Union forces back through Gettysburg to strong positions on Culp's Hill and Cemetery Hill, themselves occupying Seminary Ridge, a long partially wooded rise running north and south paralleling Cemetery Hill. Although Union forces had purchased valuable time, this came at a high cost; of 18,000 Union troops who fought that day, two-thirds were casualties.

July 2 saw the heaviest fighting. Union forces had the advantage of interior lines about three miles in length in what came to be called the Fishhook for its shape. The Confederate positions around them were about six miles long. Meade could thus shift troops and supplies more quickly than Lee and was also able to communicate more effectively than his Confederate counterpart. Stuart, however, now arrived with his cavalry. Longstreet urged Lee to secure the two Round Tops at the southern extremity of the Union line and then swing in behind the Union forces, cutting them off from the rear. Lee, however, decided on a two-prong attack on the Union flanks. They were to be semisimultaneous, but Longstreet's orders reached him late, and much time was lost maneuvering to avoid Union lookouts on Little Round Top.

As it worked out, the Confederate attack on the two Round Tops to the south came two to three hours before that of Lieutenant General Richard Ewell on Culp's Hill on the Union right. Lee gave his corps commanders great discretion, but Ewell was no Jackson, and this was the first time he had commanded a corps in battle. Longstreet took Big Round Top but failed to take Little Round Top, which would have enabled him to enfilade the Union line. His men were turned back here by Colonel Joshua Chamberlain's badly outnumbered 20th Maine Regiment. Ewell's attack on Culp's Hill was also turned back, while Major General Jubal Early's men were driven off Cemetery Hill. The latter attack occurred at 8:00 p.m. in a desperate after-dark assault.

On July 3 Lee, having tested the Union flanks, proposed a massive frontal assault on the Union center, which was commanded by Major General Winfield Scott Hancock, perhaps the best Union general on the field. At the same time, Lee ordered Stuart and his cavalry to sweep around the Union positions from the north, then close on the center from the east. But Stuart's cavalry never got into the fray; they were halted five miles east of the battlefield and defeated there by Union cavalry.

At about 1:00 some 160 Confederate guns on Seminary Ridge opened fire, answered by more than 100 Union guns on Cemetery Ridge. The firing went on for two hours in the largest artillery duel in the history of North America. The Confederate guns largely overshot, with most of their damage coming in rear areas. The guns then fell silent, and the Confederate assault began across open ground a mile away on Seminary Ridge in ranks a mile wide with battle flags flying. Three divisions took part, but the other two melted away, and only that of Major General George Pickett remained, giving the name to Pickett's Charge. The Union guns opened up when the attackers were about a half mile distant. Only several hundred Confederates reached the Union line, where there was hand-to-hand combat in what is often referred to as the high-water mark of the Confederacy. Out of about 12,000–13,500 men, Pickett lost 8,000–10,000 that day.

Lee hoped that Meade would try to attack him the next day. Lee kept his defensive line, although he shortened it from six to four miles. Meade rejected this course out of hand. He had sustained 23,000 casualties. Lee's losses, however, were at least as great and possibly as many as 28,000. When Meade failed to attack, on the night of July 4 Lee decamped, taking advantage of darkness and torrential rain to withdraw back down the Cumberland Valley. The Potomac was up, and for a time it looked as if Meade might catch Lee and pin him against the river, but the river went down, and Confederate engineers were able to construct a bridge, which Lee crossed over on July 14 with his equipment, booty, and 6,000 Union prisoners. The South claimed Gettysburg as a victory, but Lee and his men knew better. Gettysburg and Vicksburg decisively tipped the diplomatic balance in favor of the North. Confederate hopes of foreign recognition were gone.

In the western theater, General Braxton Bragg's second Confederate invasion of Kentucky brought victory over Buell in the Battle of Perryville (October 8, 1862), but a lack of support for the Confederacy in Kentucky soon forced Bragg to withdraw. Union major general William Rosecrans and his 60,000-man Army of the Cumberland then maneuvered Bragg's 43,000 Confederates out of Tennessee, defeating Bragg in the Battle of Stones River (December 31, 1862–January 2, 1863). The Union suffered 12,906 casualties, the Confederates 11,739.

The prize was Chattanooga, a key rail center and the gateway to the heart of the Confederacy. Bragg withdrew to Lafayette, Georgia, about 26 miles from Chattanooga, where he was reinforced to about

66,000 men. Rosecrans now blundered. Tricked into believing that Bragg was in full retreat, Rosecrans pushed ahead, with elements of his army sufficiently separated that they could not support each other.

Lying in wait along Chickamauga Creek, Bragg's men struck on September 19. Heavy fighting occurred along a four-mile front, but the Union lines held. On September 20 Bragg again attacked, trying to drive between the Union forces and their base at Chattanooga. The Union side held until misinformation led to a mistaken order by Rosecrans to shift an entire division, opening a gap in the Union line into which the Confederates poured and routed half the Union army. But Union major general George Thomas ("the Rock of Chickamauga") took charge of the remaining Union troops and held, preventing catastrophe. Chickamauga was one of the most costly battles of the war. The Union reported 16,160 casualties, but Confederate losses were 18,454. Although Bragg could claim victory, he failed to mount a credible pursuit, dithering for four days and then deciding to take Chattanooga by siege. Meanwhile, Union reinforcements poured into that town.

Thomas now replaced Rosecrans in command of the Army of the Cumberland, while Grant took overall command of Union armies in the western theater on October 16. On November 23–25 Grant took the offensive in the Battle of Chattanooga (Lookout Mountain–Missionary Ridge), with Union forces under generals Hooker, Thomas, and William T. Sherman defeating the Confederates under Bragg. With Union forces now in control of Chattanooga and key mountain passes, they were poised to bisect the upper and lower South by marching across Georgia to the sea. On December 3 Longstreet abandoned his siege of Union-held Knoxville, Tennessee, and ordered a retreat.

## Grant versus Lee (1864–1865)

In March 1864 Grant was promoted to the newly revived rank of lieutenant general and given supreme command of the Union armies. Halleck became chief of staff while Meade continued in charge of the Army of the Potomac, although Grant went with him in the field. Grant now proposed a methodical hammering away at Lee's army until it was defeated.

Grant planned a multifaceted and simultaneous offensive. In the western theater Sherman would move across Georgia to Savannah, while at the same time Major General Banks would try to take Mobile. The Army of the Potomac, now more than 100,000 men, would drive south from Culpepper on Richmond, while Major General Benjamin Butler's 36,000-man Army of the James would march up the south bank of the James and cut Lee off from the lower South. Other Union forces would move against the Shenandoah Valley from the west and north to seize the railheads of Staunton and Lynchburg. To oppose Meade and Grant, Lee had 60,000 men supported by Beauregard and 30,000 men in the Richmond-Petersburg area.

The Union Overland Campaign began on May 4 when the Army of the Potomac crossed the Rapidan River and entered the so-called Wilderness. Attacking the Union left flank, Lee used the heavily wooded terrain to offset the Union numerical advantage. In the ensuing Battle of the Wilderness (May 5–6), Lee inflicted some 18,000 casualties while sustaining 10,000, but for the first time after a fight with Lee, the Army of the Potomac continued south.

Grant repeatedly tried to outflank Lee, who anticipated Grant's moves and proved too quick for him. Bloody fighting occurred at Spotsylvania Court House (May 8–12), followed by a battle at Cold Harbor on the Chickahominy (June 1–3). Grant again assaulted a well-entrenched Confederate line and on June 3 sent three corps in a frontal assault against Lee; in seven minutes 7,000 Union troops were shot down. In one month of fighting Grant had suffered nearly 60,000 casualties, a figure equal to Lee's total strength, against Confederate casualties of 25,000–30,000. But the Army of Northern Virginia never really recovered from the heavy punishment inflicted.

Grant now sought to steal a march on Lee and move his army south of the James River to Petersburg, 20 miles below Richmond, in order to approach the Confederate capital from the rear and cut its transportation connections to the south and west. Butler's inept generalship prevented Grant from taking Petersburg, which withstood four days of battering on June 15–18, costing Grant another 8,000 casualties.

Both sides now dug in. A nine-month siege followed. On July 30, Union forces exploded a huge mine under the Confederate lines in a costly but unsuccessful attempt to break the siege.

Meanwhile, Union forces were endeavoring to secure the Shenandoah Valley. Major General Franz Siegel's men met defeat at the hands of Major General John C. Breckinridge in the Battle of New Market (May 15). Major General David Hunter then replaced Siegel and resumed the offensive, taking Staunton and reaching as far as Lynchburg before he was turned back by Confederate forces under General Early. When Hunter withdrew into West Virginia, Early embarked on an raid north into Maryland (June 28–July 21) that

carried to five miles from Washington. After testing and finding the Washington defenses too strong, Early withdrew back into the valley.

During March 10–May 22, 1864, the Union mounted its largest combined operation of the war. The Red River Campaign was an attempt to capture Shreveport, Louisiana, and gain access to Texas from the east. Mansfield was the decisive battle of the campaign. There on April 8, Major General Richard Taylor and some 8,800 Confederates attacked and defeated Major General Nathaniel Banks's far larger but drawn-out Union march column, of which only about 12,000 Union troops were able to join the fray. Despite numerical superiority Banks then withdraw, necessarily followed by Rear Admiral Porter's Union naval force on the Red River. The expedition was a fiasco.

In the eastern theater, Grant gave Major General Philip J. Sheridan command of the Union Army of the Shenandoah in August and ordered him to clear the valley. Sheridan laid waste to it and defeated Early in a series of battles, including the Third Battle of Winchester (Opequon, September 19, 1864), the Battle of Cedar Creek (October 19), and finally the Battle of Waynesboro (March 2, 1865), after which Sheridan rejoined Grant.

In early May 1864, Sherman had set out from Chattanooga with 100,000 men to begin his invasion of Georgia. Johnston, who had replaced Bragg, was continually forced to retreat. For two and a half months Johnston slowed the advance of Sherman's superior forces to an average of only a mile a day, but his continued retreats led to Johnston's relief on July 19 and replacement with Lieutenant General John Bell Hood. In two pitched battles, Peachtree Creek (July 20) and Atlanta (July 22), he attacked

Sherman but, after suffering heavy losses, withdrew into Atlanta's entrenchments.

Hood finally abandoned Atlanta, and Sherman entered the city on September 2. This Union victory severed Confederate communications westward and helped secure Lincoln's reelection, dashing the last Southern hopes for a negotiated settlement.

Sherman then destroyed such supplies as might be useful to the Confederates and set out with 60,000 men on a march to the sea (November 14–December 22, 1864), cutting a swath across Georgia some 300 miles in length and 60 miles in width. Union troops systematically destroyed factories, public buildings, warehouses, bridges, and railroads. Sherman encouraged foraging, and there was widespread looting. Sherman's advance was virtually unopposed, and on December 10 he reached Savannah, which fell on December 22.

Sherman's troops then moved northward through South Carolina, inflicting even greater destruction than in Georgia. Union forces burned more than a dozen towns in whole or in part, including much of the state capital of Columbia on February 17, 1865, although at least some of the fires resulted from deliberate Confederate destruction of cotton stores.

Meanwhile, Hood had set out after Union forces under Thomas and made contact with part of them under Major General John M. Schofield at Franklin, Tennessee. In a battle there on November 30, Hood with 22,000 men sustained 6,300 casualties in repeated frontal attacks against 28,000 Union troops in prepared defenses; Union losses were only about 3,100. Schofield then joined Thomas at Nashville, again defeating Hood in a two-day battle (December 15–16), with 55,000 Union troops inflicting 6,000 casualties on Hood's 30,000 men for half that number themselves.

Both sides and especially the Confederates suffered a difficult winter in the

The ruins of Mills House and nearby buildings, Charleston, South Carolina, 1865. A shell-damaged carriage and the remains of a brick chimney are in the foreground. (National Archives)

trenches at Petersburg. Grant now had an advantage of 115,000 men to Lee's 54,000. With Grant systematically hammering away at the Confederate lines, on April 1 Lee made his last assault of the war, against Grant's left flank at Five Forks near Petersburg, only to be repulsed by Sheridan coming up from the Shenandoah Valley. The next day, April 2, Lee evacuated Petersburg and Richmond and headed west, hoping to reach Lynchburg and then move by rail to North Carolina and join forces with General Johnston.

With Grant in pursuit, Lee's movement south and west was blocked by Sheridan's cavalry. Following a series of engagements and with few ration's left, Lee surrendered his remaining force of fewer than 30,000 men on April 9 at Appomattox Court House. Grant paroled Lee's men and allowed them to return to their homes. On April 26 in Durham, North Carolina, General Joseph Johnston surrendered his 37,000 men to Sherman. Some Confederate forces remained in the field into late May, and the Confederate commerce raider *Shenandoah* continued its depredations of American whalers in the Pacific until August.

Lincoln did not live to see the end of the war. After visiting Richmond on April 5, he returned to Washington to work on his plans for the peace and for reconciliation, not a popular policy in the North. On April 14 was shot by a Southern sympathizer while attending a play at Ford's Theatre and died the next day. Vice President Andrew Johnson succeeded him and tried to carry out Lincoln's reconstruction policies but was impeached in 1868 although acquitted. The war ended by declaration on May 9, although the last Confederate command surrender occurred on June 2, 1865.

SPENCER C. TUCKER

## Consequences

The Civil War was by far the costliest U.S. war in terms of casualties. It claimed between 33 and 40 percent of the combined Union and Confederate forces. Union dead are usually given as some 360,000 (110,000 killed in battle or died of wounds) and 275,000 wounded. Confederate dead came to 258,000 (94,000 in battle or from wounds) and at least 100,000 wounded. In the South, one-quarter of all white males of military age lay dead. In terms of war dead per capita, no other U.S. conflict comes close to the Civil War, with its total of 181.7 war dead per every 10,000 people. By contrast, the comparable figure for the American Revolution was 117.9 and a distant 29.6 for World War II. A recent study by J. David Hacker based on census statistics persuasively argues that the above long-accepted death tolls should be increased by more than 20 percent, to some 750,000.

The economic cost of the war was substantial. The Union spent some $2.3 billion on its war effort, or about $98 per person in its population. The Confederacy, on the other hand, expended only $1 billion in its failed bid for independence, but that came to $111 per person for Southerners. The North continued to experience prosperity during the war, with its total wealth increasing by 50 percent during the decade of the 1860s. In stark contrast, the South was impoverished by the war. On top of its military spending, it suffered another $1.1 billion in war damage, or about 40 percent of its prewar wealth, including 40 percent of its livestock and 50 percent of its farm machinery. In addition to all of this, most of the South's invested capital—some $1.6 billion—was wiped out by the freeing of the slaves. Global cotton markets had found other sources during the war, and never again would cotton from the U.S. South command the consistently high prices it did in antebellum years. All told, it took the South more than half a century to recover from the effects of the war.

The war ensured the freedom of 3.5 million slaves. Many of them were initially declared free by Abraham Lincoln in his January 1863 Emancipation Proclamation, aimed only at slaves in areas then still in rebellion against the United States. The Thirteenth Amendment of 1865, however, freed all slaves in the United States. What to do with the newly freed millions was a difficult problem for the federal government in the waning days and immediate aftermath of the war. Plans were discussed for giving each freedman a farm—the much-discussed "forty acres and a mule"— but nothing came of this. The government did establish a Freedmen's Bureau, headed by former Union general Oliver O. Howard. It helped to care for the needs of the recent slaves until they could establish themselves in their new lives. Political realities, however, made this difficult.

Although Union forces had been victorious on the battlefield, the Union was preserved, and the slaves had been freed, white southerners waged a long and ultimately successful struggle to achieve what was for many of them the chief purpose of the war: the maintenance of white supremacy in the South. The 12-year period after the end of the war is known as Reconstruction, during which federal authorities attempted to reestablish truly loyal governments in the southern states and to secure the recognition of basic civil rights for the freedmen. Yet not all northerners were united in desiring the accomplishment of these goals. Some believed that preservation of the Union and perhaps freeing the slaves were all that the war

should have accomplished. Some believed that it had already accomplished too much. This made it a constant struggle to achieve the degree of political support in the North necessary to continue to try to impose respect for black civil rights in the South. Southern whites closed ranks against anything of the sort, showing more unity in opposition to black civil rights than they ever did in defense of the Confederacy itself. Organizations such as the Ku Klux Klan waged a war of terror and intimidation aimed at persuading blacks and their white allies to refrain from voting or to leave the region entirely.

These tactics finally prevailed. In 1877 the federal government terminated its efforts at Reconstruction, and during the next few decades the South developed a system of racial segregation and second-class citizenship for blacks known as Jim Crow. The full fruition of what had been won in the Civil War—what Lincoln called a "new birth of freedom"—had to wait for another era. The unfinished promise of the Civil War was eventually fulfilled by the civil rights movement of the 1950s and 1960s, culminating in the Civil Rights Act of 1964 and the Voting Rights Act of 1965, securing the full privileges of citizenship and civil rights to the descendants of the slaves whom the war had freed.

The war also brought the modern staff system to the U.S. Army as well as the Medal of Honor, national cemeteries, and ultimately battlefield parks. Preservation of the Union also meant that the United States would be able to fill the role of a major player in the family of nations. The war also probably hastened the British government's decision to create the Dominion of Canada in 1867.

SPENCER C. TUCKER AND
STEVEN E. WOODWORTH

## Timeline

| | |
|---|---|
| **Mar 1820** | The Missouri Compromise provides that new states will be admitted to the Union on the basis of one slave and one free. |
| **1846–1848** | The Mexican-American War ends, with the United States acquiring substantial territory. The major question is whether these will be slave or free. |
| **Aug 8, 1848** | The Wilmot Proviso proposes banning slavery in any territory acquired from Mexico as a result of the Mexican-American War. Although the proviso passes in the House, it is defeated in the Senate. |
| **Sep 9, 1850** | The Compromise of 1850 is enacted, which only increases sectional tensions. |
| **May 30, 1854** | The Kansas-Nebraska Act repeals the Missouri Compromise, further hastening the slavery crisis. |
| **Mar 6, 1857** | In the U.S. Supreme Court's *Dred Scott* decision, the high court denies citizenship to slaves, making it impossible for them to petition for their freedom. |
| **Oct 16–18, 1859** | Abolitionist John Brown leads a failed raid on the Federal Arsenal at Harpers Ferry, Virginia. Brown is captured, tried, convicted, and hanged. |
| **Nov 6, 1860** | Republican Abraham Lincoln is elected president of the United States. |
| **Dec 20, 1860** | South Carolina becomes the first state to secede from the Union. Ten other states follow in 1861. |
| **Feb 9, 1861** | Jefferson Davis is unanimously elected president of the Confederacy. |
| **Mar 6, 1861** | The Confederate Congress authorizes a volunteer army. |
| **Apr 12, 1861** | Confederate batteries at Charleston, South Carolina, open fire on Union-held Fort Sumter in Charleston Harbor, beginning the American Civil War. |
| **Apr 15, 1861** | Lincoln calls for 75,000 volunteers for three months' military service. |
| **Apr 19, 1861** | Lincoln orders a blockade of all Confederate ports. |
| **Apr 19–May 13, 1861** | Rioting occurs in Baltimore, Maryland, as Union troops on their way to Washington, D.C., are accosted by secessionists. |
| **Jul 21, 1861** | In the First Battle of Bull Run (Manassas), Union forces under Brigadier General Irvin McDowell are routed by Confederate forces under Brigadier generals Joseph E. Johnston and P. G. T. Beauregard. |
| **Sep 4, 1861** | Confederate forces under Major General Leonidas Polk invade Kentucky. |

| | |
|---|---|
| **Sep 6, 1861** | Union brigadier general Ulysses S. Grant occupies Paducah and Smithland, Kentucky. |
| **Oct 21, 1861** | Union forces advancing on Leesburg, Virginia, are defeated by the Confederates at Balls Bluff. |
| **Nov 1, 1861** | Major General George B. McClellan replaces Lieutenant General Winfield Scott as commander of Union land forces. |
| **Nov 3–7, 1861** | Union naval forces under Commodore Samuel Du Pont secure Port Royal Sound, South Carolina. |
| **Jan 19–20, 1862** | Union forces under Brigadier General George H. Thomas defeat the Confederates under Major General George B. Crittenden in the Battle of Mill Springs, Kentucky. |
| **Feb 6, 1862** | Commodore Andrew Foote's ironclads take the surrender of Confederate Fort Henry on the Tennessee River. Union troops under Grant occupy Fort Henry, then proceed against nearby Fort Donelson on the Cumberland. |
| **Feb 8, 1862** | Union forces under Burnside secure Roanoke Island, North Carolina. |
| **Feb 11–16, 1862** | Union forces under Grant and Foote capture Fort Donelson, causing Johnston to abandon Nashville. |
| **Feb 24, 1862** | Union forces under Major General Don Carlos Buell occupy Nashville, the first state capital to fall to Union troops. |
| **Mar 7–8, 1862** | Union major general Samuel R. Curtis defeats Confederate forces under Major General Earl Van Dorn in the Battle of Pea Ridge, Arkansas. |
| **Mar 8, 1862** | The Confederate ironclad *Virginia* defeats the Union Navy warships *Cumberland* and *Congress* at Hampton Roads, Virginia. |
| **Mar 9, 1862** | The Union ironclad *Monitor* fights an inconclusive battle with the *Virginia*, which, however, retires. It is the first clash between ironclad warships in history. |
| **Mar 11, 1862** | Lincoln removes McClellan from command of the entire army, leaving him with command only of the Army of the Potomac. |
| **Mar 17, 1862** | McClellan commences his Peninsula Campaign to capture Richmond from the east. |
| **Mar 23–Jun 9, 1862** | Confederate general Thomas Jackson's Shenandoah Valley Campaign ties down three Union armies with four times his own number of men. |
| **Apr 1862** | The Confederacy introduces conscription. |
| **Apr 5–May 4, 1862** | McClellan besieges Yorktown and takes it only on May 4, upon the Confederate withdrawal. |
| **Apr 6–7, 1862** | In the Battle of Shiloh, Confederate forces under Johnston surprise Grant's Union forces at Pittsburg Landing, Tennessee. With the |

arrival of reinforcements under Buell, the Union troops force the Confederates to retire.

**Apr 7, 1862**     Union forces under Brigadier General John Pope and Foote capture Island No. 10 in the Mississippi River.

**Apr 26, 1862**     Union forces under Flag Officer David G. Farragut take the surrender of New Orleans. Union troops under Butler then occupy the city.

**May 31–Jun 1, 1862**     In the Battle of Seven Pines (Fair Oaks), General Joseph Johnston's Confederates attack two Union corps, but the arrival of a third corps prevents a Union defeat. Johnston is severely wounded and is replaced as commander of the Army of Northern Virginia by General Robert E. Lee.

**Jun 12–15, 1862**     In an embarrassment for the Union, Lee's cavalry under Major General James E. B. Stuart ride entirely around McClellan's army, destroying Union supplies and rattling the Union commander.

**Jun 25–Jul 1, 1862**     Lee attacks McClellan in what becomes known as the Seven Days' Campaign. Lee fails to envelop McClellan but causes him to withdraw to the James River.

**Aug 3, 1862**     Lincoln orders McClellan to return with his army to Washington.

**Aug 29–30, 1862**     In the Second Battle of Bull Run (Second Manassas), Major General James Longstreet of Lee's Army of Northern Virginia defeats Union general John Pope's Army of Virginia.

**Sep 14**     McClellan fights a series of small battles to secure the South Mountain passes.

**Sep 15, 1862**     Jackson secures the surrender of Harpers Ferry, taking 12,419 Union prisoners in the largest Union surrender of the war.

**Sep 17, 1862**     In the Battle of Antietam (Sharpsburg), McClellan trumpets a victory but fails to pursue Lee effectively.

**Sep 22, 1862**     Lincoln issues the Preliminary Emancipation Proclamation, freeing all slaves in areas of the South still in rebellion as of January 1, 1863.

**Oct 1, 1862**     Buell drives General Braxton Bragg's Confederate invaders from Kentucky.

**Oct 3–4, 1862**     An attempt by the Confederates under Major General Earl Van Dorn to retake Corinth, Mississippi, is unsuccessful.

**Oct 8, 1862**     In the Battle of Perryville, Kentucky, Confederate general Bragg's Army of Mississippi scores a tactical victory against primarily a single corps of Buell's Union Army of the Ohio. The battle is, however, a strategic Union victory.

**Nov 7, 1862**     Lincoln replaces McClellan with General Burnside in command of the Army of the Potomac.

| | |
|---|---|
| **Dec 17, 1862** | Lee wins his most lopsided victory of the war in the Battle of Fredericksburg, repelling repeated Union assaults. |
| **Dec 20, 1862** | Confederate general Van Dorn's successful raid against Grant's supply base of Holly Springs, Mississippi, forces Grant to call off his overland drive on Vicksburg from the north. |
| **Dec 26–29, 1862** | In the Battle of Chickasaw Bluffs, Confederate forces under Vicksburg commander Lieutenant General John C. Pemberton turn back Union forces under Major General William T. Sherman. |
| **Dec 31, 1862–<br>Jan 2, 1863** | In the Battle of Stones River, Tennessee, Union forces under Major General William Rosecrans rebuff two major Confederate attacks under Bragg, ensuring continued Union control of central Tennessee. |
| **Jan 26, 1863** | Lincoln replaces Burnside as commander of the Army of the Potomac with Major General Joseph Hooker. |
| **Mar 1863** | The North introduces conscription. |
| **Mar 29, 1863** | Grant begins his second campaign to take Vicksburg. |
| **Apr 16–17, 1863** | Rear Admiral David Dixon Porter's Mississippi Squadron runs south past the Vicksburg batteries. |
| **May 2–4, 1863** | Lee's Army of Northern Virginia defeats Hooker's Army of the Potomac in the Battle of Chancellorsville. |
| **May 14, 1863** | Grant's army captures the railhead of Jackson, Mississippi, then destroys it. |
| **May 16, 1863** | Grant, moving west on Vicksburg, battles Confederate forces under Pemberton and is victorious in the hard-fought Battle of Champion's Hill. |
| **May 22, 1863** | Grant commences siege operations at Vicksburg. |
| **Jun 3, 1863** | The Gettysburg Campaign begins. |
| **Jun 9, 1863** | Union and Confederate cavalry clash in the Battle of Brandy Station, Virginia. |
| **Jun 28, 1863** | Lincoln replaces Hooker as commander of the Army of the Potomac with the dependable Major General George Gordon Meade. |
| **Jul 1–3, 1863** | In the pivotal Battle of Gettysburg, Lee fails to dislodge Meade's Union forces from their strong defensive position. On the night of July 4–5, he begins his successful withdrawal back into Virginia. |
| **Jul 4, 1863** | Pemberton surrenders Vicksburg and more than 30,000 troops. |
| **Jul 9, 1863** | The remaining Confederate Mississippi stronghold of Port Hudson surrenders. The entire river is now under Union control. |
| **Jul 13, 1863** | Violence sweeps New York City as mobs attack and kill African Americans in what is known as the New York City Draft Riots. |

| | |
|---|---|
| **Sep 19–20, 1863** | At the Battle of Chickamauga, Bragg forces Rosecrans to withdraw in what is one of the most costly battles of the war. |
| **Oct 16, 1863** | Grant assumes command of Union armies in the western theater. |
| **Nov 23–25, 1863** | In the Battle of Chattanooga (Lookout Mountain–Missionary Ridge), Grant takes forces under Generals Hooker, Thomas, and Sherman to defeat the Confederates under Bragg. |
| **Dec 3, 1863** | Longstreet abandons his siege of Union-held Knoxville, Tennessee. |
| **Mar 9, 1864** | Grant receives supreme command of the Union armies. |
| **Mar 10–May 22, 1864** | In the failed Red River Campaign, Union forces attempt to capture Shreveport and gain access to Texas from the east. |
| **Apr 8, 1864** | In the Battle of Mansfield, Louisiana, Confederate major general Richard Taylor defeats Union major general Nathaniel Banks's far larger but drawn-out Union march column. |
| **May 4, 1864** | The Union Overland Campaign commences. In the ensuing Battle of the Wilderness (May 5–6), Lee inflicts more casualties than his side suffers, but the Army of the Potomac continues south. |
| **May 8–12, 1864** | Bloody fighting occurs in the Battle of Spotsylvania Court House. |
| **May 15, 1864** | In the Battle of New Market in Virginia, Confederate forces under Major General John C. Breckinridge prevent Union forces under Major General Franz Siegel from securing control of the Shenandoah Valley. |
| **Jun 1–3, 1864** | Another bloody clash occurs between Grant and Lee at Cold Harbor. |
| **Jun 9, 1864** | Grant commences what will be a nine-month siege of Petersburg, Virginia. |
| **Jun 28–Jul 21, 1864** | Early's Washington Raid comes within five miles of Washington, D.C., before it is halted. |
| **Jul 19 1864** | President Davis replaces Johnston with Lieutenant General John Bell Hood. In two pitched battles, Peachtree Creek (July 20) and Atlanta (July 22), Hood attacks Sherman but withdraws into Atlanta's entrenchments. |
| **Jul 30, 1864** | In the Battle of the Crater, Union forces explode a huge mine under the Confederate lines at Petersburg, but poor Union planning allows the Confederates to plug the resulting breach. |
| **Aug 5, 1864** | In the Battle of Mobile Bay, Farragut moves against the Confederate defenses of Mobile Bay, defeating and capturing the Union ironclad *Tennessee.* |
| **Aug 7, 1864** | Grant gives Major General Philip J. Sheridan command of all Union forces in the Shenandoah and begins driving Early's Confederates |

from the valley in the Third Battle of Winchester (Opequon, September 19, 1864), the Battle of Cedar Creek (October 19), and finally the Battle of Waynesboro (March 2, 1865).

**Sep 2, 1864**  Sherman enters Atlanta, cutting Confederate communications westward and dashing the last Southern hopes for a negotiated settlement.

**Nov 14–Dec 2, 1864**  Sherman sets out from Atlanta with 60,000 men on a march to the sea, cutting a swath across Georgia some 60 miles wide and 300 miles long.

**Nov 30, 1864**  Hood attacks Union forces under Major General John M. Schofield at Franklin, Tennessee, and nearly destroys his army in repeated frontal assaults.

**Dec 10, 1864**  Sherman's forces reach Savannah, which falls to the Union on December 22. Sherman's troops then move northward through South Carolina, inflicting great destruction.

**Dec 15–16, 1864**  Schofield and Thomas again defeat Hood at Nashville.

**Feb 11–22, 1865**  In the Wilmington Campaign, Union land forces under Schofield and naval forces under Porter capture this key port for Confederate blockade-runners.

**Feb 17, 1865**  Much of the South Carolina capital city of Columbia is destroyed by fire.

**Apr 1, 1865**  With the Army of the Potomac now enjoying a numerical advantage of more than two to one, Lee attacks Grant a last time in the Battle of Five Forks and is defeated.

**Apr 2, 1865**  Lee evacuates Petersburg and Richmond and proceeds west, hoping to reach Lynchburg and then move by rail to North Carolina.

**Apr 9, 1865**  After a series of engagements, Lee surrenders what remains of the Army of Northern Virginia at Appomattox Court House.

**Apr 12, 1865**  Union forces under Major General Edward Canby capture Mobile, Alabama.

**Apr 14, 1865**  President Lincoln is shot by a Southern sympathizer while attending a play at Ford's Theatre in Washington and dies the next day. Vice President Andrew Johnson succeeds him.

**Apr 26, 1865**  At Bennett Place in Durham, North Carolina, General Johnston surrenders to Sherman.

**May 4, 1865**  Remaining Confederate forces in Alabama and Mississippi surrender.

**May 9, 1865**  President Johnson declares the Civil War at an end.

**Jun 2, 1865**  General Kirby Smith surrenders Confederate forces west of the Mississippi.

SPENCER C. TUCKER

## Further Reading

Beringer, Richard E., et al. *Why the South Lost the Civil War.* Athens: University of Georgia Press, 1986.

Canney, Donald L. *Lincoln's Navy: The Ships, Men and Organization, 1861–65.* Annapolis, MD: Naval Institute Press, 1998.

Catton, Bruce. *The Civil War.* New York: Houghton Mifflin, 1987.

Davis, William C. *Look Away! A History of the Confederate States of America.* New York: Free Press, 2003.

Davis, William C. *Stand in the Day of Battle: The Imperiled Union, 1861–1865.* Garden City, NY: Doubleday, 1983.

Donald, David, Jean H. Baker, and Michael F. Holt. *The Civil War and Reconstruction.* New York: Norton, 2001.

Eicher, David J. *The Longest Night: A Military History of the Civil War.* New York: Simon and Schuster, 2001.

Foner, Eric. *The Fiery Trial: Abraham Lincoln and American Slavery.* New York: Norton, 2010.

Foote, Shelby. *The Civil War: A Narrative.* 3 vols. New York: Random House, 1968–1974.

Gallagher, Gary W. *The Confederate War.* Cambridge, MA: Harvard University Press, 1999.

Guelzo, Allen C. *Fateful Lightning: A New History of the Civil War and Reconstruction.* Oxford: Oxford University Press, 2012.

Hacker, J. David. "A Census-Based Count of the Civil War Dead." *Civil War History* 57 (2011): 307–348.

Hattaway, Herman, and Archer Jones. *How the North Won: A Military History of the Civil War.* Urbana: University of Illinois Press, 1981.

Jones, Howard. *Abraham Lincoln and a New Birth of Freedom: The Union and Slavery in the Diplomacy of the Civil War.* Lincoln: University of Nebraska Press, 1999.

McPherson, James M. *Battle Cry of Freedom: The Civil War Era.* Oxford: Oxford University Press, 1988.

McPherson, James M. *This Mighty Scourge: Perspectives on the Civil War.* Oxford: Oxford University Press, 2007.

Nevins, Allan. *The War for the Union.* 8 vols. New York: Scribner, 1947–1971.

Thornton, Mark, and Robert Burton Ekelund. *Tariffs, Blockades, and Inflation: The Economics of the Civil War.* Lanham, MD: Rowman and Littlefield, 2004.

Tucker, Spencer C. *Blue and Gray Navies: The Civil War Afloat.* Annapolis, MD: Naval Institute Press, 2006.

Weigley, Frank R. *A Great Civil War: A Military and Political History, 1861–1865.* Bloomington: Indiana University Press, 2004.

# Cuban Wars of Independence (1868–1878, 1879–1880, and 1895–1898)

## Causes

What is usually known as the Cuban War of Independence against Spanish colonial rule began on February 24, 1895, and lasted until February 15, 1898, but can be said to have extended to the end of fighting between Spanish and U.S. forces on August 12, 1898, in the Spanish-American War of that year. There were actually three separate revolts on the island against Spanish colonial rule in the second half of the 19th century. The other two were the Ten Years' War (1868–1878) and the 1879–1880 Little War (Guerra Chiquita). It seems logical to treat these as three separate elements in one long struggle for independence, commencing on October 10, 1868, and extending to August 12, 1898.

**Cuban Wars of Independence (1868–1878, 1879–1880, and 1895–1898)**

| Battles of San Juan Hill and El Caney (July 1, 1898)* | | |
|---|---|---|
| | **U.S. and Allied Cuban Forces** | **Spanish Forces** |
| Killed | 124 | 215 |
| Wounded | 817 | 376 |
| Captured | 0 | 2 |

*These two simultaneous battles, fought in close proximity, were the first major engagements of the Spanish-American War.

| Santiago de Cuba, Naval Battle of (July 3, 1898) | | |
|---|---|---|
| | **United States** | **Spain** |
| Killed | 1 | 323 |
| Wounded | 1 | 151 |
| Captured | 0 | 1,720 |
| Ships lost | 0 | 6 |

| Spanish-American War (April 21–August 12, 1898) | | | | |
|---|---|---|---|---|
| | **Killed in Action or Died of Wounds** | **Died of Disease** | **Wounded** | **Captured** |
| **United States** | 385 | 2,061 | 1,662 | 8 |
| **Spain** | 1,000 | 15,000 | 800 | 30,000 |

**Sources:** Trask, David F. "The Battle of Santiago." In *Great American Naval Battles*, edited by Jack Sweetman, 198–218. Annapolis, MD: Naval Institute Press, 1998; Trask, David F. *The War with Spain in 1898*. Lincoln: University of Nebraska Press, 1996; U.S. Department of Defense. *Principal Wars in Which the United States Participated: U.S. Military Personnel Serving and Casualties*. Washington, DC: Washington Headquarters Services, Directorate for Information Operations and Reports, 2003.

Explorer Christopher Columbus, sailing for Spain, discovered the island of Cuba in 1492. Its conquest was undertaken by Spaniards under conquistador Diego Velázquez in 1510 and completed by 1515. Cuba's fertile soil was ideal for the cultivation of tobacco and sugarcane, while the discovery of gold on the island's interior led to the opening of a number of mines. In order to provide labor for the plantations and mines, the Spaniards enslaved most of the island's population.

Their susceptibility to European diseases and their exploitation resulted in the near extinction within a generation of the native population. To replace the native labor, the Spaniards imported African slaves. Until the Haitian Revolution and War of Independence (1791–1804), the Cuban economy remained diversified, with tobacco, livestock, and shipbuilding as the principal industries. Owing to a precipitous drop in sugarcane production in Haiti, however, wealthy Cuban landowners sought to make Cuba the world's leading producer of sugar, and they secured concessions from the Spanish throne to accelerate this.

Cuba's economy soon became predominantly agricultural, with sugarcane the primary cash crop and the establishment of large sugarcane plantations throughout the island. The harsh conditions of sugarcane cultivation and labor-intensive methods employed resulted in a large slave population, with an estimated 90,000 slaves brought to Cuba during 1856–1860 alone. Ultimately, sugarcane cultivation enriched a small planter class along with the few who catered to the plantation owners.

The United States, only 103 miles from Cuba, would come to play a key role in its affairs. There were many Americans, especially slaveholding expansionists in the South, who wanted to make the island a state or states of the United States, in large part to help offset the growing influence in Congress of the more populous North. In 1848 President James Polk offered Spain $100 million for the island. Spain rejected the offer. During 1849–1851 there were three successive filibustering expeditions launched to Cuba from the southern United States, all of which ended in failure, with many of those who were captured either hanged or shot by firing squads. In 1852 Spain again rejected an offer to sell Cuba to the United States.

In October 1854 during the presidency of Franklin Pierce and at the behest of U.S. secretary of state William L. Marcy, key American diplomats in Europe—Pierre Soulé, minister to Spain; James Buchanan, minister to Great Britain, and John Y. Mason, minister to France—met secretly in Ostend, Belgium, to discuss how to acquire the island from Cuba. Their draft proposal, sent to Washington in October 1854, proposed that the United States purchase the island for $120 million and outlined how this would be beneficial to both parties. They also declared that the United States would "be justified in wresting" the island from Spain if that government refused to sell.

Soulé's indiscretions led to the plan becoming public knowledge before Marcy had time to try to implement it. Members of the U.S. House of Representatives demanded that it be made public, and the administration was forced to publish it. The ensuing public reaction to what became known as the Ostend Manifesto doomed any chance of success. While these U.S. efforts to acquire Cuba were unsuccessful, Cuba did attract American investments, much of it in plantations and sugarcane-processing plants.

Cuban independence leader Carlos Manuel de Céspedes y del Castillo, who began the Ten Years' War in 1868. (Library of Congress)

The plantation system dominated the island economically and politically. Spaniards, who counted only 8 percent of the Cuban population, possessed more than 90 percent of its wealth. The Cuban-born population had no political rights and was not represented in the Spanish parliament. Anger over this state of affairs led to the first major movement for independence, centered in eastern Cuba.

In July 1867 Cuba's wealthiest plantation owner, Francisco Vicente Aguilera, formed the Revolutionary Committee of Bayamo. The movement garnered support in the larger towns of Oriente Province especially Manzanillo, where plantation and sugar mill owner Carlos Manuel de Céspedes became its leader. Informed of Céspedes's activities, the authorities tried to force him into line by imprisoning his

son Oscar. When Céspedes refused to negotiate, his son was executed.

RICK DYSON, MICHAEL R. HALL, AND SPENCER C. TUCKER

## Course

### War of 1867–1868

Céspedes had planned to launch the revolt on October 14, 1868. Warned that the authorities had ordered his arrest, he was forced to proceed early. On October 10, 1868, he rang the slave bell on his plantation and, once the slaves had assembled, announced their freedom (and conscription into his revolutionary army) and proclaimed Cuban independence from Spain.

On October 11, Céspedes and a small band of supporters attacked the nearby town of Yara. Although a failure, the assault, commonly known as the Grito de Yara (Shout of Yara) and today a national holiday in Cuba, in effect unleashed the war of independence and widespread slave revolt. The revolutionary spirit quickly spread throughout eastern Cuba. By the end of the year the rebellion counted more than 10,000 followers, many of them former slaves. Indeed, for many revolutionaries, emancipation was as important as the liberation of the island. Hoping to win the support of plantation owners in the western half of the island, Céspedes, who preferred gradual emancipation, proclaimed the death penalty for any revolutionary who attacked sugarcane estates or slave property. In addition, Céspedes favored independence as a prelude to annexation by the United States, which many Cuban nationalists opposed.

On October 13, the rebels took eight towns in Oriente Province and acquired a number of weapons as well as additional recruits; by the end of the month, the insurrectionists numbered some 12,000 men. On October 20, 1868, the revolutionaries captured Bayamo, which became the seat of a provisional government. The rebels held that city until January 11, 1869, when, faced with superior Spanish forces, they burned Bayamo to the ground rather than surrender it. While enjoying moderate success in the countryside, the rebels were unable to capture many major urban centers, however.

On April 10, 1869, the rebels convened a constitutional assembly in Guáimaro. Céspedes was elected president, while Ignacio Agramonte and Antonio Zambrana were selected as its secretaries and charged with writing a constitution. Two days later, the assembly transformed itself into the Congress of Representatives. Céspedes was elected president, and Céspedes's brother-in-law Manuel de Quesada was named head of the armed forces.

In May 1869, Céspedes petitioned the U.S. government for diplomatic recognition. Washington rejected the request. The Ulysses S. Grant Administration, which was primarily focusing on Reconstruction, feared that recognition of the Cuban rebels would undermine its legal case seeking economic damages from the United Kingdom, which had recognized the belligerency of the Confederate States of America in 1861. In addition, U.S. recognition of the Cuban rebels would absolve Spain from responsibility for damages to American property in Cuba inflicted by the Cuban revolutionaries.

Regardless of the official position, many U.S. citizens and officials were openly supportive of the Cuban revolutionary cause. In 1870 Quesada, with the collusion of American John Patterson, purchased the *Virginius,* a former Confederate blockade-runner

captured by Union forces at the end of the American Civil War.

Flying an American flag and nominally owned by Patterson, the *Virginius* was used to supply the Cuban revolutionaries with weapons and other matérial. On October 31, 1873, however, the Spanish warship *Tornado* captured the *Virginius* off the coast of Jamaica and took it to Santiago. In early November following Spanish legal proceedings, the authorities condemned and executed as pirates 53 men from the *Virginius,* many of them Americans. This event, which was well publicized in American newspapers, brought the United States and Spain to the brink of war. Tensions were reduced, however, after the Spanish government promised to pay an indemnity to the families of the executed Americans.

During the revolutionary struggle, Dominican-born Máximo Gómez y Báez trained the revolutionary forces, known as Mambí warriors, in the employment of the machete in combination with firearms against the Spanish troops. Nonetheless, more Spanish soldiers died of disease, primarily yellow fever, than in battle.

By 1873, neither side in the struggle had been able to achieve notable victories. The Spaniards had, however, constructed fortifications across Camaguey Province, effectively dividing the island in half. Céspedes's inability to expand the war into the prosperous western half of the island cost him support, and on October 27, 1873, the Congress of Representatives removed him from office. Salvador Cisneros became the new president.

In 1875, Gómez launched an unsuccessful invasion of the western half of the island. The majority of the plantation owners in western Cuba refused to support the revolutionary cause, however. Most of the fighting during the war remained confined to eastern Cuba. Rebels destroyed loyalist plantations, and Spanish troops destroyed insurgent plantations.

Spain's efforts to end the fighting in Cuba had been hampered by the Third Carlist War (1872–1876). With the end of that conflict and the restoration of the Bourbons to the Spanish throne, the Spanish government was able to dedicate greater resources to Cuba. By the end of 1876, King Alfonso XII had sent 100,000 troops in to Cuba. On October 19, 1877, they captured Cuban president Tomás Estrada Palma.

In February 1878 following a number of rebel military reverses, the Congress of Representatives opened peace negotiations with Spain. On February 10 the Cuban revolutionaries signed the Pact of Zanjón, which effectively ended the Ten Years' War. Under its terms, Spain promised numerous administrative and political reforms. All revolutionaries were granted amnesty, and former slaves who served in the revolutionary army were granted their unconditional freedom. Revolutionary general Antonio Maceo rejected this and demanded complete emancipation. He continued fighting for 10 more weeks.

The failure of the Spanish government to fulfill its pledge of reform in Cuba led to the Small War in 1879. Following his release under the Pact of Zanjón, Calixto García Iñiguez, one of the revolutionary leaders, left Cuba for the United States. In New York City, Garcia met with other Cuban exiles and organized the Cuban Revolutionary Committee. In 1878, he issued a manifesto against Spanish rule.

## War of 1879–1880

Fighting in what would be known in Cuba history as the Small War began on August 26, 1879. The rebels were poorly armed, and given the perceived slim chance of their success, there was little enthusiasm among the Cuban population for a renewal of the struggle. In western Cuba most of the rebel leaders were soon arrested, and by September 1880 the Spanish authorities had completely crushed the revolt.

## War of 1895–1898

Although Madrid again promised reform, little was accomplished in that regard. In 1881 the Spanish Constitution of 1876 was applied to Cuba, and the islanders were now able to send representatives to the Spanish Cortes (parliament); however, they were staunch conservative, and thus little changed. Also, after the Small War, U.S. investors were able to purchase estates they had tried unsuccessfully to buy before and acquire others at low prices. This further tied Cuba economically to the United States, which was already taking the majority of Cuban exports.

In January 1892, Cuban José Martí founded El Partido Revolucionario Cubano (the Cuban Revolutionary Party) in New York City and immediately called for Cuban independence. The party soon became the leading voice and organizational apparatus for Cuban independence. Its demands were independence, the removal of legal distinctions based on race, amity with those Spaniards who supported the party and the revolution, and economic and land reforms. Certain elements within Cuban society, primarily the planters and a large segment of the middle class, wished to remain a part of the Spanish Empire but with increased autonomy.

This third uprising against Spanish rule, commonly known as the War for Cuban Independence, began near Santiago de Cuba in the eastern part of the island on February 24, 1895. However, attempts to coordinate the uprising across the island faltered when Spanish officials arrested en masse the rebel leaders in Havana and Matanzas. The armed struggle floundered for most of 1895, with the rebellion again confined to the eastern part of the island and with military setbacks for the insurgents across the rest of colony. The death of Martí, killed fighting Spanish troops in the Battle of Dos Ríos on May 19, 1895, was a major blow to the rebel cause.

Spain's appointment in 1895 of Arsenio Martínez-Campos y Antón, the victor in the Ten Years' War, as captain-general offered hope for a quick end to the conflict. Campos was a conciliatory figure who had appealed to those in Cuba seeking autonomy and reform. Any hope for a quick reconciliation ended when the rebel forces moved into the central and western parts of the island, however. Campos was unable to contain the rebels in the eastern part of the island or to reach any agreement with the those favoring autonomy. Spanish conservatives now gave up any pretense of a negotiated end to the conflict and were determined to crush the rebellion militarily.

It soon became clear that the rebels were actually at war with two enemies at once—the planters and the colonial regime. The planters were thrown into the arms of the latter by virtue of the need to protect their holdings and status in Cuban society.

While Martí had been the intellectual and political leader of the rebellion, the rebel army was led by Gómez and Antonio Maceo. Gomez, a former Spanish general, established the strategy of employing hit-and-run tactics while avoiding pitched battles with the better-equipped and more numerous Spanish colonial troops. Gomez also made war on the lifeblood of the Cuban

elite and colonial regime by attacking and destroying their sugarcane plantations. At the same time, the rebels received significant support from the peasants and African plantation workers in the countryside.

As the war dragged on into 1896, Cuban exile groups in the United States, known as juntas, were able to mobilize American popular opinion to the side of the rebels. The juntas were also instrumental in funneling arms and money to the rebels. That same year the rebels were able to extend the conflict to the more prosperous western portion of the colony, which was also the heart of the sugarcane industry, inflicting significant economic losses on both the Cuban and Spanish economies.

As the conflict wore on, it turned increasingly violent. The rebel invasion of western Cuba led to the replacement of Campos. Conservative Spanish premier Antonio Cánovas del Castillo appointed General Valeriano Weyler y Nicolau as captain-general of Cuba. Weyler held that post during February 1896–October 1897.

Weyler had been governor-general of the Philippines during 1888–1891. There he mounted military operations to suppress uprisings in Mindanao and other islands. Returning to Spain in 1892, he commanded the VI Army Corps, quelling unrest in Navarre and in the Basque areas of Spain. He was then captain-general of Barcelona, where he took an active role in suppressing socialists and anarchists in this increasingly industrial city.

Arriving in Cuba with 50,000 Spanish reinforcements, Weyler continued his reputation as a stern and uncompromising officer. No friend of the American press, he soon ordered the arrest and expulsion from Cuba of American journalists. In order to isolate the insurgency, he also ordered the construction of *trochas,* or fortified lines across Cuba, and notoriously, he sought to separate the insurgents from the civilian population in the countryside by the "reconcentration" of the population, removing the peasants to fortified towns. The forerunner of the British concentration camps of the South African (Boer War) and of the U.S. Strategic Hamlet program during the Vietnam War, this program uprooted some 300,000 peasants and placed them in hastily constructed and often inadequate communities where they were prey to unsanitary conditions, disease, and even starvation.

Thousands died. Meanwhile, Weyler's troops laid waste to the countryside, destroying crops and livestock and anything else that might be of use to the rebels. These policies, while they had some success against the insurgency, earned Weyler such appellations in the American press as "The Butcher," "The Mad Dog," and "The Hyena." Weyler's policies also added to the rebel ranks and greatly aroused general American opposition to Spanish policies in Cuba.

Sensitive to this criticism and to the sharp deterioration in U.S.-Spanish relations, the government of new Spanish premier Práxedes Mateo Sagasta recalled Weyler in October 1897 and replaced him with General Ramón Blanco y Erenas. That November also, Sagasta formally granted autonomy to Cuba and Puerto Rico.

The fighting continued, however. Indeed, destruction increased as the Spanish troops withdrew into the cities and fortified villages and the rebels increasingly controlled the countryside. A war of attrition ensued that was marked by deadlock, with neither side able to defeat the other. The rebels grew stronger and bolder while Spanish morale plummeted. Many now believed that the Spanish cause was lost, with Madrid desperately seeking a way out of the Cuban morass.

Following the American Civil War (1861–1865), American investment in Cuba had grown, as had American interest in Cuban affairs. There was also some renewed interest in making Cuba part of the United States, although this time the advocates were business leaders and proponents of American empire. Tensions between the United States and Spain increased as Americans became frustrated with Spanish colonial rule and economic restrictions.

Cuban exiles in the United States lobbied for American political and popular support for Cuban independence. The Cuban juntas succeeded in casting the Cuban revolt in terms of an oppressed people endeavoring to secure their freedom from oppression, often comparing their struggle to that of the American Revolution, with the Spanish government being corrupt, brutal, and repressive.

This propaganda was immensely successful, fueled by the so-called yellow press. New York newspaper publishers William Hearst and Joseph Pulitzer, locked in a battle to increase circulation at the other's expense, exploited the interest in the fighting in Cuba to their advantage. They sent reporters to the island who then filed stories of heavy-handed Spanish rule and atrocities on the part of the Spanish Army. Many of these reports, filed from the safety of Havana, lacked any notion of balanced reporting or were outright fabrications. Weyler's reconcentration policy had been a particularly fertile source for such reporting. Tensions between Washington and Madrid, spurred by the yellow press, Washington's desire to protect American commercial interests in Cuba, and the steady drumbeat of American imperialists, grew to dangerous proportions by 1898.

On January 24, 1898, U.S. president William McKinley ordered the second-class battleship *Maine* to proceed to Havana, supposedly to protect U.S. interests in Cuba but actually to pressure Spain into changing its policies there. This was certainly a provocative act, much resented by Spain, although Madrid had reluctantly agreed to it. The *Maine* arrived in Havana Harbor the next day, and on the night of February 15 the ship was ripped apart by tremendous explosions. Attributed in the American press to a mine planted by the Spaniards, the likely cause was spontaneous combustion in a coal bunker next to an ammunition locker. The blast killed 260 members of its crew, with 6 others dying as a result of their injuries. The sinking of the *Maine* led to great anger in the United States toward Spain ("Remember the *Maine,* the hell with Spain!").

Further fueling American animosity toward Spain was the so-called De Lôme Letter. Sent by Spanish ambassador to the United States Enrique Dupuy de Lôme, it contained disparaging remarks about President McKinley. Routed through Cuba, the transmission was intercepted and then published by the Hearst papers on February 9, 1898. This promoted a "Go Home De Lôme" campaign ad that brought de Lôme's resignation.

McKinley, unwilling to stand against the growing clamor in the United States for war, on April 11 asked Congress for authority to send American troops to Cuba. On April 19, the Senate and House of Representatives passed joint resolutions that demanded a Spanish withdrawal, supported Cuban independence, disclaimed any American intention to annex Cuba, and authorized the president to employ such military force as he thought necessary to assist the Cuban insurgents in securing independence. Senator Henry Moore Teller was the author of the amendment stipulating that Cuba should be "free and independent" and that the United States could not annex Cuba and would leave "control of the island to its people." The Teller Amendment also confirmed that U.S. armed forces would be removed once the war was over. The amended resolution secured passage in the Senate by a vote of 42 to 35 and the House of Representatives by 311 to 6, both on April 19. President McKinley signed the joint resolution on April 20, and the ultimatum was forwarded to Spain, where it was rejected. Spain declared war on the United States on April 23.

Congress formally declared war on April 25, a declaration made retroactive to April 21. The Spanish-American War lasted until August 12, 1898. Hostilities began almost immediately with a U.S. naval blockade of Cuba. It took time to assemble an invasion force, and there was considerable confusion in the process, but the U.S. Army V Corps commanded by Major General William R. Shaftner came ashore in the insurgent stronghold of Oriente Province during June 22–24. Cuban forces helped establish the beachhead and protect the landing at Daiquiri and Siboney to the east of Santiago de Cuba. The Cubans also provided much-needed intelligence on Spanish military dispositions.

Spanish commander Lieutenant General Arsenio Linares y Pombo made little effort to concentrate his manpower. The U.S. V Corps numbered fewer than 20,000 men and was poorly equipped. Linares had some 35,00 men under his command, but instead of concentrating them at Santiago for a decisive encounter he left some 24,000 men in scattered locations to defend against attacks by Cuban insurgent forces. Provisioning all of them there would have been difficult, but this decision meant that only limited Spanish military resources were available to oppose the Americans in the key battles for Santiago.

The initial U.S. ground objective was to capture Santiago and its Spanish defenders as well as the naval squadron that had set out from Spain under Admiral Pascual Cervera y Topete and had taken refuge in its harbor. To reach Santiago, the Americans had to secure Spanish defenses in the San Juan Heights and at El Caney.

Meanwhile, overwhelming U.S. naval strength was concentrated off Santiago. During June 6–10, a force of more than 600 U.S. marines and 300 Cuban rebels secured strategically important Guantánamo Bay, with its excellent harbor. The major naval battle of the war, that of Santiago de Cuba, was fought on July 3, when Cervera sought to break free, and ended in the destruction of the Spanish squadron of four armored cruisers and two torpedo boat destroyers by the far more powerful U.S. Navy North Atlantic Squadron, commanded by Rear Admiral William T. Sampson.

Land battles occurred between the Spaniards and Americans at Las Guasimas (June 24) and El Caney and San Juan Hill (July 1, 1898) as the Americans sought to close on Santiago. After the Spaniards successfully defended Fort Canosa, they were able to bar entry to Santiago. American and Cuban forces then undertook a siege of the city, which Linares surrendered on July 17. Much bitterness resulted from the American refusal to permit Cuban forces from entering Santiago to prevent armed clashes between the Cubans and Spaniards. General Calixto García, commanding the rebel forces in eastern Cuba, ordered his men to hold in place. Adding insult to injury, Shafter also refused to allow García to participate in the surrender ceremonies in Santiago, leading to the latter's resignation.

After having suffered defeats in both the Philippines and Puerto Rico, which had also been invaded by the United States, the Spanish government sued for peace on July 17, and on August 12 the United States and Spain signed a protocol of peace in which Spain agreed to relinquish all claims to Cuba. The two sides then opened peace negotiations in Paris.

MICHAEL R. HALL AND
SPENCER C. TUCKER

## Consequences

Spanish historians tend to claim that the Cuban insurgency would not have been successful without U.S. intervention, while Cuban historians assert that the Cubans would have defeated Spain without U.S. military intervention. Certainly the military intervention by the United States sped up the Cuban victory, with the U.S. Navy playing the key role of isolating the island from Spanish logistical assistance. The Spanish-American War marked finis to the long decline of Spain as a world power and its relegation to second- or third-rank power status. The war also saw the United States become a colonial power and marked its arrival as a great world power.

The Treaty of Paris of December 10, 1898, formally ended hostilities. Spain renounced its sovereignty over Cuba, while the United States secured from Spain the islands of Puerto Rico and Guam as well as the entire Philippine archipelago, for which acquisition the United States agreed to pay Spain $20 million. These territories were taken for strategic regions: to secure important fleet anchorages and coaling stations for the U.S. Navy as well as to prevent Germany from acquiring the Philippines. Few realized at the time, however, the impact of the latter in setting up the future confrontation with Japan.

U.S. secretary of state John Hay had described the Spanish-American War as a "splendid little war." Indeed, the United States gained much at scant cost in American lives and treasure. Certainly the outcome of the war gave a boost to American self-confidence and assertiveness. The quick victory over Spain, however, exposed major weaknesses in weaponry, organization, logistics, planning, and interservice rivalries. Much of this was subsequently addressed.

Despite the Teller Amendment, the future status of Cuba remained in doubt. President McKinley had refused to recognize the provisional government established by the Cuban insurgents in 1895 and had then negotiated peace with Spain without including Cuban representation. With many Americans believing that Cuba was not ready for self-rule, Cuba remained under U.S. military occupation from January 1, 1899, to May 20, 1902. Although U.S. governor-general in Cuba Major General Leonard Wood accomplished a great deal in restoring the Cuban economy and U.S. doctors helped bring an end to the scourge of yellow fever, many American officials believed that full independence for Cuba would cause the island to slip back into chaos.

As a consequence, Congress insisted on the Platt Amendment of March 2, 1901, attached to an army appropriations bill, that gave the United States the right to intervene in Cuba to maintain order there. Cuba was then forced to incorporate this in a treaty. Cubans discovered that there were restrictions on rights to enter into foreign treaties or take on financial obligations, and the U.S. government secured an unlimited lease on territory at Guantánamo Bay for a naval base, which continues to the present. In effect, the Platt Amendment made Cuba a protectorate of the United States.

Indeed, the United States instigated military rule in Cuba during 1906–1909, 1912, and 1917–1922. The Platt Amendment remained in force until 1934, when most of its provisions were repealed in the Cuban-American Treaty of Relations, part of U.S. president Franklin Roosevelt's Good Neighbor policy toward Latin America. The Cuban Constitutional Convention of 1940 eliminated the Platt Amendment from the new Cuban Constitution, but the threat of U.S. intervention remained, as a pro-American dictatorship headed by Fulgencio Batista controlled Cuba from 1952 until 1959. Cubans' resentment for the continued subordination of their country's interest to those of the United States helped fuel the overthrow of Batista and ensure the success of Marxist revolutionary Fidel Castro.

SPENCER C. TUCKER

## Timeline

| | |
|---|---|
| **1492** | Explorer Christopher Columbus, sailing on behalf of the Spanish Crown, discovers Cuba. |
| **1510–1515** | Spanish forces under Diego Velázquez conquer Cuba. |
| **Jun 9, 1848** | U.S. president James K. Polk offers Spain $100 million for Cuba. |

**Aug 15, 1848**    The Spanish government declines President James Polk's offer to purchase Cuba.

**1849–1851**    Three successive Cuban filibustering expeditions launched from the United States end in failure.

**Oct 22, 1852**    Spain again refuses to sell Cuba to the United States.

**Oct 1854**    The Ostend Manifesto suggests that the United States purchase Cuba for $120 million and that if Spain should refuse, Cuba would be taken by force. The plan is publicized, ultimately dooming it.

**Jul 1867**    Wealthy Cuban plantation owner Francisco Vicente Aguilera establishes the Revolutionary Committee of Bayamo, with plantation owner Carlos Manuel de Céspedes as its leader.

**Oct 10, 1868**    Warned of his impending arrest, Céspedes launches a revolt against Spain. He announces Cuban independence and frees his slaves but conscripts them into his revolutionary army.

**Oct 11, 1868**    Céspedes attacks the nearby town of Yara. The assault, commonly known as the Grito de Yara (Shout of Yara), failsm but the revolt quickly spreads throughout eastern Cuba.

**Oct 20, 1868**    Rebel forces capture Bayamo, which becomes their provisional capital.

**Jan 11, 1869**    Spanish forces attack Bayamo, which the rebels burn rather than surrender.

**Apr 10, 1869**    The rebels convene a constitutional assembly in Guáimaro.

**Apr 12, 1869**    The assembly transforms itself into the Congress of Representatives, with Céspedes as president and his brother-in-law Manuel de Quesada as head of the armed forces.

**Oct 27, 1873**    With Céspedes unable to expand the war into western Cuba, the Congress of Representatives removes him from office. Salvador Cisneros is the new president.

**Oct 31, 1873**    The Spanish warship *Tornado* captures the *Virginius,* a former Confederate blockade-runner now used by Quesda to run arms and supplies secured in the United States to Cuba.

**Nov 4–8, 1873**    Having been condemned as pirates by Spanish authorities, 53 of those captured on the *Virginius,* many of them Americans, are executed by the Spaniards.

**1875**    Rebel general Máximo Gómez mounts an unsuccessful invasion of western Cuba.

**1876**    By the end of the year, Spanish king Alfonso XII has sent 100,000 troops to Cuba.

**Oct 19, 1877**    Spanish forces capture rebel president Tomás Estrada Palma.

| | |
|---|---|
| **Feb 10, 1878** | The Congress of Representatives opens peace negotiations with Spain and signs the Pact of Zanjón, effectively ending the Ten Years' War. |
| **Aug 26, 1879** | Fighting in what is known in Cuba history as the Little War (Guerra Chiquita) begins, triggered by the Spanish government's failure to introduce promised reforms. |
| **Sep 1880** | The Small War ends with the rebels defeated. Again the Spanish government promises reforms. |
| **1881** | Madrid allows Cuba to send representatives to the Spanish Cortes (parliament), but they are wealthy conservatives, so little changes in Cuba. |
| **Jan 5, 1892** | In New York City, Cuban José Martí founds El Partido Revolucionario Cubano (Cuban Revolutionary Party). It becomes the leading voice and organizational apparatus for Cuban independence. |
| **1895** | Spain's appointment of Arsenio Martínez-Campos y Antón as captain-general in Cuba initially offers hope for a quick end to the conflict. Campos, however, is unable to contain the rebellion to eastern Cuba. |
| **Feb 24, 1895** | The third uprising against Spanish rule begins but is initially largely confined to eastern Cuba. |
| **May 19, 1895** | Martí is killed fighting Spanish troops in the Battle of Dos Ríos, a major blow to the revolutionary cause. |
| **Jun 12, 1895** | U.S. president Grover Cleveland issues an official proclamation of neutrality in regard to the Cuban War for Independence. |
| **1896** | Cuban exiles (juntas) in the United States help mobilize American support for the rebel cause and secure arms and supplies for the rebels, who are able to extend the fighting to western Cuba. |
| **Feb 1897** | General Valeriano Weyler y Nicolau replaces Camos as governor-general of Cuba and arrives in Cuba with 50,000 Spanish reinforcements. Determined to isolate civilians from the rebels, he orders the "reconcentration" of the peasants, removing them to fortified towns. |
| **Aug 6, 1897** | Spanish premier Antonio Cánovas del Castillo is assassinated. |
| **Oct 4, 1897** | Práxedes Mateo Sagasta becomes premier of Spain for the sixth time. |
| **Oct 23, 1897** | Sagasta's government informs the United States that it will grant autonomy to Cuba. |
| **Oct 31, 1897** | Sagasta recalls Weyler and replaces him with General Ramón Blanco y Erenas. |
| **Nov 25, 1897** | Sagasta formally grants autonomy to Cuba and Puerto Rico. |

**Feb 9, 1898**    Disparaging comments made by Spanish ambassador to the United States Enrique Dupuy de Lôme regarding President William McKinley are published in the American press, fueling public anger toward Spain.

**Feb 15, 1898**    The U.S. battleship *Maine* blows up in Havana Harbor, resulting in the death of 266 crew members. The event produces great anger toward Spain in the United States.

**Apr 11, 1898**    President McKinley asks Congress for authority to send American troops to Cuba.

**Apr 19, 1898**    Congress passes the Teller Amendment, demanding Spanish withdrawal, Cuban independence, and the employment of American forces to assist the Cubans. The amendment stipulates that there will be no U.S. annexation of Cuba.

**Apr 20, 1898**    President McKinley signs the joint resolution and dispatches the ultimatum to Spain.

**Apr 23, 1898**    Spain declares war on the United States.

**Apr 25, 1898**    The United States declares war on Spain, retroactive to April 21.

**Jun 6–10, 1898**    U.S. marines and Cuban rebels secure the strategically important harbor of Guantánamo Bay.

**Jun 24–25, 1898**    The U.S. Army V Corps, commanded by Major General William R. Shaftner, comes ashore at Daiquiri and Siboney. Shaftner's aim is the capture of Santiago de Cuba, where Spain's naval squadron under Admiral Pascual Cervera y Topete has taken refuge.

**Jul 1, 1898**    The Americans are victorious in the battles at El Caney and San Juan Hill on their approach to Santiago.

**Jul 3, 1898**    Admiral Cervera's efforts to escape with his squadron result in the Battle of Santiago de Cuba in which his squadron is destroyed.

**Jul 3–17, 1898**    U.S. forces besiege Santiago, which surrenders on July 17.

**Jul 17, 1898**    Having sustained defeats in Cuba as well as the Philippines and Puerto Rico, the Spanish government sues for peace.

**Aug 12, 1898**    An armistice is concluded between U.S. and Spanish forces in Cuba, and Spain agrees to relinquish all claims to Cuba.

**Dec 10, 1898**    The Treaty of Paris is concluded between the United States and Spain, formally ending the Spanish-American War.

**Jan 1, 1899–**
**May 20, 1902**    U.S. governor-general in Cuba Major General Leonard Wood accomplishes a great deal in restoring the Cuban economy and eradicating yellow fever.

**Mar 2, 1901**    The so-called Platt Amendment gives the United States the right to intervene in Cuba to maintain order and grants the U.S. government an unlimited lease on territory at Guantánamo Bay for a naval base, which it retains today.

| | |
|---|---|
| **1906–1909** | The United States imposes military rule on Cuba. |
| **1912** | The United States imposes military rule on Cuba. |
| **1917–1922** | The United States imposes military rule on Cuba. |
| **1934** | Most provisions of the Platt Amendment are repealed in the Cuban-American Treaty of Relations, part of President Franklin Roosevelt's Good Neighbor policy. |
| **1940** | A Cuban Constitutional Convention eliminates the Platt Amendment from the new Cuban constitution. |
| **1952–1959** | The threat of U.S. intervention remains, as pro-American Cuban dictator Fulgencio Batista controls Cuba. Cuba's resentment of Batista ensures the rise to power of his successor, Marxist revolutionary Fidel Castro, in 1959. |

SPENCER C. TUCKER

## Further Reading

Bradford, Richard H. *The Virginius Affair.* Boulder: Colorado Associated University Press, 1980.

Ferrer, Ada. *Insurgent Cuba: Race, Nation, and Revolution, 1868–1898.* Chapel Hill: University of North Carolina Press, 1998.

Healy, David. *Drive to Hegemony: The United States in the Caribbean, 1898–1917.* Madison: University of Wisconsin Press, 1988.

Knight, Franklin. *Slave Society in Cuba during the Nineteenth Century.* Madison: University of Wisconsin Press, 1970.

Musicant, Ivan. *Empire by Default: The Spanish-American War and the Dawn of the American Century.* New York: Henry Holt, 1998.

Navarro, José Cantón, Mayra Fernández, and Teresita Rabassa. *History of Cuba: The Challenge of the Yoke and the Star: Biography of a people.* Havana: Instituto Cubano del Libro Editorial José Martí, 2014.

Pérez, Louis A., Jr. *Cuba between Reform and Revolution.* 3rd ed. New York: Oxford University Press, 2006.

Poyo, Gerald Eugene. *Exile and Revolution: José D. Poyo, Key West, and Cuban independence.* Gainesville: University Press of Florida, 2014.

Sheina, Robert L. *Latin America's Wars: The Age of the Caudillo, 1791–1899.* Washington, DC: Brassey's, 2003.

Smith, Joseph. *The Spanish-American War: Conflict in the Caribbean and the Pacific, 1895–1902.* New York: Longman, 1994.

Tone, John L. *War and Genocide in Cuba, 1895–1898.* Chapel Hill: University of North Carolina Press, 2006.

Trask, David F. *The War with Spain in 1898.* Lincoln: University of Nebraska Press, 1996.

# Philippine War for Independence (1899–1902)

## Causes

The Philippine War for Independence is most usually known as the Philippine-American War or, until recently by Americans, the Philippine Insurrection. Fought between forces of the First Philippine Republic and U.S. occupation forces in the Philippines, the war began on February 4, 1899, and ended on July 4, 1902. It should be noted, however, that a Philippine Revolution was proclaimed with a declaration of independence on August 23, 1896.

Located in Southeast Asia and strategically situated on major world trade routes, the Philippine archipelago includes 7,107 islands covering some 115,831 square miles. The archipelago is divided into three major island groupings: Luzon in the north, the Visayas in the middle, and Mindanao in the south. Filipinos are an Austronesian people, but by the end of the 19th century there were also a number of Spaniards, Chinese, and Arab peoples living in the islands. Substantial Malay immigration in the 14th and 15th centuries brought Islam to the southern Philippines. Except for this Moro (Muslim) population, most Filipinos practiced Roman Catholicism. Although more than 100 different languages and dialects were spoken in the islands, during the

BATTLE OF MANILA BAY, MAY 1, 1898

## Philippine War of Independence (1899–1902)

| Manila Bay, Second Battle of (February 4–5, 1899) | | |
|---|---|---|
| | **Filipino Troops** | **United States** |
| Strength | 15,000 | 19,000 |
| Killed | 238 | 55 |
| Wounded | Unknown | 204 |
| Captured | 306 | 0 |

| Zapote Bridge, Battle of (June 12, 1899) | | |
|---|---|---|
| | **Filipino Troops** | **United States** |
| Strength | 4,000–5,000 | 1,500 |
| Killed | 15 | 150 |
| Wounded | 375 | 50 |

| Balangiga Massacre (September 28, 1901)* | | |
|---|---|---|
| | **Filipino Forces** | **United States** |
| Strength | 200 | 78 |
| Killed | Unknown | 54 |

* Here Filipino forces, armed only with bolos, axes, and farm implements, attacked Company C of the 9th U.S. Army Regiment.

| Filipino Civilian Deaths Resulting from the U.S. Reconcentration Effort, 1900–1902 |
|---|
| 11,000* |

*Died from disease, malnutrition, poor sanitation.

| Total Estimated Casualties of the Philippine War of Independence (1899–1902) | | |
|---|---|---|
| | **Philippines** | **United States Forces** |
| Total strength | 800,000–1,000,000 | 126,000 |
| Killed in action, died of wounds | 16,000 | 1,500 |
| Died of disease | Unknown | 2,825 |
| Wounded | Unknown | 2,818 |
| Civilian deaths | 250,000–1,000,000 | N/A |

**Sources:** Baclagon, Uldarico. *Military History of the Philippines.* Manila: Saint Mary's Publishing, 1975; Karnow, Stanley. *In Our Image: America's Empire in the Philippines.* New York: Ballantine Books, 1989; Linn, Brian McAllister. *The Philippine War, 1899–1902.* Lawrence: University of Kansas Press, 2000.

centuries of rule by Spain, Spanish and Tagalog predominated.

Trade with other Asian nations developed by the ninth century, but the first Europeans known to set foot in the islands were the members of an expedition led by Portuguese explorer Ferdinand Magellan. Sailing for Spain, Magellan landed there on March 17, 1521, and claimed the islands for Spain, but he died in battle the next month following an unsuccessful effort to convert Visayan chieftain Lapu-Lapu to Christianity. Spain sent five subsequent expeditions to the Philippines, and in 1543 Ruy López de Villalobos named the islands of Leyte and Samar as Las Islas Filipinas after Spanish prince Felipe (Philip), who became King Philip II of Spain in 1556.

Spanish colonization commenced with the arrival from Mexico on April 27, 1565, of Miguel López de Legazpi's expedition that established in Cebu the first permanent settlement. Manila, located on the excellent harbor of the same name, became the Spanish capital in 1595.

The Spaniards were greatly aided in establishing their control of the Philippines. Government in the islands was largely centered on family-based villages known as *barangays*, headed by a *datu* (chief). With church and state closely linked, Catholic priests became an important element of Spanish control, converting the natives to Catholicism and teaching them Spanish. The Philippines came under the authority of the Mexico-based Viceroyalty of New Spain until Mexican independence in 1821, after which it was directly governed by Spain.

The Spanish administration retained the *barangay* system, with the *datus* answering to Catholic priests and provincial governors. Spaniards held all senior administrative posts, with the governor-general being appointed by the king of Spain.

Filipino resentment regarding the loss of their political freedom, the forced acculturation, imposition of Catholicism, and the *encomienda* (feudal-like labor) system led to frequent uprisings against Spanish rule. In suppressing the revolts, the Spaniards were able to take advantage of the great ethnic and linguistic divisions in the islands. Thus, Catholic Filipino soldiers helped quash revolts in the Islamic southern islands. Filipino soldiers also fought the British when the latter occupied Manila during the Seven Years' War (1756–1763).

Manila was for three centuries the center of the so-called galleon trade or silver trade between Asia and Mexico, in which silver and other Mexican goods were exchanged with the Chinese for silk and porcelain. In the 19th century a number of other Europeans as well as Americans arrived in the Philippines and established business. This influx of other foreigners accelerated changes already under way there.

As in other parts of the Spanish Empire, society was highly stratified. At the top of the socioeconomic/political pyramid were the *peninsulares,* those Spaniards born in Spain or of pure Spanish descent. Next came a small middle class of insulares, Spaniards born in the colonies and the mestizos of mixed Spanish and native descent. Chinese mestizos and native Filipinos, or indios, were at the bottom. Some Filipinos were members of the landed elite, known as ilustrados, and many of these families educated their children in Europe. Not surprisingly, many of the European-educated ilustrados became advocates for the reform of the colonial government and sought representation for the Philippines in the Spanish Cortes (parliament). Other ilustrados, however, sought nothing less than Philippine independence.

On January 20, 1872, a mutiny occurred among the military personnel of Fort San Felipe, the Spanish military arsenal in Cavite. Led by mestizo sergeant Fernando La Madrid, the mutineers seized control of the fort and killed 11 Spanish officers. The mutineers believed that their actions would bring a nationwide revolt against Spanish rule. At Cavite the soldiers were joined by workers who were upset regarding their pay. Ultimately some 200 Filipinos took part. The authorities easily crushed the revolt, and a number of participants were executed, but many scholars believe that the Cavite Mutiny was a major factor behind the Philippine Revolution of 1896.

A number of ilustrado Filipinos who were members of the so-called Propaganda Movement, which held sway during 1868–1898, went to Europe in the hopes of informing Spain about true conditions in the Philippines. Many found themselves arrested when they returned home. On January 3, 1892, Filipino reformer José Rizal established La Liga Filipina, a nationalistic civic organization for Filipinos that stressed education as the means to achieve reform and independence. The Spanish government exiled Rizal to Mindanao (where he would be executed on December 30, 1896). On July 7, 1892, the day after the announcement of Rizal's exile, Andrés Bonifacio officially established the Katipunan Society (the full title being the Highest and Most Respected Association of the Sons of the Country), a secret society dedicated to Philippine independence.

The authorities soon learned of the existence of the Katipunan, causing Bonifacio to initiate the Philippine Revolution on August 23, 1896, earlier than planned.

Filipino reformer José Rizal established La Liga Filipina, a nationalistic civic organization for Filipinos that stressed education in order to achieve reform and independence. The Spanish government exiled him to Mindanao where he was executed in 1896. (Library of Congress)

This declaration of war against Spain brought uprisings throughout the Philippines including Cavite, where ilustrado Emilio Aguinaldo led the revolutionary resistance.

The charismatic Aguinaldo soon attracted a large following. His military victory over Spanish forces in the Battle of Imus on September 3, 1896, brought him to the forefront of the revolutionary movement. By late March 1897, however, infighting within the Katipunan as well as Spanish resolve to crush the rebellion led Aguinaldo to create a new revolutionary party, of which he became president.

With Bonifacio having been eclipsed, Aguinaldo's followers alleged that he was planning a coup against the new leadership. Bonifacio was then arrested, charged with treason, and executed on May 10, 1897, probably on Aguinaldo's orders (although this has never been proven). With Bonifacio dead, Aguinaldo became the unchallenged leader of the Filipino revolutionary movement.

With many of Bonifacio's followers leaving the movement and with his own forces sustaining military defeats, Aguinaldo was willing to treat with the Spaniards, who on their part sought to avoid a protracted guerrilla war. The subsequent Pact of Biak-na-Bató of December 14, 1897, saw Aguinaldo essentially betraying the revolution. He agreed to go into exile in Hong Kong with 40 followers and a pledge of neutrality in exchange for $500,000. Aguinaldo arrived in Hong Kong on December 31. As it turned out, the Spaniards were delinquent in their payments, and Aguinaldo laid plans to return to the Philippines, something he had probably planned to do in any case.

With the United States now edging closer to war with Spain over the situation in the Spanish colony of Cuba, Aguinaldo opened communications with American officials regarding the Philippines, including U.S. consul in Hong Kong Rounsevelle Wildman, who reportedly encouraged Aguinaldo's return to the islands.

On April 25, 1898, the United States declared war, beginning the Spanish-American War. Aguinaldo was convinced that these circumstance could bring Philippine independence. Then on May 1, U.S. Navy commodore George Dewey's Pacific Squadron, having steamed there from China, destroyed Spanish rear admiral Patricio Montojo y Pasarón's squadron in the Battle of Manila Bay. Soon Dewey had established a presence ashore at Cavite. He also cabled Aguinaldo and authorized his return.

Aguinaldo arrived in the Philippines in a U.S. revenue cutter on May 19. He then met with Dewey, who provided him with arms and ammunition for his followers with which to fight the Spaniards. Establishing his headquarters at Maloles some 30 miles north of Manila, on May 24 Aguinaldo proclaimed the formation of a government. This was followed by his declaration of Philippine independence from his house in Cavite El Viejo on June 12.

On June 23, Aguinaldo formed a new government, with himself as president, of what would later be known as the First Philippine Republic; he would hold this position until April 1, 1901. Neither the Spanish government nor U.S. president William McKinley's administration recognized Aquinaldo's government, however, and U.S. secretary of the navy John D. Long instructed Dewey not to have any political discussions with Aguinaldo or his followers. Meanwhile, Aguinaldo's forces easily overcame isolated Spanish garrisons in the islands and soon had the city of Manila under siege.

At the same time, U.S. soldiers were arriving in the Philippines. The first 2,500 men of U.S. major general Wesley Merrit's VIII Corps arrived in Manila Bay from San Francisco on June 25 and began coming ashore on June 30. By the end of July all of Merritt's 10,800 men had landed, including the general himself. Since U.S. objectives would be served if the insurgents were excluded from any peace talks with the Spanish, Merritt was under strict orders from Washington not to cooperate with the revolutionary forces. In any case, Merritt had a low opinion of Aguinaldo, whom he referred to as a "half-breed Chinese adventurer." Merritt refused any communication between his forces and those of the Filipino revolutionary leader.

The tenuous alliance against the Spaniards between Aguinaldo and the U.S.

military steadily deteriorated during the summer of 1898. The tense situation was exacerbated when Aguinaldo's men were excluded from participation in the First Battle of Manila on August 13, 1898, with the Spanish authorities agreeing to surrender to the U.S. side following a sham battle to satisfy Spanish honor. U.S. troops then prevented the Philippine Revolutionary Army from entering the city. With Merritt soon departing the islands to travel to Paris for the peace talks with Spain, his successor, Major General Elwell S. Otis, continued Merritt's policy of noncooperation with Aguinaldo.

The Spanish-American War had ended with the signing in Washington of a Protocol of Peace on August 12, 1898. The situation in the Philippines remained tense, however, with Aguinaldo's forces maintaining a strong presence in the Manila area. Aguinaldo moved to the town of Malolos north of Manila, and a constitutional convention was established there in September.

The Treaty of Paris of December 10, 1898, officially ended the Spanish-American War. Although there was considerable debate in the United States regarding the future of the islands, German warships were congregating off Manila, and it appeared that if the United States did not take the islands, Germany would do so. In late October McKinley sided with the imperialists and ordered the U.S. peace commissioners at Paris to demand that Spain cede the archipelago to the United States. In return, the United States agreed to pay Spain $20 million. The Treaty of Paris was formally ratified by the U.S. Senate on February 6.

Meanwhile, on January 21, 1899, at Malolos, Aquinaldo's followers ratified the Malolos Constitution of the Republic of the Philippines (First Philippine Republic), with Aguinaldo as president. Tensions between American and Filipino forces worsened. On February 4, 1899, fighting erupted at Manila and quickly turned into a full-scale war that would last three years.

SPENCER C. TUCKER

## Course

The Second Battle of Manila was fought during February 4–5, 1899, between some 19,000 American and 15,000 Filipino troops. It began on the evening of February 4 near the San Juan River Bridge in the Santa Mesa district of northwest Manila when a patrol of U.S. troops fired on some members of the Philippine Revolutionary Army (also known as the Philippine National Army), killing a lieutenant and a soldier. This was supposedly because the Filipino soldiers had moved into what the two sides had earlier established as a neutral zone.

The next day Filipino general Isidoro Torres passed through the lines under a flag of truce to deliver a message from Aguinaldo to General Otis characterizing the fighting as "accidental" and requesting an immediate end to hostilities and the reestablishment of the neutral zone. Otis dismissed the overture and replied that with the fighting having begun, it "must go on to the grim end."

That same day Brigadier General Arthur MacArthur's 2nd Division, supported by artillery and naval gunfire, advanced across rice paddies to attack and easily seize the Filipino positions. Other American units had to overcome more difficult terrain and heavy Filipino fire, but by the end of the battle the Americans had secured the high ground north of Manila. The fighting claimed American casualties of 55 dead and 204 wounded. Filipino casualties are given as 238 killed and 306 taken prisoner.

Most of Aguinaldo's forces fell back on Caloocan, a dozen miles north of Manila. MacArthur's plan to strike Caloocan was postponed because of concerns regarding an uprising in the city of Manila. Finally, on February 10 MacArthur's division, supported by the guns of Dewey's squadron, attacked Filipino positions in Caloocan, and by day's end the Americans had secured that important rail center on the line to Malolos, capital of the Philippine Republic.

Meanwhile, the uprising in Manila, which the Americans had learned about through captured documents, enabled them to shut down the revolt before it really got started by arresting known revolutionaries. Although some street fighting ensued, it fell far short of a full-scale revolt. The campaign to clear the area around Manila concluded on March 17.

Luzon, the largest Philippine island, was, with the capital city of Manila, the key both politically and economically. General Otis believed that the key to winning the war lay in securing Luzon north of Manila. He was convinced that the "insurrection" was centered in the Tagalog population, concentrated in southern Luzon. Otis reasoned that these areas would be difficult to subjugate, but the ethnic groups north of Manila would welcome the Americans, an assessment based on a misguided understanding of Filipino opposition to a permanent U.S. presence.

Otis first sought to sever the insurgents' supply lines. On March 12, 1899, Brigadier General Lloyd Wheaton led a provisional brigade in striking east and south to Laguna de Bay. Wheaton's assignment was to clear any pockets of nationalist resistance and destroy crops that might be a supply source for Aguinaldo's forces. Supported by a gunboat and artillery, Wheaton's men delivered a crippling blow to the nationalist forces south of Manila. This phase ended on March 17.

The second part of Otis's strategy was the capture of Malolos, the newly proclaimed capital of the Philippine Republic. This campaign lasted from March 24 to August 16 and was carried out by Major General Arthur MacArthur's 2nd Division of 9,000 men in three brigades under Brigadier generals Harrison Otis, Irving Hale, and Wheaton. Otis and Hale moved north along the rail line from Caloocan, supported by artillery and a section of Colt machine guns. The advance was slow with fierce fighting as the troops worked their way through nearly impenetrable brush. Meanwhile, Wheaton's brigade, designated a "flying column," was moved to the west of Otis and Hale in the hope of trapping the Filipino troops between the two U.S. forces. On March 26 Wheaton's troops captured Malinta, though not in time to seal off Aguinaldo's withdrawing forces. Then on March 31 MacArthur's troops entered Malolos, which the departing nationalists had burned and destroyed. The Americans captured Pampagna on May 5 and San Isidro on May 15. The campaign ended with the capture on August 16, 1899, of Angeles.

While MacArthur and Wheaton moved against Aguinaldo's forces, troops under Major General Henry Ware Lawton moved south in the Laguna de Bay Campaign of April 8–17, 1899. After capturing Santa Cruz on April 10, they returned to Manila on April 17.

In the San Isidro Campaign of April 21–May 30, 1899, on April 21 General Lawton's men advanced from La Lona Church on San Isidro, dispersing insurgent forces there. Lawton's forces returned to Manila on May 30. On June 2, the Philippine Republic officially declared war on the United States. On June 13, Lawton's men overran insurgent field fortifications along the Zapote River. The Battle of Zapote Bridge of that date pitted some 1,500 U.S. troops against 4,000–5,000 Filipinos. With the U.S. Navy providing valuable gunfire support, the Americans were victorious. They lost 15 dead and 50 wounded, while the Filipinos suffered 150 dead and 375 wounded. Meanwhile, General Antonio Novicio Luna, chief of staff of the Armed Forces of the Philippines and a highly effective military officer, was assassinated by rivals within the Philippine leadership.

With the arrival of the annual summer monsoon rains, active campaigning in Luzon came to a temporary halt. During this period the character of U.S. forces in the Philippines had changed. With the expiration of the term of service for Spanish-American War troops, Washington created a force of two-year U.S. volunteer regiments (rather than state volunteer units), numbering 1 cavalry and 24 infantry regiments. This period also saw the organization of the Philippine Scouts.

Soon after their arrival, the Americans had begun recruiting and organizing indigenous Filipino forces, much as the Spaniards had done earlier. These U.S.-supported forces were first the Macabebe Scouts and then the Philippine Scouts as well as police units known as the Philippine Constabulary. The Filipinos were carefully screened to ensure their loyalty and then trained and led by American officers. The Filipinos had the great advantage of knowing the terrain, culture, and language as well as being acclimatized to tropical conditions. With some Filipinos now fighting on the U.S. side, this helped

undermine insurgent morale and that of their supporters. By the end of the war Philippine Scout forces numbered some 5,000 men, while the Philippine Constabulary counted another 5,000.

The beginning of the dry season in the fall of 1898 brought a resumption of campaigning. In the Cavite Campaign on October 7–13, 1899, forces under General Wheaton and Brigadier General Theodore Schwan ended nationalist resistance in Cavite and adjacent provinces. A 400-man U.S. Marine Corps battalion also took part, attacking Filipino entrenchments at Novaleta from the land side on October 8.

That same month, General Otis began a three-pronged offensive in northern Luzon involving forces under Lawton, Mac-Arthur, and Wheaton with the primary objective of capturing Aguinaldo in the belief that this would greatly cripple the nationalist resistance. Aguinaldo's army then numbered perhaps as many as 80,000 men. Although they were certainly not as well equipped as the U.S. forces and lacked a cadre of veteran leaders, they were tough, courageous, and determined. They also had the great advantage of familiarity with the territory.

In the San Isidro Campaign of October 15–November 19, 1899, Lawton and Brigadier General Samuel B. M. Young headed north up the Rio Grande de la Pampanga, closing off the mountain passes of the Sierra Madres in order to prevent Filipino nationalist forces from escaping. U.S. troops took San Isidro on October 19.

Recognizing the importance of capturing Aguinaldo, Lawton decided to send a mixed force of infantry and cavalry from San Isidro under Young to push on in advance of the main column. Lawton also was concerned about Wheaton, from whom he had heard nothing, and feared that if their two commands did not unite as planned, Aguinaldo would be able to evade the net and escape. Lawton's command pursued the nationalist forces aggressively, covering more than 100 miles of extremely harsh terrain over a six-week period. The group skirmished with Aguinaldo's rear guard but was unable to capture the Filipino leader. Lawton's men approached San Fabian on the Lingayen Gulf on November 18.

At the same time, in the Tarlac Campaign of November 5–20, 1899, MacArthur advanced from San Fernando along a rail route that ran through the fertile valleys and plains of central Luzon. His men captured Tarlac on November 12 and reached Dagupan on November 20.

Finally, a third force under Wheaton carried out the San Fabian Campaign of November 6–19, 1899. His 2,500-man force sailed from Manila on November 6 and came ashore at San Fabian the next day. It promptly got bogged down. Routing an insurgent force at San Jacinto on November 12, it linked up with MacArthur's men at Dagupan only on November 20, despite the fact that it was only a dozen miles from San Fabian. Even though some of Young's scouts had alerted Wheaton to the urgency of the situation, he failed to act with dispatch. Finally moved to action, Wheaton did capture Aguinaldo's mother and infant son, but the Filipino leader himself escaped with some 1,000 followers.

On December 2, elements of Wheaton's command under Major Peyton March struck Aguinaldo's rear guard at Triad Pass, killing General Gregorio del Pilar, Aguinaldo's close friend and adviser. The action at Triad Pass ended the U.S. Army's major campaigns in Luzon; only scattered insurgent elements remained active in the island.

Aguinaldo proved ineffective as a field commander, and with his best units being destroyed in stand-up battles against the better-armed American forces, he was finally forced to change tactics. On November 12 he accepted the advice of General Gregorio del Pilar and dissolved the regular army, re-forming it into guerrilla units to carry out a protracted war of raids and ambushes in the hopes of wearing down the Americans. Had this been employed earlier undoubtedly it would have yielded even greater results, but in its first four months the Americans suffered almost 500 casualties.

In response to the advent of guerrilla warfare and an insurgent shadow government replete with the taxation of civilians and requisition of supplies, the Americans devoted considerable attention to efforts to isolate the rural civilian population from the guerrillas. This included intelligence gathering through civilian informants and the issuance of identity cards, but the army also sought to concentrate the rural population in towns and villages where they could be monitored by small army detachments. This "reconcentration" effort was largely accomplished through a system of incentives, including the building of markets and stipulating that food distributions be in the towns while at the same time destroying food sources and shelter that would otherwise be accessible to the rebels. Restrictions on travel and curfews were then implemented. In the process, at least 11,000 Filipino civilians died from disease, malnutrition, and poor sanitation.

The Americans also employed reprisals. Thus, soldiers might burn homes in areas from which the insurgents had mounted ambushes or had cut telegraph wires. There were also arrests of the family members of suspected insurgents, deportations, and fines. Finally, the army also executed individuals held responsible for the murder of

Americans or friendly Filipinos. On occasion the army also used torture to extract information from suspected or captured insurgents. General Otis in particular ignored a number of directives from Washington concerning the "benevolent policy" that McKinley had promised the Filipinos. Impartial press reporting found Otis's claims of torture of American prisoners held by the insurgents to be false.

At the same time, however, the Americans made a strong effort to win the hearts and minds of the Filipinos. During the course of the war, the U.S. Army built thousands of schools and detailed soldiers to serve as teachers when required. As American civil administration became operational, thousands of civilian American teachers were brought to the Philippines to run the schools and train Filipino teachers. A vigorous economic infrastructure program was also instituted and led to the construction of roads, bridges, and telegraph lines. Public health was a major area for improvement, with inoculation programs, improved sanitary practices, and hygiene regulations.

Finally, the Americans reformed the government, with a civilian judiciary and the election of local officials. William Howard Taft became the first civilian governor-general of the Philippines beginning on July 4, 1901.

Meanwhile, the fighting continued. Aguinaldo was finally captured by U.S. forces led by Brigadier General Frederick Funston. Pretending to be American prisoners escorted by supposed Filipino insurgents but actual Maccabee Scouts dressed in Philippine Revolutionary Army uniforms, Funston and his men gained access to Aguinaldo's camp in Palanan, Isabella, on March 23, 1901, and promptly fell on the guards and took Aguinaldo prisoner.

On April 1 in Manila, Aguinaldo swore allegiance to the United States. On April 19 he issued a proclamation of formal surrender to the United States and called on his followers to lay down their weapons and give up the fight. All of this came as a great shock to Aguinaldo's followers, but many of his generals refused to capitulate, and the fighting continued.

Nine days after Aguinaldo's capture, Philippine Republic vice president Mariano Trías surrendered to the Americans along with a number of officials and officers and some 200 soldiers. Succeeding to the leadership, General Miguel Malvar launched an offensive campaign in the Batangas region of southern Luzon against American-held towns. Malvar achieved several small victories but was vigorously pursued by U.S. forces under Brigadier General J. Franklin Bell.

The most infamous Filipino ambush of U.S. soldiers occurred in the town of Balangiga on the island of Samar in the west-central Philippines. C Company of the 9th U.S. Infantry Regiment had occupied Balangiga beginning in August 1901. With tensions increasing, on September 28 about 200 Filipinos wielding bolos, axes, and farm implements attacked the Americans while they were at breakfast, with their weapons in a separate building. In what was the worst defeat for the U.S. Army since the Battle of the Little Bighorn in 1876, 54 of the 78 members of the company were hacked to death, and only 4 soldiers emerged unscathed.

The following day, with the survivors having escaped with word of what had occurred, two American companies returned to now-deserted Balangiga. They recovered the American bodies and burned the town. Brigadier General Jacob H. Smith then ordered U.S. Marine Corps major Littleton

Waller to subjugate the island, instructing him to burn every settlement and kill anyone capable of bearing arms (specifying this as 10 years old and older) who failed to surrender and did not immediately collaborate with the U.S. forces. Smith's orders resulted in the deaths of thousands of civilians in Samar, either killed outright or dead from starvation when Smith ordered all trade to Samar halted.

When news of the atrocities and Smith's orders became known in the United States, there was an immediate public outcry. In 1902 both Waller and Smith were court-martialed. Smith was reprimanded and removed from command but suffered no other formal punishment. Waller was found not guilty on a charge of ordering the execution of 11 Filipino porters. The vote was 11 to 2, and a court later held that as a marine he was not subject to an army court-martial. Press reports of the torture of Filipinos and of other atrocities by U.S. forces produced understandable outrage in the United States and bought congressional investigations.

On April 13, 1902, General Malvar, the unofficial acting president of the Philippine Republic, and most of his command surrendered. He was the last major Filipino general to do so. By the end of the month, a further 3,000 of Malvar's men surrendered. Northern Luzo had already been pacified, and now southern Luzon followed suit.

From 1901, legislative power in the islands had been exercised through a Philippine Commission effectively dominated by Americans. The Philippine Organic Act, approved by Congress on July 1, 1902, ratified President McKinley's previous executive order that had established the Second Philippine Commission. This act stipulated that a legislature would be established, consisting of a popularly elected lower house (the Philippine Assembly) and an upper house formed of the Philippine Commission, largely dominated by Americans. The act also extended the U.S. Bill of Rights to Filipinos. On July 2, the U.S. secretary of war telegraphed that since the insurrection against the United States had ended and provincial civil governments had been established throughout most of the islands, the office of military governor was terminated. On July 4 Theodore Roosevelt, who had succeeded to the U.S. presidency upon the assassination of President McKinley, proclaimed an amnesty for those who had participated in the conflict and declared the war at an end. (On April 9, 2002, Philippine president Gloria Macapagal Arroyo declared that the war had ended on April 13, 1902, with the surrender of General Miguel Malvar).

Casualty figures for the Philippine-American War vary widely depending on the source, but during 1899–1902 the 80,000 to 100,000 members of the Philippine Republican Army and auxiliaries suffered some 16,000 military deaths. Filipino civilian deaths may have been 200,000–250,000, but this included those who succumbed to disease. Perhaps 100,000 Filipino civilians perished in the subsequent Moro Rebellion. One estimate puts U.S. military dead during 1899–1902 at 4,234, with as many as 1,500 of these the result of actual combat and the remainder dead of disease. Another 2,818 American soldiers were wounded. American forces continued to suffer periodic casualties in the suppression of the Moro Rebellion in the southern Philippines until 1913.

SPENCER C. TUCKER

## Consequences

Although the Philippine-American War officially ended in 1902, sporadic resistance to the American occupation continued for years thereafter, indeed until at least 1913. This was in different regions by guerrilla organizations independent of one another. General Macario Sakay led one such group. He revived the Katipunan for a new war against the United States and even established the short-lived Katagalugan Tagalog Republic in the mountains of southern Luzon during 1902–1907, when Sakay and the Katipunan leadership were captured and executed by American forces.

Mindanao, in the southern reaches of the Philippine archipelago, was the last region to be pacified by U.S. occupation forces. The Moros there resisted until 1913 in what the Americans called the Moro Rebellion. The Moros were never a part of the Filipino forces under Aguinaldo but had instead fought independently. Nevertheless, many historians consider the Moro Rebellion to have been the second front in the Philippine-American War.

When U.S. president Theodore Roosevelt proclaimed the end of the war in 1902, he noted that this did not include Mindanao, where Moro forces were still actively resisting U.S. rule. The last major engagement between American and Moro forces was the Battle of Bud Bagsak during January 11–15, 1913, when as many as 500–1,000 Moros were killed in an American assault led by Brigadier General John J. Pershing. Not long afterward much of the Moro leadership surrendered, and on March 22, 1915, the sultan of Sulu signed an agreement with the Americans accepting U.S. sovereignty.

On July 30, 1907, elections occurred throughout the islands for the first elected Philippine Assembly. The Jones Act of August 29, 1916, formally the Philippine Autonomy Act of 1916, announced the U.S. government intention to "withdraw

their sovereignty over the Philippine Islands as soon as a stable government can be established therein." The Jones Act also replaced the Philippine Commission with an elective senate and extended the franchise to all literate Filipino males who met minimum property qualifications. The law also incorporated a bill of rights.

American sovereignty was retained in that the governor-general had the power to veto any measure passed by the new Philippine legislature. Liberal governor-general Francis Burton Harrison, who held the post during 1913–1921, rarely used this power and moved rapidly to appoint Filipinos in place of Americans in the civil service. By 1921, Filipinos had effective charge of the islands' internal affairs.

The Jones Act remained in force as a de facto constitution for the Philippines until it was superseded by the Tydings-McDuffie Act of March 24, 1934. Also known as the Philippine Independence Act, it established a 10-year transition period to Filipino independence, a process that was interrupted by the Japanese occupation of the islands during World War II. In March 1935 President Franklin D. Roosevelt approved a new constitution for the islands, which the Filipinos accepted that May. In September, Manuel Quezon was elected president, and in November, when he was inaugurated, the autonomous Commonwealth of the Philippines was formally established. Quezon was reelected president in November 1941.

Wishing to strengthen Philippine defenses against a possible attack by Japan, in 1935 Quezon invited General Douglas MacArthur to the islands as his military adviser, and the following year Quezon appointed him field marshal of the Commonwealth's armed forces.

Although U.S. war plans called for defense of the Philippines, the U.S. Congress had done little to provide funding. In 1941 the Philippine Army numbered only about 90,000 men, four-fifths of them Filipinos and the rest U.S. troops. The Philippine Navy consisted of two torpedo boats, and the air force had 40 aircraft.

The Japanese attacked the Philippines Islands, beginning with air raids on Clark and Iba Airfields on December 8, 1941, one day after their attack on Pearl Harbor. Japanese forces then landed and defeated the American and Philippine Army forces, which surrendered on May 6. President Quezon then established a government-in-exile in Washington.

Japanese claims of Asian solidarity rang hollow with their practice of treating the Filipinos with contempt and brutality. The Japanese were surprised to discover that most Filipinos remained loyal to the United States. As early as 1943 Tokyo announced its plans to grant independence to the Philippines, hoping that this would diminish anti-Japanese sentiment and allow some Japanese troops to be shifted elsewhere. But the Japanese also insisted that any grant of independence be accompanied by a declaration of war by the Philippines against the United States. Under Japanese pressure, in September 1944 the puppet Philippine government headed by José Laurel, former minister of the interior, declared war on the United States. Meanwhile, Filipino resistance forces proved to an irritant to the Japanese by providing intelligence information and greatly assisting in the reconquest of the islands by U.S. troops.

U.S. forces returned to the Philippines on October 20, 1944, and the Philippine government was reestablished in the islands at Tacloban, Leyte, three days later. U.S. forces then invaded Luzon and, following two weeks of heavy fighting that devastated the city, retook Manila in February. Laurel and some other collaborators fled to Japan, where they eventually surrendered to U.S. authorities. On July 5, 1945, MacArthur announced that the Philippines had been liberated. The Philippine Congress met on June 9 for the first time since 1941, and in September it ratified the United Nations Charter.

To the surprise of many, MacArthur adopted a lenient attitude toward the collaborators and personally pardoned Manuel Roxas, a prominent collaborator who won election to the presidency in 1946.

Sporadic violence continued in the Philippines after the war, fed by serious economic problems and separatism. Some irregular warfare occurred, led by the Hukbalahap, or "Huks," communist guerrillas who had fought the Japanese. Full independence came to the islands on July 4, 1946. The Philippines then concluded free trade agreements with the United States and secured significant funding for reconstruction and, in return, granted the United States long-term leases on military and naval bases.

SPENCER C. TUCKER

## Timeline

**Mar 17, 1521**    A Spanish expedition under Ferdinand Magellan lands in the Philippines.

**Apr 27, 1565**    The first Spanish colony is established in the Philippines.

| | |
|---|---|
| **1595** | Manila becomes the capital of the Philippine Islands. |
| **Oct 5, 1762** | British forces capture Manila. It returns to Spanish control in 1763. |
| **1821** | With the independence of Mexico, Spain assumes direct rule of the Philippines. |
| **Jan 20, 1872** | The Cavite Uprising occurs among soldiers and disgruntled workers. |
| **Jul 3, 1892** | Filipino nationalist José Rizal establishes La Liga Filipina (Filipino League) in Manila, which calls for peaceful reforms in the Philippines. Rizal is arrested on July 6 and exiled to Mindanao. |
| **Jul 7, 1892** | Andrés Bonifacio establishes the Katipunan Society (Highest and Most Respected Association of the Sons of the Country) with the aim achieving Philippine independence. |
| **Aug 23, 1896** | Spanish authorities move against the Katipunan Society, forcing Bonifacio to begin the revolution earlier than planned. |
| **Aug 26, 1896** | The Filipino War for Independence begins. |
| **Sep 3, 1896** | Filipino revolutionary Emilio Aguinaldo wins the Battle of Imus. |
| **Dec 30, 1896** | Spanish authorities execute the internally exiled Filipino nationalist José Rizal. |
| **Apr 23, 1897** | General Fernando Primo de Rivera y Sobremonte replaces General Emilio Garcia de Polavieja as Spanish governor-general of the Philippines. |
| **May 10, 1897** | Filipino nationalist Bonifacio is executed by pro-Aguinaldo elements in an internal power struggle. |
| **Dec 15, 1897** | The Pact of Biak-na-Bató ends hostilities between the Filipino rebels and the Spanish. Aguinaldo and a number of his followers are exiled to Hong Kong. |
| **Apr 3, 1898** | A rebellion begins on Cebu in the Philippines. |
| **Apr 9, 1898** | Primo de Rivera is replaced by Lieutenant General Basilio Augustín as governor-general of the Philippines, whose policies fail to pacify the Philippines. |
| **Apr 25, 1898** | The United States declares war on Spain over Cuba. |
| **Apr 27, 1898** | U.S. Navy commodore George Dewey sails with his Asiatic Squadron from Mirs Bay in China for the Philippines. |
| **May 1, 1898** | In the Battle of Manila Bay, Dewey's squadron decimates the Spanish Philippines squadron under Rear Admiral Patricio Montojo y Pasarón. |
| **May 2, 1898** | U.S. president William McKinley sends American forces to the Philippines. These forces, formed as VIII Corps, are to be commanded by Major General Wesley Merritt. Dewey cuts the undersea cable linking Manila and Hong Kong. |

| | |
|---|---|
| **May 19, 1898** | Aguinaldo returns to Luzon from Hong Kong. |
| **May 24, 1898** | Aguinaldo establishes a Filipino revolutionary government. |
| **May 26, 1898** | U.S. secretary of the navy John D. Long orders Dewey not to form alliances with Filipino rebels. |
| **Jun 12, 1898** | Aguinaldo declares the independence of the Philippines. |
| **Jun 23, 1898** | Aguinaldo forms a new government with himself as president. |
| **Jun 25, 1898** | The first members of the U.S. Army VIII Corps, commanded by Major General Wesley Merritt, arrive in the Philippines. |
| **Jun 30, 1898** | U.S. troops begin disembarking at Cavite in the Philippines. |
| **Jul 29, 1898** | Merritt's men begin their march from Cavite to Manila. |
| **Aug 12, 1898** | An armistice takes effect to end fighting in the Spanish-American War. |
| **Aug 13, 1898** | In a sham battle to satisfy Spanish honor, U.S. forces capture Manila. |
| **Sep 15, 1898** | The revolutionary Filipino Malolos Congress meets. |
| **Oct 1, 1898** | Peace talks between U.S. and Spanish negotiators commence in Paris. |
| **Oct 26, 1898** | McKinley instructs the U.S. peace commissioners to demand the annexation of the Philippines. |
| **Dec 10, 1898** | The Treaty of Paris formally ends the Spanish-American War, with the United States acquiring the Philippines from Spain for $20 million. |
| **Jan 1, 1899** | The Malolos Congress declares Aguinaldo president of the Republic of the Philippines. |
| **Jan 21, 1899** | The Malolos Congress ratifies the constitution of the Republic of the Philippines. |
| **Feb 4–5, 1899** | In the Second Battle of Manila, U.S. forces clash with and defeat the forces of the Republic of the Philippines, after which the U.S. Luzon Campaign begins, lasting until December 1899. |
| **Feb 11, 1899** | The U.S. Visayan Campaigns commence, lasting until the early summer of 1901. |
| **Mar 12, 1899** | The U.S. campaign to clear Luzon commences. |
| **Mar 26, 1899** | U.S. forces capture the Philippine Republic's capital of Malolos, which the Filipinos have burned. |
| **May 5, 1899** | Secretary of State John Hay offers autonomy to the Philippines. |
| **Jun 13, 1899** | The Americans are victorious in the Battle of Zapote Bridge. |
| **Jul 3, 1899** | Schools open in the Philippines with Spanish, American, and Filipino teachers. |

| | |
|---|---|
| **Aug 10, 1899** | U.S. brigadier general John C. Bates signs a treaty with Jolo Sultan Jamalul Kiram II in the southern Philippines. |
| **Nov 12, 1899** | After a series of military defeats, Aguinaldo dissolves the regular army and re-forms it into guerrilla units. |
| **Dec 18, 1899** | U.S. Army major general Henry Lawton is killed in the Battle of San Mateo in the Philippines. |
| **Jan 26, 1900– Apr 27, 1902** | The U.S. Samar Campaign. |
| **Mar 23, 1901** | U.S. troops and Maccabee Scouts led by Brigadier General Frederick Funston capture Aguinaldo in Palanan, Isabella. |
| **Apr 1, 1901** | In Manila, Aguinaldo takes an oath of allegiance to the United States. Leadership of the revolutionary forces falls to General Miguel Malvar. |
| **Apr 19, 1901** | Aguinaldo calls on his supporters to lay down their arms. |
| **Jul 4, 1901** | William Howard Taft becomes the first American civilian governor-general of the Philippines. |
| **Sep 28, 1901** | The Balangiga Massacre occurs in which 54 unarmed Americans are slain on the island of Samar. This brings savage U.S. reprisals. |
| **Apr 13, 1902** | General Miguel Malvar surrenders, the last Filipino rebel commander resisting American occupation. |
| **May 1902** | The U.S. Lake Lanao Campaigns begin on Mindinao, lasting until May 10, 1903. |
| **May 2, 1902** | The Battle of Bayang occurs in Moro Province. It precipitates the Moro Campaigns, which occur sporadically, lasting until 1913. |
| **Jul 1, 1902** | The U.S. Congress passes the Philippine Organic Act for administering the Philippines. |
| **Jul 4, 1902** | U.S. president Theodore Roosevelt declares an end to the Philippine-American War. |
| **1921** | By now, the Filipino people have effective control of their internal affairs. |
| **Mar 26, 1934** | The Tydings-McDuffie Act (Philippine Independence Act) establishes a 10-year transition period to Filipino independence. |
| **Mar 1935** | President Franklin D. Roosevelt approves a new constitution for the Philippines, accepted by the Filipino people in May. |
| **Nov 15, 1935** | Manuel Quezon, having been elected the first president of the Commonwealth of the Philippines in September, is inaugurated. |
| **Dec 8, 1941** | Japanese forces attack the Philippines. |

**May 6, 1942**    U.S. and Philippine Army forces surrender to the Japanese in the Philippines.

**Oct 20, 1944**    U.S. forces return to the Philippines.

**Jul 4, 1946**    The Philippines is granted full independence.

SPENCER C. TUCKER

## Further Reading

Agoncillo, Teodoro, and Oscar Alfonso. *History of the Filipino People.* Quezon City, Philippines: Malaya Books, 1968.

Baclagon, Uldarico. *Military History of the Philippines.* Manila: Saint Mary's Publishing, 1975.

Bain, David H. *Sitting in Darkness: Americans in the Philippines.* Boston: Houghton Mifflin, 1984.

Karnow, Stanley. *In Our Image: America's Empire in the Philippines.* New York: Ballantine Books, 1989.

Linn, Brian McAllister. *The Philippine War, 1899–1902.* Lawrence: University of Kansas Press, 2000.

Miller, Stuart Creighton. *"Benevolent Assimilation": The American Conquest of the Philippines, 1899–1903.* New Haven, CT: Yale University Press, 1982.

Musicant, Ivan. *Empire by Default: The Spanish-American War and the Dawn of the American Century.* New York: Henry Holt, 1998.

Schirmer, Daniel B., and Stephen R. Shalom. *The Philippines Reader: A History of Colonialism, Dictatorship, and Resistance.* Cambridge, MA: South End, 1987.

Shaw, Angel Velasco, and Luis H. Francia. *Vestiges of War: The Philippine-American War and the Aftermath of an American Dream, 1899–1999.* New York: New York University Press, 2002.

Tan, Samuel K. *The Filipino-American War, 1899–1913.* Quezon City: University of the Philippines Press, 2002.

Wolff, Leon. *Little Brown Brother: America's Forgotten Bid for Empire Which Cost 250,000 Lives.* New York: Kraus Reprint, 1970.

Woods, Damon. *The Philippines: A Global Studies Handbook.* Santa Barbara, CA: ABC-CLIO, 2006.

# Arab Revolt (June 8, 1916–October 31, 1918)

## Causes

The Arab Revolt, or Great Arab Revolt as it is also known, began on June 8, 1916, during World War I and was an effort by the Arab peoples of north, central, and western Arabia to revolt against Ottoman rule in order to secure an independent Arab state formed out of the southern territories of the Ottoman Empire that would include the territory from present-day Syria to Yemen. Since the 16th century, the Ottoman government in Istanbul (Constantinople) had controlled the area of present-day Syria, Palestine, Iraq, the western provinces of Saudi Arabia, and part of Yemen. Much of the population was nomadic.

In July 1908 the Young Turks came to power in Istanbul. They promoted centralization of power but also stressed Turkish nationalism at the expense of the many other nationalities of the empire, which included Arabs, Albanians, Greek, Armenians, Jews, Bulgarians, Serbs, and Romanians. The Arabs and the other peoples of the empire greatly resented this. The new

**Arab Revolt (June 8, 1916–October 31, 1918)**

| Population by Religion, Ottoman Empire, ca. 1900 | | | |
|---|---|---|---|
| Religion | Male | Female | Total |
| Muslim | 7,499,798 | 6,612,147 | 14,111,945 |
| Greek Orthodox | 1,341,049 | 1,228,863 | 2,569,912 |
| Armenian | 546,030 | 496,344 | 1,042,374 |
| Other | 510,503 | 435,309 | 945,812 |
| Jewish | 117,767 | 97,658 | 215,425 |
| Catholic | 65,912 | 54,567 | 120,479 |
| Protestant | 22,963 | 21,397 | 44,360 |
| Totals | 10,104,022 | 8,946,285 | 19,050,307 |

| Estimated Relative Strength of Forces, Beginning of Revolt (June 1916) | | |
|---|---|---|
| | Arab Forces | Ottoman Forces |
| Combat-ready troops | 20,000 | 30,000 |

| Aqaba (Jordan), Battle of (July 6, 1917)* | | |
|---|---|---|
| | Arab/British Forces | Ottoman Forces |
| **Strength** | 5,000 men | 750 men |
| **Losses** | 2 killed | 300 killed, 300 captured |

*This battle witnessed the loss of the Ottomans' last port on the Red Sea.

| Megiddo, Battle of (September 19–25, 1918) | | | |
|---|---|---|---|
| | **Arab Forces** | **Allied Forces** | **Ottoman Forces** |
| **Strength** | 4,000-plus men | 69,000 men | 35,000 men |
| **Killed** | Unknown | 782* | 2,000–3,000 |
| **Wounded** | Unknown | 4,179* | Unknown |
| **Captured/missing** | Unknown | 382* | 21,000 |

*These figures showing Allied losses include Arab losses.

| Estimated Casualty Statistics of World War I (1914–1918) | | | | | | | |
|---|---|---|---|---|---|---|---|
| | **Total Mobilized** | **Killed in Action or Died of Wounds** | **Wounded** | **Captured** | **Missing** | **Civilians Dead** | **Ships Lost** |
| **United States** | 4,355,000 | 126,000 | 234,300 | 7,500 | 116,700 | 750 | 3 |
| **United Kingdom** | 8,904,467 | 908,371 | 2,090,212 | 140,000 | 51,650 | 292,000 | 162 |
| **France** | 8,410,000 | 1,375,800 | 4,266,000 | 175,300 | 361,700 | 500,000 | 35 |
| **Russia** | 12,000,000 | 1,700,000 | 4,950,000 | 2,417,000 | 1,221,300 | 1,500,000 | 46 |
| **Italy** | 5,615,000 | 650,000 | 947,000 | 569,000 | 31,000 | 1,021,000 | 23 |
| **Japan** | 800,000 | 300 | 907 | 0 | 3 | 0 | 5 |
| **Austria-Hungary** | 7,800,000 | 1,200,000 | 3,620,000 | 1,344,700 | 855,300 | 700,000 | 6 |
| **Germany** | 11,000,000 | 1,773,700 | 4,216,058 | 1,049,800 | 103,000 | 692,000 | 291 |
| **Ottoman Empire** | 2,850,000 | 325,000 | 400,000 | 145,000 | 95,000 | 2,150,000 | 5 |

**Sources:** Clodfelter, Michael. *Warfare and Armed Conflict: A Statistical Reference to Casualty and Other Figures, 1618–1991.* Jefferson, NC: McFarland, 1992; Hourani, Albert. *A History of the Arab Peoples.* Cambridge, MA: Harvard University Press, 1991; McCarthy, Justin. *Arab World, Turkey, and the Balkans (1878–1914): Handbook of Historical Statistics.* Boston: G. K. Hall, 1982.

government also sent troops into Arab lands and introduced conscription, both of which caused Arab ire.

Under the terms of a new Ottoman constitution of 1909, the Arab peoples of the empire sent representatives to the imperial parliament in Istanbul (Constantinople). The first parliament under the new constitution had 275 members. Turks were in the majority, with 142 representatives, but the Arabs were the largest minority, with 45 representatives. The Arab representatives in the parliament argued for reform and openly supported Arab rights.

Although the vast majority of the 10 million or so Arabs in the Ottoman Empire in the early 20th century still gave their primary allegiance to Islam, sect, or tribe, Arab nationalism was growing. Newspapers in the Arab territories as well as small political organizations, some secret, were actively promoting Arab nationalism.

Construction of the Hejaz Railroad in 1906. The railway, which ran from Damascus to Medina, was an important supply line for the Ottoman forces and thus a major target during the Arab Revolt of World War I. (Library of Congress)

Damascus and Beirut were centers of this activity but were too close geographically to Anatolia to risk overt action. Arab power was diffused and largely wielded by local chieftains who had little ability to initiate hostilities against Ottoman rule on their own.

The center of the Arab nationalist movement came to be the Hejaz region of central Arabia, which contained the Muslim holy cities of Mecca and Medina. The region was connected to Anatolia by the Damascus-Medina (Hejaz) Railway. Running for some 810 miles, it opened in 1908. Plans to extend the line an additional 210 miles to Mecca were interrupted by World War I, however.

Ottoman leaders had pushed construction of the rail line that would connect Istanbul, the seat of the Islamic Caliphate, with the holy cities of the Hejaz, and especially Mecca, the destination of the yearly hajj pilgrimage. The rail line would also have a major economic impact, but political considerations also figured prominently in its construction, for the Ottoman leaders anticipated that it would tie the distant Arab territories to the south more closely to the rest of the empire. As the Arabs were also aware, it would greatly facilitate the movement of troops southward should that need arise.

In June 1913, some two dozen Arab intellectuals from the Arab Mashriq (the Arab region east of Egypt) met in Paris. In what became known as the Arab National Congress or First Arab Congress, they drafted a series of demands that included autonomy within the Ottoman Empire as well as a guarantee that in time of war Arab conscripts in the Ottoman Army would not have to serve outside the Arab regions of the empire.

The sharif of Mecca, Hussein ibn Ali al-Hashimi (r. 1908–1924), was the nominal ruler of the Hejaz. His position was strengthened by his senior position in the Muslim religious hierarchy as a direct descendant of

Prophet Muhammad. Regarded as loyal to the Ottoman state, Hussein nonetheless saw the Hejaz Railway as an infringement on his control. He had also long hoped to rule an independent Arab kingdom.

Hussein's loyalty to Istanbul began to fray with a coup d'état in Istanbul in 1913. The Ottoman Empire had sustained a series of defeats in both the Italo-Turkish War (1911–1912) and the First Balkan War (1912–1913). The empire's steady stream of military defeats greatly discredited Mehmed V, and on January 23, a day after the major powers had convinced the Ottoman government to yield Adrianople in negotiations to end the First Balkan War, a coup d'état occurred in Istanbul. A triumvirate now came to dominate Ottoman affairs: Ismail Enver Pasha as minister of war, Mehmed Talât Pasha as minister of the interior, and Ahmed Djemal Pasha as naval minister.

The new Ottoman government set about centralizing power in Istanbul. This ran up against Hussein's belief that the Arabs constituted a separate and distinct people and that he was destined to rule over them. World War I gave him that opportunity.

Already before the start of the war Hussein had been in communication through his son Abdullah with British authorities in Cairo. In February 1914 Abdullah met with the British high commissioner in Egypt, Field Marshal Horatio Kitchener, and asked if the British would be willing to support his father militarily if he went to war against the Ottomans over further encroachments on his power. Kitchener was noncommittal and indeed informed Abdullah that this would mean meddling in the affairs of a state with which the British enjoyed friendly relations. This was especially true with the beginning of the war in August 1914, when Britain and France hoped to keep the Ottoman Empire neutral or even fight on its side.

Enver Pasha was determined to bring the Ottoman Empire into the war on the German side, however. He then orchestrated a means to bring this about, kept secret from the rest of the government, in an Ottoman naval assault on Russian bases on the Black Sea on October 29. This brought a Russian declaration of war on November 1. Russia's wartime allies of France and the British Empire followed suit on November 5.

With the Ottoman Empire and the British now at war, London's attitude toward an alliance with the Arabs changed dramatically. Both Sir Harold Wingate, British governor-general of the Sudan, and Sir Henry McMahon, Kitchener's successor as high commissioner in Egypt during 1915–1917, kept the lines of communication open with Hussein.

In the spring of 1915, Hussein sent his third son Emir Faisal to Damascus to reassure Ottman authorities there of his loyalty but also to sound out Arab opinion. Faisal had favored supporting the Ottomans in the war, but the visit to Damascus and his discovery of the profound discontent of the Arab population there reversed this view.

Hussein now entered into active negotiations with McMahon in Cairo. In an exchange of correspondence between the two men during July 14, 1915–January 30, 1916, Hussein promised to declare war on the Ottoman Empire and raise an Arab army to assist the British in return for British support for him as king of a postwar Pan-Arab state. The British agreed, and soon they were providing some rifles and ammunition to the Arabs. In late 1916 the Allies undertook establishment of the Regular Arab Army (also known as the

Sharifian Army). Its men fought in regular battles and, in contrast with the militiamen, wore regular army uniforms. By the end of the war, British assistance reached some £220,000 a month. The French also provided financial assistance, reportedly 1.25 million gold francs. The great advantage for the British in what would be the Arab Revolt was that it would tie down substantial numbers of Ottoman troops who would otherwise be available to contest British Empire forces in the Middle East.

Meanwhile, the Ottoman authorities were endeavoring to stamp out Arab nationalism in Damascus, where they executed a number of Arab nationalist leaders. Many other Arab patriots fled south to Mecca, where they urged Hussein to take up arms. The Ottomans were well aware of Arab preparations, and from May 1916 they sought to block arms shipments to the Hejaz and began a buildup of their own forces in Damascus. The Arab Revolt was initiated by the dispatch of Ottoman troops to reinforce their garrison at Medina.

SPENCER C. TUCKER

Emir Faisal, the third son of Hussein ibn Ali al-Hashimi, grand sharif of Mecca, led the Arab Revolt against the Ottoman Empire and its climactic action, the entrance into Damascus on October 1, 1918. In 1921 he became Faisal I, king of Iraq. (Library of Congress)

## Course

At the beginning of the Arab Revolt, the Ottomans enjoyed considerable military advantage. While they were initially outnumbered in the Arab territory, with some 20,000 soldiers to perhaps a maximum of 30,000 men for the Arabs, the Ottomans were far better trained and armed, largely with German-supplied modern weapons that included artillery and aircraft. The major problem for the Ottomans during the revolt was that they were forced to fight at great distance and rely on the long Hejaz Railway for their supplies.

Ultimately the Arabs would receive rifles as well as some machine guns, mortars, and explosives from Britain and France and even some artillery and a few armored cars. British air and naval gunfire support turned out to be critical to Arab military success, however.

Some confusion exists about the start of the Arab Revolt. While it may have begun on June 5, 1916, the usually accepted date for its commencement is June 8, when Hussein's eldest son Emir Ali and Emir Faisal officially proclaimed its start. Joined by 30,000 tribesmen, Faisal immediately led an assault on the Ottoman garrison at Medina, but the defenders were able to drive them off. The Arab forces did succeed in cutting the Hejaz Railway to the north of the city. To the south, on June 10

Hussein led an attack on the 1,000-man Ottoman garrison at Mecca, taking the city after three days of street fighting. Indiscriminate Ottoman artillery fire that damaged much of the holy city of Mecca provided a propaganda boost for the Arabs.

Another Arab attack shortly thereafter against the Red Sea port city of Jeddah was also successful. It received crucial air support from planes of the British Royal Navy seaplane carrier *Ben-my-Chree.* Jeddah surrendered on June 16.

Other cities also fell to the Arabs. Arab forces liberated the Al Qunfudhah and Al Laith ports on August 15, 1916. In September, the 3,000-man garrison at Taif, the last city in the southern Hejaz held by the Ottomans, surrendered to Arab forces supported by British-supplied artillery. The Arabs had now taken some 6,000 Ottomans prisoner.

On November 2, Hussein proclaimed himself "King of the Arab Countries." This created some embarrassment for the British government with the French. Finally, the Allies worked out a compromise whereby they addressed Hussein as "King of the Hejaz."

Hussein left leadership of the revolt largely to his four sons. During World War I as many as 300,000 Arabs served in the Ottoman Army, and a number of these including officers, who were taken prisoner in the fighting, helped provide a leadership cadre for the so-called Arab Army. The actual strength of the Arab's four main field forces commanded by Hussein's sons fluctuated greatly, however.

In October 1916, the Ottomans managed to drive the Arab Army south of Medina and reopen the Hejaz Railway. In June the British had sent out a number of officers to serve as advisers to Hussein. The French also sent out a military mission, which

unlike that of the British included a number of Muslim officers. The Arabist captain T. E. Lawrence, who arrived from Egypt in October, was an important figure. British citizen Gertrude Bell, an Oxford University graduate who had traveled extensively in the region, provided important information to Lawrence, who soon became Faisal's official adviser and successfully convinced the latter not to try to retake Medina but instead to undertake a series of hit-and-run raids, primarily against the Hejaz Railway, that would take advantage of support from the local populations. From the British point of view, this would have the advantage of forcing the Ottomans to divert increasing numbers of troops to the region, relieving pressure elsewhere in the Middle East.

On December 1, 1916, Ottoman general Fakhri Pasha, governor and commander of the forces in Medina, proceeded from that city with three brigades in an effort to take Yanbu, a port on the Red Sea and now in Saudi Arabia. The Ottoman troops enjoyed success against the Arabs in several engagements, and it appeared that they would indeed take the port, but Lawrence arranged support from the Royal Navy. Gunfire and aircraft from five British warships offshore proved to be key in turning back the Ottoman assault on Yanbu during December 11–12. Fakhri then turned south in an effort to secure Rabegh, but Arab hit-and-run attacks on his flanks overextended supply lines, and British aircraft strikes forced him to return to Medina on January 18, 1917. Lawrence claimed that the Ottoman failure to take Yanbu ensured their ultimate defeat in the Hejaz.

Already Faisal had set his forces in motion to take Wejh, on the Red Sea, and establish it as his principal base for raiding the Hejaz Railway. On January 3 he proceeded northward with some 10,400 men, a large number of baggage camels, 10 machine guns, and 4 mountain howitzers. Royal Navy ships resupplied the column as it moved north. The 800 Ottoman troops defending Wejh were expecting the attack to come from the south, so they were surprised when the Royal Navy landed 400 Arab soldiers and 200 Royal Navy sailors and marines and attacked Wejh from the north on January 23. Wejh fell the next day.

Their loss of Wejh caused the Ottomans to assume a defensive posture, keeping at Medina only a sufficient number of troops to hold that place while employing the remainder of their manpower in scattered strongpoints to defend the railroad.

Soon Faisal's forces were attacking the railroad, utilizing camels for their hit-and-run raids. At first these merely destroyed sections of track, but the introduction of mines and explosive charges allowed attacks on trains that were under way. The raids not only secured needed military supplies and destroyed Ottoman rolling stock but also tied down thousands of Ottoman soldiers. Although an Ottoman raid into the Hejaz did considerable damage, increasingly the Ottoman forces were obliged to stand on the defensive.

In the spring of 1917, Faisal received pledges of Arab support from Syria once military operations reached there. In July 1917 Lawrence led an attack that captured Aqaba, the only remaining Ottoman-held port on the Red Sea. It fell on July 6 and became Faisal's chief base, while forces under Abdullah and Ali contained the Ottoman garrison at Medina and protected Mecca. Faisal's northern wing of the Arab Army was the revolt's chief military force and acted on the right flank of Lieutenant General Edmund Allenby's British Empire forces in Palestine.

In the autumn of 1917 Lawrence led a series of successful attacks on Ottoman rail traffic that greatly aided the British Empire forces under Allenby. In November 1917, Lawrence raided deep into the Yarmouk River Valley. While the raiders failed to destroy the key railroad bridge at Tel ash-Shehab, they did inflict major damage to an Ottoman train.

Allenby's calls for diversionary attacks by the Arab Army produced a series of raids that diverted some 23,000 Ottoman troops from participation in the fighting in Palestine. Then in the spring of 1918, Operation HEDGEHOG destroyed some two dozen bridges on the railroad.

Faisal's Arab forces also cooperated closely with Allenby in the Megiddo Offensive in Palestine beginning on September 19, 1918. They provided much-needed intelligence on the Ottoman positions, attacked Ottoman supply lines, and struck isolated Ottoman garrisons. On September 28, Sharifian irregulars with Lawrence, now a lieutenant colonel, captured Deraa. Now numbering some 30,000 men, Faisal's forces led the revolt's climactic action, the entrance into Damascus on October 1, 1918. Fighting came to an end on October 30, 1918, with the surrender of Ottoman Empire forces in the Armistice of Mudros. The Arab forces never did retake Medina. Held by nearly 10,000 men, it was surrendered by Fashri Pasha only after the end of the war, on January 9, 1919.

SPENCER C. TUCKER

## Consequences

The Arab Revolt had immense repercussions in the Arab world in fueling Arab nationalism. Not only did it help free the Arab lands from Ottoman rule, but it also led to the formation of quasi-independent Arab states. But the victorious Allies thwarted Hussein's ambitions to rule over a unitary Arab state.

McMahon's pledge to Hussein of support for an Arab state actually preceded by six months the secret Sykes-Picot Agreement between the British and French governments, which was a clear breach of promises made to the Arabs. Negotiated from November 1915 to March 1916 between French diplomat François Georges-Picot and Briton Mark Sykes and signed on May 16, 1916, it provided for carving out of the Ottoman Empire four new states in the Middle East: Syria and Lebanon (to be controlled by the French) and Iraq and Palestine (to pass under British control). These states were hardly independent, however. Ultimately, these new Arab states were awarded as mandates to Great Britain and France under the League of Nations. A further impediment to a greater Arab state was the Balfour Declaration of 1917. It expressed British support for a Jewish "National home" in Palestine.

Faisal tried to thwart the British and French leaders, for on March 8, 1920, he established the independent Kingdom of Syria, with himself as King Faisal I. His reign was short, lasting only until July 24, when the French Army of the Levant defeated Faisal's Arab forces in the Battle of Maysalun. French troops then occupied Syria. Syria and the Lebanon were officially recognized as French mandates by the League of Nations in 1923. Meanwhile, the British agreed that Faisal would become king of Iraq under their protection. He became Faisal I, king of Iraq, on August 23, 1921. Abdullah became king of the newly created Transjordan. Hussein declared himself caliph of Islam in March 1924 but controlled only the Hejaz region of western Arabia. His reign was brief.

On August 24, 1924, Abd al-Aziz al-Saud (Ibn Saud), sultan of Nejd, invaded the Hejaz and drove on Mecca. Hussein abdicated on October 3, succeeded by his son Ali. Mecca surrendered to Ibn Saud on October 14. On December 8, 1925, Ali, who had withdrawn to Jidda, also abdicated, and Ibn Saud's forces took Jidda on December 23. Now in effective control of the entire area, on January 8, 1926, Ibn Saud declared himself king of the Hejaz. A year later, he added the title "King of Nejd," although both kingdoms were administered separately. On September 23, 1932, Ibn Saud merged his two kingdoms of the Hejaz and Nejd to form the Kingdom of Saudi Arabia.

SPENCER C. TUCKER

## Timeline

| | |
|---|---|
| **1908** | The Hejaz Railway, connecting Damascus with Medina, opens. |
| **Jul 1908** | The Young Turks seize power in the Ottoman Empire. |
| **1909** | In a new constitution, Arabs in the parliament espouse reform and Arab rights. |
| **Jun 1913** | Some two dozen Arab intellectuals in the Arab region east of Egypt meet in Paris at the Arab National Congress. They draft a series of demands that include autonomy within the Ottoman Empire and military reforms. |

| | |
|---|---|
| **1911–1912** | The Ottoman Empire suffers defeat in the Italo-Turkish War. |
| **1912–1913** | Ottoman Empire forces are defeated in the First Balkan War. |
| **Jan 23, 1913** | In the wake of Ottoman military disasters, a coup d'état in Istanbul overthrows Sultan Mehmed V and brings to power a triumvirate of leaders: Ismail Enver Pasha (minister of war), Mehmed Talât Pasha (minister of the interior), and Ahmed Djemal Pasha (naval minister). This alienates the sharif of Mecca, Hussein ibn Ali al-Hashimi. |
| **Feb 1914** | Hussein's son Abdullah meets in Cairo with British high commissioner in Egypt Field Marshal Horatio Kitchener and asks if the British would support Hussein in a war against the Ottomans. Kitchener rebuffs Abdullah, however. |
| **Aug 4, 1914** | World War I begins. |
| **Oct 29, 1914** | Determined to see the Ottoman Empire join the Central Powers, Enver Pasha arranges an Ottoman Navy assault on Russian naval bases on the Black Sea. |
| **Nov 1, 1914** | Russia declares war on the Ottoman Empire. |
| **Nov 5, 1914** | Britain and France declare war on the Ottoman Empire. |
| **Jul 14, 1915–<br>Jan 30, 1916** | In an exchange of correspondence between Hussein and British high commissioner in Egypt Sir Henry McMahon, Hussein promises to declare war on the Ottoman Empire in return for British support for him as king of a postwar Pan-Arab state. The British agree. |
| **May 1916** | Aware of Arab war preparations, Ottoman authorities block arms shipments on the Hejaz Railway and begin building up their own forces in Damascus. |
| **May 16, 1916** | The secret Sykes-Picot Agreement provides for the postwar creation of four new states in the Middle East: Syria and Lebanon (under French control) and Iraq and Palestine (under British control). |
| **Jun 1916** | The British send out a number of military advisers to Hussein. The French also dispatch a military mission. |
| **Jun 8, 1916** | Outside Medina, Hussein's eldest son Emir Ali and Emir Faisal officially proclaim the Arab Revolt and assault the Ottoman garrison in the city. |
| **Jun 10, 1916** | Hussein leads an attack on the Ottoman garrison at Mecca, taking the city after three days of street fighting. |
| **Jun 16, 1916** | Arab forces, aided by British naval aircraft, capture the port city of Jeddah. |
| **Aug 15, 1916** | Arab forces take the ports of Al Qunfudhah and Al Laith. |
| **Sep 22, 1916** | Following a brief siege the Arab forces take Taif, the last city in the southern Hejaz held by the Ottomans. |

| | |
|---|---|
| **Oct 1916** | The Ottomans drive the Arab Army south of Medina and reopen the Hejaz Railway. Arabist and British Army captain T. E. Lawrence arrives from Cairo and joins the Arab forces, becoming Faisal's adviser. |
| **Nov 2, 1916** | Hussein proclaims himself "King of the Arab Countries." The Allies work out a compromise by which they address him as "King of the Hejaz." |
| **Late 1916** | The British and French establish the Regular Arab Army (Sharifian Army). |
| **Dec 1, 1916** | Ottoman general Fakhri Pasha, governor and commander of forces in Medina, proceeds with a force of three brigades in an effort to take the port of Yanbu on the Red Sea. |
| **Dec 11–12, 1916** | Although the Ottoman troops initially enjoy success against the Arabs, they fail to take Yanbu in assaults, thanks in large part to British naval gunfire and aircraft. |
| **Jan 3, 1917** | Faisal sets out with some 10,400 men to take Wejh, on the Red Sea, and establish it as his principal base for raiding the Hejaz Railway. |
| **Jan 18, 1917** | Also failing to take Rabegh, Fakhri returns to Medina. |
| **Jan 24, 1917** | Surprising the Ottoman troops at Wejh, the Royal Navy lands 400 Arab soldiers and 200 Royal Navy sailors and marines and attack Wejh from the north on January 23. It falls the next day. |
| **Jul 6, 1917** | Lawrence leads an attack that captures Aqaba, the sole remaining Ottoman-held port on the Red Sea. It becomes Faisal's chief base. |
| **Nov 1917** | Lawrence and Arab forces raid deep into the Yarmouk River Valley. |
| **Nov 2, 1917** | British foreign secretary Arthur James Balfour pledges his government's support for a Jewish "national home" in Palestine. |
| **Spring 1918** | Operation HEDGEHOG destroys some two dozen bridges along the Hejaz Railway. |
| **Sep 19–25, 1918** | Faisal's Arab forces cooperate closely with Allenby in the Megiddo Offensive. |
| **Sep 28, 1918** | Sherifial irregulars and Lawrence capture Deraa. |
| **Oct 1, 1918** | Faisal's forces lead the Allied entrance into Damascus. |
| **Oct 30, 1918** | The Ottoman Empire concludes the Armistice of Mudros with the Allied powers. |
| **Jan 9, 1919** | Fashri Pasha surrenders Medina. |
| **Mar 8, 1920** | Faisal establishes the independent Kingdom of Syria as Faisal I. |
| **Jul 24, 1920** | The French Army of the Levant defeats Faisal's Arab forces in the Battle of Maysalun. |

| | |
|---|---|
| **Aug 23, 1921** | The British make Faisal king of Iraq, a British mandate. |
| **Mar 1924** | Hussein declares himself caliph of Islam, but he controls only the Hejaz region of western Arabia. |
| **Aug 24, 1924** | Abd al-Aziz al-Saud (Ibn Saud), sultan of Nejd, invades the Hejaz and drives on Mecca. |
| **Oct 3, 1924** | Hussein abdicates and is succeeded by his son Ali. |
| **Oct 14, 1924** | Mecca surrenders to Ibn Saud on October 14. |
| **Dec 8, 1925** | Ali abdicates. |
| **Jam 8, 1926** | Ibn Saud declares himself king of the Hejaz. |
| **Sep 23, 1932** | Ibn Saud merges his two kingdoms of the Hejaz and Nejd to form the Kingdom of Saudi Arabia. |

SPENCER C. TUCKER

## Further Reading

Erickson, Edward. *Ordered to Die: A History of the Ottoman Army in the First World War.* Westport, CT: Praeger, 2000.

Falls, Cyril. *Official History of the Great War Based on Official Documents by Direction of the Historical Section of the Committee of Imperial Defence: Military Operations Egypt & Palestine from June 1917 to the End of the War.* Vol. 2. London: HMSO, 1930.

Fromkin, David. *A Peace to End All Peace: The Fall of the Ottoman Empire and the Creation of the Modern Middle East.* New York: Avon, 1989.

Hourani, Albert. *A History of the Arab Peoples.* Cambridge: Harvard University Press, 1991.

Korda, Michael. *Hero: The Life and Legend of Lawrence of Arabia.* New York: Harper, 2010.

Lawrence, T. E. *Seven Pillars of Wisdom.* New York: Doubleday, Doran, 1935.

Murphy, David. *The Arab Revolt, 1916–18: Lawrence Sets Arabia Ablaze.* New York: Osprey, 2008.

Murphy, David. *Lawrence of Arabia.* New York: Osprey, 2011.

Tauber, Eliezer. *The Arab Movements in World War I.* London: Frank Cass, 1993.

Thomas, Lowell. *With Lawrence in Arabia.* New York: Garden City Publishing, 1924.

Wilson, Jeremy. *Lawrence of Arabia: The Condensed Edition of the Authorised Biography of T. E. Lawrence.* London: Mandarin, 1992.

# Irish War of Independence (1919–1921)

## Causes

The English conquered Ireland in 1172 and immediately subjected the Irish to harsh rule. After a period of virtual Irish independence in the 15th century, Great Britain reestablished its control in the 17th and early 18th centuries. The great contest between Catholicism and Protestantism then sweeping Europe had major consequences for Ireland, where the English disestablished the Catholic Church and established the (Protestant) Church of Ireland, which the Irish people were obliged to support financially. Because the hated English were Protestant, the Irish clung to their Catholic faith. The English also tightened their political control; the Test Act of 1672 prevented all those not taking communion in the Church of England—that is, Catholics and nonconforming Protestants—from holding public office. The act was not repealed until 1829. The Irish also found themselves deprived of other rights, including ownership of hereditary property. By the 19th century Ireland was largely ruled by wealthy Anglican landowners, many of them absentee, while most Irishmen were reduced to agricultural labor.

Natural disasters also inflicted a heavy toll. Severe winters during 1739–1741 destroyed the potato crop and other staples, resulting in the Famine of 1740. Perhaps some 200,000 people, an eighth of the population, died. The Irish Potato Famine (1845–1852) added another 1 million deaths and led more than that number to emigrate (many to the United States).

In 1782 Ireland was granted legislative independence from Great Britain, although the British government still controlled Irish affairs. In 1798, abetted by revolutionary France, the Society of United Irishmen mounted a revolt with the goal of establishing an independent Irish republic. The revolt was easily crushed and helped bring about the Act of Union (1800), by which Ireland was joined with Great Britain to constitute the United Kingdom of Great Britain and Ireland.

The continued sectarian divide, absentee British landlords, and the religious issue all fueled demands in Ireland for home rule and independence. Hatred of the English was now part of the Irish psyche, thanks to the centuries of economic exploitation and religious and political oppression.

Ireland was now also somewhat divided along other lines as well, for in the course of the 17th century the British government had taken much of the land of northeastern Ireland and granted it to Scottish and English settlers to form the Plantation of Ulster. This northern Protestant majority, the so-called Unionists, was fearful of being engulfed in a sea of Catholic Irish and wanted to continue as part of Britain. They strongly opposed home rule for Ireland, seeing it as only a step toward Irish independence.

The gulf between Ireland and Great Britain was now deep. Whereas England and Scotland were predominantly Protestant, Ireland was largely Catholic. And whereas Great Britain had become chiefly industrial, Ireland remained largely agricultural.

In the first quarter of the 19th century, the Catholic Association came to the fore. Its leader, Daniel O'Connell, was successful in his campaign to secure repeal of the

## Irish War of Independence (1919–1921)

| Easter Rising (April 24–29, 1916)* | | |
|---|---|---|
| | **Irish Independence Forces** | **British Forces** |
| **Strength** | 1,500 | 15,500 |
| **Fighters killed** | 64 | 132 |
| **Fighters wounded** | 200 | 397 |
| **Civilians killed** | 254 | N/A |
| **Civilians wounded** | 2,127 | N/A |
| **Buildings destroyed** | 200 | N/A |

*This was the first major armed clash of the Irish revolutionary period and the most significant armed rebellion in Ireland since 1798.

| Principal Commanders and Leaders, Irish War of Independence | | |
|---|---|---|
| | **Irish Republic** | **Great Britain** |
| **Military leaders** | Michael Collins | LTG Frederick Shaw |
| | Richard Mulcahy | Gen. Nevil Macready |
| | Cathal Brugha | LTG Henry Hugh Tudor |
| **Political leaders** | Éamon de Valera | David Lloyd George |
| | Arthur Griffith | Lord John French |
| | | Lord Edmund FitzAlan |
| | | Ian Macpherson |
| | | Hamar Greenwood |

| Irish War of Independence (1919–1921), Total Losses | | |
|---|---|---|
| | **Irish Republican Army** | **British Forces** |
| **Fighters killed** | 550 | 714 |
| **Civilians killed** | 759 | N/A |

**Sources:** Foster, R. F. *Modern Ireland, 1600–1972*. London: Penguin, 1988; Gregory, Adrian, and Senia Paseta, eds. *Ireland and the Great War: A War to Unite Us All?* Manchester, UK: Manchester University Press, 2002; Hopkinson, Michael A. *The Irish War of Independence*. Ithaca, NY: McGill-Queen's University Press, 2002.

Test Act. This action enabled Catholics to hold seats in the British Parliament. O'Connell failed to end the Act of Union, however. A more radical Irish organization then formed. Known as Young Ireland and mirroring other similarly named organizations throughout Europe, it attempted a revolt on July 29, 1848, during the wave of European revolutions that year but was easily put down by the British authorities.

In the 1850s the Fenian Brotherhood came to the fore. Formed among Irish in the United States, it attracted most of its support from abroad but did produce rioting in the English cities of Lancashire in 1867, which led the government to call out troops. In 1870 a new threat arose to British rule in Ireland with the formation that year of the Irish Nationalist Party, led by Charles Stewart Parnell. It took its place in the British Parliament alongside the dominant Conservative and Liberal Parties.

By 1870 there were some 600,000 Irish tenants working the lands of the great English landlords, who had the right to impose on them whatever rents they wished. To maximize their own returns, the landlords increasingly raised rents. They were able to do this because of the expanding Irish population. With the native Irish having virtually no other alternative except farming, the landlords could extract virtually any rent they wished. They could also evict tenants with no legal obligation to compensate them for any improvements they had made during their tenancy.

The short-term demands of the Irish Nationalists included the so-called Three F's of fair rents, fixity of tenure, and free sale, or the right to sell their successors any improvements that they might have made. The ultimate Irish demand, however, was an end to landlordism and the return of the land that had once been theirs.

The so-called Irish question now dominated British domestic politics. In 1868 William Gladstone, leader of the Liberal Party, became prime minister and made reform in Ireland a priority. In his first ministry (1868–1874), Gladstone in 1869 pushed through an act that disestablished the Church of Ireland. This largely removed complaints by the Irish people regarding religion. Another act, the Land Act of 1870, prohibited the arbitrary increase of rents and stipulated that an evicted tenant had to be compensated for any improvements. The state was also to help peasants seeking to buy land. Unfortunately, the act largely failed because the

landlords were able to take advantage of legal loopholes.

In his second ministry (1880–1885), Gladstone again sought to deal with the Irish question. Parnell was determined to secure home role, and in 1877 in the House of Commons he began a policy of obstructing all legislation until this was achieved. Although Parnell was opposed to violence, it occurred in Ireland and brought repressive measures. In 1881, however, Gladstone secured passage of a new land act that provided for a fixed 15-year period for rent as well as tenants' safe tenure on the land and the right to sell any improvements.

Gladstone's third ministry in 1886 was of short duration largely because of his support of home rule in a bill to give Ireland a separate parliament for its own affairs. But more than a quarter of Gladstone's own Liberal Party members of Parliament opposed home rule. Led by John Bright and Joseph Chamberlain, they established the Liberal Unionist Party and joined with the Conservatives in defeating the home rule bill. Parliament was then dissolved to allow the electorate to pass on the issue, and the Liberals went down to defeat.

Gladstone returned to power for a fourth and last time during 1892–1894. Home rule in Ireland was the chief issue. Support from the Irish Nationalists allowed the Liberals to form a government and in 1893 pass Gladstone's Government of Ireland Bill (or second home rule bill). Promptly rejected by the House of Lords, it therefore failed to become law.

Following passage of the Parliament Act of 1911 that restricted the power of the House of Lords to veto legislation, in January 1913 the House of Commons passed a bill establishing an Irish parliament, although not with complete autonomy. The House of Lords immediately rejected it. Again it was passed by the House of Commons, and again the House of Lords rejected it. Under the provisions of the Parliament Act of 1911 it appeared that nothing could prevent the eventual enactment of the law in 1914 if the House of Commons passed it a third time. By this time, however, the Protestant Ulsterites were determined to do whatever was necessary to prevent Irish home rule. In addition to fearing rule by a majority Catholic Irish parliament, there was deep concern in the wealthier and more industrial Ulster that the views of rural and poorer Ireland would prevail and that legislation would be enacted that would be harmful to the economic life of the region. Ulsterites insisted that Ireland remain part of the United Kingdom.

Sir Edward Carson, leader of the Ulsterites, believed that the Liberal government might be frightened into dropping the home rule project if Ulster showed its determination not to submit. Mass meetings and demonstrations occurred, and on January 13, 1913, a military organization of 100,000 men, known as the Ulster Volunteer Force, was organized. Also, more than 237,000 Unionist men made a solemn covenant never to submit to an Irish parliament.

All of this caused Prime Minister Herbert H. Asquith to seek a compromise, which greatly angered Redmond, who on November 25, 1913, began to raise a force of Irish Volunteers to support home rule for all of Ireland. Civil war appeared in the offing. The situation was made all the more difficult for the government in the so-called Carragh Mutiny of March 20, 1914, when a number of British Army officers chose to submit their resignations rather than be obliged to force Ulster to accept home rule.

Despite this threatening situation, the House of Commons passed the home rule bill for a third time in May 1914. In July, with conditions in Ireland growing constantly more menacing, King George V called a conference of representatives of all sides to meet at Buckingham Palace, but no agreement could be reached.

In August 1914, World War I began. The war led all sides to reach a compromise. The home rule bill became law on September 18, but the Ulster Unionists teamed with the British Conservatives to secure simultaneous passage of the Suspensory Act that delayed enactment of Irish home rule for the duration of the war. In 1913 the Irish Nationalists had established the Irish National Volunteers of some 100,000 men to counter the formation the year before of the Ulster Volunteers. At the start of the war, most of the Irish National Volunteers joined the British Army. A minority of no more than 14,000 chose not to fight for Britain and formed the Irish Volunteers. All told, some 180,000 Irishmen served in the British Army during the war.

The Irish Republican Brotherhood, the Irish Volunteers, and the Irish Citizen Army were established to protect Irish workers now resolved to revolt against British rule and establish an Irish republic. Patrick Pearse led what became known as the Easter Rising (Easter Rebellion) of April 24–29.

Irish-born Sir Roger Casement agreed to seek German support, necessary for the endeavor to succeed. The Germans sent 20,000 rifles in the Norwegian trawler *Aud* to Ireland. Intercepted by the Royal Navy, it was scuttled by its commander. Casement meanwhile returned to Ireland aboard

Irish prisoners on a Dublin quay under British guard during the bloody, and ultimately unsuccessful, Irish insurrection that began on Easter Monday in 1916. (Library of Congress)

a U-boat but was almost immediately captured. The plotters had planned to use a parade by the Irish Volunteers in Dublin on Easter Day as cover for the risings. These setbacks and dissension in the leadership caused the rebellion to be put off until Easter Monday. While this made it a surprise to the British, it also meant that few Irish Volunteers took part, and the rebellion was confined largely to Dublin.

On April 24, 1916, some 1,500 rebels (1,200 Irish Volunteers and 300 members of the Irish Citizen Army, including 90 women) seized strategic points throughout Dublin, and Pearse proclaimed establishment of the Irish Republic. Although taken by surprise, the British rushed in reinforcements and sealed off the city while cutting rebel units off from one another. On April 29 Pearse surrendered.

In the Easter Rising, government forces lost 132 killed and 397 wounded, while 64 insurgents were killed and perhaps 200 wounded. A total of 254 civilians perished, and 2,127 were wounded. Some 200 buildings in central Dublin were destroyed by

the fighting and accompanying looting, and 100,000 people were left homeless or in need of public relief.

The surviving rebels were booed as they were marched off to prison, but the public attitude changed when the British placed all of Ireland under martial law and imprisoned some 3,500 people, most of whom had not participated in the insurrection. The authorities tried 161 participants. Sixty-six were sentenced to death, and 15, including Pearse, were executed by firing squad during May 3–15 before Asquith had the good sense to halt the remaining executions. Casement was later tried for treason and hanged in London. These actions, however, turned much of Ireland against the British and destroyed any hope of reconciliation.

In Britain the Easter Rising weakened Prime Minister Asquith, while in Ireland it led to the demise of the Irish Parliamentary Party and the rise of the separatist Sinn Féin (Ourselves Alone) party, which explains why the Easter Rising was sometimes called the Sinn Féin Rebellion, although that party had no part in it. Members of Sinn Féin who were interned for taking part in the insurrection were eventually released, and most of them, notably Michael Collins and Eamon de Valera, assumed leadership positions in the republican movement.

Sinn Féin's strength was clearly shown in the December 1918 British parliamentary elections, when it secured some 70 percent of the Irish seats in the British Parliament. Sinn Féin asserted that the elections constituted a mandate in favor of independence, and on January 21, 1919, the 27 newly elected Sinn Féin members of the British Parliament, calling themselves the Teachtaí Dála, assembled at the Mansion House in Dublin and there established an Irish parliament known as the Dáil Éireann (Assembly of Ireland). Cathal Brugha was proclaimed president, as Sinn Féin leader de Valera had been rearrested in May 1918 and was then imprisoned in Lincoln Gaol in England.

SPENCER C. TUCKER

## Course

The Irish War for Independence (Anglo-Irish War) of 1919–1921 can be said to have begun on January 21, 1919, when the members of Sinn Féin elected to the British Parliament met in Dublin and organized themselves as an Irish parliament, the Dáil Éireann (Assembly of Ireland). Several hours later, members of the Irish Volunteers ambushed the transport of a cartload of explosives bound for the quarry at Soloheadbeg, County Tipperary, and killed two members of the Royal Irish Constabulary (RIC), the Irish police force. The fighting gradually spread. It was more a struggle for control of the Irish people than for territory and remained a low-intensity insurgency, consisting largely of acts of intimidation, ambushes, and assassinations.

Sinn Féin leader Éamon de Valera, having escaped prison in England in February 1919, on April 1 replaced Cathal Brugha as president of the Dáil Éireann (Assembly of Ireland, the self-proclaimed Irish parliament). The newly reconstituted Irish Volunteers, now known as the Irish Republican Army (IRA) and commanded by Michael Collins and Richard Mulcahy, concentrated on freeing political prisoners and attacking the RIC, the symbol of British authority in Ireland and a ready source of weapons.

With the British cabinet reluctant to employ military force, the job of restoring peace in Ireland largely fell to the RIC. The IRA applied social and economic pressures against the police and their families, and sometimes this turned violent. In republican areas the campaign worked well; in Unionist areas, it failed. This strategy was sufficiently effective, however, that by the end of 1919 the RIC had lost almost 20 percent of its numbers through resignation and retirement. The recruiting pool also shrank.

When the RIC began to close its outlying stations to concentrate police power in the larger towns, the British government finally authorized recruitment of World War I veterans from Britain into the force. They became known as the Black and Tans, after their polyglot uniforms. For this reason the War of Iris Independence is sometimes called the Black and Tan War or simply the Tan War. Sent directly into the existing force with little training, the Black and Tans began to arrive in March 1920. Their numbers proved insufficient, however. The British government then in the summer of 1920 began recruiting another police group, known as the Auxiliary Division of the RIC (ADRIC). ADRIC soon earned a reputation for brutality and atrocity.

With British Army support, in the autumn of 1920 the reinforced police struck out into the countryside they had abandoned months before. This put many IRA leaders on the run, but it also forced them into the role of full-time insurgents. Although fighting was sporadic, the IRA struck back in November and December 1920. On November 21, 1920, known as Bloody Sunday, the IRA assassinated 14 British intelligence agents in Dublin. That afternoon RIC members opened fire at a soccer match, killing 14 civilians and wounding another 65. A week later the IRA ambushed and killed 17 ADRIC members at Kilmichael in County Cork. London declared martial law throughout much of southern Ireland. The fighting now intensified, with no apparent end in sight. Most of the worst combat occurred in Dublin, Belfast, and Munster; these three locations accounted for some three-quarters of the casualties.

In December 1920 the British Parliament passed a fourth home rule bill. It set up two parliaments in Ireland—one for the six counties in northeastern Ulster and another for the rest of the island. Ireland's army, navy, foreign relations, customs, and tariffs all were to remain under control of the British Parliament. Both divisions of Ireland would still be represented in the British Parliament as well, although with fewer members than before. Northern Ireland accepted the plan at once and proceeded to carry it out. The rest of Ireland repudiated it, however. Sinn Féin rejected outright anything to do with an act that would appear to permanently partition Ireland.

The year 1921 brought little change except that the British Army received a mandate to engage in combat operations against the IRA, but this had little effect beyond adding to the violence. Both sides were preparing for increased fighting when on July 11, 1921, the leaders on both sides agreed to a truce. Negotiations during the next five months resulted in the Anglo-Irish Treaty that officially ended the war on December 6, 1921. The fighting claimed some 550 dead on the IRA side and 714 dead for the UK forces; 750 civilians were also killed.

The treaty provided for the establishment of the Irish Free State. The Irish Free State would have the same constitutional status in the British Empire as the self-governing dominions. It would have its own military forces and its own armed vessels for the protection of revenue and fisheries, although some harbor facilities were conceded to the British, and the Royal Navy would have responsibility for defending the Irish coast pending an arrangement to be negotiated later. Much to the chagrin of the IRA, Northern Ireland was not to be included in the Irish Free State if it declared its desire to continue under the act of 1920.

In effect, the treaty partitioned Ireland. Southern Ireland became independent as the Irish Free State, while the six northern and primarily Protestant counties were formed into the state of Northern Ireland and continued as part of the United Kingdom.

The treaty created a schism in the IRA and was not a month old when hard-line republicans began to agitate against it in the Dáil Éireann ratification debates. De Valera took the lead in denouncing it and urged its rejection. The IRA hard-liners opposed it because the new Irish state did not include Northern Ireland and because it did not make Ireland a republic and kept it within the British Commonwealth. The moderates such as Michael Collins, who had headed the delegation to negotiate a settlement, asserted that despite failings, the treaty laid the basis for peace and friendship with England and brought to a close the centuries-old conflict. On January 7, 1922, however, the Dáil Éireann approved the treaty in a vote of 64 to 57, whereupon de Valera resigned the presidency. Collins succeeded him as chairman of the provisional government.

De Valera and his followers withdrew from the parliament and now plunged the new Irish Free State into civil war. The "Irregulars," as the IRA hard-liners came to be known, subjected Ireland to an orgy of destruction. As the Free Staters formed a government, the IRA prepared to fight. Both sides took provocative actions, but neither seemed eager to engage their former comrades in battle.

On April 14, 1922, some 200 antitreaty IRA members led by Rory O'Connor seized the Four Courts (site of the Supreme Court, the High Court, the Dublin Circuit Court, and, until 2010, the Central Criminal Court) in the middle of Dublin and began to fortify it. Their aim was to spark a new armed conflict with the British that would unite the two IRA factions and bring about the scrapping of the Anglo-Irish Treaty and a republic encompassing the whole of Ireland.

The British then still had thousands of soldiers in Dublin awaiting evacuation. Despite heavy pressure from the British, the provisional government initially did nothing. This was an act of rebellion against the legally constituted Irish government, and Collins was determined that it be put down by Irishmen, not by the British.

Elections to the Dáil Éireann occurred on June 16. An overwhelming 73 percent of the vote went to protreaty candidates, but this seemed to make little difference to antitreaty IRA members who rejected the result. Two events now prompted Collins to move against the militants. The first was the assassination of British field marshal Sir Henry Wilson, who had played an important role in the Irish War of Independence and was gunned down by IRA militants on the steps of his private residence in London. The second was the kidnapping by the militants at the Four Courts on June 27 of Irish Free State Army deputy chief of staff General J. J. O'Connell.

Collins took action the next day, initiating the Battle of Dublin, a week of street battles during June 28–July 5 that also marks the commencement of the Irish Civil War. Dislodging the antitreaty forces from their Dublin stronghold entailed much destruction. The government forces suffered 16 killed and 122 wounded, while the militant IRA defenders sustained 49 killed, 158 wounded, and more than 400 taken prisoner.

The protreaty government's control over the main cities of Ireland and the lack of coordination between the different antitreaty military units meant that the latter's forces, which did not command the support of the predominantly rural Irish people or the Catholic Church, had no chance of winning the civil war. The conflict was nonetheless intense and bloody, with atrocities on both sides. On August 22 at Béal na Bláth in County Cork, antitreaty IRA members ambushed and assassinated Collins, who was determined to visit County Cork despite pleas by his advisers that it was too dangerous. There was never an official investigation into the assassination, and the circumstances surrounding his death remain mysterious. De Valera disclaimed any role in the event. O'Connor and three others were executed by the government on December 8 as a reprisal for the murder of a Dáil Éireann member.

William Cosgrave succeeded Collins as president of the provisional government. The deputies also adopted a constitution. The British king had nominal executive authority, represented in Ireland by a governor-general, but actual executive power was in the hands of an executive council, directly responsible to the lower house of the legislature. On December 6, 1922, the Irish Free State came into being by royal proclamation. Soon Ireland had been admitted to the League of Nations and had dispatched diplomatic representatives abroad.

The fighting escalated for several months before the antitreaty IRA began losing popular support. In the spring of 1923 de Valera finally admitted the impossibility of continuing the struggle, and in late April 1923 he first issued an order to his men to cease the struggle and then a proclamation ordering a cease-fire. The final death toll in the Irish Civil War was about 5,000 on the antitreaty side and some 800 for the government. The war formally ended on May 24, 1923, although the bitterness lasted for decades thereafter, and the divide between Northern Ireland and Eire continues to the present.

WILLIAM H. KAUTT AND
SPENCER C. TUCKER

## Consequences

Sporadic violence continued in Ireland, including assassinations. In 1927 Éamon de Valera—who had refused to take the oath of allegiance to the British king and had therefore been excluded from the Chamber of Deputies—announced that he would take the oath and become head of a constitutional opposition.

Despite real gains that came to the Irish Free State during the administration of president of the Executive Council William Cosgrave (1923–1932), the world economic depression inevitably affected his government's popularity. As in other countries, the voters turned against the party in power. De Valera meanwhile appealed to Irish nationalism by taking a decidedly anti-British approach. This included a demand for abolishing the oath of allegiance to the king. De Valera also won the support of small landowners with his pledge to withhold the payments they were obliged to make to the British government under the prior land-purchase agreements.

In the Irish parliamentary election of February 16, 1932, de Valera's Fianna Fáil party triumphed over Cosgrave's Cumann na nGaedheal, winning 72 seats to 57. De Valera was then elected president of the Executive Council, and in July he withheld the payments owed to Britain on the land annuities. The British Parliament retaliated by empowering the government to levy a duty of up to 100 percent on Irish goods coming into Britain in order to secure funds equal to the defaulted land annuities. De Valera then imposed his own almost prohibitive duties on British imports. This crippling tariff war continued until 1936, when de Valera admitted failure and negotiated a trade agreement with London.

De Valera meanwhile had been taking steps intended to emphasize the political independence of the Irish Free State. The oath of allegiance to the king was abolished, and he also made it unnecessary to secure approval of the British governor-general in Ireland for acts passed by the Irish parliament. Then in December 1936, the Chamber of Deputies abolished the office of governor-general altogether.

In April 1937 a new constitution was promulgated that proclaimed the Irish nation's "indefeasible and sovereign right to choose its own form of government, to determine its relations with other nations and to develop its life, political, economic and cultural, in accordance with its own genius and traditions." Nowhere in the document was there mention of Britain or the British king. The constitution provided for a two-house legislature. It also called for a president, although real executive power was vested in a prime minister and a cabinet responsible to the lower house of the Chamber of Deputies. The constitution was approved by 56 percent of those casting votes in a national referendum on December 29, 1937. The constitution took effect immediately, and the name of the Irish Free State was officially changed to Eire (Gaelic for "Ireland").

Irish nationalism found expression in official promotion of the use of the Irish language, known as Gaelic, which is spoken as a first language by only a minority of the Irish people. The constitution of Ireland recognized it as the national and first official language of the Republic of Ireland (with English being another official language), although most business is conducted in English. From the establishment of the Irish Free State in 1922, the government required proficiency in Gaelic for new appointments to any civil service position and for lawyers (although this was modified in 1974). The Irish representative to the League of Nations was even instructed to make his speeches in it. Family names and place-names were Gaelicized. The great difficulty of the language, however, has prevented its widespread adoption.

In April 1938, de Valera concluded agreements with London that removed British naval installations and troops from the Irish Republic, making Eire responsible for its own defense. Other agreements provided for Ireland to pay a final settlement of the land annuities as well as annual payments to compensate Britain for losses sustained in the violence of the 1920s. Each nation also accorded the other most favored nation status in trade. All matters of contention between the two states were thus removed except for the vexing question of partition. De Valera's success in concluding these agreements helped his Fianna Fáil party win a decisive majority in the June 1938 elections.

The outbreak of World War II provided de Valera with an opportunity to show that Eire was independent of Great Britain. In contrast to other members of the British Commonwealth, Eire declared its neutrality, a decision that had considerable public support. With an army of only 7,500 men, two naval patrol craft, and four fighter aircraft, Eire was hardly in a position to make a major commitment of military forces. The inability to utilize Eire's ports for its naval ships, however, imposed major strain on the Allies in the vital Battle of the Atlantic. During the war, de Valera steadfastly and foolishly turned down British offers, even by Prime Minister Winston Churchill, to resolve partition in return for an end to Irish neutrality. However, Eire did allow British overflights of its territory and also returned downed Allied pilots to Northern Ireland instead of interning them; Eire also allowed British patrol craft in its waters. Thousands of Irishmen also volunteered for service in the Allied armies. During the war, more than 180,000 people left Eire for Northern Ireland or the United Kingdom, and 38,544 Irish citizens volunteered for service with the British armed forces.

There was some pro-German sentiment among the Irish, however. Anti-Semitic bills were brought before the Dáil Éireann, and de Valera refused to expel Axis diplomats. Perhaps more shocking, on Adolf

Hitler's death in 1945, de Valera went in person to the German embassy to express his condolences.

Acts of violence by the illegal IRA against Northern Ireland were a problem for the Eire government, which feared that the British might use those violent acts as an excuse to intervene. To forestall such a possibility, during the war de Valera sharply increased the size of Ireland's army and auxiliary forces to some 250,000 men (albeit poorly armed and trained). Ireland suffered economically during the war, but de Valera doggedly pursued his policies.

On the other hand, Northern Ireland was an important base for Allied operations during the war. Soon after the Japanese attack on Pearl Harbor, U.S. president Franklin D. Roosevelt and Churchill agreed that Northern Ireland and Scotland would provide bases for training and the Allied troop buildup for the invasions of North Africa in 1942 and France in 1944. The Americans took over the defense of Northern Ireland, thus allowed British soldiers to be deployed elsewhere. The Eire government officially protested this agreement.

On December 21, 1948, the Government of Ireland Act was signed into law. Under it, Eire became the Republic of Ireland. The act entered into force on April 18, 1949, Easter Monday, the 33rd anniversary of the beginning of the Easter Rising. This action ended Ireland's technical link with the British Commonwealth, which at the time precluded republics from membership.

Unfortunately for the people of Ireland, sectarian violence continued in the island as the IRA sought to bring about the union of Northern Ireland with the Republic of Ireland. The British and Irish governments sought to bring about a peaceful resolution to 30 years of sectarian violence in Northern Ireland during 1968–1998, widely known as The Troubles, between the majority Protestant and the minority Catholic paramilitaries, while the British Army sought to keep order. Not until 1998 was a peace settlement secured in the Good Friday Agreement, which was approved in referendums in both Northern Ireland and the Republic of Ireland. As part of the peace settlement, the Republic of Ireland's territorial claim to Northern Ireland expressed in Articles 2 and 3 of its constitution was removed from that document.

SPENCER C. TUCKER

## Timeline

| | |
|---|---|
| **1172** | The English conquer Ireland. |
| **1782** | Ireland is granted legislative independence from Great Britain, although the British still control Irish affairs. |
| **1798** | The Society of United Irishmen mounts an independence revolt, but it is easily put down by the British. |
| **1800** | The British Parliament enacts the Act of Union by which Ireland is joined with Great Britain to constitute the United Kingdom of Great Britain and Ireland. |
| **1845–1852** | The Irish Potato Famine brings the deaths of some 1 million Irish. More than 1 million others leave Ireland altogether. |

| | |
|---|---|
| **1867** | British Army troops are called out to put down riots by the Irish in cities in Lancashire, England. |
| **1869** | British prime minister William Gladstone secures passage of a parliamentary act disestablishing the Church of Ireland. |
| **1870** | A new threat arises to British rule in Ireland with the formation of the Irish Nationalist Party, led by Charles Stewart Parnell. Gladstone also secures passage of the Land Act in a bid to aid landless peasants. |
| **1877** | Parnell's Irish Nationalists begin obstructing all legislation in the British House of Commons until Irish home rule is achieved. |
| **1881** | Gladstone secures passage of a new land act with a fixed 15-year period for rent as well as tenants' safe tenure on the land and the right to sell any improvements. |
| **1886** | Gladstone's attempt to pass a bill granting home rule to Ireland is stymied by Parliament. |
| **1913** | Attempts by the House of Commons to establish a semiautomous Irish parliament are repeatedly stymied. The Protestant Ulsterites are determined to do whatever is necessary to prevent Irish home rule, and on January 13 they create the Ulster Volunteer Force, a military formation of some 100,000 men. |
| **Nov 25, 1913** | The Irish National Volunteers, which grows to some 100,000 men, is established to counter the force being raised by the Protestants in Ulster. |
| **Mar 20, 1914** | With civil war in Ireland looming, British Army officers at Carragh, Ireland, submit their resignations rather than being obliged to force the population of Ulster to accept home rule. |
| **Aug 4, 1914** | Britain declares war on Germany in World War I. |
| **Sep 14, 1914** | The Irish home rule bill becomes law, but the Suspensory Act delays its implementation until the end of World War I. |
| **Apr 24–29, 1916** | The leader of the so-called Easter Rising, Patrick Pearse, issues a proclamation declaring an Irish republic. Events are largely confined to Dublin, and British authorities respond swiftly and crush the insurrection by April 29. |
| **May 3–15, 1916** | British authorities, having placed Ireland under martial law, execute 15 members of the Easter Rising, including Pearse. |
| **Dec 1918** | The Irish republican Sinn Féin (Ourselves Alone) party wins a sweeping victory in elections in Ireland for the British Parliament. Sinn Féin considers this a mandate for an independent Irish republic. |
| **Jan 21, 1919** | Sinn Féin members form Dáil Éireann (Assembly of Ireland) and declare Irish independence. Because Sinn Féin leader Éamon de |

Valera is imprisoned, Cathal Brugha is proclaimed president. That same day, the Irish Volunteers kill two members of the Royal Irish Constabulary (RIC). These actions begin the Irish War of Independence.

**Apr 1, 1919**     Éamon de Valera, having escaped from prison in February, takes office as president of the Dáil Éireann.

**Mar 1920**     British veterans of World War I, recruited to serve in Ireland against the Irish republicans and known as the Black and Tans, begin arriving in Ireland.

**Nov 21, 1920**     Bloody Sunday. The Irish Republican Army assassinates 14 British intelligence agents in Dublin. In the afternoon members of the RIC open fire at a soccer match, killing 14 civilians and wounding another 65.

**Dec 1920**     The British Parliament passes a fourth home rule bill for Ireland. Northern Ireland accepts the plan, but the rest of Ireland repudiates it.

**Jul 11, 1921**     Both sides agree to a truce in the fighting in order to commence peace negotiations.

**Dec 6, 1921**     The Anglo-Irish Treaty is signed, formally ending the Irish War of Independence. Britain recognizes the Irish Free State, with the same constitutional status as the self-governing dominions.

SPENCER C. TUCKER

## Further Reading

Beaslai, Piaras. *Michael Collins and the Making of the New Ireland.* Dublin, Ireland: Phoenix, 1926.

Bowman, John. *De Valera and the Ulster Question, 1917–1973.* New York: Clarendon, 1982.

Collins, Michael. *The Path to Freedom.* Dublin, Ireland: Talbot, 1922.

Coogan, Tim Pat. *Eamon de Valera: The Man Who Was Ireland.* New York: HarperCollins, 1995.

Coogan, Tim Pat. *The Irish Civil War.* Boulder, CO: Roberts Rinehart, 1998.

Coogan, Tim Pat. *The Man Who Made Ireland: The Life and Death of Michael Collins.* Niwot, CO: Roberts Rinehart, 1992.

Dwyer, T. Ryle. *Big Fellow, Long Fellow: A Joint Biography of Collins and de Valera.* New York: St. Martin's, 1999.

Fergusson, Sir James. *The Curragh Incident.* London: Faber and Faber, 1964.

Foster, R. F. *Modern Ireland, 1600–1972.* London: Penguin, 1988.

Gregory, Adrian, and Senia Paseta, eds. *Ireland and the Great War: A War to Unite Us All?* Manchester, UK: Manchester University Press, 2002.

Hennessey, Thomas. *Dividing Ireland: World War I and Partition.* London: Routledge, 1998.

Hopkinson, Michael A. *The Irish War of Independence.* Ithaca, NY: McGill-Queen's University Press, 2002.

Jeffery, Keith. *Ireland and the Great War.* New York: Cambridge University Press, 2000.

Kautt, W. H. *Ambushes & Armour: The Irish Rebellion, 1919–1921.* Dublin, Ireland: Irish Academic Press, 2010.

Lydon, James F. *The Making of Ireland: From Ancient Times to the Present.* New York: Routledge, 1998.

McGarry, Fearghal. *The Rising: Ireland, Easter 1916.* Oxford: Oxford University Press, 2010.

Stewart, A. T. Q. *The Ulster Crisis: Resistance to Home Rule, 1912–14.* London: Faber and Faber, 1967.

Townshend, Charles. *Britain's Civil Wars: Counterinsurgency in the Twentieth Century.* London: Faber and Faber, 1986.

Townshend, Charles. *The British Campaign in Ireland, 1919–1921: The Development of Political and Military Policies.* Oxford: Oxford University Press, 1975.

Younger, Calton. *Ireland's Civil War.* New York: Taplinger, 1968.

# Rif War (1921–1926)

## Causes

The Rif War, also known as the Second Moroccan War, was a war fought by Moroccan nationalists to the Rif region to drive first the Spaniards and then the French from Morocco and secure independence.

Morocco, inhabited since Paleolithic times, has a long history. The Phoenicians established trading colonies and coastal settlements here in the sixth century BCE.

Morocco then became part of the Carthaginian Empire. The earliest known independent Moroccan state was the Berber kingdom of Mauretania, which lasted from the third century BCE until it became a Roman province in 44 BCE. Morocco was under Roman rule until 432 CE, when it was conquered first by the Vandals and then by the Visigoths. From the sixth century the Byzantine Empire controlled the

## Rif War (1921–1926)

| Annoual (Anwal), Battle of (July 21, 1921) | | |
|---|---|---|
| | **Rif Forces** | **Spanish Forces** |
| **Strength** | 3,000 men | 20,000–23,000 men |
| **Casualties** | 800* | 13,363** |

*Killed, wounded, captured.
**Includes 8,000 killed and 5,363 wounded or captured.

| Abd el-Krim's Ouergha River Valley Offensive (April 1925) | | |
|---|---|---|
| | **Rif Forces** | **French Forces** |
| **Strength** | 8,000 men | 8,000–10,000 men |
| **Casualties** | Unknown, but likely under 1,000 | 5,700* |

*Includes 1,000 killed, 3,700 wounded, and 1,000 missing/captured.

| Alhucemas Bay, Amphibious Landing at (September 1925) | | |
|---|---|---|
| | **Rif Forces** | **Spanish/French Forces** |
| **Initial strength** | 11,000 men | 13,000 men, 24 artillery pieces, 17 tanks* |

*Within a month, some 90,000 men had gone ashore, helping to end the revolt within eight months.

| Total Losses, Rif War (1921–1926) | | | |
|---|---|---|---|
| | **Rif Republic** | **Spanish** | **French** |
| **Killed/died of disease** | 10,000 men | 18,000 men | 10,000 men |
| **Wounded/missing** | 20,000 | 5,000 | 8,500 |

**Sources:** Balfour, Sebastian. *Deadly Embrace: Morocco and the Road to the Spanish Civil War*. Oxford: Oxford University Press, 2002; Pennell, Charles Richard. *Morocco since 1830: A History*. London: Hurst, 2000; Woolman, David S. *Rebels in the Rif: Abd El Krim and the Rif Rebellion*. Stanford University Press, 1968.

northern part of Morocco, with the interior remaining under Berber control. In 670 Uqba ibn Nafi, an Umayyad Muslim general, began the conquest of Morocco. The Umayyads then converted most of the population to Islam. Independent Muslim states emerged in what is modern-day Morocco as early as 710. That same year the governor of North Africa, Musa ibn Nusair, sent Muslim forces across the Strait of Gibraltar to Spain in a raiding expedition, ultimately leading to the Islamic control of Spain.

In 1549 the region fell to successive Arab dynasties, but in 1666 Morocco was reunited under the Alaouite dynasty, the ruling family of the country ever since. From the early 16th century the so-called Barbary states of Morocco, Algiers, Tunis, and Tripoli were centers of corsair activity in which they sent out warships to seize the merchant shipping and hold for ransom the crews of trading nations that failed to pay them tribute.

In the late 19th century imperialism took hold among the major world powers, with a rush by these states to secure colonies in Africa and Asia. Justification was found in the issues of prestige and international power, the need for coaling stations and naval bases, and economic factors such as securing natural resources and trade. Morocco, coveted by both France and Spain, was no exception. France hoped to secure the western flank of its possession of Algeria. The French had seized Algiers in 1830 and then expanded their holdings, creating modern-day Algeria. Morocco was also important for its strategic location, across the Strait of Gibraltar from Spain, with the strait controlling access to the Mediterranean from the Atlantic. Morocco also fronted on the eastern Atlantic. Spain was, of course, the closest

European nation to Morocco and had developed toeholds there. A dispute involving Spain's small coastal enclave of Ceuta had led to the Spanish-Moroccan War of 1859–1860. Victorious in the war, Spain secured both the enlargement of Ceuta and the cession of another enclave, Melilla. The Sultanate of Morocco was also forced to pay reparations. In 1884, Spain created a protectorate in the coastal areas of Morocco.

Until 1898, Spain had been counted a major power. In that year, however, it sustained a major military defeat in the Spanish-American War. The loss of Cuba, Puerto Rico, Guam, and the Philippines as a consequence of the war saw Spain reduced to the status of third- or fourth-rate power. This led a number of Spaniards to embrace the idea of recouping their national power with the creation of a major empire in Africa. After all, while Spain had been separated from Cuba and the Philippines by vast ocean expanses, Africa lay just eight miles by water from Spain itself.

Internal turmoil in Morocco certainly invited further European penetration. This in turn brought two international crises, in 1905–1906 and 1911, that almost produced a general European war. In 1904 the French and British governments settled international points of tension between them, with the French recognizing British interests in Egypt in return for British recognition of France's paramount position in Morocco. The French and Spanish governments then agreed that they would share power in Morocco. With British and Spanish support for its anticipated takeover, in December 1904 the French government demanded concessions from Moroccan sultan Abdelaziz (r. 1894–1906) that would have given France a virtual protectorate.

At this point the German government decided to challenge the French move as part of Kaiser Wilhelm II's determination to assert German power on the world stage. In January 1905 Berlin announced its support of Abdelaziz in resisting French demands, cemented by a daylong visit to Tangier by Wilhelm II on April 1, 1905. Berlin also put pressure on Spain.

With the possibility of a general European war looming, the French sought to buy the Germans off with territorial concessions in Africa, but having posed as the champion of African independence, however dishonestly, the German government could not now back down. The Germans were then obliged to accept an international conference on Morocco, held at Algeciras, Spain, during January 16–April 7, 1906. Expecting to secure the support of a majority of the conferees, Berlin was bitterly disappointed, for only Austria-Hungary stood by it. The Algeciras Agreement gave France and Spain control of the police in Morocco's port cities, while the French came to control the Moroccan state bank. With Moroccans frustrated, attacks on foreigners increased, as in Tangier in 1906. France then moved to secure order through full control of Morocco.

In the spring of 1911 French troops occupied Fez to protect Europeans there from antiforeign agitation. The German government demanded compensation for this violation of the Algeciras Agreement and backed this up by sending the gunboat *Panther* to the Moroccan port of Agadir. This action triggered the Second Moroccan Crisis, with London giving wholehearted diplomatic support to France. War loomed, but eventually a settlement was achieved whereby Germany agreed to a French protectorate over Morocco and received two strips of territory of the French Congo added to German Kameroon.

In accordance with the Treaty of Fez of March 30, 1912, Moroccan sultan Abd al-Hafid (r. 1908–1912) was forced to accept a protectorate. Spain not only had its coastal protectorate but now also assumed the role of the protecting power in northern Morocco, which became Spanish Morocco. By an agreement signed in November, Spain gained a zone of influence in the Rif and Cape Juby areas. Although the sultan remained the nominal sovereign and was represented by a vice-regent, a Spanish high commission held real power. The Treaty of Fez also granted the Spanish Rif Mines Company rights to the iron mines of Mount Uixan. The same company was also given the right to build a railroad to connect the mines with Melilla on the coast.

France secured control of the bulk of the country. Although the Moroccan sultan theoretically was sovereign there, the French resident general held real power. Tens of thousands of Europeans now settled in French-controlled Morocco. Much of the best agricultural land passed into their hands, and they were also involved in mining, banking, and shipping. These individuals pressed France to increase its control over Morocco in order to end the nearly continuous warfare between the various tribes of Morocco. French general Louis Hubert Lyautey, who had cut his teeth in the colonial administration first in Madagascar and then in Algeria, was appointed resident general in Morocco in 1912 and served in that position until 1925. An admirer of Moroccan culture and an adroit colonial administrator, Lyautey had long pressed the French government to take control of Morocco, but he also believed that if France was to be successful in colonial affairs it would have to respect the existing civilizations and cultures and work with the native elites of the lands it sought to manage.

Lyautey continued to press French pacification of the Moroccan interior, extending French control into the Atlas Mountains region. Concurrent with military operations, Lyautey pushed the construction of roads, railroads, and bridges and was instrumental in the creation of a modern educational system. Slavery was abolished in Morocco in 1925.

The Spaniards and French did have to deal with continued armed native opposition to European control of Morocco. This was particularly true with the Berber tribesmen in the Rif, the largely mountainous region of northern Morocco. The Rif occupies the territory along the northern coast of Morocco from Cape Spartel and Tangier in the west to Ras Kebdana and the Melwiyya River in the east and from the Mediterranean Sea in the north to Wergha River in the south. In 1893 the Berbers took up arms against the Spaniards. When they threatened to take Melilla, then the most important Spanish North African port, Spain dispatched an expeditionary force of some 25,000 men, which forced the Berbers back into the interior. Still, few Europeans had dared venture into the Rif region, and even the sultans of Morocco had not been able to establish full control of the northern areas of the Rif.

Morocco was little affected by World War I. In the French area, Moroccan soldiers known as *goumiers* serving in auxiliary units attached to the French Army of Africa did not see service outside Morocco during the war, but they did enable the French to withdraw a substantial portion of their regular forces from Morocco for service on the Western Front. Still, both France and Spain (which remained a neutral in World War I) were obliged to carry out some counterinsurgency operations in their areas of Morocco during the war.

The Rif was rich in high-grade iron ore that could easily be extracted in open pit mining, and the Spaniards were anxious to take advantage. By 1920, Spaniard Don Horsvio Echevarrieta's mining firm had extracted some 800,000 tons of ore. The open pit mining resulted in considerable environmental damage and entailed the relocation of a number of Berbers, who also did not gain any financial advantage. This drew great Berber opposition, as did Spanish efforts to bring the Rif fully under their control and convert the Muslim and animist Berbers to Catholicism.

In July 1919 Mulai Ahmed el Raisuni (also known as Raisuli), the leader of the Riffian Berbers and considered by many to be the rightful heir to the throne of Morocco, mounted attacks against Spanish Morocco. A more formidable leader against the Spaniards arose in the person of Mohammed ibn Abd el-Krim al-Khattabi, usually identified simply as Abd el-Krim and who came to be known as the "Wolf of the Rif."

Born in Ajdir, Morocco, in 1882, the son of a *qadi* (*caid,* local administrator) of the Aith Yusuf clan of the Aith Uriaghel (Waryaghar) tribe, Abd el-Krim received a traditional Muslim as well as Spanish education. Fluent in Spanish, he became a secretary in the Bureau of Native Affairs in the protectorate government. In 1915 he was appointed *qadi al-qadat* (chief Muslim judge) for the Melilla district, where he also taught at a Hispano-Arabic school and served as editor of an Arabic section of the Spanish newspaper *El Telegrama del Rif.*

Disillusioned with Spanish efforts to control the Rif, Abd el-Krim began to speak out against Spanish policies, and during World War I the Spanish authorities imprisoned him in 1916–1917 for an alleged conspiracy with the German consul. Abd el-Krim returned to Ajdir in 1919.

In 1921 Abd el-Krim, joined by his brother, who became his chief adviser and commander of the rebel army, raised the standard of resistance against foreign control of Morocco. This marked the beginning of the Rif War (1921–1926), although some historians date its start from 1920.

SPENCER C. TUCKER

## Course

The Rifs had a well-deserved reputation as tenacious fighters with excellent marksmanship. Abd el-Krim's actual field army was small, however. Sources vary but place its total strength at only 2,000–7,000 men. The remainder of the Riffian forces were classified as militia, unlikely to serve far from their homes. Taken together, Abd el-Krim could probably count on only some 80,000–90,000 men. Modern weapons were also in short supply. The Riffian resistance had only some 20,000 rifles available at any one time, and many of the weapons they secured were then poorly maintained.

Initially, Spanish forces in the Rif region consisted largely of conscripts and reservists from Spain itself, who were both poorly trained and inadequately supported. Corruption among their officers brought the siphoning off of resources and led to poor morale among the rank and file. When these forces proved inadequate against the less well-armed Riffians, Spain increasingly relied on elements of its Spanish Army of Africa, the professional military force that included regiments of Moroccans. The Spaniards also copied the organization and tactics employed with success by the French in their part of Morocco and relied on the Tercio de Extranjeros (Foreigners Brigade, known in English as the Spanish Legion). Modeled on the French Foreign Legion, it was established in 1919 and had soon developed a reputation for ruthlessness. Actually, fewer than a quarter of the members of the Spanish Legion were foreigners.

In late July 1921 Spanish general Fernándes Silvestre proceeded into the Rif interior with some 20,000 men. He failed to carry out adequate reconnaissance or mount sufficient security precautions, however. At Annoual (Anwal) on July 21, his column encountered the Spanish garrison fleeing from the next post at Abaran. In the ensuing confusion, Rif forces fell on both flanks of Silvestre's column, leading to widespread panic and a disastrous defeat for the Spanish. Some 8,000 Spanish troops were killed, and Silverstre committed suicide. Several thousand Spaniards were also taken prisoner, while the rebels secured as a result of the battle and from captured Spanish outposts considerable quantities arms, ammunition, military equipment, and supplies. The rebels then drove the Spanish forces back, rolling up their outposts as they proceeded.

Some of the Riffian forces now advanced on Melilla, the principal Spanish base in the eastern Rif region and held by 14,000 Spanish troops. Other Riffian forces moved against isolated Spanish military posts, capturing more than 130 of them. By early August the Spaniards had been pushed back to the outskirts of Melilla and had by then lost by official Spanish count 12,192 dead. Fearful that an attempt to take the city might lead to a widened war in consequence of the many citizens of other European states living there, Abd el-Krim ordered his troops not to attack Melilla. In his memoirs he would characterize this decision as his biggest mistake of the war.

By late August 1921, Spain had lost all the territory secured since 1909. However, Abd el-Krim's failure to move immediately on Melilla allowed Spain to transfer additional military resources there. By the end of August there were 36,000 troops in Melilla. New Spanish commander General José Sanjurjo then took the offensive. By January 1922 the Spaniards had retaken the major fort of Monte Arruit, where they discovered the bodies of 2,600 of their soldiers.

Meanwhile, the rebels had secured their control of the inland mountains, and in 1923 Abd el-Krim proclaimed the Republic of the Rif, with himself as president and its capital at Ajdir. He endeavored to create a centralized Berber government, one that would respect traditional values but override tribal rivalries.

The Spanish even sustained losses at sea. On March 18, 1922, the passenger ship *Juan de Joanes,* chartered by the Spanish government to transport men and supplies to Morocco, was sunk in Alhucemas Bay. It had disembarked its passengers when it came under Riffian artillery fire and was hit in the engine room area. Then on August 26, 1923, the Spanish battleship *España,* which was providing gunfire support to Spanish troops ashore, ran aground off Cape Tres Forcas, Morocco. The Spanish Navy was unable to move the ship, which was then scrapped in situ, with what remained destroyed by storms in 1924. In January 1925, however, Spanish forces captured Raisuni.

Airpower played an important role in the war. During the fighting the Spanish Army of Africa employed up to 150 aircraft, including British-built Airco DH-4s bombers, to drop conventional ordnance and also considerable quantities of German-developed mustard gas on Riffian villages. Targets included *souks* (markets), livestock, and Abd el-Krim's headquarters. The Spaniards also used their aircraft to resupply encircled posts. Riffian antiaircraft fire did bring down a number of low-flying Spanish planes, however.

By 1923, a military stalemate had taken hold. At the same time a strong division developed among Spaniards, pitting Africanistas (those who favored an expanded Spanish empire in Africa) against Abandonistas (those who wanted to quit altogether as not worth the cost in blood and treasure). As Abandonista strength grew, soldiers being sent to Morocco mutinied in railway stations, and other soldiers at Malaga refused to board the ships that were to take them to Africa. In these circumstances a political crisis developed in Spain, and General Miguel Primo de Rivera, second Marques de Estellato, seized power with the support of King Alfonso XIII and established a virtual military dictatorship until his forced resignation in January 1930. Primo de Rivera initially thought that the war was unwinnable and considered pulling back all the way to the coast, but a visit to the Rif and implied threats by the military leadership there led him to modify this position.

On April 12, 1925, the war changed dramatically when an overconfident Abd el-Krim opened a major offensive with some 8,000 of his men against the French part of Morocco in what many historians hold was a major miscalculation. Lyautey had only limited resources immediately

Rif leader Abd al-Krim (left), an attendant, and a French officer in Fez, Morocco, in 1926. The Rif War of 1921–1926 pitted the Berber rebels of the Rif region against the Spanish and then also the French in a futile effort to achieve independence. (Library of Congress)

available, and Abd el-Krim's forces were initially able to overrun 45 of 66 French posts in the Ouergha River Valley. The French also sustained casualties of some 1,000 killed, 3,700 wounded, and 1,000 missing. Lyautey employed French air assets to good effect. Regular Moroccan regiments, the *goumiers* of the French Army of Africa, also provided important service and kept order in rural districts of Morocco.

In July, Lyautey was able to halt the Berber advance short of Fez. Faced with the Rif threat, on July 26 the French and Spanish governments agreed to close cooperation against the Riffian forces. The French contributed some 160,000 men in the form of French Army regulars as well as Algerian, Senegalese, and French Foreign Legion forces in addition to the Moroccan

regulars (*tirailleurs*) and *goumiers*. Marshal Henri Philippe Pétain had command. Meanwhile, General Sanjurjo assembled as many as 90,000 men.

Pétain employed a traditional military approach centered on infantry but including cavalry, tanks, artillery, and attack aircraft. By late summer, Riffian forces were essentially caught between the advancing French and Spanish forces. On September 8, 1925, with Spanish and French capital ships providing gunfire support, the allies carried out an amphibious landing at Alhucemas Bay near Abd el-Krim's headquarters. The landing force was largely Spanish with a small French contingent and numbered 13,000 men, 24 artillery pieces, and 17 tanks to deal with an estimated 11,000 Riffians. Primo de Rivera had command. Aware of Spanish preparations, Abd el-Krim fortified the area as best he could. Within a month, 90,000 Spanish and French troops were ashore in what was the most significant operation of its kind in any irregular war during the period between the two world wars.

Lyautey, worn out by his labors, retired on September 24. He was succeeded by Pétain, with General Edmund-Just-Victor Boichut taking over command of the French forces in the field. The Riffian troops were now caught between the Spaniards to the north and the French to the south.

The period November 1925–April 1926 saw both sides in winter quarters, with only limited French and Spanish air operations occurring. Now facing overwhelming odds against them of more than 10 to 1 and technological superiority in the form of modern aircraft and artillery, and with his own weapons stocks dwindling and forces melting away, Abd el-Krim surrendered to the French on May 27, 1926. This brought the Rif War to a close, although the French continued to fight various insurgent tribes in the Atlas Mountains until the early 1930s.

The war claimed some 18,000 Spaniards killed or died of disease, while the French sustained 10,000 dead, 2,500 of them killed in battle, along with 8,500 wounded. Riffian casualties are estimated at 30,000, of whom 10,000 were killed.

SPENCER C. TUCKER

## Consequences

The Rif War was a forerunner of the successful post–World War II wars of liberation in the Maghrib region of North Africa against European rule. Abd el-Krim's guerrilla tactics also influenced 20th-century revolutionary leaders in Latin America and in Asia. The Riffian defeat was largely owing to the size and technological superiority of the European armies sent against him.

Much to the ire of the Spaniards, the French sent Abd el-Krim into a comfortable exile on the island of Réunion in the Indian Ocean. Receiving permission in 1947 to live in France, he left Réunion, and when the ship carrying him to France stopped briefly at Port Said, Egypt, he slipped his surveillance and sought asylum in Egypt, which was granted. For five years in Cairo he headed the Liberation Committee of the Arab West (sometimes called the Maghrib Bureau). With the restoration of Moroccan independence in 1956, King Muhammad V invited Abd el-Krim to return to Morocco, but he refused to do so as long as French troops remained in the Maghrib (Northwest Africa). Abd el-Krim died in Cairo on February 6, 1963.

The actions of Primo de Rivera, brought to power largely by the Rif War, largely discredited the Spanish monarchy and forced King Alfonso XIII into exile.

Heightened social tensions then led to the Spanish Civil War of 1936–1939. Indigenous Moroccans played an important role in that bloody struggle fighting on the Nationalist (fascist) side. These Fuerzas Regulares Indígenas (Indigenous Regular Forces), known simply as the Regulares, were volunteer infantry and cavalry units serving in the Spanish Army of Africa that included the Spanish Foreign Legion. The Regulares were officered by Spaniards. The Spanish Army of Africa grew from about 30,000 men at the onset of the civil war to some 60,000 at its end, and the Regulares were the most decorated units of the Nationalist forces.

On the defeat of France by the Germans in June 1940 during World War II, the Vichy France government in unoccupied France retained control of French territory overseas, including Morocco, Algeria, and Tunisia. In November 1942, however, U.S. and British forces invaded French North Africa and occupied Morocco. Morocco contributed significant manpower against Axis forces in North Africa and in Europe.

World War II signaled the end of the colonial era, and despite deep ties to France and French culture, the Moroccan people increasingly embraced nationalism. In January 1943 U.S. president Franklin D. Roosevelt traveled to Casablanca, where he met with Winston Churchill to plan military strategy. At that time Roosevelt also met with Moroccan sultan Mohammed V (r. 1927–1953, 1955–1957) and proclaimed American support for Morocco's eventual independence.

With growing nationalist sentiment in Morocco, the French government exiled the sultan and his family, first to Corsica and then to Madagascar during 1953–1955. In the wake of the Indochina War and with the outbreak of rebellion in Algeria in 1954, however, France allowed Mohammed V to return to Morocco in November 1955. He then negotiated a treaty with France, which granted independence to Morocco on March 2, 1956. Spain followed suit in April, granting independence to its region of northen Morocco. Ceuta and Melilla remained Spanish autonomous cities, and Spain continued to control the Western Sahara region until the mid-1970s.

Mohammed V took the title of king in 1957. He was both Morocco's head of government and its spiritual leader, as a direct descendent of Prophet Muhammad. In this period, Morocco maintained close ties with the United States.

Upon Mohammed V's unexpected death on February 26, 1961, his son, Crown Prince Moulay Hassan, became king as Hassan II and ruled until his death in July 1999. Hassan, while lacking the charisma and unifying ability of his father, nonetheless proved to be an effective leader. He was able to balance relations with the West, whose economic and political aid helped modernize his country, and the Middle East, whose Islamic heritage was his basis for power. Serious challenges lay ahead for Morocco, however.

SPENCER C. TUCKER

## Timeline

| | |
|---|---|
| **1549** | The territory of present-day Morocco is conquered by the Arabs. |
| **1666** | Morocco is reunited under the Alaouite dynasty, the ruling family of the country ever since. |
| **1859–1860** | Spain goes to war with Morocco, caused by a dispute over Spain's small coastal enclave of Ceuta. Spain extends its control over Morocco. |
| **1884** | Spain creates a protectorate in the coastal areas of Morocco. |
| **Apr 1904** | In one of a series of agreements, France recognizes Britain's interests in Egypt in return for Britain's recognition of France's paramount interest in Morocco. |
| **Oct 1904** | France and Spain reach agreement on a power-sharing arrangement in Morocco. |
| **1905–1906** | The First Moroccan Crisis. France demands a series of reforms of Moroccan sultan Abdelaziz, which would result in a virtual protectorate. German leaders decide to challenge the French move. Berlin insists on an international conference, expecting to be able to control the outcome. |
| **Jan 16–Apr 7, 1906** | The conference on Morocco ends with France and Spain securing their aims. Moroccan frustration results in attacks on foreigners. |
| **Spring 1911** | French troops occupy Fez to protect Europeans there. Germany then demands compensation for this violation of the Algeciras Agreement and sends the German gunboat *Panther* to Agadir. In the ensuing |

|  |  |
|---|---|
|  | Second Moroccan Crisis, Britain formally supports France. A war is averted when Germany agrees to a French protectorate in return for two strips of the French Congo to German Kameroon. |
| **Mar 30, 1912** | In the Treaty of Fez, Moroccan sultan Mulay Hafid accepts the French protectorate of Morocco, allowing France to control most of the country. Spain continues its coastal protectorate and receives control of the northern and southern Saharan zones of Morocco. |
| **1914–1918** | Moroccan soldiers (*goumiers*), who serve in auxiliary units attached to the French Army of Africa, enable the French to withdraw much of their regular forces in Morocco for service on the Western Front. |
| **1921** | Muhammad ibn Abd el-Krim al-Khattabi begins a revolt against foreign control of Morocco in what becomes known as the Rif War. |
| **Jul 21, 1921** | At Annual (Anual), Rif forces defeat the Spaniards, killing as many as 8,000. By August, the Spaniards have been pushed back to the outskirts of Melilla. |
| **1923** | Abd el-Krim proclaims the Republic of the Rif, with himself as president. |
| **Sep 15, 1923** | Spanish king Alfonso XIII lends support to a military coup carried out by General Miguel Primo de Rivera, who becomes prime minister and virtual dictator of Spain. |
| **1924** | By the end of this year, Spanish authority is reduced to the coastal enclaves of Melilla and Tetuán. The Spaniards employ aircraft to drop mustard gas on Riffian villages. |
| **Apr 12, 1925** | Abd el-Krim opens a major offensive against French Morocco. Taking advantage of Lyautey's limited resources, his troops overrun 45 of 66 French posts in the Ouergha River Valley. |
| **Jul 1925** | Lyautey is able to halt the Berber advance short of Fez, with the *goumiers* providing valuable service. The Spanish and French governments also agree to cooperate and furnish additional military manpower. Riffian forces find themselves under attack by the French and Spanish from the north and south. |
| **Sep 8, 1925** | Coalition forces carry out an amphibious landing at Alhucemas Bay near Abd el-Krim's headquarters. |
| **May 27, 1926** | Abd el-Krim surrenders to the French, bringing the Rif War to a close. |
| **Aug 20, 1953** | The French exile Moroccan sultan Mohammed V and his family to Corsica and then to Madagascar. |
| **Nov 16, 1955** | Mohammed V returns to Morocco from Madagascar and in 1957 takes the title of king. He rules until 1961. |

| | |
|---|---|
| **Mar 2, 1956** | Mohammed V negotiates with the French the independence of Morocco. |
| **Apr 7, 1956** | Spain grants independence to its region of northern Morocco. Ceuta and Melilla remain Spanish autonomous cities. |
| **Feb 6, 1963** | Abd el-Krim dies in Cairo, Egypt. |

SPENCER C. TUCKER

## Further Reading

Abdelkrim. *Mémoires d'Abd el Krim, recueillis par J. Roger-Mathieu.* Paris: Librairie des Champs Elysées, 1927.

Abdelkrim. *Mémoires II, la Crise franco-marocaine, 1955–1956.* Paris: Plon, 1984.

Alvarez, Jose E. *The Betrothed of Death: The Spanish Foreign Legion during the Rif Rebellion, 1920–1927.* Westport, CT: Greenwood, 2001.

Balfour, Sebastian. *Deadly Embrace: Morocco and the Road to the Spanish Civil War.* Oxford: Oxford University Press, 2002.

Fay, Sidney B. *The Origins of the World War,* Vol. 1, *Before Sarajevo.* New York: Free Press, 1996.

Hamilton, Richard F., and Holger H. Herwig, eds. *The Origins of World War I.* Cambridge: Cambridge University Press, 2003.

Harris, Walter B. *France, Spain, and the Rif.* London: E. Arnold, 1927.

Hart, David Montgomery Hart. *The Aith Waryaghar of the Moroccan Rif.* Tucson: University of Arizona Press, 1976.

Pennell, Charles Richard. *A Country with a Government and a Flag: The Rif War in Morocco, 1921–1926.* Wisbech, Cambridgeshire, UK: Menas, 1986.

Pennell, Charles Richard. *Morocco since 1830: A History.* London: Hurst, 2000.

Woolman, David S. *Rebels in the Rif: Abd el Krim and the Rif Rebellion.* Stanford, CA: Stanford University Press, 1968.

# Indonesian War of Independence (August 17, 1945–December 27, 1949)

## Causes

The Indonesian War of Independence, also known as the Indonesian National Revolution, occurred between August 17, 1945, and December 27, 1949, and was fought between Indonesian forces and those of the Kingdom of the Netherlands and Great Britain.

Indonesia is the world's largest archipelago. Strategically situated in Southeast Asia, it straddles the equator and sits astride major strategic shipping routes from the Pacific Ocean to the Indian Ocean. The Netherlands East Indies (NEI) extends over a vast area some 2,275 miles wide by 1,135 miles long and comprises some 17,000 islands, 6,000 of which are inhabited. The largest of these islands are Java, Sumatra, Dutch Borneo, Dutch New Guinea, Celebes, western Timor, and the Moluccas. The islands comprising Indonesia are immensely rich in natural resources including oil, tin, bauxite, and coal. They also produce rubber, copra, nickel, timber, quinine, and important foodstuffs such as rice, sugar, coffee, and tea.

China and India had traded with the Indonesian islands since at least the seventh century. This trade brought foreign cultural and religious practices, leading to the

### Indonesia War of Independence (1945–1949)

| Battle of Surabaya (October 27–November 20, 1945)* | | |
|---|---|---|
| | **Indonesian Forces** | **British/Dutch Forces** |
| **Peak strength** | 10,000–20,000 men | 30,000 men |
| **Killed in action** | 6,000+ | 2,000 |

*This was the bloodiest single confrontation of the entire war.

| Operation PRODUCT (July 21–August 4, 1947) | | |
|---|---|---|
| | **Indonesian Forces** | **Dutch Forces** |
| **Strength** | 200,000 men | 120,000 men |
| **Total casualties** | 120,000–150,000 | 6,000 |

| Indonesia War of Independence (1945–1949), Total Combatants Killed | | |
|---|---|---|
| **Indonesian Forces** | **British Forces** | **Dutch Forces** |
| 100,000 | 1,200 | 3,144 |

**Sources:** Frederick, Willam H. *Visions and Heat: The Making of the Indonesian Revolution.* Athens: Ohio University Press, 1989; Kahin, Audrey. *Regional Dynamics of the Indonesian Revolution.* Honolulu: University of Hawaii Press, 1995; Vickers, Adrian. *A History of Modern Indonesia.* Cambridge: Cambridge University Press, 2005.

establishment in the archipelago of both Hinduism and Buddhism. Muslim traders also brought Islam, which became the dominant religion in Indonesia. Indeed, Indonesia now has 12.7 percent of the world's Muslims, followed by Pakistan (11 percent) and India (10.9 percent). Christianity also arrived with European traders.

The Portuguese were the first Europeans to arrive, sailing from newly conquered Malacca in 1512 and seeking spices, an immensely important trading commodity in Europe. The Dutch sent out an expedition in 1595. Its 400 percent profit return led to other Dutch expeditions. In 1602 the Dutch government combined a number of Dutch trading companies into the United East India Company (Vereenigde Oost-Indische Compagnie, VOC).

As with other such European trading companies, the VOC had full authority to conclude treaties, establish fortresses, and even wage war. The VOC's capital city was Batavia (now Jakarta and also the capital of Indonesia), located on the northwestern coast of the island of Java. The VOC's original monopolies were in such commodities as nutmeg, peppers, cloves, and cinnamon. The Dutch then added such nonindigenous cash crops as coffee, tea, cacao, tobacco, rubber, sugar, and opium.

Mismanagement, graft, and corruption eventually brought bankruptcy and an end to the VOC in 1796. The Batavian Republic (the former Dutch Republic since 1796) then took over the VOC's territorial holdings in the archipelago. These included a good bit of Java, parts of Sumatra, much of Maluku, and territory to the interior of such ports as Makasar, Manado, and Kupang. These holdings were known as the Dutch East Indies and from 1815 with the establishment of the Kingdom of the Netherlands as the Netherlands East Indies.

Dutch control of the archipelago was neither complete nor secure, however, Although Java was dominated by the Dutch, many islands remained independent during much of the period of Dutch rule, including Aceh, Bali, Borneo, and Lombok. The Dutch were also frequently at war as various groups resisted their control. Piracy remained a major problem until at least the mid-19th century. Not until the early 20th century did the Dutch have reasonable control of what constitutes modern-day Indonesia.

The islands passed briefly under French control in 1806–1813 during the Napoleonic Wars when Emperor Napoleon I took over the Dutch Republic. Great Britain remained at war with France during this period, and in 1811 British forces occupied several Dutch East Indies ports. Dutch control was restored following the end of the Napoleonic Wars in 1815. In an 1824 Anglo-Dutch treaty the Dutch secured certain British settlements in the NEI in exchange for ceding control of their possessions in the Malay Peninsula and Dutch India.

During the tenure of NEI governor-general Count Johannes van den Bosch (1830–1833), the Dutch endeavored to maximize financial return from the islands. Dutch officials dictated crops to be produced, and the peasants were then forced to hand over one-fifth of their production. The peasants received cash payments that had been arbitrarily set without relation to actual value of the goods produced.

Opposition to Dutch colonial policies and resistance to the ongoing effort by the Dutch to expand their control (justified by the Dutch as a "civilizing" mission) brought resistance. In 1821 the Dutch intervened in the Padri War (1803–1837) and largely subjugated Sumatra. A serious challenge to

Dutch rule arose in the Java War (1825–1830), essentially a revolt by much of the population of that island against Dutch rule. The war claimed perhaps 215,000 lives, most of them Javanese.

As a result of the 1859–1863 Banjarmasin War, the Dutch reestablished their authority in eastern and southern Borneo. Following unsuccessful efforts to conquer Bali in 1846 and 1848, a third effort in 1849 brought northern Bali under Dutch control. The most prolonged Dutch military operation, however, was the Aceh War in Sumatra. Beginning in 1873, it became a largely guerrilla affair that lasted until 1912 and an Acehnese surrender. Disturbances continued, especially in Java and Sumatra, even as the Dutch brought other islands, such as Lombok, under their control. Despite the natives' tremendous numerical advantage, the technological advantages enjoyed by the Dutch were simply too great for the primitively armed natives to overcome.

The Dutch imposed their rule on southwestern Sulawesi during 1905–1906. Bali was secured during 1906–1908, as were remaining independent kingdoms in Maluku, Sumatra, Kalimantan, and Nusa Tenggara. In some cases native rulers requested and received Dutch protection from independent neighboring states, thus avoiding a complete Dutch takeover and retaining a semblance of independence.

The Dutch were neutral during World War I, so that great conflict did not have direct impact on the NEI, although decolonization found expression in such pronouncements as U.S. president Woodrow Wilson's call for the self-determination of peoples. In 1920 the Dutch brought Western New Guinea under their control, rounding out what three decades later would be the territory of the Republic of Indonesia.

The 1940 population of the NEI was about 70 million people. The largest ethnic group was the Javanese. About 1 million were Chinese, while another 250,000 were of Dutch extraction. Some 70 percent of the population lived on Java. Altogether the NEI had as many as 300 different ethnic groups speaking 365 languages.

Dutch rule in the islands was paternalistic and exploitive; the Indonesians were treated as little more than children. Some 90 percent of the population was illiterate; only a minority attended school in 1940, and few jobs were available for educated Indonesians in a bureaucracy dominated by the Dutch. The authorities ruthlessly crushed any nationalist sentiment, and there was a wide psychological breach between rulers and ruled.

World War II began in Europe in September 1939. In May 1940 German forces quickly overran the Netherlands, although the Dutch royal family and some government officials escaped abroad and established a government-in-exile in London. The advisory Volksraad (People's Council), the NEI legislative body at Batavia in Java, declared its loyalty to the London government but was soon virtually autonomous. It did refuse a demand by the Japanese for trade concessions and also obeyed the decision by the Dutch government-in-exile in August 1941 to cut off the export of oil to Japan. (The NEI was by then a major oil producer, with more than 59 million barrels extracted in 1940.)

The Netherlands government-in-exile, acting in concert with the British and U.S. governments, declared war on Japan after that country attacked the United States at Pearl Harbor in Hawaii on December 7, 1941. Securing control of the NEI was a major Japanese war aim in Tokyo's decision to go to war in 1941. The Japanese hoped that by destroying the U.S. Navy's Pacific Fleet at Pearl Harbor they would be able to secure by conquest the natural resources of Southeast Asia and especially the NEI's oil, for Japan had no oil of its own and scant reserves. Tokyo then planned to establish a defensive ring and destroy the rebuilt U.S. Navy as it endeavored to cross the Pacific.

On December 20, 1941, Japanese forces landed on oil-rich Dutch Borneo as well as in Celebes (now Sulawesi) and the Moluccas. The poorly equipped Royal Netherlands East Indies Army resisted as best it could, supported by some British, Australian, and U.S. forces. With their few air assets soon destroyed, however, all the Allies could do was briefly delay the Japanese advance. The Japanese Navy crushed Allied naval forces in the Battle of the Java Sea (February 27, 1942), and on March 8 the Dutch surrendered on Java. Resistance continued in Dutch Borneo and Celebes until October 1942, and the Japanese never did conquer all the islands.

Following their victory, the Japanese sent the Indonesian soldiers home and arrested some 170,000 Europeans, including 93,000 Dutch soldiers. All were treated inhumanely on starvation rations, bringing the deaths of 40 percent of the adult males, 13 percent of the women, and 10 percent of the children.

Many Indonesians initially welcomed the Japanese as liberators. However, Japanese rule was far more ruthless and exploitive than that of the Dutch. The systematic Japanese plunder of NEI resources began immediately after the invasion. Japan also mobilized as many as 2 million unskilled laborers. More than 270,000 of these were sent abroad, and only 50,000–70,000 of them returned home.

Because of a shortage of labor and the arrest of Dutch administrators, production fell off sharply. By 1943, rubber production was at one-fifth and tea at one-third of pre-1941 levels. Rice output fell 25 percent. The occupation currency issued by the Japanese also rapidly declined in value. By 1945, it was only worth 2.5 percent of face value. Severe shortages and acute economic hardship resulted. The closing of the export market also adversely affected the economy. In any case, thanks to Allied submarines, shipment of NEI resources to the Japanese home islands, especially desperately needed oil, steadily declined during the course of the war.

The Japanese early on prohibited all political activities in the islands. They also banned the use of Dutch and English and insisted on Japanese-language instruction in the schools. Western symbols were torn down, and streets were renamed. The Japanese ruthlessly crushed all dissent but worked with Indonesian nationalist leaders to help administer the islands under their "guidance."

Clearly, Japan's leaders hoped to annex the islands outright. Thus, while in January 1943 as a means of securing support for the Japanese war effort Prime Minister Tōjō Hideki announced that Burma and the Philippines would be made independent within a year, there was no such mention of independence for the NEI, and no Indonesian representative was present at the Greater East Asia Conference in Tokyo in November 1943. Not until September 7, 1944, did new prime minister Koiso Kuniaki announce plans to grant the NEI independence, and then only at some unspecified future date.

As the tide of war sharply turned, the Japanese sought to mobilize Indonesians against the Dutch. This included heavy use of propaganda, military training for the young, and the creation of a 25,000-man auxiliary military force, the Heiho, which served with the Japanese, and the 57,000-man *giyugun* (volunteer army) under Indonesian command.

Support among Indonesians for Japan plummeted as the economy declined and the Japanese seized rice stocks and requisitioned labor. Perhaps 2.4 million Indonesians died of famine during 1944–1945. Certainly there was some brutal treatment by the Japanese Army of the civilian population. The Japanese occupation had the overall effect of crystallizing Indonesian opposition to all foreign rule, and at the end of the war the nationalists moved into the vacuum.

In March 1945 Indonesian nationalist leaders Achmed Sukarno and Mohammed Hatta, both of whom had been well educated under Dutch rule, took the lead in calling a conference to work out the constitution of the new state. The delegates wanted the new nation to include not only the NEI proper but also Portuguese Timor, British North Borneo, and the Malay Peninsula. This was the subsequent basis of the postwar Greater Indonesia (Indonesia Raya) policy pursued by Sukarno in the 1950s and 1960s.

Sukarno sought a unitary, secular state with a strong presidency. On June 1 he presented the Pancasila, the five guiding principles of the proposed Indonesian nation. These were belief in God, humanitarianism, national unity, democracy, and social justice. Hatta, however, favored a federal system and Muslim aspirations. A compromise was reached in the so-called Jakarta Charter of June 22, 1945, whereby the state was founded on the belief in one God and Muslims were required to adhere to sharia (in Indonesian, *syariah*), or Islamic law. The conference delegates selected Sukarno as president and Hatta as vice president.

The Japanese surrender of August 15, 1945, created a vacuum in the NEI. Sukarno and Hatta, pressured by the radical *pemuda* (youth) groups, reacted quickly. In Jakarta on August 17 they declared the independence of the Republic of Indonesia, and the next day they announced that the new constitution was in effect. The Dutch refused to accept these actions, and the war was on.

SPENCER C. TUCKER

## Course

It took time for word of the declaration of independence to spread throughout the islands, but when it did it enjoyed widespread public support. By September the Republican forces, aided by the *pemuda,* had secured control of most of the infrastructure in the larger cities, to include transportation systems. With the end of press restrictions, newspapers flourished and new radio stations sprang up to spread the news of the revolution. Hopeful of securing independence by peaceful means, the revolutionaries organized mass demonstrations in the larger cities, including one in Batavia (Jakarta) with more than 200,000 people.

Fearing that the Dutch would act to crush Indonesian independence, the revolutionaries moved to create governmental institutions and establish their authority. This included the formation of a national army. On November 12 Sudirman, a 30-year-old former schoolteacher, was elected commander of the new army.

Meanwhile, violence had broken out. With the Japanese surrender, the British-led South East Asia Command was assigned the task of restoring order and civilian government in Java. The Dutch, who had loyally fought with the British in the war, assumed and expected this to mean that the prewar administration would be reimposed. Pending the Dutch return to Japan, the Allies ordered the Japanese forces in the archipelago to preserve order there. British Empire forces did not arrive in Java until late September and in other parts of the archipelago until October. Lieutenant General Sir Philip Christison commanded the forces sent to the NEI, which included a number of men of the former Dutch colonial army.

In these circumstances clashes broke out among the civilians, principally in Java and Sumatra, between those favoring an independent republic and their perceived enemies, such as the Dutch, Chinese, Eurasians, racial minorities, and Japanese as well as natives thought to be pro-Dutch. The period during August 1945–December 1946 came to be known as the Bersiap (Indonesian for "get ready" or "be prepared") in which there were numerous kidnappings and executions. The number of victims certainly exceeded 3,500.

There were also military clashes as the Japanese, acting in accordance with the surrender terms, struggled to restore order in the cities and towns. On October 3 the Japanese drove the *pemuda* out of Bandung in western Java and handed it over to the British. Fierce fighting occurred in the city of Semarang on the northern coast of Java. Retreating Republican forces killed as many as 300 Japanese prisoners in their hands. Following five days of fighting the Japanese had suffered some 500 dead and the Indonesians 2,000 when the British arrived there on October 14. The British evacuated a number of Indo-Europeans.

Then on October 27, 1945, major violence occurred in the city of Surabaya, the second-largest city in the archipelago and located in eastern Java. With Muslim organizations declaring holy war on foreigners and announcing this to be an obligation for all Muslims, many students traveled to the city from Muslim schools throughout East Java. Some 6,000 British Indian troops of the lightly armed 49th Infantry Brigade, commanded by Brigadier General A. W. S. Mallaby, were ordered into the city on October 25 to restore order and rescue foreigners. Heavy fighting began two days later.

The British soldiers found themselves confronting some 10,000–20,000 poorly trained but armed Indonesian People's Army forces and mobs of as many as 140,000 people. Upwards of 200 British Indian troops were killed and the remainder were on the verge of annihilation when the British flew in Sukarno and Vice President Mohammed Hatta. They arranged a cease-fire on October 30.

The cease-fire did not last. That same day, General Mallaby was killed in Surabaya in circumstances that remain unclear. His death, however, caused General Christison to call for a massive British military buildup in Suribaya. This involved 24,000 men of Major General E. S. Mansergh's Indian 5th Division, several dozen tanks, and gunfire support from two cruisers and three destroyers offshore.

When the insurrectionists failed to heed a November 9 ultimatum to surrender their weapons, Mansergh ordered his men into the city the next day, a date now celebrated in Indonesia as Heroes' Day. Despite sharp and even fanatical Indonesian resistance, in several weeks of fighting the British, aided by air strikes, prevailed. The cost to the British and Dutch forces in the battle (October 27–November 20) was 2,000 killed. At least 6,000 Indonesians also died, but it was the loss of much of their weaponry that was most keenly felt by the nationalist side and that hampered their military efforts for the remainder of the war.

The Battle of Surabaya was the bloodiest single event of the war. Although it was a British military victory, it certainly helped galvanize Indonesian support for the republic and removed any doubts that the revolutionaries had the support of the vast majority of the Indonesian population. International public opinion, even that of Britain, now shifted sharply in favor of independence for the Dutch East Indies.

The Dutch took control of Jakarta in January 1946, with the Republican side suffering some 8,000 killed in fighting for the city. The Dutch then reestablished their administration in the city. Dutch military operations also proceeded elsewhere. Although the Dutch could claim success in securing the cities of Java and Sumatra, they lacked the resources necessary to control the rural areas.

The last British Empire forces departed the islands in November 1946, by which time there were some 55,000 Dutch troops in Java. Not all left. Some 600 Muslims in the Indian Army defected to the Republican side, bringing their weapons with them.

The British tried to broker an agreement before their departure. This was the Linggadjati Agreement, concluded between the Dutch and the Republicans on November 15, 1946. Under its terms the Dutch government agreed to recognize Republic of Indonesia rule over Java, Sumatra, and Madura. The republic would become a constituent state of the United States of Indonesia, which would be established by January 1, 1949, and form a Netherlands-Indonesian Union along with the Netherlands, Suriname, and the Netherlands Antilles. The Dutch queen would be its official head. Although both sides signed and ratified the agreement, neither was happy with it, and it soon went into the discard pile.

Claiming that the Republican side had violated the Linggadjati Agreement, on July 20, 1947, Dutch forces, now with some 100,000 men available, launched Operation PRODUCT, their first major military offensive. The Dutch dubbed this a "police action" to restore law and order. Its goal was to establish Dutch control of both Java and Sumatra. PRODUCT drove the Republican forces from much of Samatra and also East and West Java, largely confining them to the Yogyakarta region of that island.

Although the Dutch achieved considerable military success in recapturing the urban areas, they were losing the battle for world opinion. Nearby Australia and recently independent India were strong supporters of the Republican side, as were both the Soviet Union and the United States. Meanwhile, United Nations (UN) officials worked to secure a cease-fire. Both sides agreed on August 4, 1947, to a cease-fire, called for by a UN Security Council resolution of three days earlier. On January 17, 1948, the two sides signed the Renville Agreement, which had been brokered by the UN. It established a cease-fire between the Dutch and Republican forces along the so-called Van Mook Line, an artificial line connecting the advanced Dutch positions in the field. The agreement also called for referenda to be held on the political future of those areas held by the Dutch government.

At the same time, nationalist leaders were also confronted by threats from within. The first of these was the 1948 Madiun rebellion in East Java, during which the Indonesian Communist Party (PKI) proclaimed a people's republic, which had to be reversed by force. The Darul Islam movement, a militant movement based in Java seeking the establishment of an Islamic state in southern Celebes (Sulawesi), Java, and Sumatra, was another internal threat that distracted the Nationalist/Republican forces as they fought the Dutch.

Diplomatic efforts continued, but in complete disregard of the Renville Agreement, the Dutch mounted a second "police action" (general offensive) in Operation KRAAI (CROW) on December 19, 1948. The very next day the Dutch captured the republic's temporary capital of Yogyakarta as well as the republic's leadership, including Sukarno and Hatta, who were then exiled to Bangka Island off the coast of Samatra. By the end of December, Dutch forces had taken all the Republican-held cities of Java and Sumatra.

Although the Dutch held the cities and towns, they could not control the rural areas, where a guerrilla campaign led by lieutenant colonel and future Indonesian strongman Suharto achieved a number of small successes, including the brief recapture of Yogyakarta on March 1, 1949.

Internationally this second "police action" was a disaster for the Dutch, as international opinion continued to build against them. An international conference held in New Delhi in January 1949 on the Indonesian situation demanded an end to Dutch colonial rule by January 1, 1950. Also, the UN Security Council in a resolution of January 28, 1949, demanded a cease-fire. Under pressure from the UN and especially U.S. leaders (notably Secretary of State Dean Acheson), on August 23 peace talks finally opened at The Hague in the Netherlands between the Dutch government and Indonesian nationalist representatives.

On November 2, 1949, the two sides reached agreement. On December 16 Sukarno was elected the first president of Indonesia, and on December 27 sovereignty of the 16 islands that had constituted the NEI was formally transferred from the Netherlands to the United States of Indonesia, with its capital at Jakarta. The status of Dutch New Guinea, which remained apart from the new federation, was to be decided by future negotiations. Despite some unrest in the islands, notably from Islamic insurgents and the communists, both of whom sought to establish independent governments against rule from Jakarta, in August 1950 a new unitary constitution was promulgated that created the Republic of Indonesia.

The Indonesian War of Independence claimed as many as 100,000 Indonesian combatant deaths. The British suffered 1,200 deaths, and the Dutch military some 3,144 deaths.

SPENCER C. TUCKER

## Consequences

The first two decades of Indonesian independence saw economic stagnation, despite initial optimism over a democratic constitution and a brief climb in exports during the Korean War. President Sukarno followed a policy of economic nationalism tinged with socialist Marxism and anti-imperialism.

Before departing, the Dutch imposed a federal structure on the republic when they promulgated the second provisional constitution on November 2, 1949. This structure was short-lived, however, as Indonesia reverted to a unitary system under a third provisional constitution enacted on August 17, 1950. Indonesia held its first general elections on September 29, 1955, and assembled its first-ever cabinet on an elected basis. Because no single party secured a majority, a coalition of the Nationalist

Sukarno was the leader of the Indonesian struggle for independence against the Netherlands and was then the first president of Indonesia from 1945 until 1967. (Library of Congress)

Party, Masjumi, Nahdatul Ulama, and other smaller parties was formed.

The last parliamentary cabinet fell in December 1956 because the coalition splintered. Vice President Mohammad Hatta resigned, and rebellion loomed in the outer islands. Sukarno promptly denounced the party system and proclaimed martial law in March 1957. In July 1959, he dissolved the Constituent Assembly when it failed to approve his proposal to revive the 1945 constitution. He reinstated this constitution that provided for a strong presidency and introduced his "Guided Democracy," which gave to him virtually unlimited power.

In foreign policy, Indonesia became part of the Colombo Plan (1950), and Sukarno organized the Afro-Asian Conference at Bandung (Java) in April 1955. Sukarno's antipathy toward colonialism was expressed in the 1960s through his idea of *nekolim* (*neo*colonialism, *col*onialism, and *im*perialism). He also developed the concept of *oldefos* (old established forces) versus *nefos* (new emerging forces), defining the Oldefos-Nefos antithesis not in Cold War terms but instead in terms of the continued domination of the emergent nations by the former colonial powers.

Sukarno's reliance on the PKI at the domestic level was reflected at the international level when he moved from Cold War neutrality to the formation of a Beijing-Jakarta axis by 1965. Indonesia stayed out of the Southeast Asia Treaty Organization and the Association of Southeast Asia, though it initially endorsed the idea of Maphilindo, a regional grouping of Malaya, the Philippines, and Indonesia formed to reconcile differences over the proposed formation of the Federation of Malaysia. Sukarno's conception of *konfrontasi* (confrontation) was devised to repudiate the Netherlands' claim over Irian Jaya and was later used by Foreign Minister Subandrio to challenge the legitimacy of the new Federation of Malaysia, provoking Indonesia's withdrawal from the UN in 1964.

On March 6, 1960, Sukarno dissolved the elected parliament under the 1945 constitution and replaced it with one of the appointed members in June 1960. The Indonesian Army came to play an important role in internal affairs, being co-opted for an administrative role. Sukarno sought to balance the army's support with dependence on the PKI for mass support, but the contradictions between the two organizations became obvious during an abortive coup on September 20, 1965.

The attempted coup, involving leftist junior army officers, resulted in the murder of six right-wing generals. In the anticommunist pogrom that followed, an estimated 500,000 communists and communist sympathizers were killed. Suharto, tasked with suppressing the revolt, quietly utilized the opportunity to push Sukarno aside. He did this first by usurping executive control in March 1966, then by deposing Sukarno and installing himself as acting president on March 12, 1967. Suharto proclaimed himself president on March 27, 1968, for a five-year term. He stayed in power until May 21, 1998, thanks to subsequent rigged elections.

Under Suharto's "New Order," political activity was severely restricted. Political parties were forced to reorganize into three major political parties: the Golongan Karya (Golkar, Party of the Service Society), the ruling party; the Partai Demokrasi Indonesia; and the Partai Persatuan Pembangunan. The government-sponsored Golkar effectively manipulated votes in its favor for more than two decades, while parliament was weakened and then became a virtual rubber stamp for Suharto. Suharto's strength was in the military, which in turn derived its power from the doctrine of *dwifungsi* (dual function) that extended the military's influence over the socioeconomic and political spheres. In 1987 political parties were forced to accept the state ideology, *pancasilla,* as their sole guiding principle.

Suharto imposed strict controls on the media and banned the publication of news magazines that did not toe the line. This authoritarianism asserted itself most aggressively in 1975, when Indonesian troops landed in East Timor and later incorporated it as the 27th province of Indonesia. Suharto faced serious allegations of human rights abuses in putting down the independence movement in East Timor and in suppressing a separatist movement in the north Sumatran province of Aceh.

Suharto's foreign policy was calculated to be low-profile and pragmatic. He abandoned confrontation with Malaysia, helped found the Association of Southeast Asian Nations (ASEAN) in 1967, and in 1976 established ASEAN's permanent secretariat in Jakarta. Indonesia became a leader of the Non-Aligned Movement in 1991 just as the Cold War came to an end. Following the Vietnamese invasion and subsequent occupation of Cambodia in 1978, Indonesia agreed to play the role of mediator in the crisis. Diplomatic relations with the People's Republic of China were restored in August 1990 after having been severed in 1965 because of Chinese support for the PKI. Indonesia's military, which played a central role in Indonesia's War of Independence, steadily gained influence during the Cold War, as indicated by the sharp increases in defense expenditures and substantial arms acquisitions, including fighter aircraft and submarines.

Suharto was dubbed the "father of development," as Indonesia's yearly economic growth rate skyrocketed to 7.8 percent in 1996. With the help of U.S.-trained economists, he made Indonesia a welcome destination for foreign capital, and the World Bank held it up as a model borrowing nation. During the 1980s and 1990s, the number of Indonesians living below the poverty line declined substantially.

With the demise of the Soviet Union and the end of the Cold War, Indonesia could no longer isolate itself from the forces of political change, which were sweeping away outmoded political and social thinking elsewhere; soon, new demands for political reforms began to gain momentum. Bachruddin Jusuf Habibie, buoyed by popular support, succeeded Suharto, who was forced from office on May 21, 1998. Once this initial enthusiasm had subsided, however, Habibie (who was president only from May 21, 1998, to October 20, 1999) and his successors no longer felt pressured to introduce market reforms or initiate measures to arrest government corruption.

UDAI BHANU SINGH

## Timeline

| | |
|---|---|
| **1512** | The Portuguese are the first Europeans to arrive in the Indonesian archipelago. |
| **1595** | The Dutch send an expedition to the archipelago. Its great profit return brings other Dutch expeditions. |
| **1602** | The Dutch government combines a number of Dutch trading companies into the United East India Company (VOC). Its capital city becomes Batavia (now Jakarta) in Java. |
| **1796** | With the VOC bankrupt, the Batavian Republic takes over the VOC's territorial holdings in the archipelago, now known as the Dutch East Indies (DEI) and, from 1815, the Netherlands East Indies (NEI). |
| **1806–1813** | The Dutch East Indies pass under French control when Emperor Napoleon I annexes the Batavian Republic. |
| **1811** | British forces (Great Britain then being at war with France) occupy several DEI ports. |
| **1815** | Dutch control of the DEI is restored with the end of the Napoleonic Wars. |
| **1821** | Dutch forces intervene in the Padri War (1803–1837) and largely subjugate Sumatra. |
| **1825–1830** | The Java War sees much of the population of that island rise up against the Dutch. |

| | |
|---|---|
| **1849** | The Dutch bring northern Bali under their control. |
| **1859–1863** | In the Banjarmasin War the Dutch reestablish their authority in eastern and southern Borneo. |
| **1873–1912** | The Aceh War in Sumatra ends with an Acehnese surrender to the Dutch. |
| **1905–1906** | The Dutch come to control southwestern Sulawesi. |
| **1906–1908** | The Dutch establish control of Bali and also the remaining independent kingdoms in Maluku, Sumatra, Kalimantan, and Nusa Tenggara. |
| **1920** | The Dutch bring Western New Guinea under their control. |
| **May 1940** | With the Germans having invaded and conquered the Netherlands, the advisory Volksraad (People's Council) declares its loyalty to the Dutch government-in-exile in London. |
| **Aug 1941** | The Volksraad obeys the decision by the Dutch government to cut off oil exports to Japan. |
| **Dec 8, 1941** | The Netherlands government-in-exile, acting in concert with the British and U.S. governments, declares war on Japan. |
| **Dec 20, 1941** | Japanese troops land on oil-rich Dutch Borneo as well as in Celebes (now Sulawesi) and the Moluccas. |
| **Feb 27, 1942** | The Japanese Navy crushes Allied naval forces in the Battle of the Java Sea. |
| **Mar 8, 1942** | The Dutch surrender Java. |
| **1944–1945** | As many as 2.4 million Indonesians die of famine, resulting in large part from Japanese food requisitions. |
| **Sep 7, 1944** | Japan announces plans to grant the NEI independence but does not specify a date. |
| **Mar 1945** | Indonesian nationalist leaders Achmed Sukarno and Mohammed Hatta call a conference to work out the constitution for a new state of Indonesia. |
| **Jun 1, 1945** | Sukarno presents the Pancasila, a statement of five principles to govern the proposed Indonesian nation. |
| **Jun 22, 1945** | In the Jakarta Charter, nationalists agree that the new state is to embrace monotheism, with Muslims required to adhere to sharia (Islamic law). Sukarno becomes president, and Hatta becomes vice president. |
| **Aug 1945** | Republican forces aided by the *pemuda* secure control of most of the urban centers in the NEI. Meanwhile, the British-led South East Asia Command has been tasked with restoring order in Java. Pending their arrival, the Allies order Japanese forces in the archipelago to |

preserve order there. British lieutenant general Sir Philip Christison commands the forces sent to the NEI. Clashes occur among civilians, principally in Java and Sumatra, between those favoring an independent republic and their perceived enemies. The period August 1945–December 1946 is known as the Bersiap (Indonesian for "get ready" or "be prepared").

| | |
|---|---|
| **Aug 15, 1945** | Japan surrenders. |
| **Aug 17, 1945** | Pressured by radical *pemuda* (youth) groups, Sukarno declares Indonesia's independence. The Dutch refusal to accept this brings war. |
| **Oct 3, 1945** | Japanese forces drive the *pemuda* from Bandung in western Java and hand it over to the British. |
| **Oct 9–14, 1945** | Fierce fighting occurs in the city of Semarang in Java. Japanese forces suffer some 500 dead, and the Republican side suffers 2,000. |
| **Oct 27–Nov 20, 1945** | In the Battle of Surabaya, British and Dutch forces finally establish control of this NEI city but at a high cost. It is the bloodiest single battle of the war. |
| **Jan 1946** | Dutch forces take control of Jakarta and the cities of Java and Sumatra, although the Dutch lack the resources to control the rural areas. |
| **Nov 15, 1946** | The British broker the Linggadjati Agreement in which the Dutch government agrees to recognize Republican rule over Java, Sumatra, and Madura. The agreement never takes hold, however. |
| **Jul 20, 1947** | Claiming that the Republican side has violated the Linggadjati Agreement, Dutch forces launch Operation PRODUCT with the goal of establishing full control of Java and Sumatra. |
| **Aug 4, 1947** | United Nations (UN) officials help broker a cease-fire, called for by an August 1 UN Security Council resolution. |
| **Jan 17, 1948** | The two sides sign the UN-brokered Renville Agreement, establishing a cease-fire and calling for referenda on the political future of those areas under Dutch control. |
| **Sep 18, 1948** | The Madiun rebellion occurs in East Java, during which the Indonesian Communist Party proclaims a people's republic in defiance of the Indonesian Republican leaders. It is reversed by force three months later. |
| **Dec 19, 1948** | Disregarding the Renville Agreement, the Dutch mount a second general offensive in Operation CROW and the next day capture the republic's temporary capital of Yogyakarta and the republic's leadership, including Sukarno and Hatta, who are then exiled to Bangka Island. |
| **Jan 1949** | An international conference in New Delhi on the Indonesian situation demands an end to Dutch colonial rule there by January 1, 1950. |

| | |
|---|---|
| **Jan 28, 1949** | The UN Security Council demands a cease-fire. |
| **Mar 1, 1949** | Suharto's forces recapture Yogyakarta, holding it for several hours. |
| **Aug 23, 1949** | Peace talks between representatives of the republic and the Dutch government open in The Hague. |
| **Nov 2, 1949** | The two sides at The Hague reach agreement on Indonesian independence. |
| **Dec 16, 1949** | Sukarno is elected the first president of Indonesia. |
| **Dec 27, 1949** | Sovereignty over the 16 islands that had constituted the NEI is formally transferred to the United States of Indonesia, with its capital at Jakarta. |
| **Aug 17, 1950** | A new constitution is promulgated, creating the Republic of Indonesia. |
| **Sep 29, 1950** | Indonesia holds its first general elections. |
| **Apr 1955** | Sukarno organizes the Afro-Asian Conference at Bandung. |
| **Mar 14, 1957** | Sukarno denounces the party system and proclaims martial law. |
| **Jul 5, 1959** | Sukarno dissolves the Constituent Assembly, abolishes the 1950 constitution, and arranges for himself to aggregate virtually unlimited power. |
| **Sep 20, 1965** | An abortive coup occurs against Sukarno. In the anticommunist pogrom that follows, an estimated 500,000 communists and communist sympathizers are killed. |
| **Mar 12, 1967** | Suharto deposes Sukarno and declares himself acting president. |
| **Mar 27, 1968** | Suharto proclaims himself president for a five-year term. However, he will remain in power until May 21, 1998. |

Spencer C. Tucker

**Further Reading**

Abeyasekere, Susan. *One Hand Clapping: Indonesian Nationalists and the Dutch, 1939–1942.* Clayton, Australia: Monash University, 1976.

Anderson, Ben. *Java in a Time of Revolution: Occupation and Resistance, 1944–1946.* Ithaca, NY: Cornell University Press, 1972.

Aziz, M. A. *Japan's Colonialism and Indonesia.* The Hague: Martinus Nijhoff, 1999.

Baker, Richard W., et al., eds. *Indonesia: The Challenge of Change.* Singapore: ISEAS, 1999.

Cribb, Robert. *Gangster and Revolutionaries: The Jakarta People's Militia and the Indonesian Revolution, 1945–1949.* Sydney, Australia: Allen and Unwin, 1991.

Cribb, Robert, and Colin Brown. *Modern Indonesia: A History since 1945.* London: Longman, 1995.

Frederick, William H. *Visions and Heat: The Making of the Indonesian Revolution.* Athens: Ohio University Press, 1989.

George, Margaret. *Australia and the Indonesian Revolution.* Melbourne, Australia: Melbourne University Press, 1989.

Jong, L. de. *The Collapse of a Colonial Society: The Dutch in Indonesia during the Second World War.* London: KITLV Press, 2002.

Kahin, Audrey. *Regional Dynamics of the Indonesian Revolution.* Honolulu: University of Hawaii Press, 1995.

Kahin, George McTurnan. *Nationalism and Revolution in Indonesia.* Ithaca, NY: Cornell University Press, 2003.

Kingsbury, Damien. *Power Politics and the Indonesian Military.* London: Routledge, 2003.

McMillan, Richard. *The British Occupation of Indonesia, 1945–1946.* New York: Routledge, 2005.

Ricklefs, M. C. *A History of Modern Indonesia since c.1300.* 2nd ed. Stanford, CA: Stanford University Press, 1993.

Sato Shigeru. *War, Nationalism and Peasants: Java under the Japanese Occupation, 1942–1945.* Armonk, NY: M. E. Sharpe, 1994.

Taylor, Alastair M. *Indonesian Independence and the United Nations.* London: Stevens and Sons, 1960.

Vatikiotis, Michael R. J. *Indonesian Politics under Suharto.* London: Routledge, 1993.

Zainu'ddin, Ailsa. *A Short History of Indonesia.* New York: Praeger, 1970.

# Indochina War (1946–1954)

## Causes

Also known as the First Indochina War and in contemporary Vietnam as the Anti-French Resistance War, the Indochina War of 1946–1954 was a major event in Southeast Asian and French history. It led directly to the Vietnam War (Second Indochina War) of 1957–1975. Taken together as they should be, the two wars represent the longest conflict of the 20th century.

The European powers were interested in Indochina for reasons of religion, trade, and naval facilities. Vietnam, with its long seacoast, was especially vulnerable to European penetration. The first lasting contact between Vietnam and Europe came in 1535 with the arrival of the Portuguese. Both they and the Dutch soon established rival trading posts.

By 1615 there was also a permanent Catholic mission. French priest Alexandre de Rhodes made Catholicism a cultural force when he created *quoc ngu*, written Vietnamese with a Latin alphabet and diacritical marks. Previously Vietnamese had been written in Chinese ideographs. The French used *quoc ngu* to eliminate the political and cultural influence of Vietnamese Confucian scholars, but with it also came Western ideas of freedom and democracy.

Southeast Asia increasingly attracted European attention. The term "Indochina"

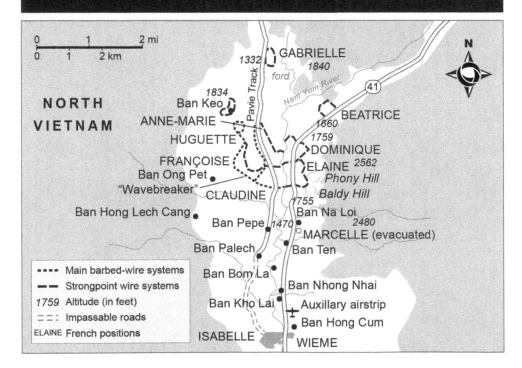

BATTLE OF DIEN BIEN PHU, MAR 13–MAY 7, 1954

**Indochina War (December 1946–July 1954)**

| Casualties for the Battle of Dien Bien Phu (March 13–May 7, 1954)* | | |
|---|---|---|
| | **France and French Allies** | **Viet Minh** |
| **Killed/missing** | 1,600 | 7,900 |
| **Wounded** | 4,800 | 15,000 |
| **Missing** | 1,600 | Unknown |

*Although the Viet Minh sustained many more casualties than the French, this battle effectively ended France's commitment to the Indochina War.

| Estimated Military Casualties, Indochina War (1946–1954) | |
|---|---|
| **France and French Allies** | **Viet Minh** |
| 172,708 (94,581 dead/missing, 78,127 wounded) | 520,000 (dead/missing/wounded) |

**Sources:** Fall, Bernard B. *Street without Joy: The French Debacle in Indochina.* Revised ed. Mechanicsburg, PA: Stackpole Books, 1994; Morgan, Ted. *Valley of Death: The Tragedy at Dien Bien Phu That Led America into the Vietnam War.* New York: Random House, 2010.

is attributed to Danish cartographer Konrad Malte-Brun (1775–1826) and was applied collectively to Burma, Thailand, Tonkin, Annam, Cochinchina, Laos, and Cambodia. At the beginning of the 19th century Catholic priest Pierre Pigneau de Béhaine helped secure European mercenaries and military equipment that enabled Nguyen Phuc Anh (from 1802, Emperor Gia Long) to reunify Vietnam. Gia Long welcomed Western military and technological assistance, but he and his successors were not interested in advancing their religion. The Vietnamese emperors regarded Catholicism as a threat to the Confucian concept of order and harmony. Catholics were not singled out, for Buddhists and Taoists were also persecuted.

The attempt by the 19th-century Vietnamese emperors to root out Christian missionaries provided the excuse for French intervention. Unfortunately for the Vietnamese, they had shown little interest in the vast improvements in weaponry since the reunification of their country, and this put them at a great disadvantage in the inevitable collision with the West.

Religion may have been the excuse, but trade was a powerful motivator for the French. In the 1840s the British had taken the lead in obtaining trading concessions in China. The French soon followed suit and hoped that Vietnam might provide access to the Chinese interior by means of the Mekong and Red Rivers. In 1845 and again in 1846, French warships were sent to Vietnam to secure the release of a Catholic priest who had been imprisoned for refusing to leave the country. During the second intervention, the French sank 4 Vietnamese warships regarded as posing a hostile intent. Then in August 1858, a Franco-Spanish squadron of 14 ships and 3,000 men arrived at Tourane (Da Nang). It proved to be no prize, and the expedition moved southward. On February 18, 1859, the French secured Saigon. A sleepy little fishing village, it had the promise of being an excellent deepwater port. Then in 1862 the French forced Emperor Tu Duc to sign a treaty confirming their conquest. It was no accident that the French chose to penetrate Cochinchina (southern Vietnam) first; it was the newest part of the country.

By 1867 the French had conquered all of Cochinchina, and by 1887 they had control over all Indochina: Cochinchina was followed by Cambodia, Annam, and Tonkin. In 1887 they were formed into French Indochina. Laos was added in 1893. Guerrilla warfare continued in parts of the country for a time, but the last major revolt was crushed in 1913. Technically only Cochinchina was an outright colony; the others were merely protectorates. The reality was that all were ruled by a French governor-general responsible to the minister of colonies in Paris.

French administration was haphazard. Ministers of colonies and governors-general changed frequently, and with each came policy changes. Indochina also did not attract the most capable civil servants, and their salaries consumed what money was available in the colonial budget, with little left for education or public works. The small French community of 40,000–50,000 people dominated the economy of what was now France's richest colony.

In education the ideal was to turn the Vietnamese into a cultural copy of mainland France, but even after World War I only 10 percent of Vietnamese of school age were attending Franco-Vietnamese schools. And as late as 1940 there were only 14 secondary schools in all of Vietnam and only 1 university (at Hanoi). This produced a talented but very small native elite aspiring to positions of influence that were nonetheless closed to them. Ultimately this drove many of them to turn against France.

Vietnamese nationalist hopes were raised by the Allied victory in World War I and U.S. president Woodrow Wilson's call for self-determination of peoples. But at the Paris Peace Conference, the Vietnamese learned that this doctrine was limited to Europe. Moderate Vietnamese nationalists now took the Nationalist Party of China as their model. Their Viet Nam Quoc Dan Dang (Vietnamese Nationalist Party, VNQDD) was established in 1927.

The VNQDD led premature uprisings in 1930–1931. Although easily crushed by the French, these opened the way for the better organized and more militant Indochinese Communist Party (ICP), formed in 1930 in Hong Kong. By World War II the ICP, led by Ho Chi Minh, was the dominant nationalist force in Indochina.

The Japanese arrived in Indochina in 1940. Having been defeated by Germany, France was in no position to resist Tokyo's demand for bases. Ironically, this brought the United States into World War II. Japan's July 1941 move into southern Indochina meant that its long-range bombers could reach Malaya, the Dutch East Indies, and the Philippines. The United States, Great Britain, and the Netherlands imposed an embargo on scrap iron and oil to Japan, and this decision caused Tokyo to embark on war with the United States.

In May 1941, ICP leader and die-hard Vietnamese nationalist Ho Chi Minh formed the Viet Minh (Vietnam Independence League), a nationalist umbrella organization dominated by the communists, to fight the French and Japanese. The U.S. Office of Strategic Services (OSS), the forerunner of the Central Intelligence Agency, supplied limited assistance to the Viet Minh during the war.

The Japanese left the Vichy French government in Indochina in place, but as the conflict neared its end, the French were determined to liberate themselves. With these plans an open secret, the Japanese struck first. On March 9, 1945, they arrested virtually all French administrators and military personnel. Tokyo created a further problem for France by declaring Vietnam independent under Emperor Bao Dai.

With the defeat of Japan, Ho moved into the vacuum. On August 16, 1945, in Hanoi, he declared himself president of a "free Vietnam," and on September 2 he proclaimed the independence of the Democratic Republic of Vietnam (North Vietnam, DRV).

World War II marked the end of European colonialism. French leaders, however, chose not to embrace the inevitable and seek accommodation with nationalist leaders. The result was a missed opportunity for orderly transition to self-rule and a close relationship with France. It is hard for the weak to be generous, and only with its empire could France hope in 1945 to continue as a Great Power.

According to the July 1945 Potsdam Agreement, the British were to take the surrender of Japanese troops south of the 16th parallel, while Chinese Nationalist troops would do the same north of that line. The British released French troops from Japanese camps, and Paris sent reinforcements to reestablish its control over southern Vietnam, Cambodia, and Laos. The French also arranged a Chinese withdrawal from North Vietnam. In October, General Jacques-Philippe Leclerc arrived in Saigon to assume command of French forces in Indochina. Reinforcements came with him.

In January 1946 Ho carried out elections in northern Vietnam. Although these were not entirely free, there could be no doubt that he had won. With the United States and the Soviet Union refusing involvement, Ho was forced, however, to deal with France, and in March 1946 he worked out an agreement with French diplomat Jean Sainteny under which the French recognized North Vietnam as a free and independent state within the French Union. France was allowed to send a limited number of troops into North Vietnam to protect its interests, although all were to be withdrawn over a five-year period. Paris also accepted the principle of a united Vietnam by agreeing to a plebiscite in southern Vietnam over whether it would join North Vietnam.

French high commissioner for Indochina Georges Thierry d'Argenlieu refused to allow the promised southern plebiscite. In a direct appeal to Paris, Ho led a delegation to France. By the time it arrived, however, the French government had fallen. June elections weakened the Left, the socialists lost seats, and the communists, who were in the government, were trying to demonstrate their patriotism. As a result, during the ensuing Fontainebleau Conference (July 6–September 10, 1946) Paris made no concessions to the Vietnamese. D'Argenlieu had meanwhile, on his own initiative, proclaimed the independence of southern Vietnam as the "Republic of Cochinchina."

D'Argenlieu's action violated the Ho-Sainteny Agreement and left Vietnamese leaders feeling betrayed. Although there is still disagreement on this point, Ho was probably a nationalist first and a communist second. Given the long antagonistic relationship between Vietnam and China, he might have become an Asian Tito. But in September, Ho left Paris predicting war.

Tensions were already high in Vietnam when, in November 1946, the French sent a war crimes commission to Lang Son to investigate a mass grave of French soldiers killed by the Japanese in March 1945. On November 20 an armed clash occurred between French troops escorting the commission and Vietnamese. Each side blamed the other. This was overshadowed by a more ominous event the same day at Tonkin's principal part of Haiphong. The French Navy had virtually blockaded Haiphong, and a patrol vessel seized a Chinese junk attempting to smuggle contraband. Vietnamese soldiers on the shore fired on the French ship, and shooting occurred in the city itself. Peace was restored on November 22 on a French pledge to respect Vietnamese sovereignty and the separation of forces within Haiphong.

At the time, d'Argenlieu was in Paris. Securing permission from Premier George Bidault to use force (Bidault probably did not realize this was imminent), d'Argenlieu cabled Vietnam and ordered a subordinate to "give a severe lesson to those who have treacherously attacked you. Use all the means at your disposal to make yourself complete master of Haiphong and so bring the Vietnamese army around to a better understanding of the situation."

On November 23 following expiration of a two-hour warning, the French opened an air, land, and sea bombardment of targets in Haiphong, with most of the firepower delivered by the cruiser *Suffren*. Estimates of the number killed in the shelling and ensuing panic vary widely, but there were probably 500 to 1,000 killed.

Although the fighting ended on November 28, whatever hopes for peace remaining had been irretrievably shattered. On December 19 the French demanded the disarmament of the Tu Ve, the Viet Minh militia in Hanoi. That night fear and mistrust, fueled by bloodshed and broken promises, erupted into all-out war.

SPENCER C. TUCKER

## Course

In September 1945 before leaving Paris, Vietnamese nationalist Ho Chi Minh had talked to an American reporter and predicted both an early start of war and how it would be fought and would end. He said that it would be the war of the tiger and the elephant. The tiger could not meet the elephant in an equal contest, so he would lay in wait for it, drop on its back from the jungle, and rip huge hunks of flesh with his claws. Eventually, the elephant would bleed to death. The war played out very much along those lines.

The French did not fight the Indochina War primarily for economic reasons; indeed, by 1950 French military expenditures surpassed the total value of all French investments there. The chief reasons were political and psychological. Perhaps only with its empire could France be counted as a Great Power. Colonial advocates also argued that concessions in Indochina would impact in the other overseas possessions, especially in North Africa, and that further losses would soon follow. French leaders also launched the domino theory. As General Jean de Lattre de Tassigny phrased it during a trip to Washington, D.C., in September 1951, "Once Tongking [*sic*] is lost, there is no barrier until Suez." Such reasoning resurfaced during the Vietnam War.

The DRV leadership planned for a long war. The Viet Minh's chief appeal was its stated goal of ridding the country of foreigners. Vo Nguyen Giap had command of the DRV's military forces, formed in May 1945 as the Vietnam Liberation Army and later the People's Army of Vietnam (PAVN), also known as the Vietnam People's Army and the North Vietnamese Army. This former lycée history teacher, self-taught in war, commanded the PAVN for 30 years. Ho and Giap wanted it to appeal to as many Vietnamese as possible. They imposed strict rules, including a 10-part oath that contained a pledge to respect, help, and protect the people, with soldiers always to be on their best behavior. Giap believed that successful warfare grew out of correct political views.

Reportedly Giap visited Mao Zedong (Mao Tse-tung) in 1941 and learned what he could about revolutionary war from the Chinese communist leader. Certainly, Giap was much influenced by Mao's writings. Giap's *People's War, People's Army* is largely a restatement of Maoist ideas with these fighting principles added on: "If the enemy advances, we retreat; if he halts, we harass; if he avoids battle, we attack; if he retreats, we follow." Giap's strategy was, however, eclectic. If it worked, he utilized it. His chief contribution to revolutionary warfare was his assessment of political and psychological difficulties that confront a democracy in waging a protracted and inconclusive war. Public opinion would at some point, he believed, demand an end to the bloodshed, and political leaders would find themselves promising an early end to the fighting. Giap made mistakes, chiefly in going over to the third phase of large-unit warfare too soon, but he also showed the capacity to learn from and not repeat his mistakes. Certainly, he proved to be adroit in logistics, timing, surprise, and deception.

Giap had no shortage of recruits. Weapons were another matter. Through 1949 the PAVN had only about 83,000 of all types. Perhaps a third were homemade, another third were World War II–vintage Japanese or OSS-supplied weapons, and the other third were purchased abroad in Thailand or Hong Kong. The DRV also purchased communications equipment from the Chinese Nationalist troops before their departure from northern Vietnam. In 1946 the DRV established training schools for officers and noncommissioned officers.

French military commander in Indochina General Jacques-Philippe Leclerc had in late 1945 used his small yet mobile force of about 40,000 men to move swiftly and secure southern Vietnam and Cambodia. The Viet Minh were soon forced out into the countryside, and life returned to normal, or almost so. There were those who dreaded the Viet Minh's retreat into the jungle. Leclerc was one; he was convinced that the Viet Minh was a nationalist movement that France could not subdue militarily. Unlike most of his compatriots, he was aware of the great difficulties of jungle warfare and favored negotiations. In a secret report to Paris, Leclerc said that there would be no solution through force in Indochina.

Although the French Socialist Party showed interest in ending the war through peace talks, the steady drift to the right of the French coalition government and increasing bloodshed prevented this. French high commissioner to Indochina Admiral Georges Thierry d'Argenlieu and other French colonial administrators opposed any meaningful concessions to the nationalists, and in the summer of 1946 Leclerc departed Indochina in frustration.

Leclerc was but the first in a succession of French military commanders. He was followed by Generals Jean-Etienne Valluy, Roger Blaizot, Marcel Carpentier, Jean de Lattre de Tassigny, Raoul Salan, Henri Navarre, and Paul Henri Romuald Ely. The frequent change in commanders undoubtedly affected the overall efficiency and morale of the French Far East Expeditionary Force.

Most French leaders assumed that the conflict would be little more than a classic colonial reconquest, securing the population centers and then expanding outward in the classic oil slick (*tache d'huile*) method that had worked effectively in Morocco and Algeria. Meanwhile, the Viet Minh steadily grew in strength and came to control more and more territory.

In May 1947 the French did make an effort at ending the war through negotiation when Paul Mus traveled from Hanoi to meet with Ho in the latter's jungle headquarters. Mus was an Asian scholar sympathetic to the Vietnamese nationalist point of view and a personal adviser to Emile Bollaert, who had replaced d'Argenlieu as high commissioner. Mus told Ho that France would agree to a cease-fire on condition that the Viet Minh lay down some of their arms, permit French troops freedom of movement in their zones, and turn over some deserters from the French Foreign Legion. Ho rejected this offer, which was tantamount to surrender, and in May Bollaert declared that "France will remain in Indochina."

Despite its stated determination to hold on to Indochina, the French government never made the commitment in manpower necessary for the army to win. The war was essentially fought by the professional soldiers: officers and noncommissioned officers who led the French Expeditionary Corps. The French government never allowed draftees to be sent to Indochina. The small number of men available to French commanders left them very few options. A shortage of noncommissioned officers, a lack of trained intelligence officers and interpreters, and little interest in or knowledge of the mechanics of pacification all hampered the French military effort.

The French held much of Cochinchina in large part because of the powerful religious sects and Buddhists there who opposed the Viet Minh. The French also controlled the Red River Delta in the north, along with the capital of Hanoi. But the Viet Minh controlled much of the country-side, and the area they dominated grew as time went on. Initially, the Viet Minh largely withdrew into the jungle to indoctrinate and train their troops. The French invested little attention and resources to pacification efforts, and their heavy-handedness alienated many Vietnamese. The French scenario had the Viet Minh eventually tiring of their cause and giving up, but it never played out that way.

To increase available manpower, attract Vietnamese nationalist support, and quiet critics at home and in the United States, Paris sought to provide at least the facade of an indigenous Vietnamese regime as a competitor to the Viet Minh. After several years of negotiations, in March 1949 the French government concluded the Elysée Agreements with former emperor Bao Dai. These created the State of Vietnam (SVN), and Paris made the key concession that Vietnam was in fact one country.

The SVN allowed the French government to portray the war as a conflict between a free Vietnam and the communists—and thus not a colonial war at all. Washington, which supported France in Indochina because it needed French military assistance in Europe, claimed to be convinced.

The problem for Vietnamese nationalists was that the SVN never truly was independent. The French continued to control all of its institutions, and its promised army never really materialized. France simply took the recruited soldiers and added them to the French Far East Expeditionary Corps, where they were commanded by French officers. In effect, there were only two choices for the Vietnamese: either the Viet Minh or the French. The French drove the nationalists into the Viet Minh camp.

In October 1947 the French mounted Operation LEA. Involving some 15,000 men and conducted over a three-week period, it was devoted almost exclusively to the capture of Ho Chi Minh and the Viet Minh leadership and the destruction of their main battle units. Operation LEA involved 17 French battalions, and while it took Thai Nguyen and some other Viet Minh–controlled cities, it failed to capture the Viet Minh leadership and destroy the main Viet Minh military units. It also showed the paucity of French resources in Indochina. The troops in LEA were badly needed elsewhere, and their employment in the operation opened up much of the countryside to Viet Minh penetration. As time went on the military situation continued to deteriorate for the French, despite the fact that by the end of 1949 Paris had expended $1.5 billion on the war.

The Indochina War changed dramatically in the fall of 1949 when the communists came to power in China. That event and the recognition of the DRV by the People's Republic of China (PRC), while helping to change Washington's attitude toward the war, in effect signaled that the war was lost for the French. The long Chinese-Vietnamese border allowed the Chinese to supply arms and equipment to the PAVN, and China provided cross-border sanctuaries where the Viet Minh could train and replenish their troops. And there were plenty of arms available from the substantial stocks of weapons, including artillery, that the United States had previously supplied to the Chinese Nationalists.

The Korean War, which began in June 1950, profoundly affected the U.S. attitude toward the war in Indochina. Korea and Vietnam came to be viewed as mutually dependent theaters in a common Western struggle against communism. Washington recognized the SVN and changed its policy of providing only indirect assistance.

In June 1950 President Harry S. Truman announced that the United States would provide direct military aid to the French in Indochina and also establish a military assistance and advisory group there. By the end of the Indochina War in 1954, the United States had furnished $2.5 billion in military aid to the French and was underwriting three-quarters of the war's cost.

The French insisted that all U.S. military assistance be given directly to them rather than channeled through the SVN. Although the Vietnamese National Army was established in 1951, it remained effectively under French control, and France continued to dominate the SVN down to the end. Regardless, the Truman and Dwight D. Eisenhower administrations assured the American people that real authority had been handed over to the Vietnamese.

The Indochina War became an endless quagmire. By 1950, it was costing France between 40 and 45 percent of its entire military budget and more than 10 percent of the national budget. During September–October 1950 the Viet Minh mounted Operation LE HONG PHONG and secured control of Route Coloniale (Colonial Highway) 4. The highway paralleled the Chinese frontier and ran from the Gulf of Tonkin to Cao Bang. In the fighting the Viet Minh captured sufficient weapons to equip an entire division. The loss of this critical frontier section gave the Viet Minh ready access to China. For all practical purposes, France had lost the war. That it was allowed to continue is proof of the lack of political leadership in Paris.

Giap now believed that circumstances were ripe for conventional large-unit warfare, and he took the offensive beginning on January 13, 1951, with Operations TRAN HUNG DAO, HOANG HOA THAM, and HA NAM NINH. These lasted until June 18 and were designed to secure Hanoi and the Red River Delta. The PAVN was, however, stopped cold by French forces led by General Jean de Lattre de Tassigny, probably the most capable of French commanders during the war. After these rebuffs, Giap simply shifted back to his phase-two strategy of engaging the French in circumstances of his own choosing.

Late that year de Lattre initiated a battle outside the important Red River Delta area. What became the Battle of Hoa Binh (November 14, 1951–February 24, 1952) was a meat-grinder battle as de Lattre envisioned but for both sides. By the end of the battle, the PAVN had paid a heavy price but had also learned how to deal with French tactics and had penetrated the French defensive ring as never before.

Giap now undertook the conquest of the Thai Highlands in northwestern Vietnam. By the end of November 1952, PAVN units had reached the Lao border. New French commander General Raoul Salan tried to halt this offensive by striking at PAVN supply lines. But Giap refused to take the bait, and Operation LORRAINE (October 29–November 8), which involved 30,000 French troops in special airborne, commando, and support formations, was soon in reverse. By December, PAVN units were still at the Lao border, and the French were back within their heavily fortified defenses in the Red River Delta.

The Viet Minh also made significant gains in central Vietnam. French control in the plateau area of the Central Highlands was narrowed to a few beachheads around Hue, Da Nang, and Nha Trang. The only areas where the French enjoyed real success were in Cochinchina and neighboring Cambodia.

In the spring of 1953, Giap assembled a powerful force to invade Laos. Laos had an army of only 10,000 men supported by 3,000 French regulars. Giap employed four divisions totaling 40,000 men and had the assistance of 4,000 communist Pathet Lao troops. Once more, the French were compelled to disperse their slender resources. They were, however, successful in preventing Giap from overrunning the Plaine des Jarres, and by late April the French halted the PAVN and inflicted heavy casualties on it. The onset of the rainy season forced the PAVN to fall back on its bases, and Laos was saved for another summer.

In July 1953, new French commander General Henri Navarre arrived in Indochina. Buoyed by pledges of increased U.S. military assistance, Navarre attempted a "general counteroffensive." The press in both France and the United States made much of the so-called Navarre Plan, but unknown to the public was Navarre's secret pessimistic assessment to his government that the war could not be won militarily and that the best that could be hoped for was a draw.

With increased resources (French forces now numbered about 517,000 men against perhaps 120,000 Viet Minh), Navarre vowed to take the offensive. He ordered the evacuation of a series of small posts and gave more responsibility to the SVN's army, although this was too little, too late.

Concurrently, Giap was gathering additional resources for a larger invasion of Laos. With five divisions he hoped to secure all Laos and perhaps Cambodia, then join up with PAVN units in the south for an assault on Saigon. In the meantime, some 60,000 guerrillas and five regular regiments would tie down the French in the north. In December 1953 and January 1954, the PAVN overran much of southern and central Laos.

The first French paratroopers arrive at the village of Dien Bien Phu in northwestern Vietnam, November 20, 1953. The defeat of the French in the ensuing Battle of Dien Bien Phu brought an end to the long Indochina War. (AP Photo)

Navarre's response was the establishment of an airhead in far northwestern Vietnam astride the main PAVN invasion route into Laos. Navarre envisioned this as either a blocking position or bait to draw enemy forces into a set-piece conventional battle, in which they would be destroyed by French artillery and airpower. The location that Navarre selected, the village of Dien Bien Phu, was in a large valley, with the French conceding the high ground around it to the PAVN. When he was asked later how he got into this position, Navarre said that at the time the French arrived PAVN forces did not have artillery, so there was no danger from the heights. Dien Bien Phu was also some 200 miles by air from Hanoi, and the French had only a very limited transport airlift capability of some 100 aircraft.

Giap took the bait, but he sent four divisions to Dien Bien Phu rather than the one that Navarre had envisioned. The siege of the French fortress lasted from March 13 to May 7, 1954, and its outcome was largely decided by the PAVN's ability to bring Chinese-supplied artillery to the heights thanks to an extensive supply network of Vietnamese civilian laborers (the "People's Porters," Giap called them) and the inadequacy of French air support. On May 7, the French garrison surrendered. Although there was some debate in Washington over possible U.S. military intervention (Operation VULTURE), President Eisenhower rejected this because the British refused to go along.

The defeat at Dien Bien Phu allowed French political leaders in Paris to shift the blame to the generals and at last bring the war to an end in a conference previously scheduled in Geneva to deal with a variety of Asian problems. The war formally ended on August 1, 1954.

SPENCER C. TUCKER

## Consequences

On June 17, 1954, Indochinese War critic Pierre Mendès-France became French premier and foreign minister. Three days later he imposed a 30-day timetable for an agreement by the Geneva Conference (April 21–July 20) and promised to resign if one was not reached. The Geneva Accords were signed on the last day of the deadline, July 20 (but only because the clocks were stopped; it was actually early on July 21).

The leading personalities at Geneva were Mendès-France, Chinese foreign minister Zhou Enlai, Soviet foreign minister Vyacheslav Molotov, British secretary of state for foreign affairs Anthony Eden, U.S. secretary of state John Foster Dulles, DRV foreign minister Pham Van Dong, and SVN foreign minister Nguyen Quoc Dinh. Dulles left the conference after only a few days. He saw no likelihood of an agreement regarding Indochina that Washington could approve, and he disliked the idea of negotiating with Zhou Enlai, as the United States did not then recognize the PRC. Dulles ordered the U.S. delegation not to participate in the discussions and to act only as observers.

The Geneva Conference produced separate armistice agreements for Vietnam, Cambodia, and Laos. Pham Van Dong found himself pressured by Zhou and Molotov into an agreement that gave the Viet Minh far less than it had won on the battlefield. The conferees established Vietnam as one state, temporarily divided at the 17th parallel pending reunification. A demilitarized zone would extend three miles (five kilometers) on either side of the line in order to prevent incidents that might lead to a breach of the armistice. The final text provided that "the military demarcation line is provisional and should not in any way be interpreted as constituting a political or territorial boundary." Vietnam's future was to be determined "on the basis of respect for the principles of independence, unity, and territorial integrity," with "national and general elections" to be held in July 1956. Troops on both sides would have up to 300 days to be regrouped north or south; civilians could also move in either direction if they so desired. The International Supervisory and Control Commission composed of representatives of Canada, Poland, and India (a Western state, a communist state, and a nonaligned state) would oversee implementation of the agreements.

Pham Van Dong was bitterly disappointed that nationwide elections were put off for two years. The DRV accepted the arrangements because of heavy pressure from the PRC and the Soviet Union and because it was confident it could control southern Vietnam. There is every reason to believe that the Chinese leadership was willing at Geneva to sabotage its ally in order to prevent the formation of a strong regional power on their southern border.

The Indochina War had really been three wars in one. Begun as a conflict between Vietnamese nationalists and France, it became a civil war between Vietnamese and was also part of the larger Cold War. In the Indochina War the French and their allies sustained 172,708 casualties: 94,581 dead or missing and 78,127 wounded. These broke down as 140,992 French Union casualties (75,867 dead or missing and 65,125 wounded), with the allied Indochina states losing 31,716 (18,714 dead or missing and 13,002 wounded). French dead or missing numbered some 20,000: 11,000 French Legionnaires, 15,000 Africans, and 46,000 Indochinese. The war took a particularly heavy toll among the officers, 1,900 of whom died. PAVN losses were probably three times those of the French and their allies. Perhaps 150,000 Vietnamese civilians also perished.

One major issue throughout the war and for some years afterward was that of prisoners held by the Viet Minh, both military and civilian. Their status was always ambiguous because they were more hostages than prisoners of war, especially as the Viet Minh did not recognize the Geneva Convention regarding prisoners of war. Their prisoners were held in barbarous conditions throughout the war and beginning in 1950 were subjected to intensive political reeducation. Only a small percentage of the 36,979 reported missing during the war returned. Depending on the source, the number of confirmed prisoners in the summer of 1954 was between 21,526 and 22,474. Only 10,754 returned home, and 6,132 of them required immediate hospitalization. Some civilians were held for up to eight years.

Regroupment of the 120,000-man French Far East Expeditionary Corps from Tonkin and 140,000 PAVN soldiers and guerrillas from the south proceeded without incident. The French had 100 days to withdraw to Haiphong and an additional 200 days to reembark them for the south. At the same time PAVN units in central and southern Vietnam carried out their own regroupment. Many northerners also took advantage of the article of the accords that allowed them free passage south during a 300-day regroupment period. The great majority of these were Roman Catholics from the Red River Delta area who often moved as entire communities. Minorities, such as the Nungs, also left. The U.S. Navy provided substantial sealift support in what was a considerable propaganda windfall for the SVN.

Former Vietnamese emperor Bao Dai, then in France, appointed Catholic politician Ngo Dinh Diem as premier of the SVN. Soon Diem brought a semblance of order, subduing the religious sects in the south and armed gangs in Saigon. His power base rested on the some 1 million northern Catholics who had relocated south.

Disagreements with Bao Dai led Diem to stage a referendum in October 1955 in which he called on the people of South Vietnam to choose between Bao Dai and himself. Diem won the vote handily, although this did not keep him from manipulating the result to make it a landslide. He then proclaimed the establishment of the Republic of Vietnam (South Vietnam), with himself as president. Diem held power until his assassination in November 1963. Claiming that he was not bound by the Geneva Accords, he refused to hold the promised elections and received strong support for his stand from President Eisenhower. When the date for the elections passed, Viet Minh political cadres in South Vietnam resumed the armed struggle, this time against the Diem government. Diem meanwhile received substantial economic aid and increasing military assistance from the United States.

In North Vietnam, Ho and other leaders were not displeased with Diem's establishment of order in South Vietnam pending the national elections. North Vietnam did face serious economic problems, for while North Vietnam contained the bulk of the industry, South Vietnam had most of the food. Ruthless moves against small landholders brought actual rebellion, crushed by PAVN troops. Then when the Viet Minh cadres left in the south to prepare for the 1956 election commenced armed struggle against Diem, the North Vietnamese leadership voted to support them, beginning the Vietnam War. The war would be extraordinarily costly to North Vietnam economically and in terms of casualties, but the desire to reunify the country overrode all other considerations. The civil war and the East-West conflict of the First Indochina War had only been suspended.

SPENCER C. TUCKER

## Timeline

| | |
|---|---|
| **1615** | By this date a permanent Catholic mission is established in Vietnam. |
| **Feb 18, 1859** | The French take possession of Saigon in Cochinchina. |
| **1862** | Vietnamese emperor Tu Duc is forced to sign a treaty with the French recognizing their conquests. |
| **1867** | The French have established their control over all of Cochinchina. |
| **1887** | The French government establishes French Indochina, consisting of Cochinchina, Annam, Tonkin (all constituting present-day Vietnam), and Cambodia. |
| **1893** | The addition of Laos completes French Indochina. |
| **Dec 27, 1927** | Vietnamese nationalists establish in Hanoi the Viet Nam Quoc Dan Dang (Vietnamese Nationalist Party, VNQDD), modeled after the Nationalist Party of China. |
| **1930–1931** | The VNQDD carries out a series of unsuccessful revolts in northern Vietnam. |
| **Feb 3, 1930** | In a meeting in Hong Kong presided over by Ho Chi Minh, Vietnamese nationalists establish the Indochinese Communist Party (ICP), also known as the Lao Dong Party. |
| **May 1941** | ICP leader Ho Chi Minh forms the Viet Minh (Vietnam Independence League), a nationalist umbrella organization dominated by the communists, to fight the French and Japanese. |
| **Mar 9, 1945** | When the Japanese learn of France's plans to liberate Indochina, they strike first, arresting and imprisoning most French administrative and military personnel. |
| **May 1945** | The Vietnam Liberation Army is formed in northern Vietnam. Commanded by Vo Nguyen Giap, it becomes the People's Army of Vietnam (PAVN), also known as the Vietnam People's Army and the North Vietnamese Army. |
| **Aug 16, 1945** | In Hanoi, Ho declares himself president of a "free Vietnam." |
| **Sep 2, 1945** | Ho proclaims the independence of the Democratic Republic of Vietnam (North Vietnam, DRV). |

| | |
|---|---|
| **Oct 5, 1945** | French general Jacques-Philippe Leclerc arrives in Saigon to take command of French forces in Indochina. |
| **Jan 1946** | Ho's supporters win elections in northern Vietnam. |
| **Mar 1946** | Ho concludes the Ho-Sainteny Agreement with French diplomat Jean Sainteny. |
| **Jun 1, 1946** | French high commissioner for Indochina Georges Thierry d'Argenlieu, on his own initiative, proclaims the formation of the "Republic of Cochinchina." |
| **Jul 6–Sep 10, 1946** | At the Fontainebleau Conference in France, the French make no concessions to the DRV. |
| **Nov 20, 1946** | Armed clashes between Vietnamese and the French occur at Lang Son and at Haiphong. |
| **Nov 23, 1946** | On d'Argenlieu's order, French forces bombard part of Haiphong. |
| **Dec 19, 1946** | Fighting begins in Hanoi, marking the beginning of the First Indochina War. Vo Nguyen Giap commands the PAVN, the military arm of the Viet Minh. |
| **May 1947** | Peace talks between French representative Paul Mus and Ho fail to reach agreement. |
| **Oct 1947** | The French mount Operation LEA, an effort to capture the DRV leadership that fails in that aim. |
| **Mar 8, 1949** | The French government concludes the Elysée Agreements with former emperor Bao Dai. These create the State of Vietnam (SVN). |
| **Oct 1, 1949** | Chinese communist leader Mao Zedong proclaims the establishment of the People's Republic of China. |
| **Jan 30, 1950** | The Soviet Union recognizes the DRV. |
| **Jun 25, 1950** | The Korean War begins. |
| **Sep–Oct 1950** | The PAVN mounts Operation LE HONG PHONG, securing much of Route Coloniale 4 in far northern Vietnam. This enables them to be supplied by China. |
| **Jan 13–Jun 18, 1951** | Giap mounts a series of offensives in Operations TRAN HUNG DAO, HOANG HOA THA, and HA NAM NIN, designed to secure Hanoi and the Red River Delta. They are halted by French forces commanded by General Jean de Lattre de Tassigny. |
| **Nov 14, 1951** | De Lattre commences the Battle of Hoa Binh. It ends on February 24, 1952, with the French proclaiming victory, but both sides suffer heavy casualties. |
| **Oct 29–Nov 8, 1952** | French commander in Indochina General Raoul Salan initiates Operation LORRAINE against Viet Minh supply areas, but Giap continues offensive operations in northwestern Vietnam. |

| | |
|---|---|
| **Mar 13–May 7, 1954** | The Viet Minh lay siege to the French strongpoint of Dien Bien Phu in northwestern Vietnam. It ends with the surrender of the French and the effective conclusion of the war. |
| **Apr 21–Jul 20, 1954** | The Geneva Accords formally end the Indochina War. The agreements establishe Vietnam as one state, temporarily divided at the 17th parallel. |
| **Jul 7, 1954** | Emperor Bao Dai appoints Ngo Dinh Diem premier of the SVN. |
| **Jul 1955** | Diem announces that the SVN will not participate in the elections mandated by the 1954 Geneva Accords. He is supported in this stance by U.S. president Dwight D. Eisenhower. |
| **Oct 23, 1955** | Diem holds a referendum in South Vietnam in which the voters overwhelming approve establishment of the Republic of Vietnam, with him as president. |
| **1957** | Viet Minh cadres left in South Vietnam reject Diem's moves, and by this date the Second Indochina War—better known as the Vietnam War—is under way. |

SPENCER C. TUCKER

## Further Reading

Buttinger, Joseph. *A Dragon Defiant: A Short History of Vietnam.* New York: Praeger, 1972.

Devillers, Philippe, and Jean Lacouture. *End of a War: Indochina, 1954.* New York: Praeger, 1969.

Duiker, William J. *The Communist Road to Power in Vietnam.* Boulder, CO: Westview, 1981.

Dunn, Peter M. *The First Vietnam War.* New York: St. Martin's, 1985.

Dunstan, Simon. *Vietnam Tracks: Armor in Battle, 1945–75.* New York: Osprey, 2004.

Fall, Bernard, B. *Hell in a Very Small Place: The Siege of Dienbienphu.* Philadelphia: J. B. Lippincott, 1966.

Fall, Bernard B. *Street without Joy.* Harrisburg, PA: Stackpole, 1961.

Fall, Bernard B. *The Two Vietnams.* New York: Praeger, 1964.

Giap, Vo Nguyen. *The Military Art of People's War.* New York: Monthly Review Press, 1970.

Gras, General Yves. *Histoire de La Guerre d'Indochine.* Paris: Éditions Denoël, 1992.

Hammer, Ellen J. *The Struggle for Indochina.* Stanford, CA: Stanford University Press, 1954.

Jian, Chen. "China and the First Indo-China War, 1950–54." *China Quarterly* 133 (March 1993): 85–110.

Kelly, George A. *Lost Soldiers: The French Army and Empire in Crisis, 1947–1962.* Cambridge, MA: MIT Press, 1965.

Le Thanh Khoi. *Le Viet-Nam: Histoire et civilisation.* Paris: Éditions de Minuit, 1955.

Maneli, Mieczyslaw. *The War of the Vanquished.* New York: Harper and Row, 1969.

Marr, David G. *Vietnamese Tradition on Trial, 1920–1945.* Berkeley: University of California Press, 1981.

Marr, David G. *Vietnam 1945: The Quest for Power.* Berkeley: University of California Press, 1995.

Porch, Douglas. *The French Foreign Legion: A Complete History of the Legendary Fighting Force.* New York: HarperCollins, 1991.

Roy, Jules. *The Battle of Dienbienphu.* New York: Pyramid Books, 1963.

Schulzinger, Robert D. *A Time for War: The United States and Vietnam, 1941–1975.* New York: Oxford University Press, 1997.

Tønnesson, Stein. *Vietnam 1946: How the War Began.* Berkeley: University of California Press, 2010.

Tucker, Spencer C. *Vietnam.* Lexington: University Press of Kentucky, 1999.

Vaïsse, Maurice, and Alain Bizard, eds. *L'Armée française dans la guerre d'Indochine (1946–1954): Adaptation ou Inadaptation?* Centre d'Études d'Histoire de la Défense. Bruxelles: Complexe, 2000.

Windrow, Martin. *The French Indochina War, 1946–1954.* London: Osprey, 1998.

# Israeli War of Independence (May 14, 1948–January 7, 1949)

## Causes

The Israeli War of Independence, also known as the First Arab-Israeli War, took place during May 14, 1948–January 7, 1949. Its causes were deep-rooted. According to the Jewish Bible, the Torah (or the Christian Old Testament), the Jews trace their origins to some 4,000 years ago. A series of Jewish kingdoms and states intermittently ruled Palestine or Israel for more than a millennium thereafter. Jews were the majority of the inhabitants of Palestine or, as the Jews called it, Israel (land of God) for many centuries, until the first century CE. Following a series of revolts against their Roman conquerors in the first century, the Romans expelled most Jews from Palestine. During the next 1,000 years, Jews settled in Western and Eastern Europe and then in the United States.

Nineteenth-century nationalism, the belief that each ethnic/linguistic grouping should have its own nation-state, impacted the Jews as well as other peoples. Persecution of Jews in Europe late in that century, especially in Russia and Poland (the pogroms) but also to a lesser extent in Central and Western Europe (for example, the Dreyfus Affair in France), led to the establishment of the Zionist movement, or the desire among many Jews to establish a national state. Called by Theodor Herzl, the First Zionist Congress was held in Basel, Switzerland, in 1897. Although other sites were discussed, Palestine, the historic homeland of the Jews before the diaspora and then part of the Ottoman Empire, was the favored and most likely location for such a state, and Jews throughout Europe contributed to the purchase of land for immigrants to settle there. Wealthy West European Jews such as the Rothschild family gave substantial sums to buy land for the Jewish settlers, most of whom were from Eastern Europe, from absentee Arab landowners. Increased Jewish immigration and continued loss of Arab lands through purchase by Jews, however, inflamed the Arab population of Palestine and led to increasing violence there.

In order to secure the support of world Jewry for the Allied cause in World War I, in 1917 the British government issued the Balfour Declaration. Named for British foreign secretary Arthur James Balfour, it expressed British support for the formation of a Jewish national homeland in Palestine. At the same time, however, in order to secure Arab support against the Ottoman Empire then at war with the Allies, the British government promised support for the establishment of an Arab state formed out of Ottoman territory in the Middle East. This found active expression in the 1916–1918 Arab Revolt in which Arab forces actively assisted British Empire forces in defeating the Ottomans in the Middle East.

As a consequence of World War I, much of the Ottoman Middle East was divided into mandates: new states that were nonetheless controlled by France and Britain under the oversight of the League of Nations. France secured the new states of Syria and Lebanon, while Britain dominated Iraq

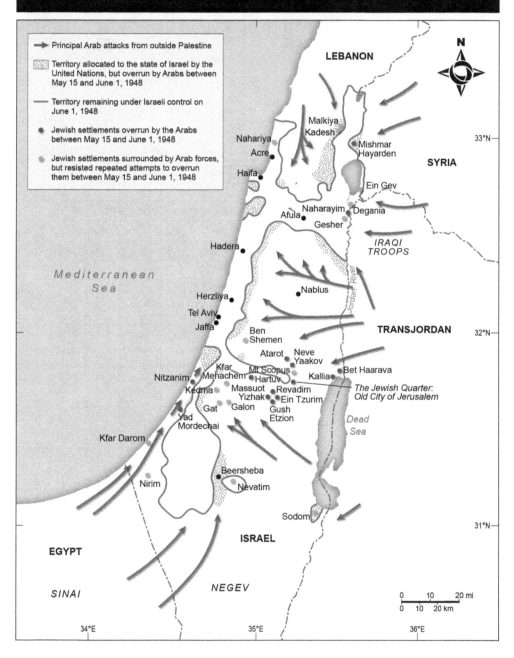

# ISRAELI WAR OF INDEPENDENCE, 1948–1949

→ Principal Arab attacks from outside Palestine

Territory allocated to the state of Israel by the United Nations, but overrun by Arabs between May 15 and June 1, 1948

— Territory remaining under Israeli control on June 1, 1948

● Jewish settlements overrun by the Arabs between May 15 and June 1, 1948

● Jewish settlements surrounded by Arab forces, but resisted repeated attempts to overrun them between May 15 and June 1, 1948

LEBANON

SYRIA

IRAQI TROOPS

TRANSJORDAN

*Mediterranean Sea*

EGYPT

SINAI

NEGEV

ISRAEL

*Dead Sea*

The Jewish Quarter: Old City of Jerusalem

and Palestine. In 1922 Britain split Palestine into Transjordan, the territory east of the Jordan River, and Palestine to its west.

Violence soon flared in Palestine in what became a triangular struggle among the British authorities, the Arabs, and the Jews largely over the matter of continued Jewish immigration there. The Arabs saw themselves becoming a marginalized minority in their own land. British policy

## Israeli War of Independence (May 14, 1948–January 7, 1949)

| Relative Strength of Opposing Forces, 1948 | | |
|---|---|---|
| | Israel | Arab States |
| May 1948 | 30,000 men | 23,000 men |
| December 1948 | 100,000 | 55,000–58,000 |

| Operation HIRAM (October 24–31, 1948) | | |
|---|---|---|
| | Israel | Arab States |
| Strength | 6,000+ men | 2,000–4,000 men |
| Losses | 100 or less | 400, killed, 550 captured* |

*As many as 50,000 Palestinians became refugees as a result of this operation.

| Peak Force Strength and Casualties, Israeli War of Independence, 1948–1949 | | | | | | |
|---|---|---|---|---|---|---|
| | Egypt | Iraq | Israel | Jordan | Lebanon | Syria |
| Population | 19,100,000 | 4,900,000 | 1,200,000 | 400,000 | 1,200,000 | 3,400,000 |
| Men mobilized | 20,000 | 15,000 | 115,000 | 8,000 | 1,000 | 5,000 |
| Men mobilized as % of population | 0.10% | 0.31% | 11.67% | 2.00% | <0.01% | 0.15% |
| Total casualties | 2,000 | 500 | 6,400 | 300 | 500 | 1,000 |

Sources: Clodfelter, Michael. *Warfare and Armed Conflict: A Statistical Reference to Casualty and Other Figures, 1618–1991*. Jefferson, NC: McFarland, 1992; Nazzal, Nafez. *The Palestinian Exodus from Galilee, 1948*. Washington, DC: Institute for Palestine Studies, 1978; Small, Melvin, and Joel David Singer. *Resort to Arms: International and Civil Wars, 1816–1980*. Thousand Oaks, CA: Sage, 1982.

vacillated, but in response to the continuing Jewish immigration, sporadic Arab attacks occurred against Jews and also British officials in Palestine. At the same time, militant Jewish groups began to agitate against what they saw as restrictive British immigration policies for Jews wishing to settle in Palestine. Armed Zionist groups such as the Lohamei Herut Israel (Stern Gang) and the Irgun carried out actions against the British administration in Palestine, and in the 1930s a three-way struggle pitted the British police and military against militant Arabs and Jews. This escalated into the so-called Arab Revolt of 1936–1939, which saw the deaths of 262 British security personnel, some 300 Jews, and perhaps 5,000 Arabs. The British government's delicate balancing act was made more difficult by the need to secure Arab (and also Jewish) support against Germany and Italy in World War II.

World War II brought the Holocaust, the Nazi effort to eradicate the Jewish people that resulted in the deaths of some 6 million Jews. The Holocaust brought heightened sympathy worldwide for the survivors. It also greatly increased the determination of Jews to establish a nation-state as the only effective means to guarantee their future survival. Sympathy for this course of action was especially strong in the United States, which now had the largest population of Jews in the world and where

Jews were an important political pressure group.

In the meantime, the British sought to restrict Jewish immigration into Palestine. During and after World War II as Jews sought to gain access to Palestine, many were forcibly turned away by British warships sent to patrol the Mediterranean coast for this very purpose. At the same time, British authorities were anxious to quit Palestine and toward that end struggled to develop a plan that would split Palestine into Arab and Jewish states. The Jews and the Arabs proved intransigent, and in February 1947 after both rejected a final proposal for partition, Britain turned the problem over to the United Nations (UN).

In August 1947, the UN recommended granting Palestine its independence. The UN also worked out a plan that would create separate Arab and Jewish states. The city of Jerusalem, holy to both Islam and Judaism, would be set up as an international area under the UN in order to preclude conflict regarding its status. Although the Arab population in Palestine was then some 1.2 million people and the Jews numbered just 600,000, the UN partition plan granted the proposed Jewish state some 55 percent of the land and the Arab state only 45 percent. Perhaps understandably, the Arab states rejected the partition plan, which included an economic union. Jews generally accepted it. The UN General Assembly approved the plan in November 1947, and the British government announced that it would accept the UN recommendation and declared that the British mandate of Palestine would come to an abrupt end on May 15, 1948.

The Council of the Arab League announced that it was prepared to prevent the creation of a Jewish state by force if necessary, and immediately following the UN vote militant Palestinian Arabs and foreign Arab fighters commenced attacks against Jewish communities in Palestine. This began what is known as the Arab-Jewish Communal War, which lasted from November 30, 1947, to May 14, 1948. The United States became the chief champion and most reliable ally of a Jewish state, a position that cost it dearly in its relations with the Arab world and greatly impacted subsequent geopolitics in the Middle East and throughout the world. It should be noted, however, that initially the Soviet Union also supported the creation of a Jewish state.

The British completed their pullout on May 14, 1948, and that same day David Ben-Gurion, executive chairman and defense minister of the Jewish Agency, declared the independent Jewish State of Israel, claiming the territory awarded to the Jewish state under the UN partition plan. Ben-Gurion became the new state's first prime minister, a post he held during 1948–1953 and 1955–1963. Immediately following Ben-Gurion's declaration, the Arab armies of Egypt, Lebanon, Jordan, Syria, and Iraq invaded Palestine, beginning the Israeli War of Independence.

SPENCER C. TUCKER

## Course

Arab forces ranged against Israeli included regulars from Egypt, Iraq, Lebanon, Syria, and Transjordan, supplemented by volunteers from Libya, Saudi Arabia, and Yemen. Officially, the Arab forces operated under the auspices of the Arab League, formed in 1945. King Abdullah of Transjordan was named commander in chief of the Arab armies, although cooperation among the Arab forces was almost nonexistent and was a chief cause of their military failure throughout the course of the war.

Abdullah I bin al-Hussein, king of Jordan, commanded the Arab forces in the Israeli War of Independence (First Arab-Israeli War) of 1948–1949. (John Phillips/The LIFE Picture Collection/Getty Images)

On May 15, the Arab League announced its intention to create a unified Palestinian state to include the Jewish and Arab regions of the UN partition plan. On May 26, the Israeli government created the Israel Defense Forces (IDF), incorporating the irregular Jewish militias that had existed under the British mandate, to include the Haganah, led by Israel Galili, and the Palmuch, commanded by Yigal Allon. The IDF initially numbered fewer than 30,000 troops, but by mid-July it had more than doubled in size. The IDF continued to grow exponentially, and by the end of 1948 it numbered more than 100,000 troops. At least initially, these forces had virtually no heavy weapons in the form of artillery, armored vehicles, or aircraft.

Although the Arab states ranged against Israel enjoyed a crushing advantage in population, their combined armies initially numbered only some 23,000 troops and increased in size to only 40,000 men in July 1948 and 55,000 by October. Still, most independent observers expected the Arabs to score a quick military victory largely because of their crushing superiority in heavy weapons at the beginning of the conflict.

The Israelis had the advantage of high morale, the fact that they were fighting on interior lines, their network of already fortified settlements known as the kibbutzim, and a unitary command structure, all of which were lacking on the Arab side. And as the fighting continued the Israeli government was able to secure some arms from abroad, beginning with a shipment of 25 aircraft from Czechoslovakia in late May. That nation continued to provide weapons to the IDF for the remainder of the war, even during UN-mandated cease-fires that prohibited arms sales to any belligerent.

During the first phase of the war, May 14–June 1, in the central part of the front, Arab armies from Transjordan and Iraq advanced on Jerusalem with the aim of driving all Jews from the city. The best Arab fighting force in the war, the Transjordan Arab Legion, secured the eastern and southern portions of the new part of the city. The legion also occupied most of Old Jerusalem and laid siege to the remainder. Although Jewish forces, ably led by American volunteer Colonel David Marcus, failed to break through the Arab roadblock on the Tel Aviv–Jerusalem road, they managed to construct a new access route (the so-called Burma Road) to Jerusalem through the mountains just before a UN-sponsored truce went into effect on June 11.

Meanwhile, Lebanese and Syrian forces invaded Palestine from the north. During June 5–6 the Lebanese captured the Jewish village of al-Malikiyya but went no farther. The Syrian invasion, which was both larger and supported by tanks and artillery, was defeated on May 20 by Jewish settlers at Degania, the oldest kibbutz in Palestine, although they possessed only light weapons. The Israelis also blunted an ineffective Iraqi invasion that crossed the Jordan River south of the Sea of Galilee. Soon the Iraqi Army shifted to a defensive posture in the regions of Jenin and Nablus.

Only in the south did Arab forces register significant territorial gains. Here two Egyptians committed some 10,000 men. These included a battalion of British-built Mark VI and Matilda tanks, artillery pieces, and aircraft in 30 Supermarine Spitfires, 4 Hawker Hurricanes, and a number of transport aircraft converted into bombers.

Two Egyptian brigades commanded by Major General Ahmed Ali al-Mwawi advanced into Palestine. The principal Egyptian force moved up the coastal road to take Gaza and threaten Tel Aviv. A smaller force moved inland from Abu Ageila by way of Beersheba toward Jerusalem. Although the Egyptian coastal force on May 29 secured Ashdod, only about 19 miles south of Tel Aviv, it bogged down shortly thereafter. The inland column was stalled by the Israelis on May 21 at the village of Ramat Rachel, just south of Jerusalem. The next day it made contact with the Arab Legion at Bethlehem. Although technically within Egyptian-conquered territory, the Israelis still held some 24 kibbutzim in the northern Negev Desert and from these harassed the Egyptian supply lines northward.

The first phase of the war ended with a UN-declared truce that went into effect on June 11. Although the truce included an

An Arab military police officer looks out on the street from a damaged Arab home in the old city of Jerusalem, on July 14, 1948, during the Israeli War of Independence. The gaping hole resulted from an Israeli mortar shell. (AP Photo/Deluce)

arms embargo for all belligerents, both sides in the war saw this as an opportunity to rest, resupply, strengthen, and reequip their forces, and the Israelis were able to smuggle in arms and ammunition from Czechoslovakia during the monthlong truce. During the cease-fire, UN mediator Folke Bernadotte advanced a new partition plan, but both sides immediately rejected it. On July 9 the cease-fire collapsed, and the IDF assumed the offensive. The second phase of the war occurred during July 9–18.

In the renewed fighting, the primary IDF objective was to regain control of the vital Tel Aviv–Jerusalem corridor in the central sector. In heavy fighting, the IDF secured the corridor after a massive assault on Lydda (present-day Lod) that included the first Israeli use of bomber aircraft. Defended by Transjordian troops and supplemented by Palestinian irregulars and units of the Arab Liberation Army, Lydda surrendered on July 11. The next day the IDF captured Ramle, another key location in the vital corridor.

In the north the IDF launched Operation DEKEL, a major push against Syrian and Lebanese troops in the lower Galilee region. The IDF captured Nazareth on July 16.

Only in the southern sector did the Israelis fail to make significant gains in the July fighting. The Egyptians had increased their strength during the cease-fire to some 18,000 men, but after preemptive attacks on July 8, just before the expiration of the cease-fire that were beaten back by the Israelis, the Egyptians abandoned plans for further offensive operations in favor of holding a series of widely scattered defensive positions. The IDF hoped to sever the Egyptian supply lines and reopen communications with the Negev, but their counterattacks were largely unsuccessful. The second phase of the war (July 9–18) ended with another UN-brokered truce, which went into effect on July 18.

Bernadotte presented yet another partition plan, this time calling for Transjordan to annex the Arab regions. It also called for the creation of an independent Jewish state and the establishment of Jerusalem as an international city. All belligerents again rejected the plan, and on September 17, the day after Bernadotte had presented his latest solution to the conflict, he was assassinated by Israeli members of Lehi, a Zionist militia.

The truce remained in effect until October 15, when the third phase of the war (October 15–November 5, 1948) began. The IDF ended the cease-fire with a series of offensives designed to drive Arab armies completely from Israeli territory. The first

strike was against Egyptian Army troops in the Negev. General al-Mwawi was well aware that his own forces, although reinforced to more than 20,000 men, were spread thin and overextended. He asked Cairo for permission to pull back and consolidate, but his request was denied.

By this time the Israelis had achieved air parity with the Arabs. Israeli Operation YOAV, commanded by Lieutenant General Yigal Allon, sought to cut off the Egyptian troops along the coast from those to the interior in the Negev. The Israelis almost cut off a large part of the Egyptian army north of Gaza, but in desperate fighting the Egyptians managed to extricate themselves while losing all the territory they had held north of Gaza. In other hard fighting the Israelis managed to cut the Ashgelon-Hebron corridor, established contact with the Negev settlements, and cut communication between the two prongs of the Egyptian forces. The Israelis also cut off some 4,000–5,000 Egyptian troops in the Negev at Fallujah, although the Egyptians there managed to hold out until the end of the war. The lack of Arab cooperation in the war was revealed when nearby Jordanian forces failed to act in support of the Egyptians. Following the Israeli capture of Beersheba on October 21, al-Mwawi was made the scapegoat for Egyptian failures and dismissed. Major General Ahmad Fucad Sadiq replaced him. The failure of the Egyptian forces in the Negev was critical to the ultimate Israeli victory.

The IDF also enjoyed success in the northern sector. On October 24 Operation HIRAM commenced in the upper Galilee region, with the IDF destroying remnants of the Arab Liberation Army, driving Lebanese forces completely out of Palestine, and pushing several miles into Lebanon. Shaky cease-fires were arranged in the north between Israeli and Syrian and Lebanese forces on November 30.

The fourth and final phase of the war occurred between November 19, 1948, and January 7, 1949, beginning with an Egyptian Army offensive on November 19. Although they failed in their design of relieving the Faluja pocket, the Egyptians were able to expand their coastal holdings around Gaza.

With cease-fires holding elsewhere, beginning on December 20, 1948, the IDF launched Operation HOREV, a major offensive designed to drive Egypt from the war. The IDF isolated Rafah on December 22 and secured Asluj and Auja, both on December 27. Halted by Egyptian forces in their effort to take El Arish, the Israelis turned to the northeast. With the IDF about to launch a major attack on Rafah, Egypt requested an immediate armistice, which the UN Security Council granted. The cease-fire went into effect on January 7, 1949.

With the cease-fire, UN mediator Dr. Ralph Bunche began armistice discussions between Israel and the Arab belligerent states. Armistice agreements, but no peace treaties, were ultimately concluded between Israel and all the Arab belligerents except Iraq. The arrangement with Egypt went into effect on February 24. It left Egyptian troops in occupation of the Gaza Strip. In the March 23 agreement with Lebanon, Israel agreed to withdraw from territory it had captured in southern Lebanon. The Israeli-Transjordan armistice of April 3 allowed Transjordanian troops to remain in control of the West Bank and East Jerusalem. The Israeli-Syrian armistice of July 20 resulted in the creation of a demilitarized zone along the Israeli-Syrian border. The costliest of Israel's modern wars, the fighting had claimed some 6,000 Israeli lives, one-third of them civilians.

Arab losses were much higher, on the order of 10,000 killed.

SPENCER C. TUCKER

## Consequences

The war ended with the new Jewish state occupying about three-fourths of the former British mandate of Palestine, or about 50 percent more land than offered in Bernadotte's original partition proposal. Although the figure is in dispute, as many as 1 million Arab Palestinians may have either voluntarily left or were driven from their homes and lands by the Israelis during the war. This is known in the Arab world as the Nakba (Catastrophe or Cataclysm). The Palestinians who had fled were forced to live in makeshift refugee camps in the adjacent Arab states, which insisted on keeping them in such camps until they were allowed to return. Refugee status has been passed on to their descendants, who have also been denied citizenship in their host countries on the insistence of the Arab League in order to preserve their Palestinian identity "and protect their right of return to their homeland." More than 1.5 million Palestinians still live in 58 recognized refugee camps, while more than 5 million Palestinians live outside Israel and the Palestinian Territories.

Meanwhile, the Israelis established their new state. The center-left Mapai Party was the dominant political force in Israel until its merger into the present Israeli Labor Party in 1968. It and the successor Labor Party were social democratic parties with strong roots in Zionism. They were hawkish on defense but favored a mixed moderate socialist and free enterprise economy and society.

The provisional government held power until February 14, 1949. Democratic elections on January 25, 1949, established a single-house parliament—later known as the Knesset—of 120 deputies. As in the British parliamentary system, the executive (cabinet) is selected by the Knesset and subject to being overthrown by it. Israel also adopted a system of proportional representation in which seats in the Knesset were based on the percentage of votes received. This meant that parties receiving very few votes in parliamentary elections would have representation in the Knesset. Typically 10 parties have been represented in the Knesset. These include those representing the minority Arab population, those espousing Orthodox Judaism, communists, and Revisionist Zionist groups. Coalition government was the inevitable result. The only faction to ever gain a majority of Knesset seats was Alignment, an alliance of the Labor Party and Mapam that held an absolute majority for a brief period from 1968 to 1969. Historically the Israeli government has alternated between periods of rule by the center-left Israeli Labor Party, in coalition with several left-wing parties, and the right-wing Likud, in coalition with several right-wing and religious parties.

On May 11, 1949, Israel was admitted as the 59th member of the UN. On July 5, 1950, Israel promulgated the so-called right-of-return law, which stipulates the right of any Jew to settle in Israel. In 1951 alone 687,000 Jews arrived in Israel, some 300,000 from the Arab states. While these new citizens from all over the world doubled the population of the Jewish state, absorbing them proved to be a daunting challenge. The immigrants included those from Eastern and Central Europe (Ashkenazi Jews), West European Jews (Sephardim), and Middle Eastern or Oriental Jews (Arabs who practice the Jewish religion). Difficulties posed by cultural differences and widely divergent economic circumstances proved daunting. Jewish communities abroad, especially in the United States, provided funds, as did the U.S. government. An unlikely and important boost came from the Federal Republic of Germany, where Chancellor Konrad Adenauer secured legislation that provided billions of dollars in assistance to Israel over a 12-year period. Israel's formative years also saw the creation of a mixed socialist-capitalist economy. Included in this were agricultural incentives to open more land to cultivation.

In foreign affairs, the relatively small and short Israeli War of Independence had immense consequences internationally. The surprising Israeli victory humiliated the Arab states and fueled demand for revenge, which continues in some quarters of the Muslim world today. The failure to reach a comprehensive peace settlement would see vast sums spent on armament (in both Israel and Arab states) rather than on infrastructure and social programs. The lack of a peace settlement also embroiled the major world powers in a series of crises, many of which revolved around securing the area's vast oil supplies, and would become a constant source of unrest in the Middle East.

At first, the interests of the United States and those of the Soviet Union regarding the Jewish state converged. Indeed, the U.S. recognition of Israel came only shortly before that of the Soviet Union. Moscow found common ground with the Jews in their suffering at the hands of the Nazis in World War II and also identified with the socialism espoused by the early Jewish settlers in Palestine as well as their anti-British stance. The Cold War, the reemergence of official anti-Semitism in the Soviet Union, and Moscow's desire to court the Arab states by supporting Arab nationalism against the West soon changed all that, with the Soviet Union becoming the major arms supplier and chief supporter of the Arabs against Israel.

The 1949 cease-fires that ended the 1948–1949 war were not followed by peace agreements. The Arab states not only refused to recognize the existence of Israel but also refused to concede defeat in the war. By 1950, they had imposed an economic and political boycott on Israel. Throughout most of the 1950s, Israel suffered from repeated attacks and raids from neighboring Arab states as well as Palestinian Arab paramilitary and terrorist groups. Aggressive Israeli retaliation failed to stop them. Continuing Arab frustration and hostility resulted in two major wars—the 1967 Six-Day War and the 1973 Yom Kippur/Ramadan War—as well as many smaller conflicts including the 1982 Israeli invasion of Lebanon and numerous incursions and terror attacks.

The perennially unstable environment of the Middle East continued into the 21st century, producing a major war in Iraq and significant rebellions in Yemen, Egypt, Libya, and Syria. It also led to the rise of extremist, fundamentalist Islamic groups such as the Islamic State of Iraq and Syria, or ISIS, which now imperils Iraq as well as Syria.

SPENCER C. TUCKER

## Timeline

**1897–1916**     The First Zionist Congress is held in Basel, Switzerland, called by Austrian Jew Theodor Herzl. It has as its goal the establishment of a Jewish national state, with the most likely location being Palestine. European Jews contribute funds to buy land for immigrants to settle there. Increased Jewish immigration and continued loss of Arab lands inflames Palestine's Arab population and leads to increasing violence there.

**1916–1918**     In the Arab Revolt, Arab forces assist the British in defeating the Ottomans in the Middle East. In return, the British pledge support for an independent Arab nation there.

**Nov 2, 1917**     The British government issues the Balfour Declaration, expressing British support for the formation of a Jewish national homeland in Palestine.

**1919**     Britain and France divide the Middle East into new states that are controlled by France and Britain as League of Nations mandates. France secures Syria and Lebanon, while Britain dominates Iraq and Palestine.

**1922**     Britain divides Palestine into Transjordan, the territory east of the Jordan River, and Palestine, to its west.

**1930s**     Violence flares in Palestine in what becomes a triangular struggle among British authorities, the Arabs, and the Jews largely over the matter of continued Jewish immigration there.

| | |
|---|---|
| **1936–1939** | The so-called Arab Revolt brings the deaths of 262 British security personnel, some 300 Jews, and perhaps 5,000 Arabs. |
| **1939–1945** | World War II precipitates the Nazi Holocaust, bringing heightened sympathy worldwide for the survivors. It also increases the Jews' determination to establish a homeland. |
| **1945–1947** | The British continue efforts to restrict Jewish immigration into Palestine. The British are also anxious to quit Palestine and toward that end endeavor to concoct a plan to split Palestine into Arab and Jewish states. |
| **Feb 1947** | With both the Jews and the Arabs having rejected a final partition proposal, Britain turns the problem over to the United Nations (UN). |
| **Aug 1947** | The UN recommends granting Palestine independence and also works out a plan to create separate Arab and Jewish states there. The Arabs reject the plan, while the Jews generally accept it. |
| **Nov 1947** | The UN General Assembly approves the partition plan, and the British government announces that its mandate of Palestine will end on May 15, 1948. |
| **Nov 30, 1947– May 14, 1948** | In the Arab-Jewish Communal War following the UN vote, militant Palestinian Arabs and foreign Arab fighters attack Jews in Palestine. |
| **May 14, 1948** | David Ben-Gurion declares the Jewish state of Israel within the territory awarded to the Jewish state under the UN partition plan. The armed forces of Egypt, Lebanon, Jordan, Syria, and Iraq immediately invade Palestine, beginning the Israeli War of Independence. |
| **May 15, 1948** | The Arab League announces its intention to create a unified Palestinian state to include the Jewish and Arab regions of the UN partition plan. |
| **May 15–17, 1948** | Iraqi forces fail to capture Gesher. |
| **May 20, 1948** | Syrian forces are stopped by Jewish settlers at the Degania kibbutz. |
| **May 21, 1948** | The inland Egyptian column driving up from the south is stalled by the Israelis on May 21 at the village of Ramat Rachel, just south of Jerusalem. |
| **May 26, 1948** | The new Israeli government creates the Israel Defense Forces (IDF), formed of the irregular Jewish militias of the British mandate. |
| **May 29, 1948** | The coastal Egyptian column driving up from the south captures Ashdod only about 19 miles south of Tel Aviv but is halted shortly thereafter. |
| **Early Jun 1948** | The Transjordan Arab Legion, having occupied much of Jerusalem, besieges the remainder. Although Jewish forces under American volunteer Colonel David Marcus fail to break through the Arab |

roadblock on the Tel Aviv–Jerusalem road, they manage to construct a new access route to Jerusalem.

**Jun 5–6, 1948**    Lebanese forces capture the Jewish village of al-Malikiyya but then bog down.

**Jun 11, 1948**    A UN-sponsored truce takes effect. During the cease-fire, UN mediator Folke Bernadotte advances a new partition plan, but both sides reject it.

**Jul 9, 1948**    The cease-fire collapses, and the IDF assumes the offensive. The second phase of the war occurrs during July 9–18.

**Jul 11–12, 1948**    In heavy fighting the IDF secures the vital Tel Aviv–Jerusalem corridor following a massive assault on Lydda (present-day Lod) on July 11 and Ramle on July 12.

**Jul 16, 1948**    The IDF captures Nazareth.

**Jul 18, 1948**    A second UN-brokered truce goes into effect.

**Sep 16, 1948**    Bernadotte presents yet another partition plan. All belligerents reject it.

**Sep 17, 1948**    Bernadotte is assassinated by Israeli members of Lehi, a Zionist militia.

**Oct 15, 1948**    With the expiration of the truce, fighting resumes in the third phase of the war (October 15–November 5, 1948). The IDF opens a series of offensives to drive Arab armies completely from Israeli territory.

**Oct 21, 1948**    IDF forces capture Beersheba.

**Oct 24, 1948**    The IDF destroys remnants of the Arab Liberation Army in the upper Galilee. Lebanese forces are driven from Palestine, and the IDF pushes several miles into Lebanon.

**Nov 30, 1948**    Shaky cease-fires are arranged between Israeli and Syrian and Lebanese forces.

**Nov 19, 1948**    The fourth and final phase of the war begins. The Egyptians are able to expand their coastal holdings around Gaza.

**Dec 20, 1948**    Taking advantage of cease-fires elsewhere, the IDF launches a major offensive designed to drive Egypt from the war.

**Dec 22, 1948**    The IDF isolates Rafah.

**Dec 27, 1948**    The IDF secures Asluj and Auja.

**Jan 7, 1949**    With the IDF about to launch a major attack on Rafah, Egypt requests an immediate armistice, which the UN Security Council grants, and the cease-fire goes into effect on this date.

**Jan 25, 1949**    Democratic elections in Israel establish a single-house parliament—later known as the Knesset—of 120 deputies. The executive (cabinet) is selected by the Knesset.

| | |
|---|---|
| **Feb 14, 1949** | The Israeli provisional government comes to an end, and Ben-Gurion becomes the first prime minister. |
| **Feb 24, 1949** | An armistice is concluded between Israel and Egypt. It leaves Egyptian troops in occupation of the Gaza Strip. |
| **Mar 23, 1949** | An armistice is concluded between Israel and Lebanon. Israel agrees to withdraw from territory it has captured in southern Lebanon. |
| **Apr 3, 1949** | An armistice is concluded between Israel and Transjordan. It allows Transjordanian troops to remain in control of the West Bank and East Jerusalem. |
| **May 11, 1949** | Israel becomes a member state of the UN. |
| **Jul 20, 1949** | An armistice is concluded between Israel and Syria. It creates a demilitarized zone along the Israeli-Syrian border. |
| **Jul 5, 1950** | Israel promulgates the so-called right-of-return law, which permits any Jew to settle in Israel and become a citizen. |

SPENCER C. TUCKER

**Further Reading**

Bowyer Bell, John. *Terror Out of Zion: The Fight for Israeli Independence.* New Brunswick, NJ: Transaction Publishers, 1996.

Bregman, Ahron. *Israel's Wars: A History since 1947.* London: Routledge, 2002.

Dupuy, Trevor N. *Elusive Victory: The Arab-Israeli Wars, 1947–1974.* Garden City, NY: Military Book Club, 2002.

Heller, Joseph. *The Birth of Israel, 1945–1949: Ben-Gurion and His Critics.* Gainesville: University Press of Florida, 2001.

Herzog, Chaim. *The Arab-Israeli Wars: War and Peace in the Middle East.* New York: Random House, 1984.

Joseph, Dov. *The Faithful City: The Siege of Jerusalem, 1948.* New York: Simon and Schuster, 1960.

Karsh, Efraim. *The Arab-Israeli Conflict: The Palestine War, 1948.* New York: Osprey, 2002.

Kurzman, Dan. *Genesis 1948: The First Arab-Israeli War.* New York: World Publishing, 1970.

Lustick, Ian. *From War to War: Israel vs. the Arabs, 1948–1967.* New York: Garland, 1994.

Morris, Benny. *1948: The First Arab-Israeli War.* New Haven, CT: Yale University Press, 2008.

Pollack, Kenneth M. *Arabs at War: Military Effectiveness, 1948–1991.* Lincoln: University of Nebraska Press, 2002.

Rogan, Eugene L., and Avi Shlaim, eds. *The War for Palestine: Rewriting the History of 1948.* 2nd ed. Cambridge: Cambridge University Press, 2007.

Sachar, Howard M. *A History of Israel.* New York: Knopf, 1979.

# Algerian War of Independence (1954–1962)

## Causes

The Algerian War of Independence (also known as the Algerian War and the Algerian Revolution) was fought between Algerian nationalists known as the Front de Libération Nationale (National Liberation Front, FLN) and the French military between November 1, 1954, and March 19, 1962. The war led to a considerable expenditure of blood and treasure, saw some 1 million Frenchmen serve in the French Army in Algeria, claimed more than a score of French ministries, and brought the end of the French Fourth Republic, replaced by the Fifth Republic. The war also did not bring peace in Algeria.

France had established its control over Algeria more than a century earlier. On June 14, 1830, a French expeditionary force of some 34,000 men commanded by Marshal Louis Auguste Victor, Count de Ghaisnes de Bourmont, landed near Algiers. The pretext for the invasion was the insult to French consul to Algiers Pierre Duval, who had been struck with a fly-swatter by Dey Husain in 1827. The French also sought to remove a threat to their Mediterranean trade, but the real reason behind French king Charles X's plan to take Algiers was to shore up his unpopular French government, headed by Prince Jules de Polignac, and enable it to win the 1830 national elections.

Algiers was duly taken on July 5, although Charles X's political gambit failed, as France experienced a revolution on July 28–30. In this July Revolution of 1830, Charles X was forced to abdicate in favor of his cousin Louis Philippe, Duc d'Orléans, who nonetheless decided to continue French military operations in Algeria.

French control was initially largely limited to the coastal areas and cities. A succession of French commanders proceeded to fight a variety of opponents and campaigns in widely differing terrain, from the Atlas Mountains to salt marshes and the *bled* (interior). Beginning in 1835 Abd al-Qadir, emir of Mascara in western Algeria, declared jihad (holy war) and fought the French. Following a number of battles, he was ultimately forced to surrender in December 1847 to French general Thomas Robert Bugeaud de la Piconnerie, who proved to be an adroit colonial administrator.

By 1847, some 50,000 Europeans had settled in Algeria. French control over the Algerian interior was not accomplished until the Second Empire of Napoleon III (1852–1870), however. European settlement increased following the French defeat in the Franco-Prussian War of 1870–1871 and the German acquisition of Alsace and Lorraine. Many of the French who had lived in the two provinces chose to settle in Algeria rather than be under German rule.

While more Frenchmen immigrated to Algeria, the imbalance between them and the Muslim population ballooned. The Pax Franca brought finis to the tribal wars and disease that had kept the population relatively static. Another factor in the burgeoning Muslim population was the greatly improved medical care that dramatically decreased the infant mortality rate.

Unique among French colonies, Algeria became a political component of France, as the three French departments of Algiers,

Algerian War of Independence (1954–1962)

| Number of People Killed, Arrested, and Executed, Sétif Uprising (May 8–June 5, 1945) | | | |
|---|---|---|---|
| | Killed | Arrested | Executed |
| French/Europeans | 100+ | N/A | N/A |
| Algerians | 1,165–10,000 | 4,500 | 99 |

| Number of Deaths during the National Liberation Front's Philippeville Offensive (August 20, 1954) | | |
|---|---|---|
| Colons | Pro-French Muslims | Army of National Liberation |
| 71 | 52 | 134 |

| Casualty and Arrest Figures during the Battle of Algiers (September 30, 1956–September 24, 1957) | | | | |
|---|---|---|---|---|
| | Killed | Wounded | Arrested | Missing |
| National Liberation Front | 1,000+ | Unknown | 24,000 | 3,000 |
| French, pro-French forces | 300 | 900 | N/A | N/A |

| Total Deaths, All Causes, Algerian War of Independence (1954–1962) | |
|---|---|
| Colons | 3,000 |
| Muslims | 300,000 |
| French and pro-French forces | 18,000 |

**Sources:** Horne, Alistair. *A Savage War of Peace: Algeria 1954–1962*. London: Macmillan, 1977; Trinquier, Roger. *Modern Warfare: A French View of Counterinsurgency*. Westport, CT: Praeger Security International, 2006.

Constantine, and Oran all had limited representation in the French Chamber of Deputies. Nonetheless, the three Algerian departments were not like those of the Metropole, as only the European settlers, known as colons or *pieds-noirs*, enjoyed full rights there. The colon and Muslim populations lived separate and unequal lives. The Europeans controlled the vast majority of the economic enterprises and wealth, while the Muslims tended to be agricultural laborers. Meanwhile, the French expanded Algeria's frontiers deep into the Sahara.

While the colons sought to preserve their status, French officials vacillated between promoting colon interests and advancing reforms for the Muslims. Pro-Muslim reform efforts failed because of political pressure from the colons and their representatives in Paris. While French political theorists debated between assimilation and autonomy for Algeria's Muslims, the Muslim majority were increasingly resentful of the privileged colon status.

World War I helped fuel Algerian Muslim nationalist sentiment, but the first Muslim political organizations appeared in the 1930s, the most important of these being Ahmed Messali Hadj's Mouvement pour le Triomphe des Libertés Démocratiques (Movement for the Triumph of

Democratic Liberties, MTLD). World War II brought opportunities for change. Following the Anglo-American landings in North Africa in November 1942, Muslim activists met with American envoy Robert Murphy and Free French general Henri Giraud concerning postwar freedoms but received no firm commitments. However, 60,000 Algerian Muslims who had fought for France were granted French citizenship.

It came as a great shock to the French when pent-up Muslim frustrations exploded on May 8, 1945, during the course of a victory parade approved by French authorities celebrating the end of World War II in Europe. A French plainclothes policeman shot to death a young marcher carrying an Algerian flag, and this touched off a bloody rampage, often referred to as the Sétif Massacre. Muslims attacked Europeans and their property, and violence quickly spread to outlying areas.

The French authorities then unleashed a violent crackdown that included Foreign Legionnaires and Senegalese troops, tanks, aircraft, and even naval gunfire from a cruiser in the Mediterranean. Settler militias and local vigilantes took a number of Muslim prisoners from jails and executed them. Major French military operations lasted two weeks, while smaller actions continued for a month. Some 4,500 Algerians were arrested; 99 people were sentenced to death, and another 64 were given life imprisonment. Casualty figures remain in dispute. At least 100 Europeans died. The official French figure of Muslim dead was 1,165, but this is certainly too low, and figures as high as 10,000 have been cited.

In March 1946 the French government announced a general amnesty and released many of the Sétif detainees, including moderate Algerian nationalist leader Ferhat Abbas, although his Friends of the Manifesto and Liberty political party, formed in 1938, was dissolved. The fierce nature of the French repression of the uprising was based on a perception that any leniency would be interpreted as weakness and would only encourage further unrest.

The Sétif Uprising, which was not followed by any meaningful French reform, drove a wedge between the two communities in Algeria. Europeans now distrusted Muslims, and the Muslims never forgave the violence of the repression. French authorities did not understand the implications of this. A number of returning Muslim veterans of the war, including Ahmed Ben Bella, now joined the more militant MTLD. Ben Bella went on to form the Organization Speciale and soon departed for Egypt to enlist the support of its leaders.

Genuine political reform proved impossible, as granting full representation to Algeria would have entailed giving it a quarter of the seats in the National Assembly. The result was the compromise Algerian Statute, approved by the French National Assembly in September 1947. For the first time, Algeria was recognized as having administrative autonomy. The heart of the statute, however, was the creation of an Algerian Assembly consisting of two coequal 60-member assemblies. Although all Algerians were classified as French citizens, the first college included all non-Muslim French citizens and those Muslims French citizens who had been so defined by virtue of military service or education. The second college provided for all other Muslims. A total of 469,023 Europeans and 63,194 Muslims were eligible to vote in the first college, and 1,301,072 Muslims were eligible to vote in the second college. Thus, for all practical purposes, the first college represented the 1.5 million Europeans, and the second represented the 9.5 million Muslims.

The deputies, while elected separately, voted together. To prevent the Muslims from having a majority by securing only one vote in the first college, a two-thirds vote could be demanded by the governor-general or 30 members of the Assembly. Designed to give the Muslims some voice in their governance while ensuring European control, the Algerian Statute proved to be a poor compromise. Still, it might have worked were it not for the fact that the mandatory elections, commencing in April 1948, were rigged. As a result, the period from 1948 to the start of the rebellion in 1954 was marked by increasing bitterness and conflict between the two Algerian communities.

Proindependence Algerian Muslims were emboldened by the May 1954 Viet Minh victory over French forces at Dien Bien Phu during the Indochina War (1946–1954), and when Algerian Muslim nationalist leaders met Democratic Republic of Vietnam president Ho Chi Minh at the Bandung Conference in April 1955, he assured them that the French could be defeated. Ben Bella and his compatriots, having established the FLN on October 10, 1954, began the Algerian War on the night of October 31–November 1.

SPENCER C. TUCKER

## Course

Early on November 1, 1954, armed members of the FLN carried out a number of small attacks across Algeria. The French government, which was then dealing with independence movements in neighboring Tunisia and Morocco, had not anticipated a similar development in Algeria. After all, Algeria had been French territory since 1830 (Tunisia had been acquired only in 1881 and Morocco in the period 1904–1911). Unlike Morocco and Tunisia, which were classed as protectorates, Algeria was held to be an integral part of France. Indeed, for some months the French people and press failed to recognize the significance of what was happening and chose to characterize the rebels as *fellagha* (outlaws).

There were valid reasons for the French to fight in order to retain Algeria. Unlike Indochina, it was in close proximity to France, just across the Mediterranean. The French had largely created modern Algeria, as the deys had only controlled a narrow coastal strip around Algiers itself. There were more than 1 million Europeans living there, and they would be unwilling to concede place to Arab nationalism. Finally, there was the French Army. Its professional soldiers had almost immediately been transferred from Indochina to Algeria. Believing strongly that they had been denied the resources necessary to win the Indochina War (1946–1954) and in the end had been sold out by their government, they were determined that this would not be the case in Algeria.

Ultimately France committed a force of 450,000 men to the war, and upwards of 1 million Frenchmen would serve there. Unlike the Indochina War, this included draftees. As the conflict intensified, French officials sought support from the North Atlantic Treaty Organization (NATO), arguing that keeping Algeria French would ensure that NATO's southern flank would be safe from communism. As a part of France, Algeria was included in the original NATO Charter, but the French government position did not receive a sympathetic response in Washington or in other NATO capitals. Only too late did a succession of

French governments attempt to carry out reform.

The FLN goal was to end French control of Algeria and drive out or eliminate the colon population. The FLN was organized in six military districts, or *wilayas*, along rigidly hierarchical lines. Wilaya 4, located near Algiers, was especially important, and the FLN was particularly active in Kabylia and the Aurés Mountains. The party tolerated no dissent. In form and style it resembled Soviet bloc communist parties, although it claimed to offer a noncommunist and non-Western alternative ideology, articulated by Frantz Fanon. The FLN military arm was the Armée de Libération Nationale (Army of National Liberation, ALN).

Any hope of reconciliation between the two sides was destroyed by a major FLN military operation on August 20, 1954. On that date, its personnel, having infiltrated the port city of Philippeville, killed 71 colons and 52 pro-French Muslims (mostly local politicians), while the French police and military killed 134 ALN troops. On the same day, the ALN attacked and slaughtered European women and children living in the countryside surrounding Constantine while the men were at work. At El-Halia, a sulfur-mining community with some 120 Europeans living peacefully among 2,000 Algerian Muslims, 37 Europeans, including 10 children, were tortured and killed. Another 13 were badly wounded. Several hours later French paratroopers arrived, supported by military aircraft. The next morning they gathered about 150 Muslims together and executed them.

The French administration now allowed the settlers to arm themselves and form self-defense units, measures that the reformist governor-general Jacques Soustelle had earlier vetoed. European vigilante

groups are reported to have subsequently carried out summary killings of Muslims. Soustelle reported a total of 1,273 Muslims killed in what he characterized as "severe" reprisals.

The Arab League strongly supported the FLN, while Egypt under President Gamal Abdel Nasser was a source of weapons and other assistance. The French government's grant of independence to both Tunisia and Morocco in March 1956 further bolstered Algerian nationalism. When Israeli, British, and French forces invaded Egypt in the Suez Crisis of 1956, the United States condemned the move and forced their withdrawal. The Algerian insurgents were emboldened by the French defeat. The French now also found themselves contending with FLN supply bases in Tunisia that they could neither attack nor eliminate. Also in 1956, the government of Socialist Party premier Guy Mollet transferred the bulk of the French Army to Algeria.

The major engagement of the war was the battle for control of the Casbah district of Algiers, a district of some 100,000 people in the Algerian capital city. With the guillotining in Algiers in June 1956 of several FLN members who had killed Europeans, FLN commander of the Algiers Autonomous Zone Saadi Yacef received instructions to kill any European between the ages of 18 and 54 but no women, children, or old people. During a three-day span in June, Yacef's roaming squads shot down 49 Europeans. It was the first time in the war that such random acts of terrorism had occurred in Algiers and began a spiral of violence there.

Hard-line European supporters of Algérie française (French Algeria) then decided to take matters into their own hands, and on the night of August 10 André Achiary, a former member of the French government's counterintelligence service, planted a bomb in a building in the Casbah that had supposedly housed the FLN, but the ensuing blast destroyed much of the neighborhood and claimed 79 lives. No one was arrested for the blast, and the FLN was determined to avenge the deaths.

Yacef, who had created a carefully organized network of some 1,400 operatives as well as bomb factories and hiding places, received orders to undertake random bombings against Europeans, a first for the capital. On September 30, 1956, 3 female FLN members planted bombs in the Milk-Bar, and in a cafeteria and a travel agency. The later bomb failed to go off owing to a faulty timer, but the other two blasts killed 3 people and wounded more than 50, including a number of children. This event is generally regarded as the beginning of the Battle of Algiers (September 30, 1956–September 24, 1957).

Violence now took hold in Algiers. Both Muslim and European populations in the city were in a state of terror. Schools closed in October, and on December 28 Mayor Amédée Froger was assassinated.

On January 7, 1957, French governor-general Robert Lacoste called in General Raoul Salan, new French commander in Algeria, and Brigadier General Jacques Massu, commander of the elite 4,600-man 10th Colonial Parachute Division, recently arrived from Suez. Lacoste ordered them to restore order in the capital city, no matter the method.

In addition to his own men, Massu could call on other French military units totaling perhaps 8,000 men. He also had the city's 1,500-man police force. Massu divided the city into four grids, with one of his regiments assigned to each. Lieutenant Colonel Marcel Bigeard's 3rd Colonial Parachute Regiment had responsibility for the Casbah itself.

The French set up a series of checkpoints. They also made use of identity cards and instituted aggressive patrolling and house-to-house searches. Massu was ably assisted by his chief of staff, Colonel Yves Godard, who soon made himself *the* expert on the Casbah. Lieutenant Colonel Roger Trinquier organized an intelligence-collection system that included paid Muslim informants and employed young French paratroopers disguised as workers to operate in the Casbah and identify FLN members. Trinquier organized a database on the Muslim civilian population. The French also employed harsh interrogation techniques of suspects, including the use of torture that included electric shock.

The army broke a called Muslim general strike at the end of January in only a few days. Yacef was able to carry out more bombings, but the French Army ultimately won the battle and took the FLN leadership prisoner, although Yacef was not captured until September 1957. Some 3,000 of 24,000 Muslims arrested during the Battle of Algiers were never seen again. The French side lost an estimated 300 dead and 900 wounded.

The Battle of Algiers had a widespread negative impact for the French military effort in Algeria, however. Although the army embarked on an elaborate cover-up, its use of torture soon became public knowledge and created a firestorm that greatly increased opposition in Metropolitan France to the war. It should be noted, however, that the French employed torture to force FLN operatives to talk, and some were murdered in the process. The FLN, on the other hand, routinely murdered captured French soldiers and civilian Europeans.

French soldiers conducting house-to-house searches in the Casbah in the Battle of Algiers during the Algerian War. (Bettmann/Getty Images)

In an effort to cut off the FLN from outside support, the French also erected the Morice Line. Named for French minister of defense André Morice, it ran for some 200 miles from the Mediterranean Sea in the north into the Sahara in the south. The line was centered on an 8-foot tall 5,000-volt electric fence that ran its entire length. Supporting this was a 50-yard-wide "killing zone" on each side of the fence rigged with antipersonnel mines. The line was also covered by previously ranged 105mm howitzers. A patrolled track paralleled the fence on its Algerian side. The Morice Line was bolstered by electronic sensors that provided warning of any attempt to pierce the barrier. Searchlights operated at night.

Although manning the line required a large number of French soldiers, it did significantly reduce infiltration by the FLN from Tunisia. By April 1958, the French estimated that they had defeated 80 percent of FLN infiltration attempts. This contributed greatly to the isolation of those FLN units within Algeria reliant on support from Tunisia. The French subsequently constructed a less extensive barrier, known as the Pedron Line, along the Algerian border with Morocco.

Despite victory in Algiers, French forces were not able to end the Algerian rebellion or gain the confidence of the colons. Some colons grew fearful that the French government was about to negotiate with the FLN, and in the spring of 1958 there were a number of plots to change the colonial government. Colon and army veteran Pierre Lagaillarde organized hundreds of commandos and began a revolt on May 13, 1958. A number of senior army officers, determined that the French government not repeat what had happened in Indochina, lent support. Massu quickly formed the Committee of Public Safety, and Salan assumed its leadership.

The plotters would have preferred someone more frankly authoritarian, but Salan called for the return to power of General Charles de Gaulle. Although de Gaulle had been out of power for more than a decade, on May 19 he announced his willingness to assume authority.

Massu was prepared to bring back de Gaulle by force if necessary, and plans were developed to dispatch paratroopers to Metropolitan France from Algeria, but this option was not needed. On June 1, 1958, the French National Assembly invested de Gaulle with the premiership; technically he was the last premier of the Fourth Republic. De Gaulle ultimately established a new French political framework, the Fifth Republic, with greatly enhanced presidential powers.

De Gaulle visited Algeria five times between June and December 1958. At Oran on June 4, he said about France in Algeria that "she is here forever." A month later he proposed 15 billion francs for Algerian housing, education, and public works, and that October he suggested an even more sweeping proposal, known as the Constantine Plan. The funding for the massive projects, however, was never forthcoming. True reform was never realized and in any case was probably too late to impact the Muslim community.

Algeria's new military commander, General Maurice Challe, arrived in Algeria on December 12, 1958, and launched a series of attacks on FLN positions in rural Kabylia in early 1959. The Harkis, Muslim troops loyal to France, guided special mobile French troops called Commandos de Chasse. An aggressive set of sorties deep in Kabylia made considerable headway, and Challe calculated that by the end of October his men had killed half of the FLN operatives there. A second phase of the offensive was to occur in 1960, but by then de Gaulle, who had gradually eliminated options, had decided that Algerian independence was inevitable.

In late August 1959, de Gaulle braced his generals for the decision and then addressed the nation on September 19, 1959, declaring his support for Algerian self-determination. Fearing for their future, some die-hard colons created the Front Nationale Français and fomented another revolt on January 24, 1960, in the so-called Barricades Week. Mayhem ensued when policemen tried to restore order, and a number of people were killed or wounded. General Challe and the colony's governor, Paul Delouvrier, fled Algiers on January 28, but the next day de Gaulle, wearing his old army uniform, turned the tide via a televised address to the nation. On February 1 army units swore loyalty to the government, and the revolt quickly collapsed.

Early in 1961, increasingly desperate Ultras formed a terrorist group called the Secret Army Organization. It targeted colons whom they regarded as traitors and also carried out bombings in France and attempted to assassinate de Gaulle.

The Generals' Putsch of April 20–26, 1961, was a serious threat to de Gaulle's regime. General Challe wanted a revolt limited to Algeria, but Salan and his colleagues (Ground Forces chief of staff General André Zeller and recently retired inspector general of the air force Edmond Jouhaud) had prepared for a revolt in France as well. The generals had the support of many frontline officers in addition to almost two divisions of troops. The Foreign Legion arrested commander of French forces in Algeria General Fernand Gambiez, and paratroopers near Rambouillet prepared to march on Paris after obtaining armored support. The coup collapsed, however, as police units managed to convince the paratroopers to depart, and army units again swore loyalty to de Gaulle.

On June 10, 1961, de Gaulle held secret meetings with FLN representatives in Paris, and then on June 14 he made a televised appeal for the FLN's so-called provisional government to negotiate an end to the war. Peace talks during June 25–29 failed to lead to resolution, but de Gaulle was set in his course. During his visit to Algeria in December, he was greeted by large pro-FLN Muslim rallies and anticolon riots. The United Nations recognized Algeria's independence on December 20, and in a national referendum on January 8, 1962, the French public voted in favor of Algerian independence.

A massive exodus of colons was already under way. Nearly 1 million returned to their ancestral homelands (half of them went to France, while most of the rest went to Spain and Italy). Peace talks resumed in March at Évian, and both sides reached a settlement on May 18, 1962. The war had claimed some 18,000 French military deaths, 3,000 colon deaths, and perhaps 300,000 Muslim deaths.

SPENCER C. TUCKER AND
WILLIAM E. WATSON

## Consequences

The formal handover of power occurred on July 5, 1962, when the FLN's Provisional Committee took control of Algeria. This day is celebrated as Algeria's independence day. In September Ben Bella was elected the first president of the People's Democratic Republic of Algeria.

Europeans living in Algeria were encouraged to leave (*la valise ou le cercueil*, meaning "the suitcase or the coffin"), and some 1.5 million did so. Perhaps half relocated in Metropolitan France, and most of the remainder went to Spain or Italy. Some 30,000 Europeans remained in Algeria. Ostensibly granted equal rights in the peace treaty, they instead faced official discrimination by the FLN government and the loss of much of their property. The FLN-led Algerian government, headed by Prime Minister Ben Bella, promptly confiscated the colons' abandoned property and established a decentralized socialist economy and a one-party state.

The Harkis, those Algerian Muslims who fought on the French side in the war, suffered terribly. Some 91,000 and their family members settled in France. At least 30,000 and perhaps as many as 150,000 Harkis and their family members, including young children, who remained in Algeria were subsequently butchered by either the FLN or lynch mobs.

Ben Bella took office on September 15, 1962. His attempt to consolidate his power, combined with popular discontent with the economy's inefficiency, sparked a bloodless military coup by Defense Minister Houari Boumédienne in June 1965. In 1971, the government endeavored to stimulate economic growth by nationalizing the oil industry and investing the revenues in centrally orchestrated industrial development. During the years that followed Boumédienne's military-dominated government took on an increasingly authoritarian cast.

Algeria's leaders sought to retain their autonomy, joining their country to the Non-Aligned Movement, and Boumédienne phased out French military bases. Although Algeria denounced perceived American imperialism and supported Cuba, the Viet Cong in South Vietnam, Palestinian nationalists, and African anticolonial fighters, it maintained in a strong trading relationship with the United States. At the same time Algeria cultivated economic ties with the Soviet Union, which provided the nation with military equipment and training. When the Spanish relinquished control of the Western Sahara in 1976, Morocco attempted to annex the region, leading to a 12-year low-level war with Algeria, which supported the guerrilla movement fighting for the region's independence.

Diplomatic relations with the United States warmed after Algeria negotiated the release of American hostages in Iran in 1980 and Morocco fell out of U.S. favor by allying with Libya in 1984.

In 1976 a long-promised constitution that provided for elections was enacted, although Algeria remained a one-party state. When Boumédienne died in December 1978, power passed to Chadli Bendjedid, the army-backed candidate. Bendjedid retreated from Boumédienne's increasingly ineffective economic policies, privatizing much of the economy and encouraging entrepreneurship. However, accumulated debt continued to retard economic expansion. Growing public protests from labor unions, students, and Islamic fundamentalists forced the government to end restrictions on political expression in 1988.

The Islamic Salvation Front (Front Islamique du Salut, FIS) proved to be the most successful of the new political parties. After victories by the FIS in local elections in June 1990 and national elections in December 1991, Benjedid resigned, and a new regime under Mohamed Boudiaf imposed martial law, banning the FIS in March 1992. In response, Islamist radicals began a guerrilla war that persisted to 2002, taking a toll of as many as 150,000 lives. Although Algeria's military government managed to gain the upper hand, Islamic groups continued to carry out occasional terrorist acts against the state, which maintains control through repression and tainted elections.

ELUN GABRIEL

## Timeline

| | |
|---|---|
| **Jul 5, 1830** | French forces capture Algiers. |
| **1835** | France finally subjugates all of Algeria. |
| **1848** | Algeria is recognized as an integral part of France and is opened to European settlement. |
| **1936** | French settlers in Algiers succeed in blocking the Blum-Viollette reform for Algeria. |
| **Mar 1937** | Algerian nationalist Ahmed Messali Hadj forms the Parti du Peuple Algerien (Algerian People's Party, PPA). |
| **1938** | Algerian nationalist Ferhat Abbas forms the moderate Union Populaire Algérienne (Algerian Popular Union). |

| | |
|---|---|
| **Jun 1940** | France is defeated by Germany in World War II. |
| **Nov 8, 1942** | U.S. and British forces land in Morocco and Algeria. |
| **May 8, 1944** | Germany surrenders, ending World War II in Europe. Independence Day demonstrations in Sétif, Algeria, turn violent. |
| **Oct 1946** | The PPA is replaced by the Mouvement pour le Triomphe des Libertés Démocratiques (Movement for the Triumph of Democratic Liberties, MTLD), with Messali Hadj as president. |
| **1947** | The Organization Spéciale (Special Organization, OS) is formed as a paramilitary arm of the MTLD. |
| **Sep 20, 1947** | The French National Assembly offers all Algerian citizens French citizenship, yet the new Algerian Assembly continues settler domination. |
| **1949** | The OS mounts an attack on the Oran central post office, netting 3 million francs. |
| **1952** | French authorities arrest several OS leaders, but Ahmed Ben Bella escapes to Cairo. |
| **1954** | Several members of the OS organize the Comité Révolutionaire d'Unité et d'Action (Revolutionary Committee for Unity and Action, CRUA) to lead the revolt against the French. |
| **Apr 21–Jul 20, 1954** | An international conference meeting in Geneva, Switzerland, ends the Indochina War. |
| **Oct 10, 1954** | The CRUA changes its name to the Front de Libération Nationale (National Liberation Front, FLN). |
| **Oct 31–Nov 1, 1954** | The FLN commences the Algerian War, having ordered the Armée de Libération Nationale (National Liberation Army, ALN), to attack police and military posts in Aurès and Kabylia. |
| **Nov 1954** | Messali Hadj, under house arrest in France, founds the Mouvement National Algérien (Algerian National Movement, MNA) as a moderate alternative to the FLN. |
| **1955** | The French administration now allows the settlers to arm themselves and form self-defense units. |
| **Jan 26, 1955** | Jacques-Émile Soustelle is appointed governor-general of Algeria and introduces liberal reforms. |
| **Feb 1955** | The ALN targets Muslims cooperating with Europeans, including farmworkers and those attending associated rural schools. |
| **Aug 20, 1955** | At Philippeville, ALN operatives kill 71 French citizens and 52 pro-French Algerian Muslims. The French kill around 130 of the FLN commandos. This same day, European women and children are slaughtered in their homes surrounding Constantine. At El-Halia 37 Europeans are slain. French paratroopers execute 150 Muslims. |

| | |
|---|---|
| **Feb 1, 1956** | Socialist Party leader Guy Mollet becomes French premier. |
| **Feb 9, 1956** | Soustelle is recalled to Paris. Robert Lacoste replaces him as governor-general of Algeria. |
| **Mar 2, 1956** | Morocco is granted independence by France. |
| **Mar 20, 1956** | Tunisia is granted independence by France. Both Morocco and Tunisia will allow the FLN to establish base camps in their territory. |
| **Sep 30, 1956** | Three young Muslim women place bombs in a European milk bar, cafeteria, and travel agency, killing 3 Europeans and wounding 50 more. This marks the beginning of the Battle of Algiers. |
| **Oct 16, 1956** | The French Navy intercepts the ship *Athos*, sailing from Egypt to Algiers with arms for the FLN. |
| **Oct 22, 1956** | FLN leader Ben Bella is arrested by French military authorities when the commercial airliner in which he is flying is diverted to France. |
| **Nov 5, 1956** | French and British forces land at Suez, part of an unsuccessful Israeli-British-French effort to unseat Gamal Abdel Nasser. This unsuccessful gambit leads Nasser to increase aid to the FLN. |
| **Dec 14, 1956** | General Raoul Albin Louis Salan is appointed commander of French forces in Algeria. |
| **Jan 7, 1957** | Brigadier General Jacques Massu's 10th Parachute Division commences operations in the Casbah area of Algiers. |
| **May 31, 1957** | FLN guerrillas massacre 303 Muslim supporters of Messali Hadj's MNA in the village of Melouza. The FLN then blames the massacre on the French. |
| **Sep 1957** | The French complete the Morice Line, a defensive barrier along the Tunisian border to prevent the movement of FLN forces and supplies from that country into Algeria. |
| **Sep 24, 1957** | FLN leader in Algiers Yacef Saadi is captured, marking the effective end of the Battle of Algiers. |
| **Dec 1957** | General Salan is appointed commander of French forces in Algeria. |
| **Feb 8, 1958** | French aircraft bomb Sakiet Sidi Youssef (Saqiyat Sidi Yusuf) in Tunisia, where the FLN has established a base. |
| **May 13, 1958** | Demonstrators in Algiers seize government buildings and then demand that Charles de Gaulle be named premier of France. |
| **Jun 1, 1958** | De Gaulle is named premier of France. |
| **Jun 4, 1958** | De Gaulle visits Algeria. |
| **Sep 19, 1958** | Ferhat Abbas is named head of the Gouvernement Provisoire de la République Algérienne (Provisional Government of the Algerian Republic). |

| | |
|---|---|
| **Oct 3, 1958** | In the course of a speech de Gaulle offers a peace and amnesty agreement to the FLN, which rejects it. |
| **Oct 8, 1958** | The French Fifth Republic is established. |
| **Dec 12, 1958** | De Gaulle names General Maurice Challe to replace General Salan as commander of French forces in Algeria. |
| **Jan 8, 1959** | De Gaulle becomes president of France. |
| **Feb 1959** | Challe begins a series of major offensives against different *wilayas*. These force the FLN/ALN to disperse into small units to avoid capture. |
| **Sep 16, 1959** | De Gaulle offers Algeria self-determination with a referendum. This greatly angers the die-hard colons determined to keep Algeria French. |
| **Sep 19, 1959** | General Massu is sacked for opposing de Gaulle's Algerian policy. |
| **Jan 24, 1960** | The Week of Barricades, an insurrection in Algiers by those wishing to keep Algeria part of France, begins. |
| **Jan 29, 1960** | Following a speech by de Gaulle, the Algiers insurrection collapses. |
| **Apr 1960** | Challe begins Operation TRIDENT, the final phase of his military offensives against the FLN. |
| **Jun 25–29, 1960** | Peace talks fail between the French government and FLN. |
| **Dec 9–13, 1960** | De Gaulle visits Algeria. |
| **Dec 20, 1960** | The United Nations recognizes Algeria's right to self-determination. |
| **Jan 25, 1961** | Those determined to keep Algeria a part of France establish the Organisation de l'Armée Secrète (Secret Army Organization, OAS). They begin a series of assassinations in France and Algeria. |
| **Apr 22, 1961** | A second attempt to seize power by those determined to keep Algeria a part of France occurs in Algiers. Dubbed the Generals' Putsch, it includes former commanders in Algeria Generals Salan and Challe, General André Zeller, and General Edmond Jouhaud. Aided by a paratroop regiment, they take power in Algiers. |
| **Apr 26, 1961** | Troops supporting the Generals' Putsch surrender. Challe also surrenders, and Zeller is captured. Salan and Jouhaud escape to lead the OAS. |
| **May 19, 1961** | OAS operatives explode a bomb in Algiers. |
| **May 20–Jul 28, 1961** | Peace talks occur between the French government and the FLN at Évian but end in failure. |
| **Sep 8, 1961** | De Gaulle narrowly escapes assassination by the OAS at Pont-sur-Seine, France. |
| **Feb 1962** | OAS bombings and assassinations kill more than 500 people, but these seriously weaken support for the OAS cause in France. |

| | |
|---|---|
| **Mar 7–18, 1962** | Peace talks between French and FLN representatives at Évian, France, reach agreement. |
| **Mar 19, 1962** | A cease-fire agreement goes into effect between the French and the FLN. |
| **Apr 20, 1962** | OAS leader Salan is captured in Algiers. |
| **Jul 1, 1962** | A referendum is held in France on the issue of independence for Algeria. The vote is some 6 million in favor and only 16,000 opposed. |
| **Jul 5, 1962** | Algerian independence is declared. Ben Bella becomes the first Algerian prime minister. |
| **Sep 15, 1962** | Ben Bella takes office as the first president of the People's Democratic Republic of Algeria. |

SPENCER C. TUCKER

### Further Reading

Alleg, Henri. *La Question.* Paris: Éditions de Minuit, 1958.

Aron, Robert. *Les Origines de la guerre d'Algérie: Textes et documents contemporaine.* Paris: Fayard, 1962

Aussaresses, Paul. *The Battle of the Casbah: Terrorism and Counter-Terrorism in Algeria, 1955–1957.* New York: Enigma Books, 2010.

Danziger, Rapahel. *Abd al'Qadir and the Algerians: Resistance to the French and Internal Consolidation.* New York: Holmes and Meier, 1977.

Derradji, Abder-Rahmane. *The Algerian Guerrilla Campaign Strategy & Tactics.* New York: Edwin Mellen, 1997.

Galula, David. *Counterinsurgency Warfare: Theory and Practice.* Westport, CT: Praeger Security International, 1964.

Gillespie, Joan. *Algeria: Rebellion and Revolution.* New York: Praeger, 1960.

Gordon, David C. *The Passing of French Algeria.* London: Oxford University Press, 1966.

Horne, Alistair. *A Savage War of Peace: Algeria, 1954–1962.* London: Macmillan, 1977.

Humbaraci, Arslan. *Algeria: A Revolution That Failed.* London: Pall Mall, 1966.

Kettle, Michael. *De Gaulle and Algeria, 1940–1960.* London: Quartet, 1993.

Leulliette, Pierre. *St. Michael and the Dragon: Memoirs of a Paratrooper.* Boston: Houghton Mifflin, 1964.

Maran, Rita. *Torture: The Role of Ideology in the French-Algerian War.* New York: Praeger, 1989.

Servan-Schreiber, Jean-Jacques. *Lieutenant in Algeria.* Translated by Ronald Matthews. New York: Knopf, 1957.

Sessions, Jennifer. *By Sword and Plow: France and the Conquest of Algeria.* Ithaca, NY: Cornell University Press, 2011.

Smith, Tony. *The French Stake in Algeria, 1945–1962.* Ithaca, NY: Cornell University Press, 1979.

Sullivan, Anthony. *Thomas-Robert Bugeaud: France and Algeria, 1784–1849: Politics, Power, and the Good Society.* Hamden, CT: Archon Books, 1983.

Talbott, John. *The War without a Name: France in Algeria, 1954–1962.* New York: Knopf, 1980.

Trinquier, Roger. *Modern Warfare: A French View of Counterinsurgency.* Westport, CT: Praeger Security International, 2006.

Tucker, Spencer C. "The Fourth Republic and Algeria." Doctoral dissertation, University of North Carolina at Chapel Hill, 1965.

Watson, William E. *Tricolor and Crescent: France and the Islamic World.* Westport, CT: Praeger, 2003.

Windrow, Martin. *The Algerian War, 1954–62.* London: Osprey, 1997.

# Portuguese Colonial Wars in Africa (1961–1974)

## Background

In February 1961 fighting began in the Portuguese African provinces of Angola, part of the Portuguese colonial empire in Africa comprising Angola, Mozambique, and Portuguese Guinea. The fighting spread to Guinea in 1963 and to Mozambique in 1964. The wider conflict is known as the Portuguese Colonial War or, in Portugal, as the Overseas War. The former colonies usually refer to the conflict in their country as the war of liberation or the war of independence. These three conflicts proved to be a tremendous drain on the Portuguese economy and came to an end when a leftist military coup overthrew the Portuguese government in Lisbon on April 25, 1974, and declared its intention to grant independence to the African provinces. Cease-fire arrangements were concluded. Guinea was officially granted its independence as Guinea-Bissau on September 10, 1974; Mozambique became independent on January 25, 1975; and Angola received its independence on November 11, 1975.

The Portuguese established Europe's first colonial empire. It was also one of the largest and most long-lived. Beginning with the 1415 acquisition of Ceuta (now an autonomous Spanish city) located on the northwest coast of Africa, the empire lasted nearly six centuries to 1999, when the Portuguese government officially handed over Macau to the People's Republic of China. At its greatest extent the Portuguese Empire (Império Português), also known as Portuguese Overseas (Ultramar

Português), included territories around the globe. The largest of these was Brazil in Latin America, followed by territorial holdings in Africa, but the Portuguese also held important lands in the Middle East, South Asia, and India.

Portuguese explorers initiated the European Age of Discovery in the 15th century. The Portuguese Crown sent ships to locate sources of gold on the eastern coast of North Africa. They also sought to discover a sea route to Asia for the lucrative spice trade. As early as 1418–1419 Portuguese sailors undertook explorations of the African coast and the Atlantic archipelagos. In 1488 Bartolomeu Dias rounded the southern coast of the African continent into the Pacific, and in 1498 Vasco da Gama reached India. In 1500 Pedro Álvares Cabral made landfall on the southeastern coast of South America in what would be Brazil. By the 16th century, its empire was accounting for perhaps 20 percent of the Portuguese economy.

In 1580 King Philip II of Spain (r. 1556–1598) inherited the Portuguese throne as King Philip I of Portugal. During the 60 years that Portugal and Spain were united, the Portuguese Empire came under attack from three major seafaring countries at war with Spain: England, France, and the Dutch Republic. With its small population, Portugal proved unable to defend its empire, which now began a slow but steady decline. Brazil broke away in 1822 as a consequence of the Napoleonic Wars and the Wars of Latin American Independence.

# AFRICAN INDEPENDENCE, 1910–1977

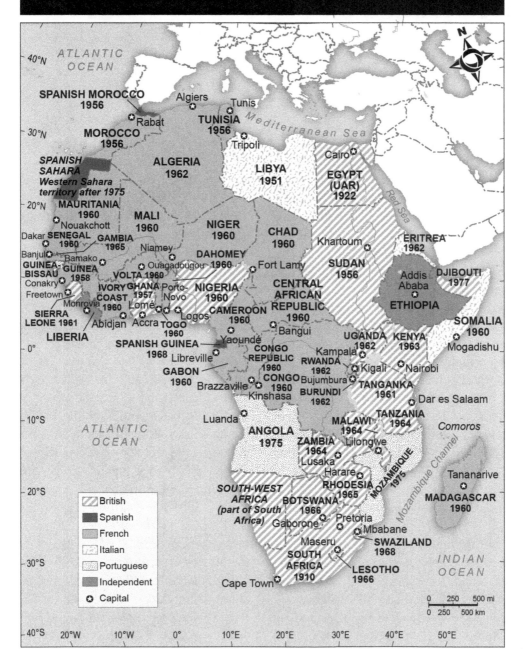

SPANISH MOROCCO 1956
Algiers
Tunis
Rabat
TUNISIA 1956
MOROCCO 1956
Tripoli
ATLANTIC OCEAN
40°N
30°N
Mediterranean Sea
SPANISH SAHARA
Western Sahara territory after 1975
ALGERIA 1962
LIBYA 1951
EGYPT (UAR) 1922
Cairo
Red Sea
20°N
MAURITANIA 1960
Nouakchott
MALI 1960
NIGER 1960
CHAD 1960
Khartoum
ERITREA 1962
Dakar SENEGAL 1960
GAMBIA 1965
Banjul
Bamako
Niamey
DAHOMEY 1960
Fort Lamy
SUDAN 1956
Addis Ababa
DJIBOUTI 1977
GUINEA-BISSAU
GUINEA 1958
Conakry
Freetown
VOLTA 1960
Ouagadougou
Porto-
Novo
NIGERIA 1960
CENTRAL AFRICAN REPUBLIC 1960
ETHIOPIA
IVORY COAST 1960
GHANA 1957
CAMEROON 1960
Bangui
UGANDA 1962
KENYA 1963
SOMALIA 1960
SIERRA LEONE 1961
Monrovia
Abidjan
Accra
TOGO 1960
Lomé
Logos
Yaoundé
CONGO REPUBLIC 1960
Kampala
RWANDA 1962
Kigali
Nairobi
Mogadishu
LIBERIA
SPANISH GUINEA 1968
Libreville
GABON 1960
Brazzaville
CONGO 1960
Kinshasa
Bujumbura
BURUNDI 1962
TANGANKA 1961
Dar es Salaam
0°
10°S
ATLANTIC OCEAN
Luanda
ANGOLA 1975
MALAWI 1964
Lilongwe
ZAMBIA 1964
Lusaka
TANZANIA 1964
Comoros
Tananarive
MADAGASCAR 1960
20°S
SOUTH-WEST AFRICA (part of South Africa)
BOTSWANA 1966
Gaborone
Harare
RHODESIA 1965
MOZAMBIQUE 1975
Mozambique Channel
INDIAN OCEAN
30°S
Maseru
Pretoria
Mbabane
SWAZILAND 1968
SOUTH AFRICA 1910
Cape Town
LESOTHO 1966

**Legend:**
- British
- Spanish
- French
- Italian
- Portuguese
- Independent
- ✪ Capital

0   250   500 mi
0   250   500 km

40°S
20°W   10°W   0°   10°E   20°E   30°E   40°E   50°E

During the late 1800s there was a great scramble by the major European powers for territorial holdings in Africa. The goals here were largely economic gain, naval bases, and international prestige. During this period the European colonial powers expanded their coastal holdings deep into the African interior. After World War I nationalism impacted the African colonies. U.S. president Woodrow Wilson's declaration of self-determination of peoples resonated in Africa and in Asia, even though Wilson was applying it only to Europe.

The Portuguese Colonial Act of June 13, 1933, recognized the supremacy of the Portuguese over all native peoples. Although blacks could pursue higher education, they were left at great disadvantage in their own land.

The end of World War II saw a considerable increase in emigration from Portugal to its African colonies, which was encouraged by Portuguese prime minister and de facto dictator António de Oliveira Salazar during 1932–1968. On June 11, 1951, owing to rising international criticism of colonialism, the Salazar government changed the status of its colonies to overseas provinces (*províncias ultramarinas*). Although it was possible for Africans to become fully assimilated Portuguese citizens this was extremely difficult, and Portuguese colonial policy was both suppressive of native rights and economically exploitative. Yet World War II had brought the winds of change throughout Africa, and the days of colonialism were clearly numbered. However, as with the French and Belgian governments, the Portuguese missed their historic cue. It is hard for the weak to be generous, and Lisbon was determined to hold onto the country's considerable colonial empire. The result,

however, was a long period of warfare from 1961 to 1974 that ended only with the overthrow of the Portuguese government in the Carnation Revolution of 1974.

SPENCER C. TUCKER

## Angolan War of Independence (1961–1974)

### Causes

The Angolan War of Independence began on February 4, 1961, in an uprising against forced agricultural labor and then became a struggle between three nationalist movements and one breakaway faction against the Portuguese Army for control of the Portugese overseas province of Angola.

In 1482 Portuguese sailors under navigator Diego Cäo landed on the northern coast of Angola and made contact with the African Kongo and Ndongo kingdoms (Angola takes its named from *ngola*, the Ndongo term for their king). By the beginning of the 16th century the Portuguese had established a number of forts along the Angolan coast, and in 1575 they founded the port city of Luanda. The Portuguese were chiefly interested in the exploitation of Angola's mineral wealth and the slave trade, with the slaves being shipped from Luanda to Brazil. During the centuries of Portuguese colonial settlement there was almost constant warfare with the indigenous tribes, and in 1623–1626 the Portuguese campaigned against and defeated the Ndongos, led by Queen Nzinga. During 1641–1648 the Dutch occupied Luanda and drove the Portuguese from their coastal enclaves.

In 1648 Portuguese forces from Brazil recaptured Luanda and the other coastal forts. By 1671 Ndongo was firmly under Portuguese control. In 1836 the Portuguese abolished the slave trade but not the

## Portuguese Colonial Wars of Independence (1961–1974)

| Angolan War of Independence, 1961–1974 | |
| --- | --- |
| Approximate Deaths, UPA Raid into Angola (March 15, 1961) | |
| Black Population | White Population |
| 6,000 | 1,000 |

| Total Approximate Deaths, All Causes, Angolan War of Independence (1961–1974) | | |
| --- | --- | --- |
| Insurgents, All Groups | Portuguese Forces | Civilians |
| 50,000+ | 4,456 | 30,000–50,000 |

| Mozambique War of Independence (1964–1975) | | |
| --- | --- | --- |
| Operation GORDIAN KNOT (July–August 1970) | | |
| | FRELIMO | Portuguese Military |
| Strength | 5,000–6,000 men | 35,000 personnel |
| Losses | 600 dead, 1,800 captured, 200 camps destroyed | Unknown |

| Total Approximate Deaths, Mozambique War of Independence, 1965–1975 | | |
| --- | --- | --- |
| FRELIMO | Portuguese Military | Civilians |
| 10,000–35,000 | 3,500 | 50,000 |

| Guinea War of Independence, 1961–1974 | | | |
| --- | --- | --- | --- |
| | Insurgents and Allies | Portuguese | Civilians |
| Peak strength | 10,000 | 32,000 | N/A |
| Killed | 6,000-plus | 2,069 | 5,000 |

**Sources:** Cann, John P. *Counterinsurgency in Africa: The Portuguese Way of War, 1961–1974.* Richmond, VA: Hailer Publishing, 2005; Coelho, João Paulo Borges. "African Troops in the Portuguese Colonial Army, 1961–1974: Angola, Guinea-Bissau and Mozambique," *Portuguese Studies Review* 10(1) (2002): 129–150; Marcum, John A. *The Angolan Revolution.* 2 vols. Cambridge, MA: MIT Press, 1969, 1978.

practice of forced labor. By 1884 the Portuguese had begun to expand their control over the interior. The Congress of Berlin of 1885 officially set Angola's borders, although Angola's present-day borders were not finally settled until after World War I, in 1921. (Angola is today Africa's seventh-largest country.)

At the close of World War II, much of colonial Africa was swept by demands for change. In 1947 a number of Angolans, notably Viriato da Cruz, established the Movement of Young Intellectuals to promote Angolan history and culture. In 1953 Angolans formed the Partido da Luta Unida dos Africanos de Angola (Party of the United Struggle for Africans in Angola, PLUA), the first Angolan political party to advocate independence from Portugal. The next year Holden Roberto and

Barros Necaca founded another independence party, the União dos Povos do Norte de Angola (Union of Peoples of Northern Angola), subsequently renamed the União dos Povos de Angola (Union of Peoples of Angola, UPA). It sought independence for the territory that comprised the former Kingdom of the Kongo, which would include other territory outside Portuguese Angola.

Roberto was born in 1923 in São Salvador, Angola, but moved with his family to Léoipoldville (now Kinhasa) in the Belgium Congo (the present-day Democratic Republic of the Congo) and there graduated from a Baptist missionary school. During the next eight years he worked for the Belgian Finance Ministry in the Congo. In 1951 Roberto visited in Angola, where he witnessed the mistreatment of an old man by the Portuguese authorities that, he said, aroused him politically. In December 1958 Roberto represented Angola at the Ghana-sponsored All-African People's Congress.

In 1955, meanwhile, Mário Pinto de Andrade and his brother Joaquin established the Partido Comunista Angolano (Angolan Communist Party, PCA). That December the PCA merged with the PLUA to form the Movimento Popular da Libertação de Angola (Popular Movement for the Liberation of Angola, MPLA). António Agostinho Neto (later the first president of an independent Angola) became its leader.

Born in 1922, Neto was the son of a Methodist minister and studied medicine at the universities of Coimbra and Lisbon in Portugal. Arrested in 1951 for his Angolan separatists activities, Neto was imprisoned by the Portuguese government. Released in 1958, he completed his medical studies and returned to Angola in 1959. Neto was again arrested by the Portuguese

António Agostinho Neto became the leader of the Movimento Popular da Libertação de Angola (MPLA, Popular Movement for the Liberation of Angola), which fought against the Portuguese. Neto was then the first president of an independent Angola. (Bettmann/ Getty Images)

in 1960. His political supporters and patients marched to demand his release, and Portuguese soldiers opened fire, killing 30 and wounding 200 in what became known as the Massacre of Icolo e Bengo. Neto was exiled to Cape Verde and then was sent to Lisbon, where he was imprisoned. Following international protests, the Portuguese government released him from prison but placed him under house arrest. Neto escaped from this and made his way to Zaire (today the Democratic Republic of the Congo).

The MPLA, based in Brazzaville in the Republic of the Congo before moving its headquarters to Zambia in 1965, was established on a nonracial, nontribal basis, with its goal the termination of Portuguese rule and the establishment of a Marxist-Leninist state. To accomplish this, the military wing of the MPLA received training in Algeria and later in Soviet bloc countries, from which it also received military assistance.

The granting of independence in 1960 by Belgium to the Congo, renamed Zaire, was a considerable boost to the nascent independence movement in Angola. The MPLA was also able to capitalize on native unrest in Angola, for on January 3, 1961, workers in the cotton fields of the Baixa de Cassanje, Malanje, region mounted a boycott of the Cotonang Company, owned by Portuguese and other foreign investors, to protest both working conditions and pay. Known as the Baixa de Cassanje Revolt, the workers also burned their identification cards and attacked Portuguese traders. The Portuguese military responded the next day, employing aircraft dropping bombs that, according to some accounts, included napalm. Estimates of casualties vary considerably, from 400 to 7,000 Angolan blacks killed.

SPENCER C. TUCKER

## Course

On February 4, 1961, the MPLA began the Angolan War of Independence by undertaking military operations against the Portuguese in northern Angola in an attack against both a police station and the São Paulo prison. Seven policemen died along with 40 of the MPLA attackers, and no prisoners were freed. The MPLA attacked a second prison on February 10. After both attacks the Portuguese authorities came down hard on blacks, especially in the slums of Luanda, killing hundreds of people.

The MPLA operated first from the Republic of the Congo, then from Zaire (the present Democratic Republic of the Congo), and then back in the Republic of the Congo. Although the MPLA had 3,000–5,000 fighters, few were actually based in Angola itself. (In 1962 Neto traveled to the United States to request aid from the U.S. government but was turned down by the John F. Kennedy administration because of his Marxist orientation.)

Soon there would be three Angolan independence organizations. The second was the UPA. Led by Holden Roberto, it was based in Zaire. On March 15, several thousand UPA militants crossed into Angola, where they attacked government outposts and raided farms and trading centers. Reportedly they killed some 1,000 whites and 6,000 blacks, including women and children. Most of the blacks were contract workers from the Ovimbundu Bantu ethnic group. That the MPLA and UPA were rivals was shown in the UPA taking prisoner 21 members of the MPLA and then executing them.

In March 1962 Roberto merged his UPA with another Angolan political organization, the Partido Democrático de Angola (Democratic Party of Angola), to form the Frente Nacional de Liberaração de Angola (National Liberation Front of Angola, FNLA). It drew its strength from among the Bakongo tribe of northern Angola and operated chiefly out of Zaire. Roberto received the support of president of Zaire Mobutu Sese Seko when he divorced his wife and married a woman from Mobuto's wife's village. Roberto also received some aid from Israel. On March 27, 1962, Roberto established the Governo Revolucionário de Angola no exílio (Revolutionary Government of Angola in Exile).

One of Roberto's key lieutenants was Janos Savimbi. Born in 1934 in Munhango, Bie Province, Angola, Savimbi was purposely vague and evasive about his early life. He claimed that he had earned a PhD from the University of Lausanne, Switzerland, and he may have spent two years in Portugal as a medical student. Returning to Angola, Savimbi accepted the post of foreign minister in the FNLA but broke with Roberto in 1964 when the latter refused to expand his movement into southern Angola. In 1966 Savimbi founded the União Nacional para a Independência Total de Angola (National Union for the Total Independence of Angola, UNITA). Whereas the FNLA base of support was among the Bakongo people, UNITA was centered in the south among the Ovimbundu and Chokwe peoples.

UNITA's first attack occurred on December 25, 1966, against the Benguela rail line on the border with Zambia. This attack angered the Zambian government, as copper from Zambia was shipped on the line, and as a result it expelled UNITA personnel from the country. Savimbi then relocated to Cairo before returning to Angola a year later. UNITA became the only Angolan insurgent group based in Angola itself but was quite small, with only several hundred fighters.

All three insurgent groups were savaged by Portuguese Army forces, particularly after the latter received helicopters. Portuguese control of the air was an immense advantage, especially in the largely open eastern part of the country. The Portuguese also carried out resettlement operations, moving the native peoples into government-controlled *dendandas* (defended villages). The Portuguese Army also employed black Angolan troops. Initially these were simply soldiers or noncommissioned officers, but as the war continued a number became officers, although they were limited to junior ranks. By the 1970s the Portuguese finally recognized the deleterious effect of

its discriminatory policies on the administration and the military in the colonies and sought to correct these, but it was a case of too little too late.

The insurgents took heavy casualties but struck back with mines, and they also employed mortars and rockets to attack important Portuguese economic targets such as the Gulf Oil operations in the Cabinda enclave, although without great success. In February 1972, the South African military crossed into Angola and engaged and destroyed MPLA forces in Moxico. Meanwhile, Portuguese army troops forced the MPLA to withdraw from Angola into the Republic of the Congo.

In 1973 Daniel Chipenda, the field commander of the MPLA's Eastern Front, split from the MPLA with some 1,500 followers and formed the Revolta do Leste (Eastern Revolt, RDL). Later Chipenda joined the FNLA but then left it to rejoin the MPLA, which he left again in July 1992. Meanwhile, president of Tanzania Julius Nyerere convinced the leaders of the People's Republic of China, which had been aiding the MPLA, to switch their support to the FNLA against the MPLA.

The Angolan War reached a stalemate in 1974. The bitterly divided Angolan resistance groups would achieve their goal of independence not because of battlefield success but instead because of a change in the Portuguese government. The economic costs of Portuguese military operations in Angola as well as in its other African colonies of Guinea and Mozambique, where it had been fighting insurgencies (Guinea since January 1963 and Mozambique since September 1964), were simply staggering. Indeed, by the late 1960s the colonial wars were consuming 50 percent of the national budget. This could simply not be sustained.

On April 25, 1974, young progressive Portuguese Army officers formed into the Movimento das Forças Armadas (Armed Forces Movement) seized power in Lisbon in what became known as the Carnation Revolution. Their new government declared its intention to grant the colonies independence and agreed to grant colonial independence, and a cease-fire was declared that October.

On January 5, 1975, leaders of the three principal factions vying for control of Angola—the MPLA, the FNLA, and UNITA—met and agreed to stop fighting each other. They then met with Portuguese government representatives at Alvor, Portugal, beginning on January 10 and agreed on January 15 to set up a coalition government for Angola, with independence for Angola to occur on November 11, 1975. Fighting continued nonetheless, although the Portuguese troops departed Angola on its independence.

SPENCER C. TUCKER

## Consequences

Angola did not enjoy a respite. Although the Angolan Civil War is usually dated from November 11, 2015, it actually began immediately after the signing of the Alvor Accords on January 15, 2015, that established a power-sharing arrangement for the new government. Two resistance organizations, the Frente para a Libertação do Enclave de Cabinda (Front for the Liberation of the Enclave of Cabinda) and the RDL, were excluded from the negotiations and never did adhere to the accords. But the key factor was that the coalition government agreement quickly collapsed amid squabbling by the three major participants of the Movimento Popular de Libertação de Angola (Popular Movement for the Liberation of Angola, MPLA), led by António Agostinho Neto; the anticommunist FNLA, led by Holden Roberto; and UNITA, headed by Jonas Savimbi.

In order to prevent the avowedly Marxist MPLA from taking power, the anti-Marxist FNLA and UNITA formed an alliance. These two groups were supported by Zaire (now the Democratic Republic of the Congo), South Africa, and the United States, through its Central Intelligence Agency. The MPLA enjoyed the support of the Soviet Union and, at its behest, Cuba.

Fighting between the three forces occurred in the Angolan capital of Luanda concurrent with the transitional government assuming office on January 15, 1975. The MPLA was able to wrest control of Luanda from the FNLA, but by March the FNLA had secured control of the northern provinces of Angola and was advancing on the capital from the north. With encouragement from the United States, at the end of April Zaire sent some 1,200 troops into northern Angola to assist the FNLA.

It seemed as if the MPLA would be forced to quit Luanda, but beginning in March the Soviet Union shipped large amounts of arms to the MPLA. The Soviets also prevailed on Cuba to assist in training the MPLA forces, and that country sent some 500 men with the goal of training 4,800 recruits within three to six months. The Cuban mission was supposed to be a short-term operation of perhaps six months only. Further complicating the mix, the South Africans intervened on behalf of the FNLA in order to protect their own economic interests in Angola and ensure their control of South West Africa (now Namibia). In Operation SAVANNAH during August 14, 1975–April 30, 1976, South African Defense Force (SADF) troops entered southern Angola, defeated the MPLA forces there, and handed over control of the region to UNITA.

On November 10, 1975, having already defeated the MPLA forces at Porto Quipiri, the FNLA was advancing on Luanda, supported by the Zaireans and South Africans, when they encountered the MPLA and Cubans at the strategically located village of Quifangondo, some six miles east of the capital. The advancing force included some 1,000 FNLA troops, 120 mostly white deserters from the Portuguese Army, perhaps 1,200 Zaireans, and about 50 South African artillerymen.

With Angola's independence to take effect the next day, November 11, Roberto was determined to take the capital city. The South Africans provided three 5.5-inch (140mm) World War II–era howitzers, while the Zaireans contributed two 130mm guns. South African Canberra bombers were to open the battle with an air strike. Just before the battle, however, the Soviets airlifted Cuban military specialists into Luanda in order to man six BM-21 multiple rocket launchers supplied by the Soviets that had escaped detection by the attackers and were to prove decisive in the battle's outcome.

The South African air strike and the artillery bombardment went as planned, but any advantage was lost in that the ground attack was delayed and then poorly handled. Some 1,000 MPLA troops and 188 Cubans caught the attacking force in the open and unleashed devastating rocket and mortar fire, which destroyed most of the attackers' Panhard armored cars as well as six jeeps mounting recoilless rifles. The rockets outranged the South African and Zairean artillery, and one of the Zairean guns blew up on its first fire as a consequence of poor maintenance. The battle saw hundreds of attackers killed for a reported one killed and a handful wounded

for the defenders. Roberto, who had not been present at the battle, arrived the next morning to discover his men in retreat.

The battle ended any FNLA attempt to take Luanda. By the end of 1975 there were some 25,000 Cuban troops in Angola, and they promptly cleared the FNLA from northeastern Angola. The Zaireans and South African gunners withdrew to Ambrizette, where they were evacuated by a South African Navy frigate.

Although the MPLA now held power with Neto as president, fighting continued. In the Battle of Bridge 14 on December 12, SDAF engineers rebuilt while under enemy fire a bridge over the Bhia River, allowing an SDAF armored column to cross to the other side and rout a far larger Cuban and MPLA force defending the opposite bank. Other inconclusive battles followed before the South African government reached an agreement with the MPLA government under which it would withdraw its forces from Angola in return for an MPLA promise of protection for South African economic interests in Angola. All SDAF forces had departed the country by the end of April 1976.

Alarmed at President Gerald Ford's support for UNITA, on January 27, 1976, the U.S. House of Representatives overwhelmingly passed an amendment to the Arms Export Control Act (the Senate had approved it earlier) proposed by Senator Dick Clark (Democrat of Iowa). The Clark Amendment prohibited U.S. aid to private groups engaged in military or paramilitary operations in Angola. Even after passage of the amendment, director of the Central Intelligence Agency George H. W. Bush refused to concede that all U.S. aid to Angola had ceased. Indeed, U.S. ally Israel agreed to step in as a proxy arms supplier for the United States.

On February 8, 1976, MPLA forces and Cuban troops captured the FNLA stronghold of Huambo, forcing Roberto and many of his supporters to seek refuge in Zambia. The United States then switched its support to Savimbi's UNITA. In early June up to 15,000 Cuban troops launched the first of several offensives that year against UNITA. While these operations forced UNITA into southeastern Angola, they failed to defeat it completely, and Savimbi was able to continue insurgent operations. U.S. support for UNITA was now minimal, however, thanks to the Clark Amendment.

Although Marxist-Leninism was the declared official MPLA doctrine, in practice Neto tended to favor a socialist, not communist, model for Angola. In 1977 he violently suppressed an attempted coup by the Organização dos Communistas de Angola (Communist Organization of Angola, OCA), with some 18,000 OCA supporters killed during a two-year span. Neto died in Moscow on September 10, 1979, while undergoing cancer surgery. His birthday is celebrated as National Heroes Day, a public holiday in Angola.

Savimbi's UNITA continued to carry out guerrilla operations against the MPLA and the Cubans, attacking supply convoys and mounting hit-and-run attacks against MPLA bases. The South African government provided some support, and by the early 1980s UNITA controlled the southeastern third of the country. UNITA lacked the resources to defeat the MPLA, however. A stalemate occurred because even with Cuban assistance, the MPLA was unable to completely defeat UNITA.

The MPLA meanwhile developed close military ties with the South West Africa Peoples Organization (SWAPO) in South West Africa and the socialist regime in Mozambique as well as with Zambia and the African National Congress in South Africa. In July 1985 the U.S. Congress repealed the Clark Amendment, and the Ronald Reagan administration then supplied UNITA with substantial assistance. Zaire and South Africa served as the major conduits for the U.S. aid.

During December 6, 1983–January 8, 1984, South Africa sent some 2,300 SADF troops on a raid into Angola. Dubbed Operation ASKARI, this sixth SADF foray into Angola was designed to disrupt plans by SWAPO, the liberation movement in South West Africa, for an offensive in early 1984. The primary battle took place outside Cuvelai during January 3–5, with the SADF defeating a combined Cuban, Angolan, and SWAPO force. The SADF claimed to have killed 324 men of the opposing force while suffering only 21 casualties itself.

On January 30, 1984, Zambian president Kenneth Kaunda invited Republic of South Africa and SWAPO representatives to meet in Lusaka to discuss a truce. With the war in South West Africa now costing the South African government some $4 million a day and anxious to disengage his country's forces, on January 31 South African prime minster Pieter Willem Botha announced that he would withdraw his nation's forces from Angola.

On February 23, 1984, representatives of the South African and Angolan governments met in Lusaka, Zambia, and signed a cease-fire agreement. All South African forces were withdrawn from Angola, and the Angolan government agreed that no SWAPO troops or Cubans would be allowed into the vacated territory.

On December 27, 1988, the Cuban government agreed to withdraw its force, which had reached some 50,000 troops, from Angola. The withdrawal was to be completed by July 1991. Still pressed militarily by Savimbi's forces, the Angolan government negotiated a cease-fire with UNITA, and Savimbi himself ran for president in the national elections of 1992, which foreign monitors declared to have been fair. Neither he nor MPLA leader and president José Eduardo dos Santos won the requisite 50 percent, however, and were therefore forced into a runoff from which Savimbi withdrew, citing electoral fraud. He then resumed the war, much of it financed by the sale of illegally mined diamonds. In 1994 UNITA agreed to a new peace accord, but Savimbi declined the vice presidency offered him and again took up arms in 1998. On November 20, 1994, UNITA representatives signed the Lusaka Protocol with representatives of the Angolan government as part of an effort to bring to an end the Angolan Civil War.

On February 22, 2002, Savimbi was killed during fighting with MPLA government troops. His death finally made possible a durable cease-fire agreement. UNITA leaders agreed to give up their armed resistance and became the chief opposition party. Although Angola now began to stabilize politically, President dos Santos refused to institute regular democratic processes, and opposition to the government continued in the northern exclave of Cabinda.

Although Angola has substantial subsoil assets especially in diamonds and oil, this wealth has yet to reach most Angolans. Angola also remains an authoritarian regime, which has been strengthened by a new constitution, with the president and vice president no longer directly elected but chosen instead by the political party that wins the parliamentary elections.

The Angolan Civil War had lasted a quarter of a century and claimed the lives of an estimated half million people. The MPLA, which subsequently abandoned Marxist-Leninism in favor of social democracy, retains power in Angola today.

SPENCER C. TUCKER

## Guinea War of Independence (1961–1974)

### Causes

Located on the Atlantic coast in West Africa and once part of the kingdom of Gabu, part of the Mali Empire, present-day Guinea-Bissau is bounded by Senegal to the north, Guinea to the east and south, and the Atlantic Ocean to the west. The Republic of Guinea-Bissau includes the Bijagós (Bissagos) archipelago and other islands off the coast.

In 1437, the Portuguese Crown sent out expeditions to explore the Atlantic coast of Africa in search of gold and other valuable trading commodities. In 1456 the Portuguese established control of the Cape Verde Islands and by 1460 had explored as far south as Sierre Leone. Coastal trading posts followed, and the Portuguese government established the Company of Guinea to oversea the lucrative trade in gold, ivory, pepper, and slaves. The slaves were first sent to work in the Cape Verde Islands and then across the Atlantic to the Portuguese colony of Brazil. This trade continued until the 1850s.

In the 1630s and 1640s the Dutch drove the Portuguese from most of the Gold Coast, but the Portuguese retained a foothold. In 1765 the Portuguese founded Bissau, the present capital city, and in 1837 they occupied the island of Bolama, control over which they contested with the British. At the same time there was some native resistance to Portuguese efforts to control and tax the natives in the interior.

From the 1930s to 1960s Guinea was a neglected backwater, with peanuts being its chief crop. Portuguese investments in infrastructure, education, and public health projects came largely after the start of the war of independence. Thus, in 1959 Guinea had only some 200 primary schools with 13,500 pupils and 36 postprimary schools with 1,300 pupils for a total population of some 500,000.

In 1956 agricultural engineer Amílcar Cabral founded the Partido Africano da Independência de Guiné e Cabo Verde (African Party for the Independence of Guinea and Cape Verde, PAIGC). At first the PAIGC organized strikes by urban workers, especially those in the port and river transport sectors. This, however, brought the deaths of 50 striking dockworkers on August 3, 1959, causing the PAIGC to shift its strategy from public demonstrations to efforts to organize the peasants. Following the failure of political efforts to secure independence, on January 23, 1963, Cabral initiated a military campaign against Portuguese rule.

SPENCER C. TUCKER

## Course

At the beginning of the war the Portuguese Army had only two infantry companies in the colony, but Portugal ultimately committed some 30,000 men to the struggle against some 10,000 insurgents.

The PAIGC adopted guerrilla tactics. In their struggle the insurgents had the significant advantage of bases, training, and weapons in neighboring Senegal and the Republic of Guinea, both of these countries having recently achieved their independence from France. Certain communist states also provided weaponry and training. Cabral also proved to be a brilliant revolutionary theoretician and practitioner

of insurgency. He sought to improve local crop yields and ordered his men to assist farmers in their fields when they themselves were not fighting. He established trade-and-barter bazaars to bring goods to the natives at cheaper cost than those available through colonial merchants, and he set up field hospital and triage stations to aid his men but also to bring improved medical care to the rural population. Cabral established a government-in-exile in Conakry, Republic of Guinea.

The Portuguese meanwhile took advantage of tribal rivalries, and ultimately half of their 30,000-man force consisted of native troops. Nonetheless, the insurgency in Guinea cost the Portuguese disproportionately higher casualties than those in Angola and Mozambique, leading to it being known as "Portugal's Vietnam." General Arnaldo Schulz, the Portuguese military commander there during 1964–1968, initiated a resettlement program, which his successor, General António de Spinola, was able to utilize to full advantage. Spinola restored Portuguese Army morale through frequent visits to the troops and indoctrination programs for his own men. He also adopted the slogan "Guiné Melhor" (Better Guinea) and began a hearts-and-minds program that included expenditures in health services and education that won back many refugees. He also took advantage of the arrival of helicopters to withdraw isolated garrisons and restore mobility.

Although the Portuguese did not mount cross-border operations, they did support an abortive landing by Republic of Guinea exiles in 1970. They may also have been involved in the assassination of Cabral in Conakry, capital of the Republic of Guinea, on January 20, 1973. The military situation was largely a stalemate by the time of Spinola's departure in 1973.

Although the Portuguese controlled the coastal areas and principal population centers, the PAIGC controlled wide swaths of the north and the south of the country (it claimed to control 80 percent of the country by 1971). At Madina do Boe next to Guinea on September 24, 1973, the PAIGC declared the independence of Guinea-Bissau.

The wars in Angola, Guinea, and Mozambique were a tremendous drain on the Portuguese economy, and the April 1974 coup in Lisbon brought negotiations with the colonial insurgents. Guinea-Bissau was granted independence on September 10, 1974.

SPENCER C. TUCKER

## Consequences

Unfortunately for the new country, Guinea-Bissau did not experience political stability. Luís Cabral, cofounder of the PAIGC and half brother of the slain Amílcar Cabral, became Guineas-Bissau's first president. He served until 1980. Following independence, members of the PAIGC took vengeance on those citizens who had fought for the Portuguese against them. Although some managed to escape to Portugal or other countries, the number of victims ran into the thousands, many of whom were buried in unmarked graves.

On November 14, 1980, Prime Minister João Bernardo "Nino" Vieira ousted Cabral in a bloodless coup and became president, with a revolutionary council ruling the country. Describing himself as "God's gift to Guinea-Bissau," Vieira was president from November 14, 1980, to May 14, 1984. In 1984 a new constitution returned the country to civilian rule. Vieira was again president from May 16, 1984, to May 7, 1999, winning the first multiparty elections in Guinea-Bissau in 1994.

On June 7, 1998, an army uprising in Bissau and other locations led to the Guinea-Bissau Civil War of June 7, 1998– May 10, 1999, and the ousting of President Vieira on May 7, 1999. After securing refuge in the Portuguese embassy, Vieira went into exile in Portugal in June.

Elections in 2000 saw Kumba Ialá become president, but on September 14, 2003, the military mounted a coup, arresting Ialá on the charge of "being unable to solve the problems" facing the country. A military mutiny on October 6, 2004, saw the assassination of head of the armed forces General Verissimo Correia Seabra, who had led the coup against Ialá. General Batista Tagme Na Waie succeeded him.

Vieira returned to the presidency for a third time on October 1, 2005, having won the election of that year. General Na Waie was killed in a bomb blast on March 1, 2009. Vieira was killed by soldiers the next day, apparently in retaliation for the death of Na Waie.

SPENCER C. TUCKER

## Mozambique War of Independence, 1964–1974

### Causes

Located in Southeast Africa on the Indian Ocean, Mozambique is bordered by the Indian Ocean to the east, Tanzania to the north, Malawi and Zambia to the northwest, Zimbabwe to the west, and Swaziland and South Africa to the southwest. The Mozambique Channel separates Mozambique from Madagascar to the east. The country's population is overwhelming Bantu people.

During the first and fifth centuries CE, Bantu-speaking peoples migrated to what would become Mozambique from the north and west. The Swahilis and later the Arabs opened commercial ports along the coast. Portuguese seaman Vasco da Gama explored the coast of Mozambique in 1498, and in 1505 the Portuguese secured the Island of Mozambique, a small coral island situated at the mouth of Mossuril Bay in northern Mozambique. They also secured the port city of Sofala. By the 1530s Portuguese traders seeking gold were working their way inland on the rivers and establishing trading posts on the Zambezi River. Slavery was endemic, with much of the native population already enslaved.

Portuguese control was tenuous, with the Portuguese operating through various powerful individuals who were accorded considerable autonomy. Until about 1700 the Portuguese controlled most of the regional trade, but afterward the Arabs staged a comeback and through forceful means reclaimed much of the Indian Ocean trade, forcing the Portuguese southward. During the 19th century other European powers, particularly the British in their British South Africa Company and the French in Madagascar, became increasingly involved in the trade and politics of Southeast Africa. Slavery was abolished in Mozambique by the end of the 19th century.

In the early 20th century, the Portuguese increasingly turned control of Mozambique over to large private companies, some of which were controlled by the British who were anxious to construct rail lines connecting to their neighboring colonies of Rhodesia and South Africa. These companies employed forced labor. The new Portuguese corporatist regime of prime minister and de facto dictator António de Oliveira Salazar, who held power during 1932–1968, ended the power of the private companies and brought stronger Portuguese government control of the economy of Mozambique.

World War II had a profound impact throughout Africa, leading to enhanced African nationalism and demands for an end to European control. The leaders of the two new superpowers, the United States and the Soviet Union, had both expressed strong opposition to colonialism, and many African nationalist intellectuals were attracted to communist ideologies. In an effort to counter the growing international criticism of colonialism, in June 1951 the Salazar government changed the status of its colonies to overseas provinces of Portugal. This did not mean any practical changes in Portuguese control or the suppressive nature of its regime, however.

Black Mozambique nationalists, dissatisfied with the exploitative Portuguese colonial regime and inspired by decolonization taking place in the rest of Africa, saw their aspirations met by repression. The Portuguese authorities imprisoned or exiled the most strident advocates of independence. In 1962, however, Mozambique nationalist groups coalesced into the Frente de Libertação de Moçambique (Front for the Liberation of Mozambique, FRELIMO). It was initially led by American-trained anthropologist Dr. Eduardo C. Mondlane and headquartered in newly independent Tanzania, a country whose leftist leadership provided sanctuary and material support for liberation movements throughout sub-Saharan Africa.

Attempts to negotiate with the government in Portugal produced no tangible results, and on September 25, 1964, FRELIMO initiated a guerrilla war against the Portuguese colonial authorities.

Spencer C. Tucker

## Course

Operating from bases in their Tanzanian sanctuary, lightly armed FRELIMO fighters conducted cross-border raids that targeted Portuguese military and police posts in northern Mozambique, planted land mines on roads, and ambushed Portuguese security forces detachments. Local conditions complicated the Portuguese military response. The insurgents enjoyed considerable though by no means unanimous support among the local population, while the small size of the guerrilla detachments of some 10–15 fighters each made detection difficult. The insurgents' tendency to intensify their attacks during the monsoon season minimized the effectiveness of the limited Portuguese air assets in the region. By 1967, FRELIMO's ranks included 8,000 fighters who began to make excursions into the central parts of the country.

At the same time, FRELIMO's ideological stance continued to shift to the left, a pattern reflected in an internal power struggle following the assassination of Mondlane on February 3, 1969, that elevated Samora Machel, an avowed Marxist, to the leadership in 1970. Machel forged closer links with the Soviet Union, China, and Algeria, which provided FRELIMO with training and weapons, including heavy machine guns and even artillery. Under Machel's guidance, FRELIMO broadened its range of activities, supplementing its guerrilla campaign in the countryside with terrorism, subversion, and sabotage in urban areas. Machel also implemented a ruthless campaign of repression against internal dissidents and defectors as well as against those Mozambican communities who displayed reluctance to join the insurgent movement.

Portuguese efforts to combat FRELIMO intensified in 1969 when General Kaúlza de Oliveira de Arriaga assumed command in Mozambique. Influenced by the American counterinsurgency experience in Vietnam, Arriaga favored a heavy-handed search-and-destroy approach epitomized by Operation GORDIAN KNOT in the summer of 1970. Intended to destroy FRELIMO's bases in the northern Cabo Delgado Province, GORDIAN KNOT combined ground, air, and riverine naval assets and a total of about 35,000 personnel.

The largest conventional operation undertaken by the Portuguese military during the colonial struggles of 1960s and 1970s, GORDIAN KNOT proved tactically and operationally successful, but its strategic and political implications were more ambivalent. It showcased the effectiveness of the combination of special forces, heliborne assaults, and close air support in eliminating guerrilla units and supply bases in difficult terrain. In spite of Portuguese claims of success, backed up by more than 600 guerrillas killed, some 1,800 captured, and more than 200 bases and camps destroyed, GORDIAN KNOT was not the knockout blow Arriaga had hoped. It diverted troops and matériel from other parts of Mozambique, a situation that FRELIMO readily exploited by stepping up its activities in locales that had been deprived of its garrisons.

Nevertheless, the guerrillas had been dealt a severe setback that bought the Portuguese a narrow time window they sought to exploit by initiating a civic action program designed to win the hearts and minds of black Mozambicans. This too proved controversial. Its centerpiece was the Aldeamentos (Resettlement Villages) Program, an effort that resembled the American Strategic Hamlet initiative in

Vietnam. Intended to separate the insurgents from their rural base of support, the program made sense as a counterinsurgency measure but was not widely popular with the Mozambicans who were subjected to it. In consequence, it was frequently perceived as little more than a forcible measure that did little to endear Portuguese security forces to the rural population.

Construction of the Cahora Bassa dam was equally beset by controversy. A high-profile project intended to showcase Portugal's commitment to improving Mozambique's infrastructure, the dam absorbed a disproportionate share of scare resources, necessitated the forced resettlement of local inhabitants, and interrupted the cyclical floods of the Zambezi River that local farmers depended on for fertilizing their fields.

In spite of the tactical and operational success of Operation GORDIAN KNOT, the protracted war was becoming deeply unpopular in Portugal itself. FRELIMO, though crippled, remained a formidable opponent, intensifying its urban terrorism campaign and launching a major operation in Tete Province in late 1972. The difficulty of combating FRELIMO had profound effects on the military effectiveness of the Portuguese conscripts, who suffered from increasingly poor morale occasioned by the low quality of their weapons and equipment, mounting casualties, and the difficulties inherent in fighting an elusive and resourceful enemy. By 1974, nearly half of the 50,000 Portuguese troops in Mozambique were locally recruited Africans organized into Flechas (Arrows) units, special forces who played an increasingly vital role in antiguerrilla operations.

Though able to hold their own against FRELIMO in the field, Portuguese security forces could do nothing to address the growing concern in Portugal about the human and material costs of the Mozambique War as well as the counterinsurgency campaigns Portugal was simultaneously conducting in Angola and Guinea. Domestic dissatisfaction with the protracted colonial conflicts ultimately led in April 1974 to the peaceful military coup known as the Carnation Revolution. Engineered by a group of left-leaning army officers who overthrew the conservative regime of Marcello Caetano, it paved the way for a ceasefire between Portugal and FRELIMO culminating in a negotiated settlement that granted independence to what became the People's Republic of Mozambique on June 25, 1975.

SEBASTIAN H. LUKASIK

## Consequences

FRELIMO now took control of Mozambique. As with Angola and Guinea-Bissau, this was not smooth sailing. Within a year most of the 250,000 Portuguese had departed, many of them fleeing in fear after the passage of a law ordering them to leave within 24 hours with only 44 pounds of luggage. As a result, most returned to Portugal penniless. Ironically, Portuguese remains the official language of the country and is spoken as a second language by perhaps half the population. Among the native languages are Makhuwa, Sena, and Swahili.

FRELIMO military leader Samora Machel became president on June 25, 1975, and held office until his death on October 19, 1986. He soon established a one-party Marxist state supported by the Soviet Union and Cuba. His policies led to a long civil war during 1977–1992 that pitted the anticommunist Mozambican National Resistance (RENAMO) rebel militias against the FRELIMO regime. With FRELIMO extending support to the South African rebels of the African National Congress and Zimbabwean rebels of the Zimbabwe African National Union, the governments of both white-led Rhodesia and South Africa gave support to RENAMO. The new Rhodesian government also did not help itself with the people by its inept governance, nationalization of private industry, and imposed central planning resulting in economic collapse and extensive famine.

During most of the civil war RENAMO controlled much of the countryside, with FRELIMO's authority largely restricted to the urban areas of the country, including the capital and largest city of Maputo (formerly Lourenço Marques). The war saw massive human rights abuses by both sides and the collapse of social services. The central government executed tens of thousands of people and sent many more to so-called reeducation camps, where thousands more perished. During the war, RENAMO proposed a peace agreement based on the secession of RENAMO-controlled northern and western territories as the independent Republic of Rombesia. FRELIMO rejected this outright, and the fighting continued.

On October 19, 1986, President Machel was returning from a meeting in Zambia when his Russian-built Tupolev Tu-134 aircraft crashed in the Lebombo Mountains near Mbuzini. Ten people survived, but the crash killed Machel and 31 others. The Soviet Union claimed that the plane had been intentionally diverted by a false navigational beacon signal employing technology provided by the South African government.

New president Joaquim Chissano carried out sweeping changes, overseeing the transition from Marxism to capitalism and also

entering into peace talks with RENAMO. A new constitution in 1990 also provided for a multiparty political system, a market-based economy, and free elections.

The civil war ended with the Rome General Peace Accords of October 4, 1992. A United Nations–sponsored peacekeeping force kept the peace. The civil war had claimed some 1 million lives, while another 1.7 million citizens of Mozambique had fled to neighboring states, and perhaps 4 million others were internally displaced. By 1993, more than 1.5 million of the refugees had returned home.

Mozambique's national elections in 1994 were believed to be generally free and fair. FRELIMO won, with Chissano retaining office, while RENAMO, led by Afonso Dhlakama, was the opposition. In 1995 Mozambique joined the Commonwealth of Nations, becoming at the time the only member state never to have been part of the British Empire. FRELIMO won the next national elections in December 1999, but this time RENAMO accused FRELIMO of fraud and threatened a return to civil war. The elections of December 2004 saw FRELIMO again triumphant, with Armando Guebuza winning the presidency and FRELIMO again controlling parliament. Guebuza served two five-year terms. His successor, Filipe Nyusi, became the fourth president of Mozambique in January 2015.

Since 2013, Mozambique has been plagued by a RENAMO insurgency in the central and northern parts of the country. In September 2014, former president Guebuza and RENAMO leader Dhlakama signed the Accord on Cessation of Hostilities, which ended hostilities before the national elections in October 2014. When FELIMO again won, Mozambique again teetered on chaos as RENAMO refused to recognize the validity of the election, demanding control of six provinces where it claimed it had won a majority of the vote.

Human rights groups have accused the government of destroying villages and carrying out summary executions.

SPENCER C. TUCKER

## Timeline

| | |
|---|---|
| **1455** | Portugal secures the Cape Verde Islands. |
| **1482** | The Portuguese establish the Company of Guinea to aid in West African trade. Portuguese ships commanded by Diego Cäo land on the northern coastline of Angola and encounter the Kongo and Ndongo kingdoms. |
| **1498** | Vasco da Gama explores the coast of Mozambique. |
| **1500** | In the early 1500s the Portuguese establish a number of coastal forts in Angola. |
| **1505** | The Portuguese secure the island of Mozambique and the port city of Sofala. |
| **1575** | The Portuguese establish the port of Luanda. |
| **1623–1626** | Portuguese forces in Angola defeat the Ndongos, led by Queen Nzinga. |
| **1630s–1640s** | The Dutch drive the Portuguese from much of the Gold Coast of West Africa. |
| **1641–1648** | The Dutch occupy Luanda and drive the Portuguese from their coastal settlements. |
| **1648** | Portuguese forces from Brazil retake Luanda and other Angolan coastal forts. |
| **1671** | The Portuguese secure control of the Kingdom of Ndongo in present-day Angola. |
| **1765** | The Portuguese found Bissau, the present-day capital of Guinea-Bissau. |
| **1836** | Portugal abolishes the slave trade but not forced labor in its colonies. |
| **1837** | The Portuguese occupy the island of Bolama off West Africa. |
| **1884** | Portugal expands its control of Angola into the interior. |
| **1885** | The Congress of Berlin establishes Angola's borders. |
| **1921** | Angola's present-day borders are set. |
| **Jul 5, 1932** | António de Oliveira Salazar becomes prime minister of Portugal. Establishing a de facto dictatorship, he rules until 1968. |
| **Jun 11, 1951** | Portugal's African colonies, including Angola, are recognized as overseas provinces of Portugal. |

| | |
|---|---|
| **1956** | The Movimento Popular da Libertação de Angola (Popular Movement for the Liberation of Angola, MPLA), led by António Agostinho Neto, is formed to affect independence. The MPLA receives material assistance from the Soviet Union. Amílcar Cabral founds the Partido Africano da Independência de Guiné e Cabo Verde (African Party for the Independence of Guinea and Cape Verde, PAIGC). |
| **1961** | Luanda and northern Angola undergo MPLA-backed rebellions against colonial rule. Portuguese authorities respond with repressive measures. Rebellions on February 4 in the coffee plantations against compulsory labor requirements mark the beginning of the Angolan War of Independence. |
| **1962** | The Frente Nacional de Liberaração de Angola (National Front for the Liberation of Angola, FNLA) in northern Angola, led by Holden Roberto, begins an insurgency. Zaire and the United States support the FNLA. |
| | Mozambique nationalist groups come together to form the Frente de Libertação de Moçambique (Front for the Liberation of Mozambique, FRELIMO), initially led by Eduardo C. Mondlane. |
| **Sep 25, 1964** | FRELIMO initiates guerrilla warfare against the Portuguese in Mozambique from Tanzania. |
| **1966** | The União Nacional para a Independência Total de Angola (National Union for the Total Independence of Angola, UNITA), formed by Jonas Savimbi in southern Angola, becomes Angola's third major nationalist movement. |
| **Feb 3, 1969** | Mondlane is assassinated by a parcel bomb. |
| **1970** | A power struggle within FRELIMO following the death of Mondlane brings to the fore Samora Machel, an avowed Marxist. Machel forges closer links with the Soviet Union, China, and Algeria. |
| **Jul 6–Aug 6, 1970** | In Operation GORDIAN KNOT, Portuguese Army commander in Mozambique General Kaúlza de Oliveira de Arriaga mounts a major search-and-destroy operation against FRELIMO in northern Cabo Delgado Province. |
| **Jan 20, 1973** | Amílcar Cabral is assassinated. |
| **Sep 24, 1973** | At Medina do Boe near the Guinean border, the PAIGC declares the independence of Guinea-Bissau. |
| **Apr 25, 1974** | coup d'état led by progressive Portuguese Army officers occurs in Lisbon. The new government announces its intention to end the wars in Portuguese Africa. |
| **Sep 10, 1974** | Guinea-Bissau becomes independent. |
| **Oct 1974** | A cease-fire goes into effect in Angola. |

| | |
|---|---|
| **Jan 15, 1975** | In a meeting at Alvor, Portugal, Angola's three principal nationalist movements (the MPLA, the FNLA, and UNITA) agree to the establishment of a coalition government. |
| **Jun 25, 1975** | Mozambique becomes independent as the People's Republic of Mozambique. Machal becomes president and soon establishes a one-party Marxist state. |
| **Nov 10, 1975** | In the Battle of Quifangondo, FNLA, Zairean, and South African Defense Force troops attempting to capture Luanda are defeated by MPLA and Cuban troops. |
| **Nov 11, 1975** | Angola achieves independence. The MPLA unilaterally proclaims the People's Republic of Angola with Neto as president, in effect beginning the Angolan Civil War of 1975–2000. |

SPENCER C. TUCKER

### Further Reading

Abbott, Peter, and Manuel Ribeiro Rodrigues. *Modern African Wars (2): Angola and Mozambique, 1961–74*. Oxford, UK: Osprey, 2013.

Cabrita, João M. *Mozambique: The Tortuous Road to Democracy*. New York: Palgrave, 2000.

Cann, John. *Counterinsurgency in Africa: The Portuguese Way of War, 1961–1974*. Westport, CT: Greenwood, 1997.

Cann, John P. *Brown Waters of Africa: Portuguese Riverine Warfare, 1961–1974*. St. Petersburg, FL: Hailer Publishing, 2007.

Coelho, João Paulo Borges. "African Troops in the Portuguese Colonial Army, 1961–1974: Angola, Guinea-Bissau and Mozambique." *Portuguese Studies Review* 10(1) (2002): 129–150.

George, Edward. *The Cuban Intervention in Angola, 1965–1991: From Che Guevara to Cuito Cuanavale*. New York: Frank Cass, 2005.

Guimaraes, Fernando Andresen. *The Origins of the Angolan Civil War: Foreign Intervention and Domestic Political Conflict*. Basingstoke, UK: Macmillan, 1998.

Henriksen, Thomas H. *Revolution and Counterrevolution: Mozambique's War of Independence, 1964–1974*. Westport, CT: Greenwood, 1983.

Hodges, Tony. *Angola from Afro-Stalinism to Petro-Diamond Capitalism*. Bloomington: Indiana University Press, 2001.

Klinghoffer, Arthur Jay. *The Angolan War*. Boulder, CO: Westview, 1980.

Laidi, Zaki. *The Superpowers and Africa: The Constraints of a Rivalry, 1960–1990*. Chicago: University Of Chicago Press, 1990.

Marcum, John A. *The Angolan Revolution*. 2 vols. Cambridge, MA: MIT Press, 1969, 1978.

Schneidman, Witney Wright. *Engaging Africa: Washington and the Fall of Portugal's Colonial Empire*. Lanham, MD: University Press of America, 2004.

Tvedten, Inge. *Angola: Struggle for Peace and Reconstruction*. Boulder, CO: Westview, 1997.

Windrich, Elaine. *The Cold War Guerrilla: Jonas Savimbi and the Angolan War*. Westport, CT: Greenwood, 1992.

Wright, George. *The Destruction of a Nation: United States Policy towards Angola since 1945*. Chicago: Pluto, 1997.

# Biafra War for Independence (1967–1970)

## Causes

The Biafra War for Independence, also known as the Nigerian Civil War and the Biafra War, was fought during July 6, 1967–January 15, 1970, by the central government of Nigeria in an effort to end the nationalist aspirations of the Igbo (Ibo or Ebo) people of southeastern Nigeria who had declared their independence as the Republic of Biafra on May 30, 1967. Nigeria is Africa's most populous country and is home to more than 500 different ethnic groups speaking as many different languages and marked by religious and cultural differences. Nigeria is bordered by Benin to the west, Cameroon to the east, the Gulf of Guinea to the south, and Niger and Chad to the north. In 1967 Nigeria had a population of some 52.5 million.

Muslims of the linked Hausa and Fulani groups dominate the northern half of Nigeria, known as the Northern Region. The Western Region, which constitutes that part of Nigeria to the south and west of the Niger River, has a majority population of Yoruba people, while the southeastern portion of Nigeria, known as the Eastern Region, is home to a large population of Igbo people.

A number of native kingdoms had ruled the territory of present-day Nigeria, and slavery had been practiced throughout much of Africa. The British government announced in 1807 that it would act to prevent the international trade in slaves. In November 1851 as a part of its antislavery campaign but also as a pretext for making inroads into the Kingdom of Lagos, the British shelled Lagos, ousted the proslavery *oba* (ruler) Kosoko, and established a treaty with the more amenable Oba Akitoye. Britain annexed the Kingdom of Lagos and established it as a crown colony in August 1861. Britain then expanded its influence along the Niger Delta in the 1870s and 1880s. In 1879 the British created the United African Company, later the Royal Niger Company, under the leadership of Sir George Taubman Goldie.

The British territorial holdings received recognition by the other European colonial powers in the 1885 Congress of Berlin. In 1900, with the British controlling virtually all the territory constituting modern-day Nigeria, the British government took control of the Royal Niger Company, and on January 1, 1901, the territory became a British protectorate. In 1914 the British united the Muslim north and the mostly Christian south under a single administration.

World War I was a considerable boost to nationalism in Africa and Asia, but the colonial populations soon discovered that U.S. president Woodrow Wilson's proclamation in 1918 of the principle of self-determination of peoples applied only to Europeans. World War II had a profound impact on Nigeria, which had provided fighting units for British Empire forces. The war also signaled the end of imperialism and heightened Nigerian nationalism.

Following the war, Britain granted more autonomy to Nigeria. British policy favored a federal structure for the rival ethnic regions while at the same time strengthening the preeminence of the Muslim north. In March 1953 in the Nigerian House of Representatives the leading advocate of Nigerian independence and democracy, Anthony Enahoro of the Acton

## Biafra War for Independence (1967–1970)

| Operation OAU (September 2–October 15, 1969) | | |
|---|---|---|
| | **Biafrans** | **Nigerian Government Forces** |
| **Strength** | 10,000–20,000 men* | 180,000 men |
| **Casualties** | Unknown | 21,500 |

*Although heavily outnumbered, Biafran forces maintained control of Umuahia and eventually recaptured Owerri and Aba.

| Estimated Losses, Biafra War for Independence (1967–1970) | |
|---|---|
| **Military deaths, both sides** | 45,000–100,000 |
| **Civilian deaths** | 2,000,000–2,900,000* |
| **Internally displaced persons** | 2,000,000–4,500,000 |
| **Refugees** | 500,000–3,000,000 |

* Most of the civilian deaths were of children lost to starvation as a direct result of the Nigerian government blockade that caused massive food shortages and a lack of medical supplies.

**Sources:** Bartrop, Paul R. *A Biographical Encyclopedia of Modern Genocide.* Santa Barbara, CA: ABC-CLIO, 2012; Phillips, Charles, and Alan Axelrod. *Encyclopedia of Wars,* Vol. 2. New York: Facts on File, 2005.

Group (AG) party, proposed Nigerian independence for 1956. The motion was supported by both the AG and the National Council of Nigeria and the Cameroons (NCNC) party. Leader of the Northern People's Congress and the Saraduna of Sokoto, Alhaji Ahmadu Bello, in a countermotion replaced "in the year 1956" with the phrase "as soon as practicable." Another northern member of the House made a motion for adjournment, which was seen by the AG and the NCNC as a delaying tactic. Sharp differences regarding the timing and nature of self-government for Nigeria brought the May 1–5 Kano Riots in the northern city of that name. These clashes between northerners (Yorubas) and southerners (Ibos) claimed many lives, caused many injuries, and led to a sharp deterioration in the relationship between the Northern and Southern Regions of the country. Meanwhile, the search for oil, begun in 1908, finally reached fruition in

1956 with the discovery by Sun Oil and British Petroleum of major oil resources in the Eastern Region.

On October 1, 1960, Nigeria became an independent republic within the British Commonwealth. A federal structure of government was installed in 1963. While meant to provide a high degree of autonomy to the different regions of the country, in practice the central federal government dominated affairs. At independence Nigeria was divided into just three regions, but over time it continued to subdivide and reapportion provinces in response to the political demands of smaller ethnic groups. There are now dozens of states.

The country elected rulers democratically until January 1966. Tensions soon arose, with the new weak central government unable to control the discord sparked by the sharp differences that had arisen among the various peoples of the country. During January 15–16, 1966, dissident army officers led by leftist Major Emmanuel Ifeajuna and Major Chukwuma Kaduna Nzeogwu overthrew the government of Prime Minister Sir Abudakar Tafawa Balewa, who was killed in the coup d'état. The coup leaders were unable to bring to power their choice of jailed opposition leader Chief Obafemi Awolowo and turned instead to army head General Johnson Aguiyi-Ironsi, who became chief of state in a military government.

On July 29, 1966, Aguiyi-Ironsi was overthrown and killed in a new military coup. The coup leaders were mostly from the northern Hausa tribe, and their motivations were chiefly ethnic and religious. The new head of state was Lieutenant Colonel Yakubu Gowon. The coup, however, brought increased ethnic tensions and violence and the execution of a number of military officers and civilians, especially those of the southeastern Christian Igbo people, many of whom had held important positions in the government, the army, and commerce. This prompted the flight of many Igbos from the north to their own tribal area in the southeastern part of the country, which only strengthened sectionalism in the country. Southeastern Nigeria was rich in natural resources, especially agriculture and oil.

It was soon clear that tribal tensions might bring the secession of southeastern Nigeria, now led by Oxford University–educated Nigerian Army lieutenant colonel Chukwuemeka Odumegwu Ojukwu. In January 1967, central government leader and northerner Colonel Gowon and Ojukwu met in the Aburi Conference to try to reach a peaceful solution to the crisis.

Lieutenant Colonel Chukwuemeka Odumegwu Ojukwu takes the oath of office as president following the proclamation of Biafran independence, in Enugu, Nigeria, June 10, 1967. (AP Photo)

Ojukwu, however, declared himself unhappy with the negotiations, which envisaged a renewed federal structure, and moved toward secession.

On May 30, 1967, the Southeastern Region of Nigeria declared itself independent as the Republic of Biafra, with Ojuwu as president. Gowon and the Nigerian central government refused to accept the secession, and Gowon sent the Nigerian Army into Biafra on July 6, beginning the war.

SPENCER C. TUCKER

## Course

On July 6 Colonel Yakubu Gowon, leader of the Nigerian central government, ordered some 12,000 troops of the Nigerian Army into the breakaway southeastern part of Nigeria, which had proclaimed itself the Republic of Biafra under new president Ojukwu. The invaders were soon driven out. The hastily organized Biafran forces then took the offensive, invading the midwestern part of Nigeria and capturing the city of Benia on August 9.

In the ensuing struggle the central government of Nigeria enjoyed the advantages of overwhelming manpower and equipment resources. In September its reorganized forces again took the offensive, and during the course of the next nine months they occupied about half of Biafra. They were finally halted by Biafran forces defending their capital city of Umuahia.

In August 1967, Biafran forces launched an offensive across the Niger River and captured Benin City. They then continued west but were stopped at Ore and pushed back to the Niger by the Nigerian 2nd Division under Colonel Murtala Muhammed. At Asaba, the Biafrans withdrew across the Niger to the Biafran city of Onitsha. The Biafrans then blew up the eastern spans of the bridge to prevent the Nigerian government forces from following.

The federal troops entered Asaba on October 5 and soon began ransacking houses and killing civilians, whom they claimed were Biafran sympathizers. The city leaders called for the inhabitants to assemble on the morning of October 7, hoping to end the violence through a show of support for "One Nigeria." Hundreds of civilians—men, women, and children, many wearing ceremonial garb—paraded along the main street singing, dancing, and chanting "One Nigeria." The Nigerian soldiers then separated the men and teenage boys from the women and young children, and in a square at Ogbe-Osawa village, Major Ibrahim Taiwo ordered the men and boys machine-gunned to death. More than 700 were killed (this in addition to those slain earlier), some of them as young as 12 yeas old, in what is known as the Asaba Massacre. Federal troops remained in Asaba for some months, destroying much of the town and committing numerous rapes and other outrages. During October 17–19 in Operation TIGER CLAW, the Nigerian forces captured the major Biafran port city of Calabar.

The fighting in Nigeria was a major problem for the British government, led by Prime Minister Harold Wilson. He called for negotiations and a peaceful settlement, but his government also sought to maintain Nigerian national unity and prevent communist inroads in the region and also agreed to supply arms to the Nigerian central government and not to Biafra. Wilson justified this because Britain was, in his words, a "traditional supplier" of weaponry to Nigeria. This position brought sharp criticism in the House of Commons. Later when the Nigerian government's blockade of Biafra brought mass starvation there, parliamentary criticism of Wilson became even sharper. Wilson was not alone in arguing, however, that Ojukwu's policy of only allowing night relief flights so he could simultaneously import arms contributed to the humanitarian catastrophe.

The Israeli government, which saw Nigeria as a major influence in Africa, turned down requests from Biafra for weapons and sold arms to the central Nigerian government. Nigeria also ultimately purchased some arms from the Soviet bloc but maintained a generally pro-Western orientation. The French government, however, supplied arms to Biafra, leading Wilson in his memoirs to sharply criticize President Charles de Gaulle for having prolonged the war. Meanwhile, peace negotiations in May 1968 in London and at Kampala in June failed to produce a settlement.

The United States, at the time very much preoccupied with the Vietnam War in Asia, recognized British predominance in the region and pursued a cautious policy of not selling arms to either side, although some private U.S. citizens did so. Washington did support the British goal of Nigerian unity and pushed for a peaceful resolution of the conflict. The leaders of the Soviet Union also abstained from intervention, clearly seeing the risks of being caught up in an unstable situation. Neither side wanted Nigeria to become a new Cold War battle zone.

As the conflict dragged on the death toll rose dramatically, especially in Biafra from starvation and disease, the result of the Nigerian government decision to employ a total blockade, including foodstuffs, in order to end the secession. The Nigerian government held that employing starvation against an enemy was a legitimate tool of warfare.

In September 1968, Nigerian central government troops again took the offensive.

Biafran refugees flee the advance of Nigerian federal troops on a road near Ogbaku, Nigeria, on August 5, 1968. (AP Photo/Kurt Strumpf)

They captured Aba on September 4 and Owerri on September 16 before Biafran forces halted them. Nonetheless, the Nigerians had cut Biafra off from access to the sea, although an airlift of some food and arms was maintained through the Spanish colony of Fernando Po.

During November 15–29, 1968, Biafran forces carried out Operation HIROSHIMA, an unsuccessful attempt to recapture Onitsha on the Niger, which had been lost earlier to Nigerian government forces. In 1969 Biafra adopted one of the most progressive national constitutions in Africa. That February Biafran forces launched a surprise counteroffensive in an effort to reopen access to the sea. They reached the outskirts of Aba on March 3 but were halted there. On April 22, Nigerian Army forces captured the new Biafran capital of Umuahiarri. A stalemate in the fighting then took hold, but much of the Biafran civilian population was now starving as a result of the blockade that included food.

On June 1, 1969, speaking in the town of Ahiara, Ojukwu delivered what became known as the Ahiara Declaration. Drafted by the National Guidance Committee of Biafra, it sought to shame the world and encourage Biafran patriotism. The declaration sharply attacked the British government, accusing "Anglo-Saxons" of sins "against the world" in numerous genocides, including against the Biafran people. It also pointed out the "racist indifference to the suffering of black-skinned noncombatants" and affirmed that Biafrans were "the latest victims of a wicked collusion between the three traditional scourges of the black man—racism, Arab-Muslim expansionism and white economic imperialism." Biafra's struggle was "not a mere resistance" but rather a "positive commitment to build a healthy, dynamic and progressive state,

such as would be the pride of black men the world over."

Also in June, Nigerian government forces, now numbering an overwhelming 180,000 men, began a final offensive to break through the Baifran defenses. During September 2–October 15 the Nigerian forces launched Operation OAU, an effort to capture the remaining Biafran cities. Although the Biafrans were heavily outnumbered, they were able to retain control of Umuahia and eventually to recapture the cities of Owerri and Aba.

On January 7, 1970, General Odumegwu Ojukwu launched Operation TAIL-WIND, the final Nigerian government offensive of the war. The fighting was centered in the towns of Owerri and Uli, both of which fell to the central government forces. On January 9, Ojukwu escaped by air to the Ivory Coast and asylum. On January 15, new president of Biafra Philip Effiong surrendered to Colonel Olusegun Obasanjo, ending the war.

SPENCER C. TUCKER

## Consequences

The former Biafra was devastated by the war in terms of infrastructure, wealth, and primarily lives. Its population of 12 million before the conflict was reduced to some 10 million by its end. Most of the 2–3 million deaths were of children lost to starvation as a direct result of the Nigerian government blockade that caused massive food shortages and a lack of medical supplies. The International Red Cross estimated in September 1968 that 8,000–10,000 people were dying daily. Some scholars have argued that the Biafran War was in fact a genocide for which no perpetrators have been held accountable.

Igbos found themselves unable to recover lost jobs and properties (the Nigerian government claimed that the latter had simply been "abandoned"). Igbos also suffered economically from the Nigerian government decision to institute a new currency, which rendered worthless prewar currency held by inhabitants of the Eastern Region. Ojukwu, the former president of the breakaway Republic of Biafra who had fled into exile at the end of the war in 1970, was, however, allowed to return to Nigeria under a special pardon in 1983.

Oil revenues helped with reconstruction in the Eastern Region, although there were accusations of Nigerian government officials diverting resources meant for reconstruction in the former Biafran areas to their ethnic areas. The war also did little to reduce ethnic and religious tensions in Nigeria. Although laws were passed requiring that political parties not be structured along ethnic lines, these have been widely evaded in practice.

Since the civil war, Nigeria has alternated between short periods of democratic government and longer periods of military rule. Strongman president Yakubu Gowon remained in power until 1975; subsequent military rulers of the country included Ramat Mohammed (1975–1976), Olusegun Obasanjo (1976–1979), Muhammad Buhari (1983–1985), Ibrahim Babangida (1985–1993), and Sani Abacha (1993–1998). A civilian, Shehu Shagari, served as president during the years of the Second Nigerian Republic (1979–1983).

The 1970s saw considerable economic growth and development, fueled in large part by the exploitation of the country's considerable oil reserves. Even today the petroleum industry accounts for more than half of the Nigerian gross national product and most of its exports. Unfortunately, the considerable corruption that accompanied this has seen much of the revenue

end up in the hands of a few rather than being used for development purposes. There have also been charges that the oil revenues have not been spread equally among the various areas of the country. Mismanagement has also retarded economic development.

Nigeria remained formally nonaligned during the rest of the Cold War years but nonetheless retained cordial relations with the United States and Great Britain. English remains Nigeria's official language. Nigeria also trades extensively with France, West Germany, and other Western nations.

In an effort to demonstrate its important position in Africa, Nigerian leaders have at times taken an important role in African crises, as in opposition to the Republic of South Africa's apartheid policies in the early 1980s. Nigeria's important contributions to the arts have been recognized in Chinua Achebe and Wole Soyinka, the first African Nobel laureate in literature. The current constitution was enacted on May 29, 1999, inaugurating the Fourth Nigerian Republic, which continues today.

Ethnic violence continues and remains a major problem. Especially worrisome is the conflict between Muslims and Christians. Since 2002, Nigeria has experienced attacks that have claimed more than 15,000 lives and resulted in the kidnapping of a number of children by the Islamic extremist Boko Haram group, which seeks to eradicate secular government and create a Muslim state under strict sharia law in northern Nigeria. There has been considerable international criticism of the central Nigerian government and especially Goodluck Jonathan, Nigerian president during 2010–2015, for the failure to adequately address this threat.

SPENCER C. TUCKER

## Timeline

| | |
|---|---|
| **1879** | The British United African Company, later the Royal Niger Company, led by Sir George Taubman Goldie, establishes control of much of Nigeria. |
| **1885** | The Congress of Berlin establishes African boundaries and formalizes the British claim to what is known as the "Oil Rivers Protectorate." |
| **1900** | The British government assumes the governance of Nigeria. |
| **Jan 1, 1900** | The territory constituting Nigeria becomes a British protectorate. |
| **Jan 1, 1914** | The mostly Muslim north and the mostly Christian south are amalgamated, although separately administered. |
| **Jan 8, 1918** | U.S. president Woodrow Wilson proclaims in his Fourteen Points the principle of "self-determination of peoples." |
| **Aug 14, 1941** | In the Atlantic Charter, U.S. president Franklin Roosevelt and British prime minister Winston Churchill pledge self-determination and sovereignty for "all peoples." |
| **1946** | The Richards Constitution subdivides the Southern Region of Nigeria into Eastern and Western Regions. The constitution also reasserts the British Crown's ownership of "all mineral oils" in Nigeria. |
| **Aug 1951** | The National Council of Nigeria and the Cameroons party calls for independence in 1956. |
| **Mar 31, 1953** | In the House of Representatives, Nigeria's leading independence and prodemocracy advocate Anthony Enahoro, of the Acton Group, party proposes that Nigerian independence occur in 1956. Leader of the Northern People's Congress and the Saraduna of Sokoto, Alhaji Ahmadu Bello, replaces "in the year 1956" with the phrase "as soon as practicable." |
| **1956** | Exploration efforts by Sun Oil–British Petroleum discover major petroleum deposits in the Eastern Region of Nigeria. |
| **Oct 1, 1960** | Nigeria becomes an independent republic within the British Commonwealth. The southern part of the British Cameroons merges with the former French colony of the Republic of Cameroun to form the Federal Republic of Cameroon. The northern part of the British Cameroons votes to join Nigeria. |
| **Jan 15–16, 1966** | Dissident Nigerian Army officers overthrow the prime minister, Sir Abudakar Tafawa Balewa, who is killed. Unable to bring to power Chief Obafemi Awolowo, the junta appoints army head General Johnson Aguiyi-Ironsi as chief of state. |
| **Jul 29, 1966** | Auyi-Ironsi is ousted by another military coup and is replaced by Lieutenant Colonel Yakubu Gowon. The coup brings increasing ethnic tensions and violence, however. |

| | |
|---|---|
| **May 20, 1967** | The Southeastern Region of Nigeria declares its independence as the Republic of Biafra, with Ojuwa as president. The Nigerian central government and Gowon refuse to accept this, and civil war ensues. |
| **May 27, 1967** | Gowon announces a planned redistricting of the Nigerian federation. |
| **May 30, 1967** | Ojukwu formally declares the independence of the Republic of Biafra. |
| **Jul 6, 1967** | In Operation UNICORD, Nigerian government forces invade Biafra. |
| **Late July 1967** | Nigerian forces capture Bonny Island. |
| **Aug 9, 1967** | Biafra captures its capital of Benin. |
| **Sep 20, 1967** | Creation of the short-lived Republic of Benin in the Northwest Region, with its capital at Benin City. |
| **Oct 1–4, 1967** | Nigerian forces capture the Biafran capital of Enugu. |
| **Oct 4–12, 1967** | The first Nigerian Army invasion of Onitsha occurs. |
| **Oct 7, 1967** | The Asaba Massacre occurs in which Federal troops round up men and teenage boys and machine-gun more than 700 of them to death. |
| **Oct 17–19, 1967** | In Operation TIGER CLAW, Nigerian forces capture the major Biafran port city of Calabar. |
| **Jan 2–Mar 30, 1968** | The second Nigerian Army invasion of Onitsha occurs. |
| **Mar 31, 1968** | In the Abagana Ambush, Biafran forces waylay a Nigerian force of 200 soldiers, killing 150 of them. |
| **May 19, 1968** | Nigerian forces capture Port Harcourt. |
| **Jun 12, 1968** | The "Save Biafra" media campaign begins in Great Britain. |
| **Jul 17, 1968** | The Israeli Knesset debates Israeli moral obligations regarding the Biafran genocide. |
| **Sep 1968** | Nigerian central government troops again go on the offensive, capturing Aba (September 4) and Owerri (September 16) before the Biafarans halt them. |
| **Nov 15–29, 1968** | Operation HIROSHIMA occurs, an unsuccessful Biafran attempt to recapture Onitsha. |
| **Feb–Mar 1969** | Biafran forces launch a surprise counteroffensive to reopen access to the sea. They reach the outskirts of Aba on March 3 but are halted, and a stalemate ensues. Meanwhile, much of the Biafran civilian population is now starving as a result of the central government's blockade. |
| **Apr 22, 1969** | Nigerian Army forces capture the new Biafran capital of Umuahiarri. |
| **Jun 1969** | Forces of the central Nigerian government begin a final offensive against the Biafran defenses and break through them. |

| **Jun 1, 1969** | Ojukwa delivers what becomes known as the Ahiara Declaration, a statement of revolutionary principles that also condemns world acceptance of the Nigerian blockade of food imports into Biafra. |
| --- | --- |
| **Sep 2–Oct 15, 1969** | Nigerian central government forces launch Operation OAU, an effort to capture the remaining Biafran cities. |
| **Sep 16, 1969** | An uprising by the Agbekoyas occurs in the Western Region of Nigeria. |
| **Jan 7–12, 1970** | Operation TAIL-WIND occurs. This final Nigerian government offensive of the war takes place in the towns of Owerri and Uli, both of which fall to central government forces. The new president of Biafra surrenders to Colonel Olusegun Obasanjo. |
| **Jan 15, 1970** | Biafra formally surrenders, bringing the war to a close. |

SPENCER C. TUCKER

## Further Reading

Achebe, Chinua. *There Was a Country*. New York: Penguin, 2012.

Diamond, Larry. *Class, Ethnicity and Democracy in Nigeria: The Failure of the First Republic*. Basingstroke, UK: Macmillan, 1988.

Draper, Michael I. *Shadows: Airlift and Airwar in Biafra and Nigeria 1967–1970*. Aldershot, Hants, UK: Hikoki, 1999.

Dudley, Billy. *Instability and Political Order: Politics and Crisis in Nigeria*. Ibadan, Nigeria: Ibadan University Press, 1973.

Ekwe-Ekwe, Herbert. *The Biafra War: Nigeria and the Aftermath*. Lewiston, NY: Edwin Mellen, 1990.

Falola, Toyin. *The History of Nigeria*. Westport, CT: Greenwood, 1999.

Griffin, Christopher. "French Military Policy in the Nigerian Civil War, 1967–1970." *Small Wars & Insurgencies* 26(1) (2015): 114–135.

Kirk-Greene, A. H. M. *The Genesis of the Nigerian Civil War and the Theory of Fear*. Uppsala, Sweden: Scandinavian Institute of African Studies, 1975.

Levey, Zach. "Israel, Nigeria and the Biafra Civil War, 1967–70." *Journal of Genocide Research* 16(2–3) (2014): 263–280.

Madiebo, Alexander A. *The Nigerian Revolution and the Biafran War*. Enugu, Nigeria: Fourth Dimension Publishers, 1980.

Njoku, H. M. *A Tragedy without Heroes: The Nigeria-Biafra War*. Enugu, Nigeria: Fourth Dimension Publishers, 1987.

Ojiaku, Uche Jim. *Surviving the Iron Curtain: A Microscopic View of What Life Was Like Inside a War-Torn Region*. Baltimore: PublishAmerica, 2007.

Osaghae, Eghosa E. *CrippledGiant: Nigeria since Independence*. Bloomington: Indiana University Press, 1998.

O'Sullivan, Kevin. "Humanitarian Encounters: Biafra, NGOs and Imaginings of the Third World in Britain and Ireland, 1967–70." *Journal of Genocide Research* 16(2–3) (2014): 299–315.

Stremlau, John J. *The International Politics of the Nigerian Civil War, 1967–70*. Princeton, NJ: Princeton University Press, 1977.

Uche, Chibuike. "Oil, British Interests and the Nigerian Civil War." *Journal of African History* 49(1) (2008): 111–135.

U.S. Department of State. *Foreign Relations of the United States 1964–1968*, Vol. 24, *Africa*. Washington, DC: U.S. Government Printing Office, 1999.

Wilson, Harold. *The Labor Government 1964–1970. A Personal Record*. London: Weidenfeld and Nicolson, 1971.

# Tamil War for Independence (1983–2009)

## Causes

The Tamil War of Independence, also known as the Sri Lankan Civil War, was fought during 1983–2009 between the forces of the Democratic Socialist Republic of Sri Lanka and the Liberation Tigers of Tamil Eelam (Tamil Tigers, LTTE), who sought an independent Tamil state. One of the longest conflicts of modern times, it lasted a quarter century, from July 23, 1983, to May 19, 2009.

Sri Lanka, known as Ceylon until 1972, is an island in South Asia. Located just 20 miles off the southern tip of India, Sri Lanka is bordered by the Bay of Bengal to the northeast, the Indian Ocean to the east and south, and the Gulf of Mannar to the west. The island's location and its excellent deep harbors made it of considerable geostrategic importance during World War II.

The ancient kingdoms of Sri Lanka were the object of frequent invasions by neighboring South Asian dynasties. In 1505 the Portuguese arrived. They named the island Ceilão. This was transliterated into English as Ceylon.

By 1517 the Portuguese had constructed a coastal fort and began to expand their holdings. In 1638 the ruler of the Kingdom of Kandy, which comprised western Ceylon and constituted more than a third of the island, concluded a treaty with the Dutch in order to expel the Portuguese, who then ruled much of the coast of Kandy. Under the treaty terms, the Dutch were to hand over to the king the areas taken from the

**Tamil War for Independence (1983–2009)**

| Operation VADAMARACHCHI (LIBERATION) (May 26, 1987) | | |
|---|---|---|
| | **LTTE** | **Sri Lankan Forces** |
| **Strength** | Unknown | 8,000 men |
| **Killed** | 631 | 689 |

| Aranthalawa Massacre (June 2, 1987) | |
|---|---|
| **Buddhist monks murdered by LTTE rebels** | 33 |
| **Civilians murdered by LTTE rebels** | 4 |

| Total Estimated Casualties/Losses, Tamil War for Independence (through May 19, 2009) | |
|---|---|
| **Total killed, LTTE and Sri Lankan forces, all causes** | 80,000–100,000* |
| **Indian peace-keeping forces** | 1,200 |
| **Displaced persons** | 290,000 |

*As many as 40,000 civilian deaths are included in this figure.

**Sources**: Mohan, Rohini. *The Seasons of Trouble: Life amid the Ruins of Sri Lanka's Civil War.* New York: Verso Books, 2014; Weiss, Gordon. *The Cage: The Fight for Sri Lanka and the Last Days of the Tamil Tigers.* New York: Bellevue Literary, 2012.

Portuguese and would be granted in return a trading monopoly. Both sides failed to honor the agreement, and by 1660 the Dutch controlled virtually all of Kandy.

The British arrived in 1796 during the French Revolutionary War, when they feared that the Dutch might yield Ceylon to the French. The Treaty of Amiens of 1802 between the British and the French awarded the Dutch part of Ceylon to the British. In 1803 British forces invaded the Kingdom of Kandy but were repulsed. A new British invasion in 1815 was successful, and the British crushed armed uprisings in 1818 and 1848. Following World War II, in 1948 Ceylon became a self-governing dominion within the British Commonwealth of Nations.

Ceylon was sharply split along ethnic lines. During the 19th century the British had settled a large number of Tamil laborers from southern India to work on the Ceylonese plantations. While Sinhalese Buddhists made up some 70 percent of the Sri Lankan population, there was a strong Tamil Hindu minority of some 20 percent concentrated in the northern and eastern parts of the island. The two ethnic groups have separate languages: Sinhala and Tamil. Tamil is the mother tongue of the nation's three largest minorities— the Indian Tamils, the Sri Lankan Tamils, and the Moors—who together were about 29 percent of the island's population. Ceylon thus faced sharp differences in ethnicity, religion, and language.

Ceylonese prime minister Solomon Bandaranaike, who held office during 1956–1959, sparked conflict between the Sinhalese and the Tamils by championing the Sinhala language and Buddhism. In June 1956 in the Sinhala Only Act, he made Sinhala the only official language. Bandaranaike also took other actions that

exacerbated communal politics. Certainly his policies profoundly impacted Ceylonese politics for decades.

The Tamils responded with civil disobedience, and occasionally this led to riots, which were especially severe in the first half of 1958 (but largely ended when Tamil was granted limited official status in August 1961.) On September 26, 1959, Bandaranaike was assassinated not by Tamils but instead by a Buddhist radical who believed that the prime minister had not done enough to establish Sinhalese dominance.

The 1960 elections were won by Bandaranaike's widow, Sirimavo Bandaranaike, the world's first female prime minister. She expanded her husband's foreign and domestic policies during two terms in office (1960–1965, 1970–1977). In May 1972 she secured a change in the name of the country from Ceylon to Sri Lanka, Sinhalese for "resplendent land," and declared it a republic as the Free, Sovereign and Independent Republic of Sri Lanka. A new constitution came into effect in 1978, and the country's name became the Democratic Socialist Republic of Sri Lanka. Buddhism became the state religion, further alienating the predominantly Hindu Tamils.

Prime Minister Bandaranaike also faced an attempt during April 5–June 9, 1971, by the Ceylonese communist party, the Janatha Vimukthi Peramuna (People's Liberation Front, JVP), to seize power. An accidental explosion in a JVP bomb factory tipped off the government and forced the JVP to launch its attempt prematurely. Although the insurgents were for the most part young, poorly armed, and inadequately trained, they were able to seize control of parts of a number of cities, including Colombo.

After several weeks of fighting, the government put down the revolt in the cities, but unrest continued in the rural areas in the southern and central ports of the island. The Soviet Union, India, Pakistan, and Britain all provided military assistance to the government. In order to end the violence, Bandaranaike offered amnesties in May and June 1971, and only the top JVP leaders were tried and sentenced to prison. On June 9 the government officially announced the end of the rebellion, which nonetheless may have claimed 15,000 lives.

Meanwhile, ethnic violence intensified. Reacting to Bandaranaike's politics of ethnic division, politicized Tamil youths began to form and ultimately co-opted the moderates. The most important of the extreme nationalist organizations was the LTTE, established on May 5, 1976, and led by Velupillai Prabhakaran. It soon began a campaign of violence against the government, targeting policemen but also moderate Tamils who were willing to negotiate with the government. Prabhakaran subsequently claimed responsibility for the earlier assassination on July 27, 1975, of Alfred Duraiappah, a prominent Tamil lawyer, the mayor of Jaffna, and a member of parliament.

Ethnic violence increased, and on the night of May 31–June 1, 1981, an organized mob of Sinhalese burned the Jaffna Public Library that contained more than 97,000 books and manuscripts including the Palm Leaf Scrolls, which were of great historical value. This event served to convince many moderate Tamils that the government was not prepared to protect them or their cultural heritage. Although the government responded with a declaration of a state of emergency, this did little to quell the violence.

The accepted date for the start of the war is July 23, 1983, when the LTTE attacked the 15-man Sri Lankan Army checkpoint Four Four Bravo outside the town of Thirunelveli in the Jaffna Peninsula. In their attack the LTTE killed 1 officer and 12 soldiers.

SPENCER C. TUCKER

## Course

With the start of the war in the July 23, 1983, attack by the extreme nationalist the LTTE on Sri Lankan Army checkpoint Four Four Bravo, ethnic violence quickly spread. Extremist Sinalese nationalists carried out pogroms in the capital of Colombo and elsewhere. As many as 3,000 Tamils were killed, and a great many more fled Sinhalese-majority areas in what became known as Black July.

Initially there were a number of Tamil militant groups, but the LTTE gained preeminence through its devastating terrorist acts. These included the Kent and Dollar Farm Massacres, an attack on two small farming communities on November 30, 1984. Hundreds of Sinhalese men, women, and children were attacked during the night as they slept and were hacked to death with axes. Another such action was the May 14, 1985, Anuradhapura Massacre, when LTTE members indiscriminately opened fire and killed or wounded 146 civilians within the Jaya Sri Maha Bodhi Buddhist shrine. Government forces responded in kind the next day with the Kumudini Boat Massacre in which they killed 23 Tamil civilians. Many Tamils rejected the violence of the LTTE terror campaign and its goal of an independent Tamil state. A number agreed to work with the Sri Lankan government as paramilitaries, while others sought to work within the mainstream political parties.

Attempts at peace proved unsuccessful. Talks between the Sri Lankan government

Merchants return to their burned-out businesses in the Pettha area of downtown Colombo, Sri Lanka, on August 1, 1983, following a week of rioting in which more than 1,000 Tamil businesses and homes were destroyed. (AP Photo/JLR)

and the LTTE in Thimphu in 1985 soon collapsed, and the war continued, with increasing numbers of civilian dead. In 1987 the fighting grew more intense. On April 21 the LTTE exploded a car bomb at the central bus station in Colombo, killing 113 people and wounding many others.

The central government responded by activating reserve forces and on May 26, 1987, mounted Operation VADAMARACHCHI (LIBERATION). Extending into June, it was a successful effort to secure military control of the LTTE stronghold of the Jaffna Peninsula. With the population of Jaffna city soon in dire straits and with the Tamil population of southern India calling for action, the Indian government of Rajiv Gandhi attempted to send relief supplies. When the Sri Lankan Navy turned back the Indian ships, on June 4 the Indian Air Force mounted Operation POOMALAI (FLOWER GARDEN), parachuting food and other supplies into the city.

On July 29, Gandhi's government pressured the Sri Lanka government into accepting an Indian "settlement" of the war. Signed by Gandhi and Sri Lankan president J. R. Jayewardene in Colombo, the accord included a pledge by the Sri Lankan government to withdraw its troops from the Jaffna area and initiate limited autonomy for the Tamil region of the country. In return, the Tamil Tigers were to surrender their arms. When the LTTE rejected this arrangement, the Indian government dispatched troops—the Indian Peacekeeping Force (IPKF) of some 50,000 men—in an effort to disarm the Tamils. This operation, which extended into March 1990 and included an unsuccessful airborne operation against Jaffna, resulted in the deaths of some 1,200 Indian soldiers, with several thousand others wounded. LTTE casualties are not known. The situation became even more complicated when Sinhalese nationalists initiated a guerrilla terrorist campaign against the government, which they believed to have given up too much to the Tamils and to India.

The religious side of the war can be seen in the Aranthalawa Massacre, one of the most notorious atrocities of the conflict. On June 2, 1987, LTTE members stopped a bus close to the village of Aranthalawa in eastern Sri Lanka and massacred 33 Buddhist monks, almost all of them young novices, along with 4 other individuals.

On July 5, 1987, the LTTE mounted its first suicide attack when 21-year-old Vallipuram Vasanthan drove a small truck packed with explosives through the wall of a fortified Sri Lankan Army camp at Nelliady in the Jaffna Peninsula. The ensuing blast killed Vasanthan and 40 soldiers. Suicide attacks became an LTTE trademark, with the organization carrying out hundreds of them during the course of the war.

Despite the presence of the IPKF the violence grew worse, as the Marxist JVP, which had attempted to seize power in 1971, again carried out an armed uprising against the government. The JVP skillfully exploited Sinhalese national opposition to the presence of IPKF troops and began a terrorist campaign against the government of Prime Minister Ranasinghe Premadsa (elected in December 1988) as well as prominent Sinhalese opposed to their philosophy. The nation underwent a severe test with many JVP-enforced strikes.

In November 1989 in Colombo, however, government forces killed JVP leader Rohana Wijeweera, and by early 1990 they had either killed or imprisoned the remaining JVP leadership and arrested some 7,000 of its rank and file. The number of dead from this insurgency is unknown because it had merged with the concurrent struggle against the LTTE. After 1990 the remaining JVP leaders entered into the democratic process, participating in the 1994 parliamentary general election.

Another side note in the war between the militant Tamils and the Sri Lankan government was the effort by revolutionaries in the Maldives to seize power there. To accomplish that end they invited in Tamil guerrilla mercenaries. The Maldivian government appealed to India for assistance, and in Operation CACTUS on the night of November 3, 1988, the Indian Air Force airlifted a paratroop battalion from Agra more than 1,200 miles to the Maldives. Landing at Hulule, the paratroopers secured the airfield there and several hours later restored the government at Malé.

In September 1989, the Indian and Sri Lankan governments reached agreement on the withdrawal of the 50,000 Indian troops. This was completed by March 1990. The withdrawal, however, left the majority Tamil-populated areas in the hands of the rebels, and fighting continued.

Brief cease-fires were unsuccessful, and in August 1989 the LTTE attacked the previously unaffected and neutral Muslim communities. The Muslims responded with a jihad (holy war) against the Tamils. On December 3 after considerable bloodshed, the LTTE proclaimed a unilateral cease-fire and announced its willingness to conduct peace talks with the Sri Lankan government. The cease-fire did not hold.

Former Indian prime minister Rajiv Gandhi became a casualty of the Sri Lankan Civil War. The LTTE held Gandhi responsible for the dispatch of the IPKF to northern Sri Lanka and the sending of troops to the Maldives to reverse the coup there led by Tamil mercenaries. In 1991 also, Gandhi had imposed direct rule on the southern Indian state of Tamil

Nadu that had been supporting the LTTE. On May 21, 1991, LTTE suicide bomber Thenmuli Rajaratnam assassinated Gandhi in Sriperumbudur, where he was campaigning for reelection. A number of others also died in the blast.

On May 1, 1993, an LTTE suicide bomber assassinated Sri Lankan president Ranasinghe Premadasa in Colombo while the president was at a May Day parade. Twenty-three bystanders were also killed, and scores more were wounded. Beginning in September, government forces launched a major offensive against the LTTE, and on October 1 they captured the Tamil Tiger naval base at Kilali and there destroyed some 120 vessels.

In August 1994 Chandrika Kumaratunga became prime minister of a coalition government that bridged both Buddhist extremists and Marxist revolutionaries. That fall she campaigned for the presidency on a pledge to negotiate with the LTTE, and in November 1994 she became the first woman elected president in Sri Lanka. Kumaratunga secured a truce in January 1995. It lasted only three months, ending when the LTTE sank Sri Lankan Navy vessels and shot down two aircraft. On January 31, 1996, an LTTE suicide bomber drove a truck filled with some 440 pounds of explosives into the Central Bank of Sri Lanka building. The ensuing blast killed 91 people and wounded 1,400 others.

On March 6, 1997, LTTE fighters assaulted a Sri Lankan military base and there killed more than 200 soldiers. In the most devastating economic loss of the war, on July 24, 2001, 14 LTTE members carried out a suicide attack on Bandaranaike International Airport. All were killed but not before they had destroyed eight Sri Lankan air force aircraft and four Sri Lankan

Airlines planes. The attack had a major negative impact on Sri Lankan tourism and thus the entire national economy. Compounding the cost of the civil war, on December 26, 2004, in the worst natural disaster in modern times, a giant tsunami, generated by a powerful undersea earthquake in the Indian Ocean, struck the coasts of India, Thailand, Malaysia, Myanmar, the Maldives, Indonesia, Bangladesh, and Sri Lanka. The official death toll was some 225,000 people, with as many as half a million people injured. The Sri Lankan toll was as many as 39,000 dead.

In November 2005 former labor activist Mahinda Rajapaksa was elected president of Sri Lanka. He was determined to use the military to wipe out the LTTE, and on September 26, 2008, the Sri Lankan government launched a major military operation with heavy artillery and air strikes toward Kilinochchi, the town the rebels considered to be their capital. On November 15 government forces captured Pooneryn, a spit of land paralleling the neck of the northern Jaffna Peninsula and a key LTTE stronghold. Control of Pooneryn enabled the Sri Lankan forces to attack the Tamil capital of Kilinochchi from three sides and cut off a Tamil supply route. Also, for the first time since 1993 the government now controlled a land route that would allow easier resupply of its own forces fighting the Tamils.

The government offensive continued, and on December 21 the Sri Lankan troops captured the important LTTE-held town of Paranthan, located on a highway connecting the northern Jaffna Peninsula with the mainland. This brought government forces within several miles of the former Tamil capital and stronghold of Kilinochchi. Following several days of heavy fighting, on

January 1, 2009, the government secured Kilinochchi. The news prompted celebrations in Colombo and other Sri Lankan cities. The Tamil Tigers meanwhile moved their operations center to Mullaitivu, on the northeastern coast.

On January 25, Sri Lankan Army chief of staff Lieutenant General Sarath Fonseka announced that the army had taken Mullaitivu, ending a dozen years of LTTE rule there. By February the LTTE fighters had been restricted to only about 60 square miles of territory, but an estimated 100,000 civilians were at risk because the government had banned aid workers from the area. On April 26 the government rejected an LTTE offer of a cease-fire but the next day ordered an end to the employment of air and artillery in order to spare civilian casualties. This followed calls by the United Nations (UN), the United States, the European Union, and India for a cease-fire.

On May 16, a Sri Lankan government spokesperson announced that government forces now controlled the entire Sri Lankan coastline, cutting off any escape by sea. President Rajapaksa declared the final defeat of the Tamil rebels, now restricted to a tiny pocket of only some 1.2 square miles. On May 19, Rajapaksa proclaimed victory in the long war in a speech before parliament. He also announced the death of LTTE leader Velupillai Prabhakaran, whose body was subsequently put on public display by the Sri Lankan military, and declared a national holiday in celebration.

SPENCER C. TUCKER

## Consequences

Although the Sri Lankan government claimed a much lower figure, especially regarding the last months of heavy fighting,

the UN estimated that the Tamil War for Independence had claimed some 80,000–100,000 lives, of whom some 40,000 were civilians. The UN also estimated that some 290,000 civilians had been displaced by the fighting.

With the end of the war, Sri Lankan president Mahinda Rajapaksa, who held office during November 2005–January 2015, oversaw an ambitious economic development program, much of it financed by loans from the People's Republic of China. Perhaps surprising given the duration of the civil war, Sri Lanka has been one of the world's fastest-growing economies. In addition to efforts to reconstruct its economy, the government had by 2015 reportedly resettled more than 95 percent of those civilians displaced by the fighting. The vast majority of former LTTE combatants who had been imprisoned were also returned to civilian society. Unfortunately, there has been little progress on such contentious matters as reaching a political settlement with elected Tamil representatives and holding accountable those individuals on both sides in the civil war alleged to have committed human rights violations.

During the war the UN had repeatedly called on the Sri Lankan government and the LTTE to make protection of civilians a priority, but little to nothing was done. After the war, with many claims of rape especially by Sri Lankan security forces, there have been repeated calls for investigations into war crimes and atrocities.

On March 31, 2011, UN secretary-general Ban Ki-moon released a report commissioned in 2010. It concluded that "a wide range of serious violations of international humanitarian and human rights law were committed by the government

Tamil refugees cross into government-held territory near Vavuniya after fleeing from fighting in northern Sri Lanka on August 21, 1996. (AP Photo/John Moore)

of Sri Lanka and the LTTE, some of which would amount to war crimes and crimes against humanity." The government was held responsible for the killing of civilians, including the shelling of hospitals and humanitarian objects in no-fire zones, the denial of humanitarian assistance, forced displacement, and torture. The LTTE was held responsible for using civilians as human shields, killing civilians attempting to flee, firing from civilian installations, forcibly recruiting children, employing forced labor, and carrying out indiscriminate suicide attacks. Despite strong opposition from the Sri Lankan government, in March 2014 the UN Human Rights Council voted to open an international inquiry into such charges and on June 25 appointed three international experts to advise the investigation. The Sri Lankan government and army commanders claimed that they had nothing to hide. During Sri Lanka's national independence day celebrations on February 4, 2016, the Tamil version of the national anthem "Sri Lanka Matha" was sung for the first time since 1949 at an official government event, an action approved by President Maithripala Sirisena as a reconciliation measure.

SPENCER C. TUCKER

**Timeline**

| | |
|---|---|
| **1517** | The Portuguese establish a coastal fortification in the Ceylonese Kingdom of Kandy. |
| **1660** | By this date the Dutch control virtually all of the Ceylonese Kingdom of Kandy. |
| **1796** | The British arrive in Ceylon and take possession from the Dutch. |
| **1802** | The Treaty of Amiens awards Ceylon to the British. |
| **1818, 1848** | The British crush two rebellions against their rule in Ceylon. |
| **1948** | Ceylon becomes a self-governing dominion within the British Commonwealth of Nations. |
| **1956–1959** | Ceylonese prime minister Solomon Bandaranaike creates conflict with the minority Hindu Tamils when he champions use of the Sinala language and Buddhism. |
| **Apr 5–Jun 9, 1971** | The communist Janatha Vimukthi Peramuna (People's Liberation Front, JVP) attempts to seize power in Sri Lanka. The government puts down the revolt, which may have cost 15,000 lives. |
| **May 22, 1972** | Ceylon officially becomes the Republic of Sri Lanka. |
| **May 5, 1976** | The Liberation Tigers of Tamil Eelam (LTTE) is established. Led by Velupillai Prabhakaran, it soon commences a program of violence against the Sri Lankan government. |
| **May 31–Jun 1, 1981** | An organized Sinhalese mob burns the Jaffna Public Library containing more than 97,000 books and manuscripts, among them important Tamil documents. |
| **Aug 17, 1981** | The Sri Lankan government declares a state of emergency. |
| **Jul 23, 1983** | The Sri Lankan Civil War begins with an LTTE attack on an army outpost outside Thirunelveli, killing 13 Sri Lankan soldiers. Sinhalese mobs respond by killing as many as 3,000 Tamils, with a great many more fleeing Sinhalese-majority areas, in what becomes known as Black July. |
| **Nov 30, 1984** | LTTE members kill hundreds of Sinalese men, women, and children in the Ken and Dollar Farm Massacres. |
| **May 14, 1985** | LTTE militants kill 146 civilians at the Jaya Sri Maha Bodhi Buddhist shrine. The Sri Lankan Army retaliates the next day, killing 23 Tamil civilians in the Kumudini Boat Massacre. |
| **1987–1989** | The Marxist JVP carries out a terrorist campaign in which thousands are killed. |
| **May 26, 1987** | In Operation VADAMARACHCHI (LIBERATION), the Sri Lankan central government sends troops against the LTTE stronghold of Jaffna in |

northern Sri Lanka. Indian prime Minister Rajiv Gandhi attempts a relief mission, parachuting food and other supplies into the city.

**Jul 5, 1987**  An LTTE member explodes a truck bomb in a Sri Lankan Army camp at Nelliady in the Jaffna Peninsula. Suicide attacks now become an LTTE trademark.

**Jul 29, 1987**  The Indian government pressures Sri Lanka to accept a "settlement" in the civil war. When the LTTE rejects this, the Indian government sends a peacekeeping force of some 50,000 men in an effort to disarm the Tamils.

**Nov 13, 1989**  Government forces in Colombo kill JVP leader Rohana Wijeweera.

**1990**  By early 1990 the government has either killed or imprisoned the remaining JVP leadership and arrested some 7,000 of its rank and file.

**Nov 3, 1998**  Revolutionaries in the Maldives invite in Tamil guerrilla mercenaries from Sri Lanka to mount a coup d'état, which the Indian government helps to quash.

**Sep 1989**  The Indian and Sri Lankan governments agree to a withdrawal of the some 50,000 Indian peacekeeping troops from the northern and eastern provinces of Sri Lanka. This leaves those areas under Tamil control.

**Aug 1990**  The LTTE mounts attacks on Muslim communities. The Muslims respond with a jihad (holy war) against the Tamils.

**Dec 3, 1990**  The LTTE proclaims a unilateral cease-fire and announces its willingness to conduct peace talks with the Sri Lankan government.

**May 21, 1991**  The LTTE assassinates former Indian prime minister Rajiv Gandhi in Sriperumbudur, India.

**May 1, 1993**  An LTTE member assassinates Sri Lankan president Ranasinghe Premadasa in Colombo.

**Sep–Oct 1993**  The Sri Lankan government launches a major offensive against the LTTE. On October 1, government troops capture the LTTE naval base at Kilali and destroy some 120 vessels.

**Jan 1995**  A truce between the LTTE and the Sri Lankan government lasts only three months.

**Jan 31, 1996**  An LTTE truck bomb targeting the Central Bank of Sri Lanka building in Colombo kills 91 people and wounds 1,400 others.

**Mar 6, 1997**  LTTE members assault a Sri Lankan military base and there kill more than 200 soldiers.

**Jul 24, 2001**  The LTTE carries out a suicide attack on Bandaranaike International Airport. This attack sharply affects tourism and has a major financial impact on the economy.

| | |
|---|---|
| **Sep 26, 2008** | In a major escalation of the civil war, the Sri Lankan government launches a major military operation toward Kilinochchi, the town that the LTTE considers its capital. |
| **Nov 15, 2008** | Sri Lankan government forces capture Pooneryn, a key LTTE stronghold. |
| **Dec 31, 2008** | Government forces secure the important northern town of Paranthan. This brings government forces within several miles of the Tamil stronghold of Kilinochchi. |
| **Jan 1, 2009** | Government forces capture Kilinochchi. The LTTE moves its operations center to Mullaitivu, on the northeastern coast. |
| **Jan 25, 2009** | Sri Lankan government forces capture Mullaitivu. |
| **Apr 27, 2009** | The government orders an end to combat operations in northern Sri Lanka. |
| **May 16, 2009** | President Mahina Rajapaksa declares that Sri Lankan forces have "finally defeated" the Tamil rebels, who are now restricted to a tiny pocket of only some 1.2 square miles. |
| **May 19, 2009** | President Rajapaksa announces victory in the civil war against the LTTE. He also announces the death of Tamil leader Velupillai Prabhakaran. |

SPENCER C. TUCKER

## Further Reading

Amato, Edward J. "Tail of the Dragon: Sri Lankan Efforts to Subdue the Liberation Tigers of Tamil Eelam." Master's thesis, U.S. Command and General Staff College, Fort Leavenworth, Kansas, 2002.

Balasingham, Adele. *The Will to Freedom: An Inside View of Tamil Resistance.* Mitcham, UK: Fairmax Publishing, 2003.

Bandarage, Asoka. *The Separatist Conflict in Sri Lanka: Terrorism, Ethnicity, Political Economy.* New York: Routledge, 2004.

Bullion, Alan J. *India, Sri Lanka and the Tamil Crisis, 1976–1994: An International Perspective.* London: Pinter, 1995.

Clarance, William. *Ethnic Warfare in Sri Lanka and the UN Crisis.* Ann Arbor, MI: Pluto, 2007.

Danayaka, T. D. S. A. *War or Peace in Sri Lanka.* Mumbai: Popular Prakashan, 2005.

Deegalle, Mahinda, ed. *Buddhism, Conflict and Violence in Modern Sri Lanka.* London: Routlege, 2006.

Dixit, J. N. *Assignment Colombo.* Delhi: Konark Publishers, 2002.

Gamage, S., and I. B. Watson. *Conflict and Community in Contemporary Sri Lanka.* New Delhi: Sage, 1999.

Gunaratna, Rohan. *Indian Intervention in Sri Lanka: The Role of India's Intelligence Agencies.* Colombo, Sri Lanka: South Asian Network on Conflict Research, 1993.

Gunaratna, Rohan, Alok Bansal, M. Mayilvaganan, and Sukanya Podder. *Sri Lanka: Search for Peace.* New Delhi: Manas Publications, 2007.

Hashim, Ahmed S. *When Counterinsurgency Wins: Sri Lanka's Defeat of the Tamil Tigers.* Philadelphia: University of Pennsylvania Press, 2012.

Hoole, R., D. Somasundaram, K. Sritharan, and R. Thiranagama. *The Broken Palmyra: The Tamil Crisis in Sri Lanka; An Inside Account.* Claremont, CA: Sri Lanka Studies Institute, 1990.

Johnson, Robert. *A Region in Turmoil.* New York: Reaktion, 2005.

Mohan, Rohini. *The Seasons of Trouble: Life amid the Ruins of Sri Lanka's Civil War.* New York: Verso Books, 2014.

Narayan Swamy, M. R. *Tigers of Lanka: From Boys to Guerrillas.* Delhi: Konark Publishers, 2002.

Rotberg, Robert I. *Creating Peace in Sri Lanka: Civil War and Reconciliation.* Washington, DC: Brookings Institution Press, 1999.

Thiranagama, Sharika. *In My Mother's House: Civil War in Sri Lanka.* Philadelphia: University of Pennsylvania Press, 2011.

Weiss, Gordon. *The Cage: The Fight for Sri Lanka and the Last Days of the Tamil Tigers.* New York: Bellevue Literary, 2012.

Winslow, Deborah, and Michael D. Woost. *Economy, Culture, and Civil War in Sri Lanka.* Bloomington: Indiana University Press, 2004.

# Contributors

Rick Dyson
Information Services Librarian
Missouri Western State University
Saint Joseph, Missouri

Dr. Elun Gabriel
Associate Professor and Department
    Chair, History
St. Lawrence University
Canton, New York

Dr. Michael R. Hall
Professor of History
Armstrong Atlantic State University
Savannah, Georgia

Dr. William H. Kautt
Professor of Military History
U.S. Army Command and General Staff
    College
Fort Leavenworth, Kansas

Dr. Sebastian H. Lukasik
Assistant Professor of Comparative
    Military History
U.S. Air Force Air University
Montgomery, Alabama

Dr. Jennie Purnell
Associate Professor of Political Science
Boston College

Dr. Udai Bhanu Singh
Senior Research Associate
Institute for Defense Studies and
    Analyses
New Delhi, India

Dr. Spencer C. Tucker
Senior Fellow
Military History, ABC-CLIO, Inc.

Dr. William E. Watson
Professor of History and Chair of the
    History Department
Immaculata University

Dr. Steven E. Woodworth
Professor, Department of History
Texas Christian University

# Index